Special Edition

Using

Oracle
Applications

By BOSS Corporation, Jim Crum

with

Ken Conway   Bob McLean
Bill Dunham   Cathy Morris
Jim Bunn   Bill Stratton
Satyakanth Abbaraju

Special Contributions by

Jan Cooper   David Gilmartin
Kathy Gates   Charles Steedley

A Division of Macmillan Publishing USA
201 W. 103rd Street
Indianapolis, Indiana 46290

Special Edition Using Oracle Applications

International Standard Book Number: 0-7897-1280-6

Library of Congress Catalog Card Number: 99-63998

Printed in the United States of America

First Printing: April, 2000

02 01 00 4 3 2 1

Trademarks

All terms mentioned in this book that are known to be trademarks or service marks have been appropriately capitalized. Que cannot attest to the accuracy of this information. Use of a term in this book should not be regarded as affecting the validity of any trademark or service mark.

Oracle® is a registered trademark of Oracle Corporation. The publisher gratefully acknowledges Oracle's kind permission to use its trademarks in this publication. Fastforward, Jinitiator, Oracle, Oracle Alert, Oracle Alliance, Oracle Application Object Library, OracleBRONZE, OracleSILVER, OracleGold, Oracle Consulting Services, Oracle Financials, Oraclemetals, Oracle MetaLink, Oracle Method, Oracle Workflow, Oracle7, Oracle8, Oracle8I, PL/SQL, SmartClient, SQL*Forms, SQL*Loader, and SQL*Plus are trademarks, registered trademarks, or service marks of Oracle Corporation. Oracle Corporation is not the publisher of this book and is not responsible for it under any aspect of press law.

This publication was produced using the Advent **3B2** Publishing System.

Warning and Disclaimer

Every effort has been made to make this book as complete and as accurate as possible, but no warranty or fitness is implied. The information provided is on an "as is" basis. The authors and the publisher shall have neither liability nor responsibility to any person or entity with respect to any loss or damages arising from the information contained in this book or from the use of the Web site.

Associate Publisher
Tracy Dunkelberger

Acquisitions Editor
Michelle Newcomb

Development Editors
Sean Dixon
Bryan Morgan

Managing Editor
Matt Purcell

Project Editor
Natalie Harris

Copy Editors
Kelly Talbot
Geneil Breeze
Kezia Endsley
Kris Simmons

Indexer
Larry Sweazy

Proofreaders
Benjamin Berg
Sossity Smith

Technical Editor
Karen Edge-Clere
Patricia Schatter
Rebecca Enonchong
Joanne Babunovic
Phil Robbins
Bill Stratton

Software Specialist
Michael Hunter

Team Coordinator
Cindy Teeters

Interior Designer
Ruth Lewis

Cover Designers
Dan Armstrong
Ruth Lewis

Editorial Assistant
Angela Boley

3B2 Interior Design
Daniela Radersdorf

3B2 Layout Technicians
Brandon Allen
Susan Geiselman

CONTENTS

ABOUT THE AUTHORS

BOSS Corporation is an Oracle Applications services company. BOSS is an acronym that stands for Better Organization Service Solutions. The consulting organization was formed in July 1995 and has focused exclusively on providing Enterprise Resource Planning (ERP) solutions, applications implementation project services, and database administration services for the Oracle Applications.

BOSS Corporation headquarters is located near Atlanta, Georgia, but our consultants provide services throughout the United States or globally as our clients require. Regional offices are located near Dallas, Texas, and Raleigh, North Carolina.

The company is proud of the quality of its consultants. It uses a combination of its own employees and associates to provide the correct skills at the right time to meet the needs of its clients.

BOSS Corporation offers many services to customers using the Oracle Applications. These services include the following:

- Expert assistance for financial applications implementations and upgrades (GL, AP, PO, FA, AR, PA)
- Expert assistance for distribution applications implementations and upgrades (PO, INV, AR, OE)
- Expert assistance for manufacturing applications implementations and upgrades (MRP, MPS, OE, INV, BOM, ENG, CST, CPP, OPM)
- Expert assistance for human resources applications implementations and upgrades (HR, PAY)
- Project management and planning for Oracle Applications implementations
- Database administration services for installation, upgrade, and tuning of the Oracle Applications
- Remote database administration services
- Technical services to convert legacy data, create interfaces, and extend or modify the basic functionality of the Oracle Applications

See the advertisements at the back of this book for more details about BOSS Corporation.

You can contact the authors at the following address:

BOSS Corporation
6455 East Johns Crossing, Suite 404
Duluth, GA 30097
Tel: 770-622-5500
FAX: 770-622-5400
Email: authors@bosscorporation.com

The company maintains a Web site with free Oracle Applications tips and techniques at http://www.bosscorporation.com.

Jim Crum is the chief operating officer and one of the original founders of BOSS Corporation. Previously, he was practice manager for consulting services at Oracle Corporation. Jim has over six years of functional experience with the Oracle Applications and thirteen years of technical experience with the Oracle database and tools. While at Oracle Corporation, Jim was a certified trainer in the Application Implementation Method (AIM). In addition, Jim has been employed as director of MIS, division financial director, plant controller, and manufacturing manager for several large international corporations. Jim has a B.A. degree from DePauw University. Jim is active in the local chapter of the Oracle Applications User Group (OAUG), and he edits the *Tips and Techniques* newsletter for the Atlanta OAUG.

Ken Conway is executive vice president of BOSS Corporation. He has thirteen years of consulting and highly technical software experience. He has been involved in the management, design, development, and installation of projects involving both custom and package software. Ken has managed many implementations of Oracle Human Resources and Oracle Payroll, including several of the first successful implementations that have gone into production in the United States. He was also involved in the Oracle BETA program during the early releases of the Oracle HR and Payroll products.

Ken has been very active in the Oracle Global Human Resource Information Systems (HRIS) Special Interest Group (SIG). He has made several presentations to the HRIS SIG and to OAUG regarding creative solutions using the Oracle HRMS product suite.

Ken has earned an M.B.A. degree from the University of Houston at Clear Lake and a B.S. degree in computer science at Sam Houston State University. He achieved both degrees in only four years.

Bill Dunham holds the position vice president, practice director, for BOSS Corporation. Previously, he was managing principal and practice manager for consulting services at Oracle Corporation. Twelve years of Bill's sixteen-year career have focused on Oracle Applications, products, and technology. He has over eight years of functional experience with various Oracle Applications and twelve years of technical experience with the Oracle database and tools. Bill has functioned as systems programmer, application developer, database administrator, technical team lead, project manager, and director of information technology for several public sector, manufacturing, and consulting organizations. While an employee at Oracle Corporation, Bill led a variety of projects. These projects include custom development projects for clients and multi-million dollar Oracle Application implementation projects for clients and Oracle Corporation. The Oracle Applications projects include two of the largest public sector projects in the United States. Bill has a B.S. degree in computer science from High Point University and an M.B.A. from Wake Forest University's Babcock School of Management. Bill has presented papers at local and regional Oracle Application and Technology User Groups, and Bill is cofounder of the Piedmont/Triad Oracle Users Group. Bill will also be presenting a paper at the Spring 2000 OAUG conference in Philadelphia.

David Gilmartin is based in Dublin, Ireland. David has fourteen years of experience working with high technology multinational corporations. During this time, his responsibilities have included quality engineering, manufacturing engineering, commodity management, and materials management. David's involvement with Enterprise Resource Planning (ERP) applications began with managing an implementation in 1995. He expanded this involvement by taking the role of project manager for a global implementation of the Oracle manufacturing, distribution, and financials applications in 1997 and 1998. His specialty is managing rapid implementations with minimal resources. He has over three years of experience with the Oracle Applications with an in-depth functional knowledge of the manufacturing and distribution applications.

David presented a paper titled "A Rapid Implementation Story (Around The World In Under 270 Days)" at the 1999 Oracle Applications User Group conference in Barcelona. He also has qualifications in electronic engineering and quality technology.

Jimmy Bunn achieved a bachelor of science degree in applied physics in 1974. He has 20 years of experience in the United States Air Force as a project manager for many software projects. After retirement from the Air Force, he worked as a member of an information technology staff for a manufacturing company where he was trained in and participated in the implementation of the Oracle financial, distribution, and manufacturing modules.

Jimmy has been working as an Oracle Applications Consultant since 1995, and he has more than four years of continuous experience with the Oracle financial, distribution, and manufacturing applications. He is currently a senior consultant with BOSS Corporation, and he specializes in implementation projects for the distribution and manufacturing applications.

Jan Cooper is the national practice director, Oracle Applications for Diversified Computer Consultants. Previously, she was a managing partner in the firm Cooper Gates Consulting. Jan has over four years of Oracle functional experience as both a user and consultant. Her Oracle Application implementation experience includes all of the Oracle Financials Applications and Oracle Projects. She has completed an Oracle Masters Certificate establishing her expertise as an Oracle Applications Functional Project Team Member. Jan has authored two articles to date: "Multi-Org Made Easy," *OAUG INSIGHT*, Spring 1999, and "Financial Software Implementation Needn't be a Nightmare for Your Clients," *Insight, The Magazine of the Illinois CPA Society*, October 1997. Jan is active in her local users group, the North Central OAUG (NCOAUG), where she has presented papers on avoiding "nightmare" implementations in February 1998 and February 1999, on Multi-Org Release 11.0 in February 1999, and on Multi-Org for Users in September 1998. She is an active member of the OAUG Publications Committee and has been a panel member and presenter at the Spring 1996 Oracle Applications Users Group (OAUG) in Orlando, FL, discussing financial implementations and communication. She has 15 years of solid accounting experience with an emphasis in cost, general accounting, payables, receivables, payroll, and project accounting. Jan is a Certified Public Accountant and has a master's degree in business administration.

Satyakanth Abbaraju is a senior consultant with BOSS Corporation, with over three years of extensive experience in Oracle financials and Oracle Process Manufacturing applications. Satyakanth has a bachelor's degree in commerce and is a member of the Institute of Chartered Accountants of India. He also has over 9 years of industry experience in various capacities as a user, manager, consultant, and auditor in several manufacturing and service industries. Prior to becoming an applications consultant for Oracle's ERP products, he worked as accounts manager and MIS manager and practiced as a chartered accountant in India. He was a key functional member of the team that converted Oracle GEMMS to Oracle Process Manufacturing release 11.

Charles Steedley has over 10 years of experience in implementing financial and manufacturing applications in both a functional and technical capacity. The last six years have been spent working with the Oracle ERP Applications. Chuck was employed by Oracle Corporation as a senior financial applications consultant, and he has worked as an independent consultant since 1995. Prior to implementing Oracle Applications, he had extensive experience implementing J.D. Edwards and Platinum financial applications. Mr. Steedley is a Certified Oracle Professional for release 11 and a Certified Public Accountant. He has a master's of science degree in information systems from Georgia State University.

Kathy Gates achieved a B.S. degree in accounting from Illinois State University and an M.B.A. in finance from Keller School of Management and has been a CPA and member of the Illinois CPA Society member since 1997. She is an editor on the Communications Committee of the Oracle Application Users Group and has given presentations on Oracle General Ledger Consolidations at the North Central Oracle Applications Users Group (NCOAUG).

Kathy has been working with the Oracle Applications since 1995. She began working with Oracle software as a user and began consulting in 1997. She has 12 years of solid accounting experience with an emphasis in general accounting, payables, cost accounting, and project costing. Currently, Kathy is president of the Gates Consulting Group.

Robert McLean holds the position of senior business analyst and project leader with American Tool Companies, Inc. with over 20 years of experience in successful project management and consulting in manufacturing systems. His experience includes designing, marketing, teaching, implementing, documenting, and supporting enterprise resource planning systems. Mr. McLean has earned a bachelor's degree in mathematics and economics from the University of Kansas. He is certified in Production and Inventory Control (CPIM) by APICS. He has been a guest lecturer at APICS meetings and Business Schools. In some of his past employment, Mr. McLean has been a senior consultant with BOSS Corporation, manager of software customer support for IBM, customer executive speaker at IBM plant sites, an author of two publications on manufacturing control systems, and an instructor in the Oracle Application Consulting "bootcamp" for new Oracle consultants.

DEDICATION

I dedicate this book to the fantastic clients, consultants, and friends of BOSS Corporation. Your support, enthusiasm, and friendship have made this endeavor especially rewarding.

Most importantly, we say thank you very much to the spouses of the authors. You gave up countless weekends and evenings so we could work on our assigned chapters. Marilynn, Avis, Lisa, Mary, Wanda, Renuka, Yvonne, Charlie, Daryl, and Conrad, thank you for your support and patience. We couldn't have created this book without your support.

Also, thank you Jyh Yi Wang for production support and development of BOSS Corporation material at the back of the book. Thank you Mike Auquier and Gloria Law for your help with the HR and Payroll chapters.

Finally, we offer special thanks to Diane McHugh for taking extra responsibility and running the BOSS Corporation business during the many hours we were writing and editing.

Jim Crum—January 2000

TELL US WHAT YOU THINK!

As the reader of this book, *you* are our most important critic and commentator. We value your opinion and want to know what we're doing right, what we could do better, what areas you'd like to see us publish in, and any other words of wisdom you're willing to pass our way.

As an associate publisher for Que, I welcome your comments. You can fax, email, or write me directly to let me know what you did or didn't like about this book—as well as what we can do to make our books stronger.

Please note that I cannot help you with technical problems related to the topic of this book, and that due to the high volume of mail I receive, I might not be able to reply to every message.

When you write, please be sure to include this book's title and author as well as your name and phone or fax number. I will carefully review your comments and share them with the author and editors who worked on the book.

Fax: 317-581-4666

Email: quetechnical@mcp.com

Mail: Associate Publisher
    Que
    201 West 103rd Street
    Indianapolis, IN 46290 USA

INTRODUCING THE ORACLE APPLICATIONS

CHAPTER 1

REVIEWING ERP AND ORACLE CORPORATION

Enterprise Resource Planning (ERP) systems evolved from the Material Requirements Planning (MRP) systems of the late 1970s. In the 1980s, businesses implemented systems for Total Quality Management (TQM), Just in Time (JIT) manufacturing, and MRP II. In the 1990s the big initiatives have been Business Process Reengineering (BPR), Enterprise Resource Planning (ERP) and Year 2000 (Y2K) compliance. Today, a business can implement a large and integrated suite of application software modules for most common business practices. Several leading software companies sell and support full-featured accounting, distribution, procurement, manufacturing, human resources, and payroll systems.

This book is about implementing and using the ERP Applications of the Oracle Corporation. Part I introduces ERP systems and the Oracle ERP Applications. Part II of this book will help you implement the applications, and Part III will help you configure and use the core financial, distribution, manufacturing, and Human Resource applications. Part IV and Part V of this book offer information about implementing software with partners, vendors and consultants.

INTRODUCTION

The Oracle suite of ERP applications is a big and complex subject. The Oracle Corporation manuals for the core financial, distribution, and manufacturing applications might easily occupy 15 feet of your bookshelf space, and the product documentation is good. If you use the detailed reference material enough, you can find almost all the answers for even complex business situations. However, the documentation and its topic are so large and complex, many users find the documentation difficult. We hope this book will serve as a more practical reference material between the high-level overviews and the detailed reference manuals provided by Oracle. Our goal is to present enough information and concepts about the Oracle applications to enable you to manage your software implementation project, configure the system, and run some functional tests in a complete conference room pilot.

Due to space requirements, we can only present so much detail on each application and business process. For specific report, screen level, field level, and technical information, you will want to consult the online help, the User Guides for each application, and the Technical Reference Manuals. Researching a concept or specific topic takes practice. Start with the material in this book, and then drill down into the Oracle reference manuals when necessary.

During the writing of this book, we had several types of readers in mind. Generally, we present material that is suitable for the intermediate or advanced user, and we assume that you already know your individual business processes, the basic Oracle vocabulary, and navigation techniques. Some readers who might find this book useful include the following:

- The implementation team project manager who must determine the scope of the project and understand the concepts and issues to be resolved for each application will want to read most chapters in this book. Start with Part II, "Implementing the Oracle Applications," to learn the details of package software implementation. Then skim through the chapters of your most important applications as you build your implementation team, set your project scope, and identify issues. Read Part IV, "Working with Partners," to understand the importance of Oracle Support, consultants, and vendors of compatible software. Finally, use the checklist in Appendix C to start planning and establish project control.

- If you are on a software implementation team and you are assigned to configure and test an application module, you will want to study the individual chapter in Part III about that application. You will obtain an understanding of how each application is configured and the main transactions the application can perform. You will also want to read the other chapters that bracket your core business functions to understand the integration points and process flow. For example, if you are implementing the Payables module, consider reading the chapters for Purchasing (Chapter 15) and General Ledger (Chapter 11) to see how Payables integrates with the other applications.

- A database administrator or a technical user can gain interesting insights into the issues and concerns of functional users by reading chapters in Part III about specific applications. Use these chapters to put your technical reference material into a business perspective and map the functional areas of the business to the internal database objects.

- If you are contemplating purchase of the Oracle ERP software, consider reading chapter 4 about how much things cost and how much effort an ERP implementation takes. Use the chapters in Part III about individual modules to prepare questions for your Oracle sales representative. Understand the compatible software of the Cooperative Applications Initiative vendors in Chapter 30, "Alliance Partners." Also, check out Chapter 28, "Working with Oracle Support."

- A functional consultant who is an expert in three or four applications could extend his skills to include another application, by reading a chapter or two in Part III.

- If you want to become a project manager, consider reading the chapters in Part II. Then consider becoming a functional expert in three or more application modules in Part III.

- If you are a power user of one or two applications and your job description is about to change, consider reading the chapters in Part III about the applications that describe your new responsibilities.

This book is organized into five parts. This is a reference manual, and you will not read it cover to cover. Just try to get familiar with the structure of the book so you will know what topics are available and how to access them quickly from the table of contents or the index. Each part has a specific purpose as follows:

- Part I, "Introducing the Oracle Applications," introduces the organization of this book, discusses the topic of Enterprise Resource Planning, and gives a high-level overview of Oracle Corporation and the Oracle software.

- Part II, "Implementing the Oracle Applications," presents project management techniques and implementation methods for packaged software and ERP systems. Oracle has an Application Implementation Method called AIM and other consulting firms have developed similar work plans and templates. We discuss the phases of a software project, key activities, and deliverables of the project team.

- In Part III, "Configuring and Using the Oracle Applications," you will read about each of the core financial, distribution, manufacturing, and human resource applications. Each chapter is generally divided into a section on configuration parameters and another section on major transactions and using the application.

- Everyone needs assistance with her ERP system. You can get this help from Oracle Support, outside consultants, and other software vendors. These topics are presented in Part IV, "Working with Partners."

- Finally, the last part has three sections including two appendixes about the careers of people that work with ERP systems. A final appendix has an implementation checklist.

UNDERSTANDING ERP CONCEPTS

ERP is a software system that is often referred to as the backbone for the entire business. However, these systems are more than just a bony skeleton. These systems have lots of brains (process logic), muscle (business transactions), and heart (business policy). The software communicates (as a nervous system) across business functions.

Also, the medical analogy is appropriate because these systems grow and evolve over time. For example, ERP systems can get soft and flabby if left unattended. The freshly implemented system is not stable like your legacy system. It can be more like a young adolescent with raging hormones, limited experience, and a contrary disposition. As with an adolescent child, your users might not like your ERP system until it matures.

Oracle ERP software is On-Line Transaction Processing (OLTP) software, and many manual or automatic transactions start coordinated and automatic transactions in other modules. For example, when the clerk at the shipping dock records the transaction that goods have shipped to a customer, integrated changes are made in the order entry, billing, and inventory systems, and new transactions for revenue recognition and cost of goods sold are started.

ERP systems attempt to replicate your business structure, processes, policies, and procedures. Because each business is different, you can't just install the programs on a computer and start business operations immediately. First, you must determine the basic nature of your business and compare that with the functionality of the software. By carefully setting thousands of configuration parameters, you can often achieve a system that meets 90 percent to 100 percent of your business needs.

Configuring an ERP system can be tricky because many of the parameters interact with each other, and you need to understand how the software works before you actually have a chance to use it. For example, your strategy for configuring your enterprise organization structure can have significant impact on the way you prepare financial statements, manage inventories, fulfill customer orders, procure materials, manage compensation and benefits, secure your data, and so forth. Your company might be centralized for fulfillment of customer orders and decentralized for procurement and inventory management. In this example, to configure your system properly, you will want to resolve the centralized/decentralized issues within each application.

UNDERSTANDING THE ATTRIBUTES OF ERP SYSTEMS

The Oracle ERP systems have the functionality to support industry standards and best practices. The recommendations of the American Production and Inventory Control Society (APICS) and Generally Accepted Accounting Practices (GAAP) are well supported by the Oracle software. Look for the following characteristics:

- These systems are composed of many modules called applications. The core Oracle Applications support three broad business functions: financial, distribution, and manufacturing transactions. For example, the financial applications are General Ledger, Accounts Payable, Accounts Receivable, and Fixed Assets. You can license only the applications you need.

- The applications are integrated and work together to pass individual transactions through an entire business process. The modularization approach gives flexibility, and the modules interact by passing data through program interfaces. A single manual transaction in one application can initiate transactions in other applications.

- ERP systems are complex, and the more applications you use, the more complexity you have. Thousands of configuration parameters interact with each other and change the logic of the programs to fit your unique business situation. It can take months to set up and learn how the programs operate. The documentation is voluminous.

- The flexibility of these systems is the upside of the complexity problem. Oracle has thousands of customers in hundreds of industries all over the world using the applications in their own special way. Manufacturing companies, utilities, service companies, governments, and others have all been able to configure the applications to meet their specific business needs.

- ERP systems often use powerful data storage mechanisms such as the Oracle Relational Database Management System (RDBMS). The database gives the transaction system the performance and scalability to process thousands of transactions per hour and store the data for years. A large ERP database can be more than 300GB in size.

- ERP software vendors are highly competitive. Each has loaded their software with every conceivable function point and business process. Typically, interfaces among vendors are proprietary solutions and must be implemented as custom extensions.

- These systems can be a mixture of online and batch processes. Many functions support a manual interactive process and an automated batch process. For example, you can apply cash receipts to your Oracle Receivables by keying the data into a form, or you can configure the system to use the AutoLockbox program to process a data file from the bank

- The systems are Y2K-compliant. During the second half of the 1990s, many companies adopted a Y2K strategy of replacing their old custom software with packages of modules from the ERP vendors. This replacement strategy allowed these companies to upgrade thousands of obsolete programs with new programs that were written to be Y2K-complaint. The Oracle Applications Release 10.7 (with patches) was the first version of the Oracle ERP applications to be accepted as Y2K-compliant. Oracle maintains an extensive Web site and support organization to help its customers solve date problems with their ERP applications.

ERP ADVANTAGES DRIVE IMPLEMENTATION PROJECTS

Companies implement ERP systems for many tangible, intangible, and strategic reasons. Many companies don't even try to calculate a total return on investment from an ERP system because there are so many intangible and strategic benefits. If you understand what you want from the new software, you might be able to obtain some of the following benefits:

- Reduce the amount invested in inventory.
- Improve worker productivity.
- Reduce processing costs per business transaction.
- Reduce the time it takes to perform a financial close and prepare financial statements.
- Reduce procurement costs.
- Install Y2K-compliant systems.
- Install systems with vendor-supported maintenance.
- Improve the scalability of business systems to support future growth.
- Upgrade systems to support globalized transactions (for example, Euro currency requirements).
- Obtain better reporting and information about your business.
- Replace a hodgepodge of old systems, and install new or improved business processes.
- Improve fiscal controls.
- Integrate and standardize processes among your business units and trading partners in your supply chain.
- Improve system performance, reliability, and fault tolerance.
- Reduce the costs of Information Technology.
- Improve order management, customer service, and on-time delivery.

ERP DISADVANTAGES MUST BE OVERCOME

However, ERP systems are not without their share of problems. ERP systems can be difficult to implement and operate. Although the odds of success have improved in the past five years, you should carefully consider the following issues as you work with ERP applications:

- Everyone in your organization from the database administrator to the receiving clerk to the CEO needs new skills to work with the new technology and business processes.

- Most companies must hire outside consultants to help accelerate and improve the implementation.

- In the early 1990s, almost half of the MRP/ERP implementation projects could be called failures. Many of these early projects were either abandoned or were finished late and over budget. An industry of software implementation specialists was created to assist businesses with implementation projects.

- Many large and costly implementation projects have produced little or no return on investment for their owners other than to solve the Y2K problem. Several companies have actually observed a reduction in productivity in the first six to twelve months after starting their new systems.

- Many companies are surprised to discover the ERP implementation wasn't just a software replacement project, but the start of a continuous process of change, evolution, and improvement.

- Many implementation team members have discovered after the ERP project is over that their old jobs either no longer exist or are dull and insignificant.

- Package software can force you to make certain choices about how your business will operate, and you might introduce some constraints on your traditional business processes.

- In the mid-1990s when customers evaluated software packages, they often selected the one with the most features. A competitive war among the ERP software vendors caused feature bloat as every possible feature and function of virtually every industry was added. The systems became a lot more flexible and capable, but many companies found themselves spending good money to turn off features or scale down systems and processes they did not need. Many users had to spend money to work around features that added overhead to their businesses.

BUSINESS ON LINE

The latest hot concept in the ERP world is the Business On Line (BOL) service model. The BOL model establishes a service provider to host your ERP applications in a centralized data center over an Internet/intranet connection for a monthly fee. Oracle has been experimenting with hosted applications for a couple of years, and in October 1999, they started launching this service so that it becomes a significant part of their future growth.

Important considerations under this model are similar to the issues and concerns you would have with any outsourcing arrangement:

- You want to make sure the application implementation meets the needs of your business.
- The support expertise of the service provider must exceed the expectations of the users.
- Data center management must be better than your own data center.
- The costs of the service must be reasonable.

When you evaluate the economics of the BOL model, compare the monthly charge per user of the BOL system to the initial investment in software, hardware, support, implementation services and the continuing costs of operating your own systems. If you have 100 users at a monthly subscription cost of $500/user, your BOL costs might be $50,000/month and might grow or shrink proportionately as your business changes. Compare that monthly charge with a $2 million up-front investment in hardware, software, and consulting, and add annual direct operating costs of $300,000+ for system administrator, support, and data center costs. Typically you must sign a multiyear deal for the BOL services, but you would pay by the month.

Oracle is committed to the success of this model and some forecasts project as much as half of revenues and future growth might come from this source. That is a big deal for a high-growth company such as Oracle. Some projections show Oracle's goal is to have 100,000 users online by the end of 2001. At 100 users per company, that would be 1,000 customers using the service.

Consider the following advantages and disadvantages when you evaluate Oracle as an Application Service Provider (ASP).

ADVANTAGES OF BUSINESS ON LINE

The advantages of the BOL model come from your relationship with Oracle Corporation and your ability to avoid the initial costs of starting up the system. Consider the following benefits of BOL.

- You know who is responsible with the single vendor solution.
- This architecture moves complexity off the desktop and on to the managed server located in a professionally managed data center.
- You avoid an investment in hardware, software, and implementation costs.
- You avoid the cost of support (which can be 20 percent of the software costs).
- You don't have to find and retain talented technical staff to run these systems.

DISADVANTAGES OF BUSINESS ON LINE

The disadvantages of the BOL model come from your relationship with Oracle Corporation and the loss of control and flexibility you need to meet current and future business requirements. Evaluate the following issues before considering the Business On Line service.

■ The solution is proprietary. If you want to rent the ERP and e-commerce applications, you must get them from Oracle.

■ Oracle is an unproven outsourcer. This is a new business for them. If they can't make their normal growth rate and profit margins, they might not sustain the business as you expect.

■ You are locked into Oracle, and it will be hard to switch vendors because you would have to switch applications, too.

■ You will be restricted to the types of extensions available. Are there additional pieces of software you need to run your business?

■ There will be little price competition or flexibility after you commit.

■ You will be locked in to a long-term contract with limited flexibility to change or terminate.

■ Application performance issues might be a concern.

■ Consider the ASP capability to implement and administer the applications.

■ When you use ASP, security concerns must be resolved. You must be sure your business data remains private and secure.

■ The ASP business model is unproven. (If it doesn't work out, where are you in three years?)

ORACLE IS A LEADING-EDGE TECHNOLOGY COMPANY

Oracle Corporation is a very successful, high-technology company. The database, programming tools, applications, services, support, and educational products from the company use modern computer hardware and software capabilities. Oracle advertises itself as the second largest software company in the world. Through its actions and alliances with other high technology companies, Oracle influences the working and computing environment for millions of users.

ATTRIBUTES

Oracle Corporation customers should understand and react to the attributes of their favorite database and ERP applications vendor. For example, in the software industry, a system might be rushed to market for competitive reasons. If the support and the quality of the product are not quite ready for release, you must deal with those problems while enjoying the improved features and performance.

RAPID GROWTH

Oracle competes aggressively and tries to grow its business rapidly. The sales force has always been considered high-powered and aggressive. Annual revenue growth for the past five years is about 35 percent, and ERP Applications and Services is a significant part of fiscal 1999's total revenue of $8.8 billion. The company strategy is aligned to take advantage of the growth in Internet technology and products.

NEW PRODUCTS AND CAPABILITIES

To sustain revenue growth rates of 30 to 40 percent, Oracle has introduced new products and services every year throughout its history. Often, the products improve dramatically over the capability of earlier versions, and the company regularly produces better-than order-of-magnitude improvements in the software performance. In 1995, 50GB was considered to be a huge Oracle ERP applications database. Now, 50GB is common, and large companies are consolidating global data centers into ERP instances ten times larger.

CONSTANT CHANGE

The technology sector is always changing, and Oracle Corporation has been the root cause of a lot of that change. Occasionally, companies such as Oracle can introduce new products and features faster than their customers can implement them. You must stay reasonably current with new releases and upgrades to the products you license.

COMPETITIVE NATURE

The ERP software vendors competed in a window of opportunity from 1994 to 1999 when most large companies replaced legacy systems and adopted the client server systems architecture. Oracle has been at the forefront of the stampede to sell loads of software, services, and education to the Fortune 1000 companies. Even though Oracle now says the client/server architecture was a flawed design, their message was quite different when they were trying to beat the competition with release 10.6 of the ERP Applications. As someone who uses packaged software to run their business, you should realize that occasionally software vendors adjust their products to meet competitive pressures. You must be prepared to deal with that change.

EXPERIMENTAL NATURE

Occasionally, products and services have been marketed and promoted before they are ready to see the light of day. More than once to close a big deal, features have been added without adequate testing. Products have been announced as "in the pipeline" simply because the competition had a similar product, feature, or service. Many long-time Oracle customers have fallen for the promise of "its in the next release"—some more than once.

Tip   If you are running a business on production software, no matter how badly you want to use the new technology, consider waiting about six months from the production release date before upgrading any Oracle software. New software is often late and, for production systems, shouldn't be considered real until it is actually shipping with production status. It will take about six months to work out the kinks and get the support staff trained. Let the implementation sites with nonproduction systems find the bugs in the new release. These rules of thumb were formulated 13 years ago when Oracle was releasing version 5.0 of the database and tools, and these rules are still appropriate today.

ADMITTING MISTAKES

Recently, Oracle has admitted several mistakes and lessons learned from the previous versions of the ERP software. These pronouncements come directly from Larry Ellison, the CEO of Oracle Corporation. Maybe admitting their mistakes over the past five years is a marketing tactic to alert the market of a major shift in direction. To properly manage your ERP system, you should understand Oracle's current direction and recent history.

THE CLIENT/SERVER MODEL IS INFERIOR TO THE INTERNET ARCHITECTURE

Oracle now clearly states the client/server architecture was a bad idea. Oracle was late with their GUI version of the software, and release 10.7 was quite a bit buggier than usual. Specifically, the client side of the software was a major problem for Oracle.

Building many high functionality systems on desktops was hard to maintain. When release 10.7 was the primary release, Oracle released the production version of the program many times. These releases were called PROD releases, and each had a number. Oracle customers updated their desktop systems regularly from release PROD8 through PROD16.1. After Oracle stopped development on release 10.7 and the PROD releases were frozen at PROD16.1, they still released many large patches to fix bugs in the individual modules.

In addition, client/server performance over wide area networks was not acceptable. The amount of data and the number of packets making round trips between the desktops and the database server were just too high to achieve good performance. The client connection could not be established over a dial-up circuit. Global companies had to establish multiple database servers to decentralize and localize the ERP software to get closer to the users.

BEST OF BREED IMPLEMENTATIONS DON'T WORK

Some companies have tried to implement best of breed modules by selecting applications from many vendors and bolting them together. Oracle supported that movement with vertical market and partner alliance initiatives. In a tightly integrated business process, that strategy can introduce many difficulties that might offset the benefits, and many companies have had mixed or unsatisfactory results. For example, you might give up a lot of benefits in payables and inventory planning if you tried to replace the Oracle Purchasing module with something less integrated by another vendor. In addition, you would be maintaining interfaces among several systems, working with multiple support organizations, and trying to coordinate differing software upgrade schedules.

However, there are several business situations that allow the profitable use of multiple vendors in your ERP system:

- A vendor might offer functionality you just can't buy from Oracle, and these extensions have just a few well-defined points of contact with the Oracle ERP systems.

- Vendor-supported software and an upgrade patch can be a better investment than modifying the Oracle programs or developing your own code to meet business requirements.

- Tools from a third-party vendor that might provide more effective and efficient administration of the system or enable users to access the data can pay for themselves at many companies.

Oracle Corporation introduced and sponsored the Cooperative Applications Initiative (CAI) program so that some standards and protocols could be established for software products that should be compatible with the Oracle applications. See Part IV of this book for additional information about the CAI vendors and their offerings.

ORACLE NEEDS TO CUT ITS COSTS

Except for an occasional opportunity, the battle is over among software vendors to win the ERP systems of the largest companies in the United States. Oracle wants to find a way to sell its products to the customer with a smaller budget and simpler requirements. In the same way, support, education, and services for its products will be streamlined, and different relationship models will be offered to the Oracle customer. The Business On Line model and rapid implementations of preconfigured modules will be used to minimize front-end investments and reduce costs for customers that can accept that level of functionality and service. Oracle forecasts that 80 percent of its products will be available via a Web store. It is hard to think of a complex and configurable system such as ERP as a commodity software package, but certain basic modules are approaching that status.

UNDERSTANDING THE ORACLE CORPORATION IMPACT ON YOU—THE CUSTOMER

Organizations allocate money and resources to change and maintain their computerized business systems in two ways, continuously and periodically. I call a company that keeps its systems and skills current with the latest technology a type one Oracle customer. I label the company that undertakes large technology projects periodically and spends only small amounts between projects a type two Oracle customer.

Your organization's spending patterns may be somewhere in between these two extremes. However, if you understand which type of customer you are, you will begin to know your relationship with Oracle Corporation.

UNDERSTANDING THE IMPACT OF ORACLE ON TYPE ONE CUSTOMERS

Type one customers invest in computer systems continuously and think of information technology as a strategic business activity. New or continuously improving systems give them a competitive edge or are strategic to the definition of the business. These companies tend to pick which technology is currently important to their business and proactively allocate budget dollars and work assignments to those activities. These companies can tolerate quite a bit of change and have a goal of continuous improvement. Change is evolutionary at the type one company.

Oracle sales and the type one customer might get along very well. The customer will be a showcase site for the latest technology and might provide enthusiastic references for the latest release of the software. The sales representative can arrange for the type one customer to participate in informal beta testing programs so the customer can experiment with the next release of the software.

Type one companies will try to employ technically aggressive people. They will set up continuing education programs to bring the targeted skills inhouse. These companies might establish the position of internal consultant to go between the information technology department and the business units. The technical people at these companies think of their users as their customers. Everyone is comfortable with continuous change and the occasional disruptions caused by new software.

The type one company will attempt every upgrade and major release of the software. They will read each statement of direction published by Oracle and eagerly anticipate using the new features and functionality. They will participate in the user group's committees to suggest ways to improve the software to Oracle Corporation. They will complain loudly when the software is late or poor in quality and affects their business.

The type one company allocates available budgets continuously across desirable technologies. Because these companies don't have unlimited funds, they pick the most important investments areas and leave the rest. Their attitude might be "last year we did ERP, and this year we will do the Internet." Because they are always improving and changing the systems to fit their needs, the type one companies might be heavily customized. These companies develop techniques for dealing with the disruptions caused by patches and new software releases.

Working with Oracle Support is a critical function at the type one company. There will be problems with new software, and problem diagnosis is an important skill to have. If you are a type one company, consider upgrading the support services that you buy.

UNDERSTANDING THE ORACLE IMPACT ON TYPE TWO CUSTOMERS

Type two customers invest in computer systems periodically and like to establish quiet periods of stability and low cost of operations between large spending projects. Type two customers often adopt a strategy of skipping every other generation of computer technology to maximize the return on investment from the previous spending program. These companies tend to think of information technology as a necessary but burdensome expense to be controlled and minimized. For example, these companies might be thankful they stayed away from that "horribly expensive client/server mess," and now, they are ideally positioned to replace their aging systems with a model based on the Internet. Or, these companies are thankful they implemented great new ERP systems in the previous two years, but they are pretty sure their company doesn't have to become a dot-com company, and they can rest comfortably for the next year on release 10.7 of the Oracle Applications.

Type two customers are only in phase with the standard Oracle marketing program when they are in their heavy spending cycle and will lose contact with Oracle sales during their stability cycle. Larry Ellison, the Oracle CEO and industry visionary, has a message for business in late 1999 that the Internet changes everything and you must throw away everything in IT to survive. The type two customers that just finished a big ERP implementation project will not feel the need to follow Mr. Ellison's leadership. These companies want to gain the benefits of the systems they just installed.

Type two companies implement systems with relatively large, periodic projects. Change is revolutionary at these companies. Typically, change happens when the cost of doing nothing is greater than the cost of the project. When the project is completed, change activity diminishes, and stability and cost management becomes important.

The type two company will disband its implementation team and send the key project team members back to their operating departments. If the project was successful, the project team members often will have added responsibility and career enhancement. They might become the power users and might be the key people who now know how the business is supposed to operate with the new software and business processes.

An employee of a type two company who really wants to work for a type one company will often leave the company when the implementation project finishes. Other companies that are about to start implementations, consulting firms, and Oracle Corporation itself will happily hire these former implementation team members who don't want to go back to their old jobs after a year of hard work on an ERP project.

Upgrades and new software releases are troublesome for the type two company because they can destabilize the production systems, and everyone who should test the new release is busy with their primary responsibility to run the business.

Tip

It is very important to stay reasonably current on major releases of the ERP applications, the operating system, and the database. If you get too far behind, you might find yourself forced into an upgrade project without the funding, people, or support from senior management. You can plan to skip release 11 and stay on release 10.7 of the applications until release 11i is stable, but you must plan to upgrade to something before the support on release 10.7 runs out in June 2001.

When you upgrade, you must almost always pay more money to someone. It is wise to plan for these expenses and set management's expectations that it can't be avoided. Oracle

Corporation doesn't always get your money unless you buy more products, use their services, or attend their education classes. However, the upgrade will utilize new technology, and you must change the system to accommodate the new release. For example, the R10.6 upgrade sold a lot of disks. The upgrade to R10.7SC required lots of desktop memory and many customers had to buy 17-inch monitors for their users. R11 requires many customers to upgrade their desktop processor speeds. Depending on your level of customization, all these upgrades might have required you to engage outside consulting help. Paying for Oracle support gets you the upgrade software, but you must set the type two company management's expectations for other expenses to fully maintain the Oracle ERP system.

At the type two company, use of Oracle Support is mostly for maintenance, access to required patches (such as Y2K), and a way to prepay for the next release of the software. The main desire is to avoid destabilizing the production systems and avoid all the testing to certify new patches and upgrades. If the type two company upgraded to premium support during the implementation of the system, they can consider capturing a cost reduction by falling back to the basic pricing plan after the project is completed.

In Summary

Enterprise Resource Planning systems are complex, configurable, flexible, and tightly integrated. You can purchase additional software to extend your ERP system from non-Oracle vendors in the Cooperative Applications Initiative program. You can achieve substantial strategic, tangible, and intangible advantages to your business by implementing these systems, but you must overcome the disadvantages.

Oracle Corporation is a really great technology company, and they have highly functional and popular software. This book is generally quite positive about the Oracle ERP software, and most Oracle customers are quite satisfied. However, ERP systems and their vendors can dramatically affect your business, and when appropriate, we will try to alert you to risks, problems, solutions, and opportunities.

Most companies are not 100 percent type one or type two in their orientation toward Oracle technology. However, it helps to know the predisposition of your management. Your company's orientation might affect the way you view the rest of this book.

In the next chapter, we will investigate the specific features and capabilities of the Oracle ERP applications.

CHAPTER 2

THE ORACLE APPLICATIONS

In this chapter, I introduce the Oracle Applications. If you are an experienced user, you can proceed directly to the chapters that interest you. If you are new to the subject, however, read this chapter to understand what kinds of business functions are available and how the Oracle Applications might meet your business requirements.

The Oracle Enterprise Resource Planning (ERP) applications are really an integrated suite of modules identified by major business function. The applications discussed in this book are online transaction processing (OLTP) applications. For example, the Receivables application is designed to bill customers, collect cash, and keep track of what amounts are owed to your company. Most functions are designed to enable you to continuously interact with the system and perform the transactions of your business. Most reports are designed to list what transactions were made, control your processes, and show what balances remain after the transaction is made.

The customer base of Oracle Applications users numbers over 8,000 sites in more than 60 countries. Over 8,000 users attend one or both of the Oracle Applications User Group (OAUG) conferences each year. The business grows about 40 percent per year.

The breadth and depth of the Applications is too great for any one book or any one user to deal with completely. For example, if you ordered a complete set of user guides, technical reference manuals, installation manuals, and upgrade manuals for all the applications, you could easily fill 15 feet of bookshelf space. If you install all the applications discussed in this book, your database might have over 20,000 objects in it. It would take you several years to understand it all, and by that time, Oracle will have released new versions and your business will have changed.

Because this is a big and complex set of modules, one of our biggest challenges when writing this book was to present the right amount of information about each topic and to limit the scope so that it would all fit in one desktop reference manual. To meet that challenge, we made some hard choices, and many topics you might find interesting had to be cut. Some applications are not present at all. For example, the Project Accounting application would have easily required 80+ pages. Also, the process manufacturing (OPM) and customer relationship management (CRM)applications are real software, but they are going through rapid and radical changes as Oracle develops these new modules. Finally, in the space allowed, we found we couldn't cover the many tightly focused applications for everything from quality to salesman compensation. For this book, we pruned the topics we could reasonably cover to four broad, core areas:

- Financial applications
- Manufacturing applications
- Supply chain management applications
- Human resource management systems

As this chapter is being written in November 1999, the vast majority of the installed Oracle customer base is running their businesses on some version of release 10.7 of the Applications. This release is promised to be Y2K-compliant and represents the end of the evolution of the client/server and server-only ERP systems that Oracle delivered from 1994 through 1999. Release 10.7 was issued in three different architectures:

- Server only. Character user interface
- Smart Client. Client/server architecture with graphical user interface
- Network Computing Architecture. Multiserver and thin graphical client

Looking forward, the current production version of the software is called release 11 of the Oracle Applications, and this version is available only in the Network Computing Architecture. The year 2000 should be a big upgrade and improvement year for most Oracle customers, and we hope this book will help you implement or upgrade to release 11 of the software.

FINANCIAL APPLICATIONS

The financial applications of the Oracle ERP suite of applications are the General Ledger and the subledgers. The financial applications discussed in this book include the following (the common shorthand abbreviation is shown in parentheses):

- General Ledger (GL)
- Accounts Payable (AP)
- Accounts Receivable (AR)
- Fixed Assets (FA)

In addition, the Inventory (INV), Cost Management (CST), and Purchasing (PO) applications can also make journal entries in the General Ledger, but these applications are more properly classified as manufacturing or distribution applications.

The General Ledger provides the capability for multiple sets of books and supports complex enterprise organizations. The General Ledger hosts the subledgers and provides the definition of the chart of accounts structure, a fiscal calendar, and a currency. Because the GL and FA applications can support multiple sets of books and the other financial applications can support multiple organizations, you can set up separate and fully functional accounting systems for each of your business organizations.

GENERAL LEDGER

The General Ledger (GL) application is the foundation for a full-featured accounting system. The GL receives journal entries from the Oracle subledgers and has an open interface for incoming journal entries from non-Oracle systems. We discuss this application in detail in Chapter 11, "Using Oracle General Ledger." Although not strictly part of the GL application, the Application Desktop Integrator (ADI) for GL enables you to perform reporting, journal entry, and budgeting functions while using an Excel spreadsheet interface. The GL application provides you with the following major business functions:

- The capability to create, change, approve, reverse, and post manual and electronic actual, statistical, and budget journal entries
- The capability to create and update budgets
- The capability to establish budgetary control and online funds checking
- Accounting for multiple companies
- Consolidation of multiple sets of books
- Financial reporting writing through the Financial Statement Generator (FSG) and the Application Desktop Interface (ADI)
- Fiscal calendar and chart of accounts maintenance
- Currency transactions, conversion, translation, and revaluation

PAYABLES

Use Oracle Payables (AP) to control and process your payments for purchases of goods and services, employee expense reports, taxes, rents, and so forth. The release 11 version of this application provides two user workbench environments for invoice and payment processing. The manual invoice entry screens can be set up for high-speed data entry. The AP application is a subledger to the GL, and it is tightly integrated and shares data with the purchasing application. There are 41 steps to set up and configure the AP application in release 11, and we discuss the following features of AP in Chapter 12, "Using Oracle Payables":

- The capability to set up and maintain supplier records
- Electronic and manual invoice entry
- Expense report processing
- The capability to create and maintain invoice holds and payment schedules
- Cash disbursements for checks and electronic transfers
- Accounting distributions
- Two-, three-, and four-way invoice matching and validation with purchase orders and receipts
- Sales tax and VAT processing
- Expense and disbursements journal entries to GL
- Foreign currency transactions
- Bank transaction reconciliation

RECEIVABLES

Use the Oracle Receivables (AR) application to recognize revenue, process cash receipts, and collect money that is owed to you. A user workbench is provided for each of these three functions. In addition, there are manual and automatic versions of programs to support billing and cash receipt transactions. The AR application is a subledger to the GL, and it is closely integrated and shares data with the Order Entry (OE) application. There are 52 setup steps to configure the release 11 AR application. You will find a discussion of these functions in Chapter 13, "Using Oracle Receivables":

- The capability to set up and maintain customer records
- The capability to process cash receipt transactions
- The capability to support collection activities with call history, statements, and dunning letters
- The capability to create and maintain revenue and adjustment transactions
- Accounting distributions
- Revenue and cash receipt journal entries to GL
- Foreign currency transactions
- The capability to archive and purge

FIXED ASSETS

The Fixed Assets (FA) application can be set up to maintain asset records and process transactions using three workbenches for assets, mass additions, and tax. FA is a subledger to the GL. There are 29 setup steps to configure the release 11 FA application, and we discuss this application in Chapter 14, "Using Oracle Assets":

- The capability to create, maintain, and retire fixed asset records
- Asset physical inventory
- The capability to compute and maintain depreciation calculations
- Depreciation and asset transaction journal entries to GL
- Tax accounting
- Capital budgeting
- Asset listings and construction in progress reports

MANUFACTURING APPLICATIONS

The Oracle manufacturing applications are used to define and value the items you produce. In addition, these applications help you plan, schedule, track progress, and manage the production process. These applications are closely integrated with the financial and supply-chain applications. These applications are at the center of your supply chain and are almost always implemented with the Oracle financial and supply-chain applications. The manufacturing applications include the following:

- Bills of Material (BOM) and Engineering (ENG)
- Work in Process (WIP)

- Cost Management (CST)
- Material Requirements Planning (MRP), Master Production Scheduling (MPS), and Capacity Planning (CPP)

BILLS OF MATERIAL AND ENGINEERING

The Bill of Material (BOM) and Engineering (ENG) applications maintain and control the specifications of your product structure and process information for products. Although these applications are relatively easy to configure, the Bills and Routings are at the heart of the planning, scheduling, and costing processes. You will want to make sure this foundation data is complete and accurate. In release 11, there are 19 tasks to configure BOM and 9 steps to set up the ENG application. We discuss these functions of BOM and ENG in detail in Chapter 18, "Using Oracle Engineering and BOM":

- The capability to create and maintain bills of material
- The capability to create and maintain manufacturing process routings
- Flow manufacturing specifications
- The capability to configure to order definition and maintenance
- Scheduling and lead-time definition and maintenance
- Engineering change orders
- Engineering prototypes

WORK IN PROCESS

The Work in Process (WIP) application supports the actual manufacturing process on the shop floor. In your factory, WIP can support combinations of discrete, repetitive, assemble to order, and work orderless manufacturing methods. There are 11 configuration tasks to set up the WIP Application. We discuss this application in Chapter 21, "Using Oracle Work in Process." The following are the main features of WIP:

- The capability to create and maintain discrete jobs
- Flow manufacturing
- The capability to create and maintain repetitive schedules
- Material control and management
- Shop floor control and transactions
- Resource management
- Job status controls
- Costing, valuation, and variances from standard
- Shop floor scheduling
- Outside processing

COST MANAGEMENT

The Cost Management (CST) application provides a full absorption-cost accounting system for use by the Inventory, Work in Process, Purchasing, and Order Entry applications. CST calculates the values and variances of each transaction and keeps a current, perpetual valuation for each item inventory balance. There are 11 setup steps you should evaluate to set up CST. You will find more details about the following topics in Chapter 19, "Using Oracle Cost Management":

- Standard, average, and activity-based costing
- The capability to create and maintain item costs by cost element and sub-element
- Bill of material cost rollup by cost type
- Inventory transaction costing
- Work in Process costing (perpetual balances and transactions)
- Revaluation for cost changes
- Valuation of perpetual inventory balances
- Project and flow manufacturing
- WIP and INV transaction and variance journal entries to GL

PLANNING

The Material Requirements Planning (MRP), Master Production Scheduling (MPS), and Capacity Planning (CPP) applications support the manufacturing planning process. The planning process attempts to balance the supply and demand for item components and products in your supply chain of vendors, factories, inventories, and customers. See Chapter 20, "Using Oracle Planning Applications," for information on these topics:

- Forecasting and management of product demand
- The capability to simulate supply and demand scenarios
- The capability to create and maintain master demand and production schedules
- The capability to generate and maintain material requirements plans
- Supply-chain planning
- The capability to create and maintain aggregate production plans
- Rough-cut capacity planning
- Planner workbench
- Demand classes
- Time fence control and planning
- Repetitive planning
- Two-level master scheduling for key sub assemblies and configure to order final assemblies
- Kanban planning

SUPPLY CHAIN MANAGEMENT APPLICATIONS

The supply-chain management applications are used for procurement, inventory, and customer fulfillment processes. These applications were called the distribution applications in release 10 of the applications and include the following:

- Purchasing (PO)
- Order Entry (OE)
- Inventory (INV)

PURCHASING

The Purchasing (PO) application is used to buy and receive all sorts of goods and services to supply the needs of your business and customers. The planning applications can make integrated requisitions for required items, and manual requisitions can procure other items, supplies, or services. The PO application is tightly integrated with Accounts Payable, Material Requirements Planning, and Inventory. There are 30 setup tasks to accomplish when you configure the PO application. We discuss these features of PO in Chapter 15, "Using Oracle Purchasing":

- The capability to create and maintain purchase requisitions
- The capability to create, source, and maintain purchase orders
- The capability to create and maintain requests for proposals and requests for quotations
- Document approval and control
- Receiving and inspection
- Returns to vendors
- Accrued receipts transactions and price variance journal entries to GL

ORDER ENTRY

The Order Entry (OE) application is the cornerstone of the customer fulfillment and customer service process. In the planning process, OE is the primary source of demand for your goods and services. This application is tightly integrated with AR to recognize revenue for shipments and control the extension of credit to your customers. There are 32 setup steps to consider when you configure the OE application. See Chapter 17, "Using Oracle Order Entry and Shipping," for information on these topics:

- The capability to create and maintain customer records
- The capability to create and maintain sales orders
- The capability to create and maintain pricing and customer discounts
- The capability to plan, pick, pack, and ship deliveries for order fulfillment
- The capability to return material authorization

- The capability to interface shipped transactions to Oracle AR
- The capability to control orders with multiple holds and credit check from Oracle AR

INVENTORY

The inventory (INV) application is an important application for the manufacturing and supply-chain management activities of the ERP system. The INV application is closely integrated with the GL, PO, MRP, BOM, WIP, CST, OE, and AR applications, and there are 53 setup tasks to perform when configuring a release 11 INV module for your business. Chapter 16, "Using Oracle Inventory," has a discussion of these features of the INV application:

- Item master and inventory organization structure definition
- Inventory transactions for customer returns, inspection, transfers among subinventories, transfers among organizations, and miscellaneous transactions
- Lot and serial number control
- The capability to maintain perpetual quantity balances and onhand availability
- Available to promise (ATP) calculations for sales order schedules
- Value of transactions journal entry to GL
- ABC Analysis
- Multiple item category groups and catalogs
- Cycle counting and physical inventory controls
- Min-max planning and purchase requisitioning for resupply

HUMAN RESOURCES APPLICATIONS

This book discusses the Human Resource (HR) and Payroll (PAY) applications of Oracle release 11. These two applications were developed after the Financial and Manufacturing applications, and they are now achieving the stability and robust functionality of a mature set of products. The HR and PAY applications are complex and somewhat difficult to implement because of their technology and your business requirements for extreme flexibility and accuracy. Your organization has a unique culture, and the relationships with its people are governed by a combination of company policies, laws, regulations, and industry dynamics. These Oracle applications provide a core system to support the basic elements, but you might have to customize them to meet your unique requirements.

HUMAN RESOURCES MANAGEMENT SYSTEMS

The Human Resources (HR) application enables you to build an information model to represent your business organizations, pay and benefit policies, and people in a system that can be used to support the payroll process and manage the human resource business functions. We discuss this application and the following features in Chapters 24,

"Implementing Oracle Human Resources and Oracle Payroll," and 25, "Using Oracle Human Resources":

- The capability to create and maintain employee (and applicant) records by date through the full cycle of hiring, employment, and termination
- The capability to create and maintain employer and other organizations for the enterprise organization model
- The capability to maintain jobs and positions
- The capability to maintain and manage pay grades
- The capability to create and maintain elements for compensation and benefits
- The capability to administrate salaries, budgets, and labor costs
- The capability to manage benefit programs
- Labor costs journal entry to GL
- Recruitment, selection, and hiring
- Reporting required by the government
- Career path management and competency tracking
- Assessments and appraisals
- The capability to match people and enterprise requirements
- Absence and paid time-off administration
- Event administration

PAYROLL

The Payroll (PAY) application is much more than just paying people for hours worked or services performed. This application builds on the information model of the HR application to support the key management and administrative processes of compensating your people. We discuss the implementation, configuration, and operation of the following Payroll application functions in Chapters 24, "Implementing Oracle Human Resources and Oracle Payroll," and 26, "Using Oracle Payroll":

- Absence and attendance
- Compensation
- Benefits
- Wage attachments
- Taxes
- Tax and wage reporting
- Worker's compensation administration
- Payroll runtime processing, corrections, and adjustments

OTHER APPLICATION FEATURES

In addition to the individual applications modules, there are four major topics you will want to understand:

- Workflow
- Multi-org
- System administration
- Applications of the vendors in the Cooperative Applications Initiative

These additional topics add many features and capabilities to the Oracle ERP system, and in release 11 of the applications, these features are an integral part of your system.

WORKFLOW

The Workflow application helps you manage business processes. For example, in the GL application, there is a new Approve Journal Entry process using an approval hierarchy and limits that can be implemented. The Workflow system uses the approval hierarchy and money limits to route journal entries to the appropriate user before posting. If you need to modify the Workflow definitions embedded within the applications, you can do so, but if you want to write new Workflow process definitions, you must license the Workflow application software from Oracle.

You can provide additional logic and process steps based on your business requirements. Workflow is a technical solution to a functional business process, and to implement Workflow, you will want to use both technical and functional resources.

Workflow consists of four major systems, and you will find detailed information in Chapter 22, "Using Oracle Workflow":

- Use the Workflow builder to create or modify workflow process definitions.
- The Workflow engine executes the process definitions and interacts with the Applications.
- The notifications system communicates with users by sending and receiving messages.
- The monitoring tool enables you to observe Workflow processes.

MULTI-ORG

The multi-org functions within the Oracle applications enable you to define a complex enterprise business model with many organizations. The multi-org model is important because it can affect how the business units interact with each other and how transactions flow through the enterprise. AR, OE, AP, and PO are the key applications discussed in this book that can use multi-org capabilities. The GL and FA applications implement an enterprise organization model through multiple sets of books. The manufacturing and human resources applications also implement an organization model but without using multi-org.

There are 13 steps to configuring and setting up the multi-org functions, and we discuss the features of multi-org in detail in Chapter 23, "Understanding Multi-Org":

The main features of multi-org include the following:

- Organization security and limited access through partitioned data tables.
- Intercompany AR invoice processing and accounting.
- Intercompany AP invoice processing and accounting.
- Many business units can use the same database instance.
- Support for six types of organizations, including set of books, legal entity, business group, balancing entity, operating unit, and inventory organization.
- Flexible purchasing and receiving by different legal entities.
- Flexible selling and shipping by different legal entities.

SYSTEM ADMINISTRATION

The system administration functions of the applications enable you to implement security, change user preferences, and set up batch jobs. Although a user might be able to perform many of these functions, not all users will be comfortable with the technical aspects of managing printers, menus, and concurrent processing. These functions are different from the administration tasks performed by a database administrator (DBA). Because there are important technical and security requirements for the system administration functions, realize that most users should not have access to this part of the system and consider carefully how you assign staff to these functions.

There are 11 setup tasks you should consider early in your implementation project, and we discuss system administration in detail in Chapter 27, "Administering the Oracle Applications." The system administration functions include the capability to do the following:

- Define security and access for the ERP applications.
- Create and maintain profile options and preferences.
- Extend the online HTML help for local policies and procedures.
- Manage concurrent processing of batch programs.
- Customize menus and interactive navigation paths for users.
- Set up and maintain printers.

CAI APPLICATIONS EXTENSIONS

The Cooperative Applications Initiative (CAI) is an organization of vendors that provide software that is compatible with the Oracle applications. When Oracle added approximately 30 Application Program Interfaces (APIs) to the first releases of release 10.x of the applications in 1994, it started a small industry of software companies that built extensions and enhancements to the core functionality provided by Oracle.

Note

Implementing "best of breed" software from many vendors is hard to do, and the compatibility among CAI solutions varies in robustness from one vendor to the next. Although Oracle does have certification standards for software and vendors to belong to the CAI program, don't assume this certification translates to automatic or even easy implementation. A multivendor implementation still produces issues with support, process flow, documentation, and so forth.

If you spent your entire software budget with Oracle Corporation and if you have no gaps in functionality, you can skip to the next chapter. But, if you have some money left and business requirements beyond the functionality you get from Oracle, consider the CAI extensions discussed in Chapter 30, "Alliance Partners." These extensions are grouped into the following major categories:

- Administration Utilities
- Implementation and Interface Tools
- Asset Management
- Business to Consumer Commerce
- Electronic Commerce and Electronic Data Interchange
- Global Commerce and Import/Export
- Data Collection and Bar Codes
- Expense Management
- Document Management and Workflow
- Payroll Processing
- Treasury Management
- Project Management
- Engineering Management
- Quality Management
- Taxation
- Automotive Industry
- Planning and Supply-Chain Management
- Warehouse and Distribution Management
- Reporting Enhancements and Business Intelligence
- Printing and Output Enhancement

SUMMARY

Therefore, the Oracle ERP Applications are a suite of modules that can provide your organization with robust transaction processing capability for accounting, distribution, manufacturing, and human resources business requirements. This chapter contains information about the high-level capabilities of the applications. If you are interested in application implementation techniques, please continue reading in Part III. If you need to understand more details about a specific business function, you will find a chapter on each application in Part IV of this book.

PART **II**

Implementing the Oracle Applications

SOFTWARE IMP METHODS

In this section of the book, we discuss techniques for implementing the Oracle Applications. This chapter discusses general strategies and differences of various implementation methods. In other chapters in this section, you will read about the following topics:

- Factors affecting how much your project will cost and how much effort it will take.
- Techniques for project management and control.
- Planning project tasks and scope definitions.
- Analysis techniques for your business and technical systems.
- Designing ERP solutions for your business.
- Techniques to enable the system.
- Managing change, migrating from old to new systems, and supporting users after your systems go live.

USING ORACLE'S APPLICATION IMPLEMENTATION METHOD (AIM)

Oracle Corporation formalized an Application Implementation Method (AIM) in 1994 to support its rapidly growing consulting organization and the first shipments of release 10 of the Applications. Prior to AIM, Oracle consultants used something called Application Implementation Plan (AIP) for release 9 implementation projects. Because AIP was really nothing more than a huge list of project tasks, AIM was a big improvement. AIM provided the Oracle consultant with an integrated set of templates, procedures, PowerPoint presentations, spreadsheets, and project plans for implementing the applications. AIM was such a success, Oracle created a subset of the templates, called it AIM Advantage, and made it available as a product to customers and other consulting firms. Since its initial release, AIM has been revised and improved several times with new templates and improved methods.

AIM IS A SIX-PHASE METHOD

Because the Oracle ERP Applications are software modules you buy from a vendor, you will use different implementation methods than the techniques you use for custom developed systems that you get from your information technology department. AIM has six major phases:

- During the *Definition* phase, you plan the project, determine business objectives, and verify the feasibility of the project for given time, resource, and budget limits.
- The *Operations Analysis* phase documents business requirements, gaps in the software, and system architecture requirements. Results of the analysis should result in a proposal for future business processes, a technical architecture model, an application architecture model, workarounds for application gaps, performance testing models, and a transition strategy to migrate to the new systems.

- The *Solution Design* phase is used to create designs for solutions that meet future business requirements and processes.

- Coding and testing of customizations, enhancements, interfaces, and data conversions happens during the *Build* phase of AIM. In addition, one or more conference room pilots test the integrated enterprise system. The results of the build phase should be a working, tested business system solution.

- During the *Transition* phase, the project team delivers the finished solution to the enterprise. End user training and support, management of change, and data conversions are major activities of this phase.

- The *Production* phase starts when the system goes live. Technical people work to stabilize and maintain the system under full transaction loads. Users and the implementation team begin a series of refinements to minimize unfavorable impacts and realize the business objectives identified in the definition phase.

> **Note**
>
> AIM tends to create large and robust project plans that are suitable for complex enterprises. Because large and robust also means costly, we discuss a modified and more reasonable version of implementation methods later in Part II of the book. The basic methods are suitable for most implementations.

DEFINED DELIVERABLES

AIM has a defined set of project tasks, and each task has one or more deliverable results. Each deliverable document has a template with some form and content, and there is a standard style to give a consistent look and feel to the templates. If you do a good job of completing the deliverables, you will have a well-documented project library.

> **Tip**
>
> Many of the deliverable documents build on each other to produce a solution. For example, analysis documents drive design, build, transition, and production project activities. Try not to skip deliverables if they are required by other project activities.

ADVANTAGES OF AIM

AIM was a great thing when it was first released in 1994. Oracle consultants took to it like a drowning man grabs for a life preserver. Since that time, Oracle has improved the product several times, and thousands of consultants have learned basic packaged software implementation techniques. Consider using AIM to gain these advantages:

- The method is usually successful and reduces the risk of an ERP project.

- AIM is a good roadmap for inexperienced customers and consultants.

- Complex projects are supported.

- Communication among project team resources is improved through the project library, presentations, and integrated activities.

- The documentation is a good source of reference for future upgrades and customizations.

- The templates look professional.

- AIM is based on the familiar MS Office suite of products.

DISADVANTAGES OF AIM

It is hard to say much that is bad about AIM. On balance, the advantages outweigh the disadvantages. However, like any tool, you can misuse it and get less than great results. Consider the following before automatically selecting this method for your project:

- AIM produces a relatively high-cost project plan.

- Several activities are appropriate only for complex projects. It takes a skilled practitioner to know how to scale AIM down for the less demanding situation.

- Like any tool, you must learn how to use AIM techniques. You can't get great results if you try to skip the learning curve. Early in the project, you must learn how to use the method and approve the deliverables.

- Many AIM deliverables are required and not flexible because they are needed for downstream activities.

- Skipping or poor execution of a required deliverable can throw off dependent project activities.

- AIM does not help you find bugs in the software, diagnose problems with the software, or learn how to work with Oracle support.

UNDERSTANDING RAPID IMPLEMENTATIONS

In the late 1990s as Y2K approached, customers demanded and consulting firms discovered faster ways to implement packaged software applications. The rapid implementation became possible for certain types of customers. The events that converged in the late 1990s to provide faster implementations include the following:

- Many smaller companies couldn't afford the big ERP project. If the software vendors and consulting firms were going to sell to the "middle market" companies, they had to develop more efficient methods.

- The functionality of the software improved a lot, many gaps were eliminated, and more companies could implement with fewer customizations.

- After the big, complex companies implemented their ERP systems, the typical implementation became less difficult.

- The number of skilled consultants and project managers increased significantly.
- Other software vendors started packaging preprogrammed integration points to the Oracle ERP modules.

> **Note**
>
> A rapid implementation of five basic financial applications using preconfigured modules and predefined business processes for 30 to 50 users can still take three or four months. When you add the manufacturing applications, rapid means six months.

DESCRIPTION OF RAPID IMPLEMENTATION TECHNIQUES

Rapid implementations focus on delivering a predefined set of functionality. A key set of business processes is installed in a standard way to accelerate the implementation schedule. These projects benefit from the use of preconfigured modules and predefined business processes. You get to reuse the analysis and integration testing from other implementations, and you agree to ignore all gaps by modifying your business to fit the software. Typically, the enterprise will be allowed some control over key decisions such as the structure of the chart of accounts. Fixed budgets are set for training, production support, and data conversions.

PART

II

CH

3

> **Note**
>
> There is an important difference between the terms *preconfigured module* and *vanilla implementation*. In a vanilla implementation, you analyze and choose your configuration parameters to use any or all of the software functionality without customization. In the preconfigured method, you gain speed by accepting a basic configuration and predefined business processes.

> **Tip**
>
> Faster implementations usually mean lower costs. If you use an experienced team of consultants, the critical factor to the speed of your implementation is probably the ability of your organization to absorb change.

ADVANTAGES

For certain customers, the rapid implementation of preconfigured modules and predefined business processes, has several advantages:

- The business can start to realize ERP benefits quickly.
- The Oracle customer will have to spend less staff time on project. This can be a big plus if the project team can't get away from their regular job assignments.
- There might be fewer business disruptions during the implementation project.

- Decisions are made quickly.
- Rapidly implemented projects can cost less.

DISADVANTAGES

When using this project method, the disadvantages often outweigh the advantages for some customers. If you are inexperienced with the Oracle software, you might be unable to predict the changes that a rapid implementation will have on important aspects of your business. Consider the following items:

- You will not have the time to customize or make interfaces to the ERP software to support your business processes the way you need them.
- If end-users cannot or will not receive changes at the rapid implementation pace, your business processes might become unstable or uncoordinated.
- Certain aspects of your corporate strategy might have to change to fit the predefined processes. Consider the effects of the software on your customers, employees, and vendors. For example, are you prepared to change your product pricing formulas and salesman compensation programs? Can you visualize how your factory will run with the news software?
- Even when the implementation project ends, end users and technical people will not understand the full capabilities of the system.
- These techniques are only appropriate for small groups of users (20 to 80 users).
- The rapid implementation might require a core group of senior people to participate and to make decisions quickly.
- This project method might require higher up-front costs over the phased implementation.
- To implement effectively, you must have good understanding of your business processes and the software capability.
- The information technology department might not have the skills to support the production software when the system is ready to go live.
- There might be more business disruptions after the system goes live.

UNDERSTANDING THE PROGRAM OFFICE

The program office method can be used in very complex situations to coordinate, control, and manage many parallel implementation projects. Using this method, the program office staff performs certain implementation tasks at an enterprise level and then issues requirements to the subprojects at each site. For example, the program office often creates a global chart of accounts and requires each business unit to translate and convert the various legacy general ledgers to the new corporate standard chart.

Typically, the program office is interested in the definition of all Key Flexfields, the definition of some of the Descriptive Flexfields, implementation of corporate policy, audit requirements, intercompany transactions, and the centralized business processes. The program office might also control the budget and master schedule for all the subprojects. Often, the program office allows local autonomy to the individual site projects for testing, end user training, data conversions, interfaces, customizations, and configuration of system parameters that support local functions or never cross organization boundaries.

Also, the program office project team monitors the local activities and deliverables of the individual subprojects. The goal of this activity is to facilitate the flow of coding and knowledge among the subprojects. For example, if one site develops a customization, the program office knows which of the other subprojects have the same requirement and are interested in the work. The program office makes the customization available to the other sites through a centralized library of project deliverables.

ADVANTAGES

The advantages of the program office method come primarily in project efficiency and control. Often, the centralized project team can accomplish centralized tasks and give the results to the subprojects. Consider the following:

- The program office method can reduce total implementation costs by 20 to 30 percent.
- The program office can consolidate buying power for enterprisewide software licenses.
- Enterprise configuration parameters are established in a uniform way.
- Many project tasks are performed only one time.
- Corporate policies and procedures can be consistently established and enforced by the new software configuration.
- The business rules for intercompany transactions are clearly defined and rationalized.
- Senior management can become involved in important aspects of the ERP software.

DISADVANTAGES

The disadvantages of program office techniques are related to the top-down nature of the method and include the following items:

- Sometimes, the program office compromises on the lowest common denominator for a configuration decision. Many sites perceive a gap relative to their specific local requirements and the enterprise configuration. The subprojects spend time and money to customize the applications or work around the gap created by the program office.
- The implementation team members in subprojects often resent the controls and decisions of the centralized authority.

- Because each site has an active implementation subproject, staff requirements and costs are still very large.
- The analysis phase of the program office can take a very long time.
- Program office project team members must travel a lot.

UNDERSTANDING PHASED IMPLEMENTATIONS

Phased implementations seek to break up the work of an ERP implementation project. This technique can make the system more manageable and reduce risks to the enterprise. In the mid-1990s, four or five was about the maximum number of application modules that could be launched into production at one time. If you bought 12 or 13 applications, there would be a financial phase that would be followed by phases for the distribution and manufacturing applications. As implementation techniques improved and Y2K pressures grew in the late 1990s, more and more companies started launching most of their applications at the same time. This method became known as the big bang approach. Now, each company selects a phased or big bang approach based on its individual requirements.

Another approach to phasing can be employed by companies with business units at multiple sites. With this technique, one business unit is used as a template, and all applications are completely implemented in an initial phase lasting 10 to 14 months. Then, other sites implement the applications in cookie cutter fashion. The cookie cutter phases are focused on end user training and the differences that a site has from the prototype site. The cookie cutter phase can be as short as 9 to 12 weeks, and these phases can be conducted at several sites simultaneously.

For your reference, we participated in an efficient project where 13 applications were implemented big bang-style in July at the Chicago site after about 8 months work. A site in Malaysia went live in October. The Ireland site started up in November. After a holiday break, the Atlanta business unit went live in February, and the final site in China started using the applications in April. Implementing thirteen application modules at five sites in four countries in 16 months was pretty impressive.

ADVANTAGES

There are several advantages to the phased implementation over the all-at-once approach:

- The enterprise is in control of how much change it must absorb at one time.
- Typically, a phased implementation has less risk than the big bang approach because problems can be isolated and complexity is reduced.
- Phases can be scheduled so new software is not going live during the busy season of the business.
- Lessons learned, project materials, and deliverables from early phases can be applied to later phases to improve performance.

- Because the user population and transaction volume grows at a slower rate, the technical infrastructure can be developed more precisely over a longer period.

- The core implementation team doesn't have to do all the work when using the cookie cutter approach. Power users from the first sites can assist with subsequent implementations. Key users at unimplemented sites can observe and learn about the production software from the already implemented locations.

- The big bang approach takes more training and coordination during the transition phase as the new systems are about to be launched. With the big bang method, it is hard to predict which groups of users will have problems with the new software and what affect those problems will have on the integrated system.

DISADVANTAGES

The phased implementation technique has a few disadvantages compared with the big bang method:

- Phased implementations can cost more and take longer to complete.

- Returns on the investment in ERP software are slower to develop.

- Oracle can release new software while the company is between phases. An upgrade might become required before a new phase can start.

- The phased approach might require creation of temporary interfaces between the Oracle system and the legacy system. As the system is completed, these temporary interfaces are thrown away.

- If any of the sites goes poorly, word will quickly spread, and the project team will have a credibility problem and a rough time when they start work on the next site.

CASE STUDIES ILLUSTRATING IMPLEMENTATION TECHNIQUES

Some practical examples from the real world might help to illustrate some of the principles and techniques of various software implementation methods. These case studies are composites from about 40 different implementation projects we have observed during the past seven years.

BIG COMPANIES

We have observed both extremely efficient and almost totally dysfunctional big company implementations of the ERP software. Each big company project is unique and has special needs. To meet those needs, the big company project manager can construct a customized project plan and implementation method to fit the situation. Phased implementations work well at big companies because it is hard to coordinate many complicated modules or handle the logistics of many sites. Sometimes the financial applications are implemented in the first phase followed by phases for distribution, manufacturing, and payroll applications.

Sometimes all the applications are implemented at one site, and each site becomes a subsequent cookie cutter implementation project.

Big companies often have a horrible time resolving issues and deciding on configuration parameters because there is so much money involved and each of many sites might want to control decisions about what it considers its critical success factors. For example, we once saw a large company argue for over two months about the chart of accounts structure, while eight consultants from two consulting firms tried to referee among the feuding operating units. Another large company labored for more than six months to unify a master customer list for a centralized receivables and decentralized order entry system.

Transition activities at large companies need special attention. Training end users can be a logistical challenge and can require considerable planning. For example, if you have 800 users to train and each user needs an average of three classes of two hours each and you have one month, how many classrooms and instructors do you need? Another example is that loading data from a legacy system can be a problem. If you have one million customers to load into Oracle receivables at the rate of 5,000/hour and the database administrator allows you to load 20 hours per day, you have a 10-day task. Can you imagine trying to load customers and train users on the same system during the week before going live? Now, combine those two nontrivial tasks with a hundred other transition activities.

Because they spend huge amounts of money on their ERP systems, many big companies try to optimize the systems and capture specific returns on the investment. However, sometimes companies can be incredibly insensitive and uncoordinated as they try to make money from their ERP software. For example, one business announced at the beginning of a project that the accounts payable department would be cut from 50 to 17 employees as soon as the system went live. Another company decided to centralize about 30 accounting sites into one shared service center and advised about 60 accountants that they would lose their jobs in about a year. Several of the 60 employees were offered positions on the ERP implementation team. Both of these projects encountered considerable delay and resistance by the affected users.

SMALL COMPANIES

Small companies sometimes have a hard time staffing their project implementation teams. However, at the end of the project, the implementation team members become very qualified power users of the system. Often, the team members retain their primary job responsibilities during the project and can only work on the new system part-time.

Small companies have other problems when creating an implementation team. Occasionally, the small company tries to put clerical employees on the team and they have problems with issue resolution or some of the ERP concepts. In another case, one small company didn't create the position of project manager. Each department worked on its own modules and ignored the integration points, testing, and requirements of other users. When Y2K deadlines forced the system startup, results were disastrous with a cost impact that doubled the cost of the entire project.

Project team members at small companies sometimes have a hard time relating to the cost of the implementation. We once worked with a company where the project manager (who was also the database administrator) advised me within the first hour of our meeting that he thought consulting charges of $3/minute were outrageous, and he couldn't rationalize how we could possibly make such a contribution. We agreed a consultant could not contribute $3 in value each and every minute to his project. However, when I told him we would be able to save him $10,000/week and make the difference between success and failure, he realized we should get to work.

Because the small company might be relatively simple to implement and the technical staff might be inexperienced with the database and software, it is possible that the technical staff will be on the critical path of the project. If the database administrator can't learn how to handle the production database by the time the users are ready to go live, you might need to hire some temporary help to enable the users to keep to the schedule. In addition, we often see small companies with just a single database administrator who might be working 60 or more hours per week. They feel they can't afford to have more DBAs as employees, but they don't know how to establish the right ratio of support staff to user requirements. These companies can burn out a DBA quickly and then have to deal with the problem of replacing an important skill.

GREEN FIELD COMPANIES

The green field company is just starting operations. They literally start with a green field, build a factory, hire some workers, and start production. In these companies, a small core group of key managers start everything. Typically this group is very busy because they are involved in all aspects of constructing buildings, setting up production lines, hiring and training workers, and so forth. However, the green field company has many advantages over other ERP implementations, and these factors can easily result in an implementation that is 25 percent more efficient. Even if you are an established company, consider the following to learn some of the dynamics behind how an implementation project progresses:

- Everyone is new to the company. Politics and departmental boundaries are nonexistent. Everyone's agenda is aligned toward getting the systems into production.

- Tolerance for change is high. Everything changes every week, and it is exciting, positive change. When things change, there is a sense of accomplishment. Employees expect problems, deal with them, and move on.

- Users are easy to train. They have no habits to unlearn, and they are eager to understand the systems of their new employer. User expectations of the new systems are low.

- There is no legacy system, and that means there are few data conversions and almost no interfaces. There are no spreadsheets, personal databases, and other isolated islands of computer processing on user desktops. In fact, the only other systems in the whole business might be a remote financial system at a parent company and some shop floor control systems.

- There are no favorite reports that have to be replicated in the new systems.

PUBLIC SECTOR

The public sector implementation project can have some unusual dynamics. These projects can be large and complex with significant numbers of users, transaction volumes, and requirements for server performance. Business processes are different in the public sector. Oracle has separate versions of the software and documentation for these customers, and some consultants specialize in the unique needs of the public sector.

In addition, the public sector project can have a different perspective from the commercially driven implementation. These projects are funded and therefore take on the characteristics of a fixed-price project. Also, change management techniques are important to the public sector project. Procedures and business processes can be difficult to change, and there are many issues to be resolved. Issues and configuration decisions might be addressed differently by the public sector project team. Communication is important as everyone tries to figure out how the new relationships and processes will work.

Often, the legacy system is in terrible shape. The data conversions and interfaces to and from the legacy systems might be difficult or involve significant programming. We were once asked to convert a 50,000 record file that held both vendor and customer information in the same record layout because it was really just names and addresses. About 70 percent of the required fields by Oracle Payables and Oracle Receivables weren't in the file. In another situation, the agency had no funding for laser printers and expected the ERP system to print reports on old daisy wheel printers. We calculated that some daily reports would not finish printing in less than 8 hours.

IN SUMMARY

There are different techniques that you can use to implement your Oracle ERP Applications. The Application Implementation Method developed by Oracle is a good place to start when you evaluate the methods you will use. However, each technique has its strengths and weaknesses and might be more or less appropriate for your enterprise. Your best solution might be a hybrid approach based on your unique needs.

In the remainder of this section of the book, we will discuss the principal activities and deliverables associated with each major phase of an implementation project.

CHAPTER 4

UNDERSTANDING WHAT AFFECTS THE DEGREE OF EFFORT AND COST

Packaged software implementation is expensive. However, progress is being made to lower the costs. In the past five years, consulting firms and Oracle have developed many techniques to control costs, project scope, and complexity. The cost, scope, and risk of an ERP project are directly proportional to the following items:

- The degree of business complexity.
- The number of applications to be implemented.
- The amount of extensions to the package software.
- The nature of the business processes.

There are trade-offs that you must make when implementing packaged ERP software. You can implement your software rapidly, cheaply, or fully featured. Usually, you cannot capture all three benefits at the same time. Because they do less, rapid implementations are often less expensive than full-featured, customized implementations. If the rapid implementation must also be full-featured and customized, the amount of implementation work is the same as the slower paced, full-featured implementation. There will be a large, coordinated, and expensive project team to accomplish both projects.

The project method you pick affects the costs and the skills required on the project. Oracle uses several methods including the following:

- Application Implementation Method (AIM)
- Program Office
- Rapidly Preconfigured Modules (RPM)
- Fast Forward
- Business Models

Other consulting firms have a wide assortment of work plans, templates, methods, and techniques to reduce cost and minimize the risks of these projects.

Tip

Remember, Oracle provides services to sell software. If you choose a low-cost implementation method, make sure the technique will actually work in your company. For example, the preconfigured module method might produce an inexpensive implementation, but if you require several interfaces to non-Oracle systems, you might not meet your business requirements.

To understand cost drivers, BOSS Corporation analyzed a complex project to determine what factors controlled the cost. The work plan for this project was over 1,500 consulting workdays and 4,000 client workdays. The method chosen for the project was similar to Oracle AIM. The people at BOSS looked at each task in the work plan, the cost factors controlling the task, and the number of planned days to complete the task. Then, they weighted the results to determine which factors contributed the most to implemented cost.

Because multiple factors might contribute to the cost of a single task, results add to more than 100 percent. Table 4.1 shows factors affecting the total cost.

TABLE 4.1   FACTORS AFFECTING TOTAL COST

Factor	Impact
Applications to be implemented	45%
Business complexity	40%
Customizations, interfaces, data conversion	31%
Business processes and reengineering	13%

USING THE NUMBER AND TYPE OF APPLICATIONS TO ESTIMATE COSTS

The number of applications to be implemented is the main cost driver for an ERP project. Implementation of each application is a miniproject within the main implementation project. A full suite of twelve manufacturing applications takes more work than a financial suite of a General Ledger plus three or four subledgers. The process analysis, setup, testing, training, and so forth must be done for each application.

In addition, when you implement more applications, you have more function points to interface, more interdepartmental relationships, and longer business processes. For example, a simple Payables implementation can involve more effort (and be more rewarding) if you implement it as part of a procurement system with purchasing and receiving. When you involve many business functions and processes, project management, issue resolution, and coordination take more effort.

UNDERSTANDING THE RELATIVE COMPLEXITY OF EACH APPLICATION

Some of the Oracle Applications are more difficult to implement than others, and you might have business conditions that will emphasize one of the more difficult applications. For example, if you have a million customers and generate 100,000 billing lines a day through the AR module, you will want to have a much more robust implementation effort than the typical AR project.

Table 4.2 shows typical relative weights for each application with GL and INV set to a degree of difficulty of 100. When you calculate your project work plan, allow more time and resources for the more complex applications and adjust the relative difficulty for your business requirements.

TABLE 4.2   RELATIVE DEGREES OF DIFFICULTY

Application Name	Difficulty Index
General Ledger	100
Payables	80
Purchasing	120
Receivables	90
Fixed Assets	80
Order Entry	170
Inventory	100
Bill of Material	80
Engineering	50
Master Production Scheduling	90
Material Requirements Planning	150
Capacity Planning	30
Work in Process	100
Cost Management	120
Human Resources	No Estimate
Payroll	No Estimate

Note

The HR/PAY applications are very complex and often use a different method for implementation. A complex payroll implementation can take more than five times the effort of a General Ledger. Your situation might vary.

BUSINESS SYSTEMS COMPLEXITY

The complexity of your business directly affects the effort and cost of the application's implementation. Complexity is the second most important cost driver of your ERP project. The type of industry, regulations, technology, integration, and company culture might dictate reduced flexibility and business requirements that can increase costs. Global companies with many sites using different currencies, languages, and systems have special requirements that affect costs and effort.

COUNTING THE NUMBER OF USERS AND SITES

The number of users and sites is often a good proxy to indicate complexity. The number of users involved in the project can impact the project in several ways. Costs for security, training, and support for each user are directly proportional to the number of users.

However, added users often bring additional requirements and agendas for what the new system must do. These requirements often result in extensions and customizations to the applications. A project with more end users is more costly than a project for a smaller group.

For projects with multiple sites, a program office method can coordinate common tasks across all sites. In a five-site implementation, the program office methods save about 20 percent of the costs in comparison to five separate projects.

In addition, multisite projects have technical architecture complexities that must match the application's architecture and business processes. The centralized/decentralized business model might constrain the implementation. For example, a multisite company with centralized payables and decentralized purchasing has a more complex implementation.

Understanding the Agendas of Users

Increasing the number of users and sites adds cost by increasing the number of agendas and issues to be addressed. Many users might not appreciate the software because their leaders were not on the software selection team. When the project leadership is from a specific group (MIS, accounting, or manufacturing) or from a specific site (headquarters, shared services, or plant X), the project inherits the attributes of the leadership.

Accountants seem to be more structured and therefore have an easier agenda during implementation than HR, OE, or Procurement users. Perhaps the financial applications have been around longer and have a better fit rate for most business processes because there is less variation from company to company in accounting systems as opposed to fulfillment, HR, or procurement systems.

Also, the political process of the organization can dramatically affect costs because the issue-resolution mechanism is affected. Package software can often redistribute work loads and information flows in an organization, and those users on the wrong side of the redistribution can use the political process to delay, change scope, or place additional requirements on the implementation.

Excellent executive sponsorship is the classic way to resolve issues, minimize the political process, and ensure end user cooperation with the change to new systems and procedures. If you can involve executives at a high level, you can reduce the costs of the project. Also, form a project team that can make efficient decisions and represent the full constituency of end users to resolve potential stumbling blocks.

Considering Other Types of Complexity

Complexity can also be brought to the project by requirements of trading partners, government regulations, industry practices, and so forth. You might simply have to activate more function points in the application to meet the minimum requirements of your business. Your trading partners might expect supply-chain management practices. You might want to activate lot and serial number tracking for raw materials and finished goods. Your industry might have intricate pricing mechanisms. When you know your business well, the trick to estimating the cost of complexity is to understand what the applications support and how to fill the gaps.

UNDERSTANDING THE EFFECT OF COMPLEXITY ON THE SIMPLE PROJECT

Complexity affects the simple ERP project too because Oracle has built the applications to service large organizations in many industries. The pressure to compete with SAP, PeopleSoft, and others forces features and functions into the applications that you might never use. However, you must cope with extensive documentation, configuration parameters, testing, patches, and so forth for these features that might be irrelevant to your requirements.

MINIMIZING CUSTOMIZATIONS AND EXTENSIONS TO LOWER COSTS

The third significant area of expense and effort is customizations and extensions to the applications. There are nine common types of customizations. Remember, to meet a business requirement or fill a gap, you might require several of these elemental customizations to meet a single business requirement:

- Modify a copy of an Oracle form
- Create a new form
- Modify a copy of an Oracle report
- Create a new report
- Modify an existing Oracle workflow
- Create a new program, package, workflow, or procedure
- Convert legacy or external data for import into an Oracle application
- Interface to external systems
- Create different menus
- Create tables, indexes, and other database objects to support other customizations

Tip

Many extensions have a system lifetime cost as well as an implementation cost. You will have the opportunity to revisit your extensions on virtually every upgrade or patch application to make sure they continue to work with the changes coming in from Oracle.

At the beginning of the project, prepare a list of each type of possible customization or extension by application, and use that list to control the scope of the project. As the project progresses, ask the steering committee to approve additions to the list.

Each customization should be evaluated by degree of difficulty:

- Very easy
- Easy
- Moderately difficult
- Complex

Also, each customization will have various work components: analyze, design, build, test, document, train, and so forth. Make sure you have the skills on the project team to accomplish each component and task. Estimate the effort for each work component for each customization.

AUTOMATING DATA CONVERSION WORK

Conversion of legacy data is a popular and potentially expensive implementation activity. If there is an Application Program Interface (API) for the incoming data, the task might be rated easy and built in three to five days by an experienced consultant. If there is no API, you might have to reverse engineer the applications and spend time mapping data elements. Conversions without an API are complex to build and have higher risks associated with them.

Tip

There are APIs for almost all the major data entities. If there is not an API, evaluate carefully the cost of analyzing, programming, and testing the conversion against the value of the converted data.

Another factor affecting the difficulty of data conversions is the cleanliness and consistency of the legacy data. Some very old legacy systems don't even have the minimum data fields to map to the required fields in Oracle. For example, one organization with very old and proprietary systems had vendors, customers, and employees in the same legacy data file because the data was little more than names, addresses, and phone numbers. If you must create required Oracle fields with program logic during data conversions, plan for highly complex analysis, programming, and testing activities.

Tip

It might be less expensive to clean and enhance the legacy data before converting to Oracle. A partial load combined with interactive query and field updates through Oracle forms can actually take longer than manually entering all the data through a data entry form.

Another popular data conversion technique uses a spreadsheet to organize the data from the legacy system. If you import the data into a spreadsheet, users can often clean up many records before the data are loaded into and validated by the Oracle interface programs. When the records are in spreadsheet format, you can rearrange the columns and export them as comma-separated values for easy insertion into the interface tables by the SQL*Loader utility.

> **Tip**
>
> Consider a combination of automatic and manual techniques to load a data set one time. For example, if 5,000 customers load correctly and 100 are rejected by the API validation routines, simply enter the rejected 100 records manually. Don't spend a lot of time modifying the load programs to handle the special cases that make up only a small percentage of the transactions.

INTERFACES

Interfaces can represent incoming or outgoing data from Oracle's perspective. Outgoing interfaces are like reports with a data format. Incoming interfaces are a lot like one-time legacy data conversions, except they occur many times and must be 100 percent reliable, well documented, self-balancing, and operable by users. You still have to map the foreign data elements to the Oracle data, write a loader program, prevalidate the incoming data, and run the Oracle interface programs.

REPORTS

Reporting and information processing are consistent problems for Oracle Applications projects. Users and executive sponsors expect the new database systems to give them valuable information about the business. However, the applications are mostly transaction processing systems, and stock reports are usually transaction listings, registers, journal entries, account balance listings, and so forth. Users and executive sponsors might expect more from the project.

Oracle provides a report developer, a browser, a financial statement generator, and desktop integration tools to help with reporting requirements. Other third-party vendors also have several query and output format utilities. Using these tools might provide production of a custom report in two to four days, but an ERP implementation easily might have 50 to 100+ reports. Reporting requirements can easily add 100 to 400 work days to a moderately sized project, and you should develop a strategy early in the project to manage these costs. Relying on end users to learn a reporting tool is usually a risky strategy because only about 20 percent of end users will learn the tool and almost all end users will have difficulty understanding how the Oracle Applications store the data. Many ERP projects don't address reporting requirements early enough in the work plan, and you might have to meet business requirements with expensive resources late in the project.

BUSINESS PROCESSES

Your business processes are the fourth significant contributors to effort and cost. The executive sponsor might support a no customizations (vanilla) implementation or changing the business to do it the Oracle way. Oracle Applications are designed to accommodate several business models, and a reasonable vanilla configuration might be an improvement over the legacy systems and processes.

Tip

> If you have a simple project, the key to controlling costs is to manage the ability of the organization to absorb the changes the new software will bring.

For the more complex business, a large part of the implementation process involves making decisions about configuration parameters that might then constrain other choices. When the constraints outnumber the available choices, an extension or workaround might be required, and costs increase. For example, the GL chart of accounts structure determines how much information is stored in the General Ledger, and this drives other requirements for a reporting strategy. Companies have implemented an account structure of from four to eleven segments. The longer structures might meet business requirements for reporting and budgeting, but they can cause difficulties or added complexity when configuring and operating the subledgers.

DOCUMENTING AND UNDERSTANDING PROCESSES

The implementation team must work with the applications on at least three levels: unit transactions inside one application, interfaces between applications, and enterprise integration. A clear understanding of processes facilitates the work of the implementation team because the applications often redistribute work and information throughout the organization. For example, Oracle developed the receiving function as part of the purchasing application. If the legacy system has receiving as part of the inventory, planning, or logistics process, there might be some adjustment or realignment of responsibilities in your organization. If the implementation team has a novice understanding of the new applications and the legacy processes are also not well understood, the implementation will be inefficient.

FLEXIBLE OR RIGID BUSINESS REQUIREMENTS AND PROCESSES

What is the organization's ability to absorb change? When the business is flexible, a workaround is usually cheaper to implement than customizing the applications. Are the business processes rigid because of regulations or corporate policies? Does the implementation team have the authority to make changes? Can policies be revised? Consider how the organization uses information and whether the standard reports can replace the familiar legacy reports.

OTHER PROJECTS IN PROCESS

Often, an organization has several systems projects in process at the same time. In the mid-1990s, some companies tried to implement radically reengineered processes or ISO9000 certification at the same time as an ERP project. Other projects can often change the scope, affect the resources, or complicate the ERP implementation.

NON-ORACLE APPLICATIONS

Integrating "best of breed" or non-Oracle applications into a suite of applications to service the enterprise is hard. Everything from interfaces to training requires extra effort. Legacy systems that will remain live might have a different data model. Data elements must be mapped, cleaned, documented, and tracked for the life of the system. APIs require support from the MIS department. The upgrade and patch cycle must be continually managed and tested. Finding and maintaining a compatible combination of release levels for the Oracle Applications, the non-Oracle applications, the database, the operating system, the desktops, and so forth can be quite challenging and force you to upgrade your schedules.

REENGINEERING AND BEST PRACTICES

Reengineered processes are theoretical, conceptual, and hard to understand in the context of the new ERP software. The user doesn't understand either system. When reengineering risk is transferred to the ERP implementation, the scope and risk of the ERP project increases. The decision-making process in combined projects is slower, and more time is spent in testing, pilots, and training.

ISO9000

Often, ISO9000 certification becomes a mission-critical application required for industry, corporate survival, or regulatory compliance. Documenting new procedures can take a lot of time because they are not well understood, and implementation team members might be required to serve both the ERP and the ISO9000 projects.

MERGER AND ACQUISITION ACTIVITY

Mergers and acquisitions can cause uncertainty and system integration issues for the implementation team. One company worked for about 14 months to implement Oracle at three sites and was then acquired by a firm that was implementing SAP. After 6 more months of creating interfaces and moving the work around the new organization, the acquired company started converting to SAP. You can't avoid merger and acquisitions activity when it happens, but be aware of the impact on implementation costs.

CAPABILITY OF THE PROJECT TEAM

The capability of the project team is important to the success and cost of the project, and you need an advanced level of business, technical, and project management experience. Cross-functional capability among project team members is a plus and can improve issue resolution. Try to staff the project team with the current or future leaders of the company. Sponsors are important to controlling costs, maintaining scope, and creating a sense of urgency and purpose. The project team should be able to communicate with the rest of the organization and fully represent their constituents. Get temporary outside help in areas where the project team needs experience.

Tip

> Experienced consultants are important. One large company spent approximately an extra 25 percent ($1-2 million) because their chosen consulting firm was large but had little Oracle Applications experience.

DEVELOPING THE ABILITY TO RESOLVE ISSUES

The decision-making process in some organizations can increase costs. Once, a client and two large consulting firms tied up four consultants and eight client team members for three months as they debated the structure of the chart of accounts. The real agenda was that a recently acquired business didn't want a lot of information to be stored in the GL where the parent could run reports and comparative analysis. Definition of the issue is 90 percent of the resolution.

Issues should be logged, tracked, and escalated when they become critical to progress. Issues can be functional, technical, procedural, managerial, political, and so forth. An issue will have one of three characteristics:

- The item will change the scope of the project.

- The item will require a decision that must come from outside the project team or through a team consensus.

- A task on the critical path of the project is late and is affecting completion of other tasks.

Tip

> There are only a few items in the Oracle Applications that cannot be changed (or are very expensive to change) after the initial setup. If the issue is caused by a lack of familiarity with Oracle Applications, try to resolve the problem by considering the pros and cons of three or four alternatives suggested by an expert. Don't get paralyzed. You can usually make changes during the conference room pilot.

Key issues in many organizations usually revolve around the following areas:

- The structure of the key accounting flexfield, the item definition, the PO approval hierarchy, and several key flexfields in HR

- Centralized versus decentralized business processes and the technical architecture model

- The reporting strategy and information flow

- Installation and testing of new releases of the software

- Change management and impact on end users

- Application function points and the degree to which they fit your business requirements

- System performance, space requirements, and bugs
- Implementation of the multi-org setup

IMPROVING AND MANAGING TOLERANCE FOR CHANGE

The ability of your organization to absorb change will affect your costs and degree of implementation effort. Improving flexibility of policy and procedure and your ability to match the Oracle Applications design model are important considerations. The impact of external constraints from trading partners, governments, industry practices, labor contracts, corporate headquarters, and so forth will cause requirements that force extensions to the basic Oracle Applications.

> **Tip**
>
> Change happens when the cost of doing nothing is greater than the cost of the change. New organizations or those with very old legacy systems often have the least resistance to change because the cost of change is very low for new companies and the cost of doing nothing might be very high for old systems.

UNDERSTANDING THE PERSONALITY OF THE ORGANIZATION

The culture and personality of your organization can affect the cost of the implementation project. Three different companies are described in this section. Six to nine months after startup, there was little difference in the satisfaction level of users, and all three companies were continuing to improve in the way they used Oracle Applications.

One company was very respectful of each user's requirements and formed a large implementation team to make sure everyone was represented. Issues were resolved well in advance of the go-live date. Everything possible was done to meet each user's expectations for the new software. Much effort was spent to communicate progress and project status to users outside the project team. At the end of the project, the project team members became users. This project was very expensive, and many users were still not satisfied at startup.

At the other extreme, another company formed a very small team and empowered them to decide for a vast constituency of users. Expectations were set early in the project that the software couldn't be and didn't have to be perfect. Major issues and proof of concepts were resolved in a conference room pilot, and a pact was made with users to address concerns and minor issues in a cleanup phase of the project. On transition, users took ownership rapidly and resolved many issues. This project was very efficient, but did not meet all the business expectations at startup.

Another company announced at the beginning of the project that the implementation would be part of a major company restructuring. The Accounts Payable function would be cut from over 50 employees to less than 20 when it was consolidated into a shared service center. Similar staff changes would be made in finance as the monthly closing and reporting processes became centralized. Two competing consulting firms were used to manage the

ERP project and the restructuring project. The project team was partially staffed with employees whose jobs would be eliminated by the new software. This project had extra costs as team members and consulting firms worked through personal agendas before dealing with issues.

These three examples demonstrate a wide variety of approaches to implementing the Oracle Applications with about the same results. Although all these projects are considered successful, the cost and effort required of the implementations was higher than expected or the results were less than expected. Your organization and ERP implementation project will have its own internal dynamics that affect the cost effort to implement the Oracle Applications.

In Summary

The effort and cost of an Oracle ERP Applications implementation project is driven by many factors, including the following:

- The complexity and culture of your organization
- The number of application modules
- The complexity of your business processes
- The amount of customizations required
- Other projects happening at the same time
- The capability of your implementation team
- The ability of your organization to absorb change

You can significantly reduce the cost and effort of your project by understanding the complexity and dynamics of your specific organization. You must consider these dynamics when you construct your project work plan. The plan that works for one company might not work well at all for another organization. If you can modify or take advantage of the the dynamics of your organization and minimize the number and magnitude of customizations, you might save quite a bit of money.

PART

II

CH

4

CHAPTER 5

UNDERSTANDING PROJECT MANAGEMENT AND CONTROL

The Oracle Applications implementation project is a significant piece of work and requires formal project management techniques. You might not require or use all of the practices discussed in this chapter, but you should choose carefully when you decide to eliminate a particular technique. Generally, an ERP Applications implementation plan should allow 7 to 10 percent of the budget for project management and control activities. Although these activities might seem to be overhead to the project, they pay for themselves. If you eliminate these activities, you lose more time in the long run.

DEVELOPING ISSUE-RESOLUTION TECHNIQUES

The ability to identify and resolve issues is an important one for the project team and a critical success factor for the project.

> **Tip**
> Definition of the issue is probably 90 percent of the requirement for solving the problem. If you are having trouble resolving an issue, look at how you have defined the problem.

We know a consulting firm that defines an issue as "any project-related concern and/or controversy that needs to be documented so that risks (if any) can be addressed, resolved, and managed." Because it can cover almost any topic, this general definition works well and creates an open communication capability among the project team members.

For Oracle ERP software implementation projects, I usually use a narrower definition of an issue to focus on the tasks at hand, and I try to identify significant issues so everyone knows that issue resolution is high-value and high-priority. We believe an issue will have at least one of three characteristics:

1. The item will change the scope of the project.
2. The item will require a decision that must come from outside the project team or through a team consensus.
3. A task on the critical path of the project is late and is affecting completion of other tasks.

> **Tip**
> The common task of creating a Technical Assistance Request (TAR) with Oracle Support is likely *not* an issue by itself unless it meets one of the three criteria above. Projects are all about solving problems, and the TAR is just another problem to deal with. Just get the support from Oracle, close the TAR, and move on to the next item on the work plan.

Issues should be recorded in a log. The log can be a simple word processing or spreadsheet document, or the log can be a relational database schema with forms and reports. All of the project team should have access to the issues log and the status reports. Key information you want to capture about an issue includes the following:

- An issue identifier such as an issue number
- Date issue is first identified
- The functional application or project area that is affected
- The type of issue (scheduling, function gap, decision, configuration parameter choice, scope change, and so forth)
- Priority (high, medium, low, or red, yellow, green)
- Status (open, closed, hold, cancelled)
- Owner responsible to resolve the problem
- Resolution date requirement
- Comments and description

IMPLEMENTING STATUS REPORTING FOR YOUR PROJECT

The project team owes periodic status reports to the project sponsors and management. If the project is big enough to have subproject teams, status reports can promote communication throughout a large team. Typically, status reports should be issued weekly or every two weeks.

Status reports should have at least four sections:

1. The executive overview section summarizes the project or subproject for the reader who is not involved with the details of the project. This section should be free of technical jargon. If you include an unresolved problem or issue in this section, you are asking the reader to get involved.
2. The specific progress made from the previous report should be listed. Often, this is a list of completed deliverables and resolved issues from the planned work section of previous report.
3. List the assignments, milestones, and planned work that will happen before the next report is created.
4. List important issues and issues where the resolution date is past due.

CREATING MEETING MINUTES

Oracle software implementation projects produce lots of formal and informal meetings as the project team works through requirements, new business processes, configuration parameters, pilot activities, issues, and so forth. Meeting minutes are a way to formalize and document the decisions, issues, action items, responsibilities, and progress of the project.

> **Tip**
>
> A very wise project manager once told me, "If it's not written down, it was never said and never agreed to."

Meeting minutes are also a great way to communicate between project teams, levels of project administration, and company management not directly involved with the day-to-day details of the project. Each meeting should have a scribe to take notes and publish the minutes. It is a good idea to establish a template so important details are not missed. The template can be set up to do the following:

- Name the meeting.
- Note the date and time.
- List who called the meeting, who led it, and who was the note taker.
- List the attendees and distribution for the minutes.
- Attach a copy of the agenda and any handouts.
- Report issues and discussion.
- Report any agreements, action items, due dates, and who is responsible for future progress.

> **Tip**
>
> If you openly and faithfully publish meeting minutes, status reports, and other project deliverables to all concerned and everyone on the distribution list is engaged in the project, you might be able to implement the "Silence = Acceptance" rule. If you achieve this level of communication, the project team should operate efficiently.

IDENTIFYING RED FLAGS

Red flags are telling warnings that might indicate the project would have trouble meeting its goals. One, two, or several of these warnings might not prevent the project from succeeding, but too many of these problems indicate a higher-than-normal degree of risk for the project. Consider objectively testing your project for these warning signals every few months or when major milestones are delivered. These warnings can be grouped in three ways:

- User red flags
- Communications red flags
- Project management red flags

User red flags indicate the degree of interest and involvement of the end users or their project team representatives. Ultimately, each successful project will transfer ownership of the new software and business processes to the end users. The following items might indicate how graceful that transfer will be:

- The user is frequently unavailable or not on-site.
- The user is not fully involved with the project.
- The user is not part of or represented by the project team.
- The user lacks full functional knowledge of the new (or old) system.
- There is an intense political atmosphere between users, a user and the MIS staff, or the client and a consultant.
- The user is looking for a quick fix and signs off too quickly on configuration parameters, design, or issue resolution.
- The user can't make up her mind.
- The user is uncomfortable with change in general. Any deviation from the current routine is resisted.
- The user wants to cut corners to make deadlines.

Communications red flags show the openness and honesty of the project. Good communications inspires trust and acceptance of the new software and business processes. An effective communications plan will eliminate surprises and facilitate the transition to the new systems. Look for these red flags:

- Project staff and users do not meet to discuss day-to-day requirements, configuration, process, and design issues.
- There are communication gaps at the user-to-user, user-to-manager, manager-to-staff, or staff-to-staff levels of the project hierarchy.
- The scope of the project is poorly defined, and user expectations are different from what the project team can deliver.
- Project leadership has not clearly explained the reasons and goals for the project. Participants do not fully understand why the project is necessary.
- All participants (project manager, user, sponsor, DBA, programmer, consultant, and so forth) are not defined clearly at the beginning of the project.

Project management red flags show the degree of control and organization of the project. A well-run package software implementation project will have several distinct phases, including plan, analysis, design, build and test, transition, and production. These red flags might appear at any time:

- No formal definition of requirements has been made for the business.
- There is no provision in the work plan for development of conversion programs, security systems, testing, revisions, project management time, and so forth.
- There is excessive overtime on the project.
- The project manager has no to-do or issues list for the project. The manager does not have a work plan in sufficient detail.

- The project manager cannot give a definitive answer when asked what is done, what is not done, and which tasks are assigned to which team members.

- The project manager does not know how the project's actual expenses and stage of completion compares to the budget and the planned schedule.

- There has been no sign-off on the plan, functional requirements, design, conversion results, or system test.

- Configuration or setup has begun prior to the sign-off on the analysis, requirements, and gap issues.

- There was no design audit performed prior to starting to build the systems.

- Project resources are double-booked between projects or between the project and their regular jobs.

- There is a sharp change in number of staff available to the project. There might be a good reason for adding resources to a project, but it is hard for the newcomers to get up to speed. If resources are transferred to other work, the software implementation project might fall behind schedule or be unable to make good progress.

MAINTAINING THE PROJECT PLAN

There should be a complete project plan, and you should measure progress against each task in the plan. The project plan should include the following:

- The task list shows the work to be done and defines the scope of the project. Tasks can be grouped into phases, and transitions between phases can be marked by milestones.

- The duration of each task has two components. The first component shows the amount of work effort in some unit of time that is required to complete a task. Because we often work on many tasks simultaneously, the second aspect of duration shows the scheduled dates between the start of work and the completion date of each task. For example, if resources aren't exclusively devoted to an activity, a four-day task might be in-progress for two weeks.

- The resource assignments schedule shows who is responsible for completing each task. Multiple resources can be assigned to a task.

- The dependencies of each task and the work schedules of the project resources establish the critical path for the project. Determine which tasks have other activities that must precede the startup of the task to understand the dependencies of each task.

> **Tip**
>
> As a rule of thumb, if the amount of effort for a task is more than four days' duration, divide the task into subtasks for better control. For example, a twelve-day task to create a legacy system interface could be scheduled as subtasks to analyze, design, code, test, document, and so forth.

As the project progresses, it is important to record progress compared to the plan. The simplest way to determine progress is to periodically estimate the percentage of completion of each task. Coordinate the completion estimate with the status report, and you will be able to determine whether you are ahead of or behind schedule and whether you have enough resources.

MAINTAINING CONTROL OF THE PROJECT SCOPE

The project scope is usually not fixed in the early phases (planning, analysis, and design) of the software implementation. However, by the time the schedule reaches the building, testing, and transition phases, you should have a precise understanding of what the project will accomplish. When the budget and implementation schedule become firm, you will want to implement change control procedures. Whoever supplies the budget and resources to the project must be involved in the project change process. For this reason, most successful projects establish a cross-functional steering committee to authorize changes in project scope that are consistent with similar changes in budget, resources, and schedule.

Tip

Because programming, or at least substantial discussion, will be involved, pay particular attention to functionality gaps in the packaged software. These gaps can radically change the scope of the project work plan.

Consider preparation of a gap analysis document to control and communicate potential changes to the steering committee and other project participants. This gap analysis document should include comments for the following topics:

- Describe the business requirement and the gap in the packaged software.
- List the people who support the proposed changes.
- List the applications that will be affected.
- Describe the current practices in the legacy system.
- Describe the proposed practices as they will be supported by the Oracle Applications.
- List the consequences of doing nothing to show the impact of the gap.
- Discuss possible workarounds or alternative processes that might fill the gap.
- Describe the extension that must be made to the Oracle applications.
- List the benefits to be obtained if the extension is authorized. If possible, assign a monetary value to quantify the benefit.
- List the costs that will be incurred to create the extension. Don't forget to include the cost of ongoing maintenance and upgrade considerations.
- Describe the impact on the project schedule.

- Describe changes (if any) that must be made to Oracle's code.
- Draw a conclusion, with a recommended course of action, and explain why various alternatives are not recommended.

MANAGING THE CRITICAL PATH

When tasks are blocked by other activities that must finish before the task can start, you have a critical path to the project. The critical path will control the software implementation schedule. If you can understand and manage the critical sequence of events, you can improve the performance and efficiency of the project team. Because each project has a different set of dynamics, you must determine and manage your own project's critical path.

> **Tip**
>
> If a resource is on the critical path of a project because you matched the best skills with each task, consider assigning some tasks to other team members. This technique is a growth opportunity for the team, and it is possible to shorten a project schedule by as much as 20 percent by managing the critical path through alternative resource assignments.

> **Tip**
>
> If possible, try to keep the technical resources off the critical path and make alternative plans when this happens. Because the new technology might introduce difficult-to-understand or unpredictable delays, avoid schedule slippage by making sure the technical tasks and issues are managed well.

ESTABLISHING QUALITY CONTROL PROCEDURES

Many Oracle Applications implementation projects are large enough to benefit from formal quality control procedures. Usually, these procedures introduce a semi-independent third party to audit the project implementation team. The auditor will typically look at the following items:

- Work should be progressing satisfactorily according to the plan and schedule. Tasks should be assigned to team members with the skills to complete the activity. Team members should not be consistently scheduled beyond normal working hours. The plan should be complete.
- Project controls, communications procedures, and issue-resolution techniques should be in place.
- The quality of deliverables should be adequate.
- Red flags and risks should appear to be under control.

Tip

> Even if your project doesn't establish formal quality control procedures, it will likely benefit from a constructive review you can conduct yourself.

TAR TRACKING, RESOLUTION, AND LOGGING

Working effectively with Oracle Support is a critical success factor for most implementation projects. A Technical Assistance Request (TAR) is created by Oracle for each problem, and they do a pretty good job of documenting the problem, the status, and the resolution. To effectively manage Oracle Support as a critical project resource, you need to be able to monitor their work. Often, you will solve the same problem in several instances as the project progresses, and we suggest you construct a log of all activity so that you can re-create the solutions you get from Oracle Support. For additional techniques for working with Oracle Support, see Chapter 28, "Working with Oracle Support."

Tip

> Even if you implemented the applications years ago and your system has stabilized, consider keeping a TAR log so that you will have a history of system problems.

UNDERSTANDING THE IMPACT OF OTHER PROJECTS

ISO9000 projects, business process reengineering, mergers, acquisitions, and other package software projects can have an impact on your Oracle software implementation. These projects often cannot be avoided, but they introduce complications that you must manage:

- Other projects compete for scarce resources that you will need for your Oracle software implementation.

- Issues become more frequent, and their resolution becomes more complex. You might have to negotiate and compromise to resolve issues.

- The external projects might not have the same implementation schedule as your project. There might be extra tasks and one-time interfaces required to synchronize each project's requirements.

- Reengineering projects often require additional analysis and prototyping of various scenarios for an Oracle software project. If the reengineering project team members are not expert in the Oracle software, reengineering projects can introduce gaps when a perfectly good Oracle-based solution already exists.

PART

II

CH

5

- ISO9000 certifications often create additional documentation requirements for the Oracle software project. This documentation is often time-consuming to create because the people writing the documentation don't quite understand yet how the Oracle software works.

- Mergers and acquisitions create restructuring pressures that can affect the users' desire to cooperate with project teams who bring process change and career uncertainty.

IN SUMMARY

Effective project management and control is a critical success factor for your implementation project that can require 7 to 10 percent of the project budget. The management and control activities are not simply overhead to the project. The effort you make to effectively manage the project is required to avoid the consequences of several kinds of project risks. For example, I know of one company with nonexistent project management, and three months before startup, they had many red flags and unresolved issues. Their management techniques consisted of several department heads meeting as a committee without an adequate leader, plan, or implementation method. After delaying their software startup several times, they decided to launch the systems even if they weren't ready. Within three weeks, they were shutting down factories, and they were unable to make shipments because the inventory, planning, and fulfillment applications were configured improperly and were not integrated. This company fixed many of the problems within six months, but the cost to the company was over two million dollars, damaged customer relationships, unhappy employees, and so forth. They spent more money recovering from the problems than they spent for all of the hardware, software, and 18 months of pre-launch consulting.

CHAPTER 6

GETTING STARTED

Each Oracle Applications implementation project must start somewhere. The start is a mix of strategy, high-level analysis, planning, and organizing. This chapter shows you how to build a good foundation for your project.

FORMING THE PROJECT TEAM

The project team is a mix of project manager, project leader(s), application consultants (technical and functional), business analyst(s), developer(s), and database and system administrator(s). The size and complexity of the project determines the number of each of the resources. Team building starts with the minimum resources required, and a complete team may be formed in phases as the project progresses.

Typically, the team starts with a project manager and project sponsor who will interact, negotiate, and finalize the project requirements with an implementation consultant. This is the project conceptualization phase. As the project progresses, the project manager, project leader(s), business analysts, application consultants, database administrators, and developers are drawn into the team depending on the input required from each of these skills. These additional team members can provide valuable insight to business and team requirements.

An understanding of the activities involved to get started, as discussed further in this section, provides a fair idea as to the composition and building of the project team.

SPONSOR

The sponsor provides the business case and funding for the project. Some enterprise resource planning (ERP) projects appear to have many sponsors because the entire enterprise is involved. Ideally, sponsorship should be focused, involved, and established at the highest level of the organization as possible. If multiple sponsors are involved, they should form a steering committee to resolve issues, provide funding, set priorities, and coordinate high-level project direction.

PROJECT MANAGER

The project manager is the formal head of the project team. In a large project where resources are formed into many groups, each group may be headed by a project leader who will discharge the role of project manager at this group level, and the project manager manages the total project based on input from project leader(s). In a small project, a project leader may be the project manager.

The project manager determines the scope and plan of the project, coordinates the activities and resources, monitors the progress, resolves issues, and implements decisions for the sponsor or steering committee.

The attributes of the project manager include the following:

- The project manager should have knowledge of the functionality of the software. She can always take the help of application consultants for finer details. The project manager should also have an understanding of integration issues with other modules and systems.

- She will be able to coordinate the resources, recognize and resolve issues on time, negotiate compromise, and make decisions.

- The project manager will have good knowledge of management and communication tools for efficient execution, monitoring, and reporting. She will have good oral and written communication skills.

- She will have a good knowledge of the implementation methods to be used.

The responsibilities of the project manager are as follows:

- Studies the requirements and works to meet the needs of the business and users

- Determines direct processes, workarounds, and customization requirements for the new systems

- Finalizes the training schedules

- Usually defines the scope of the project and possibly drafts the implementation contract with consultants

- Continuously monitors the changes required during the project and manages any changes in scope

- Selects and adapts the implementation methods for the project

- Initiates the project and forms the project team

- Coordinates the resources and activities and monitors progress and prepares status reports

- Represents the project team and interacts with the sponsor on behalf of the team. When there are issues, the project manager brings them to the attention of the sponsor and makes decisions for resolving the issues

APPLICATIONS CONSULTANT

An applications consultant is experienced with the software and determines the functionality, gaps, and related issues. An applications consultant may also be expected to have a reasonable knowledge of related third-party items such as operating systems, networking, bar code systems, electronic commerce, peripherals, desktop software, and so forth.

The applications consultant may give training and also guide the customization team according to the specifications given by the project manager.

Because each module of the applications suite serves a specialized set of business functions and no one consultant can know the full range of the Oracle Applications, it is likely that several application consultants will be on a project with many applications.

A functional consultant is expected to have the following attributes:

PART

II

CH

6

- Good understanding of the scope of the project and implementation method to be followed
- Good knowledge of software functionality including data setup and training
- Good knowledge of the business functions of the user
- Good knowledge of security issues controls and audit requirements
- Understanding of integration issues with other software
- Skills to prepare high-level and functional design specifications
- Reasonable knowledge of technology and tools to be used in customization or product extensions

A technical consultant is expected to have the following characteristics:

- Good understanding of the scope of the project and implementation method to be followed
- Good knowledge of product technology and installation
- Good knowledge of technology and tools to be used in customization or software extensions coupled with programming skills
- Good knowledge of related third-party products such as operating systems and networking
- Good knowledge of integration issues with other products
- Good understanding of the security implementation
- Skills to prepare detailed designs and technical specifications
- Reasonable understanding of the product functionality and business functions of the users

The responsibilities of the applications consultant are as follows:

- The applications consultant gives necessary input to the project manager during the project planning stage.
- The functional consultant identifies process mapping, gaps, and customization requirements.
- The functional consultant makes resource estimates and a detailed activity plan based on the gaps and customization requirements identified.
- The applications consultant collects test data from users and ensures that it is as close to reality as possible. The consultant sets up the modules with the test data.
- The technical consultant prepares the detailed design for customization and in most cases leads the group carrying out any custom development.

- The technical consultant tracks and resolves bugs in custom-developed code or extensions.

- For any bugs in the applications products, the consultant initiates a technical assistance request (TAR) with Oracle Support.

TECHNICAL STAFF

The technical members of a project team include the database administrator (DBA), applications administrator, UNIX administrator, technical consultant (discussed previously), developers, and support staff. The following paragraphs briefly discuss the roles of each technical member.

> **Note**
>
> Remember, this discussion is about technical roles. Small projects often assign multiple roles to one or two key technical individuals.

DATABASE ADMINISTRATOR

The role of DBA in an Oracle Applications implementation project is very important. Typically, there might be three or more instances of the database. The most common instances are for production, testing, and training. In addition, there might be other instances for development, demonstration, conference room pilots, and so forth. A full implementation of Oracle financial and manufacturing applications can create more than 20,000 database objects in each instance that must be maintained and monitored by the DBA.

The typical DBA performs these tasks for normal system maintenance:

- Becomes a point of contact with Oracle Support
- Allocates space and data storage needs for the database objects and plans future disk space requirements
- Plans hardware capacity requirements for the database and Web servers
- Installs, upgrades, and maintains the Oracle database, tools, and applications software
- Maintains the fault tolerance of the database (backup, restore, import, export, and so forth)
- Manages activity of the control files, rollback segments, and online redo logs
- Administers the SQL*Net software
- Starts up and shuts down databases
- Documents system administration procedures and policies

The DBA is also responsible for the performance of the system:

- Monitors and optimizes performance of the database
- Evaluates and adjusts database initialization parameters

PART

II

CH

6

- Controls fragmentation in the tablespaces
- Evaluates hardware performance
- Distributes the physical data storage to maximize hardware I/O and minimize disk hot spots
- Tunes the allocation of available memory

Also, the DBA provides security and controls access to the database:

- Enrolls new users and controls access with passwords
- Provides system uptime
- Establishes system fault tolerance and backup/recovery capability
- Maintains archived data
- Disables access for terminated users
- Controls access to database objects

APPLICATIONS SYSTEM ADMINISTRATOR

The Oracle Applications system administrator maintains the setups in the SYSADMIN module. The Oracle Applications system administrator typically performs these tasks:

- Secures access to the Oracle Applications via user accounts, menus, passwords, and environment variables
- Defines and assigns alternate menus, responsibilities, report groups, and report sets
- Registers custom programs
- Defines and sets profile options at the system, application, and responsibility levels; advises users how to set individual profile options at the user level
- Becomes a point of contact with Oracle Support to define problems and order patches
- Configures, starts up and shuts down the concurrent managers
- Defines and assigns printers and printer styles
- Assists with periodic processing (archive and purges)
- Evaluates system online response time
- Diagnoses and repairs interface problems

OPERATING SYSTEM (UNIX OR NT) ADMINISTRATOR

The operating system administrator maintains the UNIX or NT operating system. The typical operating system administrator performs these tasks:

- Manages and plans disk space usage
- Adjusts kernel parameters for tuning and sizing the system
- Becomes a point of contact for the hardware vendor's support organization

- Backs up and restores the system
- Establishes the disaster recovery plan
- Plans and manages the system architecture of servers, network, desktop devices, and peripherals
- Monitors system loads and evaluates hardware performance and bottlenecks
- Sets up user accounts and computing environment on the operating system
- Disables accounts of terminated users
- Installs peripheral equipment and networked devices
- Schedules periodic system jobs
- Writes utility scripts to automate system processes

DEVELOPMENT STAFF

The development members of the project team create enhancements, do the coding, and perform all the programming jobs in the project. The typical development staff performs these project tasks and takes on the following responsibilities:

- Develops the custom forms and reports and modifies existing forms and reports
- Writes concurrent programs using PL/SQL or UNIX shell scripts
- Writes custom database triggers, packages, or procedures
- Develops custom alerts
- Converts legacy data
- Builds interfaces to third-party systems
- Loads data from legacy systems for Oracle Applications initial balances

SUPPORT STAFF

The support staff members are involved with many activities necessary for the project to start up and progress smoothly. The typical support staff performs these project tasks:

- Communication with users
- Change management
- End user training in large projects
- Help desk and end user support
- Time keeping and tracking progress against the schedule
- Record keeping and preparation of meeting minutes and status reports
- Travel coordination

PART
II

CH
6

STARTING QUICKLY

Many activities can get an implementation project off to a quick start. When you rapidly establish high visibility with the users and sponsors, you create a good feeling about the changes that are about to happen.

SET UP A WAR ROOM

Establish an environment for the project team to work efficiently. The project team needs personal computers, network connections, printers, a white board, phones, email addresses, Internet connections, office supplies, file cabinets, bookshelves, and so forth. Try to get the project team away from their regular jobs and involved in the new activities.

> **Tip**
>
> To improve communication, consider asking the technical people to establish their work areas near the functional team members.

LIST HIGH-LEVEL BUSINESS REQUIREMENTS

List all the major business functions and processes to be performed by the proposed software implementation. Also indicate the areas where third-party products will integrate.

This listing should be grouped by business function and performing department. Show the flow of transactions and data through the entire functional cycle. Show the relationships between different functions of the cycle and relationships with other functional cycles or business processes as well.

This document forms the basis for and helps in preparing the mapping document. The business requirement listing and the mapping document allow the project team to identify gaps and draw the customization specifications. Also, you might identify special skills you will need on the project team.

ORGANIZE DOCUMENTS ON A SERVER

Establish a documentation directory structure for the project team on the network server. Create the directory and sub-directories to mirror the phases and tasks in your project work plan. Use the directory to store work-in-progress and signed-off versions of documents. Establish procedures at the start of the project to manage source and executable code changes and document versions. When you use this procedure, you create a centralized library of project work that becomes a resource for all to use. Avoid fragmentation of your documents, and don't allow project team members to store the official copies of project deliverables on their personal computers.

GATHER BUSINESS VOLUMES AND FREQUENCIES

Make a list of all transactions of the business and note the frequency and volume of each event. This analysis should cover all the business functions listed in the high-level listing of business requirements. Identify the number of users you will have for each business function. Make sure that the hardware vendor and the Oracle sales support staff use this information to help you determine the size and architecture of the hardware.

COLLECT SAMPLES OF INPUTS AND OUTPUTS FROM THE EXISTING BUSINESS PROCESSES

For each of the transactions listed previously, prepare a list of input parameters and gather samples of output data and reports. After taking sample outputs from existing system, check with the users to identify any changes or discrepancies. Determine the distribution of each report.

SELECTING AND SCHEDULING THE MODULES

The modules that are least dependent on others and need minimum information from other modules should be implemented first. Traditionally, the following order is accepted as most suitable for ERP implementations. This order is not a hard-and-fast rule, and it is possible that a unique business process of your enterprise may require a different sequence. First implement the financial and distribution modules. They are General Ledger (GL), Receivables (AR), Human Resources (HR), Payables (AP), Inventory (INV), Purchasing (PO), and Order Entry (OE) in order of least dependencies. You may prefer that OE be done with manufacturing modules. Then implement the manufacturing modules: Inventory, Bills of Material (BOM), Work in Process (WIP), Engineering (ENG), and Order Entry. Finally, implement Payroll (PAY) and Planning in any order. Assets (FA) may be implemented at any time after GL.

Many companies adopt a strategy to their ERP implementation called the Big Bang Approach. This method involves implementing all the modules at the same time. Despite the fact that all the modules start up at once, they must still resolve issues and dependencies in order of the implementation dependencies discussed previously. The most important factor in the Big Bang Approach is to estimate and coordinate the resources and users simultaneously and have adequate backup measures for any technical obstacles. This approach is suitable for projects where

- The modules involved are simple and fall in one functional business cycle—for example GL, AP, and AR.

- The implementation sites and end users are not scattered over a wide geographical area. For a successful Big Bang implementation, it should be easy to coordinate all sites and users together.

PART

II

CH

6

UNDERSTANDING TYPICAL TASKS, DELIVERABLES, AND MILESTONES

The planning and strategy phase of an implementation project has several key tasks and deliverables. Typically, you want to develop a work environment and plan an activity framework for the project. However, until you are close to completing the analysis phase, you will not have a complete definition of the scope of the project. Try to perform these tasks simultaneously with the activities of the analysis phase of the project and keep the planning deliverables open and flexible. Your consultants should be able to provide templates and master copies of most of the documents you will need to get started.

GET ORGANIZED

One of the first tasks to do (and arguably the most important) is to have all the paper work in place before attempting to start the project. Following is a typical list of necessary documents:

- A terminology and scope document to determine the boundaries of the implementation project.

- An implementation method document including formats for reporting, progress monitoring, communication of issues, minutes of meetings, deliverables, sign-off documents for each deliverable, change requests, and issue tracking (maintaining open and closed issues).

- List of requirements for all the proposed team members, possibly in the form of a resume.

- Details of the sponsors, team members, and users who will interact with the project team; know how decisions will be made and who will make them.

- Checklists for the hardware and software features and capabilities.

- List of the details necessary to contact Oracle Support.

- A tentative project work plan.

- An education plan for the project team.

- Documents, formats, and checklists to be used for analysis and user responses.

- List of quality and acceptance criteria for the software and for each project deliverable.

- Documentation about legacy systems, third-party software, and interface requirements.

- Details of any other projects, ongoing or recently completed, that are likely to impact this Oracle Applications implementation project.

CREATE THE PROJECT WORK PLAN

See Appendix C, "An Oracle Applications Implementation Checklist," for a list of project activities. Your organization may have additional requirements, or your project may be able to avoid performing some of the tasks. If you skip a task, make sure that it is really optional for your organization and not a critical success factor. Many projects try to skip tasks at the beginning of the project and then end up performing them at the last minute during the transition phase when it is discovered that the activity really wasn't optional.

HOW MUCH TIME IS NEEDED?

Every organization has different implementation requirements, and you need to understand what will control the critical path for your organization. Although many factors contribute to the time and expense of a software implementation, the controlling factor for how long it takes is usually your organization's ability to accept and absorb the changes in procedures, processes, and technology.

Generally, rapid implementations may be more successful than slow implementations. In a slow implementation, business requirements tend to change during the project, and scope is more difficult to control. Keep it simple, and you will implement faster.

CREATE AN EDUCATION PLAN

Education is different from end user training. Education is for the project implementation team. Even though your project team may be made up of employees who are end users, they need more than training in how to use the modules. The team should receive education about how the modules are configured, how the applications work together, and all available features of the applications.

> **Tip**
>
> If you have a large project with more than 100 days of education, contact education sales at Oracle Corporation. They can do much of the planning and coordinating for you.

Consider including the following in your training plan:

- Construct a worksheet with the course name, location, phone, start date, course content, and student prerequisites.
- Determine who on the project team will represent which skill sets.
- Match the team member skill sets with the course content and produce a schedule.
- If you have more than four students for a class, calculate your break-even point for onsite classes.
- Immediately after class ask students to record open issues and questions raised by the education.
- Record course attendance by student and course name.
- Document the student's evaluation of the course and evaluate comprehension and retention of the material.

PART

II

CH

6

- If you attempt onsite education, make sure that you have a technical environment with the right software installed, printers, working concurrent managers, student workstations, and so forth. Also, create a good classroom environment by providing a white board, markers, a flip chart, written login procedures, overhead projector, a keyboard mapping template, and so forth.

- Establish an education coordinator to communicate and execute the plan.

Tip

> Oracle Education has occasionally canceled classes with a small number of registrants. Try to remain flexible and plan alternative classes and schedules. Monitor future scheduled class registrations to determine the odds that a class will actually be held.

CREATE A PROJECT ENVIRONMENT AND INFRASTRUCTURE PLAN

Prepare a plan and a checklist for the hardware and software environment. It should typically include the hardware makes and models, configuration, quantities, and install locations. The plan should also include the software including operating systems, database, Oracle Applications, programming tools, word processors, spreadsheets, project management, and presentation software with their versions and installation particulars. When you document the purposes for each piece of the project environment, you will know that everything is in place before the project begins.

COMMUNICATE YOUR PROJECT STRATEGY

The implementation strategy must be communicated to the entire project team, including the sponsor and steering committee. This communication is ideally done in the form of a kick-off presentation. Answer the following questions to determine the details and agenda of the meeting:

- Determine the members to whom the presentation will be made. The list should ideally include all the members of the project team. If you plan to make more than one presentation to address specific requirements, group the members accordingly for respective presentations.

- Determine the level of detail necessary to address the audience. Consider the complexity of the project, the experience of the members of the team, the purpose of the presentation, and the time allotted. You should not only identify the final project goal in a single statement but also determine goals for major project phases. Present measurable targets and milestones for each phase. List critical success factors for each work phase.

- Include an organization chart of the project team. Identify the team members, team leaders, and project leaders, and their roles and responsibilities.

- Make sure to briefly mention the progress already made by any team members in terms of groundwork, study, infrastructure, and other arrangements.

- Determine who will make the presentation. It may not necessarily be the project manager. The presentation must be made by a person who understands the varying interests in the project and of the members present, and who can communicate the appropriate level of detail. Your consultants should be able to help, especially if they are providing most of the work plans and implementation methods.

Pay attention to following points before making the presentation:

- Plan the presentation; many details relevant to the current project or phase must be gathered and incorporated into the kick-off meeting.

- If any of the audience need exposure to information about this project or phase and its background, do this in advance.

- Plan the content and level of detail of the presentation in consultation with the sponsor and users. If users are to be at the presentation, they may want a work session or demonstration as well. Consider planning for work sessions separately.

DEVELOP A QUALITY PLAN

The quality plan forms the procedural framework to control how the project will be executed, delivered, and accepted. It typically establishes the systems to be followed during the normal course of the project as well as during abnormal situations that may arise from time to time. Your quality plan should include the details for the following topics:

- Team hierarchy with members' general roles and responsibilities
- Monitoring and reporting the status and progress
- Issue tracking and control, including procedures for escalating and addressing issues and support problems
- Change control and scope management
- Testing and software review criteria and procedures
- Acceptance criteria for deliverables in each phase
- Configuration management and version control
- Programming standards for customization work

DOCUMENT THE SCOPE AND OBJECTIVES OF THE PROJECT

The scope of your project is the outer boundary for the activities. It defines what is included in the project and how much work will be done. The objectives of your project are all that are intended to be achieved within the scope.

The scope is important because your project plan, project activities, and all cost estimates are dependent on the scope determined. If any change is proposed in the project activities, you should study its impact on the scope of the project. For any change or addition of project activity, scope control and change control procedures should be established and followed.

Also establish a procedure for issue tracking and resolution. This procedure is necessary because many issues will come up during the project that are within the scope but must be resolved. A final record of all open and closed issues should be maintained. Your quality plan will tell you how to resolve issues and acceptance criteria when there are open issues.

The objectives to be achieved by the implementation project should be identified, listed, and briefly explained in a Scope and Objectives document. Define the objectives in terms of the major business requirements to be satisfied by the current project including the following:

- Implementation of the different modules of the Oracle Applications
- New business systems that will come into operation as a result of the implementation
- Major changes in business process with intended improvement in efficiency or savings
- Training objectives
- Data migration objectives

Another important aspect of scope documentation is risk management. Clearly document all the risks perceived at this stage of the project and how or to what extent they will be addressed by the project plan. Also establish guidelines for managing other risks that may arise during the course of the project.

DEVELOP A STAFFING PLAN

Create a twofold staffing plan. One part should include the staffing requirement from the implementation consultant(s), and the other part should include the staffing requirement from the sponsor. Each of the two parts should include the following:

- The composition of the project team in terms of smaller groups such as steering committee, functional teams, development teams, documentation and training teams, and so on
- A detailed estimate of staffing requirements for each phase and activity
- A list of skills required for each role of the project team.
- The timing of staff deployment, where all activities do not begin and end at the same time
- Additional resource requirements for each staff member in terms of hardware, communications, and other supplies
- Procedures to monitor resource utilization and effectiveness

SUMMARY

There are many startup activities that you can accomplish between the time you sign the contract for Oracle software and when it is installed on your new computer system. You can select the people for the project team and establish their roles. Set up a project environment so the team will be organized, comfortable, and efficient. Perform a high-level analysis of future business requirements and transaction volumes. Start planning and coordinating the work. Develop education, staffing, and quality plans, and determine the scope and objectives for the project.

In Chapter 7, "Analyzing the Project," you will begin to study the detailed work of implementing the Oracle software.

ANALYZING THE PROJECT

PROJECT ANALYSIS OVERVIEW

The analysis phase of the project defines the business and system requirements of your business and the Oracle Applications. Work flows, policies, and procedures are documented. This stage can define the need for interfaces to external systems, customizations, or enhancements to the applications. During this phase, the project team will assess the fit of the applications to the business processes.

Often, you will want to perform the analysis from two perspectives. From your business perspective, document the special things your business does very well and your critical success factors. From the Oracle applications perspective, review the functions and capabilities of the applications and make a detailed study of how well those functions fit your business. If you employ outside consultants, they should be able to bring the applications perspective to your business. If you send your project team to classes at Oracle Education, they can compare existing business practices to the course material.

The analysis phase of an Oracle applications implementation project accomplishes several things:

- Establishes the scope and boundaries of the project
- Determines the technical and information infrastructure for the new systems
- Acquaints the project team with the new business processes and software functions
- Determines the degree of fit and gap for business requirements
- Develops a reporting and information strategy
- Educates outside consultants about business requirements and critical success factors for the project

BUSINESS PROCESS ANALYSIS

A study of your business processes has four main activities:

- Understanding the current business processes
- Defining the business requirements for the new software
- Assessing the fit and identify gaps
- Developing a vision of future business processes

UNDERSTANDING THE BUSINESS

The basic processes embedded in the logic of the Oracle Applications might be different from your legacy system processes. The implementation team members must develop an understanding of how the new enterprisewide systems will work in that context. This analysis starts with an understanding of the current business processes. If you assemble a team of functional business analysts from many areas of your company and use outside consultants, you will want to spend time to make sure everyone acquires the same view of the essential business transactions, practices, policies, controls, data flows, interfaces, reports, performance indicators, and so forth.

Draw pictures. Resolve issues. Document and communicate the results. However, because this activity represents the systems you will be leaving, don't spend too much time on it. Your new system doesn't have to copy the old system. You can meet your business requirements using the new software and techniques. Your goals are to establish a baseline to know the business requirements and to create a structure to discover weaknesses or gaps in the new software.

DISCOVERING AND DOCUMENTING THE BUSINESS REQUIREMENTS

Many years ago as a consultant, I was helping a credit manager implement Oracle Receivables. After only two interviews of four hours, we started to discuss how to configure the applications and what software features would be used. The credit manager asked how we could determine the business requirements and their special needs so quickly. She was amazed that we could be making such good progress after just a few hours when it took her several weeks to train a new recruit for the credit department. There were several good reasons for our progress:

- We had a questionnaire to organize the topic.
- The Oracle Receivables software was a good fit for this customer.
- The client was open to changing most of their processes to match the standard Oracle application process flow.
- An experienced consultant concentrated on parts of the process where this client had special business requirements. For example, because they were in the construction supply business, they placed many liens on properties where they delivered products, and Oracle Receivables had no equivalent function.
- Almost no time was lost on the process steps where the Oracle application could be set up in a standard way.

It helps to be organized when you look for business requirements. If you prepared a Request for Proposal or if you have working papers from the competitive evaluations from when you purchased the software, you could use that information to start a requirements evaluation. If you use a consultant to help with the implementation, he should have a questionnaire. If you have to discover requirements from scratch, consider running a conference room pilot to evaluate each function of the applications and make a detailed map from your legacy system to the Oracle Applications.

DISCOVERING THE DEGREE OF FIT

The degree of fit for an applications module is determined by several factors. The relationships in your supply chain, the complexity and size of the business, the regulatory environment, and the ability for your organization to accept change are all factors you will want to consider. If your business closely follows Generally Accepted Accounting Practices

(GAAP) and the teachings of the American Production and Inventory Control Society (APICS), you might have a good fit.

One of the key deliverables of the analysis phase of an implementation project is the Gap Analysis document. This document should show the differences between your current business practices and the Oracle Applications. You can resolve gaps by customizing the Applications or by changing your business processes and requirements. When the Gap Analysis is completed, you should have a pretty good idea of the project scope, and you can finalize the project cost, schedule, and work plan.

Each organization will have different gaps between their business processes and the capability of the Oracle applications. Look for three kinds of gaps: integration gaps, data conversion gaps, and functionality gaps. Sometimes, these gaps can be very strange. For example, a functionality gap was discovered many years ago when an agricultural supply company was considering implementing the Oracle Receivables module. This company shipped its products to customers in the spring during planting season and required the farmers to pay 30 days after the harvest. Because the dates for both planting and harvesting were different for each customer and could not be predicted by any formula at the time of shipment, something as basic and simple as the terms and aging formulas in Oracle Receivables were a major problem. Because of this gap, the customer actually discontinued the project to implement Oracle Receivables.

To understand the impact on the project implementation schedule, you should categorize gaps by priority and requirement. The priority classification indicates when the gap must be resolved (for example, on the go-live date, by the end of the first fiscal quarter, and so forth). The requirement to fill the gap can be categorized by an ABC analysis. For example, all "A" requirement gaps could be considered show stoppers unless some kind of extension or work around is available when the software is turned over to the users. Gaps with lower requirements might be post launch requirements (for example, year-end processing) or "nice to have" requirements that don't enhance mission-critical activities.

Tip	If the ABC analysis of gaps turns up many "C" status items, consider creating a Phase II for the implementation project to resolve these issues after the system is active. Because users might have a fuzzy idea of how the Oracle Applications really work at this point in the project, when you assign these gaps to Phase II, you might gain enough delay time for the user to realize the gap was really a training issue.

DEVELOPING A VISION OF HOW THE FUTURE BUSINESS PROCESS WILL WORK

During the analysis phase of the applications implementation, you evaluate the changes the new software will make to your business. Consider the interdepartmental relationships and how the implementation of the applications will change the way work is done. Hopefully, many process steps will be automated after you convert to the Oracle Applications, but some work might move from one department to another. When work moves in the process sequence, you might have to consider headcount staffing allowances and how your business units cooperate with each other.

For example, the back office functions of the payables and receivables departments in accounting are often the beneficiaries of improved processes after the applications are implemented. However, this improvement often comes at the expense of new process steps that will be performed in the purchasing and order entry departments.

Because implementation projects are expensive, many companies require a return-on-investment commitment from the operating units before they will buy the software. When you understand how the Oracle Applications will work in your business, you can start to determine how you will capture the return on investment and deliver the performance improvement that your project sponsorship expects. At this point in the project, you might realize some expected returns will not materialize unless you also accomplish some business process reengineering or some specialized end-user training.

Many features and functions of the Oracle Applications cannot be utilized without configuration of some of the setup parameters. When you determine which future business processes you will use and how they should work, you then will be able to select the proper settings for the configuration parameters. If you don't have a unified and integrated design of how the ERP system will work, you might have to make several conference room pilot tests. Also, your risk can be increased that you might configure something incorrectly or miss a point of integration.

Tip

Because the applications are a series of integrated modules, adopt a broad definition for basic business functions that span the boundaries of several Oracle Applications and the departments within your organization. For example, it is much better for the project team to implement the procurement process as a whole instead of implementing the planning (MRP), purchasing (PO), receiving (PO), and payables (AP) processes individually.

Create future process flow diagrams to communicate to the users outside the project implementation team how the new system will work. The process flow diagram is a picture of what the business does, who performs the process steps, and the sequence of process steps. Typically, a process flow diagram is not concerned with where, how, or why the process is performed. You can use future process flow diagrams to organize a conference room pilot and help train users.

Tip

Process flow diagrams are not like the old data flow diagrams that define the logic and flow of a computer program. See Figure 7.1 for a sample process flow diagram. Focus on the verbs that describe what business work is to be done and the sequence of steps or tasks that will define the business process.

PART

II

CH

7

Figure 7.1
Process flow diagrams show what happens, who is involved, and the sequence of events.

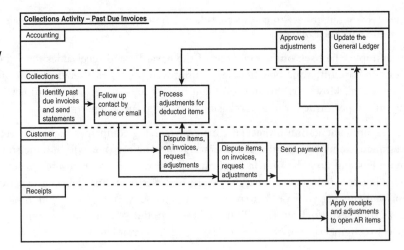

DETERMINING YOUR REPORTING NEEDS

The analysis phase of the project should determine the information flow and reporting requirements for the new software. Reporting is a continuing problem with Oracle Applications implementations because these information requirements can easily change the scope of the project. Without the familiar reports and system outputs of the legacy system, end users and sponsors feel a sense of loss, and change in the organization becomes difficult. If users don't see their familiar reports, you might have a gap list with many items on it.

> **Tip**
>
> Develop a strategy to deal with reporting issues early in the project. When reporting, information, and managerial requirements are known, determine who will be responsible for these requirements and what tools will be used. Communicate your strategy to all concerned.

The Oracle Applications are an On-Line Transaction Processing (OLTP) system that uses the powerful Oracle Relational Database Management System (RDBMS). Many users and project sponsors assume that storing transaction information in the database automatically creates all kinds of interesting reports. This assumption often causes problems because the act of storing the transaction data in the database doesn't actually create the report, and the Oracle database structure is too complicated for an end user to access the data without help. If the project sponsor expects to perform data mining or gain new knowledge about the business transactions in the Oracle database, that requirement is a sizable gap for the OLTP applications, and you will want to develop a separate strategy for that requirement.

Concerning OLTP outputs, you can classify reports in the six ways shown in the following list. The list includes the report group category and several general examples that you might find in your legacy system and your new Oracle software. You should map existing legacy system reports to the equivalent reports that Oracle provides with the software:

- *Transaction Reports.* Check registers, journal entry listings, depreciation details, WIP transactions, cost revaluation details, and so forth

- *Special Forms.* Checks, invoices, statements, purchase orders, bills of lading, packing slip, and so forth

- *Control Reports.* Financial statements, aged trial balances, AP open items, inventory valuation reports, asset listings, and so forth

- *System Configuration Listings.* Listings of customers, vendors, items, codes, cross validation rules, allocation formulas, and so forth

- *System Operation and Management Reports.* Job execution logs, menu listings, and so forth

- *Executive Information Inquiries.* Sales history by product (or time, customer, or region), key performance statistics, balanced score card, margin analysis, and so forth

---

Tip

Mapping legacy reports is time-consuming and often thought to be a thankless task. However, it must be done to help ensure end user satisfaction. This task is better done during the analysis phase than during user training.

Many implementation teams have a hard time reconciling the reports that ship with the Oracle applications and the expectations of the users and executives. For example, many users want the Order Entry and Receivables Applications in Oracle to also support the business's requirements for sales history reporting and planning. Although these applications have much interesting data stored away in the database, their primary mission is to ship products, track what is owed, and collect cash. That primary mission does not extend to answering questions such as, "How many of part number 1234 did we ship last month?"

The legacy software that is being replaced will likely have all kinds of interesting reports that users and management will not want to lose. You can deal with this situation in several ways:

- Educate the users about new processes and reports that support those processes. Determine which legacy reports will not be needed because processes are changing.

- Verify which reports are used frequently and map their content by data element to the Oracle reports.

- Use the software change as an excuse to eliminate redundant, unused, and inconsistent reports.

- Classify the important legacy reports as business requirements, and if the equivalent function is not supported in the Oracle application, add the requirements to the project work plan and scope. Deal with the requirements early in the project.

PART

II

CH

7

INFRASTRUCTURE ANALYSIS

Most implementation projects acquire and install the server hardware and the Oracle applications early in the project. Often, in simple organizations, you can easily specify and acquire the infrastructure your systems will need from the information you received when you were evaluating the purchase of the applications. However, you should still consider studying the infrastructure. The infrastructure analysis helps determine the system requirements.

For example, most Oracle Applications implementations require the purchase of additional disks within the first year of operation. It is very easy to underestimate the requirement for disk space, and you don't want to go back to your source of funding too many times.

Larger organizations will want to make sure the servers can handle the transaction volume and that response time will be adequate. Try to understand the loads your business will place on the new system. Often, it is easy to add more memory and processors to a piece of hardware, but you want to avoid exceeding the maximum configuration of your hardware and performing a "box swap" within the first two years of the system's life. Give your business some room to grow, and estimate your margin of safety.

PHYSICAL ARCHITECTURE

You must determine the physical architecture and structure of the system to serve users. Determine the volumes, frequencies, and sources of key business transactions to estimate requirements for disk space and interfaces. Map where users and functions are located to determine network, desktop, support, and education requirements. A good technical architecture baseline deliverable should include your strategy and configuration for the following:

- Processor Configuration
- Memory
- Disk Space
- Disk I/O Balance Plan
- Network
- Shop Floor Data Collection
- Printers
- Operating System
- Desktop Computers

DEVELOPING A LOGICAL SYSTEM MODEL

During the analysis phase, you should develop a model of how your business will operate with the new software. Some companies called this "Developing a Vision" until that phrase became over used. You want to understand the function points and interfaces among Oracle modules. Include non-Oracle modules, too. A brief conference room pilot can help clarify how much change your business will have to absorb when it starts using the new software.

Tip	Many companies adopt the "vanilla" implementation approach to save customization costs. Vanilla is a code word among project sponsors to mean they don't want to complicate (or pay for) the implementation project with customizations. To these sponsors, vanilla means to configure and use the software exactly as intended by Oracle Corporation; even if it changes the business. However, some sponsors only give lip service to really operating their business exactly as provided by the Oracle Applications. You need to get high-level sponsorship for the future processes, interfaces, transaction flows, controls, procedures, and so forth. If you skip this step, you run the risk of discovering all kinds of show stoppers and reports just as you are about to enter the transition phase of the project.

DATABASE INSTANCES

Determine the number, purpose, and locations of the physical Oracle database instances you will need in order to implement your system. You might determine there are different degrees of fault tolerance and performance requirements for each instance. For example, you probably won't have the same configuration parameters for a pilot database that you use in the production database. Some installations try to put all the instances on one database server, and other sites establish different machines for production and test instances.

Common instances you might consider creating during your implementation include the following:

- *Demo.* Oracle ships a fully configured demonstration database with the software. Many implementation projects use this database for the first conference room pilot. Often, this database is eliminated quickly when lack of disk space becomes a problem.

- *Pilot.* Implementation teams like to stage conference room pilots to try out various business scenarios and evaluate configuration choices.

- *Test.* Many customers rigorously analyze and test every patch and program change before making the change to the production database. Many Oracle customers set up test databases in 1999 to support Y2K certification projects.

- *Development.* This database instance is often established so the high-risk activities of programmers and consultants won't affect other project activities. Many clients restrict their outside consultants and contractors to this instance.

- *Training.* A training database can be established and periodically refreshed for inexperienced users. Some users relax and learn more when they can experiment and explore an instance where they can't hurt anything.

PART

II

CH

7

- *Production.* This instance is the online transaction processing database. It will be fully configured with security, fault tolerance, and tuned performance parameters and architecture.

- *Reporting.* Some companies make nightly copies of the production database to a different machine. To keep the load of batch reports off the production database, users are connected to the copy when they want to run long-running jobs. The Oracle applications were not created with this usage in mind, and this technique is probably a bad idea for most installations.

Tip

Remember that every instance you create requires some degree of configuration, administration, and maintenance. If you have many instances, you will need a mechanism to track the configuration setup and patch level of each instance. Also, if you regularly copy your production database to a development instance to give programmers a realistic set of data, will you have to establish new passwords, responsibilities, and so forth each time you make a copy?

Note

The basic architecture of the Oracle Applications is designed for only one physical production instance of the database. You can put multiple organizations and multiple sets of books within one instance of the applications. However, if you have the requirement to establish several production instances of the application database, please realize you are setting up a difficult architecture; you should consider every possible alternative before implementing the complexity of multiple production instances.

DETERMINING IT DEPARTMENT STAFFING

Another part of infrastructure analysis and planning relates to the structure of the information technology department. The new software and hardware will require new skills. Determine changes that might be made in job descriptions, roles, and responsibilities. Analyze your inventory of skills for new requirements and obsolescence problems. During a rapid implementation project, it is conceivable that some of the application modules might be ready for production status before the technical skills are in place to support a production system. Usually, you will want to avoid situations where the technical staff is on the critical path of the project.

CUSTOMIZATIONS

The analysis phase of the project is concerned with identifying customizations to the Applications. After you understand the business requirements and have a gap list, you can begin to address the customizations you will require. Perform a high-level analysis of each customization before you finalize the project scope and work plan. If you decide to extend the Oracle Applications, you will want to add and track tasks for design, build, unit test, integration test, and document to the project work plan. Because customizations change the scope, cost, and schedule for the implementation, your steering committee and project sponsor should be aware of all customizations.

> **Note**
>
> *Customization* is a general term to refer to almost any enhancement or extension that you make to the Oracle applications. Some customizations are ill-advised because they might impact your ability to obtain support from Oracle Corporation, and they require much work during upgrade projects. Other customizations are a normal part of Oracle Applications implementations and include reports and interfaces.

LEGACY DATA AND CONVERSION

During the analysis phase of the project, you should understand and develop a strategy for each major data entity you are going to load into the new applications. Also, consider the shared entities, such as customers and vendors, from all perspectives. For example, the purchasing and payables departments often have a completely different view of vendor data.

First, determine what to convert from the legacy system. Look at the table of contents of the reference manuals and find nouns that name objects in your business. These are the entities you will want to estimate. For example, in the table of contents for the Receivables manual, you will find transactions (invoices and memos), customers, receipts, and so forth. The following is a list of major business entities you might want to convert during your applications implementation project:

- GL Balances
- GL Transactions
- Customers
- Vendors
- Items
- Inventory Balances
- AP Open Items
- AR Open Items
- Open Purchase Orders
- Open Purchase Order Requisitions
- Open Sales Orders
- WIP Balances
- Bills of Material
- Routings

PART
II

CH
7

- AP History
- AR History
- Inventory Transaction History
- Employees
- Year to Date Payroll Balances

Next, determine a strategy for conversion of each entity for planning purposes. You can choose to manually enter 1,200 vendors because that can be accomplished with clerical labor in under 10 days and there is no Oracle open interface for vendors. However, loading 50,000 items with more than 150 attributes for each item is clearly something that should be programmed and converted from legacy data.

Consider whether the data from the legacy system is clean, consistent, and worth loading. For example, if you reorganized your entire department structure in the General Ledger a year ago, it might make no sense to load five years of legacy GL balances because there is no comparison between the current year and the prior year balances.

Tip

Inconsistent data is hard to load programmatically, and you should try to avoid putting lots of logic into your conversion programs.

Tip

Some data is not worth the trouble to convert. Consider developing alternative strategies. Some companies have left their legacy systems available to users after startup, printed everything out, or archived legacy data to a simpler database structure than the Oracle applications.

If there is an Oracle Application Program Interface (API) for the entity you must convert, that is the conversion technique you will want to use. Usually, the API will have a set of tables and an import program to process the legacy system data you put in the interface tables. Most APIs have a report to tell you about data that fails validation. APIs are not end user tools, however. It usually takes a functional analyst to map each data element in the legacy data to the Oracle interface structure. Also, you need a programmer to load the data into the Oracle interfaces and clear invalid records.

If you must synchronize a major data element in a foreign system and an Oracle application, you have a special problem that is more of a continuous interface than a data conversion task. For example, if you have a non-Oracle order entry system and must share customers with Oracle AR, you will have a customer master file for each system, and you will want to make sure that every customer in each application is replicated in the other. In this example, you might use the customer API in AR to avoid duplicate data entry by programming a recurring conversion for new order entry customers. These recurring data conversions require more analysis, programming, testing, and documentation than the one-time data loads.

UNDERSTANDING TYPICAL TASKS, DELIVERABLES, AND MILESTONES OF THE ANALYSIS PHASE

You should prepare several documents during the analysis phase of the project. These tasks and deliverables will provide a foundation for the rest of the project implementation activity. These project deliverables document the current processes and requirements, the new processes, the system architecture, the degree of fit, the data conversion strategy, and the system interface strategy. You will use these documents to support your configuration choices, conference room pilots, test plans, customization designs, and end user training.

DETERMINING EXISTING BUSINESS TRANSACTION PROCESSES

Document how your business currently operates. Work with broad processes such as procurement and customer fulfillment instead of narrow applications such as purchasing and order entry. For each application, consider producing a document to show the following baseline items:

- Draw diagrams of process flows to show what happens in the business, the sequence of events, integration among unit transactions, interdepartmental relationships, inter-company activity, and system interfaces.

- Use questionnaires to document and analyze each business function.

- Analyze the information, requirements, and format of special forms.

- Analyze information on management, transaction, and control reports.

- Document security requirements.

- Document legal and regulatory requirements.

- Determine the process inconsistencies and differences among all your business units.

DETERMINING THE EXISTING COMPUTER SYSTEM ARCHITECTURE

A good technical architecture baseline document will establish the boundaries and capabilities of the legacy system. Typically, users will expect new user interfaces, reports, procedures, and capabilities of the new systems. However, users will also expect the new systems to replace each and every function and feature of the outgoing systems. You will want to map existing capabilities to the functions of the Oracle Applications to establish a baseline and to manage user and management expectations from that basic set of requirements.

Consider the following items as you establish your technical architecture baseline:

- Document each existing application.

- Catalog databases.

- Understand existing interfaces.

- Inventory key hardware.
- Evaluate the existing network.
- Document expected changes.
- Note areas of improvement.

DETERMINING THE BUSINESS SIZE (TRANSACTION VOLUME AND FREQUENCY)

Almost every Oracle Applications installation must buy additional disk space sooner than expected. In addition, you will want to determine what history and basic data you will load into the new system and what techniques you will use to enter startup data. For example, if you have more than about 2,500 customers or vendors, you will want to consider loading them with a program instead of manually. We know of one client that loaded one million customer records into their AR system at the rate of about 5,000 per hour. At 20 hours per day, this volume required a 10-day task, lots of coordination with other systems, and lots of system resources right before the system went live. Consider producing a document to show the volumes and frequencies of each of your significant transactions. Use this information to calculate disk space requirements, balance I/O across the disk array, and evaluate expected system loads.

AGREEING ON DETAILED BUSINESS REQUIREMENTS

For each future business process, document the business requirements. Define each step of the process, who is involved, and what information they use to make each transaction. Understand corporate policies, controls, audit requirements, and management involvement with the process. Document external influences from customers, vendors, and government agencies.

Tip	Also, consider business requirements for the project implementation schedule. (For example, consider waiting until the busy season is over before launching the new systems.)

Understand the transactional, technical, cultural, informational, and managerial needs of the business in these areas:

- Business goals
- Key performance drivers
- Objectives and policies
- Definitions
- Seasonal influences
- Transaction event sequences

Every Oracle applications implementation is different and will have several critical success factors that will define the project. Even if the project sponsor proclaims your project to be a vanilla implementation, make sure you understand which application functions you must activate. For example, if you are in an industry that requires lot or serial number control and tracking for your products, the Oracle applications can likely meet that requirement. However, you should document the need and make sure that the guy who loads your item master understands what must be done.

ANALYZING TRANSACTION REQUIREMENTS

Determine which transactions are required. During the analysis phase, users might ask for every feature and function provided by Oracle Applications. However, does it really make sense to activate the AutoLockbox transactions for cash receipts on fewer than 2,000 invoices per month? You will want to determine the setup and processing overhead of activating an automatic Oracle process. Many customers disable standard Oracle application features to avoid adding overhead to their business.

PERFORMANCE AND EQUIPMENT REQUIREMENTS

Consider documenting appropriate system response time in the technical architecture deliverables if you have significant transaction volumes. For example, if you are trying to create 10,000 invoices an hour in your AR system, you will want to understand the performance issues. Response time requirements can impact the physical technical architecture of the servers, desktops, user interface, network, and so forth. Consider the space requirements for your transaction volume. For example, will the administrators be able to support a database that is growing at a rate of five percent a month?

SECURITY REQUIREMENTS

You might have strict security requirements for your Oracle applications. You should understand who has access to which menu choices for screens. You should determine whether certain reports are sensitive and which users can run which reports. If you will use the multiorg functionality, you will want to understand how partitioning the data will affect your reports and what kinds of responsibilities you will need to support.

REPORTING AND EXECUTIVE INFORMATION REQUIREMENTS

Reporting requirements are often the most neglected critical success factor for an implementation project, and you should develop a strategy for reporting after you have analyzed the requirements. Your worst nightmare is to skip this analysis and discover show stopper requirements for 50 or more reports a month before going live. If it takes two to three days to create a report, it is almost impossible to avoid postponing the launch schedule when this happens. Determine your reporting scope and strategy in a document in the project analysis phase. Make sure gaps in reporting requirements are linked to the primary gap analysis document.

AUDIT AND CONTROL REQUIREMENTS

Most large companies have established audit and control requirements, and you will have a hard time changing these policies during your implementation project. You will want to create a document if you have to work around the Oracle Applications to satisfy these policies. Examples of requirements in this area include the following:

- Auditors might need specialized reports. Consider your internal auditors, public accountants, and government auditors. Typically, these reports are not daily operating reports, and you might have to search for them.

- Most companies establish separation of duties when cash is involved. If you have a very small payables or credit department, you will have to devise a process, security, and work assignments to satisfy this requirement.

- Many companies require special approvals for certain types of expenditures, and you might have requirements for the purchasing approval hierarchy. Also, you might have to modify an Oracle Workflow process.

DETERMINING YOUR FUTURE BUSINESS PROCESSES

When you know your business requirements and process flows, you can create a map of each function to an Oracle Applications function to see how it fits. If there are gaps in the function map, you will have to start planning for user process changes or customization of the software.

Tip

Implementation team members with little Oracle Applications experience often have a hard time visualizing how Oracle Applications will work in a given business situation. An experienced consultant can often add a lot of value and help determine the degree of fit among your requirements and the applications.

A business process reengineering (BPR) project can be disruptive to an Oracle Applications implementation project. If you include BPR in your project, make sure the reengineering team is well familiar with the applications and uses the new systems as the baseline for change. Consider the Oracle capabilities before designing a reengineered process.

Tip

Some processes in the business often will change during the Oracle implementation project. Make sure to design new processes from the new software's natural process flow. Often, a legacy process is reengineered, and the improvement becomes part of the requirements for the new system. Unfortunately, the great new change is made late in the applications project, and the Oracle process might be entirely different. When this situation occurs, customization to the basic Oracle code could be required to make the reengineered solution successful, and you must deal with changes in scope late in the implementation project.

DETERMINING THE DEGREE OF FIT

Make sure to itemize and publish to everyone a document of where your business requirements and processes are different from the basic functionality provided by the Oracle applications. Consider creating an issue log entry for each gap, and assign a project team member and a resolution date to the problem. Update the project work plan to create tasks to design, build, test, and document customizations or a work-around for each gap.

> **Tip**
>
> Prepare the gap analysis document in plain language, and describe the gap in terms of the current user process. Many steering committee members, sponsors, and department heads won't be able to help resolve issues that are presented from a technical or Oracle Applications perspective.

THINKING ABOUT TRANSITION REQUIREMENTS

When you transition from your legacy systems to the Oracle ERP software, you will have many diverse tasks including end user training, data conversion, change management, and so forth. During the analysis phase of the project, you can prepare a document to outline a strategy for training and supporting users. If you get this task out of the way early in the project, you will have it already prepared and ready for reference during the more hectic time as you start the transition phase of the project.

ANALYZING AND DEVELOPING A DATA CONVERSION STRATEGY

For each entity to be converted, publish an analysis to support the conversion strategy. Consider doing the following in your document:

- Document the record layout of the legacy data.
- Determine who owns and is responsible for the source data.
- Determine whether the conversion will be manual or programmed. Estimate the time required for each technique.
- Determine whether there are problems with the legacy data.
- If the conversion is programmed, map the source data to required Oracle API columns and tables.
- Determine when the conversion will take place.
- Determine balancing and validation tests.

ANALYZING AND DEVELOPING A SYSTEM INTEGRATION STRATEGY

Often, Oracle Applications will interface with non-Oracle systems. For each interface point, determine how the system will operate. Integration can be single-directional or bidirectional. For example, you might want to send some billing data to a non-Oracle sales history system (outbound interface). You might bring in cash receipts transactions from your bank (inbound interface to an Oracle API). You might need to synchronize all kinds of shipping, receiving, and billing transactions with a non-Oracle warehouse management system. By the end of the analysis phase of the project, you should know which interfaces are part of your implementation project and how much effort will be required to build, test, and document each interface program.

In Summary

The analysis phase of an Oracle Applications implementation project is the foundation for almost all project activities that come later in the implementation. Most of the deliverables of the analysis phase are "living documents" in that they will be included in deliverables for other activities. The functional and technical analysis is important. If you skip parts of analysis, you will have to perform those parts at a later and less convenient time and at higher cost. This phase of the project should determine your project scope and will have a major influence on the total cost of the project.

The analysis deliverables are like a road map to guide you from your legacy system to your new Oracle ERP system. Implementing an ERP system can be confusing, and the analysis helps keep you from getting lost. When you have a good map and refer to it often throughout the trip, you improve your odds of success. To improve the chances of delivering your project on time and within budget, make sure you do well in the analysis phase of the project.

CHAPTER 8

CONVERTING ANALYSIS INTO SOLUTIONS

Welcome to the next chapter! This chapter discusses converting gaps from the analysis of Oracle Applications and your organization into solutions. These solutions can be customizations, setups, or specific configurations of the Oracle Applications during the implementation. This chapter provides a framework for designing solutions that utilize the Oracle Applications and technology to fulfill your organization's business requirements.

The primary purposes of this phase are to develop the design documents for the solutions that fill the gaps between the Oracle Applications and your business requirements, and develop supporting application setup documents. Many other deliverables in this phase complement the business requirements and setup documents. You will design your technical and application architecture, create data conversion scripts and programs, develop initial testing and training documents, and prepare your organization for transition to the production environment.

Each business requirement solution may have several alternatives developed that need to be further reviewed and discussed with the project team members. The alternatives presented could range from doing nothing to building a very complex customization. The pros and cons, as well as the cost and benefit, for each alternative should be presented. Selection of the most cost-effective alternative might not necessarily prove to be the best choice for your organization. The project team members need to scrutinize the solutions and select the one most suitable and cost effective for your organization. As these solutions are created, your team will begin to design the end user documentation. This documentation will be reviewed and revised appropriately as the solutions are solidified and finalized.

While you are converting your business analysis gaps into solutions, keep in mind the organizational changes and reengineering of business processes. These changes need to be considered in the future business model and included in the scope of the overall project. Downstream project activities and resources may be affected by these business changes. It is recommended to bring all new processes, policies, and procedures into the scope of the project as soon as possible to set proper expectations with your project team and management.

During this phase, the application and technical architecture is designed and documented by technical team members. The technical architecture is designed to support the standard Oracle Applications, custom solutions, ancillary applications, and third-party products. The technical team will also design and document the performance testing approach and programs.

Converting the business analysis into solutions is an iterative process. Many tasks in converting the analysis into solutions and enabling the system (discussed in Chapter 9, "Enabling the System") overlap. These overlapping tasks will appear seamless to the project team as they progress from phase to phase, continually building on the preceding tasks. This is an exciting time for all team members as the business requirements and solutions begin to shape the future business model of your organization.

DESIGNING CUSTOMIZATIONS

Designing customizations is one of the main objectives of this phase. Your team's focus will be to produce design documents for Oracle Application customizations that meet the functional requirements of the business—functionally, technically, and financially. You will design customizations to fill the gaps between the Oracle Applications, legacy systems, third-party applications, and your organization's business requirements. The overall customization approach is defined in the customization strategy prepared earlier in the project. Each design specification must be created in a way that it promotes and supports the future maintenance and support of the system. These design documents must also take into consideration the application setups and test plans for each Oracle Application module. You also need to consider your organization's security, database, and network requirements because these create additional constraints on the design of your customizations.

Customizations to the Oracle Applications can be categorized in three ways:

- Extensions
- Modifications
- Interfaces

Some project activities that can be considered customizations are the following:

- Creating a new report or form
- Renaming or modifying a copy of a standard Oracle report or form
- Creating a one-time interface to convert legacy data
- Creating an inbound or outbound interface to a non-Oracle application
- Creating an Oracle Application Alert
- Renaming or modifying a copy of an Oracle Workflow

PROJECT DESIGN AND BUILD STANDARDS

Design and build standards ensure that all project team members follow a consistent method of delivering work products to the team and end users. Normally, project team members discuss what standards they want to develop and establish prior to beginning any design work. It is highly recommended that you review the following documents before establishing your own standards. These documents have evolved over the years and are full of helpful information:

- *Oracle Application Installation Manual*
- *Application Object Library Reference Manual*
- *Oracle Application Coding Standards*
- *Building Systems Using Oracle(7/8) Programming Tools*

Many other standards need to be considered prior to any deliverables being designed or developed. Make sure to establish an application short name and custom working directory for your customizations. Consider establishing an acronym or using the first three letters of your company's name for the short name.

The short name will become a prefix on all your custom work. It will be used internally within the application as well as operating system files. For example, BOS could be the application short name for BOSS Corporation custom development. This ensures that your customizations don't get mixed up with Oracle Applications code. Register your custom application within the Oracle Applications. When your custom application has been registered, it then becomes accessible to you like any other Oracle Application module. You will begin to see it listed in QuickPicks throughout the Applications. After the custom application has been created, you have the ability to mix it with the standard Oracle modules. You can mix and match custom and standard menus and forms, creating an extraordinary customized application. Also, make sure that each new custom object that is created gets registered within your newly defined application. Doing this secures your work during future upgrades, allowing for a smoother and more successful transition to new releases of Oracle Applications.

SOURCE CODE: SQL, PL/SQL, AND PROGRAMMING LANGUAGES

As you begin to develop new code, make sure that there are common programming standards for source code. Specifically for program file headers, consider capturing information such as filename, description of the program, how the program is used, any notes that would be of importance, and a complete history of the changes, including the developer's name, date, and reason for making the change.

Also make sure that any helpful comments embedded within your source code follow a common standard. It is recommended that comments be used liberally and generously throughout the code to assist your development staff in the future. It is best to encapsulate comments in a box of hyphens (-) or pound signs (#) to help them stand out within the code. You should have comments before each step in a program, before each procedure in a program, and wherever they can assist in understanding complex program logic or algorithms.

ORACLE TOOLS

For Oracle Forms, Oracle Reports, SQL, PL/SQL, and database trigger coding standards, follow the published standards in *Building Systems Using Oracle(7/8) Programming Tools* and *Oracle Applications Coding Standards*. These products have evolved over the years and have developed natural layout conventions that can be found in the aforementioned books. You have no reason to invent your own coding standards because these have been proven successful and are widely accepted within the Oracle community.

DESIGNING NEW TABLES

When new tables are designed for your customizations, make sure to create them in an exclusive "custom only" Oracle user account. Create the user account with the same name as the application short name previously discussed. Create all new tables with the application short name prefix, so that the custom tables are easily identified and recognized by your development team. For example, a BOSS custom table would be identified as follows: BOS_LOOKUPS, where BOS is the application short name, and LOOKUPS is the table name for the custom application lookups.

SOURCE NAMING CONVENTIONS

Another mechanism for keeping objects organized within your custom working directories is the use of naming conventions. Consider using a standard approach for naming objects, such as BOSGLU10.sql. Where BOS is the application short name, GL is for the Oracle General Ledger module, U is a unique identifier for Update, which is the type of transaction being performed within the object, and 10 is a unique sequence number for the customization. The .sql is the standard Oracle extension that indicates the code as being an SQL*Plus or PL/SQL program.

> **Tip**
>
> Consider developing a one-page, high-level document that contains an example of the naming convention standard, with a description of each segment and possible values. Distribute this to your team and have them tape it up in their offices. This helps promote the standards, by making the standards readily accessible for reference.

You may want to use similar naming conventions for all your project deliverables to help keep objects organized and understood by all team members. For example, in BOSGS021.doc, BOS represents the short name, GS stands for a Getting Started phase deliverable, 2 represents the second deliverable of the phase, and 1 represents the first revision of the document. The .doc is the standard extension for MS Word documents. Be creative in designing your naming convention, but be consistent.

CUSTOM INSTALLATION ROUTINES

The creation of installation scripts is more important than the code itself. Develop scripts for your custom objects to install them with minimal steps and re-execute without errors or failure due to duplicate data. They also need to be transferable to other hardware platforms and operating systems. Generate scripts for creating your database objects, generating seed data, and creating grants and synonyms. Scripts can be created to do just about anything needed to support your customizations. Be sure that these objects are included as part of your unit and integration testing. To help put things into perspective, what if a disaster occurred and your custom application was wiped out? How would you recover? Your immediate response would be let's restore from our backups. Well, there are no backups; the tapes can't be read by your tape drive. Now what? Inevitably, you will need a way to recreate your custom application from scratch. Having these installation scripts will be invaluable in this situation. Take the time and effort required to design, develop, and test these installation scripts!

THE SOLUTION/CONCEPTUAL DESIGN DOCUMENT

This design document summarizes your business requirements that are not addressed by a specific application module and recommends one or more solution(s) for each requirement. The document is created as one of the last tasks in the Analyzing the Project phase of the implementation (see Chapter 7, "Analyzing the Project") but is reviewed in detail prior to beginning the next step of design tasks assigned to your team. It serves as a confirmation that your project team understands your business requirements and documents the solution and assumptions that are the foundation for the level of effort estimates.

A description of each business requirement should be contained in this document, along with the specific requirements and your recommended solution. Your solutions may include workarounds in the application or the use of standard features, extensions to the database, creating flexfields or customizations, or procedural changes.

Upon completion of this design document, it is followed by two more documents, the functional/high level design and technical/low level design. These documents are discussed in the following sections, and when all three have been completed, they are considered a complete design package for your customizations.

> **Tip**
>
> Suggest to end users the possibility of an application workaround or use of standard functionality prior to committing to a customization. Many times there may be an acceptable way to fulfill the users' requirements by using standard application functionality. Also, explain to your users that customizations add complexity to the implementation, as well as ongoing maintenance and future upgrades. Often, users are focused on their needs and don't see the additional burden placed on their organizations by customizations.

An estimate for the amount of time and resources for each recommended solution should be provided. Each solution should have a specific list of the customizations that are going to be created. These modules include new or modified reports, forms, and programs; conversion scripts; and database tables. A difficulty range should be determined, and an appropriate estimate calculated.

The estimates provided need to cover all work associated with the customization until the end of the project. The estimates should include functional and technical designs, creation of the custom object, associated test scripts, and installation routines. Also take into consideration how many resources will be needed to complete the customization based on your estimates. See the section "Estimating Customizations" later in the chapter for more details on providing realistic estimates.

THE HIGH-LEVEL/FUNCTIONAL DESIGN DOCUMENT

This design document is developed in layman terms and is normally written by the functional project team members. It is used as a bridging document between the end users' business requirements and the technical team design documents.

The document begins with a narrative essay that presents the requirement in layman terms and expands on the solution design document created earlier in the project. The next section of the document should cover the business needs to justify why this customization is being produced. You can also provide additional information such as the major features, end user procedures, and any supporting assumptions that will help your technical team comprehend the customization. The addition of business scenarios, which are based on real business transactions, will help the project team further understand the requirements of the customization.

The functional design document is straightforward but important and should be designed for every customization. This document needs to be reviewed and approved by your project team and end users prior to being presented to your technical staff. This project deliverable should have an acceptance certificate created and signed by the end users. Changes after the acceptance certificate would require a change order created to bring them into the scope of the project.

THE LOW-LEVEL/TECHNICAL DESIGN DOCUMENT

The technical design documents are complex in nature and are not meant to be reviewed with your end users. These documents are very technical and provide a level of detail required only by that of the technical team. This document defines the components required to support and implement the customizations. It serves as the bridge between the functional design document discussed earlier and the actual code required to support the business requirement. Both documents should be considered a complete detailed design.

The technical design document provides all the details necessary to maintain and support a customization. It contains information on the specific module names, objects that describe the customization, navigation logic on how to enter the application to execute the customization, and how to leave the applications. There should also be information that represents the relationship of database objects being used within the customization and any special logic that will help the development team understand how the customization is set up and meant to be used in a production environment. There can also be pseudo code that supports the program logic for SQL, PL/SQL, or any of the Pro languages. Overall, this document is meant to be the all-inclusive guide to a customization. Your development team needs to spend time developing code and this document to have a successful customization. To put things in perspective, if a customization works fine and there are no problems, that is excellent. However, if it doesn't, and there is minimal supporting documentation, it is going to be difficult to research and resurrect the problem. The final words on the subject—a customization is not complete without supporting detailed design documentation!

Each of the design documents should go through a peer review by the more experienced team members to ensure that quality and efficient deliverables are being developed. A good-quality control process helps further enhance your team's ability to deliver good work products. These quality reviews should be constructive and a learning experience for all team members involved.

ESTIMATING CUSTOMIZATIONS

Providing estimates for documents customizations is always difficult. This section can be used to help devise a way to estimate your project customizations or other uncertain activities.

Below is an estimating model that has been used on many Oracle projects. This formula provides a method for project planning that is easy to use and produces a realistic estimate. You must remember that this is only an estimate.

This estimating model helps provide more realistic estimates. The result field is TIME, which represents the estimated time it's going to take to complete all phases of the customization. Additional information on this model can be found in PERT/CPM estimating and project management books. This is a standard model for estimating uncertain activities and tasks.

> **Tip**
>
> Create a spreadsheet of the estimating model for your project team to use. Place it in a working directory, or have them create a shortcut on their desktop so that they can easily access and execute the estimating model. This model is not the answer to all estimating, but an approach that provides more realistic estimates.

The variable fields you ask your team members to provide estimates for are To, which represents your optimistic time estimate, Tm, your most likely time estimate, and Tp, your pessimistic time estimate. If a wide range of estimates is provided, then there is a high degree of uncertainty of the business requirements.

When providing estimates, consider many different factors that may affect your time to completion. Understand the business objectives behind what you are estimating. Also, consider the primary resources assigned to the project. An inexperienced developer might work at half the speed of an experienced developer. However, the use of certain tools such as Oracle Designer might speed up a development effort. Understanding the experience level of an organization's resources is critical to estimating. Many organizations provide estimates without taking into consideration the available skills, tools, or technology. If your estimate is for a significant amount of time or cost, consider decomposing the main task into subtasks such as analyze, design, build, document, and so forth. Don't be afraid to use estimates from prior projects. You may require additional time or resources based on the experience you've gained from completing the first customization. But it's a safe bet to use an existing estimate.

> **Note**
>
> The application developers are critical to this phase of the project. Estimates for a customization can make or break a project. If you find the time is going to push your project past the target date, add another developer to shorten the duration. If these tasks are associated with the critical path of a project, adding resources might be your only alternative.

Many professionals are too confident in their estimates and assume that no unexpected events will occur and the task or project will progress smoothly. Consider adding contingency time to your estimates, which will act as a cushion for unexpected events.

MANAGING THE PHASE

As you progress from phase to phase on your project, you will validate the accuracy and completeness of the documentation and information developed in the previous phases. One of the first things that need to be defined is the design and build standards and guidelines that will be used by your project team. Standards should be defined for each kind of object that is going to be designed to support the solutions earlier defined. For example, if no new forms are being developed, then there is no need to have a standard created for forms. After the standards have been defined, your development staff can begin to focus on creating the design documents. If there are many customizations, the module design and build process can use up a great deal of the time and budget of a project.

It is important to schedule the right technical resources and provide time for functional team members and end users to participate in testing. Many tasks between this phase and the Enabling the System phase overlap. You will find your team working on tasks in each phase simultaneously. Your work breakdown structure should allow plenty of time so that resources can be assigned to individual modules to manage and control their assignments properly.

Having a good technical team lead can provide solid technical leadership and management of the lesser experienced staff. The technical lead must assume the responsibility and accountability for creating good-quality work products that will be maintained by your organization for years to come. A systematic approach to quality control is essential to the success of a project.

> **Note**
>
> If you are implementing Oracle Applications in phases, keep in mind that you will then be supporting legacy and new systems simultaneously. You will need to think about reporting consolidation or building additional interfaces to support both applications. Now is the time to rethink your approach, or to estimate and design the reporting procedures and interfaces.

When scheduling your resources to develop design documents, take into consideration the number of available and qualified team members. Also take into consideration the productivity of the work environment. Don't put your design and development staff in a high traffic area. These people like to be heads down on activities and have a quiet place to work.

When developing schedules and the project plan you need to consider which tasks can be conducted in parallel. Take into consideration the diversity of your group when creating your estimates. Don't assign a task that has been estimated for an experienced developer to a lesser experienced individual. If you do, re-estimate your plan.

During this phase of the project, some project team members may be phased out due to budget considerations or unplanned events. Make sure that all supporting documentation is transferred to other project team members or is saved in the project repository before team members are released from the project.

PHASE SUCCESS FACTORS

The following are some critical success factors to consider during this phase of a project:

- Clear definition of business objectives
- Involvement of key executives, functional experts, and technical staff from all areas of the business
- Knowledge of key features and capabilities of the application and technology
- Complete traceability of design to specific business requirements
- Management of designs within the scope and objectives of the project
- Ensuring that proper resources and time commitments can be met
- Management and control of scope changes via a change control system
- Ensuring that there is sufficient data for performance testing of the database, application, and system
- Development of a comprehensive strategy for transitioning the organization to the new application
- Development a contingency plan to support all transition and retransition activities

REVISITING BUSINESS REQUIREMENTS

As you continue with the design of application customizations, you will continue to develop new business requirements. To help support these requirements and transition your user community later in the project, you need to create training material and user procedures that support the customizations and standard functionality of the application. Some organizations like to create process narratives that are based on the business processes that support their daily operations. These narratives lay the groundwork necessary for developing user procedures, user training material, and system and acceptance testing.

Tip

If you experience a constant change in requirements from your users during the design effort, implement a review and sign-off procedure for each design to keep control of the project scope.

DESIGNING THE TECHNICAL ARCHITECTURE

During this phase, the technical architecture begins to take shape. Detailed design documents for the application and database architectures are developed. Documents for the detailed network, hardware, and software needed to support the application's deployment in the future are designed. Identify all applications involved, including legacy and ancillary systems. This document will become invaluable later in the project and will provide management with "the big picture" of all applications being implemented.

The degree of detail needed to support the preceding documents depends on the scope of the project and required architecture. If the architecture is a localized implementation with one installation of the applications, a system administrator or technical architect can perform these tasks. The system administrator can configure and install the technical foundation for the new system without additional work.

If the architecture is at the enterprise level, designing below this level may be difficult without understanding the localized issues. In this case, architects will design only at the enterprise level and leave the detail architecture to the local system administrator or technical architect.

Tip

Consider developing a one-page, high-level design document using a business drawing tool. Design the document using objects that represent the hardware, network, and applications architecture being implemented. Also include customizations and third-party applications. Include a list of software that will reside on each server. Consider shading or coloring these objects to represent the phase or time frame in which they will be implemented. Try to keep this to one page and make sure that project team members and management receive a copy.

The application architect should develop a detailed application plan identifying key setups, logical databases, and the modules to be installed. The technical architect works closely with the application architect to design the hardware and networking needs to support the applications and ensure the business and technical architecture needs are met.

The technical architect role is critical to the success of the project. Some organizations are hesitant to use external technical architects if they feel their groups' abilities are adequate. It really shouldn't matter whether the technical architect is a consultant or employee. What matters most is that the architecture be the best for your organization.

DATA CONVERSION

One of the first tasks that need to be performed is the creation of a conversion environment. This environment will be used to prepare conversion design documents during the build and testing tasks in the subsequent phases of the project. Next, perform a data element mapping exercise where legacy data sources are mapped to the Oracle Application tables and columns. Depending on the Oracle Application module, you will have access to open interfaces and application program interfaces in which legacy data can be mapped.

Establish regularly scheduled meetings with the data conversion team and your end user community; once or twice a week should be sufficient. This meeting will keep all team members abreast of progress and issues. Your team will have many informal meetings with the end users to discuss mapping details. Also, make sure that you have legacy application technical expertise available to help with the conversion mapping exercise. Many legacy application data elements are not intuitive, and it will take someone with the proper expertise to decipher the information.

On completing the mapping exercise, the conversion programs and scripts to convert data should be created. If you plan to use automated conversion approach or tools, you may need to develop traditional code to perform the data conversion. Regardless of the approach, business rules need to be created to support the conversion effort. In addition to creating programs and supporting business rules, test plans need to be developed to ensure that all data is converted successfully. Simple programs can be written to ensure that data has been converted successfully and the integrity has remained intact.

You may determine that manual conversion of data is the best approach for your organization. Depending on the amount and complexity of the data, you will still need a conversion plan. It is best to create a plan that your conversion staff can follow to help them understand the data dependency requirements of the application. When planning your data conversion tasks, take into consideration changes caused by discovering new application requirements found while creating your design documents. For example, you would not want to enter an employee into Oracle HR until her manager's data has been entered. This is a simple example of how a manual data conversion plan will save time and money.

Data conversion design documents can be created by individuals with both technical and functional experience and good knowledge of the integration required for performing this exercise.

INITIAL PROJECT DOCUMENTATION

During this phase of the project, the initial designs for the custom user guide and reference manual, as well as the technical manual and system guide, are created. The need and time to develop these documents is often underestimated, which leads to poor or no documentation being developed. The following sections discuss the need for training and transitioning your organization to the production environment.

TRAINING DOCUMENTATION

Design the initial training material during this phase after the future process modules have been reviewed and finalized. The end user training material should be developed based on user roles and aligned closely with your business scenarios created earlier in the project. When designing the training documentation, keep in mind how training will be delivered. The following is a list of things to think about as you are designing your training material.

- What size classes are acceptable?
- Will you use onsite trainers to assist?
- Will it be a train-the-trainer approach?
- How much training will the instructors need prior to delivering the classes?
- Will classes be held in multiple sites at the same time?
- Will you need multiple training database instances?

As you design your documentation, take into consideration new policies and procedures that have been defined during the implementation. Also keep in mind that as new employees are hired into your organization, these people will need to be trained. Get them trained as part of their orientation to your organization.

> **Note**   Good training material and delivery has a direct impact on the continued success of your implementation!

TRANSITIONING TO PRODUCTION

During the transition to production, you will need a support infrastructure as well as contingency and transition plans. The production support team will act as the help desk for all application, database, and network issues during the transition. The roles and responsibilities of this team must be identified early in the project so that the team is trained and educated properly to supply adequate support.

DESIGNING THE TRANSITION AND CONTINGENCY PLANS

The development of a detailed transition and contingency plan includes the tasks associated with transitioning the organization to production. These documents are inspired by documents created earlier in the project, such as the education and training plan, performance testing strategy, and the transition strategy. The transition plan should include a series of specific tasks to assist the project team and end users. These tasks should promote and facilitate the planning and estimating activities required to guide your team through the transition to production.

Many organizations overlook the need for contingency plans prior to implementing. There is, at times, a false sense of security in implementing a solid ERP application such as Oracle. There have been many successes, as well as many failures. The design of a contingency plan should provide alternatives to your organization if the transition to production is unsuccessful.

The plan should cover all circumstances that would require its execution. The contingency plan should also include a list of implementation steps that, if failed, could be used to understand specifically what went wrong and how the team should react. It might be possible that a specific implementation step could cause the transition to stop; although, if a resolution or solution is documented, the project could resume after the problem is fixed. The plan should also include steps to retransition to the production system after the problems are resolved.

PRELIMINARY APPLICATION SETUP DOCUMENTS

These documents are perhaps the most important to be created during the project. After the business models have been developed and the final requirements determined, the application setup documents must be defined. These setup documents are detailed plans of how to set up each Oracle Application module. A typical application document should include information on data conversion, system, application, and data administration task. Do not underestimate the time required to develop these documents. You will need to review these documents with your end users on a regular basis and test the values in a SETUP only database instance of the applications prior to your final version.

Tip

> If disk capacity allows, create a separate instance for testing the values in conjunction with designing your setup document. This database instance should be for setups only, and as soon as your documents have all been created, the SETUP instance can be removed. This provides a safe and static place for application setups to be tested and documented.

Another setup task is to design a form for capturing the application sign-on profiles for your end users. This document should capture information such as the user's name, application sign-on name, role or title, responsibility, and department or group assignment. It is also good to add the network and operating system logons. Many times this information is not shared between your system administrator and applications administrator. Putting this information together in one document helps manage, control, and organize the process.

PREPARING FOR SYSTEM TEST

At this stage in the project, you need to be developing a test strategy that encompasses all testing tasks. This document should include an overview of your testing approach, the test scripts to be created and executed, a testing plan that includes resources and responsibilities, and a step-by-step review of the issue resolution process. The objective of the testing strategy is to provide overall direction and guidelines for testing all aspects of the system. This includes developing an overall approach to the testing effort, organizing and scheduling testing resources and the execution of test scripts, installing and configuring the test environment and tools as needed, and establishing the issues management process.

Tip

> Create a separate application database instance for business system testing. This database instance should be for testing the application only. This provides a safe, clean, and static place for testing the application.

The testing strategy needs to be developed based on the characteristics of the customizations. You need to take into consideration how many custom modules are being developed, how much data is being converted, any system performance concerns, the number of interfaces, the scope and types of testing to be performed, and the level of importance of the system to the business.

To facilitate testing, develop a master test plan that consolidates all detailed test scripts into a complete checklist for testing the applications. Develop detailed scripts for each type of testing to be performed. The test scripts should include unit, link, integration, and system testing. Unit tests may include checklists for the developers to check off as they execute the tests, making sure that they have performed specific activities and tasks. Integration, link, and system tests should include testing scenarios, with action steps to lead testers through the testing effort. These tests are sometimes called application thread tests because they weave themselves through a complete set of business scenarios from initial to final transactions.

When developing your business system tests, take advantage of the previously created project documentation. There is no sense developing this documentation from scratch. There are future process modules, which can lead you through the application, that can be used as direct input into the business system tests. As the project progresses there should be a continuous reuse of project deliverables. Each test will build on the previous, or if it is an initial document, you may still be able to use sections of other documents to create the draft. Most of the design documents, and the testing strategy should be completed by the end of this phase.

The business system tests are created to test, monitor, and document specific test scenarios executed within the applications. Each test scenario needs to include specific action steps, identify who is responsible for executing the steps, and identify the expected and actual results. As previously mentioned, make sure that testing is performed in an instance of the application that has sufficient and clean test data. It is important that you test in an instance that will yield valid results. These tests should be executed with data that will properly exercise the application functionality. If these tests are inadequately prepared, your team may be faced with a credibility problem. The users may think that it is the application not your tests. Be sure to spend significant time and resources in the preparation and execution of your system tests.

The preparation for business system testing is normally underestimated by inexperienced teams. Adequate preparation includes carefully planning to thoroughly and efficiently test the application. You need to determine the number of resources, locations, organizations, and the deployment schedule prior to developing your test plans. Developing your test plans should be a carefully planned and organized effort. Good test plans yield good results.

In conclusion, consider the following thoughts as you progress with your implementation. If you want to improve the productivity and quality of the documentation, it may be best to outsource the development of these documents to a technical writer or other writing professionals. Take the design and development of your project documentation seriously because the implementation, maintenance, and ongoing support of your applications will rely heavily upon it. Also, don't underestimate the time required to develop these documents; most likely it will take longer than you think.

PERFORMANCE TESTING PREPARATION

When designing the performance testing approach, you need a test database and a method for populating the instance. You need to identify special loading programs and testing transactions to load and test the application. Often, organizations use a simplistic approach to stressing the applications using minimal data. As part of performance testing, be sure to use valid volumes of data when stress testing the applications and database. Involve your users in this effort; they can add tremendous value and credibility to your testing. You also need to develop performance monitoring scripts or take advantage of tools offered by Oracle such as Enterprise Manager.

> **Note**
>
> If you experience inconsistent problems with performance testing, you may want to revisit the database, network, and server sizing estimates created earlier in the project or provided to you by your vendors. You may be experiencing symptoms of poor capacity planning. Revisit the transaction volumes and frequency numbers, as well as determine whether the concurrent user estimates are accurate.

You do not need to test every transaction in the application; that would be time-consuming and not worth the effort. You want to develop test models that will adequately test performance of the application. Your technical team can design and develop these test scripts with the assistance of your functional team members. They will work together to determine specific test scripts that simulate business transactions.

They also need to determine the amount of data and number of transactions to be tested. Normally, there is very little data in the testing instance, so you'll want to make sure that you have enough data to adequately stress test the database and system. Take advantage of the data conversion instance where data has already been loaded, or programs to load data into your performance testing instance. You can easily copy the data conversion instance to a performance testing instance to give your team the volume of data necessary for proper testing.

> **Note**
>
> If you have purchased a testing tool and don't have the expertise on staff, you may want to consider contracting or hiring someone with the product expertise to design your test scripts. Many times, testing can be flawed due to inexperience or inadequately trained project team members.

Automated testing tools can also be used for performance testing. The technical team will need to develop test scripts and configure the testing tools to simulate your user environment.

Many testing tools are available that can simulate large environments and yield excellent testing results for adequate sizing, tuning, and configuration of your servers and network. You may want to consider contacting your hardware vendor to assist with performance testing, by providing information and benchmarks.

DESIGN THE SUPPORT ORGANIZATION

Some organizations have already defined a support team, mostly referred to as the help desk, which provides support and could take on additional responsibilities of supporting the Oracle Applications. If you are lucky enough to have a dedicated and disciplined help desk, continue to use them. You may want to review their procedures and determine whether there are any areas for improvement. You need to create a method to document, manage, and control support problems, whether you use previously defined procedures or design new ones.

Tip

As you design your help desk procedures, contact your software or hardware vendors to get ideas on how they handle support problems. The more ideas you can obtain, the better support service you can provide to your end users. Don't be afraid to ask questions and seek advice from your vendors.

Your help desk team needs to have in-depth knowledge of the Oracle Applications and your business to properly support your organization while in production. In some cases, it may be best to take some of your project staff and convert them into the help desk after the implementation. Most likely, these team members have been away from their original job duties while working with the project team and could move nicely into a support role.

Note

You may also consider purchasing a help desk software product that can integrate with your in-house email product, integrating your help desk with the entire organization. For remote users, this can be a helpful and efficient way to communicate.

When the support organization and procedures are defined, remember, you need to communicate this information to your end users. Some organizations like to provide end users with this information as they participate in training. Consider designing a business card with contact information and general procedures, or develop a Web page with the help desk policies and procedures. Help desk information can be disseminated to the user community in many ways. You need to determine which approach is most effective in your organization.

SUMMARY

As you progress from phase to phase, additional requirements may be found. Consider their business value and determine whether they should be included in the scope of the project.

You may also consider holding the requirement for another phase or project. Often, these requirements are superficial and once put on the shelf, never come off.

Being a part of an implementation is exciting and a learning exercise for you and your team members. Having the opportunity to design the way your business will operate in the future does not happen often. During this phase of the implementation, take advantage of the opportunities presented to you and your team to design the most efficient and effective organization possible.

CHAPTER 9

ENABLING THE SYSTEM

Welcome to the next phase, Enabling the System! The primary objective of this phase is to "code and test" customizations, conversions of data, interfaces, and modifications that have been identified and determined to be in scope for your project. If there are no customizations, data conversion, interfaces, or modifications, this phase is still important because of the business system test, or the conference room pilot (CRP). The CRP validates solutions and simulates your production environment and configuration. Other key tasks during this phase are the development and execution of performance test scripts, unit tests, and integration tests. Each of these tasks is vital to the success of this phase as well as the overall project.

This phase may overlap the Converting Analysis into Solutions phase of the project (see Chapter 8, "Converting Analysis into Solutions"). You don't want developers waiting around until the analysts have completed all the design documents for every customization before building the customizations. This approach saves time and money. In many cases, you will have several developers on your project, each with his own skills and work pace. Don't feel as if each developer has to be synchronized, task by task, on the project. As long as the team is managed appropriately and milestones are being met, let them work at their own pace and construct successful customizations to the applications.

This phase of the project should also be used to validate any documentation associated with tasks mentioned previously. Make sure that you receive supporting documentation for each customization that is within the scope of your project. Often, organizations are left without supporting documentation and must bring resources back to finish; make sure that documentation is reviewed at the same time.

Also during this phase, refine and update the documentation for any policies and procedures that were developed during the early phases of the project.

CUSTOMIZATIONS

A customization is a change made to a standard Oracle Application object that resolves a gap between the standard Oracle Application functionality and the requirements of the user. Customizations to the Oracle Applications may be categorized in three ways:

- Extensions
- Modifications
- Interfaces

When making customizations to the Oracle Applications software, you must take the responsibility to maintain and support the code, and take into consideration what may happen during and after an upgrade to application software. Some activities that can be considered customizations include the following:

- Creating a new report or form
- Renaming or modifying a copy of an Oracle Application report or form

- Creating a one-time interface to convert legacy data for beginning balances or initial transactions
- Creating inbound or outbound interfaces to non-Oracle applications
- Creating application alerts
- Renaming or modifying a copy of an Oracle Workflow

Requirements for customizations are normally found during the Analyzing the Project phase of an implementation (see Chapter 7, "Analyzing the Project"). Some customizations are known prior to the beginning of a project and are normally documented within the scope of the overall project. It's inevitable that requirements for customizations will change as the project team learns more about the application modules being implemented. Often, customizations are removed, and new ones are added. Make sure to update your project work plan when customizations are removed from the original scope of the project. Document changes at this stage of the project with a change request form or a control log. The time for the original customizations should be substituted with new customizations or removed entirely from the scope of the project. Don't forget about these in the heat of trying to get other project tasks completed. To every customization, there is money that may be needed downstream in the project for more critical tasks or post-production support.

If you get into a situation where you have several large customizations, consider beginning work on them as soon as possible after the analysis and design are complete. Starting early on the biggest jobs helps expedite the build and test efforts. On the other hand, some implementation teams like to knock out all the easy customizations first. This all depends on the project, team, and management needs. You could also create a subproject for certain customizations. A subproject can be created to ensure more control over specific customizations. A subproject creates more finite management and control, and requires the assistance of a technical team lead to ensure milestones are met.

MODIFICATIONS

Modifications are considered to be minor changes to forms, reports, and programs to resolve application gaps between customer requirements and Oracle Application functionality. The project team should consider application workarounds before undergoing a custom modification or new development. Some modifications might be classified as a configuration versus customization, whereas configuring an application module during setup is far less expensive than a customization.

PROGRESSING FROM SIMPLE TO COMPLEX

When building customizations, start out small with some simple code or changes that will provide a fast return on investment. This will provide quick and positive feedback to your project team and management. It will build confidence in your team in its ability to deliver good-quality work products.

CREATING AND TESTING CUSTOMIZATIONS

The actual creation effort for a customization should be a heads-down activity for developers. They should have frequent build reviews with the functional users to ensure progress is being made in the right direction. Often, developers go off and develop a form and report that looks nothing like what the user requested. This should not happen!

The testing effort should take place as an iterative process during the Enabling the System phase. As developers construct a customization, they should constantly be testing. This can be considered a "desk check," where, while working at their desks, they perform iterative tests, testing and retesting what they are building. The build and testing effort should not be distinct. Developers should consider performing desk checks and unit and link testing. Unit testing can be considered the second step of testing, whereas the desk check is first. Unit testing is designed to confirm the results of the gap analysis performed earlier in the project. It ensures that the solution or approach suggested meets each business requirement identified by the project team. Unit testing is also known as the developers' formal and final testing of their assigned customizations.

The expectation is to finish the test with the customization being solid under verifiable conditions with testing being performed under normal and abnormal operations. In addition, the unit testing should evaluate the initial, standalone measurement of performance. The developer or tester should show that the customization allows correct use and excludes incorrect use. When the testing is completed, the developer or tester can submit the customization to the next stage of testing.

The testing effort should be performed for all custom modules until all have been thoroughly tested and are ready for system testing. Please review the section "Testing Strategies" found later in this chapter for additional discussion about unit, integration, and system testing.

After custom modules are complete, they should be moved from the development environment to a system test environment where they can be executed to ensure that all components work properly.

Migration of the customization depends on the type of change or new code that you are installing. Most organizations have a production load procedure where an objective team member moves custom objects from development to production.

DOCUMENTING THE CUSTOMIZATIONS

The documentation you create to support the customizations is indispensable to the ongoing maintenance and support of the application. Documentation should be constantly updated as the application is being tested and revised. All associated documents, such as the technical reference and users guide, should be finalized only after all testing has been completed. This documentation can be easily converted into HTML and placed on your project's intranet Web site, or used to develop online help text for supporting your application.

> **Tip**
>
> Many excellent developers do not have good communications skills and try to avoid documentation activities. Consider developing the documentation at the same time you develop the functional specification for the customization. If you move documentation to the front of the development process, when testing validates that the program functions as documented, then you are done.

Consider using the Oracle manuals as a template for documenting customizations. For complex customizations, documentation should consist of a users guide, a technical reference manual, and system management guide. The following documents can be created to support your customizations:

■ *Users guide.* A road map of how to use the module or customization within the application.

■ *Technical reference manual.* Can be used to support customizations after implementation team has disbanded. This document describes technically how the customization was constructed, including tables, views, and code. The document also identifies what support tools are required. This document can be generated from the high-level and detail design documents developed in the earlier phases of the project. This also contains information on how to recreate the customization in case of code being lost, database corruption, or any other emergency.

■ *System management guide.* Will be used by your system administrator, database administrator, and applications administrator to support your customizations from a technical standpoint.

The users reference manual/guide should be created to support the user and describe the features and functionality of the customization. Pay close attention to details because this document will support the customizations well after the implementation project is over.

The system management and technical reference guides discuss the technical aspects of the customization and what is required to install and maintain them. The technical documentation discusses how to execute the installation scripts required to support the customization, also the specific details of objects contained within. Keep in mind that all these documents can be derived from early documentation developed during the analysis phase of the project.

> **Tip**
>
> Don't skimp on documentation. If you need to hire a technical writer to develop all your documentation, do it. These documents will be the only representation of customizations that are created beyond the code itself.

Also, as previously mentioned, the use of installation routines can become critical to support each customization. These installation routines support the initial install as well as any future installations or upgrades. They also provide the capability to quickly recover after a system crash. The routines or documentation should be accessible to all personnel who are required to support or maintain the customizations in the production environment.

BUILDING CUSTOM REPORTS

If you understand the Oracle Applications data schema and the SQL language, building custom reports for Oracle Applications is relatively easy for a technical programmer with Developer 2000 skills. Building custom reports against the Applications database is not an end user task. Reports can use PL/SQL to perform computations, implement conditional control, format data, and restrict output. Reports can be enhanced in appearance with the graphical layout editor and can be displayed via the output viewer to see exactly how your report will look when printed. There are no layout restrictions using Oracle Reports; report objects can be positioned anywhere you want.

DATA CONVERSION, INTERFACES, AND APIS

Data conversion should be considered as early in the project as possible. The conversion of legacy data can be complex and tedious depending on the cleanliness and integrity of the data. Also, depending on the age of your legacy application, you may find that your newer staff is not familiar with the schema, file layout, or technology. Make an assessment of skills needed for data conversion and begin mapping your legacy application to the Oracle Application open interfaces as soon as you can.

During this phase of the project, the actual data conversion programs are developed. Determine which entities must be converted, such as Customers or Inventory Items. Within the legacy applications, determine what data needs to be converted and what does not. For example, it might not be a business requirement to carry closed invoice data and their payments forward into your new Oracle Application.

> **Tip**
>
> Try to anticipate the level of data cleansing that will be required before converting data to Oracle Applications. If you have cleaner data coming into the Oracle Applications, you will have a better conversion. Data cleansing can be time consuming and requires someone with in-depth knowledge of the source application to lead the effort.

DETERMINING ORDER OF APPLICATIONS TO CONVERT

Determine the order in which the legacy application modules will be converted. All legacy module dependencies need to be understood and taken into consideration prior to converting. For example, customer data needs to be converted prior to invoice data. Also decide how the data will be converted, whether manually or programmatically. Develop a simple mapping document to map each legacy application to the matching Oracle Application. This helps maintain the scope of what will be converted, and in what Oracle Application it will be converted.

MANUAL, PROGRAMMATIC, OR AUTOMATED DATA CONVERSION?

You will no doubt have some type of manual data conversion or clean up on your data conversion project. If all data is converted successfully and there is no manual effort, you're way ahead of the game!

A benefit of manual data conversion is that data validation within the application is used for all data entered. One drawback of the manual process is that it is time consuming and might not be feasible if your data set is large. Take into consideration how long it will take for the manual transaction to be entered into the Oracle Applications and multiply that times the number of records that need to be converted. This will give you a rough idea of how long it will take to manually execute data conversion. Certainly, you can add resources, and your time goes down, but the cost and mistakes go up. Think about this alternative carefully.

The programmatic approach is one of the fastest ways to fulfill data conversion requirements. It does require that programs be written from scratch to load the database directly. There is good and bad with this approach as well. The good thing is that it speeds up data conversion time when the conversion actually takes place. Therefore, automated conversion is good to use with a lot of data. Based on the volume of data to be converted, a decision needs to be made on whether to choose manual over programmatic. There will be more time spent on writing the code to populate the tables than actually converting the data itself; therefore, this method can be more expensive. Data conversion scripts and programs can be written with tools such as SQL*Plus, Pro*C, Shell scripts, and PL/SQL.

To supplement or replace these programmatic conversion programs, an automated approach can be used by using a tool from a third-party vendor. These automation tools offer reusable preconfigured templates containing validation, mapping, and transformation rules and documentation providing an integrated, faster solution. These templates are available for many Oracle Applications including Manufacturing, Financials, Human Resources, and E-commerce. If you want to find out more about third-party conversion tool vendors, see Chapter 30, "Alliance Partners."

Although they are a more expensive solution, use of these commercially available conversion products may significantly improve the resource and time requirements of data conversion.

WRITING AND TESTING DATA CONVERSION PROGRAMS

Conversion programs that are written should be integrated into unit testing when test scripts are created. Some organizations that don't look at the conversion programs as part of testing find out the hard way when data has not been converted successfully or the integrity of the data has been jeopardized.

Upon completing data conversion, the integrity of the data should be tested within each application. Also, validation tests should be executed to test the application with all this new data loaded. This performance test should cover all application modules and be included in the application integration testing.

Based on whether you are implementing in multiple phases or multiple organizations, you may need to perform and execute all data conversion tasks at different times. Coordination of this effort is important and should be scheduled according to all project implementation schedules.

DATA CONVERSION SIZING

Sizing of the application database seems to always be an issue when you are converting legacy data. There are estimating spreadsheets that are used early on in the project, or sometimes used by Oracle to recommend disk capacity.

Determine the number of records per object that will be converted. It's also helpful to indicate whether the object will be a one-time conversion or periodic.

As legacy data is converted, more of the allocated disk space is being consumed. Make sure that you have plenty of room to grow after all legacy data has been converted. Plan to revisit the disk capacity requirements for your production server during the Enabling the System phase. This gives you time to react to any unplanned disk capacity issues prior to the start of production business transaction processing.

USING THE OPEN INTERFACES

Open interfaces are provided with the Oracle Applications. They are primarily used to integrate with custom or non-Oracle applications. However, these interfaces are also used for importing historical data from legacy applications and from spreadsheets.

The following application modules have open interfaces available for use, and each has detailed information contained within the Oracle Open Interface manuals for Financials, Manufacturing, and Distribution applications:

- Oracle Assets
- Oracle General Ledger
- Oracle Inventory
- Oracle Order Entry/Shipping
- Oracle Payables
- Oracle Purchasing
- Oracle Receivables

The open interface documentation indicates which fields are mandatory and optional. It identifies key fields and whether a column should be null. The documents are helpful and should be used as a guide when converting data.

Tip

Make sure that you have the most recent version of the Oracle documentation on open interfaces when you start development. Occasionally, the specifications will

> change, and you can save a lot of testing time by developing from the information in the correct manuals.

Internally, Oracle Applications use many of the open interfaces for daily processing. These interface programs are scheduled in the Concurrent manager. The open interfaces validate the integrity of data and ensure that all business rules are met. The primary function of the open interfaces is to import data from Oracle and non-Oracle applications.

ORACLE HR APIS

The Oracle HR module has many application program interfaces or APIs that support such functions as creation of employees, creating grade rates, and payment methods. These APIs may be used to convert data, or pass transactions to the Oracle HR application. APIs pull data versus push, pulling data from a file in which you have defined, whereas the open interfaces receive, or are pushed data, from a source file. Unfortunately, APIs are not found in the Financial applications, so Financial users must continue to focus on using the open interfaces.

An advantage of APIs is that they validate data and enforce business rules that have been established by the application suite. Unfortunately, APIs can't be used directly by an end user and must be used within PL/SQL programs.

MANAGING THE PHASE

During this phase, one of the keys to success is having a strong technical team lead to manage and control the work effort. The team lead must continue to motivate and keep the team focused on tasks and achieving milestones. This person must have strong Oracle Applications and technology experience.

Managing the shift from phase to phase is difficult, more so from Solutions to Enabling the System. Normally, during this phase, you shift from functional activities to technical tasks. It's best to keep a strong functional team member on the duration of the project for the continuity of staff. Most implementation teams do not want to rotate the team members on and off the project. So, it's best to leave at least one strong functional staff member who can assist with issues and questions relating to the project. While the technical tasks are in process, the functional implementation team members can perform unit testing of customizations, validate configuration parameters, create documentation, create training materials, and perform an integrated conference room pilot during this phase of the project.

PHASE SUCCESS FACTORS

The following are some critical success factors to consider during this phase of a project:

- Obtain a clear understanding of the requirements of the project.
- Ensure accurate and comprehensive functional and technical design documentation.

- Encourage the involvement of user management.
- Assess the skills of the technical team early. If they are not what you need or are not performing at the expected level, obtain the proper skills!

PHASE MILESTONES

Activities considered milestones in this phase are the creation of a development environment, final data conversion mapping, documentation to support customizations, and a final version of each testing document. Upon successfully completing these activities, the project should be able to move onto the next phase. The following presents an overview of each milestone:

- *Development environment.* One of the most important milestones of this project phase is having a development environment readily available for the technical staff. From a technical perspective, having a separate application user where all custom objects reside is just as important but obviously can't be done without an application instance. As the project progresses, the use of modular code becomes a timesaver, as well as keeps code smaller and more organized for easier quality checks. Finally, the last technical milestone would be to have all the installation scripts and routines readily available in case of an emergency or in case the customizations need to be recreated for some reason.

- *Data conversion mapping documents and conversion programs.* Within data conversion there are a couple of milestones. The final data conversion mapping documents are of most importance. After these documents are created, the development staff can begin working on the conversion programs, which are considered the next milestone.

  After the conversion programs have been written and informal testing has been completed, unit testing of all the data that has been converted needs to take place. This helps enforce integrity constraints and ensures proper programming techniques and quality. When all data has been converted into the test or development environment, the data must be validated to its source. This can primarily be a user task, but most likely some technical assistance will be required.

- *Documentation.* Documentation is one of the most important aspects of a project and is always one of the most difficult tasks to complete. A first milestone within documentation responsibilities is having the users guide and reference manuals completed for the customizations. The task of creating technical reference material, help desk, and system administrator documentation comes next. The help desk documentation can be a boiled-down version of the system administrator document, or a complete guide. Certainly this depends on the knowledge and experience of the help desk operators.

- *Testing.* Testing milestones start with unit testing of customizations, data conversion, interfaces, or modifications as they are being developed by the applications development staff. Linking or integrating a customization into the application can be considered the next milestone for testing. This testing brings together the customization and the application into an integrated solution. System testing follows the integration testing and is the execution of thread and non-thread application tests throughout the application. Performance testing is the last testing to take place due to the overall objective it's trying to accomplish.

SETTING UP NEW HARDWARE

Each Oracle Applications implementation project must ensure that the development environment is ready on time. A development team must have the resources needed to be successful. If the hardware is not installed prior to the development team's arrival this can become costly, in dollars as well as lost personnel. Many projects try to time the arrival of technical staff as soon as the customizations have been identified and accepted. Not having the computing resources, such as workstations, connectivity to the network, access to the application and database server, and in some cases access to the IS Operations area, can cause major delays in this phase of the project.

> **Tip**
>
> Make sure that at least one development environment is set up and tested well before the technical staff starts on the project. Also, obtain technical team members' names prior to their arrival. Have the network, operating system, and application logins or accounts established for them when they walk in the door. Once on board, these folks should hit the ground running!

INSTALLING THE APPLICATIONS

At this point in the project, a test or development environment has been established for the technical staff to use all by themselves. Often, the technical staff will need to unit test a customization that may be integrated with an object within the application. It is best to have a separate instance of the application that will not affect the rest of the project team. Although some organizations like to copy the Vision Applications instance for use by the development staff, this procedure can be risky because the Vision Application doesn't contain the same configuration or functionality as the application that you are implementing. The Vision instance is primarily an Oracle sales tool used for application demos to prospective clients. The Vision Applications are a copy of the Oracle Applications that can be installed prior to your implementation. Many organizations use Vision as their temporary playground prior to having a Test or Development application instance available.

OPTIMAL FLEXIBLE ARCHITECTURE STANDARD (OFA)

The OFA concept was created several years ago by Oracle employees who decided to add some organization to the installation and support of Oracle Applications. OFA is the method for installing and organizing Oracle products on an application or database server or client. You will want to use OFA methods to organize the customizations to the applications as well.

The OFA-compliant directory structure provides a mechanism for organizing all Oracle Applications, standard or custom, under one top directory usually called $APPL_TOP. Each

Oracle Application has a default top directory name and location, such as $FA_TOP. The directory architecture provides subdirectories under each application's top directory to store programs, forms, reports, shell scripts, data, and so on.

For example, the standard naming convention for the Oracle Fixed Assets home directory is FA_TOP. Customizations to Fixed Assets would reside in CUST_FA_TOP, where CUST would represent the directory for all Fixed Asset customizations with all the appropriate, or needed, subdirectories.

Many organizations use prefixes like CUST, or a short name for their organization, such as BOSS_FA_TOP, for BOSS Corporation Fixed Assets customizations. Be creative and consistent when establishing a customization prefix.

DELIVERABLES

Some major deliverables found in this phase of the implementation are the programs, reports, test scripts, and documentation required to support each customization. Many deliverables throughout this phase will be used during the remaining phases of the project. Some deliverables can be consolidated with others based on content, time, and need. The following paragraphs describe several key deliverables that should be considered during this phase.

For all custom objects, project team members need to create technical reference manuals, users guides, and help desk documentation. Users will appreciate having this documentation for future reference, follow-up, and guidance during upgrades and installations.

Development of conversion programs and supporting documentation is essential to a project's success. Documenting the conversion programs, as well as which conversion programs have been tested and accepted by the end user community, will be needed prior to executing them in production.

All installation routines for customizations need to be documented. Often, these are not clearly documented, and when it comes time to install these objects into production, it is performed incorrectly. These routines include all shell scripts, SQL, SQL*Loader, and keystroke files that are required to install and configure customizations into the production environment. These are also good reference documents for production support, maintenance, and upgrades.

Unit, integration, and system testing of customizations are other vital steps to a successful project. Developing unit test documents for each customization will support the objects as they are transitioned into production. Your development or testing team will develop and execute these tests to ensure that quality and coding standards are met. The creation of an integration test document is written as part of the detailed design and is usually performed by several developers or test team members. These tests focus on all external application interfaces and help document associated programs and unit and link tests for the customizations.

System testing is written specifically for the business process flow and is performed by key project team members and end users. Because of the amount and complexity of these tests, additional end users are brought in to assist with the effort. The testing is performed after all unit and integration tests have passed. A combination of customizations, integration, and standard functionality is tested during these tests.

Another key deliverable found throughout the implementation, and most importantly during this phase, is the acceptance certificate. You may decide that on completion of each deliverable an acceptance certificate be signed by your end users. This certificate documents their acceptance and verification of your development team's work.

A deliverable sometimes overlooked and considered one of the most important is the end user training material. These documents are normally created by your application owners or end users. Some organizations hire technical writers or someone specifically for developing this type of documentation. This documentation is essential during the transition and production phases of your project.

TESTING STRATEGIES

The testing environment you create needs to support each type of testing that is planned, such as unit, integration, and system, and acceptance. This testing environment needs to be unique and only accessible and used by the testing team. You don't want other team members using the testing instance as, or in conjunction with, the development instance.

Consider making the Testing instance a standalone instance in which the data is only being changed by the Testing team and no one else. The integrity of the Testing data is vital to successful testing and if corrupted could invalidate all applications testing, cause inaccurate results, and create unnecessary tension within the project team.

Some testing concepts were discussed earlier in the chapter and will be solidified in the next few paragraphs. The primary emphasis during the testing activities involves testing all customizations as they move through unit testing in development to integration testing with the other application modules.

The use of test scripts is vital to the management and control of testing customizations. Test scripts guide users through the business systems testing effort as well as act as a tracking document for test success or failure. Each test script needs to be executed multiple times, preferably by different users, to be successfully tested.

On success or failure, certain activities should occur. If the test is a success, then document it appropriately and move onto the next steps or test. If the customization fails, then document the failure and notify the applications developer or team member responsible for the customization. Often, failures have a simple solution and can be resolved quickly by another team member. After the issues are thought to be resolved, re-execute the test and stay in this test loop until all testing is successful.

CONFERENCE ROOM PILOT

The APICS dictionary describes prototyping as "a product model constructed for testing and evaluation to see how the product performs before releasing the product to manufacture."

A Conference Room Pilot (CRP) is exactly that, a prototyping of the software functionality before releasing the product to the end user.

Each customization should be prototyped and executed during a series of detailed pilots or a module walk-through. Each pilot should be designed to target a specific stage, event, or business process of the implementation and determine success or failure as the outcome.

Some organizations may want to have separate module walk-through and prototyping sessions for departmental customizations. The execution of a CRP is conducted by the entire team to validate the interoperability of business processes.

This effort allows all decisions to benefit the entire organization and not just one department.

SOME ALTERNATIVES TO CUSTOMIZATIONS

Due to the cost and complexity of customizations, alternatives should be considered. Instead of building a new multirow form, maybe consider customizing a standard folder to fulfill your end users' requirements. Think of ways to utilize standard features of Oracle Applications such as folders, flexfields, and the Custom library.

FOLDERS

A folder is a special block within an Oracle Application form that resembles an Excel spreadsheet. Folder block field and record layout can be customized to retrieve a subset of records or display records in a different format.

> **Tip**
>
> When saving folders, be creative with their names. Users often name folders something that doesn't relate to what the folder does. If the folder is set up to query all open purchases orders, then save the folder as "Open Purchase Orders," not MyFolder. Each folder should be saved with a name that represents the layout of the fields or query criteria selected. If your organization uses many folders, you may want to consider developing a naming convention. If users recognize a public folder because its name is intuitive, it will be used.

On installation of the Oracle Applications, a default folder block is available. This folder can be modified and saved as a new customized folder. The customized default folder is easily distinguished from the original folder because its name appears next to the Open Folder button on the form.

The Folder Tools button is enabled when you navigate to a folder block. By selecting the button, a tools palette will be displayed. The following buttons are available for customizing a folder.

- *Open Folder*. Allows you to select another folder to open
- *Save Folder*. Allows you to save a modified folder

- *Create New Folder*. Provides capability to create a folder
- *Delete Folder*. Provides capability to select a folder to delete
- *Widen Field*. Increases field width
- *Shrink Field*. Decreases field width
- *Show Field*. Shows an undisplayed field
- *Hide Field*. Hides a displayed field
- *Move Left*. Moves field to the left
- *Move Right*. Moves field to the right
- *Move Up*. Moves field up one character height
- *Move Down*. Moves field down one character height

FOLDER QUERIES

Folders can be further enhanced by defining queries. You can customize a folder to retrieve only the records you want to see. Altering the query criteria of the folder and saving the folder can do this. When in a multirecord block, you can alter the sorting order of the records retrieved.

Defining a query is simple and is created as follows:

1. Navigate to the appropriate application folder.
2. Execute query by using Query find or query-by-example (QBE).
3. Select Save As on the Folder menu if you want to save this version of the folder.
4. Provide a name for the folder. Associating it with the query criteria provides an easy understanding of what the folder provides.
5. Select an Autoquery Option Group—Always, Never or Ask Each Time:
   - If Always is selected, the query automatically is executed each time the folder is opened.
   - If Never is selected, the query is not executed when the folder is opened.
   - If Ask Each Time is selected, the query prompt appears each time the folder is opened.
6. Select OK. The folder is now created.

Note   On saving a folder, the query criteria is saved at the same time as the default query. If data is initially retrieved on opening the folder, each subsequent query is executed on this initial subset of data. If you want to enter a new query on all data, you need to reset or remove the default query within the folder before proceeding with another query.

Occasionally, you may want to view the query criteria for a specific folder. By selecting the Choose View Query from the Folder menu, a window called Folder Contents appears.

This window may display the WHERE clause that is used for criteria to retrieve the records displayed for the selected folder. If the window is empty, then there is no SQL WHERE clause defined, and all records will be retrieved.

There may also be times when the query must be reset. In this case, choose the Reset Query option from the Folder menu. After this is selected, the WHERE clause is cleared from the current folder. Executing this only resets the WHERE clause and not the folder name or layout. On resetting the query, perform another query and choose the Save option on the Folder menu to save the current folder with the query criteria.

SORTING IN A FOLDER

As mentioned earlier, sorting the retrieved records in a multirecord folder is simple and can be done by choosing the Show Order By option from the Folder menu. After this is selected, sort buttons appear directly below the first three fields of the folder block.

The sort buttons may be clicked on for different settings, such as ascending, descending, and unsorted. Depending on which sort is selected, the folder displays the records accordingly. The sort is applied to the records from left to right when the records are retrieved. After the sorting options are selected, choose the Run option from the Query menu to execute the query to see the changes.

Folders are a powerful and inexpensive way to customize Oracle Applications. Power users who have been trained and educated on foldering capabilities primarily create folders. Folders were created with end users in mind. With a little practice and patience, you can create folders to improve your use of Oracle Applications.

MENUS

Oracle Application menus can be created specifically for your organization and may include options for Oracle Applications or custom applications that have been registered within AOL. Many organizations determine, after using Oracle Applications for a period of time, that customizing and developing their own menus is more efficient than pecking through standard application menus.

MAPPING YOUR CUSTOM MENUS

On defining a new menu structure, you must follow several steps. First, map out a logical hierarchy for a specific business function or user responsibility. This map provides a simple but easy-to-access menu structure for your users. Determine what functionality of the application is required for users to fulfill their organizational duties. It is wise to develop a matrix consisting of a list of functions and users, or functions and responsibilities. Second, develop the menu like a road map for your users. The object of a customized menu is to act as a map, easily guiding end users to their application forms. Use the predefined menus, forms, and form subfunctions to determine the new entries for the custom menu. Run the standard Oracle report called Menu Reports to provide all predefined menus.

> **Tip**
>
> Menus cannot be copied, so use predefined menus for menu entries to minimize your work. Individual functions can be excluded after menu entries are assigned to a responsibility.
>
> Also, if you want all custom menus, define and create the lowest-level menus first because they need to be available as entries to other menus. Then assign lower-level menus and functions to higher-level menus, with the higher-level menus eventually assigned to a root, or main menu.

DESIGNING MENUS

When designing application menus, keep in mind the number of keystrokes or mouse clicks users will have to enter to gain access to the specified form or menu. You want to design the menu so that typing the first letter automatically chooses the form or menu. Also when creating the menu, design the sequence of the menu prompts with the most frequently accessed functions first. Design menus for fast and easy keyboard access.

At some point, you may need to change the menu names or modify specific entries. When you change a menu's name, the entries contained within that menu are not affected in any way. The menu that was changed exists under a new name, and any menus calling it will continue to access it under its changed name. The old menu name is no longer accessible or available anywhere in the application.

PRESERVING MENUS

Custom menus are preserved during upgrades of Oracle Applications because of the unique names. As long as your menus are created under a custom application, such as Custom Fixed Assets, and are assigned an application short name, such as CFA, and the short name is prefixed to your menu, such as CFA_MENU_LEVEL_3, your menus will survive!

During an upgrade, Oracle Application standard menus can be overwritten. A good rule is to not assign your custom menus to an Oracle standard menu but to add the standard menu as a submenu to your custom menu.

> **Note**
>
> Prior to upgrading, it is recommended that you run the function security report set to document your custom menu structures. The report set contains the Function Security Functions Report, the Function Security Menu Report, and the Function Security Navigator Report.

FLEXFIELDS

Flexfields are user-defined data entry fields that are available throughout the Oracle Applications. They can be used to customize Oracle Applications without programming. The two types of flexfields are key and descriptive.

When designing a key or descriptive flexfield, take your time and create a design acceptable to all personnel affected. Organizations sometimes rush through this effort only to find that they are capturing too much information or not enough. First, create a team to design and develop your flexfield structure and values. This is time well spent and will keep all concerned parties informed and part of the definition and decision-making process. Second, design the structure such that it is flexible enough for future growth or easy expansion.

Because flexfields do not require programming, they allow you to perform significant customizations to the Oracle Applications relatively easily. These "flexfield customizations" are guaranteed by Oracle to be preserved through an upgrade. The use of key and descriptive flexfields versus customizations saves time and money and allows for a smoother and more efficient upgrade in the future.

KEY FLEXFIELDS

Key flexfields are commonly used when multisegment values such as account numbers and inventory part numbers are required. They are made up of segments that have a value and a meaning. Key flexfields are usually stored in the *segment* columns of an Oracle Applications database table. Key flexfields are referred to as an intelligent field that organizations can use to capture information represented as codes.

DESCRIPTIVE FLEXFIELDS

Descriptive flexfields are used to capture additional information in generic fields. If the Oracle Applications do not provide a field, a descriptive flexfield can provide the capability to expand application forms to capture additional information organizations may need. A descriptive flexfield is represented by a two-character unnamed field enclosed by brackets, or as some like to say, "it looks like a two-fisted beer mug."

As you're reading this, you may be wondering why are descriptive flexfields being mentioned in the Enabling the System phase? When organizations must customize a form to capture additional information on a row, or about a certain subject, they should first try to use a descriptive flexfield. Organizations can customize descriptive flexfields to include as many fields as needed. These fields are also referred to as segments and appear in the descriptive flexfield window. Descriptive flexfields are usually stored in the *attribute* columns of an Oracle Application database table.

Each segment of a descriptive flexfield has a name and associated value. The values used within the descriptive flexfield can be independent or dependent on other descriptive segment values. Descriptive flexfields are widely used by organizations and continue to be an excellent way to extend the usability of Oracle Applications.

USING THE CUSTOM LIBRARY

Use of the Custom library allows extensions of Oracle Application modules without modifying module code. The Custom library is a PL/SQL library for use throughout Oracle Applications. The Custom library can be used for customizations such as zooms, enforcing business rules, and disabling application form fields. The Custom library is available for use only by Oracle Application customers.

Procedure shells also are available for developing your own custom code. The code is written inside these shells where logic is associated with a specific form and block in which the code is to run. These procedure shells add a layer of flexibility in the use of the Custom library. There is no predefined logic in the Custom library other than the procedure shells.

The Custom library also supports application events. These events are executed throughout Oracle Applications, and custom code can be written in conjunction with them to perform various types of transactions. There are two different kinds of applications events, generic and product-specific. Generic events are available to all Oracle Application forms. The generic events are as follows:

- WHEN-FORM-NAVIGATE
- WHEN-NEW-FORM-INSTANCE
- WHEN-NEW-BLOCK-INSTANCE
- WHEN-NEW-RECORD-INSTANCE
- WHEN-NEW-ITEM-INSTANCE
- WHEN-VALIDATE-RECORD
- SPECIAL*n* (*n* represents number)
- ZOOM
- EXPORT

The Custom library can be used in three cases: for zooms, for logic for generic events, and for logic for product-specific events. Each must be coded differently. Zooms are fairly simple and straightforward. They typically consist of opening an Oracle Application form and passing parameter values to the form via Zoom logic. This can be an effective way to execute inquiry forms from an application module. An example could be to Zoom to an Inventory form from the Order Entry screen to inquire about the on-hand balance for a particular product.

Generic events actually extend Oracle Applications through the use of events such as WHEN-NEW-FORM-INSTANCE, WHEN-VALIDATE-RECORD, or WHEN-NEW-BLOCK-INSTANCE. See the complete list of events presented earlier. The product-specific events can actually augment or replace applications logic for certain products or business rules. Be cautious when using this type of event because the expected results may vary due to the complexities of the Oracle Applications code. Be sure to thoroughly test all your customizations.

BUILDING CODE WITH THE CUSTOM LIBRARY

The Custom library can be found in the $AU_TOP/res/plsql directory. After designing and developing your own code, you must replace the default Custom library. After your code has been written, you must compile and generate the library using Oracle Forms and place it into the $AU_TOP/res/plsql directory. Active Oracle Application users need to exit the applications and log back in to execute the newly written code.

> **Note**
>
> Oracle Forms always uses a . plx (complied code) for a library over the .pll. The .plx file is created when you generate a library using the Forms generator COMPILE_ALL parameter set to 'YES', not when you compile and save using Designer. The best thing to do is delete the .plx file to allow your code to run from the .pll or create your own .plx file using the Forms generator.

The Custom package within the Custom library cannot be changed. Packages added to the Custom library must be added after the Custom package and must begin with an alphabetical letter after "C". Oracle recommends that custom packages begin with "USER_" for the code to remain sequenced appropriately.

RECOMMENDATIONS AND CODING STANDARDS FOR THE CUSTOM LIBRARY

These are some supporting comments, considerations, restrictions, and recommendations when using the Custom library.

When adding code to the Custom library, keep in mind that Oracle Applications may run in many environments. The following are some considerations and restrictions you should understand when using the Custom library or any additional libraries:

- You cannot use any SQL in the library.
- PL/SQL package variables do not change between calls to the Custom library. This also has no bearing on which form actually makes the call.
- PL/SQL code contained within the Startup code (Package but not in a function or procedure) is executed only once when the Custom library is initially called.
- Global variables contained within Oracle Forms are visible to all running forms.

> **Tip**
>
> When you need to know the names of blocks, fields, or particular items within Oracle Applications, use the Examine feature from within the appropriate application form by going to the Help, Tools menu option.

The use of coding standards within the Custom library is important. The Developer/2000 products must support all code. The only exception is that you cannot call APPCORE routines from the Custom library or from within any Zoom, or other event. Almost all APPCORE routines begin with the "APP" prefix.

After an upgrade, the following items should be considered regarding customizations to the Custom library. If there are problems with forms operating with a version of the Custom library that has changed, the Custom code can be turned off temporarily by executing the menu choice Help, Tools, Custom Code, Off until the problem has been resolved. The Oracle Applications code can be evaluated while the Custom code is turned off. Earlier versions of Oracle Applications require the Custom library shipped with the applications to be replaced versus the capability to turn it on/off via the menu option.

Prior to upgrading Oracle Applications, make a backup copy of your current Custom library. If a backup is not made, you will lose all changes made to the Custom library because the upgrade will install a new version of the Custom library. After the upgrade, all custom logic should be tested to ensure that the code still operates as intended.

PERFORMANCE TESTING

The Oracle ERP Applications can consume large amounts of server, network, desktop, and disk resources, and some customers experience slow response times when a full business load is placed on the system. Performance testing is normally conducted during this phase of a project, and this testing can help to avoid response time problems. Many implementation projects make the decision to not perform performance testing tasks. This decision may cause the project schedule to slip due to inaccurate and insufficient computing resources.

Performance testing should happen early enough in the project to allow for timely resolution. Testing results should be analyzed and documented. System administrators and DBAs need to perform as much technical environment testing as possible. They need to make sure that the test environment is stable and operating at an acceptable level, so that there is no delay with system or integration testing. Delays or false starts cause frustration on the application team and erode the credibility of your technical staff.

The technical team should test all transaction programs, test scripts, and the database itself, in a test instance of the database. The testing time taken at this stage of the project may save a great deal of user time, money, and frustration in the future. Performance testing often defines some type of problem or system bottleneck.

Tuning and retuning happens on a regular basis during heavy transaction volume testing. Certain test parameters or a specific configuration may require multiple tests to be performed to properly tune for realistic results. Tuning needs to be proactive instead of reactive. If the database is being monitored proactively, there's a good chance that problems can be found prior to the users even noticing.

After performance testing has been completed, a formal report can be generated and presented to management as needed. All the code and scripts written will be useful in the future, so put them in a safe place; you'll need them. Developing a toolbox of performance monitoring code and scripts is an excellent investment in time for DBAs. Having the right tools available in a crisis can make the difference between success and failure.

The test environment can be used as a baseline environment for future testing of enhancements, reports, and so on. Try to keep the environment static so that the baseline performance numbers you generated do not constantly need to be refreshed. Following are some of the tasks your DBA and system administrator may perform during or prior to this phase.

- Preparation of hardware, software, and network
- Installation of performance monitoring tools
- Installation and configuration of a test environment
- Installation and configuration of test scripts and transaction programs

PERFORMANCE TESTING TOOLS

Many performance testing products are on the market today. Some vendors offer automated software that provides a complete testing solution for Oracle Applications. These products have the capability to predict system performance, verify functionality, and test the scalability. These products can also manage the entire testing process. Refer to Chapter 30, "Alliance Partners," for a list of vendors and their product offerings.

There is even a simplistic way to test your applications. This could be used for performance testing as well as unit, integration, and system testing. It's easy to use and is found in the graphical interface for Oracle Applications. If you're familiar with Oracle Forms, then you know of the feature for recording keystrokes. In standard Oracle Forms, if you want to capture and play keystrokes, then you need to supply the KEYIN and KEYOUT runtime parameters when invoking Forms.

Within Oracle Applications, the commands are similar, but easier to remember. For capturing keystrokes within Oracle Applications, supply the argument RECORD=*filename* on the command line found in the properties of the Oracle Applications icon. Basically, the command would look something like this, D:\ORAWIN\BIN\AIAP45.EXE RECORD=*RECORDFILE*.

After this command is in place, Oracle Applications starts up with the record script on capturing all keystrokes. All keystrokes and events are captured in a macro script that can be played again in the future.

To play the script mentioned previously, simply change your command string to D:\ORAWIN\BIN\AIAP45.EXE PLAY=*RECORDFILE* The PLAY parameter plays back what is contained within the macro file. After you have captured your keystrokes, the possibilities of how the event logger can be used are endless.

Some areas where the event logger could be used are during application setups, data conversion, unit testing, integration testing, system testing, performance testing, and many more. As you can see, this can be a simple, easy, and inexpensive way to test your applications.

Just image having your application setups stored in a file that can be edited via MS Word or vi. The macro file generated is non-procedural and is a simple series of statements. This setup macro, if acceptable, and containing final setup values, could be played in your Production instance to set up your application. This saves time and money, as well as ensures that the applications are set up the same as they were in the Testing instance.

This event logging, keystroke-capturing capability may not continue in Oracle Application releases to come. This is a relatively unknown feature; if more people knew of it, its future could probably be saved. We're not sure but would like to see it retained for continued enjoyment and success.

ADDITIONAL REFERENCE MATERIAL

This section covers additional documentation and products that can assist you in this phase as well as the entire project. Most of this documentation and reference material is not free. You must contact Oracle Documentation Sales, or your Oracle Sales representative for additional information.

TECHNICAL REFERENCE MANUALS

Oracle Application Technical reference manuals, or TRMs, are available for all Oracle Application modules. This documentation provides the entire Oracle Applications database schema with all tables, columns, indexes, and views. This documentation is propriety information and can be purchased from Oracle Corporation Book Sales. You must be an Oracle Applications customer to receive the TRMs.

APPLICATIONS REPOSITORY

The use of Designer/2000 for custom developed solutions and the Oracle Applications Repository enforces and cross-validates the design and integration of your solutions.

Many organizations are not aware of the availability of the Designer/2000 repository for Oracle Applications. This repository contains the entity relationship diagrams as well as other supporting information for Oracle Applications. A phone call to Oracle support or your local Sales Representative can initiate the process. Prior to receiving the information, the signing of a nondisclosure statement is required.

UNDERSTANDING THE POSITION OF ORACLE SUPPORT

Oracle will support customizations that follow the standards identified within the Oracle Applications Coding Standards document. Following Oracle guidelines and standards is the most logical and safest approach. Play it safe and follow Oracle's recommendations. If you want to read more about Oracle Support, see Chapter 28, "Working with Oracle Support."

SUMMARY

Customizations are a common occurrence during Oracle Application implementations. Many organizations indicate they would like to execute a "vanilla" implementation, installing the Oracle Applications with *no* customizations. This hardly ends up being the case. Because customizations will exist in varying areas of the application, from Alerts to designing your own Oracle Payables check, they will exist in some form for all implementations.

With this in mind, the use of design and build standards is critical during Oracle Application implementations. If your organization doesn't employ these practices today, consider acquiring consultants or hiring staff that can bring a method or discipline to your organization. You can also review the preceding chapter, "Converting Analysis into Solutions," for additional thoughts and ideas about creating your own customization standards and methods.

After all customizations have been created and documented and your project team has been dismantled and members returned to their real jobs, someone needs to maintain the system. The next chapter, Chapter 10, "Launching Your New System," will help you understand how to manage and control your production environment.

LAUNCHING YOUR NEW SYSTEMS

This chapter is about managing change, transitioning from old to new systems, and supporting your production applications. These activities facilitate the first use of the ERP software by your users. Typical activities include training users, converting beginning balances and historical data from the legacy system, and migrating proven solutions from a pilot database to a production system.

MANAGING CHANGE

Managing change is one of the most important things you can do to improve the success of your software implementation. The capability of the organization to absorb change is a key factor to the critical path and the total cost of the project. The *critical path* is the series of tasks that must be completed in sequence and on schedule for the project to finish on time. Because each activity on the critical path must finish without delay, you must manage the changes caused by those activities to stay on schedule. Many information technology professionals, project sponsors, and project managers view an Oracle ERP project as a technical activity involving new computers, a sophisticated database management system, and complex application software.

In reality, implementing a big ERP system is about half technological issues and half organizational and human issues. It is easy to focus on the technology and overlook the non-technical side of the project. Try to avoid that mistake.

The impact of these complex software packages will be felt throughout your company. The dynamics of your project may require action by the project team to accomplish the following:

- Manage changes in the organizational structure
- Facilitate the alteration of business processes
- Gain concurrence on process modifications
- Neutralize barriers to change
- Promote adoption of the system in various functional departments and geographical sites

COMMUNICATING

Communication is a key activity throughout the ERP project, and you should not wait until the transition phase to begin communicating. ERP systems force a lot of change on an organization, and everyone must understand what is happening, when the changes will happen, who will make them happen, and why they must happen. Consider the following techniques to establish interest, trust, and confidence in the new systems.

- Stage demonstrations for the steering committee and key users. Target certain key employees for communication and try to reach beyond just the interested users.
- Make sure you tell everyone about the boundaries and scope of your project.

- Get the users involved with resolution of issues and make sure concerns are addressed. If there were employees who wanted to participate and were excluded from the implementation team, consider trying to involve them during testing.

- Publish your project materials to the entire organization. Set up a Web page with links to the project schedule, deliverables, status reports, issue logs, meeting minutes, and so forth. Set up email distribution lists and use them to push these materials to the people who need to see them but who are too busy to pull them from the Web page. Also, consider adding general interest articles to your company newsletter to advertise the project. You must sell the project internally to get key employees to buy in to your activities.

- Be enthusiastic, open, honest, and available.

- Schedule regular steering committee meetings and make these managers work on the project. If everything is going well and they have nothing to do, invent some minor issues to keep the members interested and participating. Don't let the steering committee become an uninformed rubber stamp that just approves project activities.

- Listen to what the users are telling you and understand their agenda and concerns.

- Interface with other software projects and company programs that are causing change at the same time as your project.

ESTABLISHING USER AND MANAGEMENT EXPECTATIONS

Accurately setting user and management expectations is quite important to your successful project. If you are expected to deliver a perfectly working system that meets every desire business ever had, you will have a difficult transition. On the other hand, if your users and management understand that the complexity of these integrated systems might cause problems and if they take responsibility to resolve problems as a normal business activity, the transition to the new ERP systems will be much smoother. Frequent and honest communication is the best way to set the expectations of your constituents.

> **Tip**
>
> Many ERP projects have difficulty because the organization was not prepared to accept change or they were expecting something different or better. Deal with erroneous expectations as soon as you become aware of them—this improves the acceptance of the new software.

RESOLVING ISSUES AND CONCERNS

If you do a good job of resolving issues at each stage of the project, the transition phase will be easy and uneventful. If you don't address issues and concerns, you will have to resolve "show stopper" items at the most inconvenient time (during transition), you might lose control of the schedule, and you might have to delay the start up of the system.

There are several ways to resolve issues. Try making a master log entry for every issue to make sure all concerns are tracked. Publish the log regularly. Assign each issue to a responsible person for resolution and determine the due date. If the due date is missed, it is possible you don't have a critical resolution factor. Perhaps the responsible person doesn't have the authority or political consensus to close the item. Don't be afraid to escalate issues to the ERP project steering committee or to the sponsor.

Also, act on items that are out of the scope of your project but that your organization wants to put into scope. A common example is an immature reporting strategy. For example, if your company really wants data warehouse-like reporting from the on-line transaction processing system, you must deal with expectations that you cannot meet with a basic Oracle ERP system.

HOW MUCH TRAINING IS APPROPRIATE?

Training users is a significant change-management activity. Training provides information about change and sets new expectations for acceptable behavior. Training requirements are different in every organization. Small groups of users might be trained on the job just a few days before the production systems go live. Larger groups of users with many integrated applications require formal, cross-functional classroom training led by instructors.

> **Tip**
>
> Budget carefully for training because this activity can require significant amounts of money and time. One rule of thumb is to allow between 10-15 percent of the total project budget for training activities.

Consider special needs training for certain users of the system. For example, the high-level manager who approves a purchase order only once a week will have radically different training needs than the help desk staff who must support that manager. Consider the audience to be trained and the appropriate level of detail to present. The technical staff of database administrators, system administrators, and support staff often have special training needs, and these people must achieve a high level of proficiency before the system goes live.

TRANSITIONING TO NEW SYSTEMS

The success of your final conference room pilot—the dress rehearsal—usually dictates when it is safe to migrate to the transition phase of the project. If the pilot raises issues from key users about business process steps, missing reports, format of business forms, system response time, and so forth, you are not ready for transition.

Everyone has heard stories of failed implementations and blown budgets. If you are going to have problems, they will show up in the transition phase. An honest reappraisal of your risks and preparedness is worthwhile at this point. Listen carefully to what the users are saying as they become familiar with the new software.

This phase of the implementation should involve user training and a fairly mechanical process to migrate your legacy data and proven solutions to a production database. If you are still programming customizations, chasing bugs, formulating company policy, selecting configuration parameters, debating the best business process flow, and so forth, you are still building the system. Since these activities can disrupt the transition phase, you must proceed carefully if they are still occurring.

PREPARING FOR THE TRANSITION

Just like during any other phase of the implementation project, you should plan and prepare for the transition from legacy systems to your new Oracle ERP applications. You might have significant tasks if you have large numbers of users to train or large volumes of data to convert from the legacy system. Consider the following items as you create your transition plan.

- Define the goals of the implementation project team for the transition phase. Identify the goals of each group of users.

- Define the scope of the transition activities. For example, identify how much legacy data will be converted by the time the system goes to production status.

- Determine the sequence of events. Create a script of tasks, responsibilities, dependencies, and due dates. Since it is easy to over load your project team and your launch date is important, make sure the due dates are realistic and coordinated with work schedules.

- Identify who will perform the user training.

- Double-check the commitment and level of participation of your senior management. Will management help you to establish new job roles, create new business processes, activate new business requirements, deal with out-of-scope situations, and support user training schedules and content?

- Define the criteria you will use to accept the quality of training materials, configuration of the production instance, customization documentation, and conversion accuracy.

- Determine who will install the production software, who will configure each application, who will maintain the production system, when production maintenance officially will start, and when users should access the new system for the first time.

- Determine the activities needed to shut down and disable the legacy system.

- Identify how the user support infrastructure will work. Determine special support requirements for the first three months after the go-live date. Communicate problem resolution procedures to the users.

- Consider whether parts of the legacy system should run parallel for a number of days. For example, you might schedule full parallel runs for several payrolls.

- Perform an analysis to determine the point of no return to your legacy system. Identify your contingency options and procedures.

PART

II

CH

10

- Describe the detailed criteria to determine your organization's readiness to switch systems. Some companies simply hold a go/no-go vote and some users vote for production status because of political pressure or ignorance of what is about to happen. Detailed criteria are important to determine your true readiness status and are your true indicators that the users are ready to operate the software.

- Determine how you and the organization will respond to users' requests to change the scope of the system.

CONFIGURING THE PRODUCTION SYSTEM

You must manually install and configure your production version of the Oracle ERP Applications. Because the configuration steps for each application must be accomplished in sequence and the forms under the setup menu use a lot of logic and perform required validation, you must re-enter the configuration for each application. This manual process is required, even though you might have several working systems for pilot, test, and training, because you cannot create a production version by copying pieces of other systems.

Since this manual configuration process takes several days for the full implementation team and the schedule is tight during the transition phase, consider making a backup copy of the system after the configuration is complete. This backup copy might be valuable if problems are encountered during data conversion or when production transaction processing starts. Also, you might want to make a backup of the system, immediately before the first transactions start.

TRAINING YOUR USERS

The primary question a user has when entering a training program is "how do I do my job with this new software?" You want to be able to answer that question. Of course, since your ERP implementation may have fundamentally reengineered the user's responsibilities and business process, you might have to deal with the fundamental definition of the user's job. For this reason, the more sophisticated training activities use a role-based, process-oriented approach. If you are presenting new concepts or significant change to clerical users, ask a responsible functional leader to participate and endorse the new systems as part of the training.

> **Tip**
>
> Ease of use and training should be top priorities for an ERP project, because integrated applications reach new users who may be unfamiliar with ERP systems.

During user training, you must respond to changes in the workload caused by the new ERP systems. Depending on the capabilities of your legacy systems, some users may experience an increase in effort required to accomplish their key business function. For example, users of Oracle Order Entry and Purchasing Applications often complain of extra data-entry requirements when they first see the new software. If the instructors can explain how the expanded data entry enables new or more powerful business functions, the users can balance their complaints with appreciation for new features such as advanced scheduling or pay on receipt processing.

The users doing the additional work will still be unhappy, but they will be less unhappy than if you just blame the Oracle system for the increased workload. Try to explain the Oracle system requirements in a way that shows how they enable your business goals and meet your requirements.

Consider the following activities and items as you train users.

- If you have many users to train, prepare a dedicated training environment. Create a separate installation of the applications to isolate training from data conversion and keep untrained users away from the production system.

- Many companies adopt a "train the trainer" strategy when they start the ERP project because that phrase sounds clever and easy to execute. This approach assumes the project team or power users will become trained in the software during the course of the project, and they will be able to perform the user training for little or no cost. Since there are special skills required to be an effective trainer, consider the effectiveness of this strategy when you determine who will be instructors, and consider training the trainers in how to train.

- Review user procedures, policies, and requirements. If you are changing any business processes, be prepared to show the users how each step of their current process will be transformed in the new system.

- If appropriate, use actual business scenarios and transactions in instructor demonstrations and user laboratories. You may have extra set up requirements to use actual scenarios. For example, if you want to train the AP three way match process, you must create several purchase orders and make receipt transactions before the class starts.

- One hour of formal classroom training can require a day of preparation by a skilled instructor. A full day of instructor lead training might take a week to prepare training materials and set up data for examples and exercises.

- Prepare training aids such as quick reference cards, keyboard templates, help desk procedures, and lists of common navigation paths for users to take away from class.

- If users must retain classroom material for more than a few days before they use it in production, assign exercises to be performed between the time the class ends and the system goes live. Provide a test database for the users to practice their new skills on their own.

- Prepare an instructor and classroom schedule. Make sure classrooms are fully equipped, and that the response time of the training system is appropriate.

- Consider how some classes may be prerequisites for other training. Some users with broad business roles may require seven to ten classes. Consider providing cross-functional classes for some users with more theory and less detail than you provide to the daily users.

- Take attendance and determine how you will handle absenteeism. If you don't address absenteeism during transition, the effects will show up rapidly after the system starts business transactions.

- Collect and review feedback from the training sessions. You don't have to measure the popularity of the instructor, but you want to determine at the earliest possible time whether the users will be able to operate the system. Some organizations use a formal student survey at the end of each class. You should also talk to a sample of users to get extended feedback.

- Plan for continued training. Save materials, class notes, and the training database instance. These items may become valuable during a software upgrade or as new users are added to the system. After the system has been operational for a few months, consider providing both advanced user classes to explore underutilized features and remedial classes to improve productivity.

CONVERTING AND LOADING DATA

In the previous project phases, you analyzed, created, documented, and tested data conversion programs and scripts. During the transition phase, you perform the data conversion into the production database. Since the Oracle database generates relationships and distinct primary keys each time data is loaded, the conversion load process must be repeated on each database, and you cannot simply copy or export/import the data from the test database. For each data entity such as customers, items, general ledger balances, and so forth, perform the following tasks.

- Extract data from legacy systems. Make sure you know which data are time sensitive and observe proper transaction cut-off procedures.

- Run conversion programs, spreadsheets, and scripts to clean, validate, load, convert, and audit the legacy data.

- Check on the actual volume of data. Verify row counts, records processed, and records that did not validate.

- Repair invalid records and reload them.

- Begin maintenance of data by responsible users.

- Perform data entry on entities to be converted manually.

- Verify and reconcile balances. For example, the trial balance in the Oracle General Ledger should be the same as on the legacy system. When the change in systems forces a complex reconciliation, such as when the chart of accounts changes, involve the users to insure that all is satisfactory.

DEALING WITH THE NEW RELEASE

Since your implementation project might take longer that eight or nine months, Oracle may release a new version of the ERP software while your project is in progress and before you launch your systems.

> **Tip**
>
> Consider carefully your desire to install the new software release if you are in the transition phase. What you are really contemplating is an upgrade, and that action is a project within itself. To avoid invalidating your testing, training, configuration, customization, and documentation, you must freeze the system at some point and launch your new systems from a known and stable configuration.

PREPARING TO SUPPORT PRODUCTION USERS

In the transition phase, you determine and set up your production support infrastructure. Every organization is different and has procedures for user support. Small companies might simply establish a buddy system among implementation team power users and novice users. Larger companies may have already established a help desk organization to take over support from the implementation team. Consider the following activities to establish your support infrastructure.

- Make sure points of contact with Oracle support are well established.
- Transfer the library of project deliverables and documentation from the implementation team to the support group.
- As required, create special responsibilities within the Oracle Applications for support staff.
- Perform additional functional, cross-functional, and business process training for support personnel.
- Consider obtaining extra copies of Oracle reference manuals, technical reference manuals, and user guides.
- Train everyone to use the on-line help. In release 11 it is in Web page format, it is context-sensitive, and it is quite good.
- Implement an on-line system to track issues and problems.
- Establish a procedure for users to make change requests.
- Create a test database instance as a copy of the production instance. Use this instance as a staging area to test patches from Oracle Support before applying them to your production database.
- Establish a bug reporting and tracking procedure.
- If you have multiple sites, distribute all procedures and support materials to all locations.

SUPPORTING PRODUCTION OPERATIONS

When you put a full transaction load on the applications, the system achieves production status. Due to the nature of the business process, not all applications start transacting immediately. For example, the first payables check run may be a full week after purchasing goes live and the first fiscal close of the general ledger may be five weeks after the revenue and inventory transactions begin.

Production support involves auditing, maintaining, tuning, and improving the systems. The production launch date is not the end of the ERP project activities, and post launch tasks can easily continue for a year or more.

AUDITING THE PRODUCTION SYSTEMS

Go back to the documentation you created during the planning and analysis phases of the implementation project. Verify that you are meeting the goals and business requirements that you identified at the beginning of your project.

Determine your return on investment (ROI) for the new software. This calculation takes several months or even more than a year because you have to measure results and convert the change in your key performance indicators to hard currency. However, make sure you save key statistics from the legacy system as you shut it down so that you have something to compare. For example, if one of your project goals was to improve inventory turnover 30 percent, you need to know how the old system was performing to make a valid comparison with the Oracle software.

> **Tip**
>
> Consider conducting a formal user satisfaction survey or at least interviews with key users. Try to quantify a baseline satisfaction level and measure improvements against the baseline. Take the survey about four months after the systems go live, and use the results to start the continuous improvement activities for the system.

MAINTAINING THE PRODUCTION SYSTEMS

Within a few hours of launching the system, you must begin system maintenance and administration activities.

Make sure transactions are not hung up in the interfaces. For example, two days after start up in July 1998, I saw a new user make a simple keystroke error and enter a July 1988 date in the Ship Confirm window of Order Entry. The invoicing interface would not process the shipment because July 1988 was not in the fiscal calendar. Most interfaces produce a validation report or have a window to show unprocessed transactions and you should look for invalid transactions.

Tip

> Some interfaces require a technical person to correct the data in the transaction interface table with Structured Query Language (SQL).

Activate database and hardware fault-tolerant systems for backup, archive, and restoration of production data. Verify that the fault-tolerance systems and procedures are actually working. If required, implement changes to your disaster-recovery procedures.

Activate daily, weekly, or monthly postings of the AP, AR, PO, INV, PAY, and FA sub-ledgers to the general ledger. Balance and reconcile the sub-ledgers to the general ledger. Activate and monitor interfaces to and from non-Oracle computer systems.

Apply patches after appropriate testing and check regularly for invalid database objects. You should keep your Oracle system reasonably current to gain the most from your service from Oracle support. You must balance the production system's need for stability with the need to fix problems and remain close to the current release level of the software.

PART
II

CH
10

Note

> Invalid database objects are not the same as invalid data. An invalid database object may be a piece of a program logic that is used by a window or report. If a patch causes an object to be out of date or inconsistent with the rest of the system, the object may be marked invalid and the program will produce cryptic error messages that are hard for users to understand. Your database administrator can easily fix invalid objects.

TUNING PRODUCTION SYSTEMS

Since you may find your database is growing at more than five percent per month, you must quickly start production database administration procedures to manage disk space usage, eliminate disk hot spots, and control fragmentation. Compare your actual disk space usage with the estimates you made during the analysis phase and analyze the variances.

Tuning is a continuous process because the system is dynamic. Evaluate the following areas to improve performance.

- Look for hot spots (areas of high read/write activity) on the disk array. If you have excessive disk I/O on several disks, consider redistributing some database objects.

- Determine whether you need performance patches from Oracle Support. New releases are often tuned with patches after Oracle can observe real-world performance dynamics. Also, if you have an unusual data distribution or transaction volume, you may be able to obtain technical assistance from Oracle support that will patch your specific requirements.

- Analyze usage patterns and distribute the work schedule for the concurrent manager(s) so those batch jobs don't block interactive user activities.

- Look for the top ten resource hogs on your system. A hog may be either a single program that runs for a long time once a day or a program that runs for just a few minutes but runs hundreds of times per day. Once you have identified potential problems, you can determine which strategy you should use to minimize the load on the system.

- Analyze memory usage per real user. Sometimes users will develop the habit of opening windows for each responsibility or business function, and Oracle systems will allocate memory and a connection for each window.

- Verify that your network is performing acceptably. In release 11, a 100MB network should perform well, but you might have to analyze your routers and network configuration after you see the real loads.

- Analyze how well your processors and the server operating systems are handling the transaction loads throughout the business day. The application servers will have different capabilities than the database server. You want to determine where the system is constrained, which is where you must perform tuning.

BEGINNING CONTINUOUS IMPROVEMENT

The launch of an ERP system can be disruptive to the business. For example, inventory turnover can go down and some users may have a loss of productivity. Typically, users must work with the system for a time to fine tune everything from min-max reorder points to interdepartmental agreements about workloads and process steps. It can take from four months to more than a year for users to take ownership of the new system.

Tip	After several months, review how the users are using each function of the system and compare their actual practices to the business processes you trained them to use. You might find some radical differences when you see the real-world effects of the ERP system, and that can be a good starting point for further innovation or a return to standard practice.

If you deferred any customizations into the "nice to have but not a show stopper" category, you can start work on these business requirements after the system and business stabilize. These items could be a new report or any process change to repair the disruptions caused by the new software. The users will remember all of the scope issues from the first project and your promises to revisit each issue will come back to haunt you. Consider a proactive approach to meeting your pledges.

Evaluate profile options for each user role and responsibility. Some of the profile options affect security and user productivity. These options should be evaluated periodically as new users are added to the system and as experienced users become more common.

Since ERP systems are primarily transaction-processing systems, they do not handle certain tasks well. The best ERP implementations come from a series of continuous improvements.

This process enables the system to evolve into a stable and integrated platform for enterprise computing. These improvements are designed to extend ERP beyond the basic transactions of the initial implementation. Consider the following projects to enhance your new ERP system.

- Archive the transaction data in a data warehouse and take a new approach to reporting business information.
- Implement customer relationship management applications.
- Automate computer operations for the database and application servers.
- Create a business information and analysis system.
- Add sales force automation applications as a front end to ERP.
- Extend your supply chain with e-commerce.
- Begin using Internet/intranet-based self-service applications for customers, suppliers, and employees.
- Activate automatic versions of transactions that were implemented in manual mode. Examples include AutoLockbox in AR, Pay on Receipt in AP, and workflow enabled functions.
- Prepare for the next upgrade of the Oracle Applications.

You must decide whether you will develop these extensions yourself, buy the software from Oracle, or purchase from third-party vendors such as those described in Chapter 30, "Alliance Partners." The latter approach might buy you more functionality, but integrating products to work together can be a challenge.

SUMMARY

In this chapter, you have learned all of the details and tasks necessary to launch your new systems into production. Although Oracle software projects have a large technical requirement, an ERP project must incorporate the human and organizational requirements to be successful. You must properly set your users' expectations of the software and resolve their issues and concerns.

During the transition phase of the project, you train users, convert and load data, and develop the user support infrastructure. For many months to a year after the system goes live, you audit, maintain, tune, and improve the system as the users take ownership. At that point, the new software becomes the backbone of your enterprise and the key platform for growth and improvement.

PART III

Configuring and Using the Oracle Applications

CHAPTER 11

Using Oracle General Ledger

INTRODUCTION

Oracle General Ledger (GL) performs the accounting and budgeting functions in the Oracle Applications suite. It is the central module of Oracle Applications because it owns the set of books that forms the basis for all other Financials modules. Receivables, Payables, Inventory, and Assets are the main subledgers of GL. GL shares the setup information with subledgers.

GL only receives transaction information and does not send any transaction information to other modules. The main transactions in GL are Accounting (including Multi-Company and Multi-Currency), Budgeting, and Encumbrance Accounting. The main setups are Chart of Accounts (Accounting Flexfield Structure), Calendar, Currencies, Set of Books, Currency Conversion Rates, Journal Sources, Journal Categories, Encumbrance, System Controls, Profile Options, and Accounting Periods.

RELATIONSHIP TO OTHER ORACLE APPLICATIONS

GL has relationships to most of the modules in the Oracle Applications suite. The Inventory, Purchasing, Order Entry, Payables, Receivables, Assets, and Cost Management modules share the setup information from GL, and the accounting transactions from these modules are imported into GL. GL depends on the Applications Object Library (AOL) for responsibilities, menus, profile options, and other related setups. Figure 11.1 shows how various modules are related to GL. In each module, the information it shares is indicated. Arrows show the direction in which this information flows and to which modules the information flows.

DISCOVERING NEW FEATURES IN RELEASE 11

The following sections describe some of the important new features in release 11 of GL. These features include the Global Consolidation System, Centralized Transaction Approval, and Mass Maintenance.

GLOBAL CONSOLIDATION SYSTEM

In GL releases prior to release 11, the consolidation process consisted of a series of predefined, one-to-one company relationships. The consolidation process could become quite involved in a complex corporate structure where multiple levels of consolidation were required. It was up to the user to keep track of the structure, the proper order of consolidation, and which consolidations had been completed.

The release 11 Global Consolidation System (GCS) is a tool to make the complex consolidation process easier to manage. Within GCS is the Consolidation Workbench. This is the central control for tracking the status of all the consolidations. The Consolidation Workbench provides the means to perform the various consolidations, keep you informed of

Figure 11.1
General Ledger relationships to other applications.

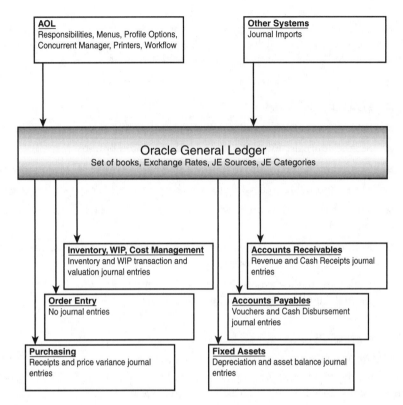

the status of each, and indicate whether transactions have been made to the subsidiary after the consolidation has taken place with the parent.

Within the Consolidation Workbench, there is a navigation tool called the State Controller. This is a set of optional buttons that can navigate you to the activities associated with the functional steps in a consolidation.

CENTRALIZED TRANSACTION APPROVAL

Centralized Transaction Approval (CENTRA) is an enhancement to the Intercompany (I/C) functionality of GL. Prior to release 11, to create an I/C entry, you needed access/security to more than one balancing segment (company). Anyone authorized to make entries into two different balancing segments could make them in the same journal entry and thereby create intercompany entries at the time of posting. There was no approval process for I/C transactions. CENTRA introduces an approval process for I/C transactions. You can create an intercompany journal entry, but it cannot be posted until an authorized person approves the I/C charge.

JOURNAL APPROVAL SYSTEM

The Journal Approval process before release 11 was handled indirectly by menu security. If you wanted someone to approve journal entries prior to posting then you gave them the

PART

III

CH

11

Journal Post screen. The posting process also became the approval process. As part of the release 11 General Ledger, Oracle delivers a workflow process for journal approvals. You do not need to have an Oracle Workflow license to use this workflow process.

To enable Journal Approval, you should do the following:

- Have Oracle Workflow installed.
- Set the Journals: Allow Preparer Approval profile option.
- Set the Journals: Find Approver Method profile options.
- Configure the GL journal approval process in Oracle Workflow Builder.
- Mark the Enable Journal Approval check box in your Set of Books window.
- Mark the Require Journal Approval check box for each journal source that needs approval.
- Employees involved in the preparation and approval of journal entries must be defined using the Enter Person window.
- Define the authorization limit for each employee involved in the process using the Journal Authorization Limits window.

MASS MAINTENANCE

The Mass Maintenance window can be used to move or merge GL account balances by specifying the source and the target accounts. You can also use the Mass Creation function to automatically create accounts based on existing accounts.

There are several restrictions on the move or merge functions:

- The move or merge is not allowed across sets of books, balancing segment values, and financial statement categories.
- The Mass Maintenance function does not allow move or merge functions for budget or encumbrance balances and balances of purged accounting periods.
- Accounts and account ranges defined for recurring journals, MassAllocations, consolidation mappings, and summary accounts are not updated.
- Historical rates, if any, must be rebuilt for the target account.
- Special rules must be followed for moving net income accounts.

This process creates move/merge audit journals and produces the Mass Maintenance Execution Report. If, however, you are not satisfied with the move, the whole process could still be reversed as long as the move/merge tables are not yet purged.

CROSS-CURRENCY RATES

Older versions of GL stated all currency exchange rates in relation to the functional (reporting) currency of the set of books. If the functional currency was US-Dollars (USD), all exchange rates were stated as a fraction of USD. You could not define an exchange rate between Japanese Yen and the French Franc.

Release 11 still defaults the To currency to the functional currency for the set of books. If your functional currency is a European Monetary Unit (EMU), GL defaults the Euro as the To currency.

SINGLE EXCHANGE RATE TABLE

Release 11 changes the way exchange rates are stored for multiple sets of books. Older versions stored the rates in each set of books with the functional currency in each being the only permitted value for the To currency. Release 11 has one rate table for all sets of books and you can maintain it from any set of books. You need only define one set of conversion rates, even if you have multiple sets of books.

DOWNLOADING EXCHANGE RATES

Release 11 provides an interface table (GL_DAILY_RATES_INTERFACE) for updating, insertion, and deleting exchange rates. This table provides for the use of a range of dates (for example, for a full accounting period) where the rate is the same every day. This interface is an excellent feature for companies using corporate-directed exchange rates. GL builds a separate rate record for each date in the range.

MULTIPLE REPORTING CURRENCIES

Multiple Reporting Currencies (MRC) resolves a common problem for global companies operating in several countries. In many cases, these companies are presented the problem of what functional currency to use: the reporting currency required by headquarters for consolidation or the local currency required by law. Many of these companies have developed customizations to copy all transactions from one set of books to a second set of books. This way, they can have two functional currencies. This customization could be quite complex when you consider the problems involved:

- Reversing journals at the original exchange rate and not the current rate
- MassAllocation differences between the books
- Consolidation and revaluation entries not to be copied

MRC handles many of these problems. Through configuration, you define what entries are copied by source and by category. GL copies the appropriate entries at the time of posting to the primary set of books. MRC will replace the dual currency functions from earlier versions of the applications.

RESOLVING ISSUES AND GAPS

The decisions made during the implementation will affect the use of the GL module for years to come. Some configuration and modification decisions cannot be reversed without a significant additional investment of time and money, and some customizations or corrective actions might cause you to lose your technical support from Oracle. All these factors are critical for an implementation and should be given due consideration at the very beginning of implementation.

SUMMARY ACCOUNTS

Summary Accounts maintain summarized balances. You can use them for online inquiries and rapid reporting. Refer to discussion on summary accounts and summary templates later in this chapter in the section "Set of Books Setup." You can assign budgetary control options to summary accounts to perform summary level budgetary control.

ROLLUP GROUPS

A Rollup Group is the sum of the values in a specified value segment. Rollup Groups are calculated by GL by adding up the child values at the time of reporting. This enables you to generate calculations at the time of reporting without having to maintain or update the values during transactions. Refer to the discussion on rollup groups later in this chapter in the section "Set of Books Setup."

PROPOSED ENHANCEMENTS

Following are some enhancements that have been asked for by users at large for some time and have been proposed for incorporation in release 11i or release 12 as indicated.

DRILL-DOWN

The current drill-down feature in Account Inquiry displays only the journal line affecting the balance. The enhancement gives the user the capability to also view all other lines in that journal entry.

INTERCOMPANY (I/C) ACCOUNTING

In respect to I/C balancing, from any balancing segment (for example, company), you can only tell what the net I/C balance for that entity is. You can neither determine what other entities owe funds nor which entities are owed funds. This proposed enhancement (release 11i) would provide the capability to determine the fund relationships between pairs of entities.

Another proposed enhancement (release 11i) is for automatic I/C elimination. This would enhance the I/C process to build consolidation elimination entries when creating I/C entries. Users would most likely register elimination types of I/C activity. GL would build the usual I/C entry but also an elimination entry in another set of books designated as the Elimination Company.

Part of this functionality is available in release 11 through GCS and CENTRA as discussed earlier in this chapter in the section "Discovering New Features in Release 11."

YEAR-END CLOSING ENTRIES

Current versions of GL close out the P&L into Retained Earnings by adjusting year-end balances and do not create a journal entry for audit trail purposes. This proposed enhancement will have GL create a journal entry for posting that can also be printed for visual verification.

AUTO STEP-DOWN ALLOCATIONS

Currently, to perform an allocation that is based on a previous allocation (step-down), users must generate the first allocation and post it prior to generating the second allocation. This can be a tedious process because someone must watch the posting concurrent request to see when it is finished before starting the second allocation process. The enhancement will add workflow capabilities to the process to specify the order of multiple events.

> **Tip**
>
> Many of the enhancements developed for new releases are made available to users of earlier releases. These are called backports and are made available to licensed users by the application of patches. To see a list of current backports, check Oracle's MetaLink Web site at `http://metalink.oracle.com`.

PART
III

CH
11

CONFIGURING THE GL APPLICATION

The following section lists all the setup tasks for a GL implementation and briefly describes each task. The tasks should be performed in the order discussed here.

RESOLVING CRITICAL SETUP ISSUES

In addition to understanding the factors discussed previously, you should identify and understand some key issues underlying a GL implementation. The issues vary depending on the business scenario and requirements. The following are some common issues that apply in all circumstances.

DETERMINING THE STRUCTURE OF THE KEY ACCOUNTING FLEXFIELD

The Key Accounting Flexfield (KAFF) structure forms an important component of the set of books and cannot be changed after transactions are entered. The requirements of transaction flow from all the modules should be considered before designing the KAFF structure. An understanding of various features, such as rollup groups, summary accounts, cross-validation rules, and set of books requirements, will help design a practical KAFF structure. Determine at this stage whether a common KAFF structure can serve the business requirements. If there is a need for multiple KAFF structures, you must create multiple sets of books.

DETERMINING THE SETS OF BOOKS FOR YOUR ENTERPRISE

This configuration task depends directly on the requirements of the KAFF structure, currency, and calendar. If the business requires more than one combination of these three components, you need multiple sets of books. See Chapter 23, "Understanding Multi-Org," to understand the role and importance of a set of books in a multiple organization structure of Oracle Applications. Understand the consolidation and reporting features with multiple sets of books and their limitations to determine the way sets of books should be configured for your implementation.

REQUIRED SETUP TASKS

Table 11.1 shows the tasks to set up the GL Application in the order they should be performed. Try not to skip tasks or perform them out of sequence because many tasks use predecessor tasks for data validation, and you might receive error messages.

TABLE 11.1 GL SETUP TASKS

Setup Task Name	Required?
Define Responsibilities	Yes
Define Value Sets	Yes
Define Flexfield Structure	Yes
Define Segment Values	Yes
Define Rollup Groups	No
Define Security Rules	No
Define Cross-Validation Rules	No
Enter Account Code Combinations	No
Enter Additional I/C Accounts	No
Enter Additional Suspense Accounts	No
Define Summary Accounts	No
Define Calendar Period Types	Yes
Define Calendar Periods	Yes
Define Transaction Calendar	No
Define Currencies	Yes
Define Daily Conversion Rate Types	Yes
Enter Daily Conversion Rates	No
Define a Set of Books	Yes
Assign Set of Books to a Responsibility	Yes
Define Historical Rates	No
Define Shorthand Aliases	No
Define Journal Sources	Yes

TABLE 11.1 GL SETUP TASKS

Setup Task Name	Required?
Define Journal Categories	Yes
Define Statistical Units of Measure	No
Define Budgetary Control Groups	No
Define Encumbrance Types	No
Set up Automatic Posting	No
Index Accounting Flexfield Segments	No
Define System Controls	Yes
Define Profile Options	Yes
Define and Assign Document Sequences	No
Open and Close Accounting Periods	Yes
Configure the Desktop Integrator	No
Administer System Issues	No
Define Concurrent Program Controls	No
Use the Optimizer to Improve Performance	No
Set System Storage Parameters	No

UNDERSTANDING EACH SETUP TASK

This section discusses the details of each setup task in the order they should be performed. They are categorized broadly into two parts: set of books setup and GL setup. The first category is necessary for the functioning of any module of Oracle Applications. The second category is directly related to the functioning of GL. Before carrying out these two sets of setups, define one responsibility to use for setup tasks.

DEFINING RESPONSIBILITIES

The responsibility definition is done in the Oracle Applications System Administration module. GL has six predefined responsibilities. Copy one of these predefined responsibilities to create a new responsibility with different capabilities.

Choose a responsibility that has access to set up functions, such as General Ledger Controller, to carry out the following setups.

SET OF BOOKS SETUP

A set of books is a combination of Currency, Calendar, and Chart of Accounts or Key Accounting Flexfield (KAFF) structure. One set of books can be shared by many organizations, and if so, they must share the same Currency, Calendar, and KAFF structure.

This section discusses the setup of a set of books that is necessary to use any module of Oracle Financials. The setups specific to the operation of GL are discussed in the next section.

CHART OF ACCOUNTS Defining a Chart of Accounts involves first defining a KAFF structure and entering Account Code Combinations (ACC) for that structure. Perform the following steps.

DEFINING VALUE SETS A *value set* contains the definition and rules that will be assigned to a flexfield segment. The values that can be entered in a segment, their validation, and other properties are determined by the value set assigned to it. Understand each segment in the KAFF with respect to the values that go into it, the validations to be performed, and other general properties. Define a value set for each combination of these requirements.

There can be two types of value sets: *parent* values and *child* values. A parent value is one that has one or more child values associated with it. A child value is one that lies in a range of values belonging to a parent value. A child value can belong to more than one parent value. A child value cannot be a dependent value; that is, the actual value of the child must not depend on the value of another segment.

You create parent-child relationships by defining a range of child values that belong to a parent value. You can use parent-child relationships for reporting and other application purposes. Parent value sets are used to create rollup groups.

> **Tip**
>
> Using a value set in multiple segments reduces maintenance. Similarly, using a value set in multiple KAFF structures improves the consolidation process. Change in the value set affects all the flexfields it is assigned to. In such a case, quickly create a new value set by copying from the existing value set and updating its properties as required.

DEFINING FLEXFIELD STRUCTURE The Key Accounting Flexfield (KAFF) structure is the GL's definition of the chart of accounts. Define a KAFF for use in a set of books definition, define segments for each flexfield structure, and assign a value set to each segment. You must designate one segment as the natural account segment and another segment as the balancing segment. Enable and freeze the structure after the flexfield definition is complete. Freeze the rollup groups after segment values have been defined in the next step. Enable dynamic inserts (see the following section, "Defining Segment Values") or enter segment values before using them in accounts code combinations.

> **Note**
>
> Changes cannot be made in a frozen flexfield definition. Uncheck the frozen box, make changes as necessary, and freeze it again.

DEFINING SEGMENT VALUES This task determines the scope within which the values entered in this segment will be validated. These values must be entered before they can be used in account code combinations.

DEFINING ROLLUP GROUPS   A *rollup group* is used to identify a group of parent values for reporting or other application purposes. Rollup groups are used to create summary templates. You can assign key flexfield segment values to rollup groups using the Segment Values window.

Rollup groups are separate from parent-child relationships. You can assign any parent value to a given rollup group, regardless of that parent value's place in a parent-child hierarchy you might create.

DEFINING SECURITY RULES   Security rules enable you to restrict data entry and online inquiry for the ranges of segment values. Each rule is defined for a specific segment. Rules come into effect only when attached to a responsibility and do not affect reporting. The rules are defined to exclude or include the absolute values restricted by the rule. When a rule is defined, by default, GL excludes all values except those specifically included. Therefore, each rule must have at least one Include rule element. Attach these rules to responsibilities in the Assign Security Rules window.

Tip

It is recommended that a rule should start with a general include element for the entire range and then have exclude elements for the ranges that should be restricted. Also, users must change responsibilities or log off and log on for security rules to take effect after you assign them to a responsibility.

PART

III

CH

11

DEFINING CROSS-VALIDATION RULES   Cross-Validation Rules enable you to restrict entry of account code combinations, as opposed to Security Rules, which restrict values entered for individual segments. Account code combinations already entered are not affected by new rules, so always define these rules before you enter account code combinations. The Cross-Validation Rules are for the entire KAFF structure and not assigned to any responsibility. When a Cross-Validation Rule is defined for a KAFF, by default, GL excludes all combinations except those specifically included. Start with a general include element. Then exclude the ranges that should be restricted.

DYNAMIC INSERTION   Use of dynamic insertion is a key issue to be determined at the beginning of your implementation. It is difficult to manually enter a long list of account combinations. Any missing combinations give rise to errors in data entry. On the other hand, having the dynamic insertion enabled always results in some unwanted account combinations, which might be due to errors in data entry.

Tip

It is easy to have dynamic insertion enabled initially when keying in or migrating initial data into GL. After a period of time, prune the list and determine a policy on usage of account code combinations. It is best to disable dynamic insertion at this stage unless the business requirement determines otherwise. Any code combination to be used subsequently should first be defined.

DEFINING ACCOUNTING CALENDAR Defining an Accounting Calendar involves defining calendar period types and defining periods for the calendar.

DEFINING CALENDAR PERIOD TYPES GL has three predefined period types: Month, Quarter, and Year. Use the predefined types or define new types. For best use, the name of a new period type should give the best possible indication of its nature or purpose. The type definition indicates the number of periods per year and the year type (Calendar or Fiscal).

DEFINING CALENDAR PERIODS Define your calendar by creating a name, and define the periods within the calendar. The periods in the calendar must be of a predefined or user-defined type. Adjusting periods can overlap, but nonadjusting periods cannot overlap.

Note

Carefully, consider the following restrictions before choosing the earliest period:
- After opening the first period, prior periods cannot be opened.
- Foreign currency translation cannot be performed in the first period.

DEFINING CURRENCIES GL comes predefined with all the currencies of ISO member countries. Enable a currency before using it in a set of books. The currency used in a set of books is called its functional currency. USD is the only currency enabled by default. You must enable other currencies and enter conversion rates before using them in transactions. Additional currencies can be defined as required. Consider some questions such as the functional currency, precision required for accounting, foreign currency transactions, use of multiple currencies in the organization (which will require multiple sets of books), dual-currency accounting, method, and frequency of foreign currency translations.

DEFINING CONVERSION RATE TYPES GL comes with three predefined rate types: Corporate, Spot, and User. Additional rate types can be defined as required.

When currency rates must be entered at the time of transactions, use the User rate type. If rates must be stored into GL and validated, use Corporate, Spot, or another newly defined rate type. Enter these rates using the Daily Rates window.

ENTERING CONVERSION RATES Use the Daily Rates window to define exchange conversion rates for combinations of foreign currency and date. The daily rates can be for corporate, spot, or other newly defined rate types.

CREATING THE SET OF BOOKS FROM A KAFF, CURRENCY, AND CALENDAR A set of books is a combination of the following three components:

- Currency
- Calendar
- Chart of Accounts (KAFF)

The set of books is the foundation of not only the GL but also of all other modules of Oracle Applications that share any kind of accounting information. You must define at least one set of books for an organization.

Define a set of books and select a Currency, Calendar, and KAFF structure for it. To complete the definition of set of books, specify the following accounts:

- A *retained earnings account* is necessary for GL to post the net balance of all revenue and expense accounts at the beginning of each fiscal year.

- A *suspense account* is necessary if Suspense Posting is enabled. In such cases, GL automatically balances the unbalanced journals by posting the difference to the suspense account.

- An *intercompany account* is necessary if intercompany balancing is enabled.

- A *translation adjustment account* is necessary to perform currency translation.

- A *reserve for encumbrance account* can be entered if budgetary control is enabled or if encumbrance accounting is to be used. If this is entered, GL posts difference of out-of-balance encumbrance journals to this account.

Note

Encumbrance journals need not be balanced like actual accounting journals.

ASSIGNING THE SET OF BOOKS TO RESPONSIBILITIES (OR SITE)   Assign the set of books to a responsibility by specifying the set of books in the responsibility's profile option. This is the set of books you will operate on when you log in as this responsibility. The set of books of a responsibility can only be changed by assigning value to its profile option and cannot be changed by selecting online.

ENTERING ACCOUNT CODE COMBINATIONS   The Account Code Combination (ACC) is a combination of segment values for the KAFF that can be used in transactions. Enter all the possible ACCs that will be used in transactions.

Note

If dynamic insertion is enabled, GL automatically creates the new ACCs as they are entered in transactions.

When new ACCs are manually entered, make sure of the following:

- The Enabled option is selected, without which the account cannot be used in transactions

- Select the Allow Posting option, without which GL will not post any transactions to the account. There might be accounts (such as summary accounts) to which you do not want to post entries directly, in which case you can leave the Allow Posting option unselected.

■ The Allow Posting option should be enabled for each segment value of the ACC.

■ Enter an optional end date only in future periods when you want this account not to be used in any transactions.

> **Tip**
>
> When preparing an exhaustive list of ACCs, it is good to start with a study of existing account codes in the system. Taking that study as a base, modifications can be made to suit the business requirements. This exercise many times leads to a completely different account coding, but it is easy to start with because the users are familiar with the existing account coding. Make sure you have a segment value blocking strategy that supports your financial reports, account hierarchy, budget organizations, summary accounts, and rollup groups.

DEFINING ADDITIONAL INTERCOMPANY ACCOUNTS   Additional Intercompany (I/C) Accounts can be defined for each combination of journal sources and journal categories. Define additional I/C accounts to indicate you want to balance I/C journal entries from specific journal sources and journal categories to different I/C accounts. The default I/C account specified in the set of books appears with the source and category "other."

GL will post a balancing I/C amount to an additional account only if the following is true:

■ The source of the journal entry matches the source in this definition.

■ The category in the journal entry matches the category in this definition.

■ The type of balancing entry (debit or credit) matches the debit/credit value specified in this definition.

To post both debit and credit amounts to one additional I/C account, set up two separate lines in the definition.

DEFINING ADDITIONAL SUSPENSE ACCOUNTS   Additional Suspense Accounts can be defined for each combination of journal sources and journal categories. If Suspense Posting is enabled in a set of books definition, GL automatically posts the difference of unbalanced journals to the suspense accounts.

DEFINING SUMMARY ACCOUNTS   A *summary account* is an accounting flexfield combination that is the sum of the balances in other accounting Flexfield combinations. Create summary accounts for your set of books using the Summary Accounts window. Enter a name, description, earliest period, and template for the summary accounts. GL uses summary templates to generate summary accounts. You denote in the template whether each segment is Detail or Total using the letters "D" or "T," respectively. This designation determines whether GL creates and maintains a detail summary account for each segment value or one summary account that sums the balances of all detail segment values.

Note

The status field displays Adding while GL is generating summary accounts by running a concurrent process. The field displays Current when the process is complete and the account is active. Similarly, the status field displays Deleting while GL is running a concurrent process to delete summary accounts.

Delete and recreate summary accounts when modifying the contents of a rollup group or moving existing child segment values between parent values.

Summary accounts are updated immediately on posting an entry to the corresponding detail accounts. Therefore, querying and reporting is possible with summary accounts and also saves time.

GL Setup

The following section discusses the GL specific setups. These setups are necessary to use the GL functions.

Defining Historical Rates   Use the Historical Rates window to assign historical exchange conversion rates or amounts to accounts. These rates override the use of a Translation Rate of accounts.

Defining Shorthand Aliases   *Shorthand aliases* are simple names to identify an account combination and considerably ease data entry. For example, "Cash" can be used to identify a complex five-segment account combination "1.10.21.30.400." An alias can represent the value for one or several segments or an entire account. When entering account combinations in transactions, invoke the account pop-up window. The shorthand window appears, enabling you to enter aliases. You can also skip the shorthand window to go ahead and enter the actual account combination.

Defining Journal Entry Sources   GL uses journal source definitions to identify the origin of journal entry transactions. Transactions can be grouped by sources for reporting and analysis. GL comes with more than twenty predefined sources. You can define additional sources as necessary. Also, additional I/C accounts and suspense accounts can be defined for each combination of journal sources and categories.

Defining Journal Entry Categories   GL enables you to group or categorize transactions by their purpose, such as accrual, payments, receipts, and so forth, by using journal categories. GL comes with more than 35 predefined categories. You can define additional categories as necessary for your business requirements. Also, additional I/C accounts and suspense accounts can be defined for each combination of journal sources and categories.

Tip

Specify a category for every transaction instead of leaving it blank. Categories help in reporting. Categorization also enables you to make good use of additional suspense accounts and additional I/C accounts.

Tip

Where it is not possible to assign a transaction to a specific category, have several general categories, and assign the transaction to one of these.

Tip

It might be sufficient to use predefined categories for most purposes and avoid managing a mass of categories. However, if your specific purpose requires a new name for better categorization, don't hesitate to define a new category; just keep the list easy to handle.

DEFINING STATISTICAL UNITS OF MEASURE Statistical Units of Measure enable you to additionally track nonmonetary measures for specific natural account segments. Examples of Statistical Units of Measure are Hours for consulting, Students for training programs, and so on. The usage of Statistical Units of Measure is explained later in this chapter in the section titled "Understanding Statistical Entries."

DEFINING BUDGETARY CONTROL GROUPS Defining budgetary control groups involves defining budgetary control rules by grouping the journal sources and journal categories with similar rules. You can establish any of the following:

- Advisory or absolute control
- Tolerance percentage or amount
- Override amount

An absolute control is where the transaction will not pass budgetary approval if it exceeds the tolerance specified. An advisory control is one where the system warns of the transaction but allows it to pass. These sets of rules can be specified for specific combinations of journal sources and journal categories.

Finally, use profile options to assign different budgetary control groups to different users.

If budgetary control is used, GL checks and reserves funds for budgetary control transactions in Payables and Purchasing. GL also creates encumbrance or actual journal entry batches for those transactions in Payables or Purchasing that pass funds reservation.

Tip

For strict budgetary control, always first include a general combination of Other journal sources and Other as the journal category to be absolute with no tolerance. This implies that for all the journal source/category combinations that are not specifically allowed, transactions will not pass if they exceed the budget, with zero percent tolerance.

DEFINING ENCUMBRANCE TYPES   GL comes with two predefined Encumbrance Types: Commitment and Obligation. Enable these types before using in budgetary control. You can define additional types as required. These names are for easy identification, and you can track total encumbrances under different names. For example, in a business function such as purchasing, encumbrances can be tracked by a different type at each stage of the process.

DEFINING AUTOMATIC POSTING OPTIONS   The AutoPost setup enables you to schedule automatic posting of journals by sources, balance types (Actual, Budget, Encumbrance, or ALL), and periods. Choose a priority between 1 (highest) and 99 (lowest) for each of the criteria. Finally, submit the automatic posting concurrent request to run on a periodic basis by selecting the Resubmit parameter of the Run Options window.

SETTING THE PROFILE OPTIONS   Profile options can be set at the Site (lowest priority), Application (second lowest priority), Responsibility (second highest priority), and User (highest priority) levels. The options default from a lower priority level to a higher priority level unless another option is specified at the higher priority level. Table 11.2 indicates which options can be set or updated at each of the levels. The System Administrator can set these profile options for each of the levels specified.

TABLE 11.2 GL PROFILE OPTIONS*

Profile Option	User	Resp.	App	Site
Budgetary Control Group	Yes	Yes	Yes	Yes
Dual Currency	No	Yes	Yes	Yes
FSG: Account	No	No	Yes	Yes
FSG: Allow portrait print style	Yes	Yes	Yes	Yes
FSG: Expand parent value	Yes	Yes	Yes	Yes
FSG: Message detail	Yes	Yes	Yes	Yes
GL Set of Books ID	No	View	View	View
GL Set of Books name	No	Yes	Yes	Yes
Journals: Allow multiple exchange rates	Yes	Yes	Yes	Yes
Journals: Allow posing during entry	Yes	Yes	Yes	Yes
Journals: Default category	Yes	Yes	Yes	Yes
Journals: Display inverse rate	Yes	Yes	Yes	Yes
Journals: Mix statistical & monetary	Yes	Yes	Yes	Yes
Use performance module	No	No	Yes	Yes

*View = allowed to view only
Yes = allowed to update
No = not allowed to view or update

The user can access only the following profile options and only at the User level:

- Budgetary control group (View only)
- Dual currency (View only)
- FSG: Allow portrait print style
- FSG: Expand parent value
- FSG: Message detail
- GL Set of Books ID (View only)
- Journals: Allow multiple exchange rates
- Journals: Allow posting during entry
- Journals: Display inverse rate
- Journals: Mix statistical and monetary

DEFINING AND ASSIGNING DOCUMENT SEQUENCES   You can choose automatic or manual document sequence numbering. The automatic numbering option numbers journal entries in ascending order, starting with a specified initial value. This can be used with all journals. You can also choose to inform the user by displaying a message of the document number generated. The manual numbering option requires you to enter a document number at the time of creating a journal entry and as such can be used only with journals created manually—not with those created automatically.

Use the Document Sequences window to define the document sequence numbering option for each of the documents including journal entries.

Assign each document sequence to an application and a journal category. Optionally assign each sequence to a set of books and/or a journal creation method. To assign a document sequence to a set of books, enable the set of books segment in the Document Flexfield.

The Sequential Numbering profile option must be set to one of the following three values:

- *Always used.* In this case, GL requires sequential numbering for journal entries.
- *Partially used.* In this case, GL allows sequential numbering for journal entries.
- *Not used.* In this case, GL does not allow sequential numbering for journal entries.

GL provides Journals by Document Number Report, which lists the journals with Number, Status, Creation Date, Batch Name, Header Name, Category, Posting Status, Posted Date, Currency Debits and Credits.

ADDITIONAL SETUPS

The following sections explain some setups to be completed outside GL.

CONFIGURING THE DESKTOP INTEGRATOR   Applications Desktop Integrator (ADI) is a spreadsheet-based extension to Oracle General Ledger that offers full cycle accounting within the comfort and familiarity of an Excel spreadsheet. ADI combines a spreadsheet's ease of use with the power of General Ledger to provide true desktop integration during every phase of your accounting cycle. ADI comes with an installer that will automatically install the ADI and chosen components on your personal computer. ADI includes the Budget Wizard, Journal Wizard, Report Wizard, and Watch Utility.

Budget Wizard enables you to automatically build a budget spreadsheet based on budgets and budget organizations set up in GL. Using Budget Wizard, you can do the following:

- Download existing budget balances from GL or create new budgets.
- Enter new budget balances manually.
- Use budget rules.
- Use spreadsheet formulas and models.
- Graph your budgets and compare budgets and actual balances.
- Save the budget on your PC and work on it locally.
- Automatically upload your budgets into GL.

Journal Wizard enables you to easily build journal entry worksheets. You can enter journals directly into Excel using the spreadsheet's calculation abilities and formulas. Then automatically upload journal entries into Oracle GL. ADI validates data against the accounts, security rules, and information defined in GL.

Report Wizard provides a spreadsheet-based interface to GL's Financial Statement Generator (FSG) and the ability to use the FSG reusable components. You can define simple reports entirely in a spreadsheet, using a combination of spreadsheet and assistance windows, or in configurable property sheets.

The Watch Utility is a tool used to monitor concurrent requests, and it provides instant status notification by flashing a message on your PC's screen. You can use it to simultaneously monitor any concurrent program submitted by any Oracle Application against any database.

PART
III

CH
11

PROCESSING TRANSACTIONS

GL is the central repository of accounting information, and it receives transactions from financial and manufacturing subledgers. When in the GL, the accounting information can be inquired, adjusted, converted, revalued, translated, consolidated, and reported on.

This section discusses GL transaction processing in nine sections dealing with the following topics respectively:

- Open/Closed periods
- Actual Journals
- Budget Journals
- Encumbrance Transactions
- Consolidation and Translation Entries

- Year End Activities
- Archive and Purge
- Understanding the Global Accounting Engine
- Financial Statement Generator reports

OPEN/CLOSED PERIODS

Calendar periods can have one of five statuses: Never Opened, Future Enterable, Open, Closed, or Permanently Closed.

- If a period is Never Opened, journals cannot be entered.
- If a period is Future Enterable, journals can be entered but cannot be posted. A fixed number of Future Enterable periods can be defined from the Set of Books window. To post journals, open periods using the Open and Close Periods window.
- If a period is Open, journals can be entered and posted. Open or close periods using the Open and Close Periods window.
- If a period is Closed, journals can neither be entered nor posted. A period must be opened again to enter or post journals. Open or close periods using the Open and Close Periods window.
- If a period is Permanently Closed, it cannot be reopened, so do not permanently close a period unless you are sure you won't want to reopen it.

PROCESSING ACTUAL JOURNALS

Actual journals refer to actual accounting journal entries as compared to budget or encumbrance entries, which are discussed in later sections.

Journals can be created in several ways by any of the following methods:

- Direct entry using Enter Journals window
- Importing using Journal Import window
- Creating reversals for existing entries
- Creating recurring journals using defined formulas
- Creating MassAllocations using defined formulas

Each of these is discussed here.

ENTERING JOURNALS ONLINE

Journals have three levels of information: Batch, Header, and Lines. Each journal has several account distribution lines, and optionally, several related journals can be grouped into a batch. Journals can be posted individually or by batch. Use the Reverse Journal button in the Enter Journal window to quickly create a reversal entry for the current journal or for all journals in the batch. Use the Post button to quickly post a journal or a batch. Set the profile option Journals: Allow Posting During Journal Entry to Yes if you want to use the online posting feature.

Following are some important points related to journals.

BATCH LEVEL INFORMATION ■ All information entered at this level is optional.

- GL enters a default name and the latest open period if nothing is entered, and it creates one batch for every new journal entered. Enter new information and override the defaults where needed.

- Optionally, enter a control total. The batch will not be posted unless the total of all the journals in that batch agrees with the control total entered.

HEADER LEVEL INFORMATION ■ All journals within a batch must have the same period.

- GL enters a default name and functional currency if nothing is entered. You can enter new information or override the defaults.

- Optionally, enter a journal control total. This works for a journal in the same way batch control total works for a batch.

- Optionally, enter reference information for the journal, which will be printed in reports.

- The Document Ordering Sequence can be configured to automatically generate a document number for each journal.

- To default a category for all journals, set up the profile option Journals: Default Category.

- Customize the Enter Journals folder by selecting columns to display and their display properties. Also consider making multiple versions of the folder.

LINE LEVEL INFORMATION ■ All Lines within a journal must have the same currency and category.

- The journal must be balanced in terms of total debits and total credits of all the lines unless Suspense Posting is allowed or the journal has a currency of STAT.

IMPORT JOURNALS

Subledgers and ADI send information into the GL_INTERFACE table. The Journal Import program imports entries into GL_BATCHES, GL_HEADERS, and GL_LINES. The Journal Import program can be run automatically from these subledgers or manually from GL. The only exception is Fixed Assets, which directly populates the GL_BATCHES, GL_HEADERS, and GL_LINES tables directly without the need to run Journal Import.

The subledger to GL transfers can be made in two ways: Detail or Summary. Detail transfer creates journal entry lines for all transactions against each account within a category. Summary transfer creates only totals for transactions against each account within a category.

Tip — If you are going to post journals in detail, make sure your Database Administrator understands this requirement and provides space in the database.

Journals can be imported from other legacy systems as well. To do this, populate the GL_INTERFACE table. For details of columns in this table, their contents and validations, refer to the Oracle General Ledger Technical Reference Manual and the Open Interfaces Manual.

REVERSING JOURNALS

The primary use of Reversing Journals is to reverse an accrual, a revaluation, an encumbrance, or an error. GL automatically creates a journal entry by reversing the amounts of the pre-existing journal entry. The Reversible option must be Yes to be able to reverse a journal. You can choose the fiscal period that will receive the reversing entry. Create reversing journals in one of the following ways:

- Use the Reverse Batch button from the More Actions screen in the Batch zone of the Enter Journals window to create a reversing entry for the pre-existing journal batch. An unposted reversal batch is created for each journal in the original batch.

- Use the Reverse Journal button from the More Actions screen in the Journals window or from the More Details screen in the Enter Journals window to create a reversing entry for the pre-existing journal entry. An unposted reversal batch is created for each such reversal entry.

- Use the Reverse Journals window to reverse journals with a predefined reversal period. Select the journals to be reversed and click the Reverse button. Journals not having a predefined reversal period do not appear in this list for selection.

RECURRING JOURNALS

With the Recurring Journal Entries function of GL, journal entries can be created using fixed amounts and/or accounts. Multiple journals can be created with the same or similar information.

The following types of recurring journals can be created in GL:

- *Skeleton Journals.* Here you enter accounts only. This creates journals without amounts, which are entered using the Enter Journals window.

- *Standard Journals.* Here the amounts and accounts are entered as constants, and journals are created with same account and amount information. Use the Enter Journals window to modify specific journals.

- *Formula Journals.* Here the amounts vary based on the formula defined. Each generation uses the specified account balances to calculate the journal line amounts. Use the Enter Journals window to modify specific journals.

Create recurring journals in two steps as follows.

DEFINE RECURRING FORMULA Use the Define Recurring Journal Formula window to create skeleton templates, standard templates, or formulas. Reuse these templates to generate journals multiple times.

GENERATE RECURRING JOURNAL ENTRIES Use the Generate Recurring Journals window to generate unposted journal entries based on the templates or formula defined as previously mentioned. The window lists defined recurring templates or formulas. Select the batches to generate from this list. Use the listed batches multiple times to create recurring journals in multiple periods.

MASSALLOCATIONS

Use MassAllocations to create multiple entries from a single account by using a formula. First define a formula for MassAllocation and then generate MassAllocation entries using the formula.

DEFINE MASSALLOCATION FORMULA Use the Define MassAllocations window to create MassAllocation definitions. GL prompts to start a concurrent program to validate the MassAllocation. Without successful validation, formulas cannot be generated.

When working with actual balances, you can choose Full Balance or Entered Currency to allocate. The first option allocates both functional currency and converted functional currency amounts, resulting in functional currency entries. The second option only posts the entered currency, ignoring the converted functional currency amount. This option results in transactions of the entered currency.

> **Tip**
>
> When working with encumbrance balances, always use full balance because GL always keeps track of budgeting in functional currency, and all encumbrance entries should be in functional currency.

GENERATE MASSALLOCATION ENTRIES Use the Generate MassAllocation Journals window to generate journals from the MassAllocation formula defined in the previous step. MassAllocations can be generated for a range of periods. To generate for one period, enter the same period in the From and To fields. To accomplish a multistep allocation, you should post the journals from preceding steps before generating allocations for later steps.

MassAllocations can be run in Full and Incremental modes. In Full mode, the allocations are run once. In Incremental mode, the allocation is made for the differential amount where there is a change in the original balances.

PART III

CH 11

USING THE DESKTOP INTEGRATOR WIZARD FOR ENTRIES

Applications Desktop Integrator (ADI) comes with a Journal Wizard to enter journals in a worksheet. You can use all the spreadsheet features for easy entry and formulas to calculate journal amounts.

ADI validates entries in the worksheet against accounts, rules, and reference information in GL.

MASSALLOCATIONS VERSUS RECURRING JOURNALS

There are some overlapping functions in MassAllocations and recurring journals and some possible business scenarios where either can be used. There are a few simple differences that can determine how to use these features for a specific purpose:

- The recurring journal definition allows skeleton entries; MassAllocation does not. However, both feature formula and standard entries.

- The MassAllocation definition allows use of Foreign Currency; recurring journals do not.

- The recurring journals definition allows one formula per line; MassAllocations can have one formula for many lines.

- Formulas in recurring journals can be of any type, but MassAllocation formulas must be in $A \times B/C$ format only.

UNDERSTANDING STATISTICAL ENTRIES

Statistical Journal Entries can be accomplished in two ways. The first way is by simply using STAT for the currency field and entering the journal normally as with other currencies.

The second method is to combine statistical amounts with normal amounts. To use this technique, define the Statistical Units of Measure for any natural account segment value. Set up the Journals: Mix Statistical and Monetary profile option. When entering a journal, you can additionally enter the statistical quantity.

UNDERSTANDING INTERCOMPANY ENTRIES

Intercompany (I/C) entries are those journal entries that record transactions between companies in the same enterprise. GL keeps the records balanced for each company by automatically creating offset entries to the I/C account you have defined for the journal source and category. Where no I/C account is defined for the journal source and category combination, GL posts the entry to the I/C balancing account specified in the set of books. GL uses the value of the company segment of the KAFF to determine the companies and the balancing accounts between them.

UNDERSTANDING CURRENCY PROCESSING

Transactions can be entered in either the functional currency (from a set of books) or in a foreign currency. GL automatically converts the amounts in foreign currency journals to functional currency equivalents using daily exchange rates. GL also saves and maintains both of the amounts for all transactions.

GL provides three standard reports showing foreign currency exchange rates:

- *Daily Conversion Rates Listing.* Lists daily rates for specific currency and accounting period.

- *Historical Rates Listing.* Lists defined historical translation rates and amounts.

- *Periodic Rates Listing.* Lists defined exchange rates for any accounting period, including the period-average and period-end translation rates and revaluation rates.

GL also provides few standard reports dealing with foreign currency account balances. For these, refer to the section titled "Understanding Reports" later in this chapter.

POSTING THE JOURNALS

Journal entries can be posted into GL individually or by batch. The Post Journals window lists the batches and displays batch information including the Post Status and Batch Status. Select the batches to be posted and post them. The Enter Journals window has a More Options zone where you can post individual journals or a journal batch.

GL balances unbalanced journals if Suspense Posting is enabled for the set of books.

GL automatically balances I/C journals if I/C balancing is enabled. GL Posting automatically generates journal lines to balance debits and credits for each balancing segment value using the specified I/C account.

Posting will not be successful, when any of the following occurs:

- A control total is used and the actual batch total does not match the control total entered.

- An attempt is made to post to unopened periods.

- Unbalanced journals exist and Suspense Posting is not allowed.

REVALUATION

When transactions are entered in a foreign currency, the currency exchange rates might change by the date the amounts are paid or realized. Revaluation reflects these changes in conversion rates. Revalue account balances to update functional currency equivalents. The most commonly revalued accounts are receivables and payables. GL posts the change in converted balances to an Unrealized Gain or Loss Account.

Revalue the necessary accounts in the following steps:

1. Define an Unrealized Gain/Loss Account for posting the gain or loss resulting from revaluation.

2. Define a Revaluation Rate (use the Period Rates window). Enter either a Period-End Rate or the Revaluation Rate. GL calculates the other automatically.

3. Run a revaluation concurrent request. This creates an unposted revaluation journal batch. After reporting, restore original balances by reversing this batch of journals.

4. When a foreign currency transaction amount is paid or received, the functional currency value of the foreign currency amount is recomputed, and the difference between this amount and the original transaction amount is posted to the Realized Gain or Loss Account.

TRANSLATION

GL allows reporting of functional currency transactions in another currency using *translation*. Translation does not affect functional currency balances, nor does it create journals. The translated values are stored by GL and used for reporting.

Translate actual or budget balances to foreign currencies for online inquiries, reports, and consolidations. GL posts the difference on translation to a translation adjustment account specified in the set of books. When different rates are used to translate different accounts resulting in an out-of-balance Balance Sheet, GL posts the discrepancy to a cumulative translation adjustment account (CTA). Define a CTA account as an owner's equity account or an income account.

CONSOLIDATION

When multiple sets of books are being used in GL, they can be consolidated for reporting. You must define a parent set of books into which the regular sets of books will be consolidated. GL enables you to define consolidation rules to map each set of books to the parent set of books. Run consolidation and journal import to create a consolidation batch in the parent set of books. Enable the consolidation audit trail to show any errors in consolidation so that the consolidation can be run again after corrections.

Tip
Consolidation can be used to consolidate sets of books with different charts of accounts, currencies, and calendars. When consolidating from subsidiary sets of books with a currency different from a parent set of books, simply revalue and translate balances as needed before transferring the consolidation data.

UNDERSTANDING REPORTS

Each transaction in GL can be traced back to the source using standard reports. GL provides a report utility tool called Financial Statement Generator (FSG) to define custom reports for specific financial purposes.

Following are some important GL standard reports, with a brief description of their purpose:

- *Account Analysis Report.* Lists the accumulated balances of a range of accounts and all journal lines that affect that range. Details listed for each journal line include source, batch name, and description.

- *Account Analysis with Payables Detail Report.* This report is same as the Account Analysis Report, and the details listed for each journal line additionally include vendor name and invoice number.

- *Budget Trial Balance Report.* Lists the GL account budget balances and activity for a specific currency.

- *Detail Trial Balance Report.* Lists the GL account balances and activity for GL accounts in detail.

- *Encumbrance Trial Balance Report.* Lists the encumbrance balances and activity for GL accounts in detail.

- *Expanded Trial Balance Report.* Lists the beginning, ending, and net balances, as well as period activity, for a set of accounts.

- *Foreign Account Analysis Report.* Lists the accumulated foreign balances of a range of accounts and all journal lines that affect that range. Details listed for each journal line include source, batch name, and description.

- *Foreign Account Analysis Report with Payables Detail.* This report is the same as the Foreign Account Analysis Report, and the details listed for each journal line additionally include vendor name and invoice number.

- *Foreign Currency Detail Trial Balance Report.* Lists the GL account balances and activity entered in a foreign currency in detail.

- *Foreign Currency General Ledger Report.* Lists beginning and ending account balances and all journal lines affecting each account balance entered in a foreign currency.

- *Foreign Currency Summary Trial Balance Report.* Lists the GL balances and activity entered in a foreign currency.

- *General Ledger Report.* Lists beginning and ending account balances and all journal lines affecting each account balance in functional currency. Details listed for each journal line include source and category.

- *Summary 1 Trial Balance Report.* Lists the GL account balances and activity for each segment value.

- *Summary 2 Trial Balance Report.* Lists the GL account balances and activity for a combination of account segment values and secondary segment values.

- *Translation Trial Balance Report.* Lists the translated account balances and period activity for a specific foreign currency.

UNDERSTANDING THE FINANCIAL STATEMENT GENERATOR

Financial Statement Generator (FSG) is GL's report-designing tool. Use FSG to design custom reports. Generate the reports using the Run Financial Reports window or GL's standard report submission. You can run reports individually, in a single set, or in multiple sets.

The FSG report definition is modular, and the defined components can be reused in more than one report. Use the following items to design simple reports using FSG:

- Identify the rows and columns in your report.
- Define rows, row sets, columns, and column sets in FSG by configuring the attributes of the rows and columns and grouping the rows and columns into sets of rows and columns.
- Define a report by simply giving it a name and assigning it a row set and a column set.

DEFINING A ROW SET   Use the Row Set window to define row sets and their format and contents. A row set normally contains the line items, accounts, and calculation row for totals. You can also create new row sets by copying from existing row sets.

Click the Define Rows button on this window to go to the Rows window and add lines to the row set. Create or modify the rows, specify their format options, assign accounts, or define calculations. If the Override Column Calculations option is selected, the row calculations take precedence over column calculations. When the similar option is checked in both row set and column set and there is a clash of priorities, refer to the Row Set Vs Column Set Override Summary matrix in the GL Reference Manual to determine which takes precedence in the given circumstances.

Select the Display Row option to display the row in a report. You might not want to display rows that you have defined for any calculations or for future use.

For each row, you can assign accounts or define calculations, but you cannot do both in the same row.

Tip

You can designate a different set of books to different rows. However, these different sets of books must share the same chart of accounts and calendar periods (currency can differ). If no set of books is designated, the row set can be used by any set of books.

Tip

Normally row numbers (sequence) can be used in calculations. You can also name the rows and use the names in calculation formulas.

DEFINING ROW ORDERS   GL enables you to modify the order of detail rows in a report in different ways. Choose the ranking method and then choose to display segment values, segment value descriptions, or both.

DEFINING A COLUMN SET   Use the Column Set window to define sets of columns and their format and contents. A column set normally contains the headings, subheadings, currency assignments, amount types, and calculation columns for totals. You can also create new column sets by copying from existing column sets.

Click the Define Columns button on this window to go to the Columns window and add columns for the column set. Here you create or modify the columns, specify their balance control options, and define calculations and/or exceptions. If the Override Row Calculations option is selected, the column calculations take precedence over row calculations. When the similar override option is checked in both row set and column set and there is a clash in priorities, refer to the Row Set Vs Column Set Override Summary matrix in the GL Reference Manual to determine which takes precedence in the given circumstances.

Select the Display Column option to display the column in a report. You might not want to display columns that you have defined for any calculations or for future use.

The Column Amount Type field defines the contents of a column. Choose from predefined amount types that reflect balances or calculated amounts; actuals, budgets, or encumbrances; and single or multiple period amounts. The Column Control Value must be entered where the amount type refers to budget or encumbrance.

If one column of a column set has a level of detail, every column in that set must have a level of detail.

Click the Exceptions button of the Columns window to enter exception flags. You can designate a one-character flag for the exception conditions listed and give a description. The description will not print in the reports.

You can create column sets, as previously described, column by column or graphically by choosing the Build Column Set button. Create headings for existing columns by clicking the Create Heading button from the Column Sets window.

PART

III

CH

11

Tip

The amounts displayed in the column default to the functional currency from the set of books. To display the entered currency in foreign currency transactions, enter a column control value. Then, you can override the currency when defining or requesting the report.

Tip

Normally, column numbers (sequence) can be used in calculations. You can also name the columns and use the names in calculation formulas.

DEFINING A CONTENT SET   Use a content set definition to do the following:

- Override segment values and display options in row sets.
- Print multiple reports in a specific order.

Use the Content Set window to do the following:

- Create or modify content sets.
- Override row set values and display options for account segments.
- Print segment ranges in separate reports

As in the case of row sets and column sets, content sets also can be created by AutoCopy from the existing content sets.

DEFINING REPORT DISPLAY GROUPS AND SETS   The display of ranges of rows and/or columns in a report can be controlled by using Display Groups and Display Sets. Define Display Groups to identify the ranges of rows and/or columns whose display you want to control in a report. You can enter the name of either a row or column set to control display range, but you cannot enter both.

Define a Display Set, which is a combination of display groups as defined previously. When the display groups included pertain to row and column ranges from different sequences, both columns and rows are controlled. However, when they pertain to the same sequence, only the intersection of the row and column is controlled.

USING THE DESKTOP INTEGRATOR WIZARD FOR REPORTS

The Application Desktop Integrator (ADI) Report Wizard provides you with a familiar spreadsheet-based interface to GL's FSG. Reports can be easily designed in a worksheet with reusable report objects from FSG. When the reports are designed, submit them for processing, and view reports in the spreadsheet.

Report templates can be saved on your personal computer, and you can inherit this formatting using Report Wizard.

PROCESSING BUDGET JOURNALS

Budget Journals are actual journal entries but are identified by journal type Budget. Simple budget journals can be entered the same way as Actual journal entries as discussed previously, using the Enter Journals window. GL also provides some special techniques to manage budgets, which are discussed in this section.

BUDGETING AND ENCUMBRANCES

Budgeting in GL implies the process starting from defining budgets, entering budget amounts, defining budgetary controls, and letting GL perform funds checks and control transactions based on availability of funds against the budget for these transactions.

Encumbrance simply is burdening or reserving funds for specific transactions. GL automatically creates encumbrances when budgetary control is enabled. You can also enter encumbrances manually like journal entries. These two topics are discussed in this section on budgeting and the following section on encumbrances.

UNDERSTANDING THE GL BUDGETING PROCESS

Budgetary control in GL or in Oracle Financials is optional and only certain types of organizations use these financial techniques. You can use budgetary control by checking the Enable Budgetary Control option in a set of books definition. To begin the budgetary control process, it is necessary to decide the degree of control by way of the following options:

- Detail or Summary
- Absolute or Advisory
- The Budgetary Control Group rules
- Limits/budget amounts

Budgetary control requires three components to be set up: periods, accounts (including the degree of control), and amounts. A budget definition has periods to which the budget applies. This is defined using the Define Budget window. Accounts are defined using Define Budget Organization window. Amounts can be entered in different ways, including entry of budget amounts and journals, Upload, MassBudgets, Formulas, and Transfer.

Finally, when you freeze Budgets and Budget Organizations, you prevent any updates to the budget. If changes must be made, you must open or unfreeze the budget.

When the preceding setup is in place, the budgetary control activity takes place online. GL allows only those journals to be posted that pass the funds check (assuming absolute control). GL, in integration with subledgers, tracks encumbrances for all the transactions and updates budgets/encumbrances online. GL prevents overspending by online notification of funds availability. You can build a budget hierarchy to control allocation of budget amount. You have the flexibility to enter Master/Detail budgets to suit the actual budgeting needs of the business.

PART

III

CH

11

DETERMINING DEGREE OF CONTROL

GL gives you the flexibility to implement budgetary control at several levels. Following is a brief description of each method.

CONTROL LEVEL

- *Detail Level.* This is for budgetary control at the individual account level.
- *Summary Level.* This is for budgetary control at the summary account level. Specify the options for the summary template.

FUNDS CHECK LEVEL

- *Absolute.* This is to prevent transactions that exceed the available funds.

- *Advisory.* This is to allow completion of transactions that exceed available funds, but with a warning message.

- *None.* Use this level if you do not select Automatic Encumbrance accounting.

OTHER CONTROL LEVELS

- *Amount types and boundaries.* Amount type determines the cumulative balance used for the funds checking interval and boundary determines the end point of the time interval. The expenditure can be controlled against a specified period, quarter, year, or project.

- *Budgetary Control Groups.* Journal sources and categories implement this control. Group your transactions and define rules for budgetary control groups. Specify tolerances for each rule, to which deviation can be allowed. Also, where there are insufficient funds, selectively enter an override amount to allow transactions exceeding the budget limits.

DEFINING A BUDGET

You can create, modify, open, or freeze a budget using the Define Budget window. The Budget Periods and Status are the most important parameters in this window and have direct impact on budgetary control.

You can also create new budgets using AutoCopy from existing budgets. However, the following restrictions apply:

- A new budget must have the same beginning and ending periods as the source budget.

- A new budget must span the same number of years as the source budget.

- A new budget cannot have any open years.

Open budgets are available for updates and frozen budgets are not. The Current budget is one in which the current date falls and is the default in the inquiry window. Open budget periods only when you need to use them. Open budget periods cannot be closed but are frozen. Use the Open Next Year button to open the next budget period. Check the Require Budget Journals option to create an audit trail.

The first period budget cannot be changed after a budget is defined. Also, the last period cannot go beyond the last calendar period of the fiscal year.

You can create a master/detail budget hierarchy using the master budget assignment. Several detail budgets can belong to a master budget. By assigning a master budget to several detail budgets, you can control the combined limit at the master budget level. This control provides flexibility between detail budgets.

DEFINING BUDGET ORGANIZATIONS GL uses budget organizations to specify budget accounts. You define budgetary control options by a range of accounts. You use common business-related budget areas such as department or cost center to define the Budget Organizations.

Use the Define Budget Organization window to create a new Budget Organization or to modify an existing Budget Organization. GL defaults the natural account segment name for the ordering segment and sorts accounts by this segment in ascending order when entering budget amounts or journals or querying accounts. You can optionally enable password protection for the Budget Organization using the Set Password button.

Enter the segment display sequence. This sequence is the order in which the account flexfield segments are displayed in the budget entry windows.

Use the Maintain button to start the concurrent process to add newly created or delete recently disabled accounts for a budget organization falling within the account ranges associated with a Budget Organization.

You can use the Delete button to delete the Budget Organization, and this action automatically deletes all the account assignments to this Budget Organization.

Use the Assignments window to review, delete, or assign accounts and budgetary control options to the Budget Organization. Enter them manually in the Account Assignments window. Alternatively, assign ranges manually in the Account Ranges window and use the Maintain button in the Define Budget Organization window to add all the available accounts within the assigned range.

Against each account in the Account Assignments window, specify a Budget Entry Method for the account/range from any of the following:

- Enter Budget Amounts
- Enter Budget Journals
- Upload Budgets
- Generate MassBudget Journals
- Transfer Budget Journals

Specify the budgetary control option (absolute or advisory). This assignment will imply detail-level budgetary control. Alternatively, specify None, and specify absolute or advisory in the summary template, which will imply a summary-level budgetary control.

Choose the Automatic Encumbrance option for GL to create encumbrances for Payables and Purchasing transactions to this account.

ENTERING BUDGET AMOUNTS

Use the Enter Budget Amounts window to manually enter and post budget amounts directly to balances. This action replaces any existing balance against the account. Use the Budget Rules button from this window to automatically distribute or calculate budget amounts for all

PART
III

CH
11

budget periods specified. Budget rules give you flexibility to derive budget amounts in one of the following ways:

- Dividing the total evenly among periods
- Repeating a fixed amount in every period
- Computing an amount from actual or budget balances for every period
- Dividing a total by ratio

However, budget rules apply to a specific period range and can be applied for up to thirteen periods at a time.

Where an audit trail is necessary, use the Enter Budget Journals window. Use the Worksheet mode, the Single Row mode, or the Journal mode for entering budget journals.

You can use Budget Formulas (discussed next) to create recurring entries for accruals or complex allocations and post calculated budget amounts to balances.

You can use MassBudgeting to create multiple allocation entries from a single formula.

Finally, you can use the Budget Transfer feature to transfer budget amounts from one account to another within the same budget. Use the Budget Transfer window to transfer fixed amounts or percentages of budget amounts. There are, however, the following restrictions that apply to Budget Transfer:

- Accounts must not be frozen.
- Accounts must be denominated in the same currency.
- Accounts must have amounts entered for the same unfrozen budget.

You can post budget journals (created by Enter Budget Journals, MassBudgeting, Budget Transfer, and Consolidations) like actual accounting journals.

You can make manual corrections to wrong budget amounts posted by Budget Upload, Budget Formulas, or Budget Carry Forward using the Enter Budget Amounts window. You can make corrections in budget journals created by Enter Budget Journals, MassBudgeting, Budget Transfer, and Consolidations using the Enter Journals window. If the journals have already been posted, enter correcting journals using the Enter Journals window.

DEFINING BUDGET FORMULAS   You can create recurring budget amounts based on other budget amounts or on actual results using Budget Formulas. Use the Define Budget Formula window to create new budget formulas or to modify existing budget formulas. Budget formulas can also be created by AutoCopy from already existing formulas. Use the Lines button on the Define Budget Formula window to enter formula lines.

You can generate budget amounts from defined formulas using the Calculate Budget Amounts window. Check the batches for which amounts are to be calculated, and click the Calculate button. GL calculates these amounts and replaces existing values for specified accounts.

DEFINING MASSBUDGETS   You can allocate budget amounts across a group of balancing segment values using MassBudgets. Use the Define MassBudgets window to define a MassBudget formula. This process is similar to MassAllocation formula definition. Use the Generate MassBudget Journals window to generate budget amounts from formulas defined. MassBudgets, similar to MassAllocations, can be run in Full or Incremental mode.

USING DESKTOP INTEGRATOR WIZARD FOR BUDGETS   The Budget Wizard enables you to prepare and work on budgets in a spreadsheet environment. Budgets, budget organizations, budget rules, and formulas defined in GL can be used in the spreadsheet. Create new budgets or download budgets from GL and modify them. You can see the familiar spreadsheet analysis and graphs before automatically uploading the budget to GL.

FREEZING THE BUDGET   Freeze a budget by specifying Frozen in the Status field of the Define Budget window. No updating is possible on frozen budgets. To make an update, unfreeze the budget by specifying Open in the Status field.

PROCESSING ENCUMBRANCES

Encumbrance implies burdening and reserving the funds. When budgetary control is enabled in the set of books, GL automatically creates encumbrance entries for Purchasing and Payables. Enabling Budgetary Control in a set of books is different from defining Budgetary Controls, as discussed in the earlier section.

Encumbrances can also be created in GL by manual entry of journals, MassAllocation, or journal import. If you do not want to use automatic encumbrances, Budgetary Control need not be enabled in a set of books unless Budgetary Controls are to be defined and implemented.

PART

III

CH

11

ENCUMBRANCE TYPES

GL has two predefined encumbrance types: Commitment and Obligation. The former implies that the funds have been reserved or committed for the transaction (for example, a requisition). The latter implies that a liability has been incurred and budgeted funds are permanently reduced (for example, a purchase). You can define additional encumbrance types.

An encumbrance type is necessary to do the following:

- Enter encumbrances manually
- Define an encumbrance allocation
- Import encumbrances using Journal Import.

Automatic encumbrance entries created by GL for Purchasing and Payables use the predefined encumbrance types.

ENTERING ENCUMBRANCES

Enter encumbrances in one of the following ways:

- Manual entries
- MassAllocation
- Journal Import
- Automatic entries from Purchasing and Payables

You can enter encumbrances manually using the Journals-Encumbrance window. These entries can be deleted before they are posted. For corrections after posting, correcting journal entries must be entered. GL validates entries online and creates a balancing entry to the Reserve for Encumbrance account (defined in a set of books). Encumbrance journals can only be created in the functional currency for the set of books. Both posted and unposted encumbrance entries can be reversed.

You can define MassAllocations for encumbrances just like for actual accounting journals and specify Encumbrance for Balance Type. Create unposted encumbrance entries using the Generate MassAllocation Journals window. Post these entries to update budget balances.

GL is fully integrated with Purchasing (PO) and Payables (AP) modules for encumbrances. Encumbrances are created and reversed as necessary when transactions are entered in PO and AP. For example, a commitment type encumbrance might become an obligation type on completion of the transaction. In such a case, the former entry is reversed, and the latter is created automatically by PO or AP.

Encumbrances created by manual entry, MassAllocation, or Journal Import can be relieved by reversing entries. Post the reverse entries to relieve encumbrances. You can specify a current or future period into which the encumbrance is to be reversed.

Funds availability can be determined by comparing actual balances against budget and encumbrance balances.

PROCESSING YEAR-END

Budget and encumbrance balances for any account can be carried forward to a new budget period using predefined rules. GL updates the new balances directly and does not create a journal entry.

Use the Year-End Carry Forward window to process the carry forward. Before doing a carry forward, do all of the following:

- Post all unposted journals.
- Close the last period of the fiscal year.
- Open the first period of next fiscal year.
- Open next budget year.
- Open the next encumbrance year.

UNDERSTANDING THE GLOBAL ACCOUNTING ENGINE

The Global Accounting Engine (GAE) is a relatively new addition to Oracle Applications. It is intended to aid in creating journal entries, adjusting existing balances, and posting entries to GL directly, avoiding the Transfer to GL program that exists in each subledger application.

Following are some important features of GAE:

- Define accounting rules per set of books.
- Post different accounting rules to different sets of books.
- Maintain legal and fiscal audit trail requirements.
- Reconcile a subledger accounting system with the General Ledger.
- Audit and control period and fiscal year closing procedures.
- Define journals rather than using hard-coded categories. These journals must be numbered sequentially to comply with legal requirements.
- Assign sequential numbers to the defined journals across applications.
- Create all accounting entries within subledgers, including miscellaneous entries and intraorganization entries. No adjusting entries are necessary in General Ledger.
- Secure subledger accounting entries. You can either secure accounts individually or secure the procedure to create accounting entries. To secure subledger accounting entries, use control accounts to define accounts. A control account is only accessible from the subledgers. Securing your entries ensures a valid audit trail is maintained. The secured posting makes sure that you are only given access to a range of steps involved in the posting cycle.
- Print legal subledger accounting reports.
- Define your own accounting entries and the accounts involved.
- Use an online drilldown to original documents in the subledgers.

SETUP STEPS

The following components must be set up before GAE can be used:

- Create Posting Manager defaults.
- Compile the GAE program. Use the Translator Program window to enter all the parameters before compiling. Also, you need to meet certain prerequisites on the GL side, such as defining the set of books, defining and assigning sequences, and defining and assigning categories.
- Set up control accounts. These are accounts whose balances are accessed by subledger programs. GAE automatically creates detailed balances for control account balances. Look in the GAE installation manual for more details on creating control accounts or changing status of existing accounts to control account.
- If Oracle Inventory is being used, set up additional accounts for Inventory Costing.

HOW THE ENGINE WORKS

The GAE has the following main components:

- *Journal Entries window.* This form enables you to make journal entries and adjust current account balances. You can enter, query, and update adjusting subledger entries. You can also delete untranslated adjusting entries.

- *Journal Entry Lines window.* This enables you to view GAE-translated transactions.

- *Closing subledgers.* Make sure to translate all subledger transactions before trying to close a subledger. If there are untranslated entries, the program will not close the subledger. This essentially involves closing your accounting period and creating balances for accounting period transactions.

- *Submit Posting Manager.* This program posts or transfers the subledger entries to GL.

REVIEWING GAE REPORTS

- *Daily Journal Book-Line Descriptions.* Lists all accounting entries for your set of books by sequence name and period. The report prints the amounts in functional currency.

- *Daily Journal Book-Header Descriptions.* Lists all accounting entries for your set of books by sequence name and period. The report prints the amounts in functional currency.

- *Account Ledger by Account/Accounting Flexfield.* Lists all accounting entry lines per account and period.

- *Supplier/Customer Subledger by Account/Accounting Flexfield.* Lists the activity per control account in your subledger for a chosen period or periods. This report reconciles to your balances in the Supplier/Customer Balance by Account/Account report.

- *Supplier/Customer Balance by Account/Accounting Flexfield.* Lists information about balances and period activities by account and supplier/customer for one or more accounting periods. This report enables you to justify your balances in General Ledger, Receivables, and Payables.

SUMMARY

The Oracle General Ledger Application is the foundation for financial transactions in the Oracle Applications. GL has close ties with the subledger applications: Payables, Receivables, Inventory, Assets, and Purchasing. You can define almost any financial organizational structure for your enterprise through multiple sets of books and the Key Accounting Flexfield structure. The GL Application can handle transactions in multiple currencies and has many features for those organizations that operate in many countries. Also, GL provides budgeting and reporting capability.

CHAPTER 12

USING ORACLE PAYABLES

Oracle Payables is the final link in supply-chain management. The primary purpose of Payables is to enable you to perform the tasks required by this last stage of the procurement cycle. The primary task is paying suppliers for goods and services received. Oracle Payables enables you to pay suppliers using every form of payment, including automatic checks, manual payments, wire transfers, bank drafts, and electronic funds transfers.

A good payables system ensures that suppliers are paid on time, but not earlier than necessary. It also gives you the ability to manage close supplier relationships and make informed price comparisons. Oracle Payables permits you to maximize supplier discounts, prevent duplicate payments, and pay for only the goods and services you order and receive.

RELATIONSHIP TO OTHER ORACLE APPLICATIONS

Oracle Payables is only part of the total procurement cycle. Its full benefit can only be realized when it is integrated with the other applications.

Integration with Oracle Purchasing ensures that you only pay for goods that have been received and are of acceptable quality. It also ensures that purchases are properly approved and that you do not pay more than the price quoted by the supplier.

Integration with Cash Management enables you to reconcile all payments with your bank statements automatically or manually, as well as forecast cash requirements.

Integration with Assets enables you to manage all capital assets purchased and integration, with Human Resources ensures that employee expenses are paid efficiently.

Figure 12.1 shows how the other applications are related to Payables. For each application, the information shared is indicated, and the arrows show the direction in which this information flows.

NEW FEATURES IN RELEASE 11

The following section describes some of the important features in release 11 of Payables. These features include EDI support, the new open interface for invoices, support for procurement cards, Web Employee expense report entry, and Multiple Reporting Currencies (MRC).

INCREASED EDI SUPPORT

Payables, with the Oracle EDI Gateway, now supports importing invoice data directly from your suppliers. If problems are encountered as a result of the import, an outbound application error acknowledgement is created.

The transaction sets for inbound invoices are X12 810 and EDIFACT INVOIC for invoices and X12 857 for shipment and billing notices. The transaction sets for outbound error acknowledgements are X12 824 and EDIFACT APERAK.

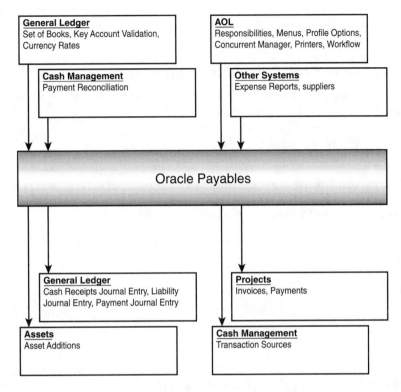

Figure 12.1
AP relation-
ships to other
applications.

PAYABLES OPEN INTERFACE

In Release 11.0, Oracle introduces a new AP Open Invoice Interface. This open interface consists of two tables, ap_invoices_interface and ap_invoice_lines_interface, that will be used instead of expense report headers and lines. This interface supports supplier EDI invoices transferred through the EDI gateway, any invoices loaded with SQL*Loader, and credit card transactions loaded with the Credit Card Invoice Interface Summary.

WORKFLOW INTEGRATION

Payables is now integrated with Workflow to automate business processes for invoices entered through the new open interface and for review and approval of procurement card transactions.

PROCUREMENT CARD INTEGRATION

The new procurement card integration feature enables you to import transaction detail from statement files provided by the card issuer. You can then use Oracle Self-Service Expenses to verify that transaction detail and automatically create invoices.

EMPLOYEE EXPENSE REPORTS VIA WEB EMPLOYEE

The new Web Employee application enables users with a Web browser and the appropriate security clearance to enter employee expense reports directly. Oracle Workflow routes the expense reports submitted for approval to the appropriate approver and automatically enforces business rules.

ENHANCED SUPPORT FOR FIXED RATE CURRENCIES

Invoices in fixed-rate currencies such as Euro or other EMU currencies can be paid in an associated fixed-rate currency.

ENHANCED TAX DEFAULTING

Setting Tax Name Defaults enables you to determine the sources you use for tax names and the order in which Payables will search through the sources for a valid tax name.

MORE FLEXIBLE ELECTRONIC PAYMENTS

With release 11.0, you can create multiple electronic payments to different bank accounts for a single invoice.

MULTIPLE REPORTING CURRENCIES

The multiple reporting currencies feature enables you to report on and manage transaction level information in any currency, not just the functional currency of your primary set of books.

CONFIGURING THE APPLICATION

Oracle Payables is a very flexible application that can be tailored to meet your business needs using the standard functionality. Planning early in the process ensures that the decisions made during configuration will not hamper the long-term effectiveness of Oracle Payables.

Oracle Payables is easy to set up and easy to change to fit your changing business requirements. The following sections discuss the issues that are most critical to successfully configuring Oracle Payables.

RESOLVING CRITICAL SETUP ISSUES

If you are implementing more than one Oracle application, you must review the systemwide setup tasks such as configuring concurrent managers and printers, setting up responsibilities, and assigning users to these responsibilities. You must also review the cross-product dependencies of setup tasks and reduce redundant ones.

You must decide whether you need to use the Oracle Applications Multiple Organization Support feature that will allow the use of more than one set of books for one Payables installation.

REQUIRED SETUP TASKS

Table 12.1 shows the tasks required to set up the Payables application. The tasks are listed in the order they should be performed. Many tasks have predecessor tasks for data validation, so they should be performed in the proper order.

TABLE 12.1   ORACLE PAYABLES SETUP TASKS

Setup Task Name	Required?
Install or Upgrade Payables	Yes
Create user sign-ons	Yes
Define Chart of Accounts	Yes
Define Period Types and Accounting Calendar	Yes
Enable Currencies	Optional
Define Set of Books	Yes
Assign Set of Books to a Responsibility	Yes
Enter Conversion Rate Types and Rates	Optional
Select Primary Set of Books	Yes
Define Payment Terms	Yes
Define Purchase Order Matching Tolerances	Optional
Define Tax Authority type Suppliers	Conditionally
Define Tax Name and Tax Withholding Groups	Optional
Define Invoice Approval Codes	Yes
Define Distributions Sets	Optional
Define Payables QuickCodes	Yes
Define Payment Interest Rates	Optional
Create Templates for Entering Expense Reports	Optional
Enter Employee QuickCodes	Optional
Enter Locations	Yes
Enter Employees	Yes
Define Reporting Entities	Yes
Define 1099 Income Tax Regions	Yes
Define Inventory Organizations	Yes
Define Financials Options	Yes
Define Payables Options	Yes
Define Payment Programs	Yes
Define Payment Formats	Optional
Update Country and Territory Information	Optional

PART

III

CH

12

TABLE 12.1 CONTINUED	
Setup Task Name	**Required?**
Define Bank Accounts	Yes
Open Accounting Period	Yes
Define Request Sets	Optional
Define Reporting Formats	Optional
Setup Printer Styles and Drivers	Yes
Define Special Calendars	Optional
Implements Budgetary Control	Optional
Implement Sequential Numbering	Optional
Define Descriptive Flexfields	Optional
Set Profile Options	Optional

UNDERSTANDING EACH SETUP TASK

The setup tasks are where you shape the application's standard features to meet your business's particular requirements. Many setup steps affect other setups, not only in Payables but in Purchasing and Cash Management as well. You need to analyze the interdependencies of theses setup steps as you are preparing to configure payables.

The following sections discusses the details of each setup task in the order they should be performed. The tasks are arranged into two loose categories; the first is concerned with tasks related to general applications installation and the creation of the set of books. If Oracle General Ledger is being used, the creation of the set of books and related tasks will be performed during the configuration of General Ledger. The second category is regarding Payables specific setups.

FIRST STEPS

The Payables application must be installed or upgraded to release 11.0. Next, you must use the System Administrator responsibility to create application user sign-ons and passwords. After the user is created, choose the General Ledger Superuser and Payables Superuser to complete the remainder of the setups.

CREATING A SET OF BOOKS

A set of books determines the functional currency, account structure, and accounting calendar for each company or group of companies. If you need to report on your account balances in multiple currencies, you should set up one additional set of books for each reporting currency. Your primary set of books should use your functional currency. Each reporting set of books should use one of your reporting currencies.

If you choose to enable budgetary control, encumbrances will be created automatically for your transactions in General Ledger, Oracle Purchasing, and Oracle Payables.

DEFINING CHART OF ACCOUNTS   If you are using General Ledger, the chart of accounts is defined there. If not, you need to define a chart of accounts.

ACCOUNTING PERIOD TYPES AND THE ACCOUNTING CALENDAR   If you are using General Ledger, the accounting period types and calendar are defined there. If not, you need to define period types and an accounting calendar.

CURRENCIES   If you are not using General Ledger, you must enable the currencies that you plan to use.

CHOOSING A SET OF BOOKS   In Payables, you must select a primary Set of Books. After choosing the primary set of books, if needed, use the Application Developer responsibility to set the GL Set of Books ID profile option to updateable. Then use the System Administrator responsibility to set the GL Set of Books profile option. For a single set of books installation, set the options at Application level for Oracle Payables. For a multiple set of books installation, set the option for each unique combination of organization and responsibility. The responsibility you choose when you log on determines the set of books you use.

ENTERING PAYMENT TERMS

You can define an unlimited number of payment terms that you assign to an invoice to automatically create scheduled payments. You can define payment terms with more than one payment line to create multiple scheduled payment lines and multiple levels of discounts. Each payment terms line and each corresponding scheduled payment has a due date or a discount date based on either a specific day of a month, such as the 20th of the month, or a number of days added to your terms date, such as 30 days after the terms date. Each payment terms line also defines the due or discount amount on a scheduled payment. When you define payment terms, you specify payment amounts either by percentages or by fixed amounts.

After you define your payment terms, you can select default system payment terms that Payables automatically assigns to the suppliers and supplier sites you enter. The payment terms for a supplier site default to the invoices you enter for the site. Oracle provides a predefined payment term called Prepayment Immediate that Payables automatically assigns to all prepayments you enter.

PART
III

CH
12

Tip

If you update the payment terms on an invoice, Payables recalculates the scheduled payment for the invoice. You must reenter any manual adjustments you made to the previous scheduled payment. For example, if you update the payment priority on a particular scheduled payment and then change the payment terms, Payables recalculates the scheduled payment using the same payment priority defaults as before, and you will need to redo your updates.

DEFINING MATCHING TOLERANCES

Payables enables you to define both percentage-based and amount-based tolerances. Matching tolerances determine whether Payables places matching holds on an invoice. When you submit Approval for an invoice you have matched to a purchase order, Payables checks that the invoice matches the purchase order within the matching tolerances you define.

If you enter a zero for a percentage tolerance and select the check box for that tolerance, Payables treats the tolerance as infinite and will never apply a hold to the invoice. You must enter a very small percentage if you want a low tolerance.

TAX AUTHORITY TYPE SUPPLIERS

To use automatic withholding tax, you need to define the Tax Authority type suppliers used by automatic withholding tax.

DEFINING TAX NAMES AND GROUPS

You define the tax names you use on invoices to record invoice taxes you pay to your suppliers and to your tax authorities. Each tax name has a tax type, tax rate, and account to which you charge tax amounts. If you assign tax names to expense or asset accounts, Payables automatically enters the appropriate tax name when you enter an account. During Approval, Payables uses the Tax Name to validate that tax distributions are correct.

The Withholding Tax type tax names can have multiple rates, effective date ranges, tax amounts limits, and taxable amount limits. You can also link a tax authority supplier to a Withholding Tax type tax name so you can create invoices to pay taxes you withheld from your suppliers

To have Payables calculate the invoice sales tax and automatically create tax distributions when you enter a Sales type tax name during invoice entry, enable automatic tax calculation. Payables uses the tax rate of the tax name to calculate the sales tax. Do not define special tax names for distributions that include tax. Simply check the Includes Tax Distribution check box when you enter the distribution, and Payables adjusts the calculation.

DEFINING INVOICE APPROVAL CODES

You can define hold codes that you assign to an invoice during entry to place the invoice on hold; you can define release codes that you use to remove the holds you place on invoices. You cannot pay an invoice that has a hold applied to it. You can define as many invoice hold codes and approval codes as you need.

You can also determine whether to allow posting for the hold codes you define. If you assign a posting hold code to an invoice, you cannot post the invoice until you remove the hold.

DEFINING DISTRIBUTION SETS

If you are not matching an invoice to a purchase order, you can use a Distribution Set to automatically enter distributions. You can assign a default Distribution Set to a supplier site so Payables will use it for every invoice entered for that supplier site. You can also assign a Distribution Set to the invoice when you enter it.

Use Full Distribution Sets to create distributions with set percentage amounts or Skeleton Distribution Sets to create distributions with no amounts. If you enable and use a descriptive flexfield with your distribution set lines, the data in the flexfield will be copied to the invoice distributions created by the Distribution Set.

Note

Distributions created by distribution sets are always exclusive of tax even if you use Automatic Tax Calculation and you have checked the Includes Tax check box at the supplier site.

DEFINING QUICKCODES FOR AP AND VENDORS

Create and maintain QuickCodes for the following items:

- *AWT Certificate Type.* Used to define withholding tax certificates.
- *AWT Rate Type.* Used to define Withholding Tax type tax names.
- *FOB.* Used as supplier default for all new purchase orders.
- *Freight Terms.* Used as supplier default for all new purchase orders.
- *Minority Group.* Used to classify suppliers for reporting.
- *Pay Group.* Used to initiate payment batches.
- *Disbursement Type.* Used to define payment documents.
- *Don't Pay Reason.* Used to modify payment batches.
- *Source.* Used to submit Payables Invoice Import and Payables Open Interface Import.
- *Tax Type.* Used to define tax names.
- *Supplier Type.* Used for supplier reporting.

Payables displays QuickCodes in the list of values for fields that require these codes. You can create as many QuickCodes for each item as you require. You can update the description and inactive date of a QuickCode at any time, but you cannot change the type or name after you enter and save it.

DEFINING PAYMENT PROGRAMS AND FORMATS

You can define payment formats for the six payment methods that Payables uses. You can define as many payment formats as you require for each payment method. Each payment format must be unique for that payment method.

You must choose a Build Payments program and a Format Payments program for each payment format. You can choose any payment program that you have defined in the Payment Programs window or any standard program Payables provides. Each Format Payments

PART

III

CH

12

program provided by Payables includes a remittance advice program, and you can control how many invoices to include on your remittance Advice.

Payables predefines one program for building payments and many standard programs for formatting payments. Payables also predefines a program for creating a separate remittance advice for payments. You can select these predefined programs when you define a payment format, or you can use these programs as templates for creating your own custom payment programs.

DEFINING PAYMENT INTEREST RATES

If you will be charging interest on overdue invoices, you must define the interest rates that Payables will use to calculate and pay the interest. Payables calculates interest only on overdue invoices if you enable the Allow Interest Invoices Payables option and enable the Allow Interest Invoices option for the supplier site of an invoice. The formula compounds monthly, up to a maximum of 365 days interest. You can add or change a rate at any time. Payables uses the interest rate that is valid on your payment date to calculate and pay interest on overdue invoices. You can specify the effective dates for each rate you define. The effective date of rates cannot overlap.

DEFINING BANK ACCOUNTS

You need to define banks and bank accounts to create payments. You must create at least one payment document before you can use a bank account to create payments.

When you define payment documents, you can only select payment formats that use the same currency as the bank account currency. If the bank account is a multiple currency bank account, you can choose foreign currency payment formats or multiple currency payment formats.

DEFINING EXPENSE REPORT TYPES

You need to define expense report templates for the different types of expense reports you use in your company. You can define default values for expense items, and you can then choose those items from a list of values when you enter expense reports. During Invoice Import, Payables uses the expense item information to create invoice distributions.

If you use Oracle Web Employees, you can define expense templates and expense items that your employees can use to enter their own expense reports using a standard Web browser.

DEFINING EMPLOYEE QUICKCODES

If you define your employees in Payables rather than Oracle Human Resources, you can also define Employee QuickCodes in Payables.

DEFINING LOCATIONS

In Oracle Human Resources, you set up each physical site where your employees work as a separate location. You can also enter the addresses of external organizations that you want to maintain in your system. When you are setting up internal or external organizations, you pick from a list of these locations. This approach enables you to enter information about each location only once, saving data entry time. It provides for central maintenance of locations to ensure consistency of address standards.

DEFINING EMPLOYEES

You can enter, maintain, and view basic personal information and addresses for employees. You can also enter work assignment information, which includes organization, job, position, work location, and supervisor's name.

> **Note**
>
> You cannot use this form if Oracle Human Resources is fully installed at your site. You must use the HR Person form, which maintains a datetracked history of any changes you make to employee records.

DEFINING REPORTING ENTITIES

A reporting entity is any person or organization that has a unique Tax Identification Number (TIN).

You can submit the following 1099 reports for a specific reporting entity:

1096 Form

1099 Forms

1099 Invoice Exceptions Report

1099 Supplier Exceptions Report

1099 Payments Report

1099 Tape

For each reporting entity, you need to assign one or more balancing segment values. Payables sums up the paid invoice distributions that have these company balancing segment values in their accounts.

DEFINING INCOME TAX REGIONS

Define tax regions if you are using 1099 Combined Filing Program reporting in the United States. If you enable the Combined Filing Payables option, when you submit the 1099 Tape, Payables produces K records for all tax regions (or states) participating in the Combined Filing Program that have qualifying payments. Payables also produces B records for suppliers with 1099 payment amounts that equal or exceed the tax region's reporting limit in qualifying states.

Payables has predefined the region abbreviations and the descriptions for all U.S. states, the District of Columbia, and some U.S. territories. Payables has also predefined the region codes for those tax regions that are participating in the Internal Revenue Service's current

Combined Filing Program. You must enter a region code for all tax regions that you want to use for the Combined Filing Program reporting and that Payables has not already defined. You must define your income tax regions so that they conform to the IRS codes. Use the 1099 Supplier Exceptions Report to identify any 1099 suppliers with state abbreviations that do not conform to the income tax regions defined here. Payables uses the tax region from the invoice distributions to determine to which tax authority Payables should report the payments when you submit your 1099 reports.

DEFINING INVENTORY ORGANIZATIONS

If you are using Oracle Inventory or Oracle Purchasing, you must define at least one Inventory Organization before you define Financials Options.

DEFINING FINANCIAL OPTIONS

Oracle Payables, Oracle Purchasing, and Oracle Assets share Financials Options. Depending on your application, you might not be required to enter all fields.

You only need to define these options and defaults once for each operating unit; you can update them at any time. If you change an option and it is used as a default value elsewhere in the system, it will only be used as a default for subsequent transactions.

You are required to enter defaults for the Accounting Financials Options in the Accounting region. If you are not using Oracle Purchasing, you do not need to enter defaults in the Supplier-Purchasing region. If you are not using Oracle Human Resources, you are not required to enter defaults in the Human Resources region. If your organization does not need to record a VAT registration number, you don't need to enter defaults in the Tax region. Most of the Supplier-Payables Financials Options are used as defaults for entering Suppliers.

DEFINING SYSTEM OPTIONS

The Control options and defaults are used throughout Payables to simplify supplier entry, invoice entry, and automatic payment processing. You only define these options and defaults once for each operating unit, but you can update them at any time to change controls and defaults for future transactions.

DEFINING AP PERIODS AND PERIOD TYPES

Oracle Payables provides you with the Period Types of Month, Quarter, and Year. You can set up additional types if needed. Use these types when you define the Payables calendar. The periods define the number of periods in the calendar year.

The possible period statuses follow:

> *Never Opened.* First status of a new period. Must be changed to Future or Open for transactions.
>
> *Future.* Invoice entry allowed.
>
> *Open.* All transactions allowed.

Closed. Transactions not allowed. Can be reopened.

Permanently Closed. Cannot be reopened.

OPEN PERIODS IN THE AP CALENDAR

Payables periods are separate from General Ledger periods. For example, you can close the January period in AP before you close the January period in General Ledger.

Payables provides for invoice entry, payment entry, and payment voiding in open accounting periods. You can enter invoices in Future accounting periods, but you cannot post any invoices in Future accounting periods until the status is changed to open. The period statuses available in Payables are Never Opened, Future, Open, Closed, and Permanently Closed.

When you update a period status to Closed, Payables automatically checks whether you have any unposted transactions in that period. If you have any unposted transactions in a period you are trying to close, Payables prevents you from closing the period and automatically submits the Unposted Invoice Sweep report. You can use this report to view all your unposted transactions for the period. You can submit the Unposted Invoice Sweep program if you want to move all unposted transactions from one period to another. Then close your period.

DEFINING REPORT SETS

Defining report sets enables you to submit the same set of reports regularly using the same request. Use the Request Set window or Request Set Wizard to create report sets.

DEFINING REPORT FORMATS

The Expense Distribution Detail Report provides you with detail expense information for both posted and unposted invoices. To define the format and sort sequence of your Expense Distribution Detail Report, use the Account Segments for Expense Reporting window. You must set up all three segments the first time you use this window. After that, the format previously set up appears as a default. You can overwrite these values to define a new Expense Distribution Detail Report format.

If you update the structure of your Accounting Flexfield, you should redefine the format and sort sequence of your Expense Distribution Detail Report.

DEFINING SPECIAL CALENDARS

You need to create special calendars to define periods that Payables will use for automatic withholding tax, recurring invoices, and for the Key Indicators Report.

DEFINING BUDGETARY CONTROL

You enable Use PO Encumbrance in the Financials Options window. This enables you to check funds before you save a transaction, and you can have Payables automatically create encumbrance entries to reserve funds for your transactions. If you use absolute budgetary control, Payables places an Insufficient Funds hold on any invoice that fails funds checking. If you use advisory budgetary control, Payables allows the invoice to pass Approval, even if it fails funds checking. During Approval, Payables creates encumbrance entries to reserve funds against the budgets you define in Oracle General Ledger.

DEFINING SEQUENTIAL NUMBERING

You can assign sequential voucher numbers to each invoice and payment in to ensure that you have a unique number for each document. For example, you might get two invoices with identical invoice numbers from two different suppliers. If you assign each a voucher number, you can locate each invoice based on its unique voucher number.

If you use sequential voucher numbers, you can confirm that no document has been lost or unposted. Each voucher number retains audit records even if invoices or payments are deleted. An audit trail is maintained so you can trace a journal entry back to the original document if you post detail journal entries in your general ledger.

DEFINING DESCRIPTIVE FLEXFIELDS

To define your descriptive flexfield, you define the segments, the descriptive information, and the value set information for each segment in a structure. You also determine the appearance of your descriptive flexfield window, including the size of the window, the number and order of the segments, and the segment descriptions and default values. The maximum number of segments possible within a single structure depends on which descriptive flexfield you are defining.

After you define or change your flexfield, you must freeze your flexfield definition and save your changes. When you do, Oracle Applications automatically compiles your flexfield to improve online performance.

After you freeze your flexfield definition and save your changes, Oracle Applications submits a concurrent request to generate a database view of the table that contains your flexfield segment columns. You can use these views for custom reporting at your site.

> **Tip**
>
> You should plan your descriptive flexfield structures carefully, including all your segment information such as segment order and field lengths, before you set up your segments. You can define your descriptive flexfields any way you want, but changing your structures after you have entered data might create data inconsistencies that could have a significant impact on the performance of your application or require a complex conversion program.

SETTING THE PROFILE OPTIONS

You set values for profile options in Oracle Financials to specify how Payables controls access to and processes data. In addition to the Payables profile options, Payables uses profile options from other Oracle Financials applications to control features, such as Budgetary Control and Sequential Numbering, which affect more than one application.

Many of these user profile options are set, using the System Administrator responsibility, at one or more of the following levels: Site, Application, Responsibility, and User. Use the Personal Profile Options window to view or set your profile options at the user level.

PROCESSING TRANSACTIONS

Transactions refer to the process of creating, approving, and maintaining invoices, credit memos, adjustments, and payments. The following sections describe how to work with the various kinds of transactions.

SETTING UP AND MODIFYING VENDORS

You might want to use a naming convention that minimizes risk of separate entries of the same supplier with slightly different spelling of the same name. If you enable the Automatic Supplier Numbering option in the Financials Options window, Payables automatically enters a sequential Supplier Number for you. You specify the beginning number when automatic Supplier Numbering is enabled. If you did not enable this option, you must enter a unique Supplier Number for each supplier.

The following information can be entered for each supplier. This information is defaulted into each supplier site created:

> Bank Information
>
> Classification Information
>
> Control Information
>
> General Information
>
> Payment Information
>
> Purchasing Information
>
> Receiving Information
>
> Tax Information

PART

III

CH

12

After entering the preceding supplier information, you must enter the Supplier Site Name and address. The Site Name will not appear on documents you send to the supplier. It is for your reference when you select a supplier site from a list of values during transaction entry. You can enter any additional Supplier Site information you want to record for each supplier site. Most of the information set at the Supplier level can also be set at the supplier site level. If supplier information has automatically defaulted to the new supplier site, you can override these defaults.

If you want to prevent invoice or purchase order entry for this supplier after a certain date, enter an Inactive date.

ENTERING INVOICES

Before payments can be made to suppliers, the suppliers invoice must be entered. Invoices can be manually entered or entered through Payable Open Interface. If invoices are entered manually, they can be entered individually or as part of a batch.

You can use batches in the following ways:

- You can enter invoice defaults at the batch level that override both system and supplier site defaults for all invoices in the batch.

- You can maximize accuracy by tracking variances between the control invoice count and total and the actual invoice count and total resulting from the invoices entered in your batch.

- You can easily locate a batch online and review the name of the person who created the batch and the date it was created.

There is much information that can be entered for each invoice; some of this information is required, and some is optional. Invoices can be matched to purchase orders or entered without matching to a purchase order. Payables supports eight different types of invoices. The data requirements might be a little different for each one. Following are the eight types of invoices:

- *Standard.* This is the typical invoice from a supplier.

- *Credit Memo.* This invoice represents a credit for goods or services.

- *Debit Memo.* This is used to notify a supplier of a credit you recorded.

- *Expense Report.* This is an internally generated invoice to record business-related expenses incurred by an employee.

- *PO Default.* When you match the invoice to a specific PO number, information is defaulted from the PO.

- *QuickMatch.* This is used when you want to automatically match all PO shipment lines to an invoice.

- *Mixed.* This invoice type can be a combination of matched to a PO or another invoice.

- *Prepayment.* This invoice is used for advanced payments. The can be entered for suppliers or employees.

Payables offers full integration with Oracle Purchasing and with other purchasing systems. Payables automatically creates distributions lines for you when you enter an invoice and match it to a purchase order. If you have set up matching tolerances, Payables validates that the match is within the tolerances defined.

Payables supports two-way, three-way, and four-way matching. Two-way matching is matching the invoice to an approved purchase order. Three-way matching is matching the invoice to an approved PO and receipt. Finally, four-way matching ensures that the invoice is for goods that are on an approved PO, have been received, and have been accepted.

USING EXPENSE REPORTS

You can use the Expense Reports window to enter, review, and modify expense reports for your employees You can review and modify expense reports entered in Oracle Projects or Web Employees and then transferred to Payables. If you have paid advances to an employee, you can apply advances to expense reports to reduce the amount you pay. You can also apply a hold to an expense report to prevent payment. You can apply advances and holds to expense reports that are from any source.

You must submit the Payables Invoice Import program to have Payables automatically create invoices from the expense reports before you can pay expense reports. You can then use Payables to pay the invoices and create journal entries for posting to your general ledger. If expense reports have been purged during the Payables Invoice Import, you can no longer view them in the Expense Reports window. If reports have not been purged, you can view them in the Expense Reports window, but you cannot make changes.

IMPORTING INVOICES

Invoice Import creates Payables invoices from expense reports entered in Payables, Oracle Web Employees, or Oracle Projects. You can then use Payables to pay these invoices and create journal entries for general ledger posting.

When you import invoices, Payables records the source of the imported invoices and the imported invoice details. Payables Invoice Import verifies all your expense report and invoice information to ensure it creates valid, fully distributed invoices that are ready for approval and payment. If the expense report fails validation, Payables Invoice Import does not create an invoice and reports the exception on the Payables Invoice Import Exceptions Report. When you submit Payables Invoice Import, Payables automatically prints the Payables Invoice Import Exceptions Report. The Payables Invoice Import Exceptions Report displays detailed information on all exceptions.

PART

III

CH

12

Tip

> If you are importing invoices from an external system, note that beginning with Payables release 12, you will be able to import external invoices only through the Payables Open Interface Import process. While using release 11, you should plan to migrate any existing processes from the Payables Invoice Import Interface Tables to the Payables Open Interface Tables. If you are implementing any new Payables Invoice Import processes, you should use only the Payables Open Interface Tables and the Payables Open Interface Import process.

If you enable the Automatically Create Employee as Supplier Payables option, Payables automatically creates suppliers and supplier sites for employees who are not already suppliers. Otherwise, you must manually enter the employee as a supplier before submitting Payables Invoice Import.

To purge expense reports from the Payables Invoice Import Interface Tables, enter the date criteria you want Payables to use. Payables deletes all records for expense reports that were entered before this date and have already been imported. Payables does not import an invoice or expense report more than once.

DEFINING AND CREATING RECURRING PAYMENTS

Recurring invoices are great for periodic business expenses such as rent, where you do not receive invoices. To create a recurring invoice, you must first create a template. The template enables you to specify the intervals in which the invoices will be created, create as many as two nonstandard invoice amounts such as deposits or balloon payments, and create invoices that increase or decrease from period to period by a fixed percentage.

APPROVING INVOICES

Before you can pay or post an invoice, the invoice must pass the Approval process. This can be done online by using the Invoice Actions window or the Approve button in the Invoice Batches window, or it can be done by submitting the Payables Approval program from the Submit Request window.

Approval validates the matching, tax, period status, exchange rate, and distribution information for invoices entered and automatically applies holds to exception invoices. If an invoice has a hold, you can release the hold by correcting the exception that caused the hold to be applied and then resubmitting Approval. You can correct the exceptions by updating the invoice or the purchase order or by changing your Invoice Tolerances. Payables automatically releases the hold when the exception is no longer an issue. You can manually release certain invoice holds even if you have not resolved the error condition. Authorized users can always correct an invoice, even if you have approved, paid, or created journal entries for the invoice.

You can check for unapproved invoices by submitting the Invoice Register for Unapproved Invoices Only or by viewing the invoice online.

Payables and Oracle Alert are fully integrated to enable you to notify approvers and purchasing agents when an invoice is placed on hold. Exception reporting in Alert is accomplished using either email or printed reports.

You can automate your approval cycle by scheduling the Approval process to run at specific intervals, such as once a day at 5 p.m. You define your submission options for the Payables Approval program in the Submit Request window.

ADJUSTING INVOICE PAYMENT SCHEDULES

If an invoice is not fully paid, you can make any adjustments you need to the scheduled payments. You can add new scheduled payments, and alter unpaid scheduled payments. You can defer payment by adjusting due dates on schedules or by applying holds to selected scheduled payments.

Payables recalculates and replaces scheduled payments if you adjust the invoice Payment Terms or if the Scheduled Payment Recalculation Payables option is enabled and you submit Approval for the invoice. If you manually adjust scheduled payments and Payables subsequently recalculates the scheduled payments, you need to reenter your changes.

ADJUSTING DISTRIBUTIONS

Authorized users can make adjustments to invoice details, distributions, and scheduled payments. These adjustments can be made even after the invoice has been posted to your general ledger or paid.

Some invoice values, such as the GL Date, are used as defaults when you create new invoice distributions. If you change an invoice GL Date, it does not affect the existing GL Dates for the invoice distributions. If you want to change invoice distribution GL Dates, you must change them in the Distributions window.

You can cancel an invoice if it has not been paid. When an invoice is canceled, no more changes can be made to it. If the invoice has never been submitted for approval, you can simply delete it.

ADJUSTING PURCHASE ORDER MATCHED INVOICES

You can reverse matched distributions or create new distributions by matching to new purchase order shipments or distributions of either the same purchase order or another purchase order. If you add or reverse invoice distributions, you must also change the scheduled payment amounts to match the new invoice total, or Payables places holds on the invoice.

If you have enabled the Allow Flexfield Override Payables option and have not yet posted the invoice, you can change the account fields to a purchase order-matched invoice distribution. You can always adjust the GL Date and Income Tax Type.

You use a price correction to adjust for a change in the invoiced unit price of previously matched purchase order shipments or distributions. You do not have to change the quantity billed.

ENTERING NOTES

Attachments can be created in the Enter Invoices window and viewed in either the Enter Invoices or Invoices Overview window. Attachments enables you to link almost any data type to your invoices. Examples would be spreadsheets, documents, or images.

WRITING OFF ACCRUALS

The Accrual Write-Off Report provides the supporting detail for the journal entries you create to write off accrual transactions. When you have identified through research all transactions that should be removed from the Accrual Write-Off Report, you use the Accrual Write-Off window to remove those transactions from the report.

ENTERING PREPAYMENTS

A prepayment is a type of invoice used to pay an advance payment to a supplier or an employee. For example, you might need to pay an employee an advance for travel expenses. You can later apply the prepayment to one or more invoices or expense reports you receive from the supplier or employee to offset the amount paid to him.

You can enter either a Temporary or Permanent type prepayment. Temporary prepayments can be applied to invoices or expense reports you receive, whereas Permanent prepayments cannot be applied to invoices. For example, you use a Temporary prepayment to pay a catering deposit. When the caterer's invoice arrives, you apply the prepayment to the invoice to reduce the amount you pay. You would use a Permanent prepayment to pay a lease deposit for which you do not expect to be invoiced. Prepayments can be changed from Permanent to Temporary if they need to be applied to an invoice.

Prepayments must be approved and fully paid before they can be applied to an invoice. You cannot partially pay a prepayment. The Settlement date controls when a prepayment is available for use. During Invoice entry, Payables notifies you if you have outstanding Temporary prepayments for that supplier or employee. You can also review the Prepayment Status Report to check the status of all Temporary prepayments.

When a prepayment is applied to an invoice, Payables automatically creates a negative distribution and a negative scheduled payment for the prepayment in the amount of the applied prepayment. Payables also reduces the amount available for prepayment by the amount applied. You can either select an invoice and apply a prepayment to it or select a prepayment and apply it to an invoice.

You apply prepayments, or employee advances, to expense reports during expense report entry. Unless you specify a specific advance to apply, Payables applies all outstanding, available advances, starting with the oldest, up to the amount of the expense report.

If you mistakenly apply a prepayment to an invoice, you can unapply it. Unapplied and unpaid prepayments can be cancelled. Prepayments that have been paid and applied to an invoice must be unapplied and the payment cancelled before the prepayment can be cancelled.

MAKING PAYMENTS

The next step after entering and approving invoices is to pay the invoices in an efficient and timely manner. Payments can be made to suppliers by any of the following means:

Automated checks

QuickCheck

Manual payments

Wire transfers

EDI

Electronic Funds Transfers (EFT)

AUTOMATED CHECKS

Automatic checks are computer-generated payments to pay a supplier for one or more invoices. Automatic checks use the payment terms and due date to select invoices for a payment batch. You follow a series of steps to create your payment batch payments, and you initiate each step from the Payment Batch Actions window. The following sequence of steps must be followed to create a payment batch:

1. Invoice Selection
2. Payment Build
3. Modification
4. Format and Print
5. Confirmation

Note   All payment batch windows display amounts in the payment currency.

SELECTING ITEMS FOR PAYMENT   The following are the steps to follow for selecting items for payment:

1. Define your invoice selection criteria in the Payment Batches window. Payables selects all approved invoices that match your invoice selection criteria.
2. Enter a unique batch name.
3. Enter or change the default bank account.
4. Select a payment document.
5. Enter or change the payment date.
6. Optionally, choose a Pay Group.
7. Verify the pay-through date.

Payables selects all invoices due for payment based on the preceding entered criteria. Payables selects invoices with a discount or due date on or before the pay-through date.

Note   If you want to save this payment batch as a template for future payment batches, check Template.

PAYMENT BUILD   When Payables builds payments, it determines which invoices will be paid with each payment document. Payables automatically builds payments when you initiate invoice selection. Payables also automatically builds payments after you modify a payment batch. You do not have to perform this task unless the build process does not complete successfully.

Choose Actions to open the Payment Batch Actions window. Depending on whether you want to be able to review and modify the payment batch before formatting, complete one of the following two options:

- If you want to format the payments without modifying them, select Format Payments to have Payables automatically select and perform the required prerequisite actions, which are Select Invoices and Build Payments. Payables then formats the payments. After formatting is complete, continue with Printing Payment Batch Checks, or if you are creating electronic payments, proceed with Confirming Payment Batches.

- If you want to review and modify the invoices selected in the payment batch before you format payments, select Select Invoices to have Payables select invoices and build payments.

After the build process is complete, you have the option to proceed with Modifying Payment Batches or Formatting Payments.

MODIFYING THE SELECTION   After selecting invoices and building payments, you have the opportunity to review and modify the payment batch. You can prevent payment of a particular invoice, modify the payment amount of an invoice, or add an invoice that Payables did not originally select. After you complete your modifications, you can review your changes on a new Preliminary Payment Register. You can continue with the next step in the process, or you can modify the payment batch as many times as needed.

> **Note**   If invoices include withholding tax, you cannot adjust the payment amount or the discount amount.

FORMATTING PAYMENTS   When Payables formats payments, it creates an output file that is used to print the checks, or if you are making electronic payments without the EDI Gateway, you can deliver the output file to your bank for processing. The output file is stored in the Payables output directory. Its name is created by appending a period and the concurrent manager request number to your AOL userID (for example, SYSADMIN.12345).

Payables uses the printer you assigned to your payment program as the default printer. If you have not assigned a printer to your payment program, Payables uses the printer assigned as your default printer in your Printer profile option.

After printing is complete, the next step is Confirming Payment Batches.

CONFIRMING PAYMENTS   Confirming is the final step in processing a payment batch. This step updates the payment history of invoices paid and associates payment document numbers with the invoices and invoice payments. You cannot close a period or use the same payment document for any other payments until you confirm the payment batch.

You must record the status of every payment document during confirmation. The four statuses are Setup, Printed, Skipped, and Spoiled. Setup is used to designate check stock that is wasted as part of the process of aligning checks in the printer; usually this is a preset number. The Printed status designates successfully printed checks. Skipped is used to designate check numbers that were skipped over or not used on a check. Lastly, Spoiled refers to checks that were damaged as part of the printing process.

If you are using check overflow, you should record the status of all the checks as Printed. Check overflow occurs when you have more invoices paid on a single check than can fit on the remittance stub and Payables voids all checks except the one on the last remittance stub for that supplier site.

From the Confirm window, you can record the status of the payments and, if necessary, restart the payment batch or cancel the remainder.

RESETTING A PAYMENT BATCH   Troubleshooting begins with identifying the current status of your payment batch so that you can determine the best course of action. You can review the payment batch status in the Payment Batches window.

Most payment batch problems are due to a printer malfunction during check printing, causing skipped or spoiled checks. If you have printer problems during check printing, you still confirm the results using the Confirm Payment Batch window.

To record a partial payment batch and restart check printing, record the checks as either Setup, Skipped, or Printed and then choose Restart Payment Batch.

To record a partial payment batch and cancel the remainder, record the checks as either Setup, Skipped, Spoiled, or Printed and then choose Cancel Remainder.

PART

III

CH

12

> Tip
>
> Do not record a damaged check as Spoiled. That results in an adjustment to the check numbering sequence, causing incorrect payment information to be recorded.

If a concurrent program does not execute successfully, you can resubmit the program by using the Payment Batch Actions window.

You can tell if a payment batch program did not complete successfully by looking at the Concurrent Requests Summary. Unsuccessful batch programs display one of the following statuses in the Payment Batches window:

- Selecting
- Building

- Modifying
- Rebuilding
- Formatting
- Confirming
- Restarting
- Canceling

When you cancel a payment batch, Payables updates the status of each invoice selected in the batch to Unpaid. In addition, canceling a payment batch makes the payment batch's payment document available for another use.

PROCESSING A QUICKCHECK

QuickCheck enables you to select an invoice and immediately create a computer-generated payment. QuickCheck enables you select an invoice regardless of the payment terms and due date.

The following restrictions apply to Quick Payments:

You can only pay as many invoices as you defined for the remittance advice of the payment document.

You can only select invoices that have the same supplier site as the payment supplier site entered for the check.

If you want to pay multiple invoices, none can be a "Pay Alone" invoice.

You must pay in the same currency as the invoice. You can enter and pay a foreign currency invoice only if your Allow Multiple Currencies Payables option is enabled and you have defined a multicurrency or foreign currency denominated bank account.

You cannot stop a Quick Payment after it has been formatted.

ENTERING MANUAL PAYMENTS

Manual Payments enable you to record payments that were created outside of Oracle Payables. For example, using a typed check or wire transfer, within Payables you can record the payment and update the invoices that you paid.

With a manual payment, you can override some payment controls. You can record a single payment for multiple Pay Alone invoices. You can also pay an invoice for a supplier that has the Hold All Payments option enabled.

WIRE TRANSFERS

Wire transfers are accounted for in the same manner as manual payments. Within Payables, you can record that the payment was made as a wire transfer and update the invoices that you paid.

EDI

You follow nearly the same steps as in creating checks in a payment batch when creating an electronic payment file. Oracle EDI Gateway formats the payment file in the outbound payment format and transfers it to your bank. The EDI translator is used to transmit the formatted payment data to your bank for disbursement.

EFT

You follow nearly the same steps as in creating checks in a payment batch to create an electronic funds transfer (EFT) payment file that you can deliver to your bank. Instead of printing the checks, you transmit an electronic copy of the formatted payments to your bank. Your bank then disburses the payments directly into each supplier's bank account.

CHANGING PAYMENT DISTRIBUTIONS

An invalid payment distribution might be created if Automatic offsets is enabled and you pay an invoice or prepayment from a pooled bank account. Payment distributions containing an invalid distribution can be corrected in the Invalid GL Accounts window.

PROCESSING STOP AND VOID PAYMENTS

Recording a stop payment status in Payables does not initiate a stop payment with the bank. You must call your bank to initiate a stop payment on a payment document. You can then void the payment to reverse the accounting and payment records. Otherwise, you can release the stop payment to reset the invoice status to negotiable to allow it to be picked up in a subsequent payment batch. You can review all current stop payments in the Stopped Payments Report.

The following restrictions apply to Stop Payments:

> You must first unapply any prepayments that have been applied to an invoice before you can initiate a stop payment on the payment document that paid the prepayment.

> You cannot initiate a stop payment on a Quick Payment that has been formatted.

When you void a payment, Payables automatically reverses the payment and its distributions. The action taken on the invoices paid by the voided payment can be selected at the time the payment is voided. You can choose to place the invoices on hold, cancel the invoices, or do nothing with the invoices, leaving them available for payment.

The following restrictions apply to voided payments:

> When you void a payment, you cannot cancel a related invoice if it was partially paid by a second payment. Instead, when you choose Cancel Invoice, the system applies an Invoice Cancel hold to the invoice for your reference. You can release the hold manually in the Invoice Holds window.

> If you attempt to cancel an invoice that has been partially paid by another payment by using the Cancel Invoice Action, instead of canceling the invoice, Payables applies an

Invoice Cancel hold to the invoice. This hold is manually releasable.

You cannot void a payment that the bank has already cleared.

You cannot void payment on a payment document that pays a prepayment that you have applied to an invoice. You must first unapply any prepayments, and you can then void the payment.

RECONCILING CASH

With Oracle Cash Management, you can reconcile payments created in Payables to your bank statements. When you reconcile payments using Oracle Cash Management, Cash Management updates the status of Payables payments to Reconciled. If you enable the Allow Reconciliation Accounting Payables option, Payables creates reconciliation accounting entries for the delay in the bank clearing of payments from the time of issuance to the time of reconciliation. It also creates entries for any differences between the original payment amount and the cleared payment amount due to exchange rate fluctuations, bank charges, or bank errors of unreconciled payments. Oracle Payables transfers these entries created by Oracle Cash Management to your general ledger when you post payments within Payables.

Note You can reconcile foreign currency payments that have no exchange rates. However, Payables does not create reconciliation accounting entries. If you enter the exchange rate in the GL Daily Rates table and then submit the AutoRate program, Payables automatically creates the reconciliation accounting entries for payments that were reconciled without exchange rates.

BALANCING THE SUBLEDGER TO THE GENERAL LEDGER

To ensure that your Trial Balance accurately reflects your accounts payable liability, you will want to reconcile your posted invoices and payments to your Accounts Payable Trial Balance. For a given period, add the current period's posted invoices (total invoice amount from the Posted Invoice Register) and subtract the current period's posted payments (total cash plus discounts taken from the Posted Payments Register) from the prior period's Accounts Payable Trial Balance. This amount should equal the balance for the current period's Accounts Payable Trial Balance. This can all be summed up in the following equation:

Prior Period Accounts Payable Trial Balance + Current Period Posted Invoice Register + Current Period Posted Payment Register = Current Period Accounts Payable Trial Balance

USING OPEN INTERFACES IN THIS APPLICATION

You can use the Payables Open Interface Import program to create invoices from invoice data imported into the Payables Open Interface Tables. You can populate the Payables Open Interface Tables with invoice data from the following sources:

- Supplier EDI invoices (ASC X12 810/EDIFACT INVOIC) transferred through Oracle EDI Gateway
- Invoices from other accounting systems loaded with a custom SQL*Loader program.
- Credit card transactions transferred using the Credit Card Invoice Interface Summary

> **Note**
>
> In Payables release 11, you still use Payables Invoice Import to import expense report data from the Payables Invoice Interface tables.

If you are importing EDI invoices through the Oracle EDI Gateway, you can submit the EDI Invoice Inbound Set. This report set submits both the EDI Gateway program and the Payables Open Interface Import Program. The EDI Gateway program populates the Open Interface Tables, and the Payables Open Interface Import program transfers the invoice data from the interface tables into the transaction invoice tables.

While trying to import invoices, you might encounter errors caused by incorrect data or program failure. If there is a problem at the invoice level, the invoice line level, or the distribution level, the invoice is rejected. The Payables Open Interface Report lists all invoices that were not imported correctly, regardless of whether the problem occurred at the invoice, line, or distribution level.

You can correct the data either by using the Open Interface Invoices window or by submitting Purge Payables Open Interface. When the interface tables are purged, you can reimport corrected data for the rejected records. If there is a failure with either the EDI Gateway Program or the Payables Open Interface Program, you can query the program in the Concurrent Requests Summary. You can read about any errors in the log file.

Use the Payables Open Interface Purge Program to purge records from the Payables Open Interface tables (AP_INVOICES_INTERFACE and AP_INVOICE_LINES_INTER-FACE). You can choose to purge only invoices that you have successfully imported; alternatively, you can choose to purge all records in the table that match the Source and Group parameters entered.

PART

III

CH

12

POSTING TO THE GENERAL LEDGER

You can initiate posting within Payables by submitting the Payables Transfer to General Ledger program. This program transfers your invoice and payment accounting distributions to the general ledger interface table. You can import the distributions into General Ledger yourself, or you can set the Transfer to General Ledger program to import the distributions automatically. With either method, the result is an unposted journal entry in the General Ledger.

Payables does not enable you to close a period having unposted invoices and payments. When you need to close a period that has unposted invoices or payments in it, you must use the Unposted Invoice Sweep Program to transfer all unposted invoices and payments from one accounting period to another. The program transfers unposted invoice distributions and payments to the period you specify by updating its GL dates to the first day of the new period. You can then close the accounting period from which Payables moved the invoices and payments.

CREATING MASS ADDITIONS TO ORACLE ASSETS

Run the Mass Additions Create program to create mass additions for Oracle Assets from invoice line distributions in Payables. After you create mass additions, you can review them in the Prepare Mass Additions window in Oracle Assets.

USING ORACLE ALERT

Payables supplies you with several predefined alerts. These alerts can be used as they are or customized. These alerts notify the appropriate person of invoice price holds and invoice receipt holds. If you install Oracle Alert, you can also create your own alerts to notify the appropriate people of specific exceptions or about key indicators occurring in the Payables database. All predefined alerts are initially disabled. You must enable the alerts you want to use.

LASER PRINTED CHECKS

Payables provides the Evergreen Check Laser Format program and corresponding Evergreen Long (Laser) Format to support your check laser printing needs. This format can be customized with variable fonts, MICR encoding, scanned signatures, and so on as needed. Just associate the customized payment format with a payment document for a bank account to begin printing laser checks.

USING ORACLE CASH MANAGEMENT

The Cash Management application enables you to control the cash cycle for your business. Cash Management is integrated with Payables, Receivables, Purchasing, and Order Entry. However, this section discusses Cash Management as it pertains to Payables. Cash Management covers basically two distinct areas: bank statement reconciliation and cash forecasting. Bank reconciliation is the method of determining whether the bank balances kept in Oracle Financials match the balances per the bank's records. Cash Forecasting enables you to project what your balance will be at some point in the future.

BANK RECONCILIATION

Cash Management enables you to reconcile the payments created in Oracle Payables against your bank statements. When you reconcile your payments, the system automatically creates accounting entries to the Cash, Cash Clearing, realized Gains and Losses, Bank Charges, and Bank Errors accounts you specified in the Bank setup.

There are two major process steps you need to follow when reconciling bank statements:

1. *Load Bank Statements.* You need to enter the detailed information from each bank statement, including bank account information, deposits received by the bank, and checks cleared. You can enter bank statements manually or load electronic statements that you receive directly from your bank.

2. *Reconcile Bank Statements.* When you have entered detailed bank statement information into Cash Management, you must reconcile that information with your system transactions. Cash Management provides two methods to do your reconciliations:

   1. *Automatic.* Bank statement details are automatically matched and reconciled with system transactions. This method is ideally suited for bank accounts that have a high volume of transactions.

   2. *Manual.* This method requires you to manually match bank statement details with accounting transactions. The method is ideally suited to reconciling bank accounts that have a small volume of monthly transactions. You can also use the manual reconciliation method to reconcile any bank statement details that could not be reconciled automatically.

AUTORECONCILIATION

You can use the AutoReconciliation program to reconcile any bank statement in Oracle Cash Management. There are three versions of the program:

AutoReconciliation. Use this program to reconcile any bank statement that has already been entered.

Bank Statement Import. Use this program to electronically import a bank statement after loading the bank file with your SQL*Loader program.

Bank Statement Import and AutoReconciliation. Use this program to import and reconcile a bank statement in the same run.

After you run the program, you can review the AutoReconciliation Execution Report to identify any reconciliation errors that need to be corrected. This report is produced automatically, or you can run it whenever needed. You can also review reconciliation errors online.

After you automatically reconcile a bank statement and correct any reconciliation errors, you can run the Bank Statement Detail Report or use the View Bank Statements window to review reconciled and unreconciled statement lines. If lines remain unreconciled, you can

PART

III

CH

12

update the bank statement and rerun AutoReconciliation or reconcile the statement lines manually.

USING CASH FORECASTING

Cash forecasting attempts to forecast a future cash position by taking the current position and adding future inflows and subtracting future outflows.

Cash Forecasting enables you to generate a cash forecast that automatically includes cash flows from other Oracle applications and external sources, as well as Payables.

Cash Management enables you to view cash forecast information online in a spreadsheet format, with the forecast periods in columns and the sources in rows. The Cash Forecast Report uses Oracle Report eXchange to export cash forecast data to a spreadsheet application. You can also print the Cash Forecast Report to review your forecasts.

RELEASE 11 FEATURES

The following sections describe the cash management features new to release 11.

BANK RECONCILIATION: BANK ERRORS AND CORRECTIONS

Cash Management now provides reconciliation of corrections and adjustments to error statement lines. You can automatically or manually reconcile correcting statement lines against error statement lines, providing an audit trail you can use to verify correction of bank errors.

BANK RECONCILIATION: MATCHING PAYMENTS AND RECEIPTS

Cash Management's AutoReconciliation program now matches payments and receipts by supplier or customer bank account number and invoice number. This feature is useful for electronic payments, for which bank statements might not include check numbers but do include invoice numbers and supplier/customer bank account numbers.

CASH FORECASTING

This release contains the production version of the Cash Forecasting feature. Cash forecasting is a planning tool that helps you anticipate cash inflow and outflow based on historical and in-process transactions from other Oracle Applications.

CASH FORECASTING INTEGRATION WITH PAYROLL   With release 11, Cash Management also provides integration with Oracle Payroll. The selection criteria for payroll payments include business group, bank account, payment method, roll forward type and period, and payroll.

FORECASTING OPEN INTERFACE AND DISTRIBUTED DATABASE INTEGRATION

Release 11 Cash Forecasting enables you to use external sources for cash inflow and outflow data. This feature requires an enterprisewide cash forecasting setup on a distributed database. For each expected cash transaction from an external system, you can specify the source, expected cash activity date, amounts, and other selection criteria values. The Forecasting Open Interface automatically retrieves the information available from the external forecast sources that you have defined.

REPORT EXCHANGE INTEGRATION WITH CASH FORECASTING   Oracle Report eXchange (RX) is a new application that enables you to download data from Oracle Applications to the desktop so that you can take advantage of desktop application features. You can use Report eXchange to submit the Cash Forecast Report and export cash forecasts to Microsoft Excel or other spreadsheet applications.

OTHER CASH FORECASTING ENHANCEMENTS

You can submit cash forecasts with user-defined currency exchange rates, providing you an enhanced multiple currency reporting option with what-if scenarios. You have the flexibility to include or exclude overdue transactions for all appropriate source transaction types in your forecasts.

CONFIGURING ORACLE CASH MANAGEMENT

Table 12.2 shows the tasks required to set up the Cash Management application. The tasks are listed in the order they should be performed. Many tasks have predecessor tasks for data validation, so they should be performed in the proper order.

TABLE 12.2   ORACLE CASH MANAGEMENT CONFIGURATION TASKS

Task Name	Required
Set Profile Options	Yes
Define System Parameters	Yes
Define Bank Transaction Codes	Optional
Setup Bank Statement Open Interface	Optional
Setup Reconciliation Open Interface	Optional
Setup Forecasting Open Interface	Optional
Define Cash Forecasting Templates	Yes
Setup Sequential Document Numbering	Optional
Define Request Sets	Optional
Define Descriptive Flexfields	Optional

PART

III

CH

12

SETTING PROFILE OPTIONS

You set values for profile options in Oracle Financials to specify how Cash Management controls access to and processes data. Many of these user profile options are set, using the System Administrator responsibility, at one or more of the following levels: Site, Application, Responsibility, and User. Use the Personal Profile Options window to view or set your profile options at the user level.

CONFIGURING SYSTEM PARAMETERS

System parameters determine defaults and controls such as which set of books Cash Management uses, the default options for manual reconciliation windows, and the control settings for the AutoReconciliation program.

CONFIGURING BANK TRANSACTION CODES

To electronically load bank statements or use the AutoReconciliation feature, you must set up the transaction codes that your bank will use to identify the different transaction types on its statement. You need to do this for each bank account from which you will be importing statements. You can make codes inactive and even delete codes that have not been used.

You can easily view the bank transaction codes you have created here by submitting the Bank Transaction Codes Listing.

SETTING UP BANK STATEMENT OPEN INTERFACE

Before you can reconcile to your bank statement, you need to enter the bank statement information into Cash Management. If your bank provides bank statements in a defined format such as BAI or SWIFT940, you can use the Bank Statement Open Interface to load this file into Cash Management.

You must first create an import program to map the structure of the bank statement file to the Cash Management bank statement open interface tables. You need a separate program for each unique file structure. Import programs are usually written using SQL*Loader. The Bank Statement Open Interface consists of two bank statement open interface tables. The first table is the Bank Statement Headers Interface Table that contains the bank statement header information. The table is named `ce_statement_headers_int_all`. The second table is the Bank Statement Lines Interface Table that contains the bank statement transaction lines. The table is named `ce_statement_lines_interface`.

SETTING UP RECONCILIATION OPEN INTERFACE

You can reconcile receipts and payments that originate in applications other than Receivables, Payables, and General Ledger. The Cash Management Reconciliation Open Interface enables you to manually or automatically reconcile transactions imported through the open interface to bank statement lines in Cash Management.

SETTING UP FORECASTING OPEN INTERFACE

There are two source transaction types for cash forecasting. The first source type is the Open Interface Inflow, which is to be used for cash receipts. The second, the Open Interface Outflow, is to be used for disbursements. The Forecasting Open Interface collects these externally generated cash flow amounts and includes them in the cash forecasts.

DEFINING CASH FORECASTING TEMPLATES

Cash forecasting templates enable you to format the incoming cash flow data to fit your needs. Among other things, you can specify the number and type of rows for the forecast data and columns for the periods for your forecast.

SEQUENTIAL DOCUMENT NUMBERING

Cash Management supports Oracle Applications' Document Sequences feature. With this feature enabled, you can assign sequential document numbers to your bank statements.

DEFINING REQUEST SETS

Defining report sets enables you to submit the same set of reports regularly using the same request. Use the Request Set window or Request Set Wizard to create report sets.

DEFINING DESCRIPTIVE FLEXFIELDS

To define your descriptive flexfield, you define the segments, the descriptive information, and the value set information for each segment in a structure. You also determine the appearance of your descriptive flexfield window. The maximum number of segments possible within a single structure depends on which descriptive flexfield you are defining.

PROCESSING CASH MANAGEMENT TRANSACTIONS

Bank statement transactions are identified by transaction codes. As you define each code, you select a Transaction Type. This transaction type determines how Payables matches and accounts for transactions having that code. The types are as follows:

PART

III

CH

12

Payment. Checks, wire transfers, EFT

Receipt. Receipts

Miscellaneous payment. Nonsupplier-related payments

Miscellaneous receipt. Noncustomer-related receipts

Stopped. Stopped or voided payments in Payables

Rejected. Rejected receipts, except for NSF

NSF. Nonsufficient funds

Cash Management-generated journal entries are transferred to the General Ledger from Payables or Receivables.

REVIEWING CASH MANAGEMENT REPORTS

You can run the following Cash Management reports from the Submit Request window.

STATEMENT REPORTS Bank Statement Detail Report

Bank Statement Summary Report

Bank Statements by Document Number Report

TRANSACTION REPORTS Cash Forecast Report

    Cash Forecast Execution Report

    AutoReconciliation Execution Report

    GL Reconciliation Report

    Transactions Available for Reconciliation Report

    Cash in Transit Report

ARCHIVING AND PURGING TRANSACTIONS

You can archive and purge the information from both your bank statement open interface tables and bank statement tables. You can configure Cash Management to automatically archive and purge records from the bank statement open interface tables during Bank Statement Import. The information is only archived and purged after successful transfer from the open interface tables to the bank statement tables.

SUMMARY

Oracle Payables, along with Oracle Cash Management, is continuously evolving to support the growing trend toward conducting business over the Web and via electronic commerce. It also supports the increasing requirements for more multinational features.

CHAPTER 13

USING ORACLE RECEIVABLES

INTRODUCTION

Oracle Receivables (AR) is a subledger to the Oracle General Ledger, and it can use the multi-org partitioning features. The main transactions in AR are billing, collections, and cash receipts. The main setup tasks involve customers, AutoAccounting, AutoInvoicing, sales tax, transactions, and receipts.

RELATIONSHIP TO OTHER APPLICATIONS

AR has close relationships to other Oracle Applications. Figure 13.1 shows that AR is dependent on GL, INV, AOL, OE, and possibly external systems for validation, input, shared objects, and so forth. AR provides outputs and services to General Ledger and Order Entry.

Figure 13.1
AR relation-
ships to other
applications.

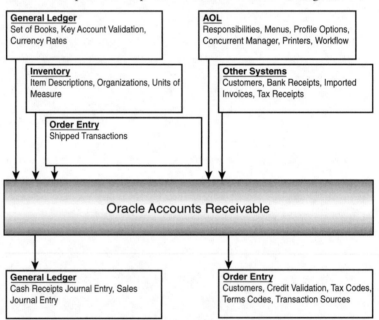

DISCOVER NEW FEATURES IN RELEASE 11

Established users and consultants who are familiar with release 10 should have no trouble with the features and functions of release 11 AR. This section discusses some new features in release 11.

> **Note**
>
> In the early versions of release 11 there was a beta version of a new transaction application programming interface (API). This interface was withdrawn during the

> beta testing and is no longer available even though you might find references to it in the release 11 documentation.

USING PAYMENT APPLICATION RULE SETS

Application rule sets for cash receipts define the default payment steps and how discounts affect the open balance of transactions. A payment application rule set defines how AR reduces the balance due for line, tax, freight, and finance charges. Three predefined rules are provided with release 11:

- The Line First—Tax Afterrule applies receipts to open line item amounts first and then remaining amounts to tax, freight, and finance charges, in that order.

- The Line First—Tax Prorate rule applies receipts proportionally to open line items and open tax amounts for each line. Remaining amounts of the receipt are applied to freight and then to finance charges.

- The Prorate All rule applies a proportionate amount of the receipt to all lines.

To define a new application rule set, complete the following steps:

1. In the Application Rule Sets window, name and describe the rule set.

2. Enter a rule sequence number. AR applies rules starting with the lowest sequence number. By default, the Overapplication rule is part of every set and is processed last in the rule set.

3. Enter rule details for at least one type of line.

4. Freeze the rule set definition, and verify that AR passes the rule set through the validation logic. A rule set must be frozen before assignment to transaction types or usage in system options. After a rule is frozen, it cannot be updated or deleted.

USING CROSS CURRENCY RECEIPTS

The Cross Currency Receipts function enables you to apply a receipt in one currency to transactions in different currencies. This feature of release 11 should be especially attractive to implementations with customers in countries participating in the European Economic Union. If you have an invoice in a national currency such as Irish pounds, and the customer pays in the new Euro currency, Cross Currency Receipts solves the triangulation problem of converting the transaction currency and the receipt currency to your set of books' functional currency.

To activate Cross Currency Receipts, set the profile option AR: Enable Cross Currency to Yes at the Site, Application, or User level. Also, define a suspense account in Oracle General Ledger for AR to use to clear multiple currency entries. The suspense account should have a category of Cross Currency and a source of Receivables.

PART

III

CH

13

Note   Defining a suspense account is sufficient to enable Cross Currency Receipts. You do not have to enable suspense accounting in GL. The entries to the suspense clearing account always net to zero when translated to the functional currency of the set of books.

USING MATCHING WITH AUTOLOCKBOX

AutoLockbox, the automated receipts processing program, uses several methods to match imported receipts with transactions. If the customer number or MICR number is not included in the receipt transmission data, AutoLockbox tries to identify the customer and transaction by matching the following fields in the following order:

- Transaction Number
- Sales Order Number
- Customer Purchase Order Number
- Consolidated Billing Invoice Number
- Other (custom defined number)

If none of the preceding match criteria are successful, AutoLockbox applies the receipts using the AutoCash rule set assigned to the customer.

USING EXPANDED CUSTOMER INQUIRY CRITERIA

Release 11 enables additional search criteria in the Find Customers window. You can now search for customers by entering a phone number, city, state, county, province, postal code, or area code.

UNDERSTANDING TAX CHANGES

Release 11 of AR enables an optional default of tax information based on the natural account segment of items on the transaction. You can enforce the relationship between the natural account and the tax to prevent updates to the transaction. This feature enhances control of revenue and tax accounting for requirements in Germany, Japan, and Scandinavia, where revenue accounts can be classified by tax rate.

In release 11, AR introduces the concept of tax-inclusive amounts. You can now enter invoice line amounts that include tax if the tax code is defined as inclusive.

USING DUNNING HISTORY AND DEFINABLE DUNNING LETTERS

In release 11, you can view the dunning history online for a specific customer, dunning letter, or letter set. You can run a dunning history report by range of collectors, by range of customers, by range of dunning levels, by dunning method, and by range of transaction types.

Also in release 11, you can create your own set of dunning letters or there are up to 10 text files you can use as your business policies require. See the setup task, "Defining Dunning Letters and Sets," later in this chapter, for more information.

REMOVING SOME R10.7 MULTI-ORG RESTRICTIONS

In a multi-org implementation in release 11, it is now possible to assign a default salesperson to the customer site level of the customer definition. Also, release 11 permits creation of centralized statement and dunning sites for each customer.

RESOLVING COMMON ISSUES AND GAPS

The AR application generally works well in its role as a subledger, a billing system, a perpetual record of open amounts due from customers, and a cash collection system. However, many customers have expectations or business requirements of the AR application that exceed the design. The following topics are often identified by implementation teams as implementation issues or gaps in functionality.

AR IS NOT A SALES HISTORY REPORTING SYSTEM

Many companies have built sales history reporting systems into their legacy billing systems. The AR application stores information about product shipments, customers, invoice details, sales allowances, and so forth. However, many of these data items are used only to print the invoice. Project sponsors are often surprised when certain key management billing reports are not available. The primary mission of AR is to recognize revenue and collect cash. Although AR can print product information on an invoice, there are no revenue reports by product, by customer, by accounting period, and so forth.

If you also have Oracle Order Entry, General Ledger, and Inventory, the Margin Analysis Report can help resolve this gap. The Margin Analysis system is really two programs: a report and a data collection module. The data collection module can gather revenue, cost, accounting period, customer, and sales representative information into a temporary table called cst_margin_temp. You can then generate fairly simple reports from the temporary table with a data browser or an end user reporting tool.

Tip

If your sales history reporting needs are significant, consider reviewing the separate Sales Analyzer application. This application is like a data warehouse product and runs in a separate database from the AR application.

PART

III

CH

13

AR IS A SUBLEDGER TO THE GENERAL LEDGER

The AR application creates journal entries for revenue and cash receipts. AR maintains perpetual balances for many balance sheet accounts. Make sure all receivable activities are transacted in the AR system and allow the AR application to update the General Ledger.

AR MIGHT IMPACT YOUR CUSTOMERS

Any system that directly touches your customers automatically could be classified as strategic. Know your business processes and policies before setting up AR. Consider carefully the content of invoices, statements, and dunning letters. Many AR users customize these documents to meet their business requirements. Look at these documents early in your implementation project.

Because Order Entry provides billing data and customer/banking information is the foundation for cash receipts, make sure you map and understand each data element coming into the AR application. Make sure the billing, credit authorization, and collection systems can support the variety of deals that will be made with your customers.

The customer merge utility is infrequently used because it has a spotty record of reliability. You should test it before you use it to make sure you understand and agree with what it does. For example, the utility merges an entire customer into a target customer structure.

THE REMIT-TO STRATEGY IS NOT ALWAYS GEOGRAPHICAL

AutoInvoice selects a remit-to address on invoices it creates by looking at the country code and postal codes of the bill-to address. The logic of the program tries to pick the geographically closest address to the bill-to customer. However, many AR users have a customer-driven strategy for selecting the remit to address and believe the remit-to address should always be the same for a customer.

THE DUE DATE IS USED IN AGING CALCULATIONS

Many companies make deals with their customers so that each transaction has its own terms. For example, "Buy this software by the end of the quarter and take 90 days to pay." AR supports overriding the default terms code at the transaction level. However, the management of these companies usually wants to measure their aged invoices by the transaction date, and a report showing an 89-day old invoice in the current column is a problem.

> **Tip**
>
> AR is a collection system, and any invoice not yet due must appear in the current column so the collector and dunning system won't erroneously ask the customer for payment.

PERFORMANCE AND ACCESS ISSUES

AutoInvoice is usually the critical performance issue for AR. AutoInvoice is a batch program that converts rows in the ra_interface_lines_all table into validated invoices. System performance is dependent on many factors, but the largest and most efficient release 10 systems have achieved between 10,000 and 20,000 invoice lines per hour.

Oracle Support has performance patches to help customers with high volumes. Because AutoInvoice performs extensive validation, efficient access to configuration data, Quick-Codes, and customer data is critical for high throughput. In addition, indexes on the flexfield columns of the ra_interface_lines_all table are important so that rows can be rapidly grouped into complete invoices.

CONFIGURING THE APPLICATION

The following section of this chapter describes the setup tasks and sequence required to configure the AR application. The tasks should be performed in the sequence listed.

RESOLVING CRITICAL SETUP ISSUES

Customers, billing, collections, and cash receipt transactions are the essence of the AR application. If you get these items right, the AR application should do well for your business.

DETERMINING HOW TO SET UP CUSTOMERS

The customer definition is critical to the smooth operation of the AR application. Customers are grouped by profile classes. A customer can have many addresses, and an address can have multiple business purposes. However, a customer can have only one name, and that name must be unique. Consider the setup carefully. If you have the same customer trading with you under more than one name, you set up multiple customers for the same customer entity, and you might have to develop techniques or even extensions to relate or combine them for reporting, credit checking, collections, and cash applications. If you have many customers with the same name that actually represent separate entities, you must develop a naming convention to differentiate the customer records.

If you have distinct groups of customers, consider how to set up the profile classes. Profile classes are groups of customer attributes that can be assigned to customers with similar attributes. Attributes can be overridden at the customer level, but that might involve lots of maintenance. In all but the simplest customer setups, it is best to develop a matrix of key profile options to determine how many profile classes will be needed and the procedures for applying them to individual customers.

In multi-org implementations, the customer is shared by all organizations, but the customer details (addresses, business purposes, contacts, and phones) are specific to each operating unit. Transactions with customers are partitioned by operating unit. Therefore, if you have decentralized customer fulfillment processes in many operating units and centralized credit, collection, and cash receipts functions, you might have to coordinate how customer records are created.

GENERATING GL ACCOUNT DISTRIBUTIONS

Because AR is a subledger to the General Ledger, it is important for the AutoAccounting setup to generate revenue, tax, receivable, freight, and other account distributions for

PART
III

CH
13

transactions. AutoAccounting provides some degree of control over the value that will be assigned to each segment of the Key Accounting Flexfield for each distribution line of each transaction.

AutoAccounting can use account distributions from the definitions for transaction types, sales representatives, standard memo lines, and tax codes. If you have specific business requirements to distribute revenue to the GL accounts, you might have to evaluate how to set up transaction types, sales representatives, or standard memo lines to accomplish the distribution.

Note

The revenue account distribution is determined by the AutoAccounting function in AR. However, when Order Entry (OE) sends shipped transactions to Inventory, Flexbuilder in release 10 and the Workflow Account Generator in release 11 determine the cost of goods sold account distribution. You will want to ensure that distributions for revenues and costs of goods sold are matched.

USING MANUAL OR AUTOMATIC RECEIPTS

Your invoice transaction volume and customer payment patterns determine whether it makes sense to set up AutoLockbox processing. If receipt transaction volume is less than 2,000 to 3,000 invoices per month, you will probably use the manual or QuickCash processes. If you can't justify the overhead of AutoLockbox processing, don't set it up.

UNDERSTANDING TAXATION

Sales Tax and VAT calculations are made with a fairly complex logic. There are tax codes and rates, geographical locations, exemptions, and exceptions. Various combinations of transaction types, customers, and items can be defined to affect the result of the tax calculation. If you have taxable transactions, products, or customers, you will want to develop an implementation strategy to make sure the application is set up to handle the wide variety of taxation requirements. If you collect tax, make sure you test these calculations completely.

SETUP TASKS

Table 13.1 shows the tasks required to set up the AR application in the order that they should be performed. Try not to skip tasks or perform them out of sequence because many tasks use predecessor tasks for data validation, and you might receive error messages.

Note

Some tasks are not required for proper system operation in manual mode. However, if you want to use some of the automated functions, such as AutoLockbox, you might be required to perform additional setup tasks. Also, if you are implementing many applications, some tasks are best set up in other applications. For example, defining the sets of books is commonly the responsibility of the GL implementation team.

TABLE 13.1 AR SETUP TASKS

Setup Task Name	Required?
Define Sets of Books	Yes
Use the Account Generator	Yes
Define the System Item Flexfield Structure	Yes
Define Organizations	Yes
Define the Territory Flexfield	No
Define the Sales Tax Location Flexfield Structure	Yes
Set Up Flexible Address Formats	No
Maintain Countries and Territories	No
Define the Transaction Flexfield Structure	No
Define AutoCash Rule Sets	No
Define QuickCodes	No
Define AutoInvoice Line Ordering Rules	No
Define AutoInvoice Grouping Rules	No
Define System Options	Yes
Define Payment Terms	Yes
Define Accounting Rules	No
Maintain Accounting Periods	Yes
Define AutoAccounting	Yes
Set Up Cash Basis Accounting	No
Define Transaction Types	Yes
Define Transaction Sources	Yes
Define Collectors	Yes
Define Adjustment Approval Limits	Yes
Define Remittance Banks	Yes
Define Distribution Sets	No
Define Receivables Activities	Yes
Define Receipt Classes	Yes
Define Payment Methods	Yes
Define Receipt Sources	Yes
Define Aging Buckets	No
Define Statement Cycles	No
Define Statement Messages	No
Define Dunning Letters	No
Define Dunning Letter Sets	No

TABLE 13.1 CONTINUED

Setup Task Name	Required?
Define Territories	No
Define Salespeople	Yes
Define Profile Options	Yes
Define Tax Codes and Rates	Yes
Define Customer Profile Classes	Yes
Define Customers	Yes
Define Remit-To Addresses	Yes
Define Customer Relationships	No
Define Customer Banks	No
Define Lockboxes	No
Define the Transmission Format	No
Define Receipt Programs	No
Define Unit of Measure Classes	No
Define Units of Measure	Yes
Define Standard Memo Lines	No
Define Item Tax Rate Exceptions	No
Define Tax Exemptions	No
Define Document Sequences	No

UNDERSTANDING EACH SETUP TASK

This section discusses the details of each setup task in the order they should be performed.

DEFINING A SET OF BOOKS

The Receivables application is a subledger of the Oracle General Ledger and must be attached to a book set definition from the General Ledger. The set of books defines for the AR application the Chart of Accounts, the Fiscal Calendar, and the Functional Currency of the application. When you define a set of books, use the setup process described in Chapter 11, "Using Oracle General Ledger." These tasks are the following:

1. Define the Key Accounting Flexfield structure, segments, segment values, and code combinations.

2. Define the Fiscal Calendar period types and periods.

3. Enable currencies and define rate types and conversion rates.

4. Create the set of books by assigning a name to a combination of the Key Accounting Flexfield, a Calendar, and a Currency.

5. Assign the set of books to the site or individual responsibilities.

SETTING UP THE ACCOUNT GENERATOR

The Workflow Account Generator is new in release 11 and is used to determine the correct balancing segment in the account distribution when AR generates finance charge transactions or currency exchange rate gains and losses. This setup step is required even if you will never charge finance charges or recognize currency gains or losses.

> **Note**
>
> The Workflow Account Generator in release 11 replaces Flexbuilder in release 10 of AR. Determining the balancing segment in finance charge and currency gain/loss transactions is the only place in AR where the Account Generator or Flexbuilder is used. All other account distributions use the AutoAccounting setup.

> **Tip**
>
> If you are setting up release 10.x of AR and must use Flexbuilder, copy the example in the *Oracle Flexfields* manual.

Oracle AR provides a default Account Generator Workflow process to derive the balancing segment. If this default process does not meet your requirements, you must use the Oracle Workflow Builder to create a new process.

> **Tip**
>
> You can copy the default AR process to a different name and then make modifications to the copy (see Chapter 22, "Using Oracle Workflow"). If you develop an alternative process, make sure to test it in a development database by running the GL Interface program.

If you change the Account Generator process, you must implement the process in AR for it to take effect. Follow this procedure to assign your newly named process:

1. Go to the Account Generator Process window.
2. Choose the appropriate Key Accounting Flexfield and structure for AR from the lists of values.
3. Specify the workflow item type as Replace Balancing Segment.
4. Specify the name of your new Account Generator Process.

> **Note**
>
> There is a new profile option in release 11 called Account Generator: Purge Runtime Data. It should be set to Yes unless you are debugging an Account Generator Process.

DEFINING THE ITEM FLEXFIELD

The Item Flexfield is required to transact and report item information. Usually, the Item Flexfield is defined in the Inventory application, and you should see Chapter 16, "Using Oracle Inventory," for a detailed description of this process.

> **Tip**
>
> After you have defined the Item Flexfield, there are several profile options that should be configured. These include the OE: Item Flexfield and the AR: Item Flexfield Mode profile options.

DEFINING ORGANIZATIONS

Organizations are often defined in another application (usually Inventory), and these definitions are shared with AR so you won't have to perform this task if it has already been done. If organizations have not been previously defined, follow these steps:

1. Define at least one organization. This step is required so that you can use the shared Inventory forms and tables without having Inventory fully installed.

2. Define the organization parameters for the organization. You need a three-character short code for the organization name and the account distribution defaults for item transactions.

3. Configure the profile option called OE: Item Validation Organization.

4. Finally and optionally, you can define items to be used by AR transactions.

DEFINING THE TERRITORY FLEXFIELD

Defining the Territory Flexfield is optional in AR. Territories are used in reports, and you should review the standard reports to see whether you have a business requirement to define the Territory Flexfield. You can refer to territories with salespeople, invoices, and customer purposes.

DEFINING THE SALES TAX LOCATION FLEXFIELD

AR provides six possible default Sales Tax Location Flexfield definitions for various combinations of city, county, state, province, and country. If none of these definitions is acceptable for your requirements, you can define a Location Flexfield by defining value sets, a structure, and segments as with any other key flexfield.

> **Note**
>
> If you are implementing Value Added Taxation (VAT), Oracle recommends the Country Flexfield structure. If you are implementing Sales Tax in the United States, Oracle recommends the State.County.City flexfield structure.

The Tax Account and Exemption qualifiers for the Flexfield should be set to the correct level for your business requirements. Double-check these levels for all classes of customers and taxing authorities. Usually, the State.County.City flexfield structure predefined by AR is adequate for United States-based sales tax calculations. However, assigning taxation boundaries on state, county, and city geographical boundaries or postal codes is not perfect. There are third-party vendor solutions that will compensate when geography doesn't work for every one of your customers.

Next, define tax locations and rates for each segment of the flexfield. AR uses these locations to validate the customer shipping address. Optionally, you can use the Tax Rate Interface program to load large quantities of locations.

DEFINING FLEXIBLE ADDRESS FORMATS

The standard AR address format is composed of a country, four lines of address, city, state, postal code, province, and county. If this format is adequate for your purposes, setting up flexible formats is optional.

In addition, AR provides address formats for Japanese, Northern European, Southern European, South American, and UK/Asia/Australia. You can define additional formats by defining other descriptive flexfield structures.

DEFINING COUNTIES AND TERRITORIES

Use the Maintain Countries and Territories window. Oracle ships AR with almost every country already defined.

> **Note**
>
> The territories mentioned here are not related to the territories enabled by the Territory Flexfield.

> **Tip**
>
> The AR responsibilities can't create new countries. To create a new country, you must use the sysadmin responsibility.

CREATING TRANSACTION FLEXFIELDS

The AutoInvoice program uses the Transaction Flexfield to uniquely identify incoming transactions to be invoiced through the ra_interface_lines table. If you are processing large volumes of transaction lines through AutoInvoice, the Transaction Flexfield is important for tuning because the validation portions of AutoInvoice must efficiently access rows in the ra_interface_lines table. Consider creating indexes on the segments to improve AutoInvoice performance.

> **Tip**
> Oracle support has a performance patch available to help if you are importing transactions from Oracle OE.

If Oracle OE is the source of your incoming transactions, the release 11 Transaction Flexfield is contained in the columns interface_line_attribute1 through interface_line_attribute10.

> **Tip**
> If Oracle OE is the transaction source, use the Manufacturing, Distribution, Sales, and Service Open Interfaces manual to determine how to set up the Transaction Flexfield. The documentation is found in the Order Entry/Shipping section of the manual. There is no documentation in the AR manuals.

If you are importing transactions from a non-Oracle system, the Transaction Flexfield should uniquely represent one interface line. You can use as many interface_line_attribute columns as necessary to achieve a unique combination.

Defining AutoCash Rule Sets

AutoCash rule sets are used to configure the AutoCash program. If you are not using AutoCash or QuickCash, this setup step is optional. Assign an AutoCash rule set to one or several customer profile classes.

> **Note**
> You can override the AutoCash rule assignments at the customer and customer site levels.

AutoCash rules are part of a default hierarchy and can be partially configured (in descending order) at the system options level, default customer profile, customer profile, customer, and customer site.

To define an AutoCash rule set, do the following:

- Name and describe the rule set in the AutoCash Rule Set form.
- Enter the type of discount option (earned, earned and unearned, or none).
- Indicate whether disputed items are to be included in calculating the customer balance.
- Indicate whether finance charges are to be included when calculating the customer balance.
- Define the automatic matching rule.
- Mark Unapplied or On-account if you use the oldest-invoice-first rule. This selection determines processing for remaining amounts if none of the rules in this rule set apply.

- Determine whether you will allow application of partial receipts.

- Use a sequence number to set the order of each rule in the rule set. Lower numbered rules are applied first.

- Select a rule from the available rules (apply to oldest first, clear the account, clear past due items, clear past due items by payment term, and match with invoice).

DEFINING QUICKCODES

Oracle AR defines more than 30 QuickCode types that you can update. Generally, you add values to expand the validation and available choices in a List of Values (QuickPick). QuickCodes can be grouped as follows:

Customer codes include address categories, business purpose codes, customer categories, customer class codes, demand classes, FOB codes, freight carriers, customer contact job titles and business titles, communication types, and document types.

Customer profile codes include account statuses, credit rating codes, and customer risk codes.

Transaction codes include adjustment reasons, approval types, batch status codes, Canadian province codes, credit memo and invoice reason codes, tax classifications, tax exemption reasons, tax type codes, statement message and text usage types, and special instruction values.

Collections codes include collector actions, collector follow-up action codes, customer response codes, call outcome codes, and line type codes for aging buckets.

Receipt codes include mandatory field prompt and reverse payment reason codes.

DEFINING AUTOINVOICE LINE ORDERING

Line-ordering rules can be used to affect the way the AutoInvoice program sequences invoice lines. The line ordering rules are a component of the AutoInvoice grouping rules. To create a line ordering rule, do the following:

- Name a rule in the line-ordering rules form.

- Enter effective dates and an optional description.

- Enter the priority of the transaction attribute in the sequence field. Lower numbers receive first priority.

- Enter the transaction attribute for this priority. Commonly used attributes are sales order and sales order line number, waybill number, and various components of the Transaction Flexfield.

- Indicate whether the attribute values should be processed in ascending or descending order.

PART

III

CH

13

DEFINING AUTOINVOICE GROUPING RULES

Definition of AutoInvoice grouping rules is an optional setup step and can be used to control how the AutoInvoice program assigns invoice numbers to imported invoice transactions. Several mandatory rules come seeded with the Oracle Applications. For example, only one currency or Bill To customer is allowed for each invoice.

AutoInvoice uses a four-level hierarchy to determine the sequence for applying grouping rules to imported transactions:

1. The rule attached to the transaction source.
2. The rule attached to the Bill To site for the transaction.
3. The rule attached to the customer profile class for the Bill To customer.
4. The rule specified as the default in the AR system options setup.

You can assign an invoice line ordering rule to each grouping rule.

DEFINING SYSTEM OPTIONS

Define system options to control the configuration for accounting, tax, miscellaneous parameters, invoices, and customers. For installations using multi-org, each operating unit gets its own set of system options, and you must define as many system options as you have operating units.

Definition of system options is a required setup task, but the following option values are optional:

- Unallocated revenue account (if the accounting method is not cash)
- AutoCash rule set
- Tax registration number
- Accounting flex tuning segment
- System items tuning segment
- SQL Trace
- Purge interface tables

DEFINING PAYMENT TERMS

AR provides two seeded payment terms: 30 NET and IMMEDIATE. If you need other terms or offer cash discounts, use the Define Payment Terms form to add other choices.

DEFINING ACCOUNTING RULES

Accounting rules are used to determine how to recognize revenue in multiple accounting periods. This setup task is optional, but if you use accounting rules, associate them with an invoicing rule. Invoicing rules determine when to record the receivable (in arrears or in advance).

If the accounting basis is cash, accounting and invoicing rules do not apply, and AutoInvoice rejects imported transactions with these kinds of rules.

MAINTAINING ACCOUNTING PERIODS

Before using AR, change the status of accounting periods in the AR calendar. Available period statuses are Not Open, Future Transactions Allowed, Open, Close Pending, and Closed. Periods with a Future Transactions Allowed status can receive transactions but cannot post those transactions. Open periods can write journal entries and post transactions. Not Open, Close Pending, and Closed periods cannot make journal entries, postings, or transactions.

A Close Pending or a Closed period can be reopened. The AR application checks for and prevents closure of a period with unposted transactions.

DEFINING AUTOACCOUNTING

AutoAccounting structures are used to determine how AR creates the GL accounting flexfield combinations for the revenue, receivables, freight, tax, suspense, unbilled revenue, and unearned revenue accounts. You can control how AutoAccounting determines the value of each segment of the Accounting Flexfield. For each of the seven AutoAccounting structures and for each segment in your GL Accounting Flexfield, you can enter a constant or select where AutoAccounting looks for the correct segment value.

AutoAccounting is capable of using the account distributions from the definitions for transaction types, salesreps, standard lines, and tax codes (on tax lines). The standard lines choice also gets account codes from the inventory item definition.

For example, if your GL Key Accounting Flexfield was defined as company.account.cost-center.region.productline, you could set up AutoAccounting to derive a revenue account as follows:

- The company and account segments come from the transaction type.
- The costcenter segment is a constant.
- The region segment comes from the sales representative.
- The productline comes from the inventory item (standard lines).

PART

III

CH

13

Installations using multi-org define AutoAccounting structures for each operating unit.

DEFINING CASH BASIS ACCOUNTING

If your system option is set to cash basis accounting, this step is required. Otherwise, the step should be skipped.

Cash basis accounting recognizes revenue when cash is actually received. If you sell to customers on credit but choose cash basis accounting, AR provides a system for creating invoices and tracking amounts due without making the accounting entries until cash is received.

DEFINING TRANSACTION TYPES

Use the transaction type definition to assign a default payment term, revenue account, tax account, freight account, and creation sign to a transaction. In addition, posting and receivables information can come from the transaction type. Define transaction types in the following order:

- Credit memo types
- Invoice, debit memo, and chargeback types
- Commitment types

AR comes with two transaction types already defined: invoice and credit memo. Installations using multi-org define transaction types for each operating unit.

If any AutoAccounting structures depend on transaction type, AR uses the Accounting Flexfield values you enter here. You can devise an elaborate series of transaction types to support multi-company, intercompany, and other account distribution requirements.

> **Tip**
>
> Before setting up a complex transaction type naming convention, consider how the transaction source system will generate the transaction type names. If the transaction source is Oracle OE, you might make the order entry process more complex.

> **Tip**
>
> If you define a transaction type of VOID with the open receivables and post-to GL fields set to No, you can easily cancel a transaction with no activity against it by changing the transaction type to VOID.

The Natural Application and Allow Overapplication fields add controls to determine how applications can affect the balance remaining on a transaction. For example, if Allow Overapplication is set to No and Natural Application is set to Yes, AR only enables you to make an application that brings the balance remaining on the original transaction closer to zero. These fields can improve control of the cash applications function but might be restrictive based on certain payment practices of your customers.

DEFINING TRANSACTION SOURCES

Transaction batches can be either manual or imported. Transaction source definitions are used to control transaction processing, transaction batch numbering, a default transaction type, and validation options for imported transactions. To properly define a transaction source for an imported transaction, you must understand precisely what data elements the import-processing program is placing in each column of the open interface table.

> **Tip**
>
> Much of the AutoInvoice validation logic is defined in the Other Information window. When you choose ID, your import program must supply the internal AR identifiers for the validation item. If you specify VALUE, AR uses the common values or names to look up the validation. Oracle OE generally uses IDs, and non-Oracle transaction sources generally use values.

> **Tip**
>
> If your implementation also includes Oracle OE and Inventory, use the shipment date as the transaction General Ledger date. This setup ensures that the revenue and cost of sales entries will be made in the same accounting period as required by generally accepted accounting principles (GAAP).

Installations using multi-org define transaction sources for each operating unit.

DEFINING COLLECTORS

Collectors are used by credit profile classes and are assigned to customers when the credit profile class is assigned. Several key reports can be sorted or grouped by collector, and the collector name and phone number can be printed on dunning letters.

SETTING ADJUSTMENT APPROVAL LIMITS

Adjustment limits are used in the Receipts, Adjustments, and Approve Adjustments windows. You can assign a control limit for each user for each currency.

DEFINING REMITTANCE BANKS

Banks have a shared definition with the Payables application and can be defined in either application. Define all banks and accounts that receive deposits from remittances. Each bank account refers to one currency, but you can enable multiple currency receipts in the account. In this case, because receipt and bank account currencies could differ, use manual payment reconciliation to avoid the exceptions that automatic reconciliation creates.

PART

III

CH

13

DEFINING DISTRIBUTION SETS

Distribution sets can speed data entry of accounting flexfield values for miscellaneous receipt transactions with a predefined accounting distribution. Distribution sets can be assigned to receivable activities with a type of miscellaneous cash.

> **Tip**
>
> The total of the distribution lines must equal 100 percent before you can save your work.

DEFINING RECEIVABLES ACTIVITIES

Use Receivables Activities to link accounting information to adjustments, finance charges, and miscellaneous cash transactions.

After you define a receivable activity, you cannot change its type, and it will appear in a list of values in the Receipts and Adjustment windows. The definition provides default accounting information and distributions to go with the activity. There are four kinds of activity types: adjustment, bank error, finance charges, and miscellaneous cash. The activity type determines whether it is a distribution set or an accounting flexfield value.

DEFINING RECEIPT CLASSES

Use a receipt class definition to specify the processing steps for manual or automatic receipts. Manual receipts must be either entered manually in the Receipts or Quick Cash windows or imported using AutoLockbox.

Automatic receipt definitions specify a remittance and clearance method and whether the definition requires confirmation. The processing steps include confirmation, remittance, and reconciliation. If you define a class to confirm and reconcile, you must also remit. If you choose No for all three steps, AR automatically creates your receipt as reconciled.

If you choose to require confirmation, also choose a remittance method to determine the accounts that AR uses for automatic receipts. Available methods are standard, factoring, standard and factoring, and no remittance.

AR uses the payment method assigned to a receipt class definition to determine the accounting distribution.

DEFINING PAYMENT METHODS

Define payment methods to account for receipt entries and determine a customer's remittance bank information. This task is a required setup step. AR requires a payment method to create automatic receipts through the Receipt Batches window. You can choose from five receipt rules: one per customer, one per customer and due date, one per site, one per invoice, and one per site and due date.

Defining Receipt Sources

Receipt batch sources are used to provide default values for the receipt class, payment method, and remittance bank account yields when you create a receipt batch. You can create receipt sources with the type value of manual. AR provides an automatic receipt source. You can set the last number of field on the automatic receipt source provided.

Installations using multi-org define receipt sources for each operating unit.

Defining Aging Buckets

Define aging buckets so that the statement report and the aging reports can group open invoices by age. Common aging buckets for a company with 30-day terms might be named Current, 30-59, 60-89, and Over 90. You can define four types of aging buckets: 4-bucket aging, 7-bucket aging, credit snapshot, and statement aging. Oracle provides a seeded 4-bucket aging definition.

- Current buckets display transaction values where the due date is less than the current date.

- Past Due buckets display transaction values where days past due falls into the day range specified.

- A Dispute Only bucket shows transaction values that are marked in dispute. You can have only one Dispute Only or Pending Adjustment entry per bucket definition.

- A Pending Adjustment Only bucket shows transaction values that are marked pending adjustment.

- A Dispute and Pending Adjustments bucket shows both disputed and pending transactions. Because you define only one dispute or pending entry per bucket definition, it is not necessary to specify day ranges.

- Future buckets show transactions due in the future as specified by the day range.

Defining Statement Cycles

Define a statement cycle to determine and control how statement reports are sent to customers. You choose a statement cycle when you print statement reports. Assign a customer to a particular statement cycle by giving the customer a profile class and assigning the statement cycle to the profile class.

Defining Statement Messages

Statement messages are optional and might print at the bottom of the statements. There are two types of standard messages: holiday and promotional. You can control when a message prints by assigning start and end dates. 255 characters is the maximum length of the standard message text.

Part

III

Ch

13

DEFINING DUNNING LETTERS AND SETS

If you send letters to your customers to advise them of past-due items and finance charges, consider defining dunning letters. AR provides three predefined dunning letters and ten user-defined dunning letters. The dunning letter files reside in the $AR_TOP/srw directory. There is a body and footer text file for each dunning letter definition. The dunning letter is composed of the remit-to address, the customer name and address, the text from the letter body file, a list of past-due invoices, and the text from the letter footer file.

You can create sets of dunning letters to show a progression of urgency and severity to the series of letters. Proceed carefully with automatic communications to your customers. Before designing a series of letters, consider customer setup data, transaction data, profile options, and system parameters to determine how the letter-writing program will process receipt grace days, items in dispute, finance charges, on-account receipts, and unapplied receipts. Dunning letter sets are assigned to groups of customers by assigning a set to a customer profile class.

DEFINING TERRITORIES

AR enables you to assign a territory flexfield value to salespeople, invoices, and customer business purposes. However, there are no reports or transactions processed by territory in the basic AR system. You must write your own reports to effectively use territory categorization of customers and transactions.

DEFINING SALESPEOPLE

Definition of salespeople is a required setup task. If AutoAccounting depends on the salesperson, consider making salesrep mandatory in the system options setup because the General Ledger accounts that you enter in the salesperson definition are used for revenue transactions.

Note

If you use Oracle Order Entry and AutoAccounting uses salesreps, note there are two levels of salesrep credit on the sales order. The order header salesrep is used to determine the receivables account distribution. The order line sales credits distribution is used to determine revenue account distribution.

Installations using multi-org define receipt sources for each operating unit.

SETTING THE PROFILE OPTIONS

Setting profile options is a required and important task. Many AR programs use profile options to determine fundamental logic in the way that they process transactions. Table 13.2 shows the profile options in AR that can affect user and system productivity.

Tip

Don't skip a profile option simply because it is optional. Some of the profile options can improve your corporate controls over cash and enhance user productivity.

TABLE 13.2 AR USER/SYSTEM PRODUCTIVITY PROFILE OPTIONS

Profile Option Name	Required?	Level*	Comment
AR: Automatic Contact Numbering	Yes	SARU	
AR: Close Periods - Run Effectiveness Report	Yes	SARU	
AR: Customer Merge Commit Size	No	SAR	Default is 1
AR: Customers - Enter Alternative Fields	No	SAR	Default is Yes
AR: Debug Level for PostBatch	No	SARU	
AR: Default Exchange Rate Type	No	SAR	
AR: Item Flexfield Mode	No	SARU	Default is segments
AR: Receipt Batch Source	Yes	SARU	Can be set by the user
AR: Sort Customer Reports by Alternative Fields	No	SAR	
AR: Transaction Batch Source	Yes	SAR	
AR: Transaction Flexfield Quick-Pick Attribute	No	SARU	
AR: Use Invoice Accounting for Credit Memos	Yes	SARU	Default is Yes
Default Country	No	SARU	
Journals: Display Inverse Rate	No	SARU	Default is No

Levels can be Site, Application, Responsibility, or User. The system administrator sets most profile options.

Another group of profile options helps you establish corporate controls and implement policy. These profile options appear in Table 13.3.

TABLE 13.3 AR CORPORATE CONTROL PROFILE OPTIONS

Profile Option Name	Required?	Level*	Comment
AR: Allow Update of Existing Sales Credits	No	SARU	
AR: Change Customer on Transaction	Yes	SARU	Default is Yes
AR: Change Customer Name	Yes	SARU	Default is Yes
AR: Create Bank Charges	No	SAR	Default is Yes

TABLE 13.3 CONTINUED

Profile Option Name	Required?	Level*	Comment
AR: GL Transfer Balance Test	Yes	SARU	Default is Yes
AR: Invoices with Un-confirmed Receipts	Yes	SARU	Default is None
AR: Override Adjustment Activity Account Option	Yes	SARU	Default is Yes
AR: Update Due Date	Yes	SARU	
Enable Transaction Codes	No	SAR	Default is No; only used in public sector AR
Sequential Numbering	No	SR	Default is Always Used
OE: Item Flexfield	No	S	
OE: Item Validation Organization	Yes	S	

Another group of profile options controls how the collections and cash receipts functions work. These options are listed in Table 13.4.

TABLE 13.4 AR PROFILE OPTIONS FOR COLLECTIONS AND CASH RECEIPTS

Profile Option Name	Required?	Level*	Comment
AR: Alternative Name Search	No	SAR	Default is Yes
AR: Cash - Allow Actions	Yes	SARU	
AR: Cash - Defaut Amount Applied	Yes	SARU	Can be set by user
AR: Commit Between Validation	No	SARU	Default is Yes
AR: Dunning Letter Remit To Address Label Size	No	SAR	
AR: Enable Cross Currency	No	SAU	Default is No
AR: Zengin Character Set	No	S	

There is one profile option that influences the invoicing function. It is shown in Table 13.5.

TABLE 13.5 AR PROFILE OPTIONS FOR INVOICING

Profile Option Name	Required?	Level*	Comment
AR: Show Billing Number	No	SAR	

Finally, several important profile options affect the way the system handles taxation. These options are listed in Table 13.6.

TABLE 13.6 AR PROFILE OPTIONS FOR TAXATION

Profile Option Name	Required?	Level*	Comment
Tax: Allow Ad Hoc Changes	Yes	SARU	Default is Yes
Tax: Allow Manual Tax Lines	Yes	SARU	Default is Yes
Tax: Allow Override of Customer Exemptions	Yes	SARU	Default is No
Tax: Allow Override of Tax Code	Yes	SARU	Default is No
Tax: Calculate Tax on Credit Memos	No	SAR	
Tax: Inventory Item for Freight	No	SARU	Can be set by the user
Tax: Invoice Freight as Revenue	No	SARU	Can be set by the user
Tax: Use Tax Vendor	No	SAR	Default is Yes

DEFINING TAX CODES AND RATES

AR supports two kinds of revenue-based taxes: VAT and sales tax. Generally, do not try to enable both taxation types in the same organization. Both tax types require you to create tax codes and rates. Tax codes can be assigned to customers at all levels of address and Bill To or Ship To business purposes. A tax code can also be assigned to a product and to standard memo lines.

If your system option tax method is VAT, define a code and rate for each tax authority. Declare a default tax code in the system options setup.

If your system option tax method is Sales Tax, you need at least one tax code with a type of Location for each date range. When you enter the accounting flexfield value for the location type, it might not be updated, but you can set up various date ranges for several accounts if the account distribution changes. The location code does not have a rate associated with it but creates a link for the tax calculation programs to the rates.

> **Tip**
>
> To control the tax calculation, many users set up tax codes of Exempt, Intercompany, or International with a tax rate of 0 percent. Assign these tax codes to customers with no tax liability.

PART

III

CH

13

Installations using multi-org define tax codes and rates for each operating unit.

DEFINING CUSTOMER PROFILE CLASSES

Customer profile classes enable you to group and categorize customers. Unless set at the customer, customer site, or customer business purpose level, many configuration parameters default to the customer from the profile class. This step is required, but AR provides a default profile class. Customer profile information can be grouped into the following seven major categories:

- *Credit parameters* enable you to record a default collector and credit limit tolerance percentage. You can also activate new order credit checking or order hold by Oracle OE.

- *Terms parameters* enable you to record a default payment term for customers with this profile class. If the override box is checked, you are enabled to change the terms code during transaction entry. Discounts for prompt payment and receipts can be adjusted by entries in the Grace Days fields.

- *Receipt parameters* control the number of clearing days, the AutoCash rule set, the Match Receipt rule, the Remaining Amount rule, and the Include Disputed Items for customers with this profile class.

- *Statement parameters* determine whether customers receive statements and what statement cycle is used.

- *Finance Charge parameters* determine whether customer accounts are charged interest on outstanding balances.

- *Dunning parameters* determine whether the customer receives dunning letters when invoices, debit memos, and chargebacks in the account become past due. If you check the Send Letters box, you can also enter a Dunning Letter Set for this customer class.

- *Invoicing parameters* control how tax is printed on the invoice and which grouping rule is used for customers in this class. If you don't specify a Tax Printing value, AR uses the value from the System Options, or if that value is not set, AR defaults to the Total Tax Only value. Detail or summary consolidated invoice billing can also be specified.

Finally, customer profile classes are currency-sensitive. Use the profile class amounts region of the form to enter the currency, currency rates and limits, minimum invoice balance for finance charges, minimum dunning amount, and credit limit.

DEFINING CUSTOMERS

Customer data may be entered into the AR application manually or through the customer application program interface (API). The API is discussed later in this chapter in the section called "Converting Data for Major Entities." If you have more than about 2000 customers to enter into AR, consider using the API to load them programmatically.

However, if you have a smaller number of customers to enter, navigate to the Customer or Customer Summary window to begin manually defining a set of customer records. Customers are a major data entity in the ERP applications, and there are five major areas to fully define a customer.

- *General.* This area includes the customer name, customer number, and a few global fields that set defaults for the rest of the customer records that might represent your customer's different addresses or business purposes.

- *Addresses*. You may have multiple addresses for each customer record. In the address record, you have the opportunity to override customer profile options that you attached to the customer at the general level.

- *Business purposes*. You may have multiple business purposes for each customer address. For example, an address may be both a Bill To and a Ship To customer site. However, it might not be a site that receives dunning notices. The business purposes recognized by the system include Bill To, Ship To, Statements, Dunning, Legal, and Marketing. Also on the business purpose records, you have the opportunity to set default values for carrier, demand class, fob term, freight terms, inventory location, order type, payment terms, price list, sales territory, ship partial indicator, and tax code.

- *Contacts*. You may have multiple contacts for each customer and also multiple contacts for each customer address. You may assign a contact to a specific business purpose.

- *Telephone numbers*. You can assign one primary phone number to the customer, and you may have multiple phone numbers for each contact.

The data storage structures for defining customers are quite flexible and can handle a wide variety of organizational and corporate relationships. However, most common problems that users have with the way AR handles customers are caused by the way AR uses the customer name. AR requires the name of the customer to be unique in the same way most legacy systems have a unique customer number. The unique name facilitates easy inquiry but can cause problems for customers with many sites. In release 11 of AR you can activate an alternative names feature by setting the profile option AR: Customers-Enter Alternate Fields to Yes. That feature gives you an alternative name on both the customer record and the customer address record. However, you will still want to test the system to make sure you have access to the alternative name whenever your business requirements dictate.

Tip

Use the online help as you enter customer data to get a precise definition of each field's purpose. This is one of the fastest and surest ways to understand field-level requirements.

PART

III

CH

13

In addition, there are other data records you can create to further define your customers. You can add these three items from the Customers or Customer Summary window.

- *Relationships*. If you define relationships among any of your customers, you are defining a one-way or reciprocal relationship to control payments and commitments. For example, you can define a one-way relationship where a parent customer could pay the invoices you send to a child customer.

- *Banks.* You can assign bank accounts to customers. If you are using the Automatic Receipts function, this feature facilitates transfer of funds from the customer bank accounts to your remittance bank account.

- *Payment Methods.* If you are using the Automatic Receipts function, you can attach payment methods to the customer. The payment methods define the processing steps for the Automatic Receipts function.

Tip

Customer entry is a tempting place to take a false shortcut because most fields are not required. The AR application provides lots of customer related fields so that you can set up defaults to speed up transaction processing. If you leave the optional customer fields blank, you will have to supply the data on each transaction, and that can be inefficient. If you set up customers completely, the transaction processing system will usually work more efficiently for you.

DEFINING REMIT-TO ADDRESSES

Remit to addresses print on invoices, statements, and dunning letters and designate where customers should send payments. Each remit-to address is associated with a state, country, and postal code combination. The bill-to address is used to determine the remit to address.

Tip

Make sure to declare a default remit to address by selecting DEFAULT from the list of values in the State field. If you do this, when you set up new customers in the future, you won't have to check whether the Bill To address fits an already defined state, country, and postal code combination.

Because a geographical association is the only way AR can determine the remit to address, many companies make an extension to allow assignment of remit to addresses to a customer. Briefly, the specification for the extension is as follows:

- Define a descriptive flexfield on the business purpose for the customer. Make it conditional to be required when the business purpose is Bill To.

- Load the desired remit to address into the descriptive flexfield for each customer.

- Write a post processor program to run in a report set behind the AutoInvoice program. The postprocessor program should replace the remit to address ID selected by AutoInvoice with the one stored on the Bill To business purpose flexfield. Remember, this data is org-specific in multi-org implementations. The remit to addresses are stored along with the customer addresses in the ra_addresses table (where customer_id = -1).

Installations using multi-org define remit to addresses for each operating unit.

DEFINING CUSTOMER RELATIONSHIPS

Applications of receipts can be restricted to related customers only when you set the system option Allow Payment of Unrelated Invoices to No. If you choose this option, consider defining customer relationships to allow application of receipts to related customer invoices. Relationships can be one-way (a parent can pay a child's invoice) or reciprocal.

> **Note**
>
> The application-level profile option OE: Customer Relationships controls whether relationships are enforced when entering sales orders. Set it to Yes to make sure only related customer addresses are available in Bill To and Ship To fields.

DEFINING CUSTOMER BANKS

If you create automatic receipts, define customer banks and bank accounts; otherwise, this task is optional. Usually, an automatic receipt requires an agreement between you and your customer.

DEFINING LOCKBOXES

If you use the AutoLockbox program to process receipts, define at least one lockbox. The lockbox definition controls the receipt batch size, the GL date, the currency exchange rate type, the receipt method, the billing location requirement, the match receipts by method, the AutoAssociate technique, and unapplied amounts.

DEFINING THE TRANSMISSION FORMAT

If you use the AutoLockbox program to process receipts, define the transmission data file format. The format definition controls the import of receipt information from the bank into AR. AR provides two standard formats that can be modified to conform to your bank's format. The two formats are SQL*Loader control files and are named ardeft.ctl and arconv.ctl. The ardeft.ctl file processes a standard Bank Administration Institute (BAI) file.

DEFINING RECEIPT PROGRAMS

If you use automatic receipts, define the receipt programs that will be used to send documents to customers and remittance banks. AR provides sample receipt and remittance document programs. You might want to copy the sample programs as a template for your own. If you create your own program, its name must be eight characters or less.

DEFINING UNIT OF MEASURE CLASSES AND UNITS OF MEASURE

Unit of Measure classes and Units of Measure definitions are described in Chapter 16. See that chapter for a complete discussion of units of measure.

PART

III

CH

13

> **Note** AR does not perform unit of measure conversions, and the price is not affected if the unit of measure is changed.

DEFINING MEMO LINES

Standard memo lines are predefined lines for debit memos, on-account credits, and invoices. There are four types of lines:

- Line
- Freight
- Tax
- Miscellaneous charges

If AutoAccounting structures use standard memo lines, the revenue, freight, AutoInvoice clearing, tax, unbilled receivable, unearned revenue, and receivable account segments can come from this definition.

You can optionally enter a standard invoicing rule, accounting rule, tax code, unit list price, and unit of measure for each standard memo line.

Installations using multi-org define memo lines for each operating unit.

DEFINING TAX EXCEPTIONS

Tax exceptions can be used to assign specific tax rates to products shipped to a specific address location. Do not assign tax codes to customers or customer sites if you use tax exceptions.

Installations using multi-org define tax exceptions for each operating unit.

DEFINING TAX EXEMPTIONS

Tax exemptions can be used to stop taxation for customers or items from specific tax codes. To use customer or product exemptions, set the system options for tax to Yes to allow these transactions.

> **Note** To exempt a customer or item from all taxes, assign the customer or item to a tax code with a zero tax rate.

Installations using multi-org define tax exemptions for each operating unit.

DEFINING DOCUMENT SEQUENCES

You can optionally assign unique document numbers to comply with some countries' requirements to account for each transaction and the document associated with it. These document numbers are in addition to the invoice and memo numbers generated by the system. To enable document sequence numbering, set the sequential numbering profile option to either Always or Partially Used. Then define and assign categories and sequences for each activity that you use.

CONVERTING DATA FOR MAJOR ENTITIES

Before processing transactions, you can choose to load three major data entities from legacy systems. AR has open interfaces to accomplish these tasks. Because each open interface requires programming, the effort to manually enter the data might be less than the effort to extract data from legacy systems, map data elements to the AR interface tables, load data into the interfaces, and balance the transactions. The major entities are as follows:

- Customers
- Open Balances

CREATING OR MODIFYING CUSTOMERS

AR provides an open interface program to help convert customer records from other systems. The open interface program can process a one-time conversion of legacy data, or it can be used to maintain and synchronize the Oracle AR customers with another system. If you have more than 2,500 to 3,000 customers, consider automatic conversion of historical data. If you have fewer customers, consider entering them manually in the Enter Customers form.

> **Tip**
>
> You should complete the setup tasks for the AR application before loading the customers. The open interface program uses the setup data to validate incoming customer data.

If you choose to convert customer data using the open interface program, use the following process:

- Load your data into the five customer interface tables.
- Run the customer interface program from the Submit Requests window.
- Analyze the Customer Transfer Report to resolve problems of records that did not load.

The customer interface tables include the following:

- ra_customer_interface
- ra_contact_phones_interface

- ra_customer_banks_interface
- ra_customer_profiles_interface
- ra_cust_pay_method_interface

The automated customer interface validates many of the columns in the interface tables and does not import records that do not pass the validation described in the customer interface table description documentation.

If you enter customers manually, only the customer name, the customer number, and an address are required. However, the customer definition provides defaults for many transactions and enables you the specific control to adjust the system behavior and activate AR functions by customer.

Tip

Entering a complete customer record when you create the customer might seem like a lot of work, but it is more efficient than creating the record with minimum information and making several updates.

Note

If you implement Oracle Order Entry, the customer definition is shared between AR and OE. Consider the effect of each field on the OE application.

CREATING OPEN BALANCES

Open balances can be created from legacy system data with the AutoInvoice program. To use this interface, you must insert rows into the ra_interface_lines_all table and then run the AutoInvoice program. The programmer must consider the AutoInvoice setup to properly map legacy data to the interface table columns. Many columns are validated against setup data, and AutoInvoice produces errors if validations fail. Refer to the AutoInvoice validation table and column descriptions to determine the proper values for the interface table.

Other conversion techniques include the following:

- Many companies define special transaction types specifically for the one-time conversion of their open invoices, credit memos, and debit memos.
- Because the actual invoice was created and printed and revenue was recognized on the legacy system, many companies do not convert line-item details. Because AR is only concerned with the amount receivable for the total invoice, a single-line invoice for

the invoice total is adequate for open balances. There are no revenue, tax, or balance sheet issues, and converting a total amount is enough to activate AR's collection and cash receipt functions.

- AR creates a sales journal for the revenue, tax, and receivable amounts when you load open items. Generally, this sales journal is not needed or desirable because the legacy system already updated the General Ledger when the item was originally created. Consider creating the open items in an accounting period earlier than the first live transactions. In this way, you can easily identify and reverse (or delete) the unnecessary sales journal entry.

Tip

Make sure you coordinate with the owners of the GL accounting calendar to open the accounting periods you need for data conversion. When the first GL period is opened, it is not possible to open earlier periods.

CREATING TRANSACTION HISTORY

Conversion of transaction history (closed items) is an optional implementation task and should be justified by business requirements. Closed items are created just as open items, discussed previously. Then AutoCash is used to simulate receipt history and close the items.

PROCESSING TRANSACTIONS

AR uses three workbenches to organize transaction processing:

- Use the Transactions workbench to create and maintain invoices, memos, on-account credits, chargebacks, and commitments.
- Use the Receipts workbench to create batches and enter, apply, correct, and delete receipts. You also use this workbench to create adjustments and chargebacks.
- Use the Collections workbench to assist credit and collection activity. You can view customer account balances, place credit holds, place items in dispute, record call history, and view dunning history.

CREATING INVOICES TRANSACTIONS

Invoices in AR can be created manually or automatically. The AR system can process invoices from many sources, including Oracle and non-Oracle Order Entry and customer order fulfillment systems.

MANUALLY CREATING INVOICES OR MEMOS

To manually create a receivable transaction, use the Transactions window and create a batch of transactions or a single invoice or memo. First, enter the transaction header information, including date, currency, transaction type, Bill To customer, terms, salesperson, remit-to address, and header freight information. Next, enter line-item details, including items, quantity, tax code, line freight, and price.

When you complete the transaction, AR performs a validation to make sure the transaction conforms to the requirements of that transaction type. For example, the GL date must be in an open or future enterable period, taxes must be correct, freight lines must have account distributions, and the sign of the transaction must agree >with the creation sign of the transaction type.

RUNNING AUTOINVOICE FOR BATCHES OF IMPORTED TRANSACTIONS

The AutoInvoice program can be used to create large batches of invoices without data entry. The AutoInvoice program processes data in three tables:

- ra_interface_lines_all
- ra_interface_sales_credits
- ra_interface_distributions

Someone must write a program to load the invoice data into these tables. The table and column descriptions for the interface tables in the Oracle documentation show the requirements and validation for each column. If you are using Oracle's Order Entry module, a few setup steps activate the interface.

PROCESSING RECEIPT TRANSACTIONS

In release 11, you can use the Receipts Workbench to apply cash receipt transactions and update your customers' open balance items. Because customers often pay amounts other than the full open item balance, the Receipts Workbench is able to make transactions for adjustments, chargebacks, manual receipts, and automatic receipts.

APPLYING RECEIPTS MANUALLY

You can apply cash receipts to open AR items, including invoices, debit memos, credit memos, chargebacks, deposits, guarantees, and on-account credits. To apply receipts, use the receipts or receipts summary window and a receipt type of Cash. Enter information about the receipt, including receipt number, currency, amount, GL date, and payment method. Identify the customer by entering a transaction number or customer name and Bill To location.

Because the payment method determines the default bank account, verify whether this account is correct or select an alternative account assigned to that payment method.

If the customer is paying many open items, use mass-apply techniques. If you choose Apply, AR marks for application open items until the full amount of the receipt is consumed. If you choose Preview, AR displays a list of open items, and you can mark which transactions are to be closed.

Tip Sort the list of open items to match the customer remittance details. Many customer AP systems print the remittance advice in document number order or date order.

If the customer is paying one or just a few open items, choose applications in the receipts window and select the transaction from the list of values window. Repeat for all transactions. To place an amount on account, enter On Account in the transaction number field.

AR uses the transaction type of the debit item and several user profile options to control the application process. If the transaction type does not allow overapplication, you cannot enter a transaction that would reverse the sign of the debit item. If the transaction type specifies natural application only, you must enter transactions that always progress the open item balance toward zero.

PROCESSING LOCKBOX TRANSACTIONS AUTOMATICALLY

If you can get a data file of lockbox activity from your bank, you can use AutoLockbox to eliminate manual data entry for cash receipt transactions. The AutoLockbox process involves three steps:

- Use a SQL*Loader script to import the bank data file.
- Run the AutoLockbox validation program. Validated data is transferred to the QuickCash tables.
- Submit the Post QuickCash process to actually update the customer balances and open items.

Tip Evaluate your cash application process carefully before implementing AutoLockbox. If your customers make lots of deductions or if manual cash applications takes only an hour a day (2,000 to 3,000 invoices per month), you might not save enough work to make this process worth automating.

CREATING CHARGEBACKS

You can create chargeback transactions during receipt processing. A *chargeback* is a new debit item that you can assign to a customer when you close an old debit item. This transaction is effective when the customer pays an invoice short, you want to clear the original invoice, but you believe the customer still owes the full amount in the account.

To create a chargeback while entering receipts, choose Chargebacks, enter the transaction type and amount, and change the account distribution provided by the transaction type if necessary. Complete the chargeback by adding a due date, a reason, and comments.

CREATING ADJUSTMENTS

You can create manual adjustments to invoices, debits, chargebacks, on-account credits, deposits, and guarantees in your customer accounts. Adjustments are subject to approval. Subject to approval limits, you can approve adjustments that you create.

An adjustment can have one of the following four approval statuses:

- An *approved* status is complete, and the debit or credit item is updated.
- A *more research* status is a hold status waiting on new information.
- A *rejected* status closes the item without updating the debit or credit item.
- A *pending approval* status indicates the adjustment is outside the approval limits of its creator and must be processed by a user with greater authority.

> **Note**
>
> If the transaction type of the item to be adjusted does not permit overapplication, you cannot create an adjustment that will reverse the sign of the debit item.

You can apply an adjustment to an entire invoice or select an adjustment type for the line, miscellaneous charges, freight, or tax. To create an adjustment during receipts processing, choose adjustments, enter an activity, choose an adjustment type, and enter an amount. To complete the adjustment, enter the GL date, enter the adjustment date, and adjust the account distribution if necessary.

Also, you can create automatic adjustments when you run the AutoAdjustment program. You can specify selection criteria to limit adjustments to a specific remaining amount, due date, customer, or transaction type.

PERFORMING COLLECTION ACTIVITIES

In addition to billing and cash receipts, the third major activity of the AR application is to support collection efforts. AR uses the Collections workbench to organize and assist collection activities. You can record calls and customer contacts, produce customer contact documents, and analyze a customer's account with inquiry screens and reports.

RECORDING CALLS

When you contact a customer about scheduling a payment for any open item, you can record the details of the conversation in the Customer Calls form. For example, this form can document items in dispute or promises to pay past-due items.

> **Tip**
>
> It is a good idea to record customer contacts and phone numbers in the customer master record. This information assists you when contacting the customer.

For each call, enter the collector, the customer name, the contact, the customer's response, the outcome of the call, and additional notes. If the customer makes a commitment to pay, enter the promise information to improve the accuracy of cash forecast reports. Finally, enter a call action to schedule future collection actions.

ANALYZING A CUSTOMER ACCOUNT

You can review open balances and activity in a specific account in several ways. There is an Account Summary window that quickly shows the total amount overdue. For more details, you can drill down in the Account Details window, which shows all past due items. In the Customer Accounts window, you can view account balances by aging bucket and drill down to view detailed items in each aging bucket.

In addition, there are several reports of interest:

- The Past Due Invoice report shows information about past due invoices, debit memos, deposits, chargebacks, and guarantees. This report does not include on-account or unapplied cash. Review the On Account/Unapplied Payments Balance report for these items.

- The Account Status report lists all open items and the total balance due in your functional currency.

- The Customer Credit Snapshot report shows key customer setup values, open-item aging, credit history, a 12-month summary, and recent transactions.

- The Aged Trial Balance listings show account details of open items and can be run by range of customers, by amount, by collector, and by salesperson. Four- and seven-bucket aging reports are available.

PLACING AN ACCOUNT ON CREDIT HOLD

If you are also using the Oracle Order Entry application, you can place a customer account on credit hold. When an account is on hold, you can still create transactions for that customer in AR, but you prevent creation of new sales order and shipping transactions for that customer. Place or release a credit hold from the Customer Accounts window. If you place and release a lot of credit holds, use the Credit Hold report to summarize the customers on credit hold, the balances due and past due by currency, contact information, and days on hold.

CREATING STATEMENTS

AR can produce specific statements for each customer billing location. Each customer can be assigned a statement cycle in his credit profile. The statement cycle controls when a statement will be produced. You can print a statement, a draft statement, or reprint a statement from the Print Statements window.

PART

III

CH

13

Note   Because the statement is designed for a preprinted form, AR creates the formatted output file but does not route it to the printer immediately. You must issue the printer command for your computer's operating system when proper forms are in the printer.

Tip

Many Oracle users are using print output format programs to laser print or fax statements and avoid the need for preprinted forms.

CREATING DUNNING LETTERS

Some AR users send dunning letters in addition to, or instead of, statements to advise customers of past-due items. When you submit the Dunning Letter Generate program, AR prints dunning letters using dunning letter sets, customers, and collectors that meet the selection criteria.

BALANCING THE AR APPLICATION INTERNALLY

Use the following six reports to collect the reconciliation totals. Make sure all of these reports are created for a consistent set of dates:

- Use an Aging report to determine beginning and ending balances.
- Use the Transaction Register to obtain the total of transactions.
- Run the Adjustment Register report to obtain the sum of adjustments for the period.
- Check out the Invoice Exceptions report to get the sum of invoice exceptions.
- Use the Applied Receipts Register to obtain the total of receipts.
- Run the Unapplied Receipts Register to determine the amount of unapplied receipts.

Use this formula to verify that your AR balances are correct:

Period Beginning Balance + Transactions + or - adjustments - Invoice Exceptions - Applied Receipts - Unapplied Receipts = Period Ending Balance

BALANCING THE SUBLEDGER TO THE GENERAL LEDGER

The AR application is a subledger to the Oracle General Ledger application. You can reconcile and balance the two applications by verifying reports and constructing a progression of transaction totals from the beginning balances of an accounting period to the ending balances. All transactions in AR are date-stamped with a GL date.

Tip

Make sure the AR reports you use to reconcile to the General Ledger are all run for the correct accounting period dates. Use the Detail By Account option to conveniently group amounts for reconciliation purposes.

Use the Sales Journal and Receipt Journal reports to verify the General Ledger transfer process. Look at the Unposted Items Report to determine whether AR is holding transactions that cannot be sent to the General Ledger.

USING OPEN INTERFACES IN THIS AR

The AR application has six major Application Program Interfaces (API):

- Inbound billing transactions
- Inbound customer records
- Inbound bank receipts
- Outbound update to the General Ledger
- Inbound sales tax rates
- The Tax Vendor Extension

Many of these Application Program Interfaces require some programming to use them. Typically, an inbound interface consists of a SQL*Loader program to load the external data into one or more database tables that mirror the record layout of the external data. Also, a PL/SQL program is used to validate the external data, clean up the external data, and migrate it to the Oracle Applications open interface tables. In addition, you can also program one or more operating system scripts and reports to control the interface, provide a user interface to the interface, and provide an audit trail of records processed.

INCOMING TRANSACTIONS TO BE INVOICED

AR uses three tables to store data for processing by the AutoInvoice program:

- ra_interface_lines
- ra_interface_salescredits
- ra_interface_distributions

The ra_interface_lines table uses the Line Transaction Flexfield as its primary key to uniquely identify each invoice line. If you are using Oracle Order Entry as the source of the incoming transaction, the Transaction Flexfield uses the first 10 interface_line_attribute columns.

PART
III

CH
13

> **Tip**
>
> This setup is documented in the Order Entry chapter of a reference manual titled *Oracle Manufacturing, Distribution, Sales and Service Open Interfaces Manual*. This manual is also found in the file mfgopen.pdf on the release 11 documentation disk.

If you are processing many rows through this interface, it is a good idea to create indexes on the columns of the Transaction Flexfield and the corresponding columns in the ra_customer_trx_lines and ra_customer_trx tables to improve performance.

IMPORTING AND MAINTAINING CUSTOMER RECORDS

The Customer API can be used to initially load a large quantity of customers on system startup, or it can create and update customer records as a slave to a non-Oracle customer master. To use the customer API, load data into five interface tables:

- ra_customer_interface
- ra_contact_phones_interface
- ra_customer_banks_interface
- ra_customer_profiles_interface
- ra_cust_pay_method_interface

When you submit the customer interface program, the data in these tables is validated and transferred to the customer tables as if it had been entered by a data entry function. Each time the customer interface API is run, AR creates the Customer Interface Transfer report to document records processed and show validation errors.

> **Note**
> The interface does not create location combinations for foreign locations (when the country code is not the same as the country code defined in your system options).

IMPORTING BANK RECEIPTS

If your bank can produce a data file of lockbox cash receipts, the AutoLockbox API processes receipt data that you load into the ar_payments_interface table. Each row in this table can accommodate payments for eight invoices and amounts. An overflow record type is available if your customer is paying more than eight transactions.

> **Note**
> AutoLockbox does not process miscellaneous or non-invoice cash receipts.

Each time the AutoLockbox API runs, you automatically receive the AutoLockbox Execution Report. This report shows invalid transactions as follows:

- The receivable item does not match the currency of the receipt.
- The receivable item belongs to an unrelated customer.
- The receivable item is not an invoice, debit memo, chargeback, credit memo, deposit, or on-account credit.

- The receivable item is a duplicate or is invalid for this customer.
- The receivable item has already been selected for automatic receipt.
- The installment number or the receivable item is invalid.

Updating the General Ledger

The General Ledger interface is an outbound interface from AR to transfer Sales and Cash journal entry data from the AR subledger to the General Ledger. This API places the journal entry data into the gl_interface table in the General Ledger. If you are using the Oracle General Ledger, no programming is necessary to implement this interface.

> **Tip**
>
> You can choose to run journal import as part of the transfer of AR data to the gl_interface table. The journal entry name contains the word "Receivables" and the concurrent process request ID number for the transfer job.

Importing Sales Tax Rate Data

The Sales Tax Rate interface is an API to load locations and tax rates into AR. Because there are about 60,000 different sales tax rates in the United States, if you have many customers in a wide variety of tax locations, you might want to buy a subscription service to get data file updates to maintain current tax data. This API processes data stored in the ar_tax_interface table and AR provides two SQL*Loader control files, aravp.ctl and arvertex.ctl, to help with the loading process.

You can run the interface in one of three modes:

- Load all data in the ar_tax_interface table.
- Load changed data only.
- Review mode prints the report without actually loading any data from the API.

Using the Tax Vendor Extension

The tax vendor extension is an interface to allow integration with an external tax calculation program. The tax extension program is called whenever AR computes a tax in any of the following windows, programs, or workbenches:

- OE Sales Order Workbench
- OE Sales Acknowledgement Report
- AR AutoInvoice
- AR Transaction Workbench
- AR Copy Transactions

- AR Credit Memos Window
- AR Adjustments Window

The tax extension passes the AR data to the vendor programs and returns a tax rate or tax amount from the vendor's program. AR is then able to use the returned information to construct the appropriate tax lines and accounting information.

> **Note** If you are implementing the tax extension in the U.S., select State.County.City or State.City for your Sales Tax Location Flexfield structure.

UNDERSTANDING KEY REPORTS

The AR application provides more than 100 reports to assist with accounting, collections, execution, printing documents, listings, tax reporting, and miscellaneous activities. In addition, because they have a variety of run parameters and sort sequences, many reports serve multiple purposes.

Accounting reports (see Table 13.7) assist with recording the history of transactions, balancing the AR subledger internally, and recording entries into the General Ledger.

TABLE 13.7 ACCOUNTING REPORTS

Report Name	Description
Adjustment Approval Report	Use this report to see information about transaction adjustments.
Adjustment Register	Review approved adjustments with this report. This is one of the reports used to balance the system.
Aging - By Account Report	This is a variation of the aging reports to show open items in summary or detail by accounting flexfield value. This is one of the reports used to balance the system.
Applied Receipts Register	This report shows all activity of a receipt. This is one of the reports used to balance the system.
Automatic Receipt Batch Management	This report is used to review the status of Automatic Receipt Batches.
Automatic Receipts Awaiting Confirmation	This report lists automatic receipts that have been formatted and have been assigned a payment method with a receipt class with Require Confirmation.
Bad Debt Provision Report	This report can calculate a bad debt exposure from the percent collectable value in the customer profile class.

TABLE 13.7   CONTINUED

Report Name	Description
Bank Risk Report	If a receipt has been factored but the collection risk has not been eliminated, it can be included on this report.
Billing and Receipt History	Use this report to see a detailed list of transactions for a date range.
Billing History Report	This report shows a summary of transactions in an account.
Commitment Balance Report	This is a summary listing of information about commitments.
Cross Currency Exchange Gain / Loss Report	If you have set up AR to use cross-currency settlements, use this report to review detailed information about these transactions.
Customer Balance Revaluation	This shows customers with negative balances for use in some countries where these balances must be adjusted.
Discount Projection Report	This report calculates and estimates your potential exposure when customers take discounts.
Invoice Exception Report	This report shows transactions where Open Receivables is equal to No. These transactions do not appear on an aging report but are on the transaction register.
Invoices Posted to Suspense Report	This is a listing of invoices where the revenue account is a suspense account.
Journal Entries Report	Use this report to reconcile the AR subledger to the General Ledger.
Journal with GL Details Report	Use this report to show journal entries for specific transactions in AR.
Miscellaneous Transaction Report	List miscellaneous receipts activity with this report.
Notes Receivable Report	This reports general information about notes receivable.
Open Items Revaluation Report	Use this report to calculate and revalue open items for currency exchange fluctuations.
Other Applications Report	This report shows information for invoices against guarantees, invoices against deposits, and credit memos for these transactions.
Projected Gains / Losses Report	Use this report to calculate potential gains and losses for currency revaluation.
Receipt Analysis - Days Late	This is a report to show customer payment patterns.
Receipt Register	This is a listing of receipts for a date range.
Receipts Awaiting Bank Clearance	This report includes automatic and manual receipts that have been remitted but have not cleared the bank, and the receipt class requires clearance.

PART

III

CH

13

TABLE 13.7   CONTINUED

Report Name	Description
Receipts Awaiting Remittance	This is a listing of receipts that have been confirmed, and the receipt class requires remittance.
Receipts Journal Report	This report lists the details of the receipts that have been included in a journal entry.
Remittance Batch Management	This is a listing to show the status of remittance batches.
Reversed Notes Receivable	Use this report to see information about reversed notes receivable.
Reversed Receipts Report	This report lists information about receipt reversals.
Sales Journal by Customer Report	This report lists all transactions by customer.
Sales Journal by GL Account	This report is similar to the transaction register by GL account. Use this report when you balance the AR aging to the General Ledger.
Transaction Reconciliation Report	This is a report to show GL journal entry lines created from specific AR transactions.
Transaction Register	Use this register to verify that postable items are included in the sales journal. This is one of the key reports used to balance the system.
Unapplied Receipts Register	This report lists the details of on-account and unapplied receipts.
Unposted Items Report	Use this report to see items not posted to the General Ledger for a date range.

COLLECTION REPORTS

Collection reports (see Table 13.8) assist with the collection, tracking, and management of open items.

TABLE 13.8 COLLECTION REPORTS

Report Name	Description
Account Status Report	For each customer, this report lists all open debit and credit items in the functional currency.
Aging - 4 and 7 Bucket Reports	The bucket reports are really a series of reports. The series shows open items in either four or seven aging buckets. The report can be sorted by customer, transaction type, balance due, or salesperson.
Call Actions Report	This report shows a detailed list of actions entered by collectors in the Customer Calls window. Review this report to see which actions require follow-up.
Collection Effectiveness Indicators	Use this report to track customer payment history and patterns.

TABLE 13.8 COLLECTION REPORTS

Report Name	Description
Collection Key Indicators	This report shows collector effectiveness. The report shows the number of calls, information about customer responses, and the outcome of the calls.
Collections by Collector Report	Use this report to tabulate payment applications for each collector.
Collections Receipt Forecast Report	This report projects the collector's estimates of cash collections into a cash receipts forecast.
Collector Call History	Use this report to see collector call information for a date range.
Collector's Follow Up Report	This report lists items that require follow-up action.
Credit Hold Report	Use this report to review customer accounts with a credit hold status.
Customer Credit Snapshot Report	This report shows a customer's credit history.
Customer Follow Up History Report	This report is used to review the history of collection calls to a customer.
Disputed Invoice Report	This report lists information and totals for debits you place in disputed status.
Invoices Awaiting Automatic Receipt	Use this report to list transactions assigned to an automatic payment method.
Past Due Invoice Report	This is a listing of past-due open items by customer.
Receipt analysis - Days Late Report	This report shows an analysis of the timing of customer payments and terms.
Receipt Promises Report	This is another report to show information from the Customer Calls window.

EXECUTION REPORTS

Execution reports (see Table 13.9) show transactions, validation results, and activity made by the batch transaction processing programs.

TABLE 13.9 EXECUTION REPORTS

Report Name	Description
Archive Detail and Summary	These reports are created automatically when you perform archive activities.
AutoAdjustment Reports	These reports list the effect of running AutoAdjustment. You can run and review the preview report before running Create Adjustments.
AutoInvoice Reports	When you run AutoInvoice, these reports are created automatically to show the effect of the batch process.

TABLE 13.9 EXECUTION REPORTS

Report Name	Description
Automatic Clearing Receipts Execution	These reports are created each time you run the automatic clearing process.
Automatic Receipts and Remittances Execution	This report is generated when automatic receipts or remittances are created, approved, or formatted.
Lockbox Execution Report	This report is created automatically whenever you run the AutoLockbox process.
Posting Execution Report	Use this report to review transactions that are transferred to the General Ledger.

INVOICE PRINT REPORTS

Invoice Print reports (see Table 13.10) are used to prepare the documents to send to your customers' accounts payable department.

TABLE 13.10 INVOICE PRINT REPORTS

Report Name	Description
Invoice Print Preview Report	Use this report to preview items that will print.
Print Invoice Reports	Use this report to print a batch of invoices, memos, chargebacks, deposits, guarantees, invoices against deposits, invoices against guarantees, on-account credits, and adjustments.

LISTING REPORTS

Listing reports (see Table 13.11) show the way your system is configured and document the various codes, profiles, lists of values, rules, and so forth.

TABLE 13.11 LISTING REPORTS

Report Name	Description
Accounting Rules Listing	This is a report to document accounting rules.
AutoCash Rules Listing	Use this report to document the sequence of AutoCash rules assigned to an AutoCash rule set.
Customer Listing	The customer detail listing produces a very long report and lists the configuration for each customer site.
Customer Profiles Report	This report shows the profile information for each customer or customer site.

TABLE 13.11 LISTING REPORTS

Report Name	Description
Customer Relationships Listing	Use this report to document all active and inactive relationships that have been defined among customers.
Duplicate Customer Report	This report locates possible redundant customer records.
European Sales Listing	This report shows sales to customers in the European Union.
Incomplete Invoices Report	This report locates and reports invoices with an incomplete status. These invoices do not update the General Ledger or receivable balances.
Ordering and Grouping Rules Listing	This report lists rules used by AutoInvoice to sort and group billing transactions.
Payment Terms Listing	This is a listing of term codes in the system.
Receipts Without Sites Report	Use this report to review all receipts that do not have an address assigned to them. The address is required to determine on which Bill To site's statement the receipt should appear.
Standard Memo Lines Listing	This report documents anything you enter in the Standard Memo Lines window.
Transaction Batch Sources Listing	This report shows all batch sources that are defined for the system.
Transaction Types Listing	This report shows the details of what you enter in the Transaction Types window.

TAX REPORTS

Tax reports (see Table 13.12) assist with the reporting, collection, and payment of tax collections.

TABLE 13.12 TAX REPORTS

Report Name	Description
Canadian GST/PST Tax Report	This report supports the reporting requirements of Canadian taxes.
Country Specific VAT Reporting	Specialized reports are available when you install Belgium, Chinese, Czech, German, Hungarian, Italian, Korean, Norwegian, Polish, Portuguese, Spanish, Swiss, Taiwan, or Thai localizations.
Customers with Invoices at 0 and no VAT Registration Number	Use this report to locate customers who are not paying VAT but have not documented their exemption.
Sales Tax Listing	This report lists the details of each sales tax location.

TABLE 13.12 TAX REPORTS

Report Name	Description
Tax Code Listing	This report lists the details of each tax code in the system.
Tax Exceptions Listing	This report documents what you enter in the Item Tax Rate Exceptions window.
Tax Exempt Customer Report	This report documents customers marked tax-exempt in their configuration.
Tax Exempt Product Listing	This report documents products marked tax exempt.
Tax Interface Report	This report is automatically generated when you run the Sales Tax Rate Interface program.
Tax Received Report	This report shows in each currency the amount of tax received for each item.
Tax Only: Open Invoices Report	Use this report to locate open invoices where the balance open is equal to the amount of the tax.
US Sales Tax Report	This report shows tax liabilities by taxing authority for invoices, credits memos, and adjustments. This report is the basis for a tax return.
VAT Exception Report	This is a report to list various AR transactions that meet VAT exception conditions.
VAT Reconciliation Report	Use this report to support periodic VAT returns.
VAT Register Report	This report is used to show VAT tax liability.

MISCELLANEOUS REPORTS

Miscellaneous reports (see Table 13.13) are provided for a variety of purposes.

TABLE 13.13 MISCELLANEOUS REPORTS

Report Name	Description
Audit Report by Document Number	Use this report to identify discrepancies in document number sequences.
Bank Charges Report	Use the Bank Charges report to list all bank charges entered in the Bank Charges window.
Deposited Cash - Applied Detail	Use this report to help reconcile daily cash transactions and bank statements.
Inter Company Invoices and Receipts Reports	Use this report to verify unposted transactions from one company and applied to another company.
Key Indicators - Daily and Summary	Use this report to compare and measure change in key indicators for two periods.
Supplier Customer Netting Report	This is a report to show the net balance of customers and vendors with exactly the same name, NIF code, or VAT registration.

TROUBLESHOOTING

In summary, the AR application is a subledger to the General Ledger, and the application processes revenue transactions, adjustments to billed items, and receipts. In addition, the AR application has a robust set of reports and windows to assist you with collection of open receivable items. It is a relatively complex financial application, and you should consider the following as you work with the setup, transactions, and reports:

- If you have a large number of billing lines, you will want to place indexes on the ra_interface_lines_all table for your Transaction Flexfield columns. Oracle Support can provide your DBA with a performance patch.

- Because AR is a subledger to the General Ledger, it will normally maintain an accurate balance among the details in AR and the accounting flexfields in the GL. A small window of vulnerability exists if the journal entry is destroyed in the GL interface before it can be imported and posted to the GL accounts. AR will not let you simply rerun a month-end posting. However, you can get a program from Oracle Support to undo the effects of closing the month, so that you can create a new month end journal entry.

- To keep the accounts in the AR subledger and the General Ledger in balance, always make adjusting entries to the detailed transactions in AR and let AR make the journal entry in the GL.

- Reversing a receipt and starting again is often the fastest way to undo a receipt entry that is causing you problems.

- If the receipt entry programs don't allow you to make adjustments or process customer overpayments and adjustments, check the settings on your profile options and the setup for the transaction type.

- AR reports are date-sensitive, and this might affect your ability to balance the subledger to the GL at period end. For example, AR can create an open item trial balance for an earlier date even though some of those items now have been paid off and new open items have been created. To balance properly at the period end, make sure that all your balancing reports use the period end date.

- If you implement the multi-org feature (see Chapter 23), realize that customer records are not partitioned by organization. However, customer addresses and business purposes are partitioned by each of your organizations.

- Most AR reports do not show the province, county, or the fourth address line of the customer record.

- Do not change the Sales Tax Location Flexfield structure after you enter customer addresses or create transactions.

- The customer API does not import Territory Flexfield information.
- You cannot adjust the exchange rate on a foreign currency invoice after it has been posted or after a receipt has been applied. To use a different exchange rate you would have to delete or credit the transaction.

CHAPTER 14

USING ORACLE ASSETS

RELATIONSHIP TO OTHER APPLICATIONS

Oracle Assets (FA) generally receives information from interfaces with either the Oracle Payables (AP) and/or the Oracle Project (PA) module. Oracle Assets can also receive information manually from users who enter it directly into the fixed asset system or upload it from a spreadsheet using ADI (Application Desktop Integrator). In addition, Oracle Assets can receive information from outside feeder systems (non-Oracle applications) through the Mass Addition Interface.

Oracle Payables sends invoices that are charged to an asset clearing account into the Mass Additions table. At various intervals during the month, the mass additions process can be run to transmit the data into the fixed asset module. Construction in Progress (CIP) assets can be tracked and analyzed in either the PA or FA module. If Oracle Projects is used, the CIP asset is tracked as defined in the project. After it is completely built, you can send it to Oracle Assets for capitalization. Note that if you are using Oracle Projects for CIP purposes, you will not need to duplicate the effort in Oracle Assets.

Oracle Assets sends fixed asset additions, depreciation, adjustments, transfers, gain/loss, and retirement information in journal entry form to Oracle General Ledger (GL). Fixed asset journal entries are created after the monthly depreciation expense process has been completed. This is accomplished by running the Standard Journal Entry process. This process should only be run once during a month. The gain/loss report can be run repeatedly during the month, but the depreciation expense process can only be run once (note that running the depreciation expense process also initiates the gain/loss process). After the entire process completes successfully, Oracle automatically closes the previous month and opens the next month in the fiscal year. There is no way to reopen a period in Oracle Assets, so you want to be sure that you are ready to proceed before you run depreciation for the month. Note that the reason that you cannot reverse the depreciation process is because FA updates the GL base tables directly. It does not go though the GL Open Interface table as the other applications do.

DISCOVERING NEW FEATURES IN RELEASE 11

This section covers the new features found in Oracle Assets release 11. The new version of the software provides more ways to track and analyze asset information.

USING ASSET PHYSICAL INVENTORY

The asset physical inventory feature is a tool to reconcile on-hand capital assets to your asset system. Data for the physical inventory can be collected either manually or by bar code scanning. If bar code scanning is used, the information can be downloaded into your asset system using an Excel spreadsheet.

There are a couple standard reports you might find helpful when reconciling your physical inventory. The first report is the Physical Inventory Comparison Report. This report indicates discrepancies in location and number of units. The second report is the Physical

Inventory Missing Asset Report. This report highlights those items that appear on your asset system but were not accounted for when you took your physical inventory.

USING WHAT-IF ANALYSIS

What-if analysis is achieved by running the What-if Depreciation Analysis report. This report helps you make depreciation projections based on parameters that you enter into the system. It is useful if you would like to evaluate the effects of a Mass Transfer or change before actually making the change. Examples of what-if scenarios include extending depreciable life of a group of assets, adding a salvage value%age to a range of asset numbers, or changing the depreciation method for a specific category of assets. The report also provides a comparison to actual current depreciation projections for analytical purposes. The information is available to compare against other what-if scenarios until you purge it from the system.

The What-if analysis differs from the Projection report because you can change asset parameters without affecting your actual asset data. Projections can only be run using the parameters that have already been set up in Oracle Assets.

To run this report, you specify which book you want to perform the analysis on. Only one book can be analyzed at a time. You must enter a start date and the number of months for which you want the analysis to be performed. Optionally, you can indicate an asset number range, dates in service, category, or description. If you choose not to specify anything in the optional fields, Oracle defaults to all assets available for that particular book.

TRACKING ASSET WARRANTIES

Manufacturer warranties for specified assets can be tracked within the Oracle Assets application. The information to be tracked is entered through the Asset Warranties window. More than one asset can be assigned the same asset warranty, and you can assign a different warranty to an asset at any time.

Warranties cannot be changed or deleted if they are currently attached to an asset. Before setting up warranties, you might want to consider developing a naming convention policy for your warranties because the warranty number and description field can be freely used.

TRACKING LEASE AMORTIZATION

Oracle Assets enables you to enter a lease payment schedule or create a lease amortization table within the application. Note that you cannot change or delete a lease after it has been entered into the system. Oracle Assets can also track information relating to nondepreciable leased assets. This information can be captured for information-gathering purposes only.

There are two functions that you can access to maintain leases: Lease Payments and Lease Details. The Lease Payments screen enables you to define a payment schedule by providing the system with an interest rate, compounding frequency, start date, number of payments, amount, and payment type (such as balloon, annuity, and bargain purchase option). The

PART

III

CH

14

Lease Details screen is where you track the actual leases, including information such as your lease number, lessor, payment schedule (from Lease Payments form), lease type, and terms.

This feature enables you to test your asset leases based on Generally Accepted Accounting Principles (GAAP) to decide whether you can capitalize and depreciate the lease. When you initially set up your lease, you are prompted to enter the information that Oracle uses to determine net present value and whether the asset qualifies for capitalization. If Oracle determines that the information you entered meets its criteria, it changes the lease type to "capitalized" and changes the asset cost to the lessor of net present value (NPV) or fair market value (FMV).

FIXED ASSET DESKTOP INTEGRATOR (ADI)

The Fixed Asset Desktop Integrator provides a method for you to load information from an Excel spreadsheet directly into the Oracle Asset tables. The two tables it interfaces with are the Mass Addition table and the Physical Inventory table. It also provides a means to download information from Oracle into a spreadsheet in Excel and also a method to print FA reports in various formats including HTML.

The Mass Addition table is generally used in this way during initial data conversion of the system. It provides a place to hold data before transferring it into Oracle Fixed Assets. The Mass Addition table is also used if additions need to be transferred from a system other than Oracle Payables or Oracle Projects.

The Physical Inventory table is used to load information gathered during the physical inventory process through an Excel spreadsheet. This is where you compare inventoried assets to the assets on the books.

USING MULTIPLE REPORTING CURRENCIES FOR TRANSACTIONS

If you use multiple currencies for reporting assets, you can set up Oracle to enable you to maintain information on each currency at the transaction level. You simply designate a primary General Ledger set of books that you maintain in your functional currency. Then, you set up separate sets of books for each currency that you report in. Note that the Asset books derive their currency designation from the General Ledger book they are associated with, not from the Asset Book.

There are several business reasons why you might need to report assets in multiple currencies. First, you might be operating your business in a country where the currency is highly fluctuating or inflationary and you need to report based on some stable standard. Second, you might be operating in one of the countries that are part of the European Monetary Union and you still need to report transactions in both the euro and local currency. The final reason you might need to report in multiple currencies is that your business might have locations in multiple countries and for consolidation purposes you need to report your information in a currency that is not your primary currency.

RETROACTIVE DATES ON AMORTIZED ADJUSTMENTS

In previous versions of Oracle Assets, you were required to use the system date as your start date for amortized adjustments (such as a change in recoverable cost). Oracle now enables you to date an amortized adjustment using a previous period. Any amount that should have been taken between the amortization start date and the current period is caught up in the current period.

This feature can be activated for one set of books or all books, depending on your specific needs. The way to activate this feature is through the Book Controls form in the Asset Set Up screen. It is a check box called Allow Amortized Changes found in the Accounting Rules screen.

CRITICAL IMPLEMENTATION FACTORS

The next section will cover some of the items you should consider before setting up your Assets module. Take special note of the critical setup issues.

ISSUES AND GAPS

When you begin to define your implementation process, there are a number of questions that you need to ask yourself. Some of the more important questions are the following:

- What depreciation methods do you use? Are any of these methods unique to your company/industry?

- What prorate conventions do you use? Do all assets in a specific category use the same prorate method?

- What naming convention should be in place for assets? How can naming conventions be used to standardize asset entry and format?

- How do you track assets (using Capital Acquisition Requisition Numbers)? Does this numbering system need to follow through from a feeder system into Oracle Assets?

- How do you handle Construction in Progress (CIP)?

- What will be the feeder system used to populate Oracle Assets?

- Do your corporate and tax books use the same fiscal year?

- How do you categorize assets? To what level do you need to be able to transfer assets (balancing segment, cost center)?

- Do you organize your assets by physical location? Do you assign assets to specific employees?

- Do you need to track assets in different currencies?

- How many tax books do you need? What are they?

- What is the oldest asset that you are tracking?

- What type of asset numbering process is being used? If automatic, what is the last asset number in place?

- What type of security do you need on your asset system?
- Do you tag your assets? Are your tag numbers available in your legacy system? Are any of your tag numbers duplicated in your legacy system?

It is best to set up a database to keep track of issues and gaps that evolve as you enter the setup phase of the project. You might want to segregate your issues by sets of books (corporate and tax).

REVIEWING TOP ENHANCEMENT REQUESTS

Following is a list of the top enhancement requests:

- Ability to perform multiple depreciation runs in a single month
- Depreciation preview report
- Ability by FA to allow depreciation process to proceed even if it encounters an error
- Ability to run a projection for individual or a range of cost centers
- Ability to "cancel" an asset and provide reversing journals
- Allow mass asset reclassifications
- Provide ability to secure FA in a multi-org environment
- Consistency between depreciation projection report and final actual depreciation
- Property tax report to sort on both City and State (currently it only sorts by State)
- Provide location information on more of the standard asset reports

Most of the preceding requests are slated for future releases of Oracle. As you can see, there are several issues that relate to the depreciation process. This process can only be run once a month, and if the system encounters any problems, it aborts the process. After you successfully run the process, it automatically closes the current month and opens the new month. Any problems that you uncover with depreciation must be corrected in the new month. If you have any questions or additional suggestions, please contact Oracle directly.

RESOLVING CRITICAL SETUP ISSUES

Probably one of the most important issues that need to be resolved during setup is that of data conversion. Data conversion efforts can take a great deal of time if not planned properly. Experience has shown that many companies are still tracking assets manually on spreadsheets, which can cause difficulties in consistency and form. The other problem with data conversion relates to mapping issues. Many times, the FA module is being configured at the same time or right after the GL module. Given that many companies choose to revise their chart of accounts when setting up GL, this creates mapping issues that need to be addressed in FA.

When setting up legacy data in FA, one trick that I have used in the past is to change your units to be equivalent to your currency total. Typically, an accounting department spends the least amount of time maintaining their FA system. This translates into many old items that are sitting on FA without any meaningful way to determine their location, description, serial number, and so on. For those items, you can set up the units to be equivalent to the dollars of the asset. This provides an easy way to retire portions of those assets over a period of years.

If you discover during data conversion that some assets have been added erroneously, they can be deleted through the Assets Workbench. Find the asset and select the Open button. When you have the asset on the screen, use the delete button (red ×) on the toolbar to delete the asset from the system. This process only works for those assets that have never had depreciation run against them. After you run depreciation, the only way to remove an asset from the system is to retire it.

When setting up this application, keep in mind that the requirements of both the Corporate and Tax departments need to be met. Tax individuals need to be kept in the loop to ensure that all regulatory needs are being fulfilled. It is critical that both areas contribute up front to the setup decisions because some of the setups cannot be changed after they are used.

Table 14.1 describes each setup task and the order in which they must be performed.

TABLE 14.1   SETUP TASKS

Task Number	Optional Setup Step	Description
Step 1		GL Setup: Define chart of accounts, period types, calendars, currencies, and set of books for general ledger
Step 2		Set up Asset Category Flexfield
Step 3		Set up Location Flexfield
Step 4		Set up Asset Key Flexfield
Step 5		Set up System Controls
Step 6	Optional	Define Locations
Step 7	Optional	Define Asset Keys
Step 8	Optional	Define Standard Asset Descriptions and Other QuickCode Values
Step 9		Define Fiscal Year
Step 10		Define Calendars (Depreciation and Prorate)
Step 11	Optional	Define Additional Journal Entry Sources
Step 12	Optional	Define Additional Journal Entry Categories
Step 13		Define Book Controls
Step 14		Review Account Generator Default
Step 15	Optional	Define Additional Depreciation Methods and Rates
Step 16	Optional	Define Depreciation Ceilings
Step 17	Optional	Define Investment Tax Credits
Step 18		Define Prorate and Retirement Conventions
Step 19	Optional	Define Price Indexes

PART

III

CH

14

TABLE 14.1 CONTINUED

Task Number	Optional Setup Step	Description
Step 20	Optional	Define Units of Measure
Step 21		Define Asset Categories
Step 22	Optional	Define Distribution Sets
Step 23	Optional	Define Leases
Step 24	Optional	Define Warranties
Step 25	Optional	Define Supplier and Employee Numbering Schema
Step 26	Optional	Define Suppliers
Step 27	Optional	Define Employees
Step 28	Optional	Define Descriptive Flexfields
Step 29		Review Default Profile Options
Step 30	Optional	Define Additional Responsibilities

UNDERSTANDING EACH SETUP TASK

Following is a step-by-step description of how to complete each task that needs to be done to configure Oracle Assets. In this chapter, I do not cover in detail the setups that normally occur in other modules. If you need assistance setting up those items, please refer to the specific modules noted for setup procedures.

CREATING THE GENERAL LEDGER SET OF BOOKS

This step only needs to be done if you have not or will not be using Oracle General Ledger. If Oracle GL is going to be used, this should be completed prior to configuring FA. If Oracle GL is not going to be used, please refer to Chapter 11, "Using Oracle General Ledger," for a detailed description of how to define a set of books, calendar, currency, period types, and chart of accounts.

CREATING THE ASSET CATEGORY KEY FLEXFIELD

Deciding how to set up the category key flexfield is probably one of the most critical setup decisions that needs to be made in FA. Asset categories are what generate most of the accounting entries that are created by FA. The more complex the accounting needs of the company, the more asset categories that will need to be created. Asset categories can be shared by more than one set of books (corporate and tax), but the accounting for each book must be set up separately. For example, the ABC Corp Book can have a category of Software.Oracle (Software is the major category, the period is the segment separator and Oracle is the minor category). ABC Federal Tax Book can also share the same category, but it will need to have its own series of GL accounts set up for it. Although this is a nice feature if you are using multiple fixed asset books that require different accounting flexfield codes, it can be cumbersome if you have the same accounting rules for multiple sets of FA books.

The category flexfield can accommodate up to seven segments and can be a total of thirty characters wide. Dynamic insertion is *not* allowed for this flexfield. (Dynamic insertion is a feature that allows the system to automatically build valid code combinations based on rules that you provide). The only requirement when setting up the category flexfield is that you must define at least one major segment. Optionally, you are allowed to define up to six additional minor segments (for a maximum of seven segments total).

Typically, the category flexfield is set up with at least two segments enabled. The segments are usually set up to delineate major and minor category information. To limit the pick list for each major category, you might make your minor category a dependent segment. When planning your category flexfield, think about grouping your segments based on depreciation rules. One note of caution: You cannot have subdependencies. For example, you cannot add a third segment and make it dependent on the second (minor category) segment.

Remember that when you have set up a flexfield and begun using it, any changes could significantly impact the integrity of your existing data. Like the accounting flexfield in GL, you will not want to make changes to this flexfield after it has been established.

CREATING THE LOCATION KEY FLEXFIELD

The location key flexfield is used to track the specific physical location of each asset. Locations can be defined as departments, floor numbers, buildings, counties, cities, states, countries, and so on.

The location flexfield can have up to seven segments and a total of thirty characters (including segment separators). Dynamic insertion can be enabled for this particular flexfield.

Oracle requires that one segment of the location flexfield must be designated as the state qualifier. One purpose for this designator is that it is a parameter in the property tax report. All other segments are optional for this flexfield.

CREATING THE ASSET KEY FLEXFIELD

This flexfield is used to group assets using nonfinancial information. Examples of an asset key might be a budget-tracking number or a project number. This flexfield has no impact on the financial activities of the asset, but it does come in handy when you want to query a group of similar assets in the Assets Workbench.

You must define one segment of the asset key even if you decide not to use it. If you do not want to use it, simply set up one segment and uncheck the Displayed and Enabled boxes on the Asset Key Flexfield form. This satisfies the system requirements of having the flexfield set up without causing the users any additional data entry work. This flexfield can be re-enabled at any time in the future by going back to the form and checking the Displayed and Enabled boxes.

PART

III

CH

14

The asset key can be up to 10 segments with a total of 30 characters, including segment separators. Dynamic insertion is also available for this flexfield.

DEFINING SYSTEM CONTROLS

To set up the system controls, you must designate the enterprise (company) name, asset numbering scheme (manual or automatic), key flexfield structures for the category, location, and asset key flexfields that were used. You must also designate the oldest date placed in service for the assets.

> **Tip**
>
> After you assign calendars to a set of depreciation books, you cannot change the Oldest Date Placed in Service. Be very sure that the date you choose reflects the oldest asset you plan on entering.

DEFINING LOCATIONS

If you have elected to use dynamic insertion for the location flexfield, you do not need to do this step. If you have not set dynamic insertion to Yes, you need to define each valid location combination that you want to use. If you have set up dependencies between your location segments, I recommend having the system create the combinations through dynamic insertion. The dependencies serve as a checkpoint and limit the possible errors that can occur with dynamic insertion on. Remember, the dynamic insertion check box can be found on the Key Flexfield Segments form.

One thing to understand about dynamic insertion is that it only enables users to choose values that have been previously defined in the Key Flexfield Values screen. It does not enable users to arbitrarily select any value of their choosing.

CREATING ASSET KEY FLEXFIELD COMBINATIONS

If you have elected to use dynamic insertion for the asset key flexfield, you do not need to do this step. If you have not set dynamic insertion to Yes, you need to define each valid asset key combination. Note that it doesn't matter whether you have elected to assign only one segment to your asset key; you still have to perform this step if dynamic insertion is not enabled.

DEFINING QUICKCODES

There are various types of QuickCodes that you can define additional values for. Some QuickCodes are restricted, and you cannot add new values, but often, you can change the description of the current codes to better suit your needs. QuickCodes generally provide a pick list of values in various forms within the Oracle application. They can be invaluable because they can reduce the amount of typing a user has to do (thus also reducing the potential typing errors that can occur). Table 14.2 lists the Asset QuickCode descriptors, whether they can be changed, existing sample values, and examples of values you might choose to add.

TABLE 14.2 ASSET QUICKCODES

QuickCode Type	Sample QuickCode Values
Asset Description	Some sample values you might want to add include Desktop Computer, Laptop Computer, Chevy Vehicle, Conference Room Table, and so on. Oracle does not come with any asset descriptions predefined.
Journal Entries	You cannot add new codes, but you can change the description of the existing codes to better suit your needs. Examples of existing codes include Addition Cost, Depreciation Expense, Retirement Cost, and Tax Expense. There are 66 predefined Journal Entry Quickcodes.
Queue Name	Sample values to add might include Category Hold and Location Flexfield Hold. You cannot change the existing value names.
Property Type	Additional values you might want to add include Long Term Lease, Short Term Lease, Residential, and so on.
Retirement Type	Sample values you might want to add to describe your retirements include Abandonment, Charitable Contribution, and Write Off. The two Oracle predefined values are Extraordinary and Sale.
Asset Category	This is only used if the Asset Category (major category) was set up utilizing table-based validation. (If it was not, you define the categories using the Asset Categories form).
Asset Subcategory	This is also only used if the Asset Subcategory (minor category) was set up using table-based validation.
Unplanned Depreciation Type	This is used to describe depreciation adjustments that were not planned at the time the asset was added to the system. Examples you might want to add include stolen, accelerated, obsolete, and so on.
Lease Frequency	You cannot enter or alter existing values, but you can change the description of them. Existing values include monthly, quarterly, semiannually, and annually.
Lease Payment Type	Existing sample values include Balloon Payment, Annuity, Bargain Purchase Option, and Bargain Renewal Option. You can add as many additional types as you deem necessary.

DEFINING FISCAL YEARS AND CALENDARS

Fiscal years must be defined beginning with the oldest asset placed in service. You determine the beginning and ending dates of the month. If you are using the standard month (as opposed to a 4-4-5 month), Oracle automatically generates the calendar for the next fiscal year.

PART

III

CH

14

Tip

When you are initially setting up your first fiscal years and calendars, fill in the first line and then hit Enter. Oracle automatically generates the next available period for you. You can then edit this line if you have any changes to make. It saves you quite a

> bit of typing, especially if you are using standard calendar months and years. Remember that you must be sure to include every day in your fiscal calendar. If you miss any dates, you can wreak havoc on your system.

You can set up as many depreciation and prorate calendars as you deem necessary because there is no limit to the number that you can use. I have set up various prorate calendars for special depreciation expense purposes. For example, I was asked to provide a setup to take depreciation based on a flat%age no matter what the date was that the asset was purchased during the year. I called my prorate calendar "Full Year," and a portion of my setup is shown in Table 14.3.

TABLE 14.3 SAMPLE PRORATE CALENDAR

Convention:	Full Year	
From Date	To Date	Prorate Date
01-APR-1996	30-APR-1996	01-APR-1996
01-MAY-1996	31-MAY-1996	01-APR-1996
01-JUN-1996	30-JUN-1996	01-APR-1996
01-JUL-1996	31-JUL-1996	01-APR-1996
01-AUG-1996	31-AUG-1996	01-APR-1996
01-SEP-1996	30-SEP-1996	01-APR-1996
01-OCT-1996	31-OCT-1996	01-APR-1996
01-NOV-1996	30-NOV-1996	01-APR-1996
01-DEC-1996	31-DEC-1996	01-APR-1996
01-JAN-1997	31-JAN-1997	01-APR-1996
01-FEB-1997	28-FEB-1997	01-APR-1996
01-MAR-1997	31-MAR-1997	01-APR-1996
01-APR-1997	30-APR-1997	01-APR-1997

The preceding prorate calendar, combined with a special depreciation method, enabled me to take a flat 25% depreciation during year 1, regardless of when the asset was actually purchased.

One other thing to keep in mind with prorate calendars is that there is a check box on the form that enables you to Depreciate when Placed in Service. What this means is that you want your depreciation to be based strictly on the date you set up the asset. This is typically used for assets that are leased such as computer equipment or leasehold improvements. If this box is checked, Oracle begins to depreciate the asset on the date you placed it in service, not the prorate date. For example, if an asset was placed in service on June 1 and your prorate calendar indicated that it should use a prorate date of April 1, it would use June 1 because the check box takes precedence over the prorate date.

It is important to note that your corporate and tax book calendars must have the same fiscal year. If you have different fiscal years (for tax and book purposes), there is no simple, clean way to accommodate this using standard functionality. The only workaround that I have seen involves customization of the Oracle product. You must set up multiple corporate books and calendars and then either develop a script to add mass additions to the second corporate book or reenter the assets manually to each additional corporate book. Remember that one corporate book does not have any relationship to another corporate book in FA. Information cannot be systematically transferred from one corporate book to another using standard functionality.

DEFINING JOURNAL ENTRY FORMATS

The journal entry sources are used to identify the types of journal entries being created by Oracle Assets. Oracle comes with many predefined journal entry formats, but additional types can be created if necessary.

Journal entry categories are used to define the type of journal entry being processed. For example, addition, depreciation, adjustment, and retirements are a few types of categories. As with journal entry sources, Oracle comes predefined with many of these values, so unless you have special reporting needs, you will probably not change any of these.

DEFINING BOOK CONTROLS

The book controls are used to set up and direct all the corporate and tax depreciation books that you need. This is where you control whether a particular asset book can post journal entries to the general ledger. Each tax book you define must be associated with a corporate book. To access each of these forms, simply click the blue drop-down box on the left side of the screen.

CALENDAR INFORMATION

To set up calendar information, you need to choose one of your previously defined depreciation and prorate calendars. Enter the current open period name for this book. Be sure that you set up the depreciation calendar for *at least* one period before the current period. For the current period, I usually choose a date that corresponds to the last month of the previous fiscal or calendar year. This enables me to run the depreciation process for the data conversion items that will provide a year-end reserve amount for reconciling purposes.

Choose whether to divide depreciation Evenly (evenly each period) or By Days (to divide based on the proportion of days per period). You must also decide whether to depreciate assets that are retired during the first year of life. Oracle Assets automatically updates the Last Depreciation Run Date after you run the depreciation process for the first time.

ACCOUNTING RULES

This form enables you to tighten or loosen controls for each asset book. For example, you can allow mass changes in your tax book but disallow mass changes in the corporate book. You

PART

III

CH

14

also designate the minimum amount of time an asset must be held in order to qualify for a capital gain when it is retired and whether you want to allow amortized changes to assets.

The Tax Rules and Allow Mass Copy options are not available to update if you are defining a corporate book. These options are only available if you are defining a tax book.

NATURAL ACCOUNTS

In this screen, you enter natural, retirement, intercompany, and depreciation accounts. These can be unique or identical for each set of fixed asset books. Even if you do not want more than one asset book posting entries to your general ledger, you still have to set up accounts for every book you define because these are required fields. I recommend that you use a unique accounting flexfield code combination for the books that have no posting ability in case something happens to go wrong. If you do this, it will be readily apparent to the user where to look if a problem arises.

JOURNAL CATEGORIES

This is where you enter the source category that you want to show up in GL when you transfer journal entries from Oracle Assets. Each asset transaction type can have a unique journal category associated with it. I have found that the standard list of categories provided by Oracle is quite extensive, and I use the categories provided. You can, however, decide to set up unique categories if desired.

CONFIGURING FLEXBUILDER FOR ASSETS

Flexbuilder automatically configures itself for each new set of books entered in Oracle Assets. If you are on a version of Oracle prior to release 11, this is where you can customize the accounting entries that are made by each set of books (corporate and tax). In general, Oracle Assets only builds accounting entries based on balancing segment. If you need your entries to include cost center information, you will need to customize Flexbuilder. In case you find yourself in the position of having to customize Flexbuilder, Table 14.4 provides you with some basic details on what the default information means.

TABLE 14.4 KEY FLEXBUILDER INFORMATION

Flexbuilder	Accounting Flexfield Developed
Default CCID (flexfield)	Taken from the Book Controls form
Account CCID (flexfield)	Taken from Asset Categories form
Account Segment (segment)	Taken from the Book Controls or Asset Category form (depending on what account it is trying to build)
Distribution CCID (flexfield)	Taken from Transfer form (expense combination set up in Assets Workbench)

Initial Flexbuilder settings use the Default CCID for all fields except the natural account. The natural account is generated based on Account Segment, and the balancing segment is taken from the Distribution ID. What this means is that if you have an accounting flexfield with a balancing segment, cost center, and natural account, the default combination would get the balancing segment from your expense combination, the natural account from your GL account, and the cost center from your book controls form. Needless to say, Flexbuilder is a very complex product that you would probably want to take a training class on before attempting to modify system generated defaults.

For version 11.0 Assets, you have the Oracle Workflow product to customize your accounting entries. Oracle Workflow is a lengthy topic that you can find covered in Chapter 22, "Using Oracle Workflow."

DEFINING DEPRECIATION METHODS

Oracle comes with a considerable number of predefined depreciation methods including Straight line, Sum of the Years Digits, MACRS, and ACRS. If you are using a unique method, you can define your own using one of four different depreciation types: calculated, table-based, units of production, or flat rate. You determine which type you need based on *how* you want Oracle Assets to calculate depreciation.

If you want to depreciate assets over a fixed period of time using specified rates, choose the calculated or table-based depreciation methods. Common examples of this type of depreciation are Double Declining Balance, Sum of the Years Digits, Alternative Minimum Tax, or ACRS.

Units of production depreciate an asset based on usage, not the passage of time. This is especially useful for equipment that is being used on a factory floor or for assets that are used up over time such as oil wells. Note that if you are using this method, you can either maintain your production information manually or track it in another system and import it into FA using the FA_PRODUCTION_INTERFACE table.

A flat rate method is used if you want to allocate a fixed rate over a specified period of time. This method is typically found in use outside of the U.S. An example of this type of depreciation is Japan Declining Balance.

Keep in mind that after you have begun using a particular method, you cannot make any changes to it. If you need to revise it, simply create a new one and assign or mass change it for the assets that need to utilize this method.

An example of the table-based method would be if you require Oracle Assets to depreciate an asset based on a different%age each year. Table 14.5 illustrates part of the setup if you wanted a method in FA to depreciate based on 25% in year 1, 35% in year 2, and 40% in year 3.

PART

III

CH

14

TABLE 14.5   SAMPLE DEPRECIATION METHOD

Year	Period	Annual Rate
1	1	.25
2	1	.35
3	1	.40

TABLE 14.5   CONTINUED

Year	Period	Annual Rate
4	1	0
1	2	.25
2	2	.35
3	2	.40
4	2	0
1	3	.25
2	3	.35
3	3	.40
4	3	0

To access the rate table, you have to click the Rates button in the lower right corner of the screen. Table 14.5 is telling Oracle that any assets purchased in period 1, year 1, should be depreciated at an annual rate of 25%. Year 2 should be depreciated at 35%, year 3 at 40%, and year 4 would have zero depreciation expense. Note, if you indicate to Oracle that you are depreciating an asset for 3 years, it automatically assumes that depreciation will occur over a four-year time frame to take into account the half-year convention. To get around that, use zero% in year 4.

For example, Asset 123 purchased for $10,000 and placed in service in period 3. Using Table 14.5 creates the yearly expense to be taken that is shown in Table 14.6.

TABLE 14.6   ASSET 123 DEPRECIATION EXPENSE SAMPLE

Year	Period(s)	Total Depreciation Expense Taken
1	3-12	$2,500
2	1-12	$3,500
3	1-12	$4,000
4	1-12	$0

The preceding example is based on a prorate calendar that takes depreciation based on a full year.

DEFINING DEPRECIATION CEILINGS

Depreciation expense ceilings are used to limit the amount of depreciation you can take for an asset. This is typically used for tax purposes to limit such things as depreciation on luxury vehicles.

There are also special depreciation cost ceilings that are in effect in some foreign countries. If you use a cost ceiling, Oracle Assets limits the cost basis to the lesser of the asset cost or cost ceiling. Remember that you can only use this option if you have checked the Allow Expense Ceilings and Allow Cost Ceilings boxes in your book controls form. The Depreciation Ceiling box can be found in the default depreciation screen when you are setting up your asset categories.

DEFINING INVESTMENT TAX CREDITS

If your company has investment tax credits, investment tax recapture, or investment tax ceilings, you would enter that information in the ITC forms. There are actually two forms involved: ITC Rates and ITC Recapture Rates. Both forms require virtually identical information except that the IRC Rate Form uses a Basis Reduction Rate where the ITC Recapture Rate form needs a Recapture Rate. These forms also require you to enter the Tax Year, Years and Months (of the Assets Life), and ITC Rate (as a percentage).

Remember that you can only use this option if you have checked the Allow Investment Tax Credits box in your book controls form. The ITC eligible box is found on the default depreciation screen of the asset category form.

DEFINING PRORATE CONVENTIONS

A prorate convention is nothing more than a way to tell Oracle Assets when to depreciate an asset during the first year and last (retirement) year of its useful life. Oracle does not come with any prorate conventions predefined because they are unique to every company.

You can define prorate conventions with prorate dates that have the effect shown in Table 14.7.

TABLE 14.7   PRORATE CONVENTIONS

Convention	What It Means
Actual Months Convention	Takes one month of depreciation in month acquired asset. No depreciation taken in the last month or month you retire the asset.
Half-Year Convention	Takes half-year of depreciation in year acquire asset and last year of asset life. Half-year of depreciation taken in the year that the asset is retired, regardless of date retired.
Standard Modified Half-Year Convention	Takes full year depreciation in year acquired, if acquired during first half of year. No depreciation if asset is acquired in second half of year. For retirement, if retired in first half of year, no depreciation taken. If retired in second half of year, full year depreciation is taken.
Alternate Modified Half-Year Convention	Retirement convention that takes one quarter of a year's depreciation in the year the asset is retired.
Following Month Convention	No depreciation taken in month asset is acquired but takes one month for the last month of the asset's life. As retirement convention, it takes one month's depreciation in the month retired.
ACRS Half-Year Convention	Full-year depreciation in year acquired asset, no depreciation in the last year of the asset's life. As retirement convention, it takes no depreciation in year asset is retired.

TABLE 14.7   CONTINUED

Convention	What It Means
Mid-Month Convention	Half a month depreciation taken in month acquired and last month of assets life. For retirement, takes half of a month's depreciation in the month it is retired.
Mid-Quarter Convention	Half a quarter taken in quarter that asset was acquired and last quarter of the assets life. Same for retirement convention.

One sample prorate calendar was shown in Table 14.3 in the section that discusses setting up calendars and fiscal years. Table 14.8 shows examples of a couple more prorate calendars.

TABLE 14.8   SAMPLE PRORATE CALENDARS

Convention: HALF YEAR

From Date	To Date	Prorate Date
01-APR-1996	30-APR-1996	01-SEP-1996
01-MAY-1996	31-MAY-1996	01-SEP-1996
01-JUN-1996	30-JUN-1996	01-SEP-1996
01-JUL-1996	31-JUL-1996	01-SEP-1996
01-AUG-1996	31-AUG-1996	01-SEP-1996
01-SEP-1996	30-SEP-1996	01-SEP-1996
01-OCT-1996	31-OCT-1996	01-SEP-1996
01-NOV-1996	30-NOV-1996	01-SEP-1996
01-DEC-1996	31-DEC-1996	01-SEP-1996
01-JAN-1997	31-JAN-1997	01-SEP-1996
01-FEB-1997	28-FEB-1997	01-SEP-1996
01-MAR-1997	31-MAR-1997	01-SEP-1996
01-APR-1997	30-APR-1997	01-SEP-1997
01-MAY-1996	31-MAY-1996	01-SEP-1997
01-JUN-1996	30-JUN-1996	01-SEP-1997
01-JUL-1996	31-JUL-1996	01-SEP-1997

Convention: HALF YEAR

From Date	To Date	Prorate Date
01-APR-1996	31-MAR-1997	01-SEP-1996
01-APR-1997	31-MAR-1998	01-SEP-1997
01-APR-1998	31-MAR-1999	01-SEP-1998
01-APR-1999	31-MAR-2000	01-SEP-1999
01-APR-2000	31-MAR-2001	01-SEP-2000

As you can see, depending on how you handle your accounting, you can set up the prorate calendars to take depreciation based on years, quarters, months, or even days. Note that if you check the Depreciate When Placed in Service box, Oracle Assets begins taking depreciation the month you indicated the asset was placed in service, regardless of the prorate dates chosen.

If you have more than one fiscal year defined, you have to set up more than one prorate calendar. Prorate calendars can be shared, but only if the different books have the same fiscal years.

DEFINING PRICE INDEXES

A price index enables you to calculate gains and losses for retirements using current value instead of historical cost. This feature is most commonly used in countries that require you to base gains and losses on current value rather than historical cost. Oracle Assets enables you to set up price indexes to calculate the gains and losses for your asset upon retirement.

This form is very simple to fill out. You choose a name for your index, enter the value (percentage) that you want Oracle Assets to use for the conversion, and save the form. You can also provide From and To Dates so that the %age can be changed as you deem necessary.

Oracle Assets enables you to associate a different index for each asset category or use the same index for all categories. To associate an index with an asset category, enter the name of the price index in the Price Index field of the Asset Categories window.

DEFINING UNITS OF MEASURE

Units of measure are typically set up in the Inventory or Purchasing modules. If you are not using Oracle Inventory or Purchasing and are planning on using a units of production depreciation method, you can define units of measure in this form. For more information on how to do this, please see the Chapter 16, "Using Oracle Inventory."

DEFINING ASSET CATEGORIES

Because Asset Categories is the only Asset flexfield not eligible for dynamic insertion, this is the form you have to use to set up each asset category combination. It is where you define asset information that is unique to a particular category such as general ledger accounts, depreciation life, and depreciation method.

One thing to keep in mind here is that you are setting up category *defaults*. There might be times when company policy dictates the use of different choices for a specific category or item. Remember that this change can be made when you actually set up the asset. If you find that you have one category combination that rarely utilizes the default information, you probably should look at adding additional default categories to your system.

The only tricky part about this form is that in order to set up multiple books under a single category combination, you must query the initial book combination. Navigate down to the lower block where you see "book," and place your cursor on that field. Click the green — on

PART

III

CH

14

your toolbar to indicate to the system that you are adding information for another book. The lower block of the screen should clear out and enable you to pick another existing book from your list of values (LOV). Choose the additional book and complete the form, including the back screen, where you indicate what the default depreciation information should be.

Note that it is critical this setup step be done correctly. If it is not, errors made in this form can have serious repercussions throughout the application. Mistakes discovered after you have associated an asset with them cannot be changed.

DEFINING FINANCIAL OPTIONS

The financial options would be set up while configuring Oracle General Ledger and Oracle Accounts Payable. If you are not using Oracle GL or AP, please refer to Chapters 11 and 12, "Using Oracle General Ledger" and "Using Oracle Payables," for more detailed instructions.

DEFINING VENDORS

Typically, vendors would be set up in either Oracle Payables or Oracle Purchasing. If you are not using either of these modules and you want to track vendor information, vendors can be set up in Oracle Assets. Oracle uses the terminology vendors and suppliers interchangeably, and you will find this option under Suppliers in FA.

The only way you can assign an asset to a supplier is if they exist in the vendor file. Note that to use the vendor, Oracle requires setup of at least one pay site for the vendor. The pay site is an alternative region reached by clicking the blue box on the left of your screen. For more detailed instructions on how to set up vendors, please refer to Chapters 12 and 15, "Using Oracle Payables" and "Using Oracle Purchasing."

DEFINING EMPLOYEES

If you want to assign assets to particular employees, you must define the employees. This is typically done in the Oracle Human Resources, Purchasing, or Payables modules. Note that if you are using the Human Resources or Purchasing module, this feature is not accessible from Assets. If you are not using those modules, set up the minimal amount of employee information necessary and save the form. For more detailed information on how to set up employees, please review Chapters 24, "Implementing Oracle Human Resources and Oracle Payroll," or 15, "Using Oracle Purchasing." Please be aware when you set up your employees that you need to take into account any requirements from the modules that share this information (Human Resources, Purchasing, and Payables). Even if you do not plan on implementing them right away, setup decisions made here will impact the future timeline and ease in which these modules can be set up.

DEFINING DESCRIPTIVE FLEXFIELDS

Descriptive flexfields are used to track information that you might need to capture but that is not available on standard forms. There is space available on a specific form for a descriptive flexfield wherever you see a blank white box with brackets around it. Setting up specific descriptive flexfields should be reviewed with your system administrator. Remember that even though you set up a descriptive flexfield, the information will not necessarily print on standard reports, nor will it necessarily carry through to other applications.

One common use for descriptive flexfields is tracking old fixed asset numbers from conversion data. If you are changing your asset-numbering schema and you decide to renumber your old assets, you might need to retain the old numbering information for reference purposes. A descriptive flexfield is an example of how you might accomplish this.

SETTING THE PROFILE OPTIONS

A system administrator generally controls profile options at the system level. Users can change their personal profile options for such things as print parameters. Most of the Oracle Assets profile options are controlled from a responsibility level, and changes should be discussed with your System Administrator.

Note that if you need to set your profile option FA Print Debug to Yes, you might see error messages coming up when you save data in various forms. The message that I have frequently seen is Error: FA_CACHE_RESULTS. Do not be alarmed; this does not harm anything and will stop happening when you change the print debug setting back to No.

CONVERTING DATA FOR MAJOR ENTITIES

This section covers the topics relating to entering your assets into Oracle. It also discusses general maintenance functions.

UNDERSTANDING THE MASS ADDITIONS INTERFACE

Oracle provides an interface table for creating mass additions from outside systems. It is the same table that Oracle uses when transferring assets from Oracle Payables.

> **Tip**
>
> You might want to assign some unique identifier in the table to distinguish the assets set up during data conversion.

When converting assets from an outside system, you can bypass the Create and Prepare part of mass additions by transferring them in with a status of Post.

ADDING ASSETS MANUALLY

Assets can be added using either the Quick or Detail asset forms. Quick is exactly what you would expect: It is a form with limited fields to enter data. Most of the information is set up using predefined system defaults, and most of the default information is derived from the category assignment. The only required fields in the quick form are asset category, assignment to a book, cost, depreciation expense account, location, and asset key (if you made it a required field).

PART

III

CH

14

Detail additions enable changes to be made when adding the asset by providing access to the system defaults. If you need to change the category defaults such as life and depreciation method, you want to enter the asset using the detail addition form. Note that there is no way to change the asset cost account and accumulated depreciation account except by changing the asset category assignment.

Assets can be added with a negative cost. If an asset is added as a credit, the journal entry Oracle creates is a credit to monthly depreciation expense and a debit to accumulated depreciation.

ASSIGNING ASSETS TO DEPRECIATION BOOKS

When entering assets, you determine which corporate book they are to be assigned to. Remember that you do not assign assets to Tax books; they are transferred there using the Initial or Periodic Mass Copy function. A specific asset can be assigned to only one corporate book, but it can be assigned to many tax books.

TRANSFERRING ASSETS

Assets can be transferred between employee assignments, expense accounts, and locations. They can be transferred either individually or using the Mass Transfers form. Individual transfers can be made from the Assets Workbench. Simply query the asset in question and open it up. To transfer between expense accounts and employee assignments, use the Assignments button.

If you want to perform Mass Transfers, use the Mass Transfer form (not the Assets Workbench). Provide the To and From fields for locations, expense accounts, or employees. Before you actually commit your transfers, I recommend that you run the Mass Transfer Preview Report. When you are certain the changes are impacting your system the way you want them to, commit the transfer.

The only way to change asset categories is to query the asset in Assets Workbench. All you need to do is choose the category that you want the asset to be assigned to and save the changes. Oracle Assets creates journal entries to transfer the cost and accumulated depreciation into the new general ledger accounts. Note that it does not reclassify any previously taken depreciation expense. One thing to be aware of, however, is that it will *not* change the default depreciation rules to the default rules of the new category. You must do that manually in the Mass Change window or Books form.

RETIRING ASSETS

To retire a single asset, query the asset in the Assets Workbench. Choose the Retirements button and then indicate which book you are retiring the asset from. At this point, you can also choose to retire any subcomponents that are associated with the asset. When you are finished indicating your retirement details (such as units retired, retirement type, cost retired, and proceeds of sale), choose the Done button to save your information. Note that Oracle Assets does not enable you to retire an asset added in the current period.

When an asset is retired before it is fully reserved, Oracle FA calculates the gain or loss on the asset retirement. The calculation is based on the following formula: Proceeds of Sale minus Cost of Removal minus NBV Retired plus Revaluation Reserved Retired equals Gain/Loss on Retirement.

> **Tip**
>
> There was a problem that I ran into relative to retirements that I would like to warn you about. It will occur during the testing phase of the process or while you are in production if you begin using the application during a fiscal year. It occurs when you try to retire an asset that has a half-year (or similar) retirement convention. If the date that the system needs to go back to occurs before the first month that you actually ran depreciation within the application, you get an error when running the Gain/Loss Report. The fix is to change the prorate convention assigned to the asset so that it falls in a period where depreciation has been run. The preventive measure is to start your application on the first day of your fiscal year.

MAKING MASS TRANSACTIONS

Most of the Standard Transactions found in Oracle Assets have Mass Transaction counterparts. These functions can save you a tremendous amount of time if your changes have some commonality. Following are the Mass Transaction functions and how they work.

MASS ADDITIONS

The mass addition process is fairly simple. After assets are created in a feeder system (such as Oracle Payables or Projects), run the Create Mass Additions process to send them into the FA Interface table. After they are in FA, review them and make any changes necessary. When they arrive in FA, they have a queue name of NEW.

If you decide to proceed with the additions, add the location, category, assignment, and asset key information. When you are satisfied that they are complete, change the queue name on each one to POST. The next step is to run the Post Mass Additions process. Finally, after you are sure that everything has processed correctly, you use the purge function to clear them back out of the interface table. Note that the purge function can only purge an asset with a queue designation of SPLIT, MERGE, ADJUST, or POSTED.

The available queue names are NEW, SPLIT, MERGE, ADJUST, POST, POSTED or ON HOLD. The queue name changes automatically if you perform a split, merge, or adjustment on the asset. To put an asset on hold, you must click the queue name box and change it yourself. You must also manually change the queue name to POST when the asset is ready to be transferred. When the transfer is complete, Oracle automatically changes the queue name to POSTED.

You can also add costs or invoice lines to an existing asset. The queue name for this type of addition is ADD TO ASSET. If you try to use any other queue name, the Mass Additions process rejects the row because it expects the item to be a new asset.

PART

III

CH

14

MASS COPY

The Initial Mass Copy program is used to populate your tax book with assets from a corporate book. The Periodic Mass Copy program can then be run to transfer new additions, adjustments, and retirements into the tax books. Note that the corporate book period must be closed before you can copy information into the related tax book. Whether the mass copy transfers adjustments and retirements is determined when you set up your book controls for each tax book.

Mass copy must be run separately for each tax book that is associated to the corporate book. The assets in the tax books use the category defaults from the tax book that you are copying into.

MASS TRANSFERS

Mass transfers enable you to transfer a group of assets from one employee name, employee number, expense account, or location to another. You enter the value that you want to transfer from and also the value that you want to transfer to. There is also the option of previewing the change before you commit the action.

MASS CHANGE

The Mass Change form enables you to make changes to a group of assets. It is one way to correct or update the financial or depreciation information for a group of assets. Note that after you have run depreciation for an asset, not all fields can be updated.

To initiate a mass change, you choose the Mass Transactions form in Oracle. To change the transfer date, open the box and enter the date on which you want the change to occur. (This date is automatically filled with the system date when you open the form.) You can change the date to any time during the current fiscal year, but you cannot backdate transfers to a previous fiscal year. You also need to indicate which book the change needs to occur in. Next, decide whether you want to preview the changes before you actually make the changes. Then choose Run to actually submit the process.

MASS RETIREMENTS

You can retire assets based on category, key, location, depreciation expense account, employee, asset number range, or the date placed in service range. You can also choose whether you want the subcomponent assets to be retired with the parent assets. Assets can be retired from one book without affecting their status in any other book where they might appear. Note that assets added in the current period cannot be retired.

MASS REVALUATION

Revaluation of assets typically occurs when the book is for a country with a highly inflationary economy. The revaluation is calculated by multiplying the asset cost by the revaluation rate you entered and a cost adjustment is made.

The process provides for review of changes prior to committing them to the system. There are also revaluation reports that can be run to evaluate the changes after committing them. Revaluations do not affect assets added in the current period, CIP assets, assets pending retirement, or fully retired assets.

MASS DEPRECIATION ADJUSTMENT

You can adjust the depreciation taken for one or all assets for a previous fiscal year in a tax book. To adjust the depreciation expense taken for all assets in a tax book, use the Mass Depreciation Adjustments form. Note that some taxing authorities allow you to prorate the depreciation expense you recognize.

To adjust tax book depreciation between minimum and maximum depreciation expense amounts, enter a factor for the calculation. Oracle Assets calculates the minimum and maximum amounts by comparing the accumulated depreciation in your tax book to a control tax book and the associated corporate book.

MASS ADDITIONS PURGING

To delete mass additions from the FA_MASS_ADDITION table, you must run the Delete Mass Additions program. The process automatically removes those assets with queue statuses of Posted, Delete, and Split. If there were any assets added erroneously, all you have to do is change their queue status to Delete.

It might be a good idea to run the Delete Mass Additions Report before running this process. This provides you the opportunity to review those items that will be deleted prior to actually removing them. Note that this process is not reversible, so you will want to be sure that you remove only those items that need to be purged. Purge accessibility should be limited to only those individuals who understand the ramifications of this process.

DATA ARCHIVE AND PURGE

Asset data such as depreciation expense and other transactions can be purged out of the Oracle Assets tables to free up disk space if the information is no longer needed for reports. The Allow Purge option must be set to Yes in the Book Controls form for each book you want to purge. It is generally best to leave it set at No until you are ready to purge to avoid causing an irreversible mistake. Oracle Assets is the only one of the Oracle Applications modules that has Archive *and* restore capability. After you have archived data, Oracle Assets removes it completely from the base tables, but references are made in some archive history tables. So if you need the information again later, you have the ability to restore. This is generally done by the technical team.

USING CONSTRUCTION IN PROGRESS

Construction in Progress (CIP) is used to track assets that are in the process of being built. Typical examples include large equipment purchases or new leasehold locations that are assembled over a period of time. You can track raw materials, labor, and overhead charges.

PART

III

CH

14

Oracle Assets identifies mass additions as CIP-based on the general ledger account they are assigned to in Payables. If they are assigned to a CIP clearing account, they are brought over as CIP assets. You can decide to capitalize them whenever you are ready to place them in service. CIP assets can also be tracked in the Oracle Projects module and transferred to Oracle Assets when they are complete.

Oracle Assets automatically creates the appropriate journal entry transactions when you move an asset from CIP to Asset Additions. At the time when an asset is transferred, you can change the date placed in service. Oracle defaults the depreciation rules to those associated with the asset category. If you need to reverse an asset that was previously capitalized, Oracle changes the asset type back to CIP and creates the adjusting entries.

There are a couple of reports that you will want to use to reconcile your CIP accounts to the general ledger. These reports are the CIP Detail and CIP Summary reports. Both of these reports can be sorted by balancing segment, asset, or CIP account.

UNDERSTANDING INVESTMENT TAX CREDITS

Investment Tax Credits (ITC) affect assets in the U.S. that were placed in service before 1987. Oracle Assets calculates the ITC amount, depreciable basis, and basis reduction amount.

Note that for an asset to be ITC eligible, ITC must be allowable by both the corporate and the tax book categories. If you are having difficulties, check the default depreciation rules for the category in question.

UNDERSTANDING UNITS OF PRODUCTION

The Units of Production method of depreciation is used to allocate the cost of an asset based on usage instead of time. Examples of assets that would be appropriate for the Units of Production depreciation method might be manufacturing equipment, oil wells, and coal mines. For more detailed information on this topic, please see the section "Defining Depreciation Methods" earlier in this chapter.

UNDERSTANDING CAPITAL BUDGETING

Capital budgets are used to track anticipated asset purchases. To track budget information, a budget book must be created. Budget information can be tracked by full category combination or by major category only. To use this feature, you must have some working knowledge of SQL*Loader, which is used to populate the interface table. Budget information can be changed at any time, but you must delete existing budget information before uploading a new capital budget from a spreadsheet.

UNDERSTANDING DEPRECIATION

Depreciation is calculated based on the depreciation method, life of the asset, and prorate convention chosen. Also, the salvage value of an item is taken into account when depreciation is calculated. The depreciation process must be run separately for each set of asset books.

When you run the depreciation process, Oracle automatically closes your books for the month, so make sure that you have completed all your transactions prior to running this process.

Following is an example of how Oracle calculates depreciation for an asset. For this example, assume that the asset will be set up using the straight-line depreciation method, with an in service date of September 22, 1999, and the prorate calendar that indicates depreciation in the first year of life will be calculated based on a half-year convention. The company uses a standard calendar year and the prorate date is July 1, 1999. The initial cost is $2,000, and the asset has a four-year depreciable life. Based on this information, the asset will have a total depreciation expense of $250 for calendar year 1999. The calculation is $2,000 divided by four and multiplied by .50 (for the half-year convention indicated by the pro-rate date of July 1, 1999).

In this scenario, when depreciation is run for the month of September 1999, Oracle will take the $250 and divide it by the six months in the prorate period (July through December), which is $41.67 per month. In September, Oracle will catch up the depreciation expense by booking $125.01. In October, the monthly depreciation expense will revert back to $41.67. By December 31, the total for the year will be $250. Beginning in the second year, Oracle will take $2,000 divided by four and allocate the full $500 (or $41.67 per month) to depreciation for this particular asset.

BALANCING THE SUBLEDGER TO THE GENERAL LEDGER

To reconcile the cost and CIP accounts, use Cost Detail and Cost Summary. Use the CIP Detail and CIP Summary reports to reconcile your CIP cost accounts to your general ledger. To reconcile with Oracle General Ledger, compare the Cost or CIP Summary report with the Account Analysis Report.

Other reports that provide supporting detail include the Asset Additions Report, Cost Adjustments Report, Asset Retirements Report, Asset Reclassifications Reconciliation Report, and Asset Transfer Reconciliation Report. The detail reports are sorted by balancing segment, asset, or CIP cost account, cost center, and asset number, and print totals for each asset or CIP cost center, account, and balancing segment. Both of the summary reports can be sorted by your balancing segment and asset or CIP account.

The Journal Entry Reserve Report can be used to determine how much depreciation expense Oracle Assets charged to a depreciation expense account for any accounting period. The report lists all active (not yet retired) capitalized assets, as well as any assets that you have retired in the period's fiscal year. The report is sorted by balancing segment, expense and reserve accounts, and cost center. It prints totals for each cost center, account, and balancing segment.

Use the Accumulated Depreciation Balance Report to reconcile your reserve accounts to your general ledger.

PART

III

CH

14

USING OPEN INTERFACES IN THIS APPLICATION

There are a number of Open Interfaces found in Oracle Assets. Please find them below along with a brief discussion on how they are used.

IMPORTING ASSETS USING THE MASS ADDITIONS INTERFACE

The database definition of the FA_MASS_ADDITIONS table does not require that you provide values for any columns, but for the Mass Additions Posting program to work properly, make sure you follow the rules in the list of column descriptions. The Mass Additions Posting program uses some of the columns in the FA_MASS_ADDITIONS table, so these columns are marked NULL. Do not import your data into columns marked NULL. You must fill columns marked REQUIRED before you run Mass Additions Post.

The FA MASS ADDITIONS table can be loaded directly using SQL*Loader, ADI (Application Desktop Integrator), or another program. If you decide to load the column directly from another system, fill in some values in the Mass Additions window before you post. Columns marked OPTIONAL are for optional asset information that you can track if you want. VARCHAR2 columns are case-sensitive. For columns marked PREP, you can either import information into the column directly or enter it in the Mass Additions window before you post.

Note that if you are using Oracle Payables, the FA MASS ADDITIONS table will be populated automatially when you run the Mass Additions Create process in Payables.

USING THE BUDGET INTERFACE

If you maintain your budget information in a spreadsheet, you can upload it to Oracle Assets using the budget interface. You can transfer budget data from any software package that prints to an ASCII file and then use SQL*Loader, ADI, or another program to load the FA_BUDGET_INTERFACE table.

USING THE PRODUCTION INTERFACE

You can enter or update production amounts for assets depreciating under units of production. You can enter production information online, or you can load it automatically from a feeder system using the Upload Periodic Production program. Enter production more than once a period if necessary.

USING THE ACE (ADJUSTED CURRENT EARNINGS) INTERFACE

You can either have Oracle Assets calculate ACE (Adjusted Current Earnings) information for you or enter it yourself. If you want Oracle Assets to calculate ACE-accumulated depreciation for you, enter historical asset information beginning no later than the last period of fiscal 1989. Start your depreciation books in Oracle Assets before the end of fiscal 1989, and enter asset transactions through the current period.

If you have ACE information from another asset system, you can load it into Oracle Assets using the ACE interface. Define the initial open period of your ACE book as the last period of the last fiscal year you completed on your previous system. Then load the accumulated depreciation for your ACE assets using this interface.

USING THE INV INTERFACE

The physical inventory interface is used to transfer the physical inventory data you have collected. This form and how to utilize it are best tackled by a technical analyst because it requires an understanding of SQL*Loader, ADI, or another program.

UNDERSTANDING KEY REPORTS

Oracle FA reports can be run either singly or by using a request set. A request set enables you to streamline your printing process by grouping reports that you frequently run together. Request sets can be run either in parallel or in sequence. Running in parallel simply means that you do not need them to be run in any particular order, and conversely, running in sequence means that they must be run in a particular order or sequence. The form to set this process up is very self-explanatory and can be used by even the most inexperienced individual.

During the testing phase of your project, it is best to review all available reports in Oracle and run them at least once to determine whether they fulfill any of your reporting needs. Prior to running them, you should make a list of the reports that you use on your current system to compare them against the standard reports. This enables you to develop a list of reporting needs that are not going to be fulfilled with standard reports.

Reports can be run using two different methods. First, you can run them directly from the application using the Submit Requests window. The second method is by running them using the Request Center in ADI. If you choose to use ADI, you can save them in Excel, text, or HTML format. You can then store the output on your hard drive or to a network directory.

In reviewing the reports that Oracle provides, there seem to be five distinct classifications of FA reports. I have grouped these into the following categories: additions, depreciation, mass, reconciling, and other. I will highlight some of the reports that I found to be most helpful and indicate what each one can provide for you.

Probably the most frequently used type of report is the Asset Additions Report. Oracle comes with about eight reports that provide information on asset additions. Depending on how you want to see them sorted and what parameters are most important to you, there are a variety of standard reports to choose from. When initially configuring your system, you will probably use either the Annual Additions Report or the Asset Additions Report to tie out your cost and accumulated depreciation. The major difference between the two reports is that the Asset Additions Report provides a lot more detail and sort capabilities. If you are looking for more summarized information, use the Annual Additions Report.

There are a few reports that relate to the depreciation expense process. The Journal Entry Reserve Ledger Report and the Gains & Losses Report are actually generated whenever you run the depreciation process in Oracle Assets. In addition to those reports, there are two additional reports that you should be aware of, and they are the Assets Not Assigned to Any Books Listing and the Assets Not Assigned to Any Cost Centers Listing. You should be sure that you run these every month prior to initiating the depreciation expense process. Because the depreciation process aborts when it encounters problems, these reports alert you to some potential problems that might exist prior to running your depreciation process.

There are also many different predefined Mass reports that come standard with Oracle. You can review mass additions that you created, posted, split, deleted, and purged. You can also print reports that provide mass retirements, transfers, and change information. These reports are very self-explanatory to run and most of them only require date parameters and a book designation to process.

The reports that are most commonly used to reconcile back to the general ledger start with the Unposted Journal Report. This report is generated automatically when you run the depreciation process. If additional copies are desired, it is accessible from the concurrent manager. There are also two drill-down reports available in general ledger called Drill Down Report and the Account Drill Down Report. Both can assist in reviewing entries created by Oracle FA.

To reconcile the cost accounts with GL, you can run the Cost Summary and Cost Detail reports (the CIP Summary and Detail reports to reconcile your CIP cost accounts). The summary report can only be sorted by balancing segment and asset account. The detail report can be sorted by balancing segment, cost center, asset number, and asset account. If there are any discrepancies, you can also print the asset additions, cost adjustment, asset transfers, and asset retirement reports. These reports provide details to assist you in determining where any balancing problems might have occurred.

Depreciation expense reconciliation can be done using the Journal Entry Reserve Ledger report. This report provides details on all active assets in addition to those assets that you might have retired during the current fiscal year. It is sorted by balancing segment, expense accounts, and cost center. Any assets that have been transferred or adjusted during the fiscal year are shown on the report with a marking to indicate that they have been changed in some way.

There are a vast number of miscellaneous reports that can be used to analyze different types of information. There are many standard tax reports that can be used to provide details for specific tax forms such as Form 4562 Depreciation and Amortization Report and Form 4626 AMT Detail and Summary Report. There are also standard Property Tax Report, Investment Tax Credit, and Tax Additions reports that specifically target the needs of your tax department. There are also reports to review setup data such as calendars, prorate conventions, asset categories, asset descriptions, asset tags, and price indexes.

One miscellaneous report that will probably be of interest is the Fixed Asset Projection report. This report is not available through the standard report submission; it is found under the depreciation menu path. When you initiate the projections process, it automatically runs the report. The report can be sorted by cost center and provides summary or detailed asset information. You must select the number of periods, start date, and the book that you want the projection to be run against.

SUMMARY

In summary, Oracle Assets is a very powerful tool for managing and keeping track of your assets. The key to success is spending the time up front analyzing your business needs. The program can be set up to accommodate many different requirements, and sometimes the solution might not be readily apparent but is available nonetheless. I hope this chapter has shown some of the ways this can be accomplished.

The next chapter is "Using Oracle Purchasing," and this topic is closely related to Oracle Assets.

CHAPTER 15

USING ORACLE PURCHASING

Oracle Purchasing provides numerous features that enable you to set up your system to reflect your business practices and manage the requisition and purchase of products and services required to run your business. The Purchasing application interfaces with Oracle Payables to assist in bill paying. Through Purchasing, you also interface to Inventory to replenish stock. You also use Purchasing to assist the material planning process in the purchase of goods and services required for the manufacturing schedule.

HOW PURCHASING RELATES TO OTHER APPLICATIONS

Purchasing has relationships to many of the modules in the Oracle application suite. The Inventory, General Ledger, Order Entry, Accounts Payable, Accounts Receivable, Fixed Assets, and Cost Management modules share the setup information from Purchasing. Purchasing depends on the Applications Object Library (AOL) for responsibilities, menus, profile options, and other related setups. Figure 15.1 shows how various modules are related to Purchasing. Each module indicates the information it shares. Arrows show the direction in which the information flows and to which modules the information flows.

Figure 15.1
Purchasing relationships to other applications.

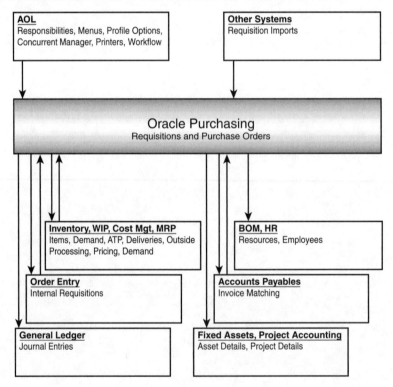

DISCOVERING NEW FEATURES IN RELEASE 11

Release 11 provides many new financials features to include multiple reporting of currencies, support for the euro, and expanded globalization. Release 11 also provides the following new manufacturing features to include mixed-mode manufacturing, flow manufacturing, and integrated-process manufacturing. Finally, Release 11 provides new capabilities for the integration of the manufacturing floor with the Internet.

ADVANCED WORKFLOW TECHNOLOGY

The new advanced workflow technology automates the procurement process through the use of rule-based processes designed for your specific business needs. Employees can use the Web, email, or the applications interface to receive and respond to workflow notifications.

Purchasing comes with the following three predefined workflows:

- Document approval process: This replaces all the approval procedures in previous releases of Purchasing.

- Automatic document-creation process: This automatically creates purchase orders or releases from approved requisitions.

- Change orders process: This processes the changes made to purchasing documents to determine which documents require re-approval on change.

For detailed discussion of workflows, such as creating new workflows or modifying predefined workflows, refer to Chapter 22, "Using Oracle Workflow."

SUPPLIER DROP SHIPMENTS

The supplier drop shipments enhancement provides the capability to ship products directly from your supplier to your customer. You can track the status of the order through the purchase order or sales order information and invoice your customer when you've been notified that the order has shipped. This enhancement can improve customer service and reduce lead times and inventory costs.

ADVANCED SHIPMENT NOTICE SUPPORT

The advanced shipment notice support enhancement is an   electronic data interchange (EDI) transaction that provides immediate visibility to your supplier's shipments. The combination of real-time shipment notice and the streamlined receiving process gives you the capability to anticipate and respond to potential delivery problems before they occur and improve transaction accuracy and throughput—thereby reducing your receiving cost and capturing carrier information automatically.

MULTIPLE REPORTING CURRENCY

The multiple reporting currency enhancement allows you to view requisitions, purchase orders, and receipts in other accounting currencies. Purchases entered in any currency are automatically converted to your primary and all reporting currencies.

ENHANCED PURCHASING OPEN INTERFACE

The enhanced purchasing open interface allows you to load and validate electronic catalogs and supply agreements. Full functional validation of inbound price/sales catalogs, quotes, and agreements is also provided. Also, the item master creates items as the information is loaded into the system.

INTEGRATION WITH ORACLE QUALITY

Purchasing is integrated with Oracle Quality through receiving inspections. You can include information on the supplier, shipper, rejections, and packaging conditions at the time of receipt. This enhancement allows you to better assess supplier quality.

> **Tip**
> Many of the enhancements developed for new releases are available to users of earlier releases. These backports are available to licensed users through patches. Check Oracle's MetaLink Web site to see a list of current backports.

CRITICAL IMPLEMENTATION FACTORS

In addition to understanding the factors discussed here, you should identify and understand some key issues underlying a Purchasing implementation. The issues vary depending on the business scenario and requirements. The following common issues apply in all circumstances.

DEFINING YOUR ACCRUAL OPTIONS

The define accrual option allows you to determine whether to accrue expense items upon receipt or at period end. For inventory items, you can only accrue on receipt.

> **Note**
> If you use cash basis accounting, the accrual option should be set to Period End. You will not normally run the Receipt Accrual-Period End process.

DEFINING YOUR CONTROL OPTIONS

The define control options allow you to define the percentage by which the autocreated purchase order line cannot exceed the requisition line price. You can also define whether to close a shipment once it has passed inspection, once it has been delivered, or once it has been received. Additionally, you can require the system to notify you when you create a requisition line if a blanket purchase agreement exists for the item. You can also define whether the item description can be updated when a requisition, request for quotation (RFQ), quotation, or purchase order line is created. Through this option, you can prevent the approval of purchase orders created with suppliers that are on hold.

DEFINING YOUR DEFAULT OPTIONS

The define default options allow you to determine how your requisitions imported through the requisition open interface are grouped. You can also determine the currency rate type that is shown on requisitions, purchase orders, RFQs, and quotations. Additionally, you can define the minimum release amount for blanket, contract, and planned purchase orders. You can define what type of invoice matching your organization uses: Two-way matching must match the purchase order and invoice quantities within the tolerance; three-way matching matches the purchase order, receipt, and invoice; and four-way matching matches the purchase order, receipt, inspection, and invoice quantity.

DEFINING YOUR NUMBERING OPTIONS

The define numbering option allows you to determine whether your organization uses automatic or manual numbering

> **Note**   You can change the method of entering document numbers at any time.

You can also define whether your organization uses numeric or alphanumeric numbering.

> **Note**   If you choose automatic document numbering, you can generate only numeric document numbers. However, you can import either numeric or alphanumeric document numbers.

ISSUES AND GAPS

Purchasing is an extensive module with many capabilities. Although the Review of the Top Enhancement Requests show some unresolved issues with Purchasing, it is for the most part a fairly complete module for the functions it covers.

REVIEWING TOP ENHANCEMENT REQUESTS

Users have requested that they be allowed to override the supplier and supplier site on approved purchase orders. Sometimes in the dynamics of today's business environment, the supplier or supplier site information might must change. Also, the fact that a purchase order has been approved does not mean that the purchase order has been printed and executed. Users need the flexibility of last-minute changes.

Users have also requested the capability to change a line type from goods to contracts. This is an important enhancement in that what might begin, for example, as a request for software can turn into a request for contract services. This is another enhancement that provides additional flexibility to the user.

Another enhancement requested by users is that cancelled purchase order lines not be printed on the printed purchase order. Cancelled purchase order lines on a printed purchase can be confusing to both the buyer and the supplier. This confusion can lead to the supplier sending items that have been cancelled.

Users have also requested the ability to enter returns against a cancelled purchase order. A cancelled purchase order might have had activity against the purchase order even though the purchase order had been cancelled.

Also, users have requested the ability to select which changes to a purchase order or requisition require reapproval. This is an enhancement of both flexibility and efficiency. The requirement that the entire requisition must be reapproved slows down the reapproval process and clutters the process.

CONFIGURING THE APPLICATION

The Purchasing module requires extensive setup for the module to be configured properly to function as advertised. The following section lists all the setup tasks for a Purchasing implementation and briefly describes each task. You should perform the tasks in the order discussed here.

RESOLVING CRITICAL SETUP ISSUES

Prior to setting up Purchasing, you must resolve several critical issues. First, you must determine the set of books and accounting structure. Second, you must set up the organizations, positions, jobs, and users so employees can purchase items. Table 15.1 shows the setup steps you must consider to configure the Purchasing application.

TABLE 15.1   PURCHASING SETUP CHECKLIST

Step	Requirement
Define set of books	Required with defaults
Define descriptive flexfields	Optional
Define organizations	Required
Define cross-reference types	Optional
Define profile options	Required
Define financials options (part 1)	Required
Define accounting flexfields combinations	Optional
Define tax names	Optional

TABLE 15.1 CONTINUED

Step	Requirement
Define payment terms	Optional
Open and close General Ledger (GL) accounting periods	Required
Open purchasing and inventory accounting periods	Required
Define locations	Required
Define location associations	Optional
Define job flexfield	Required
Define jobs	Required
Define position flexfields	Required
Define positions	Optional
Define position hierarchies	Optional
Enter employee	Required
Define item categories flexfield	Required
Define category	Required
Define category sets	Required
Define default category set	Required
Define control rules and groups	Required
Define position controls	Required
Fill employee hierarchy	Optional
Define user names	Required
Define purchasing lookup codes	Optional
Define freight carriers	Optional
Define inspection codes	Optional
Define hazard classes	Optional
Define United Nations (UN) numbers	Optional
Define standard notes	Optional
Define unit of measure classes	Required
Define units of measure	Required
Define unit of measure conversions	Required
Define system items flexfield	Required
Define item attribute controls	Required with defaults
Define item templates	Optional
Define item catalog flexfield	Required
Define item catalog groups	Optional

TABLE 15.1 CONTINUED

Step	Requirement
Define buyers	Required
Define item	Optional
Define item relationships	Optional
Define line types	Optional
Define document controls	Required with defaults
Start autosubmit	Required
Define financials options (part 2)	Required
Define purchasing options	Required
Define receiving options	Required
Enter vendors	Required
Define your transactions reasons	Optional
Set up Oracle Workflow	Required
Request your receiving transaction processor	Optional
Define your concurrent process resubmission interval	Optional

UNDERSTANDING EACH SETUP TASK

Setup tasks fall into three categories. First are those setup tasks that the Oracle system requires for the application to operate. In the Purchasing application, you must have employees defined before you can create requisitions. Additionally, you must have buyers defined before purchase orders can be created from requisitions and purchase orders can be processed. Second are those tasks that, although required, contain certain default values which you can allow the system to use. Finally, some steps are completely optional, based on your particular implementation.

DEFINING THE SET OF BOOKS

Before you can implement Oracle Purchasing, you must set up at least one set of books. The set of books defines for the Purchasing application the chart of accounts, the accounting calendar, the functional currency, and the accounting flexfield structure. When defining the set of books, use the setup process described in Chapter 11, "Using Oracle General Ledger." You need not tackle this step if you have already set up the Oracle General Ledger application.

DEFINING DESCRIPTIVE FLEXFIELDS

Oracle Applications have a feature known as descriptive flexfields. Descriptive flexfields place information into the Oracle system that might not be provided otherwise. The descriptive flexfield has global segments that always appear on a flexfield pop-up window of a form and context-sensitive segments that are dependent on other information which appears on the form.

> **Note**
>
> To avoid slowing down data entry, do not set up mandatory descriptive flexfields in the Enter Purchase Orders and Enter Purchase Agreements windows.

DEFINING ORGANIZATIONS

Before you can implement Oracle Purchasing, you must set up the organizations. The organization defines the structure within which the Purchasing application allows employees to buy and receive goods or services. You do not need this step if you have already set up the Oracle Inventory application. When defining organizations, use the setup process described in Chapter 16, "Using Oracle Inventory."

DEFINING CROSS-REFERENCE TYPES

Cross-reference types define the types of relationships between items and other entities. As an example, you can create a relationship to track your old part numbers or to track your customer's part number. You then can assign any number of cross references to items.

SETTING THE PROFILE OPTIONS

Profile options give you control over the behavior of certain application features. Profile levels are a hierarchy, where user (U) is the highest level of the hierarchy, followed by responsibility (R), application (A), and, at the lowest level, site (S). Refer to table 15.2 as you set profile option values.

TABLE 15.2 PURCHASING USER/SYSTEM PRODUCTIVITY PROFILE OPTIONS

Profile Option Name	Required?	Level	Comment
MRP: Default sourcing assignment set	Yes	SARU	Default PO assignment set
HR: Business group	Yes	SAR	Default setup business group
PO: Allow category override in autocreate	Yes	SARU	Default is yes
PO: Change supplier name	No	SARU	Yes/no
PO: Default supplier item catalog option	No	SARU	Negotiated sources
PO: Display autocreated quotation	No	SARU	Default is yes
PO: Display find on open catalog	No	SARU	Default is yes

TABLE 15.2 CONTINUED

Profile Option Name	Required?	Level	Comment
PO: Display the autocreated document	No	SARU	Default is yes
PO: Warn RFQ required before autocreate	No	SARU	Default is no
PO: Item cross-reference warning	No	SARU	Default is disposition
PO: Legal requisition type	No	SARU	Default is both
PO: Release during reqimport	No	SARU	Yes/no
PO: Supplier pricing method	No	SARU	Catalog price/last price
RCV: Allow routing override	No	SARU	Yes/No
RCV: Print receipt traveler	No	SARU	Yes/No
RCV: Processing mode	Yes	SARU	Batch/immediate/online

DEFINING FINANCIAL OPTIONS

The financial options are used throughout the Oracle Applications. You define the set of books Purchasing uses as well as defaults to simplify vendor entry, invoice entry, and automatic payments. You do not need this step if you have already set up the Oracle Payables application. When defining financial options, use the setup process described in Chapter 12, "Using Oracle Payables."

DEFINING ACCOUNTING FLEXFIELD COMBINATIONS

Your accounting flexfield defines the account structure of your general ledger accounts. The accounting flexfield combinations enable you to take advantage of the applications' flexible tools for recording and reporting accounting information. You must define all acceptable accounting flexfield combinations if dynamic insertion is not allowed. This step is not required if dynamic insertion is allowed. You do not need this step if you have set up the Oracle General Ledger application. When defining accounting flexfield combinations, use the setup process described in Chapter 11.

DEFINING TAX NAMES

You must define the taxes you use to record the invoice taxes paid to your vendors. You also define your tax authorities here. You do not need this step if you have set up the Oracle Payables application. When defining tax names, use the setup process described in Chapter 12.

DEFINING PAYMENT TERMS

Define the payment terms that reflect the way you do business. Payment terms are used to calculate the payment schedules for invoices. Payment terms can be defined either as a percentage due or as an amount due. You can also define discounts. There is no limit to the number of payment terms you can define. You do not need this step if you have already set up the Oracle Payables application. When defining payment terms, use the setup process described in Chapter 12.

OPENING AND CLOSING PERIODS IN THE ACCOUNTING CALENDAR

You must open GL periods to allow posting of accounting entries into the general ledger from a PO. Similarly, you can close a GL accounting period to prevent posting of accounting entries. You do not need this step here if you have already set up the Oracle General Ledger application. When defining opening and closing periods, use the setup process described in Chapter 11.

OPENING AND CLOSING PERIODS IN THE PO AND INV CALENDARS

Purchasing has its own periods that you must open and close separately from the General Ledger periods. You must open a purchasing period before any transactions can be entered in that period. You can close a purchasing period to prevent transactions in that period. A closed purchasing period can be opened later to allow transactions. However, if a period is permanently closed, you cannot open it again. Use caution before permanently closing a period. A permanent close ideally happens after an annual close when you are sure that there are no more transactions or corrections. You create general ledger journal entries when encumbering requisitions or purchase orders or accruing receipts.

DEFINING LOCATIONS AND LOCATION ASSOCIATIONS

Locations are defined in your organization for where you ship, receive, deliver internally, or bill for goods and services ordered. Additionally, if you group your locations by their Ship To sites, you can have your vendors ship everything to a central receiving location. You can also associate a location with vendors, vendor sites, or inventory organizations.

> **Note**
>
> Define your Ship To locations before defining other locations. Define your vendors before doing any location associations.

> **Tip**
>
> A location can be its own Ship To location. If you want to define a location to be its own Ship To location, do not enter anything in the Ship To field; Purchasing saves the location with the Ship To location as itself.

DEFINING THE JOB FLEXFIELD

Jobs are generic or specific roles within the enterprise. Jobs are independent of organization structures and are generally used where there is flexibility in employee roles. You do not must perform this step here if you have installed Oracle Human Resources. When defining the job flexfield, use the setup process described in Chapter 25, "Using Oracle Human Resources."

Caution

> Proceed carefully and coordinate with human resources if Oracle Human Resources is to be installed.

DEFINING JOBS

You must define the jobs that each employee has. Additionally, you can also define the skills that jobholders require and the grades to which they can be assigned. You do not need this step if you have installed Oracle Human Resources. When defining jobs, use the setup process described in Chapter 25.

Note

> You must coordinate the definition of jobs with human resources.

DEFINING THE POSITION FLEXFIELD

You should use positions to manage fixed establishments of posts that exist independently of the employee assignment. A position is a specific occurrence of one job, fixed within one organization. You do not must perform this step if you have installed Oracle Human Resources. When defining the position flexfield, use the setup process described in Chapter 25.

Caution

> Proceed carefully and coordinate with human resources if you install Oracle Human Resources.

DEFINING POSITIONS

You do not must define positions if you have installed Oracle Human Resources. When you define the positions within your organization, you should place them in the organization's position hierarchy. You can also maintain position holders' skills and grades. When defining positions, use the setup process described in Chapter 25.

> **Note**
>
> You must coordinate the definition of positions with human resources.
>
> You cannot change the organization or job once you have saved the definition. You can set up several positions that have the same job in the same organization. Each position name must be unique.

DEFINING POSITION HIERARCHIES

Position hierarchies are much like organization hierarchies. You can set up one primary hierarchy and multiple secondary hierarchies showing reporting lines, including "dotted line" reporting, to control access to information. The Purchasing position hierarchy is defined within a business group. The Purchasing application uses the hierarchy to determine the approval paths for your purchasing documents.

> **Note**
>
> To use position hierarchies for document approval, you must set the Use Approval Hierarchies Profile option to Yes.

ENTERING EMPLOYEES

In Purchasing, an employee can requisition goods and services—but she must first be recognized by the system as a user and she must also be a member of the requisition or purchasing hierarchy. You do not need this step if you have already installed the Oracle Human Resources application. Each employee should be assigned a job and position for document control and approval. When defining employees, use the setup process described in Chapter 25.

DEFINING THE ITEM CATEGORIES FLEXFIELD

You must design and configure your item categories flexfield before you can start defining items. Oracle Applications requires that all items be assigned to categories. You need not tackle this step if you have installed Oracle Inventory. When defining the item categories flexfield, use the setup process described in Chapter 16.

DEFINING ITEM CATEGORIES

A category is a logical classification of items that have similar characteristics. Categories are often the primary sort and/or grouping parameter for major purchasing reports. You do not need this step if you have installed Oracle Inventory. When defining item categories, use the setup process described in Chapter 16.

> **Tip**
>
> You can enter purchase order lines with only a category specified and without a item number. This is useful for one-time items that you do not want to define in your item

master. When you define general categories that you can use directly on purchase orders, give them appropriate names to print on the purchase orders.

DEFINING CATEGORY SETS

A category set is a distinct grouping scheme that consists of categories. Category sets are used in reporting for grouping together items with similar characteristics. You do not need this step if you have installed Oracle Inventory. When defining category sets, use the setup process described in Chapter 16.

SETTING THE DEFAULT CATEGORY SET

Each item you define must be assigned to a category set. You do not need this step if you have already installed Oracle Inventory. When setting default category sets, use the setup process described in Chapter 16.

Note
> The default category set used in Purchasing always enforces the list of valid categories.

DEFINING CONTROL RULES AND GROUPS

Document control rules set approval limits for your employees for requisitions, purchase orders, and releases. You can assign document controls by the document total, account range, location, item range, or item category range. To approve documents, you must have a document total and account range rule.

DEFINING POSITION CONTROLS OR CONTROLS FOR JOBS

You can assign individual positions or jobs to control groups. The employees assigned the job or position take on the authorization abilities of that job or position. The rules associated with control groups are used as a part of your hierarchy to control the flow of the approval process of your documents.

FILLING THE EMPLOYEE HIERARCHY

The fill employee hierarchy process creates a direct mapping between the defined position hierarchies and the employees holding the positions in each hierarchy. You must run this process anytime you make a change to the hierarchy for the change to take effect.

SETTING UP THE USERS

You must set up users to assign an employee to a job or position; you do so in the System Administration module. An employee assigned in human resources is matched to the user. You do not need this step if you do not use positional hierarchies for document routing.

> **Caution**
>
> Proceed carefully and coordinate with human resources if Oracle Human Resources is to be installed. If two users are assigned to the same employee, problems with the approval process could occur. Notifications might be sent to the wrong user.

SETTING UP PURCHASING QUICKCODES

Purchasing uses lookup codes to define the lists of values throughout the system. Although there are a large number of lookup codes seeded in Oracle Purchasing, you can add quickcodes that meet your specific business needs.

> **Note**
>
> You cannot change or delete codes once you have added and saved them, but you can change the code descriptions or disable them by entering an end date.
>
> Warning: Before you change the description of a quickcode, you must ensure that you do not run reports that contain previous transactions with the quickcode. Otherwise, any reports generated from the previous transactions can show quickcode descriptions inappropriate for the context.
>
> The safest option is to disable the quickcode you do not want to use and create new quickcodes with appropriate descriptions.

DEFINING FREIGHT CARRIERS

Freight carriers handle internal transfers between organizations and shipments to and from customers and suppliers. You must set up a general ledger account for collecting costs associated with using the carrier. You do not need this step if you have installed Oracle Inventory. When defining freight carriers, use the setup process described in Chapter 16.

DEFINING INSPECTION CODES

You use inspection codes when you receive and inspect items that have been ordered. Each code requires a numerical ranking, which provides an inspection scale. You do not need this step if you have installed Oracle Inventory. When defining inspection codes, use the setup process described in Chapter 16.

DEFINING HAZARD CLASSES

Purchasing places hazardous material information you've defined onto your purchase orders, request for quotes, and receipt travelers.

> **Note**
>
> You can assign a hazard class to multiple UN numbers to identify hazardous items. Follow the next step to define UN numbers.

DEFINING UN NUMBERS

United Nations (UN) numbers provide identification to hazardous materials. UN numbers have descriptions that allow the shipment of hazardous material within the US or internationally.

> **Note**
>
> You can also assign an identification number and a hazard class to each item you define.

DEFINING STANDARD NOTES

You can create attachments for your purchasing documents. The Purchasing module offers the following attachment capabilities:

- Provide unlimited text attachments on your purchasing documents.
- Designate the appropriate people who can review the attachments.
- Print attachments on your purchase orders and request for quotes for the supplier to review.
- Reuse attachments on different documents.
- Copy and modify existing attachments to speed up data entry.
- Copy attachments from your requisitions to your request for quotes and purchase orders.
- Provide standard attachments for an item that you can reference whenever you create a purchasing document for that item.

DEFINING UNIT OF MEASURE CLASSES AND UNITS OF MEASURE

Unit of measure classes are groups of units of measure with similar characteristics. Units of measure express the quantity of items. You do not need this step if you have installed Oracle Inventory. When defining units of measure, use the setup process described in Chapter 16.

> **Tip**
>
> Purchasing prints the first four characters of the unit of measure description on the purchase order. Try to make these characters representative of the unit of measure.

DEFINING UNIT OF MEASURE CONVERSIONS

Unit of measure conversions enable you to perform transactions in units other than the primary unit of the item being transacted. You do not need this step if you have installed Oracle Inventory. When defining unit of measure conversions, use the setup process described in Chapter 16.

DEFINING THE SYSTEM ITEMS KEY FLEXFIELD

The system items key flexfield records your item information. You do not need this step if you have installed Oracle Inventory. When defining the system items key flexfield, use the setup process described in Chapter 27, "Administering the Oracle Applications."

DEFINING ITEM ATTRIBUTE CONTROLS

Item attributes are information about an item. Before you can define an item, you must set attribute controls. The control-level attribute type determines whether you have centralized (master level) or decentralized (organization level) control of item attributes. The status control attribute type describes whether certain status attributes have default values that appear when you assign a status code to an item and whether status codes control those attribute values after the defaults are assigned to an item. You do not need this step if you have installed Oracle Inventory. When defining item attribute controls, use the setup process described in Chapter 16.

DEFINING ITEM TEMPLATES

Templates are standard sets of attributes that you can use over and over to create similar items. Templates make item definition easier. You do not need this step if you have installed Oracle Inventory. When defining item templates, use the setup process described in Chapter 16.

DEFINING THE ITEM CATALOG FLEXFIELD

You do not must define item catalog flexfields if you have installed Oracle Inventory. When you do define them, use the setup process described in Chapter 27.

DEFINING ITEM CATALOG GROUPS

An item catalog group has descriptive elements that are used to describe items. You can group items by these descriptive elements and then use these groupings in reporting. You do not need this step if you have installed Oracle Inventory. When defining item catalog groups, use the setup process described in Chapter 16.

DEFINING BUYERS

Buyers can review all requisitions. Also, only buyers can enter and autocreate purchasing documents. Before you can define buyers, you must define your employees and locations.

DEFINING ITEMS AND ITEM RELATIONSHIPS

Prior to requisitioning anything, you must define your items. In Purchasing, you must create item relationships for items you receive as a substitute for the original item. You do not need this step if you have installed Oracle Inventory. When defining items and item relationships, use the setup process described in Chapter 16.

DEFINING LINE TYPES

You create line types to reflect the different characteristics for the items you purchase. You might want to define one line type for items you order by quantity and unit price. A second line type might be services you order by hour. A third type might be a line for outside processing operations in Oracle Work In Process.

Note

When the outside processing line type is selected on a document line, you can only enter outside processing items, and the destination type can only be the shop floor.

Before you can define line types, you must define categories and units of measure.

STARTING THE AUTOSUBMIT PROGRAM

The autosubmit process is a concurrent program that resubmits itself every 24 hours to purge obsolete notification information from the system. Starting autosubmit is a required step.

DEFINING PURCHASING OPTIONS

You define default values and controls used throughout Purchasing through the purchasing options. The categories are

- Accrual options, such as whether to accrue expense items at period end or upon receipt.

Note

When using cash basis accounting, you should set this option to Period End, but you will not normally run the Receipt Accrual - Period End process.

- Control options, such as the receipt close point.
- Default options, such as the minimum release amount.
- Internal requisition options, such as the required order type and order source for internal requisitions.
- Numbering options, such as the numbering method, numbering type, and next number for each of your documents.

Note

You can override purchasing options when you are creating documents. You can change the method of entering document numbers at any time. If you choose automatic document number entry, you can generate only numeric document numbers.

> If you import purchasing documents that reference alphanumeric numbers, you must choose alphanumeric as your number type, regardless of your numbering method. You must set up internal requisitions if Order Entry is installed.

DEFINING RECEIVING OPTIONS

Receiving options govern the receipt of items in your organization. Most of the options set here can be overridden for specific suppliers, items, and purchase orders. You must set up receiving options for each organization.

DEFINING TRANSACTION REASONS

Transaction reasons are a standard means of classifying or explaining the reason for a transaction. You do not need this step if you have installed Oracle Inventory. When defining transaction reasons, use the setup process described in Chapter 16.

CONFIGURING FLEXBUILDER

In Release 10, you used flexbuilder to derive the account code combinations in Purchasing. In Release 11, flexbuilder has been replaced by the account generator workflow. Prior to using the account generator in a production environment, you must define your accounting flexfield structures for each set of books. You also must define your flexfield segment values and validation rules. Then, you must set up Oracle Workflow, using the process described in Chapter 22.

REQUESTING THE RECEIVING TRANSACTION PROCESSOR

If the profile option RCV: Processing Mode is set to Batch, the receiving transaction processor performs the following functions:

- Creates receipt headers for in-transit shipments
- Creates receipt lines for all receipts
- Maintains transaction history information
- Maintains lot and serial transaction history
- Accrues uninvoiced receipt liabilities
- Maintains purchase order quantities
- Closes purchase orders for receiving
- Maintains requisition information
- Maintains supply information
- Maintains inventory information
- Maintains outside processing information

DEFINING CONCURRENT PROCESSING INTERVALS

You define concurrent processing intervals to determine how often certain processes automatically run. Some of the recurring processes are the requisition import used for creating internal sales orders and the receiving transaction processor.

CONVERTING DATA FOR MAJOR ENTITIES

As your organization transitions from its current system to Oracle Purchasing, you will want to move much of the data you've gathered over the years. Currently, importing purchase orders is not supported through the Oracle Applications program interfaces. An organization can enter new and transition purchase orders directly into the applications.

ENTERING VENDORS

Vendors are individuals and companies from whom you purchase goods and services. Employees you reimburse for expense reports can also be entered as vendors. You do not need this step if you have installed Oracle Payables. When entering vendors, use the setup process described in Chapter 12.

PROCESSING REQUISITIONS AND EXPRESS REQUISITIONS

Processing requisitions online in the Purchasing module is easy and efficient in the Oracle system. Once you set up the requisition hierarchy, the requisition approval cycle makes the flow of requisitions very direct. The Purchasing module offers the following features of the online requisition process.

You can create, edit, and review requisition information online. You can review the current status and action history of your requisitions. You can route requisitions according to your approval structure. You can review and approve requisitions that need your approval. You can print requisitions (with status approved, cancelled, rejected, in process, pre-approved, and returned) for offline review and approval.

You can import requisitions from other systems such as material or distributions requirement planning applications. You can perform online funds checking before creating requisitions. You can automatically source requisitions from outstanding blanket purchase agreements or quotations you have received from suppliers. You can create requisitions quickly and easily for commonly purchased items.

You can provide attachments as notes on requisition headers and lines. You can assign requisition lines to buyers and review buyer assignments for requisition lines. You can forward all requisitions awaiting approval from one approver to an alternate approver. You can record suggested foreign currency information for each requisition line.

PROCESSING REQUESTS FOR QUOTATION

You can identify requisitions that require supplier quotations and automatically create a request for quotation. You can create a request for quotation with or without approved requisitions so that you can plan ahead for your future procurement requirements. You can record supplier quotations from a catalog, telephone conversation, or response from your request for quotation. You can review, analyze, and approve supplier quotations that you want available to reference on purchase orders and requisitions. You should be able to evaluate your suppliers based on quotation information.

You can receive automatic notification when a quotation or request for quotation approaches expiration. You can review quotation information online when creating purchase orders or requisitions. You can identify a supplier that you want to use only for receiving RFQs and quotations. You can hold all purchasing activity on a supplier at any time. You can create, change, and review supplier information online. You can review the purchase history for a specific item. You can simplify the sourcing of commonly purchased items. You can automatically source the items for which you negotiated purchase agreements.

PROCESSING PURCHASE ORDERS

You can review all of your purchases with your suppliers to negotiate better discounts. You can create purchase orders simply by entering a supplier and item details. You can create standard purchase orders and blanket releases from both online and paper requisitions. You can create accurate and detailed accounting information so that you charge purchases to the appropriate departments. You can check your funds availability while creating purchase orders.

You can review the status and history of your purchase orders at any time for all the information you need. You can print purchase orders flexibly by using a number of print options. You can inform your suppliers of your shipment schedule requirements. You can record supplier acceptances of your purchase orders. You can create your purchase orders by providing a quantity and price for each item you are ordering.

ENTERING PURCHASE ORDERS

You can enter standard and planned purchase orders as well as blanket and contract purchase agreements. You can enter purchase orders from paper requisitions or without a requisition. You can take approval actions on individual purchase orders and agreements online. You can also enter preference information for purchase order lines, shipments, distributions, and releases.

ENTERING RELEASES

You can create releases for requisition lines if they meet the following criteria:

- The releases are approved and already sourced to an existing blanket release.

- The autosource rule for the item, supplier, and blanket indicates that the release generation method is either automatic release or automatic release/review.
- The requisition line is not already on a purchase order.
- The source blanket is still active, and the release will not put the blanket over the amount limit.
- The item and item revision on the requisition match the item and item revision on the blanket.

USING AUTOCREATE

Autocreate allows you to create new standard or planned purchase orders, blanket releases, RFQs, and quotations with a minimum number of keystrokes. You can review all approved requisition lines before placing specific requisition lines on a purchase order or RFQ. You can review RFQ headers, lines, and shipments before creating a quotation from a specific RFQ. You can collect all requisition lines that meet a certain set of criteria that you establish.

You can split one requisition line into several requisition lines. You can consolidate multiple like requisition lines into single purchase order lines. You can review or change your purchase orders, quotations, or RFQs immediately after creation. You can use document security to control whether buyers can add to certain document types. You can specify foreign currency details during autocreation. You can review requisition lines by currency type.

APPROVING AND FORWARDING DOCUMENTS

You can change the default forward-from employee for requisitions if Allow Change Forward-From is enabled for the document type in the Document Types window. You can change the default approval hierarchy if Allow Change to Approval Hierarchy is enabled for the document type in the Document Types window. You can change the default forward-to employee if Allow Change to Forward-To is enabled for the document type in the Document Types window. You can enter a brief note to either record information about your approval action or provide instructions for the next approver if your document requires additional authorization. You can launch a print request.

USING MASSCANCEL

You can specify the criteria for canceling groups of requisitions or purchase orders that you no longer want to honor. You can specify a range of accounting flexfields for which to cancel requisitions or purchase orders. You can define multiple ranges of accounting flexfields, including both a low and high value for each key segment.

ENTERING RECEIPTS AND RECEIVING TRANSACTIONS

You can use routing controls at the organization, supplier, item, or order level to enforce material movement through receiving. You can define receiving tolerances at the organization, supplier, item, and order level, with the lowest level overriding previous levels. You can use blind receiving to improve accuracy in the receiving process. You can use Express

Receipt to receive an entire purchase order with a few keystrokes. You can use the Cascade function to distribute a given quantity of an item from a single supplier across multiple shipments and distributions.

You can specify invoice-matching controls. You can print the receiving and inspection documentation you need. You can track, update, and record the receipt of in-transit and inter-organization shipments. You can enter different types of receipt transactions based on your organization's needs. You can record receipt of unordered items based on your item, supplier, or organization defaults. You can record receipt of predefined substitute items if you set your receiving options to allow this feature. You can automatically update related supply information, inventory balances, work in process (WIP) operations, requisition details, and purchase order details while entering a single receiving transaction.

You can record transfers of inventory items from receiving and inspection to inventory or to the shop floor. You can record receipts against services and labor. You can receive services, inventory, expense, and outside processing items using one screen. You can distinguish closed for invoicing from closed for receiving. You can decide how you accrue uninvoiced receipts. You can identify and handle hazardous materials. You can track the quantity and destination of internally delivered items. You can define detailed rules for locator within subinventories for the disposition of inventory receipts.

You can track lot and serially controlled items. You can define which of your items require inspection. You can record returns to suppliers. You can correct receiving transaction errors. You can use flexible search criteria to choose receipts for review. You can view receipts details. You can perform transactions with minimal effort. You can use attachments throughout the receiving process to more completely identify transactions and to inform users of special requirements. You cannot process corrections and returns on an internal order.

Processing Returns to Vendor

You can return delivered items to receiving and return received or delivered externally sourced items to the supplier if the purchase order has neither been cancelled nor finally closed. If the item is controlled, you must specify lot numbers, serial numbers, or locators, as appropriate. When you are entering a return, you must first identify the purchase order number or item that you want to return. You can also return to the supplier unordered receipts that have not been matched.

Writing Off Accruals

Purchasing records an accounts payable liability to an AP accrual account for goods received but not invoiced if the perpetual accrual method is selected. The account is cleared in payables when the invoice is matched and approved.

PURGING PURCHASING AND AP TOGETHER

You can purge invoices, purchase orders, suppliers, and related records such as invoice payments and purchase receipts to free space in your database. After a record is purged, the record cannot be queried. The system does maintain summary information to prevent the duplication of invoices or purchase orders.

IMPORTING REQUISITIONS

You can import requisitions from other Oracle Applications or from non-Oracle systems. Requisitions you import can be placed on purchase orders just as you would any other requisition. Requisition import lets you integrate Purchasing with new or existing applications.

REVIEWING TOPICS OF INTEREST

The Purchasing module allows you to maintain control over your purchasing documents and to put into place a flexible approval system designed specifically for your organization. You can allow your employees to enter requisitions online. You can set up an autocreate capability within the Purchasing module. You can also provide a flexible receiving capability within your organization.

USING ORACLE ALERTS AND WORKFLOW

You can establish expiration and release control notification conditions and specify the number of days before the condition is met that you want to be notified.

Amount Not Released alerts let you know that the total planned amount released to date against a planned purchase order, blanket purchase agreement, or contract purchase agreement is insufficient. Amount Released alerts let you know that the total amount released to date against a planned purchase order, blanket purchase agreement, or contract purchase agreement meets or exceeds specified amounts. Expiration alerts let you know that a planned purchase order, blanket purchase agreement, or contract purchase agreement is about to expire. Approved Standard Purchase Orders alerts show the number of approved purchase orders created by each buyer during the past n days.

Blanket Notification Expiration alerts show the blanket purchase agreements that are about to expire. Blanket Notification Not Released alerts show the blanket purchase agreements for which an insufficient amount has been released. Blanket Notification Released alerts show the blanket purchase agreements for which the desired amount has been released. Blanket Purchase Releases over Threshold alerts look for blanket purchase releases that exceed a certain dollar amount.

Contract Notification Expiration alerts show the contract purchase agreements that are about to expire. Contract Notification Not Released alerts show the contract purchase agreements for which an insufficient amount has been released. Contract Notification Released alerts show the contract purchase agreements for which the desired amount has been released.

Planned Notification Expiration alerts show the planned purchase orders that are about to expire. Planned Notification Not Released alerts show the planned purchase orders for which an insufficient amount has been released. Planned Notification Released alerts show the planned purchase orders for which the desired amount has been released.

Small Business Suppliers alerts show your suppliers who are identified as small businesses. Standard Purchase Orders over Threshold alerts look for standard purchase orders created in the past n days that exceed a certain dollar amount. Suppliers on Hold alerts show the suppliers that you have placed on hold.

UNDERSTANDING KEY REPORTS

The Accrual Reconciliation report is where you analyze the balance of the Accounts Payable (A/P) accrual accounts. The Accrual Write-Off report provides supporting detail for your write-off journal entries. The Backordered Internal Requisitions report details information on your back-ordered internally sourced requisition lines. The Blanket and Planned PO Status report is where you review purchase order transactions for items you buy using blanket purchase agreements and planned purchase orders. The Buyer listing shows the buyer name, default purchasing category, Ship To location, and effective dates of all buyers or a selected set of buyers. The Buyer's Requisition Action Required report identifies all or specific approved requisition lines that buyers have not placed on purchase orders.

The Cancelled Purchase Order report is where you review information on cancelled purchase orders. The Cancelled Requisition report is where you review information on cancelled requisitions. The Contract Status report is where you review the status of your contracts and list purchase order information for each contract. The Create Internal Sales Orders processis where you send requisition information from approved, inventory-sourced requisition lines to the Order Entry interface tables.

The Create Releases processis how you create releases for requisition lines that meet one of the following conditions:

- They are approved.
- The requisition is already sourced to an existing blanket release.
- The autosource release generation method rule for the item, supplier, or blanket release is either automatic release or automatic release/review.
- The requisition line is not already on a purchase order.
- The source blanket is still active, and the release will not put the blanket over the amount limit.

The Encumbrance Detail report is where you review requisition and purchase order encumbrances for a range of accounts. The Expected Receipts report is where you review all or specific vendor-sourced expected receipts for a particular date or a range of dates. The Fill Employee Hierarchy process is how you create a direct mapping between the defined position hierarchies and the employees holding positions in each hierarchy. The Financials/

Purchasing Options listing is where you review the options set for your system in the Financials Options and Purchasing Options windows. The Internal Requisition Status report is where you print status information for internal requisitions. The Internal Requisitions/Deliveries Discrepancy report is where you list requisition documents with items whose source type is inventory.

The Invoice Price Variance report shows the variance between the invoice price and the purchase price for all inventory and work-in-process related invoice distribution lines. The Invoice Price Variance by Vendor shows the variance between the invoice price and the purchase price for all inventory and work-in-process related invoice distribution lines. The Item Detail listing shows detail information for items defined as purchasing items in the Item window as well as unit of measure conversion, notes, manufacturer part numbers, and dispositions assigned to the item. The Item Summary listing shows the inactive or active status of items.

The Location listing shows internal organizations locations and addresses. The Matching Holds by Buyer report is where you review all or selected invoices that Purchasing or your AP system placed on matching hold. The New Vendor Letter report is where you print letters you send to your vendors to ask for information about the nature of their businesses. The Open Purchase Orders by Buyer lists all or specific open purchase orders that relate to buyers. The Open Purchase Orders by Cost Center report reviews all or specific open purchase orders relating to one or more cost centers.

The Overdue Vendor Shipments report is where you follow up with vendors. The Overshipments report lists purchase order receipts with a quantity received greater than the quantity ordered. The Payment on Receipt automatically creates standard, unapproved invoices for payment of goods based on receipt transactions.

The Printed Change Orders report (landscape) and Printed Change Orders report (portrait) print changed purchase orders. The Printed Purchase Order report (landscape) and Printed Purchase Order report (portrait) print purchase orders. The Printed RFQ report (landscape) and Printed RFQ report (portrait) print requests for quotes.

The Printed Requisitions report prints the requisitions that have the status of approved, rejected, in process, pre-approved, or returned. The Purchase Agreement Audit report is where you review purchase order transactions for items you normally buy using blanket purchase agreements. The Purchase Order Commitment by Period report is where you show the monetary value of your purchased commitments for a specified period and the next five periods. The Purchase Order Detail report is where you list all, specific standard, or planned purchase orders. The Purchase Order Distribution Detail report shows account distributions for a range of purchase orders.

The Purchase Order and Releases Detail report shows detail information for your blanket purchase agreements and planned purchase orders. The Purchase Price Variance report shows the variance between the purchase price on the purchase order and standard cost for all items you receive and deliver into inventory and work in process. The Purchase Requisition Status report is where you review the approval status of the requisitions you create. The Purchase Summary Report by Category shows the amount of orders you place with vendors for a given category of item. The Purchasing Activity Register shows purchase order monetary activity carried out for a time interval, such as a day or month.

The Purchasing Database Administration process initiates concurrent processes that purge notifications for RFQs with close dates before the current date, notifications for quotations with expiration dates before the current date, and lot and serial numbers that were entered for receiving transactions that were ultimately not committed. The Quality Code listing shows inspection quality codes. The Quotation Action Required report lists quotations that require follow-up action. The RFQ Action Required report lists RFQs that require follow-up action. The Receipt Accruals - Period End process is how you create period-end accruals for your uninvoiced receipts for Expense distributions.

The Receipt Adjustments report lists purchase order shipments or internal requisition lines with corrections or returns to vendor. The Receipt Traveler facilitates the receiving inspection and delivery of goods within your organization. The Receiving Account Distribution report lists the accounting distributions for your receiving transactions. The Receiving Exceptions report is where you review receipts for which there is a receipt exception. The Receiving Transaction processor processes your pending or unprocessed receiving transactions. The Receiving Transactions Register lists detail information about your receiving transactions.

The Receiving Value report shows item quantity, valuation, and detailed receipt information for your receiving inspection location. The Receiving Value Report by Destination Account lists received items by purchase order destination and distribution account. The ReqExpress Templates listing shows ReqExpress template detail information. The Requisition Activity Register shows requisition activity and monetary values. The Requisition Distribution Detail report lists requisitions, distributions, and charge account information.

The Requisition Import process imports requisitions from other Oracle or non-Oracle systems. The Requisition Import Exceptions report shows errors from the Requisition Import process. The Requisitions on Cancelled Sales Order report shows information on internally sourced requisition lines for which a sales order has been generated and subsequently cancelled. The Reschedule Requisitions process updates requisition information for the rows that Master Scheduling/MRP has inserted into the rescheduling interface table.

The Savings Analysis report (by Buyer) shows buyer performance by purchase order. The Savings Analysis report (by Category) shows buyer performance by category. The Set Flexbuilder Account Flex Structure process assigns an accounting flexfield structure (chart of accounts) to the flexbuilder parameters. The Standard Notes listing shows your standard notes and their start and end dates. The Substitute Receipts report lists all or specific substitute receipts. The Tax Code listing shows the tax authorities and rates that you use when you enter purchase orders or invoices.

The Uninvoiced Receipts report is where you review all or specific uninvoiced receipts for both period end and online accruals. The Unit of Measure Class listing shows the classes of measurement you have defined. The Unit of Measure listing shows the unit conversions you have defined in the Unit of Measure Conversions window. The Unordered Receipts report lists all or selected unordered receipts. The Vendor Affiliated Structure listing shows information about your vendor's parent-child relationships. The Vendor Price Performance Analysis report is where you compare the price of an item from different vendors.

The Vendor Purchase Summary report lists the numbers and amount of orders you have placed with various vendors during a particular period. The Vendor Quality Performance Analysis report is where you review your vendors' quality performance. The Vendor Service Performance Analysis report lists late shipments, early shipments, rejected shipments, and shipments to wrong locations. The Vendor Volume Analysis report shows the dollar value of items you purchase from a vendor. The Vendors on Hold report lists all vendors placed on hold.

TROUBLESHOOTING

The Oracle Purchasing application is at the center of your procurement process. This application is tightly integrated with the planning, inventory, payables, and ledger applications. Consider the following items as you set up and use the Purchasing application:

- Coordinate the way you close purchase orders. If you close documents too early, you can disrupt the payables matching process.

- If you choose automatic document numbering, Oracle can only create numeric document numbers. However, you can still import both numeric or alphanumeric document numbers from a non-Oracle purchasing system.

- Make sure your job/position hierarchy structure supports all the approval levels of your organization.

- The security hierarchy controls which positions have access to certain document types. However, the security system does not grant approval authority.

- When a document is in the approval process, no one can access it from an entry window.

- If the Human Resources application is installed, you must use the Enter Person window in that application to maintain employee information.

- If you customize a workflow, existing documents will not be affected by the change. The change will act only on those documents submitted for approval after the workflow changes.

- You cannot change the supplier after a purchase order is approved because it is a legal document. To change suppliers after approval, you must cancel the existing document and issue a new one to the correct supplier.

- During the fiscal period-end processing, close the Oracle Payables application before closing Oracle Purchasing. Close Oracle Inventory after you close Purchasing.

CHAPTER **16**

USING ORACLE INVENTORY

INTRODUCTION

The purpose of the Oracle Inventory application is to assist an organization in defining and tracking inventory items or parts. It helps the organization answer such questions as how many of a particular part are on hand and where the parts are located. It provides support for recording the receipt and disbursement of items as well as the physical and cyclical counting of those items. Oracle Inventory also provides for the replenishment of items using either min-max or reorder point planning or replenishment support for items using kanbans.

Inventory items within an organization are stored in locations called subinventories. In these subinventories, you can specify storage locators that can consist of aisles, rows, and bins. You can specify that an item be restricted to specific locators within specific subinventories or that the part can be stored anywhere within the organization. You can specify that an item be lot- or serial-number controlled or have no controls. In addition, you can indicate that a part be revision controlled.

One of the key tasks in the implementation of the Oracle manufacturing applications is the setup of the Oracle Inventory application. This setup process consists of a number of steps wherein you define such things as the structure of your organization and your inventory items. These setup steps customize the Oracle Inventory application to your unique requirements. This chapter lists the required tasks in order to set up the Oracle Inventory application and points out some of the details for consideration in the key areas of the setup process.

In addition to the setup tasks, this chapter also highlights some of the key Oracle Inventory transactions with considerations for use of these transactions.

ORACLE INVENTORY RELATIONSHIPS TO OTHER APPLICATIONS

The Oracle Inventory application is the foundation for all the other Oracle manufacturing applications. The inventory item definition and the associated on-hand inventory balance of an item are used by the other Oracle Applications. Figure 16.1 indicates the interrelationships that Oracle Inventory has with the other Oracle Application products.

DISCOVERING NEW FEATURES IN RELEASE 11

Following are the features in the Oracle Inventory application that are new to release 11 of the product. Also included is a short description of each of the new capabilities:

- *Support for kanbans.* Support is now provided for kanbans, which are pull-based replenishment signals. You can generate kanban cards for an item, subinventory, or optionally for a locator. Support is provided to read these kanban cards and trigger a

Figure 16.1
Oracle Inventory relationships to other applications

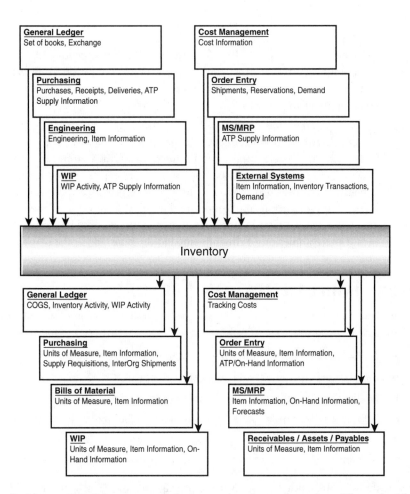

replenishment signal from external devices such as bar code readers. The replenishment trigger can be supplier sourced, generating a purchase request, or "inter-org" sourced, resulting in an inter-organization transfer.

- *Cycle counting by serial number.* You can cycle count serial-number controlled items. You can specify whether you want to just verify quantities so that if the quantities match, you do not have to verify serial numbers, or you can specify that you want to verify both quantity and serial numbers. Another option you can specify is that you want to exclude counting any serial-controlled items for a cycle count.

- *Support for project manufacturing.* Inventory provides support for tracking the inventory by project. You can segregate inventory by project using project locators. A project or task can be referenced for all of the material transactions, including the issue, backflush, and completion of project-related WIP jobs. The transfer of inventory between projects or from common inventory to project inventory is also supported.

- *Support supply chain planning from ATP forms.* Inventory offers support for viewing Available To Promise (ATP) information, taking into account all possible supply sources for a customer order line, ship set, or configuration. A global view covers material availability for the requested demand. This provides a detailed view of all of your supply chain sources.

- *Oracle Applications Implementation Wizard.* A new tool assists in the implementation of the Oracle Application products. It is particularly helpful if you are implementing more than one Oracle Application product. The Oracle Applications Implementation Wizard guides you through the implementation steps required for installing the applications in the correct order. The structure provided reduces the complexities of implementing multiple application modules that have some of the same setup steps. The wizard also assists in documenting your Oracle implementation, letting you record the completion of the implementation steps and append any special notes.

CRITICAL IMPLEMENTATION FACTORS

A number of factors contribute to the successful implementation of any manufacturing planning and execution system. Among the most important are the following:

- High-level executive commitment to the project
- Good user involvement and support of the project
- Availability of application product and process expertise
- Adequate information technology resources, including hardware and system personnel
- Good fit of the application product to the manufacturing process
- Keeping the number and size of modifications to the application product minimal

Successfully implementing an application package such as Oracle Inventory also requires several key activities:

- Educating users to ensure the application product is set up to accurately reflect the manufacturing environment
- Providing good user procedures and training to ensure the successful operation of the system
- Comprehensively testing the application product and making any necessary modifications to ensure the product performs as required to support the manufacturing process and to ensure users can perform the application transactions

In addition to the factors and activities here, another consideration that contributes to the rapid and successful deployment of Oracle Inventory is the philosophy of simplicity. For instance, when setting up Oracle Inventory, you can make a number of choices between many alternatives. Often, the best choice is the simplest one. The simplest choice can be easily understood and tested. Often, the simplest choice requires less user input and reduces the chance for errors.

An example might be managing tool room inventory. To start, the users might want to simply be able to control the issuing and receiving of tool room inventory and know how many tools are available. This might mean starting with item records for the tools and a subinventory for the tool room. Issues and receipts could be handled with miscellaneous inventory receipt and issue transactions, perhaps with account aliases to ensure the correct accounts are charged.

When users get more familiar and confident with the system, they could add slightly more advanced techniques, such as performing cycle counts or physical inventories of the tool room items using the system. You could implement the simple technique of min-max planning for the replenishment of the tool room inventory. If you have enough data and confidence in the system, you could consider more advanced techniques such as reorder point planning.

Using the simplest alternatives often leads to the quickest and most successful implementation of a system.

REVIEWING TOP ENHANCEMENT REQUESTS

Oracle Corporation attempts to continually enhance its application products. Following are some of the top potential enhancements to the Oracle Inventory application. The first two items might be included in R11.i, and other items might be included in future releases:

- Provide an option to include the on-hand quantity on the cycle count listing report and allow a cycle count frequency of less than one count per year.
- Provide a simple requisitioning process to issue or subinventory transfer material.
- Provide an option to open accounting periods in all organizations with a single command or process.
- Provide an option to cycle count by location.
- Print all category segments on Inventory reports.
- Support cycle counting of zero on-hand items without requiring item-subinventory relationship definitions.
- Provide the ability to use the same locator code in different subinventories.
- Provide an excess inventory report.
- Provide a data-archiving option for Inventory data.

Other application enhancements to Oracle Inventory that are being considered for inclusion in release 11.5 are the following:

- Subinventory transfer orders
- Material shortage message
- Cycle count open interface
- Kanban support for replenishment from stores inventory
- Kanban support for replenishment from WIP

- Improved serial-number tracking
- Synchronous transaction open interface
- Business intelligence reports
- Business views

CONFIGURING THE APPLICATION

The setup process for Oracle Inventory consists of a number of steps whereby you define such characteristics as the structure of your organization and your inventory items. These setup steps customize the Oracle Inventory application to your unique requirements. You must perform a preliminary step before you can set up Oracle Inventory. You need to set up an Oracle Applications System Administrator responsibility. Consult the *Oracle Applications Systems Administrator's Guide* for information on how to perform this step. Following are all of the setup steps. This chapter describes these setup steps in additional detail.

REQUIRED SETUP TASKS

- Create a set of books (required).
- Define the system items key flexfield (required).
- Define the item categories key flexfield (required).
- Define the item catalog group key flexfield (required).
- Define the stock locators key flexfield (required).
- Define the account aliases key flexfield (required).
- Define the sales orders key flexfield (required).
- Define locations (optional).
- Define employees (optional).
- Define the organization calendar and exceptions (required).
- Define organizations (required).
- Define organization inventory parameters (required).
- Define receiving options (optional).
- Change to a valid organization (required).
- Define picking rules (optional).
- Define available to promise (ATP) rules (optional).
- Define planners (optional).
- Define unit of measure classes and units of measure (required).
- Define unit of measure conversions and interclass conversions (optional).
- Define subinventories (required).
- Define stock locators (optional).

- Define item attribute controls (required).
- Define categories (required).
- Define category sets (required).
- Define default category sets (required).
- Define statuses (required).
- Define item catalog groups (optional).
- Define item types (optional).
- Define item templates (optional).
- Define cross-reference types (optional).
- Define item delete constraints (optional).
- Define cost types (required).
- Define cost activities (optional).
- Define material subelements (optional).
- Define material overheads (optional).
- Define default material overhead rates (optional).
- Define freight carriers (optional).
- Define organization shipping network (optional).
- Define movement statistics parameters (optional).
- Define account aliases (optional).
- Define transaction source types (optional).
- Define transaction types (optional).
- Define transaction reasons (optional).
- Define purchasing options (optional).
- Open accounting periods (required).
- Start material and cost interface managers (optional).
- Set profile options (required).
- Define container types (optional).
- Define commodity codes (optional).
- Define customer items (optional).
- Define customer item cross references (optional).

CREATING A SET OF BOOKS

The set of books defines for all of the Oracle Applications the accounting flexfield structure (chart of accounts), the fiscal calendar, and the functional currency of the applications.

You must define the set of books before you can perform any of the other setup steps. When you define a set of books, use the setup process described in Chapter 11, "Using Oracle General Ledger."

The tasks in this process are

- Define the key accounting flexfield structure, segments, segment values, and code combinations.
- Define the fiscal calendar period types and periods.
- Enable currencies, and define rate types and conversion rates.
- Create the set of books by assigning a name to a combination of the key accounting flexfield, a calendar, and a currency.
- Assign the set of books to the site or individual responsibilities.

DEFINING THE SYSTEM ITEMS KEY FLEXFIELD

The systems items key flexfield is sometimes called the item flexfield. This flexfield is an Oracle Application key flexfield that contains the definition of the structure of your item or part number field. You need to define whether your item number is a single segment or multi-segmented field and the length of each segment. If your part number is more than one segment, you also need to specify the order of the segments and the segment separator. All Oracle Application products that reference items share the item flexfield definition and support multi-segmented implementations. Every item defined requires this item number, which is also required to transact and report item information. You need to define the system items key flexfield before you can define any items.

Note	An increasing number of manufacturing enterprises use a single segment (field) nonmeaningful item number. The capability of the Oracle Application software to retrieve item information by a number of different methods, including item catalogs, manufacturer's part numbers, and item cross references, has reduced the requirement for the use of a meaningful multisegmented item number key.

To define the system items flexfield, you need to provide the following information:

- How many separate segments your item number has.
- The length of each one of the separate segments and their sequence as well as the segment separator (the character used to separate segments, such as a period or hyphen).
- Whether any of the segments will be validated.

In addition to the structure of the flexfield, you need to define any applicable value sets for validation of the flexfield, and then, you need to freeze and compile the flexfield.

For help in defining this flexfield, you can reference the *Oracle Flexfields User's Guide*.

DEFINING THE ITEM CATEGORIES KEY FLEXFIELD

A category is a logical classification of items that have similar characteristics. A category set is a way of grouping together categories. In Oracle, you can define various item categories and category sets to facilitate retrieval and reporting to meet your unique requirements. For any report or inquiry that you can specify a range or list of items, you can specify a category set and range of categories. This capability is one of the most important and powerful features of the Oracle Application products.

PART
III

CH
16

You must design and configure your item categories flexfield before you start defining items because all items must be assigned to categories. The tasks to define item categories follow:

1. Define the flexfield structures for the item categories flexfield.
2. Define categories. See the section "Defining Categories" later in this chapter.
3. Define category sets. See the section "Defining Category Sets" later in this chapter.
4. Assign default category sets for each functional area. When you install Oracle Inventory, you must assign a default category set for each of the following applications areas: Inventory, Purchasing, Order Entry, Costing, Engineering, Planning, and Service. The default category set can be the same or different for each application area. As you add new items, Oracle Inventory automatically assigns them to the default category sets with a default category value. See the section "Defining Default Category Sets" later in this chapter for additional detail on defining default category sets.

To define the flexfield structure of an item category, you need to provide the following information:

- How many separate segments your item category has.
- The length of each one of the separate segments and their sequence and segment separator.
- Whether any of the segments will be validated.

In addition, you can specify the prompts for entering the data in each of these segments, as well as the values for any of the value sets that will be used in validating the categories. You also need to freeze and compile the flexfield. For help in defining this flexfield, you can reference the *Oracle Flexfields User's Guide*.

Tip

One of the best ways to understand the process and various individual steps in defining item categories and their flexfield structures and values is to look at a sample. When you install Oracle Inventory or Oracle Purchasing, Oracle provides two category flexfield structures by default: item categories and PO item category. Examining these two category structures and their definitions can be educational and informative.

> **Note**
>
> You can use item categories to do the following:
>
> - Summarize a history of demand and generate forecasts for all items in a selected item category
>
> - Perform min-max and reorder point planning for a range of item categories
>
> - Select items from requisitions to be automatically created into purchase orders by purchasing item category
>
> - Run reports and inquiries for a single item category or range of item categories
>
> - Assign material overhead rates by item category

DEFINING THE ITEM CATALOG GROUP KEY FLEXFIELD

Oracle Inventory enables you to create multiple catalog groups to aid in item classification. Each catalog group can have its own set of item characteristics, called descriptive elements. You can define as many descriptive elements as necessary to describe your items and specify whether an entry for the element is optional. Once you have cataloged your items, you can search on one or more descriptive elements to assist in locating items for order entry or group technology purposes.

To define the item catalog group flexfield, you need to indicate how many separate segments are contained in your flexfield, how long each segment is, and whether you want to validate any of the values that you assign to the segments. After defining the structure of your flexfield and any applicable valuesets, you need to freeze and compile your flexfield definition to enable the Item Catalog Group Flexfield pop-up window.

> **Note**
>
> Even if you decide not to use item catalogs, you still must enable at least one segment in the item catalog flexfield and then compile the flexfield before you can define any items.

DEFINING THE STOCK LOCATORS KEY FLEXFIELD

A stock locator is a physical area within a subinventory where you store material (such as a combination of row, aisle, bin, or shelf).

To define the stock locator flexfield, you need to provide the following information:

- How many separate segments your stock locator has
- The length of each one of the separate segments
- Whether any of the segments will be validated

- In addition to the structure of the flexfield, you need to define any applicable value sets for validation of the flexfield, and then you need to freeze and compile the flexfield.

For help in defining this flexfield, you can reference the *Oracle Flexfields User's Guide*.

> **Tip**
>
> The stock locators key flexfield definition is global across all of the subinventories in an organization. This means that you can't have the same locator (such as Aisle 1, Row 1, Bin 1) in two different subinventories. If you have the requirement to use the same locator in several subinventories, you can make the locator unique by putting the subinventory identification in the first segment of the locator flexfield definition.

> **Note**
>
> Even if you will not be using locator controls, you still need to compile and freeze the stock locators flexfield because all of the Oracle Inventory transactions and reports require a frozen flexfield definition. You don't, however, have to configure the flexfield in any specific way.

DEFINING THE ACCOUNT ALIAS KEY FLEXFIELD

The account alias flexfield is a key flexfield that allows you to use a shorthand label for a general ledger account number combination when entering Inventory transactions. This can reduce keystroke entries as well as the chance of entering the wrong account numbers for your inventory transactions.

To configure your account alias flexfield, you need to indicate the number of separate segments your flexfield has, how many characters each segment has, and whether you want to validate the segments. In addition to defining the structure of your flexfield and any applicable value sets, you need to freeze and compile the flexfield definition. This compilation enables the Account Aliases Flexfield pop-up window.

> **Note**
>
> Even if you decide not to use account aliases, you still need to compile and freeze the account aliases flexfield. All of the Oracle Inventory transaction inquiries and reports require a frozen flexfield definition. However, you don't need to configure the flexfield in any specific way.

DEFINING THE SALES ORDERS KEY FLEXFIELD

The sales order flexfield is a key flexfield used by Oracle Inventory to uniquely identify sales order transactions that Oracle Order Entry interfaces to Oracle Inventory. If you are using Oracle OE, you should define this sales order flexfield as order number, order type, and order source. This combination makes sure that each order entry transaction interfaced to Inventory is unique.

Note

Even if you don't ship items against sales orders, you still need to compile and freeze the sales orders flexfield because all the Oracle Inventory transaction inquiries and reports require a frozen flexfield definition. You don't, however, have to configure the flexfield in any specific way.

DEFINING LOCATIONS

You should define the names and addresses for the locations you use within your organization as well as for the location of your inventory organization itself. A number of Oracle Applications, including Inventory, use locations for requisitions, receiving, billing, shipping, and employee assignments.

For each location that you are going to use, enter the following information: name, organization, description, address style (such as United States), contact, and all of the address data lines and fields such as city, state, and Zip. You also need to indicate, by way of check boxes, whether the location is a ship-to site, office site, receiving site, bill-to site, and internal site.

Tip

The standard Oracle Purchasing purchase order print program prints the bill-to and ship-to location you have defined for your organization in the bill-to and ship-to lines on your purchase order. It does not print a company or organization name in the first line of this location address. Therefore, you probably want to include your company name as the first line of the location definition that you will be associating with your inventory organization.

DEFINING EMPLOYEES

Oracle Applications use defined employees as the list of values source for employee fields in the applications. Within Oracle Inventory, employee information is used primarily to record the employees who perform cycle count and physical inventory count transactions.

You need to enter the names, addresses, and other pertinent information for all of the employees who will be performing these inventory count transactions. See Chapter 25, "Using Oracle Human Resources," for additional information on defining an employee.

DEFINING THE ORGANIZATION CALENDAR AND THE CALENDAR EXCEPTIONS

A workday calendar defines the valid working days for a manufacturing organization and consists of a pattern of repeating days on and off and exceptions to that pattern. You specify the start and end dates and the weekend schedule for each calendar. You can define any number of workday calendars and assign them to any number of organizations, and any number of organizations can share a calendar.

You can apply exceptions to the workday calendar by specifying individual days, loading them from an exception template, or copying a set of exceptions from another calendar.

For any workday calendar, you can also specify any number of shifts. Each shift can have a different weekend schedule and a list of specific work interval start and end times. Shifts inherit workday exceptions and workday patterns from the base calendar. You can specify shift exceptions that can either override or add to those of the base calendar.

For each organization, you specify the calendar to use. All scheduling functions use the calendar's available workdays to plan and schedule activities. For additional details on defining the organization calendar and the calendar exceptions, see Chapter 18, "Using Oracle Engineering and Bills of Material."

DEFINING ORGANIZATIONS

An inventory organization is an organization for which you track inventory transactions and on-hand balances and that manufactures or distributes parts and products. Some examples of organizations are manufacturing plants, warehouses, distribution centers, and sales offices. In a number of the Oracle Applications, information is secured by the inventory organization. You need to choose an organization that has been classified as an inventory organization in order to run any of the following applications: Oracle Inventory, Bills of Material, Engineering, Work in Process, Master Scheduling/MRP, Capacity, and the receiving functions in Purchasing.

Before defining organizations, you need to understand the item definition process in Oracle Inventory. You define items in a single organization sometimes referred to as the item master organization. Other organizations (child organizations) refer to the item master for item definition. Once an item has been defined in the master organization, it can be enabled or assigned to any of the other organizations.

> **Note**
>
> It is possible to define and operate the Oracle Inventory application with a single inventory organization. However, this is not recommended. The primary reason is that it limits future application flexibility and growth. It is recommended that you define, at a minimum, a separate master and child inventory organization even if you only have a single organization presently.

To define an inventory organization, you need to specify the organization name, the organization type, and a three-character abbreviation for the organization. This unique code is used to identify the organization with which you want to work. In addition, you need to specify which set of books the organization will be tied to.

DEFINING ORGANIZATION INVENTORY PARAMETERS

A number of inventory, costing, control, and movement parameters are associated with an inventory organization. This section outlines some of the areas and associated parameter data you need to specify for an inventory organization.

You must provide the following default inventory parameters:

- The master organization where items will be initially defined.
- The workday calendar for planning, scheduling, and determining days to perform cycle counts.
- Optionally, specify the demand class to be used in forecast consumption, shipment, and production relief.
- Indicate whether negative inventory balances will be allowed.

> **Note**
>
> There is an Inventory profile option called INV: Override Neg for Backflush. If you specify Yes for this option, Oracle WIP, when it backflushes components with assembly or operation pull, will ignore the preceding setting and drive inventory negative if there is not enough inventory on-hand in the supply subinventory specified on the bill of material.

Choose from the following settings for the locator control option:

- *None.* Locators not required anywhere in this organization for inventory transactions.
- *Prespecified Only.* All transactions require a valid, predefined locator for each item.
- *Dynamic Entry Allowed.* All transactions require a locator for each item, but the locator can be either predefined or dynamically entered at the time of transaction.
- *Determined at Subinventory Level.* Transactions use locator controls defined at the subinventory level.

You must specify the following costing information:

- The costing organization can be either the current organization or the item master organization.
- The costing method can be standard or actual.
- Indicate whether all GL transactions are posted in detail.
- Indicate whether to reverse encumbrance entry upon receipt into inventory.
- See Chapter 19, "Using Oracle Cost Management," for further detail on defining the default material subelement and the other cost information organization parameters.

You need to specify default valuation accounts for the organization that will be the default accounts for the subinventories you define:

- *Material.* An asset account that tracks material cost.

- *Material Overhead.* An asset account that tracks material overhead cost.

- *Resource.* An asset account that tracks resource cost.

- *Overhead.* An asset account that tracks resource and outside processing overheads.

- *Outside Processing.* An asset account that tracks outside processing cost.

- *Expense.* The expense account for tracking a non-asset item.

You need to specify the following default general ledger accounts to be associated with this organization:

- Sales

- Cost of Goods Sold

- Purchase Price Variance

- Inventory A/P Accrual

- Invoice Price Variance

- Encumbrance

- Average Cost Variance

For the revision, lot, and serial number parameters, specify information in the following areas:

- *Starting Revision.* Enter a starting revision to be the default for every new item.

- *Lot Number Uniqueness.* Pick either None where unique lot numbers are not required or Across Items where unique lot numbers for items are required across all organizations.

- *Lot Number Generation.* Pick At Item Level when you will specify a starting lot number prefix and starting lot number when you define the item; User Defined when you will enter a lot number when you receive the item; or At Organization Level when you will define the starting prefix and lot number in the following fields (the lot number will be generated by the system and be assigned to the item when it is received):

  - *Zero Pad Suffix.* Indicate whether to add zeros to right-justify the numeric portion of lot numbers.

  - *Prefix.* Optionally, enter an alphanumeric lot number prefix to be used for system-generated lot numbers.

  - *Length.* Optionally, enter a maximum total length for the prefix and number that WIP will validate if the WIP parameter for lot number is based on inventory rules.

- *Serial Number Uniqueness.* Pick either Within Inventory Items when you want unique serial numbers within an inventory item; Within Organization for unique serial numbers within the current organization; or Across Organizations for unique serial numbers across all organizations.

- *Serial Number Generation*. Pick At Item Level when you will specify a starting serial number prefix and starting serial number when you define the item or At Organization Level when you will define the starting prefix and serial number in the following fields:
  - *Prefix*. Optionally, enter an alphanumeric serial number prefix to use for system-generated serial numbers
  - *Starting Serial Number*. Enter a starting serial number to use for system-generated serial numbers.

You must supply the following ATP, pick, and item sourcing parameters:

- Select a default ATP rule. If you use Order Entry, the default is the ATP rule for the master organization.
- Select a default picking rule.
- Enter a default subinventory picking order. The value here displays when you define a subinventory.
- Enter a default locator picking order. The value here displays when you define a locator.
- Select an item sourcing replenishment type. Choose None for no default source for item replenishment; choose Supplier if you will be replenishing items from suppliers; or choose Inventory if you will replenish items from another subinventory in this or another organization. If you specify Inventory, you need to specify an organization in the next organization field and a subinventory in the subinventory field if you specify the current organization in the organization field.

You must provide inter-org information parameters to correctly transfer charges between organizations when items are moved between organizations:

- *Inter-Organization Transfer Charge Option*. Specify None if you don't want to add transfer charges to a material transfer between organizations; Predefined Percent to automatically add a predefined percent of the transaction value for inter-organization transfers (and also enter that percent); Requested Value to add a discrete value for inter-organization transfers; or Requested Percent to add a discrete percent of the transaction value when performing an inter-organization transfer.
- *Inter-Organization Transfer Accounts*. Enter the default inter-organization cost accounts, which will appear by default in the Inter-Organization Shipping Networks window when you set up shipping information between organizations.

If Oracle Project Manufacturing is installed, you need to specify additional organizational information regarding projects:

- Check whether Project Reference Enabled will be activated.
- Check whether Project Cost Collection Enabled will be activated.
- Select the project control level: project or task.

DEFINING RECEIVING OPTIONS

You need to specify which receiving options are applicable when you are receiving items from other organizations. If Oracle Purchasing is installed, you can also receive purchased items into inventory using these options. Some of the options that you can specify include

- The action to take when an item is received early or late
- The action to take if more than the quantity ordered has been received
- One of the following three options for how items will be received into inventory:
  - *Direct* if items will be received directly into their inventory location with a single step transaction
  - *Standard* if items will first be received and then in a second step delivered to their inventory location
  - *Inspection* if items will first be received, then inspected, and in a third step delivered to their inventory location
- An indication if unordered items can be received or if substitute items can be received
- Specifications for the processing of receipt numbers, express receipts, cascade transactions, blind receiving, and Advance Shipping Notice (ASN) control

These options are the default receiving options for the organization. However, most of these receiving options can be overridden at the supplier, purchase order, or item level. For additional details on specifying the receiving options for an organization, see Chapter 15, "Using Oracle Purchasing."

CHANGING TO A VALID ORGANIZATION

Normally when you sign into an Oracle Inventory transaction session, the system requires you to pick an organization. Oracle then associates your session with this inventory organization. However, when you first set up the inventory application, there are no inventory organizations defined. To associate the following setup steps with the correct organization, you need to either log off and then log back in and pick your organization or perform the Change Organization transaction that is available under the Special pull-down list.

DEFINING PICKING RULES

When you use Oracle Inventory and Order Entry to ship items against customer sales orders, you need to define picking rules. You assign a picking rule to an item to define the priorities that Inventory uses to pick units of that item for a sales order. You specify the sources and prioritization for subinventories, lots, revisions, and locators to be used when the item is pick released. You can specify None for any of the criterion fields, and Inventory will ignore that criterion when picking. You can define a unique picking rule for each item or use a generic picking rule for the organization.

If the subinventory, lot, or revision is assigned before pick release, the assignment is used rather than the picking rule. For example, if a subinventory is assigned on a lot-controlled item before pick release but the lot isn't assigned, the picking rule is used to assign the lot.

> **Note**
>
> A picking order of 1 on a subinventory or locator means that Order Entry will pick items from that subinventory or locator before others with a higher number such as 2, 3, or 4.

DEFINING AVAILABLE TO PROMISE RULES

ATP (Available to Promise) rules define supply and demand sources, time fence parameters, and available to promise calculation methods. You can give the ATP rule a meaningful name. You assign an ATP rule to an item to define the options that Inventory uses to calculate the available quantity of an item on a requested date or the first date on which a requested quantity is available for an item. If there is no ATP rule for the item, Order Entry/Shipping uses the default ATP rule for the organization.

The *Oracle Inventory User's Guide* has several good examples to illustrate the effect on ATP of picking various options in the ATP rules.

DEFINING PLANNERS

You can specify a material planner code for every item defined. The Oracle Master Scheduling/MRP and Supply Chain Planning applications use this planner code to group items together for planning and reporting purposes. For example, you can specify when using the planner workbench that you only want to work on items associated with a single planner code. Several material planning reports can be sorted by a single or range of planner codes. You need to define your planner codes first before they can be assigned to items. To define a planner code, you just need to specify up to 10 characters for the planner code and enter a description for the planner code. See Chapter 20, "Using Oracle Planning Applications," for additional details on using planner codes.

DEFINING UNIT OF MEASURE CLASSES, UNITS OF MEASURE, UNIT OF MEASURE CONVERSIONS, AND INTERCLASS CONVERSIONS

Oracle Inventory provides a flexible way of defining and transacting items in their units of measure. The process of defining units of measures to use in Oracle Inventory involves several steps:

1. Define unit of measure classes and the base unit of measure (UOM) for each class.
2. Define multiple units of measure for each unit of measure class.
3. Define conversions between units of measure of the same and of different classes.

For example, you might want two classes for UOM for quantity and weight. The base UOM for quantity might be "each" and weight might be "pound". You might want additional quantity class units of measure to be dozen and weight class units of measure to be kilogram. For each unit of measure, you must specify a label or code such as EA, DZ, LB, or KG. The following steps outline the process for defining the sample information:

1. Define the two UOM classes of Quantity and Weight and identify their base UOM of EA and LB.
2. Define the additional UOM of DZ in the class Quantity and the UOM of KG in the class Weight.
3. Specify the conversion between EA and DZ to be 1DZ=12EA and the conversion between LB and KG to be 1KG=2.2LB.

Table 16.1 shows the results of the preceding definition process.

TABLE 16.1   DEFINING UNITS OF MEASURE

UOM Class	Class Description	Base UOM	UOM Description	Other UOM	UOM Description	Conversion
Quantity	Quantity	EA	Each	DZ	Dozen	1DZ=12EA
Weight	Weight	LB	Pound	KG	Kilogram	1KG=2.2LB

When you define an item, you indicate its primary unit of measure, such as each (EA), which is the item's stocking unit of measure.

If you require, you can also specify an item-specific unit of measure conversion. For instance, you could specify that 1EA of this item = 5LB. Then, you could transact in pounds, and Inventory would convert a transaction of 50LB back into the primary unit of measure of quantity of 10EA for the item.

An entire chapter in the manual *Oracle Inventory User's Guide* describes in detail the process of defining units of measures.

Note

Units of measure in Oracle are global, which means they are used by all organizations and they only need to be defined once.

Oracle supplies no seeded values for units of measure. This means that you have to define at least one unit of measure class and its base unit of measure. This also means that you need to define all the rest of the unit of measure classes and units of measure that you think that you will require.

Tip

You can change almost any item attribute on an inventory item. About the only exception is the item's unit of measure. Once an item has been created and saved, you cannot change its unit of measure. Therefore, when you are creating inventory items, you need to be careful to define the correct unit of measure. If you do happen to create an item with an incorrect unit of measure, see the tip in this chapter in the section "Setting the Profile Options," later in this chapter, to recover the item record.

DEFINING SUBINVENTORIES

A subinventory is a subdivision of an organization, representing either a physical area or a logical grouping of items (such as a storeroom, receiving dock, or discrepant material area). All inventory transaction activity must reference a subinventory, and all material within an organization must be stored in a subinventory. It is therefore required that you define at least one subinventory. For each subinventory, you need to define both inventory and accounting information.

Some of the inventory information you need to provide when defining a subinventory includes

- A subinventory name
- Whether the inventory is quantity tracked
- Whether items are valued as assets
- Whether items in this subinventory will be used in ATP calculations
- Whether items will be used in available to reserve calculations
- Whether to include on-hand item quantities in the planning process

If you specified that the locator control is Determined at Subinventory Level when you defined your organization, you have to specify a type of locator control for the subinventory:

- *None.* No locator information is required for transactions in this subinventory.
- *Prespecified.* Inventory transactions require a valid prespecified locator for each item.
- *Dynamic Entry.* Inventory transactions require you to enter a valid predefined locator, or you can define a locator dynamically at the time of the inventory transaction.
- *Item Level.* Locator control information for inventory transactions is defined at the item level.

Specify Inventory or Supplier as the source type for replenishment in this subinventory. If you choose Supplier, it means you plan to replenish items from a supplier. If you choose Inventory, it means you plan to replenish items from another subinventory in this or another organization. You have to additionally specify the organization used to replenish items and the subinventory if you specify the current organization.

You can optionally provide the following additional inventory information when defining a subinventory:

- You can choose a picking order value that indicates the priority of picking from this subinventory relative to another subinventory. Note: A picking order priority value of 1 means that Order Entry will pick from this subinventory before other subinventories with a higher value.

- If you are using min-max planning at the subinventory level, you can enter preprocessing, processing, and postprocessing lead times for items in the subinventory.

You need to specify the following general ledger accounts to accumulate the following types of costs for items in this subinventory:

- Material
- Outside processing
- Material overhead
- Overhead
- Resource
- Expense
- Encumbrance (if using in Oracle Purchasing)

Note

The general ledger accounts listed here for each of the subinventories will default from the organization definition, and they only need to be overridden if they are different from the organization accounts.

After you define the subinventory, you can specify the stock locators for this subinventory. (Click the Locators button.) You can also assign items to this subinventory. (Click the Item/Subinventory button.)

DEFINING STOCK LOCATORS

A stock locator is a physical area within a subinventory where you store material (such as a row, rack, aisle, bin, or shelf). You can turn on locator control for the whole organization, for a specific subinventory, or for a particular item. Item quantities can be tracked by locator. You can restrict an item to a specific locator.

You must first define the structure of the stock locator flexfield before you can define any specific stock locators. See the section "Defining the Stock Locators Key Flexfield" earlier in this chapter for guidance on this task. The tasks in the process to define a specific stock locator are

1. Enter the locator and its description.

2. Enter the subinventory where the locator resides. (Optionally, you can specify the stock locator/subinventory relationship using the Define Subinventory screen.)

3. Optionally, enter a picking order value for Order Entry picking priority. (A priority of 1 gets picked before 2, 3, and so on.)

4. You can also optionally enter capacity constraint information such as maximum weight, volume, or number of items that can be stored in this locator.

Note

Using locators in Oracle Inventory has advantages and disadvantages. Some of the advantages are the following:

- You can restrict an item to a specific locator if required.

- You can locate items by locator within a subinventory, which should make it easier to locate the item in a large subinventory.

The disadvantages of using locators are:

- Every transaction into a locator-controlled subinventory requires not only the keying of the subinventory but also the keying of the locator.

- You must set up and maintain the list of locators for each item restricted to a prespecified list of locators, and the item can't be stored anywhere in the system until this maintenance has been performed. In addition, if you want to store this item in another locator, you must add the locator to the prespecified list before you can store it there.

DEFINING ITEM ATTRIBUTE CONTROLS

Each item has a number of item attributes such as lead time, cost, unit of measure, item status, revision control, and so on. You need to specify for each of these attributes the level at which Oracle Inventory will maintain the item attribute, the item master level or at the item/organization level. This means that you can choose between centralized or decentralized control of your item attributes.

You can specify that a particular item attribute, such as unit of measure, be maintained at the item master level. This means that Oracle Inventory will maintain this value at the item master level, the value will be the same in every organization where this item has been enabled, and the value cannot be updated at the item/organization level. For another item attribute such as lead time, you can specify that the value be maintained at the item/organization level. This means that each organization can have the same or a different lead time for obtaining the same item.

When you define item attribute controls, you specify only the level at which the item attribute is controlled, master level or org level, and not the value of the attribute. Some attributes can only be set at a specific level, and in those cases, you have only one option.

There are eight specific item status attributes. You can set all eight of these attributes for an item with a status code. For each of these item status attributes, in addition to specifying the control level of master or org level, you also need to specify the status setting of Defaults Value, Not Used, or Sets Value. This status setting determines whether a particular attribute can be set by the status code and, if so, whether it can be changed. See the section "Defining Statuses" later in this chapter for additional detail regarding these status attributes and their status settings.

DEFINING CATEGORIES

One of the key strengths of the Oracle Inventory application is the capability to allow the user to attach several user-defined categories to an item and inquire and report on the items using these categories.

After you define the Item Categories Key flexfield, the next step in the category definition process is the definition of the names for each one of the categories. To define a new category, you have to specify both the category flexfield structure name and a unique category name.

DEFINING CATEGORY SETS

After defining both the Item Categories Key flexfield and the categories, the next step in the category definition process is the definition of category sets.

To define a category set, you must provide the following information:

- A unique category set name.
- A category flexfield structure.
- A control level of Master Level if you want items assigned to this category set to have the same value in all of the organizations to which the item is assigned or Org Level if you want items assigned to this category set to be able to have a different value in each of the organizations to which this item is assigned.
- A default category, which is the value that Oracle Inventory assigns to an item when it is initially created. You can override this default category with an appropriate category just after creating the item.
- Indication of whether to enforce a list of valid categories. If you turn on this feature, you can only assign an item to those categories that you define as valid categories for this category set.
- A list of valid categories. If you indicate that you want a list of valid categories enforced, you enter the list of valid categories.

DEFINING DEFAULT CATEGORY SETS

The last step in the definition process for categories is the assignment of default category sets for each application functional area. You need to assign a default category set for each of the following applications areas: Inventory, Purchasing, Order Entry, Costing, Engineering, Planning, and Service. The default category set can be the same or different for each of these application areas.

As you add new items, Oracle Inventory automatically assigns the items to the default category sets with a default category value. You can override the category sets default category, and in addition, you can manually assign an item to additional category sets.

> **Note**
>
> It is recommended that you pick a value for the default category of a category set that allows you to determine that an item has not had a category assigned to it. For example, if you chose a default value of Unassigned or Unknown and the user forgets to override the default category with a valid item category, it is easy to identify those items that have not had a valid category assigned to them.

DEFINING STATUSES

There are eight key controlling item attributes called status control attributes. They are highlighted in the item attribute list in the section "Item Definition" later in this chapter and also listed here:

- BOM Allowed
- Build in WIP
- Customer Orders Enabled
- Internal Orders Enabled
- Invoice Enabled
- Transactable
- Purchasable
- Stockable

You can set all eight of these attributes with a user-defined item status. For each of the status attributes, you can specify whether the value of the attribute should be Yes or No. You specify these values with the Define Item Status Codes screen. For instance, you might want to define a status code of Production and give a value of Yes to all of the attributes. Another status you might choose to define is Preannounce with all of the attributes Yes except Customer Orders Enabled. This allows you to apply this status code to a new part and start purchasing and making the part and putting it into inventory without taking orders for the part yet. After announcement of the product, you can update the part with a status of Production and start taking customer orders.

In addition to specifying the status value of Yes or No for each of the status attributes, you can also specify a status setting for each of the status attributes. The status settings are

- *Defaults Value.* The status value will be set by the status code and can be later changed
- *None.* The value is not set by the status code
- *Sets Value.* The status value will be set by the status code and it cannot be changed.

You define these status settings at the Item Attribute Controls screen. See the section "Defining Item Attribute Controls" earlier in this chapter for further details on this activity.

DEFINING ITEM CATALOG GROUPS

Item catalogs group items that share similar descriptive elements. Oracle Inventory lets you create multiple catalog groups to aid in item classification. Each catalog group can have its own set of item characteristics, called descriptive elements. You can define as many descriptive elements as necessary to describe your items and specify whether an entry for the element is optional. Once you catalog your items, you can search on one or more descriptive elements to assist in locating items for order entry or group technology purposes.

To define catalogs, you set up as many catalog groups as you need. Each group has characteristics called descriptive elements that describe items belonging to the group. The steps involved in setting up item catalogs follow:

1. You must first define the structure of the item catalog group key flexfield. See the section "Defining the Item Catalog Group Key Flexfield" earlier in this chapter for guidance.
2. Define item catalog groups.
3. Define descriptive elements within each group.
4. Optionally, define aliases for items in the catalog group.
5. Optionally, specify recommended categories associated with the group.
6. Assign items to groups and enter descriptive element values.
7. Optionally, you can update an item's description with concatenated catalog group information.

To define an item catalog group, you need to

1. Use the Item Catalog Groups screen.
2. Enter a unique name for the catalog group.
3. Enter a description of the catalog group.

To define descriptive elements for the catalog group, follow these steps:

1. Click the Details button on the Item Catalog Groups screen when defining the catalog group or query the catalog group on the screen and choose Details.
2. Select the descriptive elements alternative region.
3. Enter a sequence number.

4. Name the descriptive element such as size, speed, or color.

5. Specify whether the descriptive element is required.

6. Specify whether the descriptive element will be automatically used to create the catalog description. When you define a descriptive element for a catalog group, you can specify that this element be concatenated with other descriptive elements and used to update the description of the item.

To assign an item to a catalog, follow these steps:

1. Use the Master Items Summary window and select an item. Choose Catalog on the Special menu.

> **Note**
> Item catalog information is created and maintained at the master level and not at the organization level. This feature prevents conflicting values in different organizations.

2. On the Item Catalog window that appears, enter a catalog group. The descriptive elements for this catalog group display in the Name field.

3. Enter a specific value for each of the descriptive elements that pertain to the item.

4. Indicate whether to include a descriptive element in a catalog-derived item description.

5. Save your work and choose Update Description if you want the item description updated with the descriptive element values you defined.

DEFINING ITEM TYPES

An item type is a user-defined field that you can attach to every item. After you define an item type, it appears in the list of values for the user item type attribute. You can use the item type field to assist in the retrieval of items. However, Oracle Applications do not print or group any of their reports by the item type field. Oracle has already predefined some item types that you can use, and you can add your own. Some examples of item types that have already been predefined are purchased item, finished good, subassembly, kit, and outside processing item.

> **Note**
> You can specify the item type with an item template. A number of customers use the item type to indicate which template was used to define an item. Oracle also uses this convention in the creation of its sample items.

> **Note**
> Remember, Oracle Applications do not use the item type field to group items for reports. The item category field is used for this purpose. If you require reports grouped by item type, you need to create your own custom reports in addition to those already provided by Oracle.

DEFINING ITEM TEMPLATES

When you define an item, you can specify more than 150 item attributes about the item. To simplify this process, you can use item templates. An item template is a set of item attributes that you can use over and over to assist in defining similar types of items.

After you define an item template, you can use it to create an item, and then you only have to specify the item attributes not already supplied by the item template.

Oracle Inventory provides a number of predefined item templates that you can use to assist in creating items. Some examples of item templates already predefined are purchased item, finished good, subassembly, kit, and outside processing item. For additional details regarding the item attributes specified in each one of these supplied templates, refer to the *Oracle Inventory User's Guide*. Alternatively, you can print the supplied Inventory report entitled Item Template listing.

PART
III
CH
16

> **Note**
>
> It is highly recommended that you use either the predefined templates supplied by Oracle or those you define yourself to assist in the process of item creation. When creating items, using templates can reduce keystroke entries as well as the chance of entering incorrect data.

DEFINING CROSS-REFERENCE TYPES

You can use cross references in Oracle Inventory to retrieve an item by attributes other than its part number. For instance, you might want to retrieve an item by its old part number or by its blue print number. To be able to do this, you first must define the cross reference types such as Old Part Number or Blue Print Number. You do this by giving each cross-reference type a name and description with the Cross-Reference Types window. Then, you assign the cross references to items using the Cross References List of Value under the Special menu when defining the item using the Master Items or Organization Items definition window. You can make the cross-reference assignment to an item applicable to all organizations or to just a specific organization.

You can assign multiple cross references to an item. For example, you might want to assign an Old Part Number of OLD123 to an item and a Blue Print Number of B1234 as well. This allows you to retrieve this item by using either reference with the Item Search window. You can also look up this reference information at any time with either the Master or Organization Item definition window for the item and looking under Cross References under the Special menu.

DEFINING ITEM DELETE CONSTRAINTS

Oracle Inventory predefines a number of item delete constraints to check for conditions that should prevent you from deleting an item. For instance, several of the delete constraints prevent the deletion of an item if there are jobs, repetitive schedules, purchase orders, or sales orders referencing the item. You can specify additional delete constraints to supplement the standard item delete constraints.

> **Note**
>
> You don't normally need to specify any additional item delete constraints unless you have additional tables or fields in your system that reference items the Oracle Inventory application is not aware of. If you do have this condition, see the section on creating custom delete constraints in the *Oracle Bills of Materials User's Guide*.

DEFINING COST TYPES

Before you can enter item costs, you need to define cost types. A cost type is a set of costs used for costs for future, current, historical, or simulation purposes. Oracle Inventory comes predefined with three cost types: frozen, average, and pending.

If you use standard costing in your organization, Oracle uses the frozen cost for all transactions at the time of the transaction. You can update frozen costs by running a standard cost update. If you use average costing, Oracle uses the average cost type and updates your average costs after the appropriate transactions.

You can also define cost types for your own use such as for simulation or historical purposes. Many of the cost reports can be submitted based on the cost type that you specify. For details regarding the definition of cost types, see Chapter 19.

DEFINING COST ACTIVITIES

In addition to cost types, you can also optionally define cost activities. Cost activities are processes or procedures that consume costs and time. Some organizations use activity-based costing to more accurately identify their product costs, particularly in the area of indirect costs. The definition of cost activities is described in more detail in Chapter 19.

DEFINING MATERIAL SUBELEMENTS

Cost subelements are a smaller classification of cost elements. You can optionally define material subelements if you want further cost breakdowns for your material costs. For each material subelement, you need to indicate the method of allocating the cost to the subelement (basis type). See Chapter 19 for further details on defining material subelements.

DEFINING MATERIAL OVERHEADS

You need to define material overheads if you want to keep track of overhead rates. If you are using standard costing, you can optionally define a material overhead for things such as purchasing or freight. Each overhead is charged when an item is received into inventory. See Chapter 19 for further details.

DEFINING DEFAULT MATERIAL OVERHEAD RATES

If you have decided to use material overheads, you can optionally enter default rates for your organization or categories. Then when you define your items, Oracle Inventory automatically uses the defaults. See Chapter 19 for further details.

DEFINING FREIGHT CARRIERS

A freight carrier is an organization or company that provides item transportation services between your organization and your customers, between your suppliers and your organization, and between several of your organizations for an inter-organization item transfer. To define a freight carrier, you need to provide a unique name for the carrier and the carrier description. You also need to specify a general ledger distribution account for the carrier that collects costs associated with using that carrier.

DEFINING THE ORGANIZATION SHIPPING NETWORK

You can use the Shipping Networks screen to define the accounting information and the relationships that exist between shipping and destination organizations. When you define a new organization relationship, the shipping information you specified in the Organization parameters appears by default on the Shipping Networks screen. For each organization relationship, you specify for an organization whether it is a shipping organization, a destination organization, or both.

You also specify for each organization relationship whether the shipping transfer type is direct or in-transit. You normally use the direct type if the shipping time is small and the in-transit type if the time to transfer between the organizations is a significant amount of time. When you move items between organizations with a transfer type of in-transit, Oracle moves material to in-transit inventory before it reaches the destination organization. If you specify the in-transit transfer type, you also need to indicate which organization owns the material while it is in-transit. You also need to indicate the type of receipt routing that is performed (direct, standard, or inspection) at the destination organization when the material is transferred in-transit.

You need to indicate whether internal requisitions are required from the destination organization when you perform inter-organization transfers of items. You also need to define an inter-organization charge type. You can specify to automatically add a predefined percentage to the transaction value, not add any transfer charges, add a discrete value, or add a discrete percentage to the transaction value. You can specify different discrete values or percentages for each of the organizational shipping relationships that you have defined.

You have to provide general ledger account codes to record charges associated with an inter-organization transfer. You can also optionally specify shipping methods and lead times associated with the shipping methods. The lead times are used by MRP when planning inter-organization supply.

> **Note**
>
> The definition of the organization shipping network is not bidirectional. If you have to move goods from a sending organization to a receiving organization and also move goods from the receiving organization back to the sending organization, you need to define two interorganizational relationships.

DEFINING ACCOUNT ALIASES

An account alias is a shorthand label for a general ledger account-number combination that you can use when entering inventory transactions such as miscellaneous issues or receipt transactions. When you enter an inventory transaction, you can enter the account alias instead of the multi-segmented account number. Using account aliases can reduce the number of keystroke entries as well as the chance of entering the wrong account number for your inventory transactions. In addition to a user-friendly reference to a particular account number, an account alias is also a transaction source type of its own. This means you can query and report on transactions using the account aliases.

To set up account aliases, you first need to define the account aliases key flexfield as detailed in an earlier section in this chapter. You then use the Account Aliases window to define an account alias and its associated general ledger account number.

DEFINING TRANSACTION SOURCE TYPES

Transaction source types enable you to classify transactions according to their origins, such as a purchase order or physical inventory. When you perform a transaction, you specify a transaction type and a source. For example, for a PO receipt, the transaction source type is Purchase Order and the actual purchase order number is the source.

Oracle Inventory provides a number of predefined transaction source types, including purchase order, sales order, account, job or schedule, internal requisition, internal order, cycle count, account alias, physical inventory, standard cost update, RMA, and inventory. In addition to these predefined source types, you can define your own source types. You can also associate a list of valid sources with your transaction source type.

You can define additional transaction source types in the Transaction Source Types window. This window also allows for the specification of a list of valid sources. You can then use these user-defined source types along with predefined transaction actions to define a new transaction type.

DEFINING TRANSACTION TYPES

Oracle Inventory provides transaction reporting and querying capabilities by transaction type. A transaction type is the combination of a transaction source type and a transaction action. Oracle Inventory provides for a number of predefined transaction types. In addition to those transaction types provided by Oracle, you can use the Transaction Types window to define additional transaction types. A user-defined transaction type is a combination of a user-defined transaction source type and a predefined transaction action such as Issue from Stores.

DEFINING TRANSACTION REASONS

A transaction reason is a way of classifying or explaining the reason for a transaction. Oracle Inventory provides for transaction reporting and inquiring by transaction reason. You can define your own transaction reason codes that you can enter when you perform an inventory transaction. To define a transaction reason, you use the Transaction Reasons window.

An example is that you want to take a number of your new low-cost, high-quality material items to a trade show for display and then give the items away at the show to customers. You can create a transaction reason of Trade Show and use this reason for all material issues for the show. You can later report on all of the items issued for the show by this transaction reason.

DEFINING PURCHASING OPTIONS

If you will be using inter-organization shipments with in-transit inventory, you need to use the Enter Receipts transaction to receive items into the destination organization. To perform this transaction effectively, you should define certain default control options in the Purchasing Options window to save you time when you create your receipts. Refer to Chapter 15 for further details.

OPENING ACCOUNTING PERIODS

Oracle Inventory uses accounting periods to group material and work-in-process transactions for accounting purposes. An accounting period must be open for you to be able to perform an inventory transaction. That means that the inventory transaction date must fall within the beginning and ending dates of the open accounting period. You first need to define your accounting periods in Oracle General Ledger. Then before you can enter transactions in Oracle Inventory, you need to open an accounting period. You use the Inventory Accounting Periods window to perform this function.

STARTING THE MATERIAL AND COST INTERFACE CONCURRENT MANAGERS

Transaction managers in Oracle execute a number of processes, including material transaction, demand reservation, move transaction, resource cost transaction, remote procedure call, and material cost transaction. These managers run at periodic intervals that you specify. You can also specify the number of transaction workers and the number of transactions processed by each worker during each interval. You need to start the material transaction and material cost interface managers if you want to perform transactions in the background or in concurrent processing mode or if you use custom forms and data collection devices to enter transactions. You also need to start the demand reservation manager if you place demand in Oracle Order Entry in the background processing mode. You can use the Interface Managers window to view the status of the transaction managers, and from the Special, menu you can launch the transaction manager that you have highlighted.

You do not have to launch these transaction managers if you decide to process all of your transactions online and if you do not use the transaction interface.

SETTING THE PROFILE OPTIONS

Each of the Oracle Applications has a set of profile options that allow you to indicate how the application should access and process application information. The Oracle Inventory profile options all have an indicator of INV. In Oracle Inventory, you can indicate what the application uses when creating, processing, or transacting an inventory item. For example, you can specify with profile options what the default unit of measure for an item should be or what the default item status should be.

You can also indicate the processing control that the Inventory application uses for transacting items. The profile option labeled TP:INV Transaction Processing Mode allows you to specify for all inventory transactions that the processing control should be via background processing, concurrent processing, or online processing. You choose online processing if you want your transactions processed immediately. You choose the other processing options if you want your transactions processed after you save your work, freeing your terminal to allow you to continue with other tasks. You can also specify form-level processing, which allows you to specify for each type of inventory transaction the type of processing control you want.

For additional information on the various profile options and the choices that you can make for each of these options, see the Oracle manual *Oracle Inventory User's Guide*.

> **Tip**
>
> A profile option called INV:Updatable Item Name defaults to a value of No and generally should be left with this value. However, you might have created an item record with bad data in it that can't be corrected; for example, units of measure on an item cannot be modified once entered. You want to be able to reuse this item number and rekey in the correct data. You can update the INV:Updatable Item Name profile option to Yes, change the bad part's item number to some obsolete number, and then recreate the item with correct data. Remember to change this profile option back to No so that you don't inadvertently update an item number key by mistake.

LOADING SYSTEM ITEMS

Oracle Inventory provides for two different methods of loading inventory items. One method uses online windows described later in the section "Item Definition." This method is appropriate for loading new items and for the initial creation of inventory items when the number of items is relatively small (several thousand or less). When an organization has a large number of inventory items to load (in the tens of thousands or more), it becomes advantageous to load these items in a more automated manner.

Oracle Inventory provides for the mass creation of items through the use of an item interface. Before you use the item interface, you need to write and run a custom program that extracts item information from your legacy system, formats this information, and inserts it into the MTL_SYSTEM_ITEM_INTERFACE table. If you will be using item revisions, you also need to insert the revision detail into MTL_ITEMS_REVISIONS_INTERFACE table. You then run the item interface to import the data. The item interface validates your data and imports the new items. You need to first import your items into the item master organization before you can import your items into any specific organization or into all the children organizations. In addition to item attributes and revision details, you can also import item material cost and material overhead through the item interface.

PROCESSING TRANSACTIONS

Oracle Inventory provides a number of online transactions to support the tracking of inventory items. Following are some of these transactions.

ENTERING RECEIPTS AND RECEIVING TRANSACTIONS

Oracle Purchasing and Oracle Inventory both allow for the receipt processing of purchased material. You can also use the Enter Receipts window to receive items shipped in-transit between organizations. This processing includes the receipt, inspection, and delivery of incoming material. For a detailed explanation of the transactions that support the receiving process, see Chapter 15.

ENTERING RETURNS AND ADJUSTMENTS

In addition to being able to receive incoming purchased material, it is sometimes necessary to correct or adjust a receiving transaction and to return a purchased item back to the vendor. The Oracle Applications Inventory and Purchasing both allow for returns and adjustments of received materials. For additional details regarding these transactions, see Chapter 15.

TRANSFERRING MATERIAL BETWEEN SUBINVENTORIES

To transfer an item from one subinventory to another, or from one locator within a subinventory to another locator within the same or a different subinventory, you use the Subinventory Transfer window. This transaction also allows for material transfers between asset and expense subinventories and from tracked to nontracked subinventories. It also allows you to use a user-defined transaction type when performing the subinventory transfer.

To perform a subinventory transfer, you navigate to the Subinventory Transfer window and then enter the following information:

- Date and time of the transaction. The present date and time appears by default on the screen. However, depending on the setting of the profile option INV:Transaction Date Validation, you can override this with an earlier date and time.

- Transaction type. Specify either a predefined transaction type or one that you have defined.

- Optionally, enter the source of the transaction type and whether inventory information should be defaulted from the serial number.

Then, to enter the item to transfer, you select Transaction Lines and enter the following information:

- The inventory item to transfer or serial number if you specified default inventory information from serial number.

- The revision of the item (optional).

- Subinventories from and to which to transfer the item.

- The locators from and to which to transfer the item (optional). You must enter locators here if you specified the item or subinventory is under locator control.

- A lot number for the item (optional)

- A unit of measure. Inventory defaults to the primary unit of measure for the item, but you can enter an alternate unit of measure.

- The quantity of item to transfer based on the unit of measure specified.

- A reason code for the transaction and up to 240 characters of text to describe the transaction (optional).

- Lot or serial number information. Click the Lot/Serial button and enter the lot or serial number information for the item to be transferred.

- After entering the information for the item to be transferred, remember to save your work.

TRANSFERRING MATERIAL BETWEEN ORGANIZATIONS

To move inventory items from one organization to another, you can use either a direct or in-transit shipment. You normally use a direct transfer if the time to move items between the organizations is small. In this type of transfer, the item goes directly in a single transaction (Inter-organization Transfer window) from a subinventory in one organization to a subinventory in another organization.

If the transportation time between two organization is significant, you transfer material from a subinventory in the shipping organization to in-transit inventory using the Inter-organization Transfer window. Then when the material reaches its destination, you use the Enter Receipts window to receive the material into a subinventory in the destination organization. The Free On Board (FOB) point defined in the Shipping Networks window determines the ownership of the material while it is in-transit. If the FOB point is set to Shipment, the destination organization owns the material when the shipping organization ships it and while it is in-transit. If the FOB point is set to Receipt, the shipping organization owns the shipment until it is received in the destination organization.

To transfer material from your current organization to another organization or to in-transit inventory, you use the Inter-organization Transfer window and enter the following information:

- The date of the transaction. The present date appears by default on the screen. However, depending on the setting of the profile option INV:Transaction Date Validation, you can override this with an earlier date.

- The organization to which to transfer the material.

- The transaction type. Specify either a predefined transaction type or one that you have defined.

- The source of the transaction type or whether inventory information should be defaulted from the serial number (optional).

- Shipping information such as shipment number (required if the To Org uses in-transit inventory), freight carrier, waybill number, and so on (optional).

Then, to enter the items to transfer, you select Transaction Lines and enter the following information:

- The inventory item to transfer. You can specify the same item more than once if you want to transfer the item to different subinventories or locators.

- For a direct transfer, if the item is under revision control in either organization, enter a revision that is common to the item in both organizations.

- The subinventory the item is from.

- The subinventory the item is going to (optional only for in-transit).

- The locators. If you specified locator control for the item, enter from and to locators.

- The lot number. If the item is under lot control, enter lot number for the item. If there are multiple lots to transfer, complete the remaining steps and then choose the Lot/Serial button to display the Lot Entry window.

- The unit of measure. The primary unit of measure for the item appears by default but can be replaced with any valid alternate unit of measure.

- A reason code and up to 240 characters of text in the reference field to describe the transaction (optional).

You can also enter transfer charges to assign to the To organization, freight costs and GL account numbers to charge to the From organization, and lot and serial numbers for each one of the items being transferred.

Remember to save your work to process the inter-organization transfer transaction.

MAINTAINING SHIPMENTS

You can use the Maintain Shipments window to find, view and update inventory in-transit shipping information. You can also use the Maintain Shipments window to view or cancel Advanced Shipment Notices (ASNs). Some of the information you can view or update includes the packing slip and bill of lading numbers, ship-to location, number of containers, receipt routing, and reason code.

MISCELLANEOUS TRANSACTIONS

The miscellaneous transaction in Oracle Inventory is one of the most powerful and flexible transactions in the system. It allows you to receive and issue material that is not a normal purchasing/receiving, work-in-process, or order entry/shipping transaction. You can use this transaction to

- Issue items and charge the material issue to a department such as marketing, charge to a special expense account such as scrap, or charge to a project.
- Make manual adjustments to the general ledger by receiving material from one GL account to inventory and then issuing the material from inventory to another GL account.
- Receive items into inventory other than from a purchase order from a supplier. For example, you might discover some items hiding in an out-of-the-way place that need to be put into a subinventory and charged to an inventory adjustment account.
- Initially load quantity on-hand information for items when you start to implement Oracle Inventory.

To perform a miscellaneous transaction, follow these steps:

1. Select the Miscellaneous Transaction screen.
2. Enter the date and time of the transaction.

> **Note** The present date and time appears by default on the screen. However, depending on the setting of the profile option INV:Transaction Date Validation, you can override this with an earlier date and time.

3. Enter a miscellaneous transaction type for the transaction. This can be a system-defined transaction type such as Miscellaneous Issue or Account Alias Issue or a user-defined transaction type.
4. You can optionally enter the following information:
   - The source of the transaction type.
   - The general ledger account number to which the material is issued or received.
   - An indication of whether item information should be defaulted from the serial number.

Then, you choose transaction lines on the Miscellaneous Transaction window to enter the item information that you want to issue or receive. This step opens the Transaction Lines Detail folder window, where you can enter such information as

- An item number that you want to issue or receive and a revision number if required.
- The subinventory, locator, and lot number, if required.
- The quantity to issue or receive.
- The unit of measure. You can replace the default.

You can enter additional information for the transaction, such as a reason code, an additional 240 characters of free text, a different GL account for the item than entered on the header screen, and the unit cost of an item if using average costing. If you have additional items to transact against the same miscellaneous transaction criteria entered on the header screen, you can continue to enter additional lines for those items on the same screen. Remember to save your work so that Oracle Inventory will process your miscellaneous transaction.

RECEIVING AND INSPECTING CUSTOMER RETURNS

If a customer wants to return an item that has been ordered from your organization, you must first enter a return material authorization (RMA) in Oracle Order Entry. The next step in the customer item return process is to determine whether the item needs to be inspected before a receipt can be performed. You specify this with the item attribute of RMA Inspection Status. A status of Inspection Required means that you must first perform an inspection of the returned items before you can perform the RMA Receipt transaction to put the items back into inventory. Even if you have specified Inspection not required, you can optionally perform the inspection step.

To perform the inspection process on a customer return, you first enter the item in the Inspect Customer Returns window. The information required to be specified to perform this transaction is the date of the transaction (which can default from the system), the RMA number and the line item number on the RMA of the item to inspect, a unit of measure (which will default from the RMA and can be overridden), and the quantity of the item to inspect or return. You also need to specify Receive or Return for the inspected items. Receive means you have successfully inspected the items, the items are now in the inspection area, and the next step to perform is the RMA Receipt transaction to put the items into inventory. Return means you are rejecting the items and either returning the items to the customer or scrapping the items. For those items you are rejecting with Return, you then want to cancel the return line in Oracle Order Entry.

After the successful inspection of the customer return, if it is required, your next step is to perform an RMA Receipt transaction. You need to provide the following information: the RMA number, the line item of the RMA, the quantity of the item to be received, and the subinventory in which to receive the material. In addition, you need to specify the date and time of the transaction, which you would usually let default from the system date and time. You can also let the unit of measure of the item being returned default from the RMA, or you can override it. Optionally, you might have to specify such information as the locator of the subinventory in which to store the items, the revision number of the item returned, and the lot or serial numbers of the returned items. You can also optionally enter a reason for this transaction as well as up to 240 characters of reference text about the return transaction.

RETURNING ITEMS TO CUSTOMER

If you have the requirement to return repaired or substituted items to your customer after the customer has sent them to you, you would accomplish this with the RMA Return transaction. Before you can return items to a customer, you must first receive the items with the RMA Receipt transaction described previously. The information required to perform the RMA Return transaction is the date and time of the transaction (which can default from the system), RMA number for the item to be returned, the inventory item number, the line item number of the RMA, the subinventory from which to return the item, a unit of measure (which will default from the RMA and can be overridden), and the quantity of the item to return. You might also have to specify the locator for the subinventory and the lot or serial numbers of the items being returned. You can also optionally enter a reason for this transaction as well as up to 240 characters of reference text about this RMA return transaction.

> **Note**
>
> Use the RMA Return transaction to only return substitute items or repaired items that you have received on an RMA. If you need to reject a customer return, do a Return using the Inspect Customer Returns transaction as described previously in the section "Receiving and Inspecting Customer Returns."

PURGING TRANSACTIONS

Oracle Inventory provides for the capability to purge transaction history and associated accounting information.

> **Note**
>
> You should use this transaction purge capability with a great deal of caution because once the information is removed, you can no longer query or report on this information. For example, the job lot composition, accrual reconciliation, or transaction register can no longer retrieve purged transaction information and report on it.

To purge transactions, you specify Transaction Purge in the Name field of the Purge Transactions or All Reports window and then specify a purge date. The date specified must be in a closed period.

RESERVING INVENTORY

You can set aside inventory of an item to reserve it for an account, an account alias, or a user-defined source such as a particular type of customer order. Reservations prevent the issue of the inventory that is set aside to anything other than that reservation's source type. To reserve an item, navigate to the Reserve Available Items Summary folder window and enter the following information:

- The origin of the transaction.
- The source against which you want to make the reservation.
- The line number that indicates the item quantity to reserve.
- The date you expect to use the material.
- The inventory item to reserve.
- If required by the attributes on the item, enter
    - The revision if item is under revision quantity control.
    - The lot number if item is under lot control.
    - The subinventory from which to reserve the item.
    - The locator if item is under locator control.
- The unit of measure in which to reserve the item.
- The quantity of item to reserve. This must be greater than zero and less than or equal to the available quantity of the item.

Save your work to reserve the specified quantity of inventory of the item.

PART

III

CH

16

> **Note**
>
> Be cautious in reserving inventory for a specific requirement that is far into the future. This could prevent you from issuing the reserved material for a different near-in requirement even though in the future, a supply of inventory might arrive and meet the inventory needs of your far-out requirement.

ENTERING STATISTICS

Oracle Inventory features a capability to gather, review, and report statistical data associated with material movements. This capability has been primarily developed to assist in the Intrastat reporting requirements of the European Union. If you have the requirement to meet these reporting requirements, you should consult the *Oracle Inventory User's Guide* for additional detailed information regarding this capability.

ITEM DEFINITION

The steps to defining an item follow:

1. Key in the item key or part number and the item description.
2. Use templates or existing items (copy items) to define items in the master organization.
3. Enter values for item attributes that were not set by templates or copying items.
4. Enter values for item categories and catalogs.
5. Enable the item in the organizations where you will be using the item.

6. Update organization-level item attributes that are different for each one of the organizations; examples are the lead time of the item or planner code or WIP supply subinventory.

To define an inventory item, you always must enter at least two pieces of information: the item key or part number and the item description. All of the other item information can default, such as the unit of measure and item status with the attributes associated with item status. In addition, you can individually specify each one of the item attributes. You don't need to specify any of the item attributes that don't apply to the item.

Oracle Inventory has an extensive list of item attributes to help you describe and control how your items are used. For ease in data entry, these item attributes are separated into application areas. Table 16.2 lists item attributes by application area.

TABLE 16.2   ATTRIBUTES FOR AN INVENTORY ITEM

Application Area	Item Attribute
Bill of Materials	Base Model
Bill of Materials	BOM Allowed
Bill of Materials	BOM Item Type
Bill of Materials	Engineering Date
Costing	Cost of Goods Sold Account
Costing	Costing Enabled
Costing	Include in Rollup
Costing	Inventory Asset Value
Costing	Standard Lot Size
General Planning	Carrying Cost Percent
General Planning	Fixed Days Supply
General Planning	Fixed Lot Size Multiplier
General Planning	Fixed Order Quantity
General Planning	Inventory Planning Method
General Planning	Make or Buy
General Planning	Maximum Order Quantity
General Planning	Min-Max Maximum Quantity
General Planning	Min-Max Minimum Quantity
General Planning	Minimum Order Quantity
General Planning	Order Cost
General Planning	Planner
General Planning	Source Type
General Planning	Safety Stock

TABLE 16.2   CONTINUED

Application Area	Item Attribute
General Planning	Safety Stock Bucket Days
General Planning	Safety Stock Percent
General Planning	Source Organization
General Planning	Source Subinventory
Inventory	Cycle Count Enabled
Inventory	Inventory Item
Inventory	Locator Control
Inventory	Lot Control
Inventory	Lot Expiration
Inventory	Neg Measurement Error
Inventory	Pos Measurement Error
Inventory	Reservation Control
Inventory	Restrict Locators
Inventory	Restrict Subinventories
Inventory	Revision Control
Inventory	Serial Number Control
Inventory	Shelf Life Days
Inventory	Starting Lot Number
Inventory	Starting Lot Prefix
Inventory	Starting Serial Number
Inventory	Starting Serial Prefix
Inventory	Stockable
Inventory	Transactable
Invoicing	Accounting Rule
Invoicing	Invoice Enabled
Invoicing	Invoiceable Item
Invoicing	Invoicing Rule
Invoicing	Payment Terms
Invoicing	Sales Account
Invoicing	Tax Code
Lead Times	Cumulative Manufacturing Lead Time
Lead Times	Cumulative Total Lead Time
Lead Times	Fixed Lead Time
Lead Times	Lead Time Lot Size

TABLE 16.2 CONTINUED

Application Area	Item Attribute
Lead Times	Postprocessing Lead Time
Lead Times	Preprocessing Lead Time
Lead Times	Processing Lead Time
Lead Times	Variable Lead Time
Main	Conversions
Main	Descriptive Flexfield
Main	Item Description
Main	Item Status
Main	Primary Unit of Measure
Main	User Item Type
MPS/MRP Planning	Acceptable Early Days
MPS/MRP Planning	Acceptable Rate Decrease
MPS/MRP Planning	Acceptable Rate Increase
MPS/MRP Planning	Calculate ATP
MPS/MRP Planning	Demand Time Fence
MPS/MRP Planning	Demand Time Fence Days
MPS/MRP Planning	End Assembly Pegging
MPS/MRP Planning	Forecast Control
MPS/MRP Planning	MRP Planning Method
MPS/MRP Planning	Overrun Percentage
MPS/MRP Planning	Planning Exception Set
MPS/MRP Planning	Planning Time Fence
MPS/MRP Planning	Planning Time Fence Days
MPS/MRP Planning	Reduce MPS
MPS/MRP Planning	Release Time Fence
MPS/MRP Planning	Release Time Fence Days
MPS/MRP Planning	Repetitive Planning
MPS/MRP Planning	Rounding Control
MPS/MRP Planning	Shrinkage Rate
Order Entry	Assemble to Order
Order Entry	ATP Components
Order Entry	ATP Rule
Order Entry	Check ATP
Order Entry	Collateral Item

TABLE 16.2   CONTINUED

Application Area	Item Attribute
Order Entry	Customer Ordered Item
Order Entry	Customer Orders Enabled
Order Entry	Default Shipping Organization
Order Entry	Internal Ordered Item
Order Entry	Internal Orders Enabled
Order Entry	OE Transactable
Order Entry	Pick Components
Order Entry	Picking Rule
Order Entry	Returnable
Order Entry	RMA Inspection Status
Order Entry	Ship Model Complete
Order Entry	Shippable Item
Physical Attributes	Container
Physical Attributes	Container Type
Physical Attributes	Internal Volume
Physical Attributes	Max Load Weight
Physical Attributes	Min Fill Percentage
Physical Attributes	Unit Volume
Physical Attributes	Unit Weight
Physical Attributes	Vehicle
Physical Attributes	Volume Unit of Measure
Physical Attributes	Weight Unit of Measure
Purchasing	Allow Description Update
Purchasing	Asset Category
Purchasing	Default Buyer
Purchasing	Encumbrance Account
Purchasing	Expense Account
Purchasing	Hazard Class
Purchasing	Inspection Required
Purchasing	Invoice Close Tolerance
Purchasing	List Price
Purchasing	Market Price
Purchasing	Outside Processing Item
Purchasing	Outside Processing Unit Type

PART

III

CH

16

TABLE 16.2 CONTINUED

Application Area	Item Attribute
Purchasing	Price Tolerance Percent
Purchasing	Purchasable
Purchasing	Purchased Item
Purchasing	Receipt Required
Purchasing	Receive Close Tolerance
Purchasing	RFQ Required
Purchasing	Rounding Factor
Purchasing	Taxable Item
Purchasing	UN Number
Purchasing	Unit of Issue
Purchasing	Use Approved Vendor
Receiving	Allow Express Delivery
Receiving	Allow Substitute Receipts
Receiving	Allow Unordered Receipts
Receiving	Days Early Receipt Allowed
Receiving	Days Late Receipt Allowed
Receiving	Enforce Ship-To Location
Receiving	Over Receipt Qty Action
Receiving	Over Receipt Qty Tolerance
Receiving	Receipt Date Action
Receiving	Receipt Routing
Service Item	Serviceable Product
Work In Process	Build in WIP
Work In Process	WIP Supply Locator
Work In Process	WIP Supply Subinventory
Work In Process	WIP Supply Type

You can set all eight of the status control attributes with a user-defined item status. See the section "Defining Statuses" earlier in this chapter for additional detail regarding defining item status control.

To assist in the item definition process, you can copy existing items. You can also use predefined or custom templates that attach a whole list of attributes to your items rather than require you to enter each item attribute individually.

Note	When you copy an item, Oracle does not copy all of the data associated with the item. Categories, organization assignments, catalog group information, and costs are not copied from one item to another.

DEFINING LOT AND SERIAL NUMBER INFORMATION

You can assign either lot or serial number information to your inventory items. For those items you have specified that you want to be under lot control, when you enter receipt or issue transactions, you need to specify the lot control information for those items so that the system will assist you in tracking the lots associated with the items. Likewise, if you have specified serial number control for any of your items, you need to specify the serial numbers for those items when you transact those items into and out of inventory.

You can specify for each of your inventory items that you want the item to be lot-controlled, to be serial number-controlled, or to have no lot or serial number control. When you use Oracle Work in Process, you cannot specify that an item be both lot-controlled and serial number-controlled.

For an item to be defined as lot-controlled, there can be no on-hand quantity of the item. When you specify that you want an item to be lot-controlled, you can also specify a starting lot prefix to be used when you define a lot number for the item. You can also specify a starting lot number suffix. Afterward, this number will be incremented for each succeeding lot. For every item that you specify that you would like to be lot-controlled, you also need to specify the type of lot expiration (shelf-life) control: for no shelf life control, "No control"; for a specific number of days for all lots of this item, "Shelf life days"; and to specify an expiration date as you receive each lot, "User-defined". For items with shelf-life days control you need to specify the number of days each lot is to be active.

For an item that you want to be serial number-controlled, you need to specify whether the serial numbers for the item will be created and assigned when you receive the item ("At inventory receipt"), created and assigned when you ship the item ("At sales order issue"), or assigned predefined serial numbers when you receive the item ("Predefined"). For all the serial numbers that you define, you can specify a starting alpha prefix and a starting serial number suffix to be used when generating the serial numbers for the item.

DEFINING ITEM AND SUBINVENTORY INFORMATION

You use the item/subinventory relationship to specify a number of different pieces of information about the item and the subinventory. You can restrict an inventory item to a list of subinventories with the Restrict Subinventories attribute on the item. Then you can assign a list of subinventories to an item. You can specify valid subinventories for zero quantity cycle counts for an item. You can also specify items for an ABC analysis at the subinventory level. If you want to perform min-max planning and replenishment processing for an item at the subinventory level rather than the organization level, you can specify planning information and locators for the item in its assigned subinventories.

To specify item/subinventory relationship information, you can specify the item on the Master Items or Organization Items Summary window, then choose Item Subinventories from the Special menu, and then enter the subinventories for the item.

Alternatively, you can specify the subinventory on the Subinventories Summary window and then choose the Item/Subinventory button to enter the items associated with this subinventory on the Item Subinventories window. For each of the item/subinventory relationships specified, you can also specify whether you would like to min-max plan this item in this subinventory and the min and max quantities for the item. You can also specify order modifiers to be used for the item in this subinventory including minimum order or repetitive rate, maximum order or repetitive rate, and fixed lot multiple quantity or repetitive rate. You can enter lead-time information for the item in the subinventory. You can also specify sourcing information for the item in the subinventory. You specify Supplier if you want to fill requisition requests for this item in this subinventory from a supplier, and you specify Inventory and the organization if you want to fill requests by internal requisitions from existing inventory.

If you want to also restrict an item to specific locators, you specify the Restrict Locators attribute on the item, and you enter the locators to which to assign the item in the subinventory in the Locators for this Item Subinventory window.

DEFINING ITEM RELATIONSHIPS, CROSS REFERENCES, AND MANUFACTURER PART NUMBERS

Oracle Inventory enables you to establish several different ways to report and inquire on an item. You can define relationships for an item, you can establish cross references for an item, and you can specify manufacturer part numbers for an item.

You can establish that an item is related to another item. You do this by using the Item Relationships window and specifying the item that is the From part of the relationship and a different item that is the To part of the relationship. In addition, you specify the type of relationship: Related just means the two parts are related in a nonspecific way, and Substitute means one item is a substitute for the other. You also indicate whether the relationship is Reciprocal. A substitute relationship that is reciprocal means that you can use the From item as a substitute for the To item and vice versa.

> **Note**   Item relationships can normally only be used for inquiry and reporting purposes. However, in Oracle Purchasing, once you define a substitute item for an item, you can receive the substitute item in place of the originally ordered item. You need to make sure that the ordered item and the substitute item share the same base unit of measure.

To establish a cross reference for an item, you must first define the cross-reference types you want to use, such as Old Part Number or Blue Print Number as defined in the section

"Defining Cross-Reference Types" earlier in this chapter. You can then assign these cross references to items by using the Cross-References Types screen or choose Cross References from the Special menu when you are using the Master Items Summary screen. After you select the item and the cross-reference type, you need to indicate whether this cross reference will apply to all organizations or just to a specific organization. You then enter the cross-reference value. For example, this is the actual value for the Old Part Number for the item.

In addition to cross references and item relationships, you can also specify manufacturer part numbers for an item. You can use the manufacturer part number for reporting purposes and for searching for an item. You do this first by defining the manufacturers in the Manufacturers window. Then, you enter the manufacturer part number and the item. You can assign the same item to multiple manufacturer part numbers.

PART

III

CH

16

DEFINING ITEM TRANSACTION DEFAULT SUBINVENTORIES AND LOCATORS

You can define a default shipping and receiving subinventory and locator for an item. Oracle Order Entry displays the default shipping information when you ship the item. Oracle Purchasing and Inventory display the default receiving information when you receive the item. You use the Item Transaction Defaults screen to specify the item, the subinventory, and whether this is to be the default shipping or receiving subinventory. If you are using locators for the item, on the same Transaction Defaults screen in the Locators alternative region, you can also specify a default locator to be used in addition to the subinventory.

ADDITIONAL APPLICATION FUNCTIONS

The primary purpose of this chapter has been to assist in the configuring of the Oracle Inventory application by describing how to perform the setup of the Oracle Inventory application. In addition, a few of the basic inventory transactions have been described. There are a number of additional application functions included in the Oracle Inventory application module. Following are some of these additional application functions and a short description of these functions:

- *Item inquiry.* There are a number of online inquiry functions provided for items including on-hand inventory, lot and serial numbers, available-to-promise inventory, item cost, item attributes, and status. The supply and demand for an item can be viewed online. Searches for items can be performed by item number, description, catalog, category, status, and item cross-references.

- *Inventory transaction inquiry.* Inventory transactions can be reviewed online. The transactions can be viewed in detail or summarized by date, item, subinventory, locator, category, or transaction type.

- *Planning and Replenishment.* Support is provided for planning of inventory items using min-max and reorder point planning. When inventory planned items get below a minimum or reorder point, an inventory planning function generates purchase requisitions for purchased items and jobs for manufactured items. Support is also provided to calculate safety stocks and to develop forecasts. Also provided is a means to support replenishment of items when doing manual replenishment counts from a nontracked subinventory. New to release 11 is a kanban system of pull-based replenishment. Support is provided to read kanban cards and trigger a replenishment signal.

■ *Counting.* There are a number of transactions and reports provided to support the counting of inventory items. The functions of taking a physical inventory and cycle counting are both supported. ABC analysis can be performed to determine the high-volume items so that faster-moving items can be counted more frequently than slower-moving items.

■ *Interface to Accounting.* All the inventory transactions generate general ledger accounting transactions. There is support provided to transfer summary or detailed inventory transactions for a given period to the General Ledger.

■ *Reports.* Inventory reports are included in the areas of transactions, items, costing, ABC analysis, counting, planning, forecasting, receiving, safety stock, and application setups.

SUMMARY

The Oracle Inventory application helps you to define and track the inventory items for your organization. The application can be used to perform these tasks for a simple, one-subinventory warehouse. Oracle Inventory can also be used as the base for a complex, multi-organizational, material planning and supply system fully integrated with a complete financial accounting system. To efficiently and accurately perform these tasks, it is necessary to customize the application to fit your requirements. This customization process is called application setup. The purpose of this chapter has been to assist the application implementation team in the application setup process. Descriptions of some of the basic Inventory transactions have also been provided.

A reminder for a successful implementation of Oracle Inventory is to start with the simplest approach whenever possible, educate and train the users, and test rigorously. When these suggestions are used along with good management support and a dedicated implementation team, success can almost be ensured.

CHAPTER 17

Using Oracle Order Entry and Shipping

Oracle Order Entry/Shipping provides numerous features that enable you to set up your system to reflect your business practices and manage the entry and shipping of your products. The Order Entry/Shipping application interfaces with AR to assist in the management of customer invoicing. Order Entry/Shipping also interfaces with Inventory through the Demand Interface. Additionally, Order Entry/Shipping interfaces to Purchasing for internal orders. Order Entry/Shipping is also used to assist the Material Planning process. Figure 17.1 shows how Order Entry/Shipping relates to the other Oracle Modules and the key types of information the modules share with each other.

Figure 17.1
OE Relation-
ships to Other
Applications

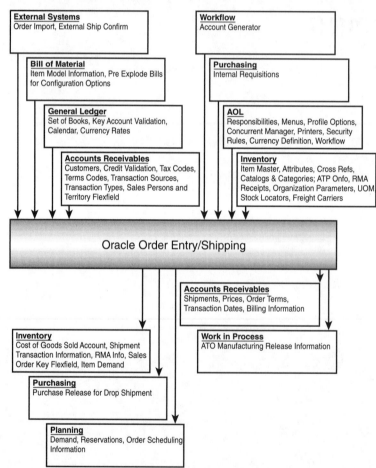

DISCOVERING NEW FEATURES IN RELEASE 11

Several new features that can be found in release 11 of the Order Entry/Shipping Module. Some of these features, such as the Departure Planning Workbench, are new features in release 11, whereas others, such as Pick Release Controls, are enhancements to the current process. The features are as follows:

Define price discounts by item, item category, customer, or customer class

Define container-load relationships

Schedule, track, invoice, and process returns for drop shipments

Schedule vehicle departures in the departure planning workbench

Control pick releases through release sequence rules and pick slip grouping rules

Capture quantity and serial number information for specific containers

Enhanced order import to dupport Oracle release management

REVIEW OF THE TOP ENHANCEMENT REQUESTS

Oracle Applications customers are looking for Oracle Order Entry/Shipping Application to include the following enhancements, among others:

Provide the capability to update pricing up to ship time with Order Entry/Shipping.

Archive order change history for management reporting for ISO9000.

Provide Customer Part Number registration.

Enforce multipliers for specific item quantities.

Add controls for the reapplication of holds.

Allow the change of Freight Carriers at Ship Confirm.

Provide the capability to maintain volume discounts across time and orders.

Maintain freight terms in lines and shipment schedule lines.

UNDERSTANDING THE DATABASE DESIGN

When you purchase the Oracle Applications including Order Entry/Shipping, the database consists of the tables, views, modules, and objects required for you to successfully implement the Order Entry/Shipping application. The database is also designed with interface tables and foundation tables so that you can easily convert existing application data, integrate Order Entry/Shipping with other applications, develop custom reports, define new alerts, create new views, and use external query tools. The following sections dig into the details of database design.

MAJOR RELATIONSHIPS

Within the Oracle Applications, major relationships exist between Order Entry/Shipping and the following modules:

■ *General Ledger.* This maintains all the accounting information for Order Entry/Shipping—in particular, the Cost of Goods Sold Account.

- *Inventory.* This maintains all the item information for Order Entry/Shipping. There is an interface to the Inventory Module that is used by Order Entry/Shipping to place demand on items being shipped.

- *Receivables.* This module interfaces with Order Entry/Shipping so that items that are shipped to a customer can be invoiced to that customer automatically.

The following are some things to keep in mind when you are working with these relationships:

- The DBA should monitor the SO_EXCEPTIONS table and delete items from this table as necessary because Order Entry/Shipping does not automatically delete rows from this table.

- Holds are not effective between Pick Release and Ship Confirmation.

- Do not change the OE: Unit Price Precision Type profile after orders have been placed into the system.

- You cannot change revision control or stock locator control when you have quantities onhand.

SIZE CONSIDERATIONS

You can enter the amount of memory that you want to allocate to the Oracle Order Entry/Shipping tax program. This memory is used to store sales and value-added tax rates to speed tax calculations.

You can purge old data through the Order Purge programs. Space in your database can be reclaimed through the purging of old orders and can further improve the performance of transactions and maintenance.

PERFORMANCE AND ACCESS ISSUES

Closing orders that are complete enhances performance because many queries retrieve open orders only. Closed orders are not selected in these queries, increasing system speed and efficiency. Many of the standard reports are also limited to the active orders only.

You can also use the database trace option to trace and evaluate the database activity for the Order Entry/Shipping transactions. The database trace feature enables you to do performance analysis and to get diagnostic information in the debugging of errors.

Turning off the Include Tax Option during setup improves the performance of credit checking. You can also improve the performance of credit checking by turning off whether to include payments at risk when calculating a customer's outstanding balance.

When you add a new order or line approval in an order cycle, system performance can be enhanced by having the appropriate database indexes rebuilt.

Indexes on certain columns of the Headers and Lines tables will also improve the query performance of the Find Order and Line Approvals window.

Include the standard actions of Complete Line and Complete Order at the end of all order cycles so that your orders and returns will close to improve the performance of your queries.

CRITICAL IMPLEMENTATION FACTORS

You should be aware of the following critical implementation factors:

- Secondary price lists only go one level deep. Discounts that apply to the primary price list do not apply to the secondary price list.
- The OE: Item Validation Organization profile should not be changed when you have open orders in your database.
- The OE: Reservations profile should not be changed when you have open orders in your database.
- When you copy orders, the Standard Value Rule Set is not copied.
- An accounting rule is required for each order. This accounting rule is provided through the Standard Value Rule Set.
- Pick-released line details cannot be modified unless they are back-ordered.
- Fully back-ordered-released lines cannot be modified unless they are back-ordered.
- Each shipping document must be assigned at least one printer.

ISSUES AND GAPS

Order Entry/Shipping is a very extensive module with many capabilities. Although there are still some issues with Order Entry/Shipping (as can be seen in the Review of the Top Enhancement Requests), it is for the most part a fairly complete module for the functions it covers.

REQUIRED SET UP TASKS

The following items are required to be set up before the Order Entry/Shipping Application will function properly:

- Inventory Organizations
- Profile Options
- AutoAccounting
- Invoice Sources
- Units of Measure
- Order Number Sources
- Shipping Document Printers
- Order Cycles
- Item Information
- Enter Items

- Pricing
- Sales Persons
- Enter Customers and Define Customer Relationships
- Order Types
- Inventory Accounting Flexbuilder

CONFIGURING THE APPLICATION

The Order Entry/Shipping Module requires extensive setup for the module to be configured properly to function as advertised. There are 41 steps to the setup of the Order Entry/Shipping module. Additionally, before the Order Entry/Shipping module can be set up, it also must have a Set of Books and Inventory set up.

RESOLVING CRITICAL SETUP ISSUES

Prior to the setup of Order Entry/Shipping, several critical issues must be resolved. First, the Set of Books and Accounting Structure must be determined. Second, the Organizations from which the Customers can order products must be set up. Finally, before a customer can order any items, he must be set up in the Inventory module.

Table 17.1 is an Order Entry/Shipping setup checklist that provides you many flexible features enabling you to efficiently set up your system and quickly begin processing orders for your company.

TABLE 17.1 ORDER ENTRY/SHIPPING SETUP CHECKLIST

Step	Requirement
Define Set of Books	Required with defaults
Define Key Flexfields	Required with defaults
Define Inventory Organizations	Required
Define Profile Options	Required
Define Payment Terms	Required with defaults
Define Invoicing and Accounting Rules	Required with defaults
Define Transaction Types	Required with defaults
Define AutoAccounting	Required
Define Territories	Optional
Define Customer Profile Classes	Optional
Define Invoice Sources	Required
Define AutoInvoice Line Ordering	Optional
Define AutoInvoice Grouping Rules	Optional
Define QuickCodes	Required with defaults

TABLE 17.1 CONTINUED

Step	Requirement
Define Freight Codes	Optional
Define Units of Measure	Required
Define Order Number Sources	Required
Define OrderImport Sources	Optional
Define Freight Charges	Optional
Set Up Shipping Document Printers	Required
Define Sales Credit Types	Required with defaults
Define Order Cycles	Required
Define Security Rules	Required with defaults
Define Item Categories	Required
Enter Items	Required
Define Configurations	Optional
Set Up Pricing	Required
Enter Salespersons	Required
Enter Customers and Define Customer Relationships	Required
Enter Customer Agreements	Optional
Define Standard Value Rule Sets	Required with defaults
Define Order Types	Required
Define Discounts	Optional
Set Up Credit Checking	Optional
Define Inventory Accounting (Flexbuilder)	Required
Define Holds	Optional
Define Notes	Optional
Define Document Sets	Optional
Define Descriptive Flexfields	Optional
Define Tax Codes and Rates	Optional
Define Tax Exceptions and Exemptions	Optional

PART

III

CH

17

UNDERSTANDING EACH SETUP TASK

Setup tasks fall into three categories. First, there are those Setup tasks that the Oracle system requires for the application to operate. In the Order Entry/Shipping application, you must have Items defined before you can place orders. Additionally, you must have Customers defined before you can ship any items. Second, there are those tasks that, although required, contain certain default values that you can allow the system to default to. Finally, there are steps that are completely optional, based on your particular implementation.

DEFINING A SET OF BOOKS

Before Oracle Order Entry can be implemented, you must set up at least one Set of Books. The Set of Books defines for the Order Entry/Shipping Application the Chart of Accounts, the Accounting Calendar, the Functional Currency and the Accounting Flexfield Structure. When defining the Set of Books, use the setup process described in Chapter 11, "Using Oracle General Ledger."

DEFINING KEY FLEXFIELDS

Oracle Applications share Key Flexfields. Key Flexfields are a major feature of the Oracle Applications as a whole and provide a mechanism for the Oracle Applications to provide you a flexible way to define how the Oracle Applications should represent objects such as accounting codes and part numbers. Key Flexfields can be set up from any Application. The Key Flexfields are usually set up during the Financial or Manufacturing Applications Implementation. Order Entry/Shipping has no Key Flexfields of its own, therefore the Key Flexfields in General Ledger, Inventory, and Accounts Receivable should be set up before setting up Order Entry/Shipping.

DEFINING THE STOCK LOCATORS FLEXFIELD The Stock Locators Flexfield is used to capture more specific stock location information about your inventory such as aisle, row, and bin item information. This Flexfield is set up in the Inventory Application Implementation. Refer to Chapter 16 for a detailed description of this process.

> **Note**
>
> The OE: Inventory Stock Location profile option specifying your Stock Locators Flexfield must be set.

DEFINING THE SALES ORDER FLEXFIELD The Sales Order Flexfield is set up in the Inventory Application and is used by the Inventory application to uniquely identify sales order transactions that Order Entry/Shipping interfaces to Inventory. This Flexfield must be set up prior to placing demand or making reservations in Order Entry/Shipping. Refer to Chapter 16 for a detailed description of this process.

> **Note**
>
> Before you can place demands or make reservations in Order Entry/Shipping, this Flexfield must be set up.
>
> This Flexfield contains three segments with the segments defined as Order Number, Order Type, and Order Source. This guarantees that each transaction to inventory is unique.
>
> To guarantee uniqueness, the profile OE: Source Code must be set up to determine the source code used in the third segment of the Flexfield.

Tip

> The value set associated with the Flexfield must be alphanumeric with a maximum size of 40, no padding of zeros on sales order numbers, dynamic inserts allowed, no validation, and a value required to be supplied.

DEFINING THE ITEM FLEXFIELD The System Items Flexfield is required for the transacting and reporting of item information. This Flexfield is defined during the Inventory Application Implementation. See Chapter 16 for details of this process.

Note

> The OE: Item Flexfield profile must be set to specify the Flexfield structure to be used in the application.
>
> The OE: Item Flexfield Entry Method profile should be set to specify your preferred your method of entry.
>
> The OE: Item View Method profile should be set to specify how to display items on the Enter Orders form.

DEFINING THE TERRITORY FLEXFIELD The Territory Flexfield is owned by the Accounts Receivable Application and is an Optional step in the Accounts Receivable Implementation. The Territory Flexfield is used in reporting and is only required if you have a sales person, invoice, or customer purposes business requirement. Refer to Chapter 13, "Using Oracle Receivables," for details of this process.

DEFINING THE SALES TAX LOCATION FLEXFIELD The Sales Tax Location Flexfield is owned by the Accounts Receivable Application and is an optional step in the Accounts Receivable Implementation. The Sales Tax Location Flexfield is used in establishing the sales tax for your customers based on their shipping address. Refer to Chapter 13 for details of this process.

ITEM CATEGORIES FLEXFIELD The Item Categories Flexfield is owned by the Inventory Application and is a required step in the Inventory Implementation. You cannot start defining items until the Item Categories Flexfield is set up because all items must be assigned to categories. Refer to Chapter 16, "Using Oracle Inventory," for details of this process.

ITEM CATALOG GROUP FLEXFIELD The Item Catalog Group Flexfield is owned by the Inventory Application and is required with defaults step in the Inventory Implementation. Item Catalog Groups are used to group your items in a standard industry catalog or grouping according to certain descriptive elements. Refer to Chapter 16 for details of this process.

DEFINING INVENTORY ORGANIZATIONS, ORGANIZATION PARAMETERS, SUBINVENTORIES, AND PICKING RULES

Inventory Organizations, Organization Parameters, Subinventories, and Picking Rules are owned by the Inventory Application, and defining them is a required step in the Inventory Implementation. Organizations are distinct distribution entities, referred to in Order Entry/Shipping as *warehouses*. You must also define the control options, account defaults, Set of Books, Master, and Costing Organizations associated with this organization. At least one subinventory is required with each Organization. A *subinventory* is a physical or logical grouping of your inventory. Finally, you must define the priorities that Oracle Inventory uses to pick items for a sales order. Refer to Chapter 16 for details of this process.

DEFINING YOUR PROFILE OPTIONS

Defining profile options is a required and important task. Many Order Entry/Shipping programs use profile options to determine fundamental logic in the way that they process transactions.

> **Tip**
>
> Do not skip a profile option simply because it is optional. Some of the profile options can improve your corporate controls and enhance end user productivity.

TABLE 17.2 ORDER ENTRY/SHIPPING USER/SYSTEM PRODUCTIVITY PROFILE OPTIONS

Profile Option Name	Required?	Level*	Comment
OE: Action QuickPick Method	Yes	ARU	Default is Dual
OE: Autobackorder	No	SAR	Active if OE:Reservations is Yes
OE: Customer Relationships	No	A	Default is Yes
OE: Cycle Action Changes Affect Existing Orders	No	A	Yes
OE: Debug	No	ARU	No
OE: Debug Trace	No	ARU	Default is No
OE: Default RMA Status	Yes	ARU	Default is Entered
OE: Default Picking Document Set	No	ARU	Default:Pick Release Documents
OE: Default Shipping Document Set	Yes	ARU	Default:All Shipping Documents
OE: Discounting Privilege	No	ARU	Default is Full
OE: GSA Discount Violation Action	No	A	Default is Warning

TABLE 17.2   CONTINUED

Profile Option Name	Required?	Level*	Comment
OE: Immediate Inventory Update	No	ARU	Default is No
OE: Included Item Freeze Method	No	A	
OE: Inventory Stock Location	No	A	
OE: Item Flexfield	Yes	S	
OE: Item Flexfield Entry Method	No	ARU	Always pop a Flexfield window
OE: Item Validation Organization	Yes	S	Do not change with open orders
OE: Item View Method	Yes	ARU	Default is Description
OE: Reservations	No	A	Must be set to Yes to use ATO
OE: Schedule Date Window	No	A	Pick Release Ignores Profile
OE: Set of Books	Yes	A	
OE: Source Code	Yes	S	Default is ORDER ENTRY
OE: Transaction Manager	Yes	ARU	
OE: Transaction Manager Debug Level	No	ARU	
OE: Tune for Large Number of Discounts	No	A	Default is No
OE: Unit Price Precision Type	Yes	A	Default is Standard
OE: Validate Option Line Item	No	A	
OE: Validate Standard Line Item	No	A	
OE: Verify GSA Violations	No	A	
OE: Weight Unit of Measure Class	No	A	
SHP: Release Online Exception Report	No	A	
SHP: Release Online Pick Slip Report	No	A	
SHP: Release Single Orders Online	Yes	A	Default is Yes

PART **III**

CH **17**

TABLE 17.2 CONTINUED

Profile Option Name	Required?	Level*	Comment
WSH: Invoice Delivery Number Method	No	S	
WSH: Shipment Method	No	A	
AR: Use Invoice Accounting for Credit Memos	Yes	SARU	Default is No
Tax: Allow Ad Hoc Tax Changes	Yes	SARU	Default is Yes

Levels can be Site, Application, Responsibility, or User. The system administrator sets most profile options.

If you are using a multiple organization structure, your system administrator must change the OE:Item Validation Organization and OE:Set of Books profile options to be visible and updatable at the responsibility level. These changes allow Order Entry/Shipping to correctly default tax code and revenue account information. See Chapter 23, "Understanding Multi-Org," for details concerning multiple organization structures.

DEFINING PAYMENT TERMS

Payment Terms are defined in Accounts Receivable Implementation. You specify the payment terms that you want to associate with your orders to determine your customer's payment schedule. Refer to Chapter 13 for details on the set up of these terms.

DEFINING INVOICE AND ACCOUNTING RULES

Invoice and Accounting Rules are defined in Accounts Receivable Implementation. You need to define your Accounting Rules if you want to recognize revenue over multiple accounting periods. Refer to Chapter 13 for details on the set up of these rules.

> **Note**
>
> If you use an Accounting rule, you must also use an Invoicing Rule. Invoicing Rules determine when to book your receivables. Oracle comes seeded with the Advance Invoice and Arrears Invoice rules.

DEFINING TRANSACTION TYPES

Transaction Types are defined in the Accounts Receivable Implementation. Transaction Types are used to determine your default payments term, account, taxes, freight, creation sign, posting, and receivable information. Transaction Types are assigned to invoices, debit memos, commitments, chargebacks, credit memos, and on-account credits. Oracle comes seeded with the Invoice and Credit Memo Transaction Types. Refer to Chapter 16 for details on the setup of Transaction Types.

DEFINING AUTOACCOUNTING

AutoAccounting is defined in the Accounts Receivable Implementation. AutoAccounting is used to dynamically create the General Ledger accounts for Order Entry/Shipping transactions that interface to Accounts Receivable. Accounts Receivable creates revenue, receivables, freight, tax, suspense, unbilled revenue, and unearned revenue accounts based on Order Entry/Shipping to Receivables transaction information. Refer to Chapter 13 for details on the setup of AutoAccounting.

DEFINING TERRITORIES

Territories are defined in the Accounts Receivable Implementation. Territories can be assigned to your customers and salespersons. When Accounts Receivable is installed, you can also assign territories to your invoices and commitments. Refer to Chapter 13 for details on the set up of Territories.

DEFINING CUSTOMER PROFILE CLASSES

Customer Profile Classes are defined in the Accounts Receivable Implementation. You define Customer Profile Classes to be assigned to customers or customer site uses. Order Entry/Shipping then uses the order and total order limits during credit checking.

DEFINING INVOICE SOURCES

Invoice Sources are defined in the Accounts Receivable Implementation; however, an invoice source is required to be set up in Order Entry/Shipping for use with the Order Entry Receivables interface. You define the batch sources that you assign to your invoices, debit memos, commitments, credit memos, and on account credits. You must first define a credit memo batch source and then an invoice batch source. Additionally, you are required to define at least one Invoice Source. This is required so order information can be interfaced to Accounts Receivable. Refer to Chapter 13 for details on the setup of Invoice Sources.

DEFINING AUTOINVOICE LINE ORDERING

AutoInvoice Line Ordering is defined in the Accounts Receivable Implementation. If AutoInvoicing is being used, you need to specify how your transaction lines are to be ordered and numbered after they have been grouped into invoices, debit memos, and credit memos.

DEFINING AUTOINVOICE GROUPING RULES

AutoInvoice Grouping Rules are defined in the Accounts Receivable Implementation. You use like attributes of shipping orders to determine how to order the transactions that get invoiced. For example, you might want to group all transactions associated with each shipment to a single invoice for the customer.

DEFINING QUICKCODES

QuickCodes are used to create the references that you use in your business in your Order Entry/Shipping. The QuickCodes that you define are the basis for many of the List of Value windows that you will see in Order Entry/Shipping.

QuickCodes can be defined for the following Order Entry/Shipping QuickCode Types:

Agreement Types

Cancellation Codes

Credit Cards

Freight Terms

Hold Types

Note Usage Formats

Release Reasons

Sales Channels

Shipment Priorities

The following QuickCode Types are shared between Oracle Order Entry/Shipping and Oracle Receivables:

Customer Business Purposes

Credit Memo Reasons

Customer Class

Customer Relationship Types

FOB

Responsibilities for the primary customer contact

Tax Exemption Reason

Tax Rate Exception Reason

Types of Communications used in contacting customers

DEFINING FREIGHT CARRIERS

Freight Carriers are defined in the Financials or Manufacturing Application Implementation. Freight Carriers are used to identify all the carriers that you use to ship items from your organization to external customers, internal customers, and interorganizational transfers.

Note Freight Carriers must be defined in each Inventory Organization.

DEFINING UNITS OF MEASURE

Units of Measure are defined in the Manufacturing Application Implementation. Units of Measure are used for tracking, counting, storing, weighing, and moving items. Each item that is defined must have a primary Unit of Measure, and each line of an order must have a Unit of Measure associated with the quantity of the item.

DEFINING ORDER NUMBER SOURCES

Order Number Sources are used to automatically number your Orders as you enter them. Order Number Sources can be used to uniquely number all your orders, or you can use a different order source for each order type.

DEFINING ORDERIMPORT SOURCES

If you have a requirement to import sales order information from other computer systems that share the same platform as Order Entry/Shipping, those sources can be identified during implementation. The OrderImport source then becomes a parameter in the OrderImport program. You can also identify an OrderImport source to transfer internal requisitions from Oracle Purchasing as internal sales orders.

DEFINING FREIGHT CHARGES

You can define your allowable freight charges used in your business. Freight charges are assigned to shipments during shipping confirmation. You can have multiple freight charges assigned to a shipment, and you can override the suggested freight amount at shipping confirmation. You can use either your functional currency or the order's foreign currency.

Note   All freight charges should be defined in your functional currency for uniformity. You can modify the currency and amount to match the order at shipping confirmation.

DEFINING SHIPPING DOCUMENT PRINTERS

You assign printers to shipping documents so that you can control which printers are used for preprinted shipping documents. Printers can be assigned at the site, application, responsibility, or user level.

Note   It is required that each shipping document be assigned at least one printer at the application level.

DEFINING SALES CREDIT TYPES

Sales Credit Types are used by Order Entry/Shipping to determine whether the sales credit for an order is a quota or nonquota amount. The sales credit types you define here are a reflection of how you award your Sales Credits in your business.

DEFINING ORDER CYCLES, CYCLE ACTIONS, CYCLE RESULTS, AND ACTION ASSIGNMENTS

Order Cycles are a powerful feature used by Order Entry/Shipping to control the steps that an order takes from entry to completion. To define Order Cycles, you must define the Cycles Action and Cycle Results, assign the Actions to Results, and then define the Order Cycle. Order Cycles provide you the flexibility to do manual or online approvals. You also have the flexibility of order-level or line-level order and return activities.

First, define all the allowable order actions that can occur for an order. The following standard order cycle actions are provided by Oracle:

Backorder Release

Cancel Line

Cancel Order

Complete Order

Complete Line

Demand Interface

Enter

Inventory Interface

Manufacturing Release

Pick Release

RMA Interface

Receivables Interface

Ship Confirm

Second, define all the allowable results for a defined action. The following standard order cycle results are provided by Oracle:

Backordered-Partial

Backordered-Complete

Booked

Cancelled

Closed

Completely Accepted

Configuration Created

Confirmed

Eligible

Entered

Fail

In Progress

Interface Error

Interfaced

Interfaced to Receivables

Not Applicable

Partial

Partially Accepted

Pass

Released

Work Order Completed

Work Order Opened

Work Order Partially Completed

Third, you assign the Action Results to the Cycle Actions to provide your necessary Order Cycle links. Each cycle action must have at least one result.

Finally, you define the Order Cycle containing cycle actions and at least one result. You can define as many Order Cycles as are required to handle the different processing requirements for different order types.

> **Note**
>
> You can determine when changes to cycle actions in an order cycle take effect through the setting of the profile option OE: Cycle Action Changes Affect Existing Orders.

DEFINING SECURITY RULES

Security Rules are used to specify where users are no longer allowed to add, delete, or cancel order or return lines; or to modify order or return information. Order Entry/Shipping provides the minimum security necessary to prevent data integrity violations. You can also develop your own rules.

You begin the development of Security Rules by choosing the object. Object names generally correspond to the part of the Order for which you want to define a rule (for example, Lines, Line Schedule Details, Shipment Schedule Lines, and so on).

DEFINING ITEM INFORMATION

Items are defined in the Oracle Financial or Manufacturing Implementations. Items must be set up before Order Entry/Shipping will function. Orders cannot be placed for items that do not exist.

DEFINING ITEM CONFIGURATIONS

Item configurations are set up using Oracle Bills of Material configuration functionality. Each model, option class, option item, standard component, and included item must be defined as an item. To provide your customers the capability to order unique configurations of a model, you must define model and option class Bills of Material.

> **Note**
>
> To control the date and time that Order Entry/Shipping uses to determine the included items for a configuration's Bill of Material, the profile option OE: Included Item Freeze Method should be defined.

MANAGING PRICING

Order Entry/Shipping provides you with a powerful and feature-filled pricing capability to allow you great flexibility in managing your pricing to reflect your pricing policies. You can define a single master price list, or you can have any number of price lists. You can also use standard value rule sets to default prices into an order from your agreements, customers, or order types. In support of sales to other countries, you can assign a currency to each price list.

Order Entry/Shipping has numerous streamlining and maintenance-reducing features to assist you in managing your price list. You can easily update pricing by a percentage or fixed amount for an entire price list or a subset of items in a price list. You can easily create new price lists using the copy feature within Order Entry/Shipping. Order Entry/Shipping enables you to copy an entire price list or a subset of items from a price list. Inventory Items can be added to a price list by item category, by item status, or from a range of items. When items are added, they can carry no price or the inventory cost as the price. Order Entry/Shipping enables you to create groups of items that can then be added to the price list as a group with effective start and end dates. You can create pricing formulas for your price list that can change prices of other items based on price fluctuations of a particular item. Also, should your pricing policy result in a rules change, Order Entry/Shipping will automatically recalculate the prices. Finally, you can easily create customized discount programs, prorated discounts, and GSA discounts.

To set your pricing, you need to first define your Pricing Attributes Descriptive Flexfield, which is used to modify the price of an item. Second, you enable your parameters for your pricing components that are used in your pricing rules. Third, you define your pricing rules to support your pricing policy. Finally, you define your price list to include all orderable inventory items.

DEFINING SALESPERSONS

Sales Credit is assigned to a salesperson when you enter orders and returns. A salesperson is assigned to one or more territories, and each salesperson has a revenue, freight, and receivables account assigned to him. You can also designate whether a salesperson receives quota or nonquota sales credits.

Note

You are required to enter a salesperson for each order and return. Order Entry/ Shipping provides a predefined value of No Sales Credit for orders and returns for which there is no salesperson.

MANAGING CUSTOMERS, CUSTOMER PROFILES, AND CUSTOMER RELATIONSHIPS

Customers are set up in the Accounts Receivable Implementation. Refer to Chapter 13 for details on the implementation of Customer, Customer Profiles, and Customer Relationships.

You should enter as many customers as you want before you begin order entry. When you enter customers, you define the primary customer address, contact, and telephone. To speed order entry, you also enter information such as the order type, sales channel, and price list associated with the customer.

PART

III

CH

17

Note

The following System Options must be defined before customers can be entered:

Receivables accounting set of books

Default tax account

Default tax method (Sales Tax or Value Added Tax)

Default tax code (Only entered if your Tax Method is VAT)

Sales Tax Location Flexfield Structure

From-To Postal Code Range

Address Validation (Error, No Validation, Warning)

Tax Cache Size

Use Tax Code for Customer Site (Yes/No)

Use Tax Code for Customer (Yes/No)

Use Exception Rate for Location (Yes/No)

Use Tax Code for Product (Yes/No)Use Customer Exemptions (Yes/No)

Use Product Exemptions (Yes/No)

Calculation Level

Rounding Rule

Reporting Currency

Precision

Minimum Accountable Unit

Allow Override (Yes/No)

Automatic Customer Numbering (Yes/No)

Automatic Site Numbering (Yes/No)

Create Reciprocal Customer (Yes/No)

Default Address Country

When you set up your customers, each one is assigned a profile class. These profiles are used in credit checking to set tolerance percentages, total limits, and per-order limits. Finally, you need to define one-way and reciprocal relationships between customers. You can use these relationships to restrict addresses, agreements, and commitments that appear, as well as to allow payment application for related customers.

Note
To determine whether customer relationships are honored, you must set the pricing profile option, OE: Customer Relationships.

ENTER CUSTOMER AGREEMENTS

In Order Entry/Shipping, you can define binding and nonbinding agreements. Agreements are referred to during the entry of an order to obtain relevant default values for a particular customer, such as assigned pricing, accounting, invoicing, and payment terms.

DEFINING STANDARD VALUE RULE SETS

Standard value rule sets are used to improve efficiency and accuracy when entering orders. Standard value rules are used to determine the source and prioritization for defaulting order information. If you modify a standard value rule set, those changes become effective immediately for any orders that use that standard value rule set. An existing order is only affected if you update a particular attribute on the order that was part of the modification. You can create new standard value rule sets by copying an existing standard value rule set, making modifications to the rule set, changing the rule set name, and saving the new rule set.

Note
A standard value rule set must be entered for order types that you assign to regular orders. The standard value rule set is the only way that an accounting rule can be designated for an order. Returns do not use standard value rules sets; instead, they use the RMA Default Sources.

DEFINING ORDER TYPES

Processing rules and entry defaults are specified on orders and returns through the use of Order Types. The order cycle and standard value rule set that are assigned to an Order Type control the order processing and provide default values.

DEFINING DISCOUNTS

Discounts are assigned to price lists. Order Entry/Shipping enables you to set up many discount types and methods to meet all your company's pricing needs. You can assign the same discount to many price lists through the copy feature. Discounts can be based on the order type, agreements, purchase order, purchase quantity, specific products, or specific customers.

PART

III

CH

17

Note

To indicate whether users are allowed to manually enter prices on orders, the OE: Discounting Privilege must be set. If you allow manually entered prices, you must also be able to override discounts, and they must be appropriate for the order and order line.

To determine how GSA discounts should be handled, the OE: GSA Discount Violation Action and OE: Verify GSA Violations profile options should be set.

DEFINING CREDIT CHECKING

A customer's outstanding credit balance is calculated through the use of credit-checking rules. You can have as many different rules as your business needs. Order Entry/Shipping uses the currency of the order to determine credit limits.

When the credit-checking rules are defined, you can implement the automatic credit checking of your orders. With this feature you can check credit at order time, shipment time, or both, thus preventing the shipment of products to customers with unacceptable outstanding credit exposure.

To activate automatic credit checking, you must first define your credit-checking rules. Second, you assign the credit-checking rules to an order type. Third, in the customer profile class, you enable credit checking and set your individual order limits, the customer's outstanding credit balance limit, the percentage by which a customer can exceed his order limit or total limit, and the currency used for his orders. Fourth, you create a Customer Profile to implement credit limits for individual customers or customer sites.

Note

Credit checking does not occur on an order if the credit limit is not defined in the same currency as the order uses.

> Credit checking does not occur on any orders for the customer or site, regardless of other credit-checking parameters, unless Credit Check is set to Yes on the Customer Profile.
>
> Credit checking does not occur on an order using payment terms unless Credit Check is set to Yes on the Customer Profile.

DEFINING FLEXBUILDER FOR COST OF GOODS SOLD ACCOUNTING

The Inventory Interface determines the Cost of Goods Sold (COGS) Account for each transaction. You can use Flexbuilder to dynamically create the COGS Account based on one or more attributes such as order type, salesperson, item, and so on. Each COGS Account is validated against the chart of accounts associated with the OE: Set of Books profile. If the generated COGS Account is valid for the rules for the set of books, the transaction is interfaced. If the COGS Account is not valid, the transaction is rejected.

In release 11, Flexbuilder is replaced with the Account Generator to provide greater flexibility and a better interface with Oracle Workflow.

DEFINING HOLDS

You can stop an order, order line, return, or return line from continuing to progress through the order cycle through the use of a hold. You can apply holds manually, such as an individual order hold, or automatically based on a set of criteria you define, such as a credit check hold. These holds can be applied at specific steps in your order cycle or to a customer or item at any step in the order cycle.

The General Services Administration (GSA) hold is a type of hold used to ensure that a specific group of customers always receives the best pricing. If an order is placed for a customer not in the group but is given the same level of discount as the group, that order is automatically placed on hold until a review is accomplished.

Another type of hold is the credit check hold. With the credit check hold, you can limit a customer's orders to preset limits, for either all orders or individual orders. Using the credit limits and credit rules you define, Order Entry/Shipping performs an automatic credit check on your customers. Additionally, you can exclude certain customers, types of orders, or payment terms from credit checking entirely.

A third type of hold utilizes hold sources to apply a particular hold to a group of existing orders, returns, or their lines and to new orders meeting your hold criteria. The key feature of hold sources is that you can hold all current and future orders for an unreleased item. You can take orders for an item, recognize the demand, and yet hold the order line until the item is ready. When the item is available, the hold source is removed, and the individual order lines can be released.

> **Tip**
>
> You control who can define, apply, and remove holds through the use of responsibilities.

DEFINING NOTES

Order Entry/Shipping enables you to attach notes to your orders, order lines, returns, or return lines. These notes can then be printed on your Sales Order Acknowledgement, Pick Slip, Pack Slip, Bill of Lading, and Commercial Invoice.

DEFINING DOCUMENT SETS

Order Entry/Shipping enables you to group shipping documents and other reports in a set. In Order Entry/Shipping, you can print document sets from the Confirm Shipment window or the Release Sales Orders for Picking window.

Three documents come seeded in the application: The Pick Release Document is printed when you release your sales orders for the products to be picked from the warehouse shipping. The Pack Slip is used to list the contents of the shipment for the receiver. The Bill of Lading is used to list the contents of the shipment for the freight carrier. You can print All Shipping Documents or the Pack Slip Only when you Confirm your Shipment.

The OE: Default Shipping Document profile option specifies the default Document Set during Confirm Shipments. The OE: Default Picking Document Set profile option specifies the default Document Set during Release Sales Orders.

DEFINING DESCRIPTIVE FLEXFIELDS

The Order Entry/Shipping comes seeded with the Pricing Attributes Descriptive Flexfield. This Flexfield is used to capture specific product pricing information. Pricing attributes modify the item's price, but they do not modify the item's physical characteristics.

You define the Pricing Descriptive Flexfield segments for the Enter Orders form's Lines zone. The Pricing Descriptive Flexfield title is Pricing Attributes. When defined, these attributes display on the Enter Orders form's Lines zone; Define Price Lists form's Lines zone; and the Define Item Groups form. Your price list line must exactly match your order lines to find a list price.

DEFINING TAX CODES, RATES, TAX EXCEPTIONS, AND TAX EXEMPTIONS

Order Entry/Shipping enables you to quote an estimated tax for orders at order entry time. The tax estimate can be based on the tax status, address information for the customer, and Value Added Tax (VAT) codes assigned to items, sites, and customers. The actual tax value that appears on the customer's invoice in Oracle Receivables can vary.

You can use the Sales Tax Rate Interface to import locations and postal codes used in address validation.

PART

III

CH

17

Generally, all your taxing parameters, including customer and item exemptions and exceptions, are defined in Oracle Receivables, and as each order is invoiced, tax is applied based on those rules. Exemptions entered during Order Entry/Shipping are subject to approval by the Receivables department through the Tax Exemptions window.

PROCESS TRANSACTIONS

The Update Shipping Information process updates order lines with shipped quantity, sets the ship confirmation status, and backorders unshipped quantities on picking lines. All pick slips having a status of Closed-Pending Update Shipping Information, are evaluated by this process. The Update Shipping Information process also creates a backordered picking line where the quantity confirmed is less than the total released for closed picking lines.

Note

If an item is not a shippable item, the Update Shipping Process automatically sets the order line's cycle status to Not Applicable for Ship Confirm.

The Material Transaction Manager creates inventory transactions, updates balances on shippable items, relieves demand on shippable and nonshippable items, and cancels reservations placed on shippable and nonshippable items.

The Close Orders process purges the MTL_DEMAND_INTERFACE and MTL_SUPPLY_DEMAND_TEMP tables. The process also updates the statuses for the Complete Order and Complete Line cycle actions.

Note

Holds that specify no cycle action or a cycle action of Complete Line or Complete Order must be removed before running the Close Orders process.

MAINTAINING CUSTOMERS

Customer Merge is used to combine duplicate customers. You can also transfer site use activities from a customer or site that is no longer active or has been taken over by another customer or site. The merge takes all activities that were associated with the old customer or site and associates them with the new customer or site. These activities include invoices, debit memos, commitments, credits, receipts, adjustments, and chargebacks.

The customer merge process also automatically merges all transactions associated with the merge candidates in the Order Entry, Payables, Inventory, Project Accounting, Master Scheduling /MRP Planning, Purchasing, Sales and Marketing, and Customer Service applications as well.

ENTERING AND MAINTAINING ORDERS

The Order Entry/Shipping Application enables you to enter, view, and update sales orders. You can enter both complex and simple orders. You can also order standard items, shippable and nonshippable items, and configurations. Order Entry/Shipping enables you to adjust pricing, assign sales credits, record payment information, attach notes, schedule shipments, enter model options, and make material reservations, including selection of item revisions, subinventories, or lots.

PICK RELEASE ORDERS

The Pick Release process releases orders for shipment. You can create picking lines for one order line, one order, or many orders depending on your release criteria. Additionally, you can run as many releases as you want. Orders can be released by warehouse, order, requested or scheduled dates, customer, item, shipment priority, order type, subinventory, ship sets, or combinations of these criteria.

PART

III

CH

17

CONFIRM SHIPMENTS

Confirm Shipments defines the shipped quantities, inventory control information for picking lines, and pick slip header information. Confirm Shipments also assigns freight charges and defines whether released picking line items are shipped or backordered when running Update Shipping Information.

Confirm Shipments consists of the portions Confirm and Close. The Confirm portion enables you to update pick slip header information and picking line information without closing the pick slip or batch. You can also define shipped quantities for picking lines, inventory controls, and pick slip header information. The Close portion involves accepting the information that has been entered for the pick slip or batch, making the pick slip or batch eligible for Update Shipping Information.

Note   When a pick slip or batch is closed, it cannot be reopened.

PRINTING SHIPPING DOCUMENT SETS

The Bill of Lading shipping document prints a list of each confirmed pick slip, customer name, both shipping and billing addresses, purchase order number, waybill number, and a listing of each item, along with the quantity shipped on a preprinted form. Shipping notes you have created are also printed on the Bill of Lading.

The Commercial Invoice shipping document is used as a customs document. It provides a list of each confirmed sales order, the customer name with both the shipping and billing addresses, the ship date, the commercial invoice ID, and the shipper identification number. Also included are the carrier name, the customer reference number, and a listing of each shipped item, along with the quantity shipped, unit value, and extended value. One Commercial Invoice is printed for each pick slip in the batch you select.

A maximum of two lines is maintained for notes at the header or footer for the fixed footer information that prints at the bottom of the Commercial Invoice. The Commercial Invoice ID is the pick slip number.

The picker in the warehouse uses the Pick Slip to collect all items included in shipments. The Pick Slip lists each item, the line number, the unit of measure, the quantity requested, and whether the item is required for shipment. The Pick Slip also lists each sales order, including customer name, shipping address, order number, order date, purchase order number, freight and payment terms, and salesperson associated with the items. Also included are the pick slip number, FOB point, planned freight carrier, requisition number, requestor, and any shipping notes associated with the order.

The Consolidated Pick Slip shipping document is used to pick items for several orders at once. The Consolidated Pick Slip picking lines are sorted by batch, subinventory, locator, item, and lot number.

The Pack Slip shipping document prints one pack slip for each pick slip in the selected picking batch. Pack Slip also prints customer name with both the shipping and billing addresses, order number, order date, purchase order number, freight and payment terms, and salesperson. The waybill number, ship date, freight type, freight amount, FOB point, and freight carrier are also included.

The Mailing Label shipping document prints out the ship-to information for your customers on labels. The customer name, ship-to address, purchase order number, order number, weight, number of packages in the shipment, customer contact name, phone number, and date of shipment are included on the Mailing Label.

The Sales Order Acknowledgement provides to your customers the items, prices, and delivery dates for orders they place with you.

MAINTAINING PRICING

Order Entry/Shipping enables you to manually add price list lines, copy from one price list to another, or add a group of inventory items to a price list.

You can create a new price list by copying from an existing price list. However, only active price list lines or those with an effective end date greater than the current date are copied. You can also copy the discounts associated with the old price list.

You can always change the price on an existing price list line. You can also set an effective end date on the existing price list line and create a new line with the new price and an effective start date to maintain a historical record of your pricing for a given item. Additionally, you can increase or decrease the list price on a group of manually added price list lines by an amount or percentage.

PURGING ORDERS

The Order Purge process selects and purges orders based on criteria you specify. Purging old data creates space in your database and can improve performance of transactions and maintenance.

To purge any orders, the orders must be closed, and no open demand can exists for the order.

You can purge orders by order number or a range of order numbers, by order date or a range of order dates, creation date or a range of creation dates, order category, order type, or customer.

RELEASE ORDERS TO MANUFACTURING

The Manufacturing Release process releases demanded order lines or line details for assemble-to-order (ATO) items and configurations to Oracle Manufacturing for processing by Oracle Work in Process if the order lines have successfully completed all the prerequisite cycle actions.

PART
III
CH
17

Note

Only items with the Assemble to Order item attribute set to Yes are processed by Manufacturing Release.

SENDING SHIPMENTS TO ORACLE ACCOUNTS RECEIVABLE FOR INVOICING

The Receivables Interface transfers shipped item information to Oracle Receivables. This includes quantities, selling prices, payment terms, and transaction dates. You can also process credit memos and credits on accounts created from returns.

IMPORTING ORDER INFORMATION INTO ORDER ENTRY/SHIPPING

You can use OrderImport to import sales orders from other sales order systems or to import internal orders created from internal requisitions in Purchasing.

With OrderImport, you can import order entry data from both Oracle and non-Oracle systems. You can import order entry data from your previous order entry system, making the transition to Order Entry/Shipping as smooth as possible.

The following profiles affect OrderImport:

OE: Included Item Freeze Method. Controls when included items are determined for a configuration's bill of material.

OE: Item Validation Organization. The organization used for validating items and bill of material structures.

OE: Reservations. Enables you to request reservations on imported order lines.

OE: Set of Books. Indicates the currency used for the imported orders.

OE: Verify GSA Violations. Applies GSA holds on imported orders where appropriate.

Items need to be defined for them to be orderable using OrderImport. Bills of material also need to be defined for models if you have any complex items that customers can order in various configurations.

Holds are automatically applied to imported orders and order lines that meet the hold criteria.

USING THE DEMAND INTERFACE

The Demand Interface places demand for shipments. The Manufacturing applications use this information for forecasting and planning product and schedule requirements.

The OE: Source Code profile option affects the operation of the Demand Interface.

The following item attributes affect the operation of the Demand Interface:

Assemble to Order. If set to Yes, ATP is only successful as long as any components with the BOM attribute Check ATP set to Yes are available on the date requested.

ATP Components. If set to Yes, the Demand Interface searches for components of the bill with Check ATP set to Yes to include in an ATP inquiry. Order Entry/Shipping continues searching down the bill structure until it reaches a level where all items have the BOM Item Type attribute of Standard or the ATP components attribute is set to No.

Check ATP. If set to Yes, Order Entry/Shipping automatically performs an ATP inquiry on the item before placing demand.

OE Transactable. If set to Yes, you can have demand placed.

Ship Model Complete. If set to Yes on a PTO model or kit, ATP is only successful if all the components with the BOM attribute Check ATP set to Yes are available on the date requested.

Only holds that specify the Demand Interface in the Cycle Action field prevent the Demand Interface from processing the records. The Demand Interface ignores all other holds, including those for credit checking.

USING THE INVENTORY INTERFACE

The Inventory Interface transfers information on the shipped picking lines for any eligible order lines. If an order line item is nonshippable but has shippable included items, the shipped included items are interfaced when the order line is eligible.

> **Note**
> You must remove any unreleased holds that specify no cycle action or a cycle action of Inventory Interface on orders or order lines that you want to interface to Oracle Inventory.

The Inventory Interface determines the Cost Of Goods Sold (COGS) Account for each transaction. Flexbuilder is used to dynamically create the COGS Account.

USING THE RMA INTERFACE

The Return Material Authorization (RMA) Interface transfers authorized return information to Inventory and obtains receipt information from Inventory. The profile option OE: Source Code is used by the RMA Interface to uniquely identify each return transaction.

To process a return line, an item must be Returnable, Shippable, Stockable, and Transactable.

If an RMA return line references a sales order, purchase order, or invoice, the following item attributes affect an RMA:

Assemble to Order. When set to Yes and the item attribute BOM Item Type is set to Model, the RMA Interface interfaces the ATO configured item.

Pick Components. When set to Yes, the RMA Interface also interfaces any shippable items, transactable items, and stockable included items.

USING THE SHIP CONFIRM INTERFACE

The Ship Confirm Open Interface loads externally derived shipping data into picking tables and closes the pick slip without using Confirm Shipments. The Ship Confirm Open Interface takes data loaded into three interface tables; validates the information contained within the interface tables; loads the valid data into the picking header, picking line details, and freight charges tables; and closes the pick slip.

REVIEWING TOPICS OF INTEREST

The Order Entry/Shipping Module enables the users to do the following:

- Enter and maintain their customer base
- Build and customize price lists and discounts for their customers
- Efficiently ship items to their customers
- Receive items returned from their customers

UNDERSTANDING KEY REPORTS

Oracle Order Entry/Shipping provides a number of reports to help improve your productivity. The following list is an overview of the reports in Order Entry/Shipping:

The Action Result Listing report reports all actions and results you have defined for use in your order cycles.

The Descriptive Flex Listing report reports descriptive Flexfields that you have defined.

The Discount Details listing shows all the details about a discount, including the discount type, price list, currency, any pricing column or customers associated with the discount, whether the discount is manual or automatic, the amount or percent, and the effective dates.

The Order Cycle listing provides the cycle action name, its level, and any prerequisite cycle actions and results.

The Price List Listing provides details on each price list, items contained within a price list, the pricing rule associated with the item, the effective dates of the price list line, the currency, and Pricing Attributes Descriptive Flexfield information.

The Pricing Rules Listing reports all pricing rules that have been defined.

The Security Rules Listing reports the security rules that you have defined for various objects and attributes.

The Standard Value Rules Listing reports the standard value rules that you have defined for various objects and attributes.

The Comprehensive Order Detail Report reports the comprehensive details of all orders.

The Order/Invoice Detail Report reports detailed invoice information for orders that have invoiced.

The Open Return Detail Report reports detailed information about open Return Material Authorizations (RMAs), including line reference, credit to invoice, and expected, received and accepted quantities.

The Open Returns Report reports summary information about open RMAs.

The Orders on Credit Check Hold Report is used to identify all the credit holds currently outstanding for a customer within a date range or to identify why a particular order is on hold.

The Hold Source Activity Report is used to report holds placed and removed under a hold source during the time period you specify.

The Outstanding Holds Report reports order holds for the customers you choose.

The Pending Order Approval Report reports all orders that are waiting for approval.

The Pending Order Line Approval Report reports all order lines that are waiting for approval.

The Order Discount Detail Report reports discounts applied to orders by order line detail.

The Order Discount Summary Report reports discounts applied to orders.

The Unbooked Orders Report is used to report on orders you have entered but not booked.

The Backorder Detail Report reports on all customer orders that have been backordered.

The Shipments Report reports on all orders that have been shipped.

The Open Batch Report reports detailed information about open picking batches awaiting shipment.

The Backlog Summary Report lists all unshipped orders, including backorders.

The Backorder Summary Report reports on all sales orders that have any backordered lines.

The Agreement Activity Report reports on all agreements that have been defined.

The Cancelled Orders Report reports on all orders that have been cancelled.

The Orders by Item Report reports on all sales for a particular item or group of items.

The Order Cycle Picture Report is used to verify the movement of orders through the appropriate order cycle actions.

The Order/Invoice Summary Report reports on summary invoice information about orders that have invoiced, including ordered amount, invoiced amount, adjusted receivables, and balance due.

The Returns by Reason Report reports on all return material authorizations for various return reasons.

The Salesperson Order Summary Report reports all orders for one or more salespersons.

The U.S. Sales Tax report provides you information on your tax liability to the various tax authorities around the US.

TROUBLESHOOTING

Sometimes in the Oracle Order Entry system, you can receive undesired results. Here, we will discuss an area where you could receive an undesired result, how to determine where the problem occurs, and how to correct the problem. A problem that can create havoc in an organization is an improperly built order cycle.

Order Cycles consist of both order-level and line-level cycle actions. Enter is an example of an order-level action. When you book an order, all lines on the order receive the result of Booked. Line-level actions, on the other hand, allow the individual lines of an order or return to move through the order cycle independently of each other. Pick Release is an example of a line-level action. Cycle actions can create problems when during setup an action result is set up as "or" instead of "and." An example is where the cycle action results allow for Pick Release or Inventory Demand. A situation like this could allow for an order to be Pick Released before the item is ever built. This situation actually occurred at an implementation. The result was a large number of orders that were Picked Released and Shipped Confirmed and were then backordered because they had not been built. When building Order Cycles, ensure that cycle actions perform the proper logic as they go through the cycle. You should always put one order through your new order cycle before putting it into full production. You can monitor your order through its cycle actions to ensure that you see the results you expect by using the View Orders window. If you complete a cycle action and your order does not appear eligible for the next cycle action, there is a problem with your order cycle. Some additional reasons why an order cycle will not complete include the following: A cycle action is not listed as a prerequisite for any subsequent cycle actions, or a cycle action's prerequisite is not a cycle action included in the order cycle.

CHAPTER 18

USING ORACLE ENGINEERING AND BILLS OF MATERIAL

USING ORACLE ENGINEERING

Oracle Engineering provides a means to control item revisions and Bill of Material changes using Engineering Change Orders (ECOs). It also provides an environment to manage Engineering prototype information and to smooth the transition of this information to Manufacturing when it is required.

Figure 18.1 shows the major relationships between Oracle Engineering and the other Oracle Applications. These relationships affect the setup and operation of the Oracle Engineering application.

Figure 18.1
This diagram shows how the Oracle Engineering application interacts with the other Oracle Applications.

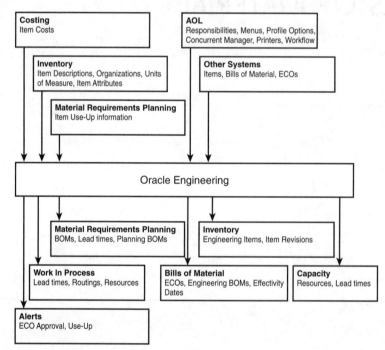

DISCOVERING NEW FEATURES IN RELEASE 11

If you have had experience implementing earlier releases of Oracle Engineering, much of what you see in release 11 will be familiar.

Oracle Workflow came into being with later releases of the 10.7 Applications. If you are implementing or upgrading to release 11, it is important to have some understanding of its operation. It is particularly important within Oracle Engineering because it provides the facility to control an Engineering Change Order (ECO) approval cycle using a Workflow.

Oracle Workflow is dealt with in detail in Chapter 22, "Using Oracle Workflow."

Release 11 also provide an ECO open interface. This interface allows for ECO information to be imported to the Oracle Engineering application from an external source.

CRITICAL IMPLEMENTATION FACTORS

The following factors should be considered before undertaking an implementation or upgrade of the Oracle Engineering application.

ISSUES AND GAPS

There have been a number of enhancements identified for Oracle Engineering that would improve functionality. Although these might not necessarily be seen in future releases, there has been consensus among users that these potential changes are important. These are some of the opportunities:

- In the Define ECO window, you cannot currently see the Purchase Orders and Discrete Jobs that relate to the revised items.

- Transferring an Engineering BOM from Engineering to Manufacturing involves transferring each sub-assembly level independently. There is no global transfer function for an Engineering BOM.

- ECO revision tracking is a manual process. There is no link between changes made to an ECO and the ECO's revision level.

- The capability to record costs associated with an ECO is available for information only. There is no automated process to collect implementation cost information for ECOs.

- Item revisions in Oracle Manufacturing must follow an ASCII sequence. There is currently no capability to create a user-defined revision sequence.

CONFIGURING THE APPLICATION

The following section describes the setup tasks and sequence to configure Oracle Engineering. The tasks should be performed in the sequence listed.

With release 11 of the Oracle Applications, a new tool called the Oracle Applications Implementation Wizard was made available. Its purpose is to improve the way in which the setup and configuration of the applications is managed. It is particularly useful for ensuring that conflicts do not arise with setup steps that overlap two or more applications. The wizard technology is built on Oracle Workflow.

RESOLVING CRITICAL SETUP ISSUES

Before setting up the Oracle Engineering application, some thought needs to be given to the existing processes for controlling changes and prototyping activity.

- Decide if Oracle Engineering will be the primary mechanism for controlling engineering changes within your organization. It is possible to manage changes outside of Oracle and only keep a record of the changes within the system.

- Carefully consider the approval process you want to use for changes. Oracle Engineering provides a number of options, with Oracle Workflow providing the most flexibility for creating and managing an approval process.

- Decide how much control you need over access to change order information. There are several Profile Options and Security Functions that can be set for each user that determine which pieces of data can be changed.

- Determine whether you will use Engineering Items and BOMs. If you choose to, you need to also decide how you will manage the transition of this information to manufacturing.

Table 18.1 shows the sequence of tasks involved in setting up Oracle Engineering and whether they are required.

TABLE 18.1 ORACLE ENGINEERING SETUP TASKS

Setup Task Name	Required?
Set Profile Options	Yes
Enter Employees	Yes
Define Change Order Types	No
Define ECO Departments	No
Define Autonumbering	No
Define Approval Lists	No
Define Reasons	No
Define Priorities	No
Start AutoImplement Manager	No

UNDERSTANDING EACH SETUP TASK

This section provides detail on each of the setup tasks and the order in which they should be performed.

SETTING THE PROFILE OPTIONS   Table 18.2 shows the profile options that directly affect the operation of the Oracle Engineering application.

TABLE 18.2 ENGINEERING PROFILE OPTIONS

Profile Option Name	Required?	Level*	Comment
ENG: Change Order Autonumbering-System Administrator Access	Yes	SARU	Default is No
ENG: ECO Department	No	SARU	
ENG: ECO Revision Warning	No	S	Default is No

TABLE 18.2   CONTINUED

Profile Option Name	Required?	Level*	Comment
ENG: Engineering Item Change Order Access	No	SARU	Default is Yes
ENG: Mandatory ECO Departments	No	S	Default is No
ENG: Model Item Change Order Access	No	SARU	Default is Yes
ENG: Planning Item Change Order Access	No	SARU	Default is No
ENG: Require Revised Item New Revision	No	SA	Default is No
ENG: Standard Item Change Order Access	No	SARU	Default is Yes

Levels can be Site, Application, Responsibility, or User. The system administrator sets most profile options.

ENTERING EMPLOYEES   To use Oracle Engineering, you must enter employees. These will be used to create and approve changes. If you have not installed Oracle Human Resource Management Systems, the installer will create the employee tables for you. You can enter the employees through the Enter Employee form in Oracle Engineering.

DEFINING CHANGE ORDER TYPES   You can define a number of change order types to facilitate easy identification of your ECOs. A typical application would be the creation of an ECO type for manufacturing items only and a separate type for ECOs that affect both manufacturing and engineering items and assemblies.

You can associate a change order type with an ECO approval workflow (see Chapter 22, "Using Oracle Workflow"). You can optionally assign a priority to the change order type (see the following section). If this is the case, Oracle Workflow takes control of the approval process based on the business rules you have associated with the approval flow. If the type and priority have not been linked to a workflow, Oracle Engineering automatically designates the ECO as Approved.

> **Tip**
>
> Consider creating a change order type for temporary deviations or waivers. If you are using workflows, you can create a separate workflow for these changes. They typically require different approvals to regular ECOs.

DEFINING ENGINEERING CHANGE ORDER DEPARTMENTS   Oracle Engineering provides access control for ECOs by enabling you to group employees into departments. Any ECO created can be assigned to a department, and the department ownership can then be changed to move the ECO between departments. An example would be moving an ECO from a Design/

Development Engineering department to a Manufacturing Engineering department. To apply this control, the ENG: ECO Department profile must be set for the user to ensure that each user is associated with an ECO department. You can require a responsible department to be assigned to all ECOs by setting the profile option ENG: Mandatory ECO Departments to Yes.

DEFINING AUTONUMBERING   You can choose to number your engineering changes manually or have the application create the numbers for you following a sequence. Change numbers can be assigned a prefix, which will become part of the number suggested by Oracle.

The use of prefixes can be controlled across your business. You can choose to specify prefixes by any of the following:

- Specific user in the current organization
- Specific user across all organizations
- All users in the current organization
- All users across all organizations

This feature will be useful to businesses with decentralized engineering functions where change tracability is important. Different prefixes can be assigned depending on the origin of the change. It will also be useful if there is a centralized engineering function with multiple manufacturing entities. The same prefix can be enforced across all organizations.

Even if autonumbering is active, you can assign a number manually. Be aware that Oracle will consider that suggested change number to be used and will offer the next one in the sequence when you define the next engineering change.

DEFINING APPROVAL LISTS   Apart from using Oracle Workflow to control the approval process, Oracle Engineering also provides basic ECO approval using Oracle Alert. This function is available in releases prior to release 11. To use the approval function, you must create approval lists using the employee names of the approvers.

DEFINING REASONS   To assist you in categorizing your changes, Oracle Engineering supports the creation of ECO Reasons. If you have been using ECOs with a legacy system, these probably exist. Typical reasons would be Customer Requested Change, Product Safety Change, Cost Reduction, and so on.

DEFINING PRIORITIES   You can define priorities that can be assigned to your changes. Again, these are for your own information only. Typical priorities would be Mandatory, Production Convenience, Urgent, Immediate, and so on.

RUNNING THE AUTOIMPLEMENT CONCURRENT MANAGER PROGRAM   Oracle Engineering provides functionality to automatically implement ECOs based on the effective dates assigned to the change. If you choose to use this functionality, you must run the AutoImplement Concurrent Manager Program. It automatically implements any change that has an effective date less than or equal to the current date and a status of Scheduled. You must specify the frequency at which this program should be run.

CONVERTING DATA FOR MAJOR ENTITIES

With release 11 of the Oracle Engineering application, an ECO open interface is provided. This simplifies the process of importing historical ECO information from legacy systems. Details of the open interface tables are provided in the "Oracle Manufacturing, Distribution, Sales and Service Open Interfaces Manual".

If you are converting data from a legacy system, you can use the Oracle Bills of Material Open Interfaces to populate Engineering data. These interfaces can also be used to import Manufacturing BOM data. The conversion process is described later.

You can use these interfaces to import primary and alternative Engineering BOMs and Engineering Routings.

Engineering item data can be imported using the Open Items Interface. This interface is also used to import Manufacturing item data (see Chapter 16, "Using Oracle Inventory"). The data to be converted from a legacy system must first be extracted and formatted for use in the interface tables. These tables are the following:

- MTL_SYSTEMS_ITEM_INTERFACE
- MTL_ITEM_REVISIONS_INTERFACE

Oracle maintains a third table to record errors resulting from the import process (MTL_INTERFACE_ERRORS). All records being imported are validated against the setup parameters that have been defined in Oracle Inventory.

PROCESSING TRANSACTIONS

The following sections deal with the operation of the Oracle Engineering application and the transactions that are involved.

MAINTAINING ENGINEERING CHANGE ORDERS

Change orders are created and updated using the Engineering Change Orders window.

The following sections explain the transactions that are involved in creating and managing an ECO.

DEFINING AN ENGINEERING CHANGE ORDER   When you create the ECO using the Engineering Change Orders window, you must enter the ECO identifier. If you have selected Autonumbering in the setup steps, the next available number defaults. You then need to select the ECO type. Depending on how the ENG: Engineering Item Change Order Access profile option has been set, you can allow or deny access to Engineering items and BOMs. This profile option needs to be set for each User, and it only affects ECO types that change Engineering items.

You can choose to enter a responsible department for the ECO. As discussed in the setup steps, this information can protect ECOs from updates by Users outside the specified department. It can be particularly useful if you need to transfer ownership for a change between departments—for example, from Design Engineering to Manufacturing Engineering.

> **Tip**
>
> If you do not set the ENG: ECO Department profile option for a particular User, users then have access to *all* ECOs. If no department has been specified on the ECO, any User with the correct responsibility also has full access to this ECO. If this is of concern to you, be sure to set the profile option *and* ensure that the correct department is specified on the ECO. You should set the profile option ENG: Mandatory ECO Departments to Yes.

You can then select your ECO reason and priority for the change. As discussed in the setup steps, Oracle Engineering evaluates the ECO type/priority combination if it has been assigned to a Workflow and then passes control of the approval cycle to that Workflow. If you are not using Oracle Workflow to manage the approval cycle, you can select an approval list that was defined in your setup. This approval list is used with an Oracle Alert, which is discussed later in the section "Using Engineering Alerts". If you do not select an approval list and you are not using a Workflow for approval, your ECO approval status defaults to Approved.

> **Tip**
>
> Consider carefully the level of control you need over your ECOs. Oracle Engineering provides numerous options to restrict access to changes and to control the approval cycle. Do you really want your changes to have a default approval status of Approved? If you currently have a paper-based approval process, this might not seem like an issue. If you truly want to benefit from the functions Oracle Engineering provides, you might want to reconsider this.

If your ECOs are likely to go through numerous changes during their life cycle, you might choose to assign a revision to the ECO and continue to update this as you make subsequent changes.

You can enter the implementation costs associated with your ECO. Currently, this information is only used for reference and is not derived from Inventory, Planning, Purchase Order, or Costing information.

Your Engineering Change Orders can be applied to items or BOMs. These are termed *Revised Items*. You can choose to use Oracle Engineering to control the release and update of items. In this case, you can also control the revision of the item using your ECO. The profile option ENG: Require Revised Item New Revision can be set to Yes to force a new item revision each time a change is created.

If you are changing an existing BOM, you can also choose an alternative BOM as the revised item. If a BOM does not currently exist and your ECO is creating the BOM through the change, you can add the BOM parent item as the revised item and then add the components using the Revised Components window.

> **Tip**
> If you are using Oracle Engineering and Oracle Bills of Material together, you should consider using an ECO to create and release *all* new BOMs and their component items. This process provides traceability to the original ECO through Oracle Bills of Material.

When the revised items are being entered, you need to assign the effective dates that will be used for the items and any components that might exist. You can choose to assign the date and implement the change regardless of onhand inventory balances, or you can make the change dependent on a "use-up" date. This date is calculated by the Material Requirements Planning (MRP) process for all items. It is based on the date by which the onhand quantity will be completely depleted by existing gross requirements. If the use-up date changes as a result of onhand quantity or if requirements change, you can have an alert send the ECO Requestor a message (see the section "Using Engineering Alerts" later in this chapter). Obviously, this only impacts changes that have not yet been implemented.

> **Tip**
> Oracle does not consider any material supply (for example, Purchase Orders or Discrete Jobs) in the calculation of the use-up date. It is based solely on onhand inventory and gross requirements. Your Planners and Buyers have to review pending changes to ensure that the supply is cancelled or rescheduled as necessary.

You can make your change dependent on the use-up date for the revised item or for any of the revised components. You can also indicate whether the change to the revised item should be MRP Active. If it is active, MRP considers the pending change in its requirement calculations. If you have made the change dependent on the use-up date for a revised component and its use-up date changes, MRP suggests a revised effective date. However, it continues to use the current effective date in planning component requirements.

> **Tip**
> The only case where MRP makes use of a revised effectivity date is when the use-up component is the revised item itself.

You can determine whether the component requirements on unreleased WIP discrete jobs or repetitive schedules should be updated when your change becomes effective. The component requirements on jobs and schedules that have already been released will not be affected by an ECO.

If you need to add disposition information for the revised items and components, Oracle Engineering provides scrap, rework, and use-up dispositions that can be applied to WIP and Inventory. These are for information only.

When entering the revised component information, you must specify whether the ECO is going to add, change (modify), or disable the component. If you are modifying component information, Oracle enables updates to quantity and other parameters associated with the component usage on the BOM.

Release 11 provides the capability to attach files to your ECO. These can be text, spreadsheet, or graphics files. You might find it useful to attach copies of part or assembly drawings to your changes.

Finally, you need to submit your ECO for approval. As discussed previously, how this happens depends on the process you have chosen to use. If you are using Workflow, you can submit the ECO to the approval workflow as soon as it has been created. If you are using approval lists, an alert is forwarded to the individuals on the list requesting their approval. If you use neither of these methods, your ECO defaults to Approved status.

IMPLEMENTING ENGINEERING CHANGE ORDERS   To implement the ECO, the approval status must be Approved. Implementation can be either manual or automatic. The changes to revised items on an ECO can be scheduled concurrently or can have different effectivity dates. Oracle marks implemented changes and updates the implemented date. When all your changes on an ECO have been implemented, Oracle marks the ECO as implemented. You cannot change ECO information for a revised item that has been implemented.

Using the manual implementation process, you implement all or individual revised items. The effective date for all components of a revised item is updated to reflect the implemented date, and status of the component item is now implemented. Even if the revised component has a future effective date, Oracle Engineering modifies this when the change has been implemented.

To use the automated implementation process, you must change the revised item status to Scheduled. Oracle Engineering now uses the revised item effective date to manage the change for you.

Tip

Nothing happens until the AutoImplement Concurrent Manager Program runs. You must schedule this program as discussed in the setup steps.

MASS CHANGES USING ENGINEERING CHANGE ORDERS   The mass change function enables you to make changes to several BOMs simultaneously (add, disable, or modify components). When used with Oracle Bills of Material alone, this function can be used to make the changes immediately. If you are also using Oracle Engineering, you can use the mass change function to create an ECO. You can then approve and implement the ECO or any part of it, as discussed previously.

There is further discussion of the mass change functionality in the section "Using Oracle Bills of Material"

PURGING ENGINEERING CHANGE ORDERS   Over time, you might end up with a substantial number of implemented ECOs. Oracle Engineering provides a Purge function to enable you to remove ECO information that is no longer required. Purging ECOs removes all the information apart from the revision information already stored with items and BOMs.

MANAGING ENGINEERING PROTOTYPES

Oracle Engineering provides an environment for managing Engineering prototype information. This information includes Engineering items, Engineering BOMs, and routings. This information is stored alongside the Manufacturing data. The items, BOMs, and routings can be transferred to Manufacturing when the Engineering activities are complete.

All the functions that can be performed with Manufacturing items, BOMs, and routings can also be used with their Engineering counterparts. This includes planning, purchasing, costing, selling, WIP transactions, inventory transactions, and revision control. The use of these functions for an Engineering item is controlled through the item attribute values set for the item. A full explanation of the use of item attributes can be found in Chapter 16, "Using Oracle Inventory."

If you want to control your Engineering items as they move through a development cycle, you can use item statuses to do this. You should create item statuses that reflect the level of control you need at each stage of the development cycle. Certain item attributes can be placed under status control and their values predetermined for that status. This could be used, for example, to prevent prototype assemblies from being sold to customers but to allow for the purchase of their components. Item statuses are discussed in detail in Chapter 16.

To prevent the proliferation of item numbers, Oracle Engineering also enables you to use item catalogs to attach characteristics to your items. Design or Development Engineers can use this feature to search for existing item numbers based on certain characteristics. The creation of item catalogs is discussed in Chapter 16.

DEFINING AN ENGINEERING ITEM AND REVISIONS   Engineering items are created in the same way as Manufacturing items (see Chapter 16, "Using Oracle Inventory," for information on how to define an item). Setting the Engineering item attribute to Yes differentiates these items from Manufacturing items. You should also set the BOM Allowed attribute to Yes (Chapter 16 explains the use of Item Attributes).

PART

III

CH

18

Revision control operates in the same way as for Manufacturing items. You can manually assign and track revisions, or you can use Oracle Engineering to manage the revisions using ECOs, as described earlier.

DEFINING AN ENGINEERING BOM AND ROUTING Engineering BOMs are created in the same way as Manufacturing BOMs. Both the Engineering Item attribute and the BOM Allowed attributes must be set to Yes. Depending on how the BOM will be used, you must also set the BOM Item Type item attribute (see the section "Using Oracle Bills of Material" later in this chapter).

One application would be the creation of an alternative Engineering BOM for an existing Manufacturing BOM to enable prototyping of changes to take place. The use of alternative BOMs is discussed in the Oracle Bills of Material section of this chapter.

A similar situation exists for Routings. In much the same was as Manufacturing Routings, you can create an Engineering Routing that can be used to prototype new or modified process flows. Another option is to create an alternative Engineering routing for an existing Manufacturing routing. The creation and use of routings is discussed in the Oracle Bills of Material section.

DEFINING ITEM/ORGANIZATION ATTRIBUTES Having created an Engineering item, you must set the item and item/organization attributes. The assignment of item attributes is covered in detail in Chapter 16.

TRANSFERRING ENGINEERING DATA When the development and prototyping activity is complete, you can transfer or copy the Engineering item, BOM, or routing to Manufacturing.

You can not transfer an item or BOM that already exists in Manufacturing, and you can only transfer or copy Engineering data within the same inventory organization.

If you copy an Engineering item, you must assign a new name and description because the original information remains in Engineering.

If you are transferring an Engineering BOM, the component items must already have been transferred, or you can transfer them at the same time as the BOM. The copy function copies BOM and component information simultaneously.

> **Tip**
>
> Oracle only transfers components on the first level of an Engineering BOM. If you are transferring a multilevel BOM, you need to transfer each of the subassemblies separately, starting with the lowest level assembly.

If there is an Engineering Routing associated with the Engineering BOM, you can transfer both together. All the components on the BOM will continue to be associated with the relevant operations on the routing. If you don't transfer the routing, you lose this relationship.

USING OPEN INTERFACES IN THIS APPLICATION

Open interfaces were mentioned earlier in this chapter in relation to converting data. These interfaces can also be used to allow data from external sources to be incorporated into the Oracle Engineering application.

Release 11 of Oracle Engineering adds an ECO open interface. This allows you to import ECO information from an external application or data source.

Bills and components can be created, updated, or deleted using the Open Bills of Material Interface. Routings can be created, updated or deleted in a similar manner using the Open Routing Interface. These interfaces can have applications in your organization when design-related data is created and maintained externally to Oracle Engineering—for example, in a Product Data Management (PDM) system. You could create your Engineering BOMs or routings using these interfaces and then use Oracle Engineering to manage the transfer of the BOMs and routings to Manufacturing.

Full details of the operation of the interfaces can be found in the Oracle reference manual *Oracle Manufacturing, Distribution, Sales and Service Open Interfaces Manual, Release 11*.

IMPORTING ITEM INFORMATION

The Open Item Interface was discussed in the section "Converting Data for Major Entities" and in Chapter 16. This interface would also have an application in the creation of new item data based on imported data from an external system.

USING ENGINEERING ALERTS

Oracle Engineering comes with two standard alerts:

■ *ECO Approval Notification.*In the discussion of ECO approval, one of the processes available uses an approval list to route an ECO for approval. This alert sends a message to each individual defined on the approval list, letting her know that an ECO requires her approval.

■ *ECO Use-up Date.* When a revised item's effectivity date is based on the use-up date of another item, this alert sends a message to the ECO requestor if the use-up date becomes different from the effectivity date.

These alerts need to be enabled, and alert-checking needs to be scheduled if you intend to use them.

UNDERSTANDING KEY REPORTS

Table 18.3 lists the standard reports provided with the Oracle Engineering application and a short description of each.

TABLE 18.3   ORACLE ENGINEERING REPORTS

Report Name	Description
Engineering Change Order Approval List Report	Lists the approvers for ECOs based on defined approval lists.
Engineering Change Order Detail Report	Reports on Engineering changes with the option to include changed component information.
Engineering Change Order Priorities Report	Reports the change order priorities that have been defined for use with Oracle Engineering.
Engineering Change Order Reasons Report	Lists the change order reasons that have been defined for use with Oracle Engineering.
Engineering Change Order Schedule Report	Reports on schedule information for pending ECOs up to a specified date.
Engineering Change OrderTypes Report	Lists the change order types that you have created.

USING ORACLE BILLS OF MATERIAL

Oracle Bills of Material provides the tools required to create and manage product structures and the manufacturing processes that are related to them. It includes the capability to create and manage complex product configurations to satisfy unique customer requirements, and with release 11, it includes tools to implement flow-manufacturing concepts in your business.

It has relationships with the Costing, Purchasing, Inventory, Order Entry, MRP, WIP, Engineering, and Capacity applications (see Figure 18.2).

DISCOVERING NEW FEATURES IN RELEASE 11

With the introduction of release 11, Oracle has added significant Just-In-Time (JIT) functionality. The most important feature is the introduction of Flow Manufacturing functionality. This has a significant impact on Oracle Bills of Material.

Although Flow Manufacturing is not based on new concepts, the fact that it has now been integrated into the applications is recognition of the benefits that it can provide in a modern manufacturing environment.

Flow Manufacturing is based on *pull* concepts:

- Customer demand pulls product through manufacturing rather than driving a production schedule based on anticipated demand.
- Raw materials are pulled through the manufacturing process (starting with the supplier) instead of being pushed onto discrete jobs.

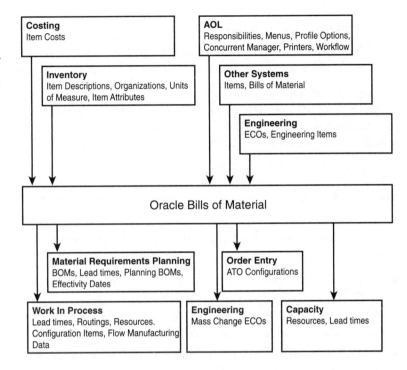

Figure 18.2
This diagram shows the major relationships between Oracle Bills of Material and the other applications.

- Material is back-flushed to relieve inventory when assemblies have completed manufacturing.
- Production lines are arranged by families of similar products rather than by process flow.

Some of the basic concepts of Flow Manufacturing are the following:

- Products and parts are grouped into product families.
- Product families are made up of products that have similar product synchronization (sync). The processes used to produce these products are similar.
- Product sync is assigning processes to product and then defining the sequence in which they are carried out.
- Production lines must be defined for parts and product families.
- You can define standard processes to be used with flow manufacturing.
- A *Flow Routing* is used to create product sync. This is similar to a regular routing in that it includes processes and resources.
- A *Mixed Model Map* is used to assist in the design of the manufacturing line. Flow manufacturing is concerned with the balancing of manufacturing lines against a forecasted daily rate. This tool calculates several pieces of information to assist with the balancing task. You can regroup "events" (similar to operations on a routing) and regenerate the map to ensure that the line is balanced.

CRITICAL IMPLEMENTATION FACTORS

Although most manufacturing operations already use Bills of Material, some of the functionality available within the Oracle application does require careful consideration.

Attempting major changes in manufacturing technologies while implementing Oracle Bills of Material might not be too successful. Consider waiting until you have a stable business system implemented before moving towards flow manufacturing or a configure-to-order environment (unless these are already part of your business processes).

ISSUES AND GAPS

Although Oracle Bills of Material does provide adequate functionality for most businesses, there are always opportunities to improve.

Some of the enhancements to the Oracle Bills of Material product that users have suggested might make their way into future releases of the product:

- The capability to perform mass changes to routings. This is currently available for BOMs.

- Sorting the BOM Structure report by item number. It can currently be sorted by item sequence or operation sequence only.

- The capability to view reference designators in a BOM comparison.

- Being able to view costing, where-used, and routing information from the Indented BOM inquiry window.

- The capability to view usage of substitute components in the where-used inquiry window.

CONFIGURING THE APPLICATION

The following section describes the setup tasks and their sequence to configure Oracle Bills of Material. Because some tasks are dependant on others, you should perform them in the sequence shown.

As mentioned in the section on Oracle Engineering, the Oracle Applications Implementation Wizard is available with release 11 of the applications. Consider using this to ensure that the setup steps are managed properly.

RESOLVING CRITICAL SETUP ISSUES

Access to create and update Bills of Material is a consideration. Oracle Bills of Material does provide some control through the Profile Options listed in the setup. You can allow access to certain BOM item types by setting these profiles at the User or Responsibility level.

Table 18.4 lists the tasks involved in setting up Oracle Bills of Material.

TABLE 18.4   BOM SETUP TASKS

Setup Task Name	Required?
Set Profile Options	Yes
Define Exception Templates	No
Assign Workday Calendar to Organization	Yes
Define Bill of Material Parameters	Yes
Define Department Classes	No
Define Resources	No
Define Resource Groups	No
Define Simulation Sets	No
Define Locations	No
Define Departments	No
Assign Resources and Resource Shifts to Departments	No
Define Overheads	No
Associate Overheads with Departments	No
Define Alternatives	No
Define Standard Bill of Material Comments	No
Define Standard Instructions	No
Define Change Order Types	No
Define Delete Constraints	No

PART

III

CH

18

UNDERSTANDING EACH SETUP TASK

This section provides details on each of the setup tasks for Oracle Bills of Material and the order in which they should be performed.

SETTING THE PROFILE OPTIONS

Table 18.5 shows the profile options that directly affect the operation of the Oracle Bills of Material application.

TABLE 18.5   BILL OF MATERIAL PROFILE OPTIONS

Profile Option Name	Required?	Level*	Comment
BOM: Check for Duplicate Configuration	No	S	Default is No
BOM: Component Item Sequence Increment	No	SARU	Default is 10
BOM: Configuration Item Delimiter	No	S	Default is No
BOM: Configuration Item Type	No	S	Default is No

TABLE 18.5 CONTINUED

Profile Option Name	Required?	Level*	Comment
BOM: Days Past Before Starting Cutoff of Order Entry Bills	No	S	Default is 0
BOM: Default Bill of Material Levels	No	SARU	Default is 1
BOM: Default WIP Supply Values for Components	No	S	Default is Yes
BOM: Hour UOM	No	S	Set to the hour UOM you will be using
BOM: Inherit Option Class Operation Sequence Number	No	S	Default is No
BOM: Model Item Access	No	SARU	Default is Yes
BOM: Perform Lead Time Calculations	No	S	Default is No
BOM: Planning Item Access	No	SARU	Default is Yes
BOM: Standard Item Access	No	SARU	Default is Yes
BOM: Update Resource UOM	No	S	Default is No

Levels can be Site, Application, Responsibility, or User. The system administrator sets most profile options.

DEFINING EXCEPTION TEMPLATES Exception Templates are used to indicate nonworking day exceptions and shifts within the Workday Calendar. Typically, these are used for national holidays, shutdowns, and so on. The process for creating these is described in Chapter 16.

DEFINING AND BUILDING THE WORKDAY CALENDAR The Workday Calendar is usually created as part of the Oracle Inventory setup (see Chapter 16). It holds information on the organization's working patterns, including nonworking days and/or shifts.

> **Tip**
>
> If you choose to set up your workday calendar from within Oracle Bills Of Material, you should be aware that effective use of Oracle Master Scheduling/MRP requires you to define a 445 or 544 weekly quarter pattern. If you use calendar months or a 13-period calendar, your MRP resolution goes to monthly buckets only (which is not necessarily a good thing if you are a Master Scheduler).

ASSIGNING A CALENDAR TO AN ORGANIZATION When the calendar has been created, it must be assigned to an inventory organization. If you are creating more than one organization, you should assign a calendar to each. One calendar can be shared across multiple organizations.

DEFINING BILL OF MATERIAL (BOM) PARAMETERS   BOM parameters must be set for each organization that you are creating. The BOM parameters window enables you to set the BOM level and configuration item options. Set the maximum number of BOM levels to be used for explosions, implosions, and loop checking. This should be considered along with the BOM: Default Bill of Material Levels profile option. Oracle Bills of Material allows a maximum of 60 levels. This should be more than adequate for most implementations!

> **Tip**
>
> If you are converting legacy data, this would be an appropriate time to consider the depth of existing BOMs.

If you will be using configure-to-order, you can also set a number of BOM defaults using this window. An inactive status can be set and used to tag completed configuration items. In a configure-to-order environment, Oracle enables you to specify the numbering segment to be used in creating configuration item numbers. This assumes that you have created a numbering segment in the System Items flexfield (see Chapter 16, "Using Oracle Inventory").

For configure-to-order, you can also define one of three numbering methods to be used for your configuration items:

- *Append a sequence.* A sequence number internally generated by Oracle is appended to the numbering segment that was previously assigned.
- *Replace with sequence.* The numbering segment is replaced with the internally generated sequence number.
- *Replace with Order, Line Number.* The Sales Order number and line number are substituted for the item segment.

DEFINING DEPARTMENT CLASSES   Department classes are used for reporting purposes only. If you need to group departments for shop floor scheduling or control reports, this can be done with the Department Classes window.

DEFINING RESOURCES AND RESOURCE GROUPS   Resources are required to enable shop floor scheduling and collection of cost information when routings are used. Resources are also required if you intend to use Outside Processing functionality.

Oracle enables you to create resources to account for most things used in a manufacturing operation, including people, equipment, cash, outside processing services, and floor space.

To correctly use routings, you need to assign the required resources to departments and then assign the departments to operations, including the resources and usage you require.

There are two prerequisites before you can define resources:

- You must set up the units of measure to be used and any conversions that will be required. This is part of the Inventory setup (see Chapter 16, "Using Oracle Inventory").

- A site-level profile option (BOM: Hour UOM) must be set to the Unit Of Measure (UOM) that will be used to represent one hour. Resources can only be scheduled when their UOM is the same as this setting or if there is a UOM conversion defined for it.

Each department resource can also be assigned to a resource group. This allows for the creation of bills of resources, which are used in Oracle Capacity (see Chapter 20, "Using Oracle Planning Applications").

DEFINING SIMULATION SETS   This is an optional setup step. Simulation sets are used with Oracle Capacity. They enable you to define modifications to available capacity for your routing-based resources (see Chapter 20).

DEFINING LOCATIONS   You must define delivery locations if you have defined departments with Outside Processing resources (see Chapter 15, "Using Oracle Purchasing").

DEFINING DEPARTMENTS   Departments are required if you will be using routing-based manufacturing.

ASSIGNING RESOURCES AND SHIFTS TO DEPARTMENTS   If you are using routing-based manufacturing, you need to assign your resources to a department. You can also assign shifts to these resources.

If you plan on using Oracle Capacity, you can group the department's resources by resource group and then assign simulation sets for each resource shift.

DEFINING OVERHEADS AND ASSOCIATING OVERHEADS WITH DEPARTMENTS   As part of the department setup, you define any overhead costs that might be related to the department and then associate these overheads with the department.

DEFINING ALTERNATIVES   An alternative BOM is a separate list of items that can be used to produce an assembly. Although there is still only one assembly item, one or more alternative BOMs can be associated with the assembly. Some applications could be the following:

- Manual and automated processes for producing the same assembly require different component items. The components might differ because of packaging or for other reasons.

- An assembly might be built using different key component items based on availability. Alternative BOMs would be applicable here if the choice of other components varied based on the choice of the key component.

You create the alternative names using the alternative window. The name chosen can be alphanumeric, but ensure that it relates in some way to its function.

> You may reuse the same alternative name on any number of assemblies. The relationship between BOM and alternative is unique to a particular assembly item number. So an alternative name of "MANUAL" can be used on several assemblies with different components being used each time.

DEFINING STANDARD BOM COMMENTS   You can define standard BOM comments that can then be assigned to any BOM you create.

DEFINING STANDARD INSTRUCTIONS   Standard instructions can be created and then used with any routing operation or standard operation.

DEFINING CHANGE ORDER TYPES   You can define change order types that can be used to tag mass changes to your Bills of Material. If you will be using Oracle Engineering, you might want to define these as part of that setup.

DEFINING DELETE CONSTRAINTS   Deleting a BOM or routing could have huge implications for your organization. Oracle Bills of Material comes with a set of predefined deletion constraints. These should prevent you from doing the unthinkable. However, operational requirements vary from business to business, and the Define Deletion Constraints window enables you to specify customized constraints. This same mechanism can be used to specify constraints for the deletion of items, bills, components, routings, and operations.

You must enter your criteria in the form of a SQL select statement specifying whether to delete if rows are found.

> To specify custom delete constraints, you should have a thorough understanding of the Oracle Application database tables and the relationships between them. For most organizations, the default constraints provided are adequate.

CONVERTING DATA FOR MAJOR ENTITIES

Oracle provides two tools with the Oracle BOM application that provide for conversion of legacy data:

- Open Bills of Material Interface
- Open Routing Interface

The operation of these interfaces is fully described in the Oracle documentation.

There are some basics that you need to consider. If you are fortunate to be in a "green field" situation, conversion of legacy data is not a concern. For most people, there is legacy data to contend with. Using the open interfaces requires some programming to extract the data from the legacy system, format it correctly, and then insert it in the interface tables. You should consider the amount of effort required to develop and test the extract programs compared to the volume of data to be converted. If there are a small number of BOMs and routings and if the number of items per BOM is small, manually entering the data could be an option.

In most cases, manually entering your BOMs and routings is not a viable option.

Tip

Before attempting to populate the interface tables, ensure that the following has been done:

- All required inventory items (parent items, component items, planning items, and so on) have already been loaded.

- All required BOM setup tasks have been completed.

Oracle provides full validation of the data being loaded through the open interfaces. You will save yourself time and effort in identifying and correcting errors if both these steps are complete.

If you choose to use the open interface program to convert your BOMs and Routings, use the following process:

- Extract your data from the legacy system.
- Populate the interface tables.
- Run the BOM/Routing import program using the Import Bills and Routings form.
- Review any errors in the interface tables using SQL*Plus or a custom developed report. (The Process_Flag is not set for any rows that have had errors.)
- Correct the problems associated with any failing rows.

The Open Bills of Material Interface tables are the following:

- BOM_BILL_OF_MTLS_INTERFACE
- BOM_INVENTORY_COMPS_INTERFACE
- BOM_REF_DESGS_INTERFACE
- BOM_SUB_COMPS_INTERFACE
- MTL_ITEM_REVISIONS_INTERFACE

The Open Routing Interface tables are the following:

- BOM_OP_ROUTINGS_INTERFACE
- BOM_OP_SEQUENCES_INTERFACE
- BOM_OP_RESOURCES_INTERFACE
- MTL_RTG_ITEM_REVS_INTERFACE

PROCESSING TRANSACTIONS

The following sections cover the transactions that are involved in the operation of the Oracle Bills of Material application.

MAINTAINING BILLS OF MATERIAL

Oracle Bills of Material provides for five distinct types of bill:

- *Standard Bill of Material.* Is the most commonly used type. Lists components and usage quantities.
- *Model Bill of Material.* Is used to configure to order. Defines options and option classes.
- *Option Class Bill of Material.* Groups optional components on a BOM. Becomes a component of the Model Bill of Material.
- *Planning Bill of Material.* Is used with Oracle Master Scheduling. Planning percentages can be assigned to components.
- *Engineering Bill of Material.* An Engineering BOM can be defined as an alternative to a manufacturing BOM. It provides for Engineers to prototype variations of a product without affecting the manufacturing BOM.

Bills of Material are created, maintained, and viewed using the same Bills of Material window.

DEFINING A BILL   There are three prerequisites to defining a BOM:

- The parent item and all components must already be defined as inventory items.
- The BOM Allowed item attribute must be set to Yes for the parent item and components.
- The parent item BOM Item Type attribute must be set to model, option class, planning, or standard. This depends on the function of the BOM.

To define a Bill, navigate to the Bills of Material window and enter the assembly item number. If you want to create an alternative BOM, you should choose the alternative name from the list created in the earlier setup steps. If you choose to use revision control for your Bills, you should also enter the revision and revision date.

In the Components region of the window, enter the item sequence number (which can be used to dictate the sort order of components when printing the BOM), the operation sequence number (which is used in conjunction with a routing), and the component item number.

In the Main region of the window, enter the quantity of the component required for the assembly.

There are other regions available to enter additional information for the component and assembly combination:

PART

III

CH

18

- *Effectivity.* Enter the in and out effectivity dates that apply to this component. This is optional when creating a new BOM.

- *Component Details.* Enter the planning percentage (if this is applicable), the yield factor (used in MRP, 1=100% 0.9=90%), and whether the component should be included in cost rollups (the material cost, not the routing cost, is used).

- *Material Control.* You can choose to specify the Supply Type for the component on this particular assembly rather than use the Supply Type specified for the component item. The available types are Assembly Pull, Bulk, Operation Pull, Phantom, Push, or Supplier. These are described in detail in Chapter 21, "Using Oracle Work in Process." If you set the profile option BOM: Default WIP Supply Values for Components to Yes, Oracle Bills of Material defaults the component values for Supply Type from the item master. In this region, you can also specify the supply subinventory to be used for this component and the locator if the subinventory is under locator control.

- *Order Entry.* If the BOM is a model, option class, or kit, you can enter min and max order quantities to be used with Oracle Order Entry. You can also specify whether Available to Promise (ATP) should be checked for the component. You must set the Check Component ATP item attribute to Yes for the assembly if you want to do this. The component can be set to Optional or Mandatory. The Mutually Exclusive field applies to option class BOMs and determines whether the option should be the only one available for selection or part of a list. The Basis field affects the way in which the quantity of the component is treated. If it is set to Option Class, it is not possible to override the quantity for the option when entering a sales order. (Oracle uses the component quantity $\times$ the option class extended quantity.)

- *Shipping.* You can specify whether the component is shippable. The value defaults from the component item attributes. If you want to have this component show on the shipping documentation, you can set Include on Ship Docs to Yes. The Required to Ship field affects Pick to Order (PTO) items only. The item must be available to allow shipment of the order. The Required for Revenue field affects Receivables. If the component has this field set to Yes, an invoice cannot be created for the parent item until the component has shipped.

To speed up the creation of a Bill for an assembly that is similar to another, Oracle provides a BOM copy function. When creating the BOM, you can simply specify the assembly that's BOM you want to copy. The components, usage quantities, and other characteristics can be modified as required when the BOM has been copied. Any revision of a BOM can be copied. A similar function is available for use with routings.

Tip

The copy function operates on a single BOM level *only*. It does not copy the components of assemblies below the first level of the BOM you are copying.

If you are copying the BOM from another Inventory Organization, you must ensure that the components of the BOM exist in the destination organization. You can only copy from another organization that shares the same item master as the destination.

Tip

The copy function is particularly useful if you are creating alternative BOMs. These are typically very similar to the primary BOM with only minor modifications.

Oracle Bill of Material enables sharing of BOM information across organizations using a Common Bill of Material. This is useful if the same assembly structure and components are to be used in more than one organization and you want to administer the BOM from one central location.

Before you reference a common BOM, you must ensure the following:

- The BOM you are referencing as a common BOM cannot reference another BOM as a common BOM.

- If you reference an alternative BOM as a common BOM, both must share the same alternative name.

- If the BOM you are creating is a manufacturing BOM, the common BOM referenced must also be a manufacturing BOM.

Tip

Your current Inventory Organization and the one in which the Common BOM resides must share the same Item Master organization. If there are components already assigned to your new BOM, you cannot reference a Common BOM.

If you are referencing a Common BOM in an Inventory Organization other than the one in which you are creating the new BOM, all the components must exist in the current organization.

Common Routings can be referenced in a similar manner.

For Model and Option Class BOMs, you can enter item catalog descriptive elements that can be used in conjunction with Order Entry to select options based on description. Item Catalogs are described in Chapter 16.

Oracle Bills of Material provides for the use of reference designators. These enable references to be made on the BOM to written instructions or drawings that, for example, indicate the location of a component. The reference designators are assigned to the component when it is added to the BOM. To speed up data entry, Oracle can append prefixes and suffixes to your designators. You can choose to have Oracle require separate designators for each component usage (for example, a quantity of five per assembly of a component requires five separate designators), or you can choose to add as many as you need.

> **Tip**
>
> If you intend to share the reference designator information with a Computer Aided Manufacturing (CAM) system or to share the reference designators from a Computer Aided Design (CAD) system, please ensure that you are consistent in the formats being used when creating BOMs.

Substitute components can be added to any component on a standard BOM. More than one substitute component can be assigned per component on the BOM. The usage quantity of the substitute can be different from that of the original component, and there are no restrictions on using the same substitute for several components on the same BOM.

> **Tip**
>
> The use of substitute components can confuse people. Although they will appear on some of the Oracle Master Scheduling/MRP reports, they are only there as a *reference*. Oracle assumes that when you are aware of an issue with the standard component, you will use the substitute information to take whatever action you need to. *Unfortunately, nothing will happen automatically!*

With release 11 of Oracle Bills of Material, you can attach files to any BOM or routing you create. This opens up the possibility to include text files, drawings, spreadsheets, graphics, and so on.

Oracle provides a loop-checking facility when you have created and saved a new BOM. BOM loops occur when the parent assembly includes itself as a component. The loop can be created through any subassembly, not just on the first level of the BOM. BOM loops cause serious problems with MRP and Cost rollups. As well as having loop-checking available when a BOM is created, Oracle Bills of Material provides a concurrent program to check for BOM loops on a range of assemblies.

> **Tip**
>
> If you are importing BOMs and components from a legacy system, take extra care to ensure that BOM loops are not created inadvertently.

MASS CHANGING SEVERAL BILLS   The Mass Change functionality enables you to apply changes to a number of BOMs based on parameters you specify. Changes can be made to add, delete, or replace components. In addition, you can change a component quantity, yield factor, or other information for a component of a BOM.

If you are using Oracle Bills of Material on its own, you can generate and execute the change directly. Oracle only allows you to make future changes on Engineering BOMs in this way. If you are also using Oracle Engineering, you can use the Mass Change functionality to create an Engineering Change Order (ECO) that can be implemented using a future effectivity. This type of change can be applied to both Manufacturing and Engineering BOMs.

In executing your Mass Change, Oracle enables you to specify limits for the assemblies to be affected. There might be reasons why you would want to apply a change to *all* assemblies, but in most cases, you will want to operate with a subset of your assemblies. You can specify a range based on item number, item category, or item type.

> **Tip**
>
> Consider creating an item category that groups your assemblies by product family. This enables you to use BOM and ECO functions limited to a particular product family. The creation of item categories is discussed in Chapter 16.

> **Caution**
>
> Mass Changes can be drastic measures. This is a powerful function that could affect every single assembly in your database. Consider carefully the desired end result and even more carefully the limits you specify for the assemblies to be affected.

> **Tip**
>
> In the unlikely event that a Mass Change is made in error, it is possible to create another mass change (using the same limits) to undo the damage.

DELETING ITEM INFORMATION In the section on setups, I discussed the creation of deletion criteria. Oracle Bills of Material comes with a set of predefined deletion criteria to control the deletion of BOM, routing, and item information. These constraints are described in detail in the Oracle documentation but include checks for the following conditions:

- Open Sales Orders for the assembly
- Open Work Orders for the assembly
- Repetitive Schedules referencing the assembly
- Demand exists for the assembly

You can begin to see that the deletion of BOM, routing, or item information could wreak havoc in your database if the information is already being used or referenced elsewhere.

From the Deletion Groups window, you can specify the type of deletion you want to perform. The type of deletion you can perform depends on the modules you have installed. In a typical manufacturing environment with Oracle Inventory and Oracle Bills of Material installed, you

PART
III

CH
18

can delete items, bills, components, and routings from this window. You can choose to archive BOM and Routing information for future reference. You need to specify a name for the deletion group.

> **Tip**
>
> Resist the temptation to name your groups "AA", "AB", and so on. Over time, the number of groups will build up, and it will be difficult to remember what exactly you were doing. Make the names meaningful.

There are two ways to operate the delete function:

- You can specify the BOMs, routings, or items you want to delete and perform a CHECK. Oracle reports any error conditions that would occur if you continue with the delete process, giving you an opportunity to take whatever action you need to.

- If you have checked the deletion and are happy with the results, you can go ahead and execute it.

DEFINING ROUTINGS AND STANDARD OPERATIONS

Routings list the sequence of operations required to manufacture a product. As with Bills of Material, Oracle enables you to define alternative routing names. These can be used to describe alternative process flows to be used when manufacturing an assembly. You can also create an Engineering routing as an alternative to a Manufacturing routing and use it for prototyping an alternative process flow. You can share any alternative labels you create between your BOMs and routings. If you do create an alternative BOM with the same label as an alternative routing, the components are added to the operations on the alternative routing.

When you create a Bill of Material that is associated with a routing, you can choose the operation sequence number to which a component should be issued. This flexibility provides for components to be issued only to the operations where they are required. You can choose to issue *all* material to first operation of the routing if you want.

Oracle Work in Process provides for the back-flush (inventory relief) of components in the process as assemblies are completed. When a routing is being created, you have the option to specify at which operations the back-flush transaction can happen.

If the routing is being created for model or option class items, you can specify the operations that are required for that particular model or option. This allows a customized routing to be created when a particular option is selected in a configuration.

Resources are associated with the operations on a routing. You can select one or more resource for each operation. For each resource being assigned to an operation, you have the choice to include the resource in scheduling and lead-time calculations. If the resource has been defined as cost, you can also collect the cost information using the routing.

Resource usage can be specified as lot-based or item-based. A lot-based usage can be useful for tasks related to the setup of a manufacturing operation. Item-based usages vary depending on the number of items being processed.

Resources can be scheduled based on resource units per item or item units per resource, depending on the resource and how it is being used. The costs associated with a resource can be manually charged or automatically charged, based on move transactions or Purchase Order receipts in the case of outside processing items.

You can specify a completion subinventory to be used with the routing. This is the default subinventory used by Oracle Work In Process when the assembly is being completed.

In defining a routing, you can also define how move transactions are recorded and resources are consumed using the Autochargeand Count Point fields. Their usage is described in the *Oracle Bills of Material User's Guide, Release 11*.

A Standard Operation is an operation that is created as a template to be used repeatedly on routings. It is created in much the same way as any other operation. When the Standard Operation has been set up, it can be copied into a new operation on any routing you are creating. You can change any of the detail copied to the new operation to suit your needs.

CALCULATING LEAD TIMES

Lead times play an important part in the planning process and in the calculation of available to promise (ATP) dates.

You can calculate lead times for manufactured items using Oracle Bills of Material. There are two types of lead time calculated:

- *Cumulative Manufacturing Lead Time.* This is the total time it would take to manufacture an item if all the components were onhand but all the subassemblies had to be manufactured level by level.

- *Cumulative Total Lead Time.* This is the total time it would take to manufacture the assembly if there were no components onhand. The calculation assumes that all components have to be purchased and all subassemblies are to be manufactured level by level.

Item categories (see Chapter 16) can be used to limit the manufacturing items that are affected by the recalculation programs. There might be groups of items whose lead times you want to manage manually.

If you modify a routing by adding or deleting operations or by changing resource usage, you need to recalculate the lead times for the assemblies using the routing.

Also, changes to the BOM structure or individual-component lead times can affect the assembly-cumulative lead times. These should be rolled up after BOM changes.

UNDERSTANDING CONFIGURE TO ORDER

For many products, customers are demanding a greater degree of customization. Oracle Bills of Material provides the tools required to support customizations of this kind.

The Configure to Order tools allow options to be defined that can be grouped into unique product configurations to satisfy a customer requirement.

There are two ways in which this can be done:

- *Assemble to Order.* A unique configuration to satisfy the customer order is created from Assemble to Order (ATO) models and options that are defined through BOMs, manufactured, and then shipped to the customer.
- *Pick to Order.* The customers' order is made up of Pick to Order (PTO) Models and option classes, which are picked from stock and then shipped to the customer.

The distinction between both methods blurs because of the flexibility Oracle Bills of Material provides in structuring model and option class BOMs. Various combinations of ATO and PTO models and options are possible to support many business scenarios. These BOMs can also include purchased items, phantom assemblies, and standard BOMs as part of their structure.

In the section on defining a BOM, I discussed models and option classes. To define an ATO Model, the Assemble to Order item attribute must be set to Yes. The BOM Item Type attribute will be set to Model. ATO option classes also require the Assemble to Order item attribute to be set to Yes, but the BOM Item Type will be Option Class. PTO models and options have the Pick Components item attribute set to Yes. The use of item attributes is discussed in Chapter 16.

> **Tip**
>
> ATO models can only have ATO option classes structured to them. Similarly, PTO models can only have PTO options structured. It is possible to combine elements of ATO and PTO items on a BOM. Set the Pick Components attribute for the parent model to Yes and add ATO models to the BOM as components.

You can make the components of your model optional or mandatory. This enables you to specify items that must always be included as part of a configuration. The use of the Mutually Exclusive field was covered in the section on defining a BOM. When used with the Optional field, you can force the selection of one or more options, or no options if you want.

BOMs made up of multiple levels of PTO and ATO models and options can become complex and can make planning an interesting activity. You can assign planning percentages to your models and options. In this way, you can use forecast or historical usage to predict the mix of options that are likely to be used in you configurations. Master Scheduling uses this information to derive planned orders and suggest reschedules of existing orders for the components required to support this.

If your company will have multiple inventory organizations, you can use Common Bills of Material to share models and options across the organizations. In this way, it is possible to have a remote site take complete Engineering responsibility for a product and have the other sites that are building the product reference it as a Common Bill. You ECOs will only have to be applied in the organization that owns the common BOM.

> **Note**
>
> As with all usage of common BOMs, all the organizations must share a common Item Master Organization. Your models and options will have to be defined in that organization and then assigned to the other organizations.

Available to Promise (ATP) checking can be used at Order Entry time. Oracle evaluates the earliest date that an item will be available to satisfy an order requirement. To enable ATP checking, you use two item attributes:

- *Check ATP*. An ATP check can be performed on this item.
- *ATP Components*. There are components of this item that require ATP checking.

In this way, ATP can navigate through your model and option BOM structure, evaluating only the components that you have selected for checking.

With ATO configurations, the order entry and manufacturing process is more complex. When entering the order, you have to choose from the options that are available on the model being ordered. This unique configuration must be released to manufacturing to allow it to be built (Manufacturing Release). This configuration remains linked to the sales order. To identify the unique configuration, you can choose to autocreate a configuration item. Oracle creates the item and assigns a BOM and routing. How the configuration item number looks depends on the options you selected for the configuration item numbering method when you set the BOM parameters (see the BOM Parameter setup step earlier in this section). Oracle Bills of Material do a cost rollup for the single-level bill of the configuration item.

When the configuration has been released to manufacturing, the Production Planner or Scheduler can use the AutoCreate Final Assembly Orders process to create a discrete job for the configuration. Creating the job establishes a reservation from the sales order to the job. When you complete a quantity from the final assembly order to inventory, you also create a reservation from the job to the finished goods inventory. As quantities are completed to inventory, the reservation on the discrete job is relieved.

> **Note**
>
> If there are multiple sales orders linked to a discrete job, you should be careful to specify which one the completion is for. Otherwise, Oracle picks the sales order with the earliest ship date and uses that for the relief.

To ensure that all items on a configuration are available to ship, order entry does not allow pick release of the order if there are discrete jobs for configuration components linked to the sales order that are still in process. If you have multiples of the configuration on the sales order, you can pick release quantities as they arrive in your finished goods inventory.

Over time, you will accumulate configuration items for all the unique configurations you have manufactured. In the setup section, I discussed the Inactive Status for configuration items. This was part of the BOM parameter setup. Using the Deactivate Configuration Items concurrent program, you can apply this status configuration to items that have zero onhand inventory or where there have been no recent sales orders for the item. Use the item delete process to purge these items from your system when the status has been updated.

USING OPEN INTERFACES IN THIS APPLICATION

Apart from their application in converting legacy data, the same open interfaces can be used to import BOM data from external systems.

USING THE BILL AND ROUTING IMPORT INTERFACE

In a manufacturing environment, a typical application using the open interfaces would be the import of product data from a Product Data Management (PDM) system or a Computer Aided Design (CAD) system. The interfaces can be used to create, update, and delete BOMs and Routings. The function being performed through the open interfaces is dependent on the value set in the TRANSACTION_TYPE column (Create, Update, or Delete). Full details of the operation of the Open Interfaces can be found in the *Oracle Manufacturing, Distribution, Sales, and Service Open Interfaces Manual, Release 11*.

> **Tip**
>
> If you are in a multiple site situation and are not able to run the application's multi-org in a single database instance, you should consider using the open interfaces to move critical BOM data between databases.

UNDERSTANDING KEY REPORTS

Oracle Bills of Material provides a comprehensive set of reports that will support most business needs. Before you consider these in detail, it is worth mentioning that there are some powerful online inquiries that eliminate the need to run some printed reports.

The Indented Bill of Material inquiry window provides a useful tool. It has applications for Design/Development Engineers, Manufacturing Engineers, Materials Professionals, Manufacturing Management, and Cost Accountants. Enter the assembly item number, the BOM alternative name (if applicable), and the revision and effectivity information. You also need to specify the number of levels of the bill that you want to explode. This value defaults based on the profile option BOM: Default Bill of Material Levels. You can also specify whether you want to see costing, material control, and lead-time information. When the bill is exploded, you can view the entire BOM structure with component effectivity information and choose to view material control, costing, and lead-time information. You can choose to expand and collapse BOM levels to suit your needs.

Another extremely useful inquiry window is theBill Components Comparison.This can be used to compare any two bills. Typical applications would be comparing primary and alternative BOMs or comparing the BOMs for the same assembly across two inventory organizations. You can choose to view the differences only or to view all components of both BOMs. The differences will be tagged within the window.

The third inquiry window to consider is the Item WhereUsed. This implodes the BOM structure, following the usage of a component upward through all the using assemblies in the structure. You can specify how many levels you want to implode. The window provides an indented view of the structure that can be expanded or collapsed as required.

Table 18.6 provides an overview of the reports provided with Oracle Bills of Material and a summary of their function.

TABLE 18.6   ORACLE BILLS OF MATERIAL REPORTS

Report Name	Description
Bill of Material Comparison Report	Similar to the inquiry screen. Compares two bills to highlight differences.
Bill of Material Listing	Reports on Engineering or Manufacturing bills but without component or routing details.
Bill of Material Loop Report	Checks an assembly or range of assemblies for BOM loops. Reports No Data Found if there are no loops.
Bill of Material Structure Report	Shows the detailed structure for an assembly or range of assemblies. You can choose how many levels to explode.
Bill of Material Parameters Report	Shows the values set for the BOM parameters. Useful when setting up Oracle Bills of Material.
Consolidated Bill of Material Report	Summarizes component usage from all levels of a bill.
Delete Items Report	Shows the deletion history for items, components, BOMs, operations, and routings.
Department Classes Report	Shows department classes and the departments that belong to these.
Department Report	Provides detail of department and overhead information.
Item Where Used Report	Similar to the Online Inquiry, this report provides information on the using assemblies for a component.
Resource Report	Provides detail of resource cost and overhead information.
Resource Where Used Report	Similar to the Item Where Used report. Shows the routings that use the selected resources.

TABLE 18.6   CONTINUED

Report Name	Description
Routing Report	Shows detailed information on routings based on the items specified.
Standard Comments Report	Reports all standard comments that have been defined.
Standard Instructions Report	Reports all standard instructions that have been defined.
Standard Operation Report	Provides information on Standard Operations that have been created. You can choose to display resource information.
Workday Exception Sets Report	Shows all workday exception sets that have been defined to be used with the workday calendar.

TROUBLESHOOTING

- If you choose to use Oracle Engineering to manage your ECO approval process, you can use an Oracle Alert or a workflow to do this. Alerts have been available in previous releases of the applications and are still of value. An ECO approval workflow provides more complete functionality in describing your process by allowing conditional branching. The trend in the development of the Oracle Applications is to increase the integration of workflow technology. If you want to "future-proof" your implementation, you should consider using a workflow for the approval process (see Chapter 22, "Using Oracle Workflow," for an explanation of how workflows operate).

- The Autoimplement Manager is a critical part of your ECO process if you choose to have Oracle Engineering manage the implementation of your engineering changes. Make sure that this concurrent program is running at all times and is scheduled to run daily at a minimum. You should monitor this concurrent program to ensure that it does not fail.

- ECOs can affect discrete jobs and repetitive schedules that are created in the Work In Process application. You need to coordinate your change activity with the users in your organization who are responsible for planning and scheduling (see Chapter 21, "Using Oracle Work In Process," and Chapter 20, "Using Oracle Planning Applications").

- Although it is covered earlier in this chapter, it is worth mentioning again that the Mass Change functionality is a very powerful tool. You should use it carefully. Although it is possible to undo changes that go wrong, it is better to avoid having to do this.

CHAPTER 19

Using Oracle Cost Management

UNDERSTANDING THE STRUCTURE OF THE COST MANAGEMENT APPLICATION

The Oracle Cost Management application provides an organization with a full-absorption, perpetual cost system for purchasing, inventory, work in process, and order entry transactions. This application provides comprehensive valuation and variance reporting and supports activity-based costing. It also provides extensive cost simulation, copying, and editing capabilities. Cost Management supports both standard and average costing.

The application is built around five predefined cost elements: material, material overhead, resource, overhead, and outside processing. Product costs are the sum of the elements used. If you use manufacturing costing, you can define an unlimited number of cost subelements.

UNDERSTANDING DEFINITIONS OF COST ELEMENTS

Cost elements and subelements are defined as follows:

- *Material.* The Material Cost Element is the raw material or component cost at the lowest level of the bill of material. It is determined from the unit cost of the component item.

- *Material Subelement.* These elements are used for detailed classification of material costs, such as plastic, steel, or aluminum. Determine the basis type (allocation charge method) for the cost and assign the appropriate amount.

- *Material Overhead.* Use the Material Overhead Cost Element for the overhead cost of material, calculated as a percentage of the total cost, or as a fixed charge per item, lot, or activity. If you use the Work in Process application, you can apply material overhead at the assembly level, and you can use several allocation methods.

- *Material Overhead Subelements.* You can define and assign Material Overhead Subelements to item costs to further categorize material overhead. For example, this assignment can include purchasing, freight, duty, or handling cost.

- *Resource.* The Resource Cost Element is used for direct costs required to manufacture products. It is calculated as the standard resource rate times the standard units on the routing, per operation, or as a fixed charge per item or lot passing through an operation. Resources can be people, machines, space, or miscellaneous charges.

- *Resource Subelements.* Use resource subelements to identify specific machines, people (labor), floor spaces, and so forth. See Chapter 18, "Using Oracle Engineering and Bills of Material," for additional information.

- *Overhead.* The Overhead Cost Element is used to record overhead costs of resources and outside processing. This cost element is calculated as a percentage of the resource or outside processing cost, as a fixed amount per resource unit, or as a fixed charge per item or lot passing through an operation. You can define multiple overhead subelements to cover both fixed and variable overhead. Each subelement can have its own rate. You can assign multiple overheads to a single department.

- *Overhead Subelements.* Overhead subelements are usually applied in the routing and represent a detail breakdown of production overhead.

- *Outside Processing.* This cost element is the cost of processing purchased from an outside supplier. It can be a fixed charge per unit or the standard resource rate times the standard units on the routing operation. To implement outside processing costs, you must define a routing operation in the Bills of Material application and use an outside processing resource.

- *Outside Processing Subelements.* These cost elements can be configured to charge actual or standard costs and can generate a purchase price variance when charged.

ACTIVITIES

Activities are an action or task you perform in a business that uses a resource or incurs cost. You can associate all product costs to activities, and you can define activities and assign them to any sub-element. You can also assign costs to your activities and build your item costs based on activities.

BASIS TYPES

Costs are assigned to an item with basis types to establish a cost allocation formula. Each sub-element cost must have a basis type. Predefined basis types in the Cost Management application are the following:

- *Item.* Use the item basis type with material and material overhead subelements to assign a fixed amount of cost per item. This basis type is usually used for purchased components. This basis type is used with resource, outside processing, and overhead subelements to charge a fixed amount per item moved through an operation.

- *Lot.* The lot basis type is used to assign a fixed lot charge to items or operations. The cost per item is calculated by dividing the fixed cost by the item's standard lot size for material and material overhead subelements. For routing steps, the cost per item is calculated by dividing the fixed cost by the standard lot quantity moved through the operation associated with a resource, outside processing, or overhead subelement.

- *Resource Value.* Use the resource value basis type to apply overhead to an item, based on the resource value earned in the routing operation. This basis type is used with the overhead sub-element only.

- *Resource Units.* The resource units basis type is used to apply overhead to an item, based on the number of resource units earned in the routing operation. This basis type is used with the overhead subelement only.

- *Total Value.* You can use the total value basis type to assign material overhead to an item, based on the total value of the item. This basis type is used with the material overhead subelement only.

- *Activity.* The activity basis type is used to directly assign the activity cost to an item. You can use this basis type only with the material overhead subelement.

COST MANAGEMENT'S RELATIONSHIP TO OTHER APPLICATIONS

The Cost Management application is tightly integrated with many Oracle applications that define products or create transactions for products. See Figure 19.1 for a diagram that shows which applications are related to the Cost Management application. Directional arrows show the flow of transactions or source data to or from the Oracle Cost Management application.

Figure 19.1
Cost Management relationships to other applications.

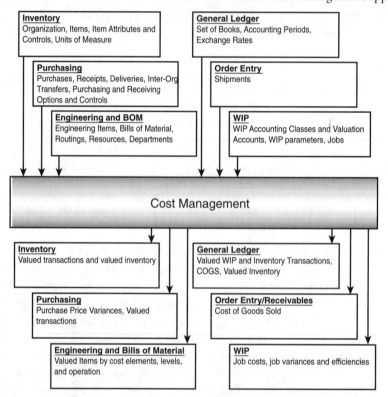

DISCOVERING NEW FEATURES IN RELEASE 11

Release 11 includes several significant improvements over release 10.7 of the Cost Management application:

- *Average costing in manufacturing.* In release 11, you can cost manufacturing transactions in an average costing organization.

- *Average cost history.* If you are using average costing, you can use the new Item Cost History window to see how an item's average cost has changed over time. In other words, you can see the transactions that make up the end result.

- *Cost element visibility in standard costing.* Cost element visibility is maintained in transfers to the General Ledger application when you assign the same account to multiple cost elements.

CRITICAL IMPLEMENTATION FACTORS

Because the Oracle Cost Management application is tightly integrated with several manufacturing applications that define and value the company's products and business transactions, a project team that works closely together produces best results. Don't treat the Cost Management module as simply an accounting responsibility. Consider the following:

- Get commitment from all levels and departments in your organization. Accounting, engineering, purchasing, inventory management, and information technology must work together to implement the Cost Management application.

- Make sure your company's engineering function is involved and understands the requirements of the Cost Management module. Certain costs and variances required by the accounting and reporting functions can impact the structure of the Bills of Material and routings.

- You should have your cost accountant involved in the configuration and testing of the BOM, WIP, and Inventory applications.

CONFIGURING THE APPLICATION

To ensure that the application works correctly for you, it must be configured to suit your business needs. There are many setup steps in the Oracle Inventory, Bills of Material, Work in Process, and Purchasing applications that must be configured before Cost Management, and these steps have a large impact on the Cost Management application. After you complete the required setup tasks in the other applications, there are nine setup steps in the Cost Management application.

REQUIRED SETUP TASKS

If you are responsible for configuring Oracle Cost Management, make sure you understand how the following items are configured in the other applications:

- Inventory
  - Define Daily and Period Rates
  - Define Organizations and Organization Parameters
  - Define Units of Measure
  - Define Subinventories

- Define Categories, Category Sets, and Default Category Sets
- Define Accounting Periods
- Define Items and Item Attribute and Controls
- Define Account Aliases
- Launch the Transaction Managers
- Define Receiving Options and Controls
- Define Purchasing Options
- Bills of Material
  - Define Bills of Material Parameters
  - Define Resources
  - Define Departments
  - Define Departments and Associate with Resources
  - Define Overheads and Assign them to Departments
  - Control Overheads by Resource
  - Define and Review Routing and Bill of Material Structures
- Work in Process
  - Define WIP Accounting Classes and Valuation Accounts
  - Define WIP Parameters

After you configure the required items in the other applications, you can set up the Oracle Cost Management module. There are nine setup steps in Cost Management (see Table 19.1 later in this chapter for the full list), and four are required as follows:

- Set Profile Options
- Set Security Functions
- Define Cost Types
- Define Material Subelements

RESOLVING CRITICAL SETUP ISSUES

Please see Chapters 15, "Using Oracle Purchasing," 16, "Using Oracle Inventory," 18, "Using Oracle Engineering and Bills of Material," and 21, "Using Oracle Work in Process," for more details about how to set up the configuration steps owned by those applications. The following topics are presented here because they are especially important to the Cost Management application:

- Costing Organization Parameters
- Default Interorganization Information
- Inventory or Manufacturing Costing
- WIP Accounting Classes

COSTING ORGANIZATION PARAMETERS

The definition of organizations is a central concept for Oracle Applications. Because organizations must be defined early in the configuration of the Inventory application and Inventory usually precedes Cost Management in the implementation schedule, you should try to identify the Cost Management business requirements before setting up the Inventory application. When you define the Costing Organization parameters in the Inventory application, consider carefully the following items:

- The costing organization can be either the current organization or the Item Master Organization.

- Choose standard or average costing:
  - Standard costing uses predefined costs for valuing inventory, WIP, and interorganization transactions. Variances are recorded for differences between standard and actual costs. When you use Bills of Material, each organization maintains its own item costs.
  - Average costing uses the average weighted value of all receipts of the purchased items. For manufactured items, this method uses a weighted average of all resources and materials consumed. You cannot share costs between organizations in an average costing organization, and average costs are maintained separately in each organization.

> **Note**
> You cannot change the costing method after transactions have been performed.

- Indicate whether GL transactions will be posted in detail.

> **Note**
> If you post in detail, the system creates large journal entries to post a line for each transaction. It is often better to post journal entries in summary, keep the detail out of the general ledger, and use subledger reports for detailed analysis.

- Indicate whether to reverse an encumbrance entry upon receipt into inventory.
- Select a default material sub-element to be used when you define item standard costs. This default enables faster entry of item costs.
- Specify Default Valuation Accounts for the organization. These Default Valuation Accounts will be the default accounts for the organization's subinventories. There are six default accounts to define:
  - *Material.* An asset account for material cost.
  - *Material Overhead.* An asset account for material overhead cost.
  - *Resource.* An asset account for resource cost.
  - *Overhead.* An asset account for resource and outside processing overheads.

- *Outside Processing.* An asset account for outside processing cost.
- *Expense.* An expense account for non-asset items.

■ You should specify the following general ledger accounts that will be the default values associated with the inventory organization:

- *Sales.* Enter an income statement account to be used as the default revenue account.
- *Cost of Goods Sold.* Use an income statement account for the default cost of goods sold entries.
- *Purchase Price Variance.* Enter a variance account that will be used to record the difference between purchase order price and standard cost. (This account is not used with average costing.)
- *Inventory A/P Accrual.* Enter a liability account to represent all purchase order receipts that are not matched in Accounts Payable.
- *Invoice Price Variance.* Use a variance account that will be used to record the difference between the purchase order price and the actual invoice price.
- *Encumbrance.* Enter an expense account that will be used to recognize the reservation of funds when a purchase order is approved. This entry is only used if you use encumbrance accounting.
- *Average Cost Variance.* If you use average costing, this account represents the inventory valuation error caused by issuing your inventory before your receipts.

DEFINING DEFAULT INTERORGANIZATION INFORMATION

If you have multiple locations or organizations, the following setup steps are important to your material movement activities. Accounting rules are designed to govern intercompany shipments and receipts. You can implement those accounting rules when you configure interorganization information.

DEFAULT INTERORGANIZATION OPTIONS When you determine the Default Inter-Organization options, you configure how you charge your internal cost to transfer material between organizations. For example, this cost transfer could be a handling or paperwork charge. The options are the following:

- *No transfer charges.* Self-explanatory.
- *Predefined percent of transaction value.* A default percentage is defined in Define Organization Parameters.
- *Requested added value.* The system requests a discrete value that is added to the material transfer at the time of the transaction.
- *Requested percent of transaction value.* The system requests, at the time of the transaction, a percentage of the transfer value to add to the material transfer.

DEFAULT INTERORGANIZATION TRANSFER ACCOUNTS   The Default Inter-Organization Transfer Accounts are default general ledger accounts that are defined for each organization. The appropriate accounts from each organization are used when you define an interorganizational relationship. The accounts are described as follows:

- *Inter-Inventory Transfer Credit.* This account collects the transfer charge cost. These charges reduce expenses for the sending organization.

- *Inter-Organization Payable.* Set this account to the clearing account used by the receiving organization. It represents an intercompany payable liability.

- *Intransit Inventory.* This account represents the value of transferred inventory that has not arrived at the receiving organization.

- *Inter-Organization Receivable.* Use this account to represent the clearing account for the shipping organization. It represents an intercompany receivable asset.

- *Inter-Organization PPV.* When you use the standard cost method, the receiving organization uses this account to recognize the difference (price variance) between the standard cost of the shipping organization and the standard cost of the receiving organization.

INVENTORY OR MANUFACTURING COSTING

Inventory and manufacturing costing are broad terms used by Oracle to describe costing functionality that has been expanded and improved in release 11. Because both the standard and average costing methods are now available to manufacturing organizations in release 11, you must determine whether you are a distribution or manufacturing organization and whether you will use the standard or average cost method.

Inventory costing is specific to distribution organizations that do not use Work in Process but might use Purchasing, Order Entry/Shipping, and Bills of Material. Manufacturing costing is applicable to organizations that specifically use the Work in Process application but might also use other applications.

Consider the following standard costing scenarios:

- If you use standard costing in a distribution organization, the costing method is standard, and all transactions are valued at the frozen standard costs. Two cost elements are used: material and material overhead.

- If you use standard costing in a distribution organization with Bills of Material, the costing method is standard, and all five cost elements are used if costs are rolled up.

- When a manufacturing organization uses standard costing, the costing method is standard, and all five cost elements are used.

Consider the following average costing scenarios in release 11:

- If you use average costing in a distribution organization, the costing method is set to average, and all five cost elements are used.

> **Note** Before release 11 of the applications, when the costing method was set to average, only one cost element, material, was used.

- If you use average costing in a manufacturing organization, the costing method is set to average, and all five cost elements are used. In this scenario you also set the CST: Average Costing profile option to Inventory and Work in Process.

If you are upgrading from release 10 to release 11, Oracle includes the release 10 cost processor for backward compatibility. However, if you want to change cost scenarios at the same time you upgrade, you will begin using the release 11 cost processor, and that event will be inconsistent with your ending inventory balances. For example, if you use manufacturing standard cost in release 10 and you want to begin using manufacturing average costing after the upgrade to release 11, you have a complex upgrade. To keep the system's perpetual records in balance, you will have to proceed carefully.

DEFINING WIP ACCOUNTING CLASSES

WIP Accounting Classes are defined in the Work in Process application. These classes control the accounting distributions for work in process activities and the details of costing information from production that you receive in the general ledger.

TYPES OF DISCRETE PRODUCTION   You can define accounting classes for three types of discrete production: standard discrete, asset nonstandard discrete, and expense nonstandard discrete.

STANDARD DISCRETE   You can define accounting classes for standard discrete jobs and use these accounting classes to group job costs. By using different accounting classes, you can separately value and report the costs associated with subassembly and finished goods production.

When you create jobs using the Planner Workbench, you can specify the discrete WIP Accounting Class. The way you select the WIP Accounting Class determines the account distribution for the job and could give you various cost breakdown scenarios. If you do not specify an accounting class, the system uses the accounting class defined by the Default Discrete Class parameter.

The account codes associated with the WIP Accounting Classes are used to make accounting entries throughout the production cycle. The valuation accounts are charged when material is issued to a job. When a job is closed, final costs and variances are calculated and posted to the variance and valuation accounts associated with the job. When the accounting period is closed, these journal entries are automatically posted to the General Ledger application.

You can use nonstandard discrete accounting classes to group and report transactions for various types of nonstandard production. For example, field service repair or engineering projects could use nonstandard discrete accounting classes.

For recurring expenses that you are tracking using nonstandard jobs, such as machine maintenance or engineering projects, define your accounting class with a type of expense Nonstandard. The valuation accounts carry the costs incurred on expense jobs as an asset during the period and automatically write them off to the variance accounts when the period closes.

For nonstandard production activities that you want to carry as an asset, define your accounting class with a type of asset nonstandard job. Asset nonstandard discrete jobs are costed the same as standard discrete jobs. Valuation accounts are charged when material is issued to a job, and final costs and variances are calculated and posted to the appropriate variance and valuation accounts when the job is closed.

REPETITIVE ACCOUNTING CLASSES   You must define accounting classes for each repetitive line/assembly association that you create. The schedule for an assembly and line association uses accounts from the Repetitive Accounting Class, and whenever you transact against the line/assembly association, those accounts are charged.

If you use a different accounting class for every line/assembly association, you will achieve detailed cost management reporting. However, you can use accounting classes to group production costs. For example, you can analyze repetitive manufacturing costs by assembly regardless of the line on which the assembly was manufactured by using the same accounting class for all lines that build the assembly. Alternatively, you can use the same class for all assemblies on a line to do line-based cost reporting.

WIP ACCOUNTING CLASS ELEMENTAL ACCOUNTS   You can enter separate accounting codes by cost element and by WIP accounting class. You can also share accounts across elements and classes to summarize an account distribution detail.

If you use the standard costing method, the accounts are debited at the standard cost when material is issued and resources are charged to a job or schedule. Outside processing is debited when the items are received into the job or schedule from the Purchasing application. Account codes are credited or relieved at the standard cost when you complete assemblies from a job or schedule, close a job, or close an accounting period.

If you use the average costing method, the accounts are debited at the average cost in effect at the time of the issue transaction. The accounts are credited when you complete assemblies from a job.

You can define the following elemental accounts or valuation accounts for WIP accounting classes:

- Material
- Material overhead
- Resource
- Outside processing
- Overhead

There are cost differences (called variances) when the actual costs charged to a valuation account do not equal the credits to the account when assemblies are completed from a job or schedule. The following variance accounts are supported in Work in Process:

- Material variance
- Resource variance
- Outside processing variance
- Overhead variance
- Standard cost adjustment variance

For more information on the setup of these accounts, see Chapter 21, "Using Oracle Work in Process."

SETUP TASKS

Table 19.1 shows the setup tasks to be completed for the Cost Management application. The tasks are influenced by the type of costing methods, standard or average, inventory or manufacturing, that you use.

TABLE 19.1 ORACLE COST MANAGEMENT SETUP TASKS

Setup Task Name	Required?
Set Profile Options	Yes
Set Security Functions	Yes
Define Cost Types	Yes
Define Activities and Activity Costs	No
Define Material Subelements	Yes
Define Overheads	No
Define Material Overhead Defaults	No
Define Category Accounts	No
Associate WIP Account Classes with Category Accounts	No

UNDERSTANDING EACH SETUP TASK

This section describes the tasks that must be performed and some of the decisions that you will need to make.

SETTING PROFILE OPTIONS

The profile options that directly affect the operation of the Cost Management application are listed in Table 19.2.

TABLE 19.2 Cost Management Profile Options

Profile Option Name	Required?	Level*	Comment
CST: Average Costing	N/A	N/A	System Derived Option
CST: Cost Rollup—wait for Table Lock	Yes	SAR	Default is None
CST: Cost Update Debug Level	Yes	SARU	Default is None
CST: Exchange Rate Type	Yes	S	Default is None

*Levels can be Site, Application, Responsibility, or User. The system administrator sets most profile options.

CST: Average Costing Option The Average Costing Option profile option is derived by the system and should not be updated by users or system administrators.

CST: Cost Rollup—Wait for Table Lock This indicates whether the cost rollup waits until the desired information is available or ends with an error after 10 attempts. The system administrator can update this option.

CST: Cost Update Debug Level The cost update program creates a log file, and this profile option determines the level and type of messages to print in the cost update log file. This option should be defined as Regular at the site level because that is the least level of detail. Consider defining it to Extended or Full at the application, responsibility, or user level. The system administrator can update this profile option at all levels. The effect of each option is as follows:

- *Regular.* Log every subroutine.
- *Extended.* Log every SQL statement.
- *Full.* Log every SQL statement and keep any temporary data in the database.

CST: Exchange Rate Type This profile option indicates whether to convert foreign currency using the end-of-period or period-average rate. The system administrator can update this option at the site level. Use this profile to control the exchange rate type used for the Margin Analysis Report.

Setting the Security Functions

During implementation, the system administrator sets up security functions. Because many organizations consider cost information to be highly sensitive and confidential, the administrator might give privileges to add, update, delete, or view costs. Privileges are implemented with function security, and the function names are listed in parenthesis.

Privilege to View Cost (CST_VIEW_COST_INFORMATION) The privilege to view cost information determines whether a specific user can see costing information. The Resources, Departments and Indented Bills of Material windows are governed by this function.

Tip

> If you exclude the privilege to maintain costs from a user, you can allow that user to print reports, but not change any costs, by leaving the Privilege to View Cost function as part of the user's responsibility.

PRIVILEGE TO MAINTAIN COST (CST_MAINTAIN_COST_INFORMATION) The Privilege to Maintain Cost function determines whether costing information can be created, updated, or deleted. This function affects the Bills of Material and the Routing windows. Because a cost rollup will save costs in the database, the Privilege to Maintain Cost function must be included as part of the responsibility for those users who perform roll ups.

OTHER PRIVILEGES THAT MIGHT BE IMPLEMENTED WITH SECURITY FUNCTIONS The functions shown in Table 19.3 determine whether costing information can be created, updated, or deleted from various windows.

TABLE 19.3 PRIVILEGES AND FUNCTION SECURITY

Privilege	Function Name	Window
Maintain Activities	CST_CSTFDATY_MAINTAIN	Activities
Maintain Cost Types	CST_CSTFDCTP_MAINTAIN	Cost Types
Maintain Item Costs	CST_CSTFITCT_MAINTAIN	Item Costs
Material Subelements	CST_CSTFDMSE_MAINTAIN	Material Subelements
Overheads	CST_CSTFDOVH_MAINTAIN	Overheads

DEFINING COST TYPES

A cost type is a group of costs with a specific name. You can define and update an unlimited number of simulation or unimplemented cost types. For example, you might want to create a cost type called "Lower of Cost or Market." The Cost Management application has three predefined cost types:

■ *Frozen Standard Costs.* The Frozen cost type is used to value transactions and inventory balances for organizations that use the standard cost method. This cost type is not available for organizations using average costing.

■ *Average Costs.* The Average cost type is used to value transactions and inventory balances for organizations that use the average cost method. It holds the average unit cost of items on hand. This cost type is not available for organizations using standard costing.

■ *Pending and all types that you define.* You can use all other cost types for any purpose. For example, you can create a cost history, perform a product cost simulation, or develop future frozen costs. Because these cost types are not implemented (frozen), you can create and update them at will. If you use the standard cost method, you can transfer costs from pending and all other cost types to update the frozen cost type.

If you are using the average cost method, you must also define at least one Average Rates cost type to hold sub-element rates or amounts. Select this Average Rates cost type when you define the Average Rates Cost Type parameter in the Organization Parameters window of the Inventory application. The Average Rates cost type is not used by organizations that use the standard cost method.

DEFINING ACTIVITIES AND ACTIVITY COSTS

Use activities to assign indirect costs to items based on the effort expended to obtain or produce the item. In your business, activities are processes that consume costs and time. In addition to cost elements and subelements, you can associate costs with an activity. Activities can be directly related to producing items, such as runtime or setup time, or, activities might be indirect in nature, such as engineering efforts.

DEFINING MATERIAL SUBELEMENTS

Material subelements are used to classify your material costs, such as plastic, steel, or aluminum. You can define material subelements, determine the basis type (allocation charge method) for the cost, and assign an appropriate amount. A material sub-element has a default activity and a default basis type assigned to it.

DEFINING OVERHEAD AND OVERHEAD COST SUBELEMENTS

When you use the standard cost method, you can use material overhead and overhead cost subelements to add indirect costs to item costs. You can add cost on a percentage basis or as a fixed amount. The Cost Management application enables you to separate overhead costs associated with materials from other overhead costs:

- *Material Overhead Subelements.* Define material overhead subelements and assign them to item costs. To control the cost allocation, determine the basis type for the cost and define an appropriate rate or amount. For example, you might use a sub-element such as purchasing, freight, or material handling.

- *Overhead Subelements.* Define overhead subelements and assign them to your item costs. Determine the basis type for the cost and define an appropriate rate or amount. Overhead subelements are applied in the routing and usually represent production overhead. You can define overheads based on the number of units or the lot moved through an operation, or based on the number of resource units or the value charged in the operation.

PART

III

CH

19

> **Tip**
>
> Each overhead sub-element has a default basis, a default activity, and an absorption account. Set up a pool of cost accounts in the general ledger and use the overhead absorption account as an offset account.

You can allocate the overhead cost amount based on the number of resource units or a percentage of the resource value earned in a routing operation. With the item or lot basis types, you can create overheads where the rate or amount is charged when each item is moved into an operation.

You can apply each of these subelements using different allocation methods or basis types. Material overhead is absorbed when an item is received into inventory or is completed from work in process. Resource overhead is absorbed as the assembly moves through routed steps in work in process.

Note When you use the Bills of Material application, you must configure the bill of material parameters before you can use the overhead cost element in the Overhead window.

DEFINING RESOURCES   Use the Define Resources window in the Bills of Material application to define the time an assembly spends at an operation and the cost of the operation. A resource can be anything that is required in your production process. For example, resources can be employees, machines, outside processing services, or physical space. The routing requires a resource and usage rate for all scheduled activities. Resources are defined in the Bills of Material application. For more information on defining resources see Chapter 18, "Using Oracle Engineering and Bills of Material."

When you define a resource, you can select the Costed check box in the Resources window to collect and assign costs to the resource. If the resource is costed, use the Standard Rate check box to indicate whether to charge jobs and repetitive schedules based on a standard rate.

If the resource is costed, enter an absorption account that is used to offset resource charges in work in process. Also, enter a variance account to collect resource rate variances for a job or repetitive schedule.

Tip If you are defining an outside processing resource that interacts with the Purchasing application, do not change the accounts that default into the field because Purchasing controls your receiving valuation account.

In the Resource Overhead Associations window, you can attach overhead subelements to the resource, choose a cost type, and enter a rate based on the resource unit of measure.

ENTERING EMPLOYEES AND EMPLOYEE LABOR RATES   If you have defined people resources and want to collect labor costs, you must define the employees and their labor rates. If you have installed the Oracle Human Resources Management application, you can define the employees through that application; otherwise, the Work in Process application provides a window to enter the employees and the rates. See Chapter 21 for more information.

DEFINING MATERIAL OVERHEAD DEFAULTS

To help speed up your data entry when you define items, you can define and update default material overhead subelements and rates. When you define items, the system enters these default values for you into the frozen costs if you are using the standard cost method or into the average rates if you are using the average cost method.

For items that you purchase, enter the material costs. For items that you produce, enter the rolled up costs. You can specify a default inventory organization and category for the same material overhead sub-element. If you have more than one default for a sub-element, the category default takes precedent over the organization default. If you have two category level defaults, the default that matches the item's planning code takes precedence.

> **Tip**
>
> You must define material overhead defaults from the master cost organization.

DEFINING CATEGORY ACCOUNTS AND ASSOCIATE CATEGORY ACCOUNTS WITH WIP ACCOUNTING CLASSES

If you use the product line accounting setup, Cost Management enables you to use categories to drive the selection of WIP Accounting Classes. You can use product line accounting when you use either the standard or average cost method. See Chapter 16, "Using Oracle Inventory," for more information on categories. The setup for product line accounting is a four-step process:

1. Create categories for each of your product lines and associate them with the product line category set.

2. Enter general ledger accounts for each category and subinventory combination in the Category Accounts Summary window. If you don't enter a subinventory, the accounts will apply to all subinventories that use the category. You can enter accounts to accumulate costs for material, outside processing, material overhead, overhead, resource, encumbrance, analytical invoice price variance, analytical purchase mirror, non-invoiced sales order, non-invoiced revenue, analytical revenue mirror, analytical margins of cost of goods sold, and average cost variance.

3. Create definitions for the WIP Accounting Classes that will be used as your default WIP Accounting Classes.

4. Make associations of the WIP Accounting Classes with the product line categories. Use the Default WIP Accounting Classes for Categories window to make the associations.

> **Tip**
>
> If you use the standard cost method, you can define WIP Accounting Classes at the category level for each organization. If you use the average cost method, you define WIP Accounting Classes at the cost group/category level for the organization.

PROCESSING TRANSACTIONS

Cost Management information can be viewed, defined, rolled up, updated, copied, purged, and so forth. This section describes the following transaction processes:

- Defining Item Costs
- Copying and Mass Editing Items and Accounts
- Roll Up Assembly Costs
- Updating Standard and Average Costs
- Maintaining Accounting Periods
- Closing Discrete Jobs
- Purging Cost Information
- Purging Margin Analysis Load Run
- Purging Standard Cost Update History

DEFINING ITEM COSTS

If you use the standard cost method in the Item Costs window, you can enter costs for purchased items or enter additional costs for products with costs generated from the cost rollup.

If you share costs among organizations, you can only define costs in the master organization. When you define a new item, Cost Management determines your costing method (standard or average) and creates a frozen or average cost type record respectively. If no inventory transactions have occurred, you can modify the frozen cost type record. This feature enables you to directly set the frozen standard cost for the item. However, if inventory transactions have occurred for this item, the system has a set of perpetual records that are already valued at the old item costs. To revalue the perpetual balances, you must define a cost in a cost type other than frozen and then perform a cost update to adjust the perpetual values and load a new frozen cost for the item. Although you can use any cost type you have defined, many companies use the pending cost type as the staging area for changes to item standard costs.

> **Note**
> If you use the average cost method, you cannot edit average costs in the Item Costs window as described previously. Instead, use the Update Average Costs window to perform maintenance on average costs.

If you use the Bills of Material application, you can run the Costed Bill of Material Explosion Reports for any cost type to see the effect of pending cost changes on an item. If you want to use the resource, outside processing, and overhead cost elements when you define item costs, you should define the Bill of Material parameters first so you will have access to the material and material overhead cost elements. See Chapter 18 for details.

COPYING AND MASS EDITING ITEM COSTS AND ACCOUNTS

Because most companies that use the Cost Management application have thousands of items stored in the database, maintenance of costs and account values could be difficult if each record had to be updated individually. Cost Management provides two utilities to perform mass edits on item costs and item accounts.

MASS EDITING ITEM COSTS

When you use the Mass Edit Cost Information window, you can apply mass edits for the following elements of cost information:

- You can apply new activity rates to item costs.

- You can change item shrinkage rates to a specified rate, or you can copy percentages from your planning shrinkage rates.

- You can use mass edits to make new costs and change existing costs by a percentage or an absolute amount.

- You can create new costs by averaging data from purchase orders or payables transactions.

You must plan carefully and develop a strategy to restrict mass edits to subelements with similar basis types. Do not mix rate-based and amount-based subelements in the same mass edit because the basis formulas calculate differently, and the values you enter in the Fixed Rate and Change Amount fields will be plugged into the formulas in drastically different ways. For example, if you enter 5.00 in the Fixed Rate field, an amount-based sub-element will increase by 5 units of your currency. However, a rate-based sub-element will multiply the cost by 5.

There are five kinds of mass edits available in release 11. You select the request name in the Mass Edit Cost Information window. These edits are named as follows:

- The Apply Last Activity Rates name is used to update item costs after you change rates on activities.

- Use the mass edit name called Change Cost Shrinkage Rates to change cost shrinkage rates for items.

- Select the name Mass Edit Actual Material Costs to create costs for your items from actual purchasing or accounts payable transactions or documents.

- The Mass Edit Material Costs name can be used to update costs by a fixed amount or percentage as determined by the basis type.

- Use Mass Edit Material Overhead Costs to change material overhead subelements by a fixed amount or percentage as determined by the basis type.

PART

III

CH

19

MASS EDITING ITEM ACCOUNTS

You can perform mass edits on account assignments for selected items in the Mass Edit Item Accounts window. You can edit the following accounts:

- Cost of Goods Sold
- Encumbrance
- Expense
- Sales

Although you can share standard costs among organizations, Cost Management does not share the item accounts. If you must change your accounts, you must make the change in each organization.

Tip

Because you edit account assignments for all items, a category of items, or a specific item, categories are essential to mass editing item accounts. If you can't use categories, your options to mass edit are limited to a single item or all items.

COPYING COST BETWEEN TWO COST TYPES

You can copy from one cost type to another and specify an item or category range. For example, you could initialize a new cost type by copying from the frozen cost type. Because the copy does not perform a cost update, you cannot copy to the frozen or average cost type. You can copy item costs within an organization or across organizations. If you are copying within an organization, you can also copy activity costs, resource and overhead costs, or resource and overhead associations.

There are three copying options that control how the copy is made:

- If you select Merge and Update Existing Costs, costs that exist in the source will be created when they don't exist in the target cost type. Costs that exist in the target but are not found in the source cost type are left unchanged. Where items exist in both cost types, the target is updated with the cost of the source item.

- Use the Copy Over New Information Only option to add item costs in the source cost type to the target cost type. Items that exist in both cost types or that exist only in the target cost type are left undisturbed.

- The option Remove and Replace All Cost Information simply replaces all item costs from the source cost type in the target cost type. If an item cost existed in the target cost type that was not in the source cost type, it will be deleted from the target.

Tip

The cost rollup function copies costs for rollup items (assemblies). When the assembly does not exist in the target cost type you roll up, the cost rollup program automatically copies the assembly information from the source cost type.

ROLLUP ASSEMBLY COSTS

If you use the Bills of Material application, you can perform either a full cost rollup or a single-level cost rollup from the Assembly Cost Rollup window. A full cost rollup explodes the complete bill of material for assemblies. The rollup process starts at the lowest level of the bill of material and builds the cost of each assembly. The rollup follows the hierarchy of the bill of material structure and calculates the costs for higher level assemblies. The full rollup uses the most current bill of material structure and component costs to make all calculations.

You can optionally select a single-level rollup if you want to calculate costs only at the first level of the bill structure for each assembly. This rollup method does not reflect changes in the bill of material structure or cost changes that have occurred at a level below the first level of your assemblies. A good use of the single-level rollup is to quickly assign new costs to the top-level assembly when you don't want to change costs on existing subassemblies.

You can control the reports that come from the rollup program, and you have the option to print the Consolidated Bills of Material Cost Report, the Indented Bills of Material Cost Report, or no report.

> **Tip**
>
> A loop in a bill of material is caused when a bill is assigned as a component to itself. Because a bill loop can cause rollup errors, before performing a full rollup, you should verify the structure of the Bills of Material. Run the Bill of Material Loop Report for the range of items in your rollup to quickly get a list of assemblies with problems.

> **Note**
>
> Phantom assemblies only include material costs in the cost rollup process. Routing costs are not included in the cost of higher level assemblies.

UPDATING STANDARD AND AVERAGE COSTS

Use the standard cost update process to define and roll up pending costs and then roll over pending costs to the frozen standard cost type. The cost update program is a batch program that you launch from a concurrent request submission. The update program waits on jobs that perform a period close, a job close, or a transfer to the General Ledger application. The update delays processing of accounting transactions until the cost update completes.

> **Note**
>
> If you want a standard cost of zero for an item, you must set it to zero. If you simply don't define a cost in the pending cost type, the update does not update the frozen cost to zero for those items.

Cost Management produces a journal entry to revalue the general ledger accounts for perpetual inventory balances to the new standard costs. The update revalues the on-hand balances in the organizations that share the updated costs. If you use the Work in Process application, the cost update revalues the discrete job balances

> **Tip**
>
> To accurately reflect standard cost variances in the current period, try to run your cost update at the beginning of the accounting period before inventory transactions are processed.

If you use the average cost method, you can update the average cost of items to include additional costs, such as job variances, freight, or invoice price variances. Navigate to the Update Average Costs window to perform the cost maintenance. You can implement a total cost change (prorated proportionately across all elements), a percentage change to selected elements and levels, a new average cost for selected elements and levels, or a value change to increment or decrement on-hand inventory balances.

REPORTING PENDING ADJUSTMENTS You can simulate the effects of a pending cost adjustment by running reports. Navigate to the Report Pending Cost Adjustments window and enter the cost type for the cost update in the parameters field. This concurrent process launches two jobs: one to simulate a cost update from the cost type you specify to the frozen cost type and the other to launch the Inventory, Intransit, and WIP Standard Cost Adjustment Reports. From these reports you can analyze the revaluation changes the standard cost update would perform for current inventory balances.

REPORTING COST UPDATE ADJUSTMENTS Cost Management enables you to optionally save cost update history records. You can print Historical Inventory and Intransit Standard Cost Adjustment Reports, and if you use the Work in Process application, you can print the Historical WIP Standard Cost Update Report. These reports show the adjustments made by the cost update to inventory and work in process perpetual balances.

MAINTAINING ACCOUNTING PERIODS

Cost Management uses the same periods, fiscal calendar, and other financial information found in the General Ledger application. See Chapter 11, "Using Oracle General Ledger," for more details about the general ledger. Because each inventory organization opens and closes periods in its fiscal calendar independently, this feature provides flexibility in financial controls and scheduling the fiscal closing for each organization. You must open a period before inventory, Work in Process, or costing transactions can be processed, but it is not necessary to close one period before opening the next.

You might get messages as you begin the period close process in the Inventory application. These messages can be caused by unprocessed transactions. Because these transactions will never process after their period is closed, you must examine and repair these transactions before continuing the close.

> **Tip**
> Check the transaction interfaces each week and fix any records that the interface cannot process. If you keep the transaction interface clear, the month-end period close will go more smoothly.

When you close the period, you accomplish several tasks:

- The system closes the open period for inventory and work in process transactions. When a period is closed, it cannot be reopened.

- The system automatically creates inventory and work in process accounting journal entries in the general ledger interface. You can perform a general ledger transfer at any time during an open period without closing the period. Interim transfers enable you to reconcile and transfer information weekly or more frequently so there will be less work during the month-end processing cycle.

- Cost Management calculates all the subinventory values for the end of the period.

Follow these steps to properly close and process all your inventory and work in process transactions:

1. Make sure everyone in your organization has completed entering all inventory and work in process transactions.

2. Verify that there are no transactions hung up in the inventory and work in process transaction interfaces.

3. Check the transaction cost manager process in the concurrent manager. If you use the Work in Process application, perform the same check on the resource transaction cost manager.

4. Verify that the Order Entry application has transferred all shipment details to Inventory.

5. Run the Material Account Distribution Report for the period and audit the contents for abnormally high transaction volumes or quantities. Also, perform a sanity check that you have made the right accounting distributions.

6. Verify that the perpetual inventory value at the end of the period matches the value you report in the general ledger.

7. If you use the Work in Process application, verify that the inventory balances with the WIP Account Distribution Detail Report.

8. Close the Payables and Purchasing applications before closing the Inventory and Work in Process applications.

9. Close the accounting period in the Inventory application. The system automatically closes the Work in Process application and transfers the accounting entries to the general ledger interface.

10. Import and post the journal entry in the General Ledger application.

> **Note**
>
> It's often easier to make a correction in the subledger before you close the fiscal period than it is to make a reconciliation in the general ledger and then make an adjusting journal entry.

CLOSING DISCRETE JOBS

Job closures are an important event for the Cost Management application. Until you close a job or change the status of the job to Complete—No Charges, you can make material, resource, and scrap charges to the job. Closing a discrete job prevents any further activity on the job. If you use the standard cost method, the Work in Process application recognizes variances when you close a job. The job closure process writes off any balances in any cost elements to the variance accounts. Using the Work in Process application, you can select which jobs to close or unclose. Choose Close or Unclose from the Special Menu to submit the request. The status of jobs submitted for close changes to Pending Close until the close process completes. If for some reason you have an abnormal termination of a request to close jobs, the status might be Pending Close. To clear the process, these jobs must be manually resubmitted.

The close process runs the Discrete Job Value Report for the standard and nonstandard asset jobs after job variances are computed.

> **Tip**
>
> Run the Discrete Job Value Report before closing a job so that you can fix any inaccuracies.

COSTING REPETITIVE SCHEDULE PERIOD CLOSE TRANSACTIONS

You do not close a repetitive schedule. The closing of the accounting period causes the system to zero WIP accounting balances and recognize variances. Use the Repetitive Value Report to check your transactions and balances before you close an accounting period.

If you have positive balances in the repetitive schedules when the period closes, the system debits the WIP Accounting Class variance accounts and credits the WIP Accounting Class valuation accounts.

For more information about closing jobs, see Chapter 21, "Using Oracle Work in Process."

PURGING COST INFORMATION

You cannot purge frozen costs if you are using the standard cost method or average costs if you are using average costing. However, you can purge other cost types and all or part of the costs within the cost type. For example, you might want to purge only purchased items from a cost type. Use the Purge Cost Information window to initiate a purge. This program removes the selected cost information permanently from the database, and these records are not retrievable after you run the purge. If you disable the Allow Updates check box when you define a cost type, you can prevent accidental loss of data through purging.

PURGING MARGIN ANALYSIS LOAD RUN

If you use the Receivables, Inventory, and Order Entry, applications, you can use the Margin Analysis Report. Before running this report, you must run the Margin Analysis Load Run, which, based on your parameters, creates temporary data in tables that are used by the report program. When they are no longer needed, you can purge the temporary data from previous margin analysis load runs by navigating to the Purge Margin Analysis Run window.

PURGING STANDARD COST UPDATE HISTORY

When you update costs, the system enables you to save the details for historical reporting and to rerun adjustment reports. When you no longer need such information, use the Purge Standard Cost History window to purge it.

UNDERSTANDING KEY REPORTS FROM COST MANAGEMENT

There are many reports available to help monitor your costs. Table 19.4 describes some of the major reports.

TABLE 19.4   ORACLE COST MANAGEMENT REPORTS

Report Name	Description
Cost Type Comparison Report	Use the Cost Type Comparison Report to show the differences in item costs for two cost types. You can compare by cost element, activity, sub-element, department, this/previous level, or operation.
Elemental CostReport	Use the Elemental Cost Report to report and summarize item costs by cost element.
Indented Bills of Material Cost Report	This report shows item costs by bill of material level. The report lists the detailed assembly costs by sub-element to the lowest level of the bill.
Intransit Value Report	Use the Intransit Value Report to report the value and quantity of items in the intransit inventory.
Inventory Value Report	Use the Inventory Value Report to show quantity, valuation, and detailed item information for each subinventory.

TABLE 19.4 CONTINUED

Report Name	Description
Margin Analysis Report	If you have the AR, OE, and INV applications, the Margin Analysis Report is a major analysis tool. The report shows revenue, cost of goods sold, and gross margin information for each item shipped or invoiced within a date range. This report can show summary or detail information by customer, order, and line number.
Item Definition Summary Report	If you use average costing, this report provides a summary listing with more information.

TROUBLESHOOTING

The Cost Management application can be difficult to set up because it is dependent on the configuration of four other applications: Inventory, Work in Process, Purchasing, and Bills of Material. In addition, this application doesn't get much respect from the implementation team because it is viewed as a minor application or assigned second class status. Consider the following as you configure and use the Cost Management application:

- Make sure a cost accountant is involved in the parts of the configuration of the four applications that precede the Cost Management setup.
- Understand the business requirements of your organization for Cost Management before you configure the Inventory, Work in Process, or Bills of Material applications.
- Try to perform cost updates at the beginning of a month before transactions start in the new month.
- Don't include a mix of rate-based and amount-based basis types in a mass edit.
- Perform the fiscal month-end closing on the applications in the following order: Payables, Purchasing, and Inventory/WIP.
- Do not create journal entries in detail unless you have very low transaction volumes.
- Make sure you follow good job closure procedures to recognize variances on discrete jobs. If you have a lot of jobs to close, consider performing that action during off-peak hours.
- Transfer inventory transactions to the general ledger periodically to minimize processing at month end.
- Verify that inventory transactions are not getting hung up in the transaction processing interfaces. Do this regularly. Make sure the transaction interfaces are clear before closing the fiscal period.

CHAPTER 20

Using Oracle Planning Applications

INTRODUCTION

This chapter covers the setup and use of the Oracle planning applications. There are two separate sections to deal with Oracle Master Scheduling/MRP (including Oracle Supply Chain Management) and Oracle Capacity.

USING ORACLE MASTER SCHEDULING/MRP

The Oracle Master Scheduling/MRP application provides a capable forecasting and planning solution for most organizations. When used with the Supply Chain Planning functionality and Oracle Capacity, these capabilities can extend to a support a multisite/multiorganization manufacturing and distribution planning process.

Figure 20.1 shows the major relationships between Oracle Master Scheduling/MRP and the other Oracle applications. The relationships affect the setup and operation of the Oracle Master Scheduling/MRP application.

Figure 20.1
This diagram shows how the Oracle Master Scheduling/ MRP application interacts with the other Oracle applications.

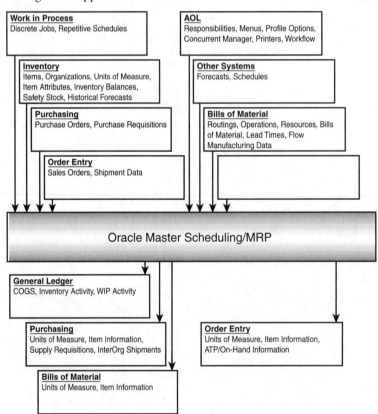

DISCOVERING NEW FEATURES IN RELEASE 11

Release 11 introduces some new features that enhance the operation of the Oracle Master Scheduling/MRP applications:

- *Support for Kanban Planning.* Kanbans are typically used as part of the pull-based replenishment process in just-in-time or flow manufacturing processes. They were originally cards that indicated when an item needed to be replenished. You can use Oracle Master Scheduling/MRP to calculate Kanban sizes and the number of Kanbans based on planning data.

- *Product Planning.* In release 11, you can plan at an aggregate product family level. To do this, you need to create a product family item (see Chapter 16, "Using Oracle Inventory") and then assign the family members (see Chapter 18, "Using Oracle Engineering and Bills of Material"). You can also associate planning percentages for each family member. You can track forecast consumption and master demand schedule reliefs for both the product family and its members.

- *Online Capacity.* If you have also installed the Oracle Capacity application, you can generate and review capacity planning information along with a material requirements plan.

- *Capable To Promise (CTP).* You can extend Available To Promise (ATP) information by using CTP calculations to consider the availability of both materials and resources (see the section "Using the Planner Workbench" later in this chapter for an explanation of CTP).

- *Supply Chain ATP.* If you are using Oracle Supply Chain Management, you can view ATP information for organizations within a supply chain from the Oracle Inventory or Oracle Order Entry applications. You need to do the following:

  - Create the sourcing rules or bills of distribution (see the section "Using Supply Chain Planning" later in this chapter).

  - Assign the sourcing rules or bills of distribution to customer and organization combinations.

  - Set up supply-chain ATP inquiries to return the receipt dates based on all possible sources of supply.

PART

III

CH

20

CRITICAL IMPLEMENTATION FACTORS

You should consider the following factors before you undertake an implementation or upgrade of the Oracle Master Scheduling/MRP application.

REVIEWING TOP ENHANCEMENT REQUESTS

Companies implementing and using the Master Scheduling/MRP application have identified some areas that require enhancement. These are some of the enhancements that have been requested through the Oracle Applications User Group (OAUG):

- The Planner Workbench should show item descriptions when using the supply/demand view.

- A process is required to eliminate MPS entries with zero quantities without overwriting the entire MPS.

- All reschedule recommendations should be shown on the Planner Workbench, including suggested purchase order cancellations.

- There should be automatic rescheduling of purchase orders.

- The forecast should be included in the supply/demand view.

- Pegging should allow end demand to be displayed immediately.

CONFIGURING THE APPLICATION

The following section describes the setup tasks required to configure the Oracle Master Scheduling/MRP application. If you are implementing release 11 of the applications, you can use the Oracle Applications Implementation Wizard to manage the setup tasks.

RESOLVING CRITICAL SETUP ISSUES

Before you begin the setup of the Oracle Master Scheduling/MRP application, there are some key issues that should be considered.

MPS VERSUS MRP PLANNING FOR ITEMS

If you are converting data from a legacy system, you will probably have already decided on whether items should be MPS planned or MRP planned. If not, you need to consider at what level you want to plan items.

Traditionally, MPS planning was reserved for items that required close attention and manual intervention to manage supply quantities. In many organizations, this would include items that are manufactured and some purchased items on allocation or with long lead times. MPS planning within the Oracle Master Scheduling/MRP application provides for this level of control.

The decision should be based on how closely you want to manage an item. When you know which direction you want to take for an item, you need to set the Planning Method item attribute appropriately (see Chapter 16 for an explanation of item attributes). If you are converting legacy data, you can set this attribute when importing data through the Open Item Interface (see the section "Converting Data for Major Entities" later in the chapter).

DETERMINING THE PLANNING PROCESS FOR YOUR ORGANIZATION

Before getting your team involved in the setup of the Master Scheduling/MRP application, you need to understand how the planning processes currently operate within your business. This application provides capabilities to address the needs of a wide range of organizations.

The Forecasting, Master Scheduling, MRP, and Supply Chain Planning tools are complex by themselves. When you start to put them together to build a planning process for an enterprise that consists of a number of organizations, the task might seem daunting.

There is no one way to structure a planning process. As you prototype the planning process, pay particular attention to the options available for loading forecasts, loading schedules, and managing relief/consumption. There will be some degree of trial and error involved before you arrive at a process that works for you.

ORACLE MASTER SCHEDULING/MRP SETUP TASKS

Before you proceed with setting up the Oracle Master Scheduling/MRP application, you should complete the setup of the following applications:

- Oracle Inventory
- Oracle Purchasing
- Oracle Bills of Material
- Oracle Work in Process

Table 20.1 shows the steps required to set up the Oracle Master Scheduling/MRP application. Because there are dependencies between steps, they should be completed in the sequence listed.

TABLE 20.1 ORACLE MASTER SCHEDULING/MRP SETUP TASKS

Setup Task Name	Required?
Define Master Scheduling/MRP Parameters	Yes
Define Deliver-to Locations	No
Define Employees	No
Set Profile Options	Yes (Required with defaults)
Define Forecast Sets	No
Define MDS Names	No
Define MPS Names	No
Define MRP Names	No
Define DRP Names	No
Define Sourcing Rules and Bills of Distribution	No
Create Assignment Sets	No
Define Interorganization Shipping Network	No
Define Shipping Methods and in-transit lead times	Yes
Run Information Audit Report	No (but recommended)
Define Planning Parameters	Yes
Start the Planning Manager	Yes

TABLE 20.1 CONTINUED

Setup Task Name	Required?
Define Planners	No
Define Planning Exception Sets	No
Define Demand Classes	No
Create Source Lists	No
Set Up the Planner Workbench	Yes
Set Up Supplier Planned Inventories	No

UNDERSTANDING EACH SETUP TASK

This section provides detail on each of the setup tasks and the order in which they should be performed.

DEFINING PLANNING PARAMETERS

Set system values for the planning module in the Planning Parameters window. When you work with this window, consider checking the Snapshot Lock Tables box to ensure data consistency of on-hand quantities and order quantities during a planning run. Select the system execution defaults and enter repetitive planning parameters as required.

> **Note**
>
> You must enter safety stock information for individual inventory items before MPS/MRP will calculate a safety stock for the item.

DEFINING DELIVER-TO LOCATIONS

If you will be creating purchase requisitions from planned orders, you must define at least one deliver-to location. This will be used in the creation of a purchase order from the requisition. If you are implementing Oracle Purchasing, you can define thedeliver-to location while setting up that application.

DEFINING EMPLOYEES

Employees need to be set up to allow the creation of purchase requisitions from planned orders. These requisitions are imported into Oracle Purchasing to create purchase orders. You must define individuals who will create requisitions, create purchase orders, approve purchases, and perform receipt transactions.

If you have installed Oracle HRMS, you can use this application to set up your employees. Otherwise, you can use the Enter Employee form provided with the Master Scheduling/MRP application.

SETTING THE PROFILE OPTIONS

Table 20.2 shows the profile options that directly affect the operation of the Oracle Master Scheduling/MRP application.

TABLE 20.2 ORACLE MASTER SCHEDULING/MRP PROFILE OPTIONS

Profile Option Name	Level*	Comment
MRP:ATP Assignment Set	S	No Default
MRP:Calculate Excess Exceptions on Time Fence	S	Default is No
MRP:Compute Sales Order Changes	S	Default is Yes
MRP:Consume Forecast	S	Default is Yes
MRP:Consume MDS	S	Default is Yes
MRP:Consume MPS	S	Default is Yes
MRP:Cutoff Date Offset Months	SU	No Default
MRP:Debug Mode	SAR-U	Default is No
MRP:Default DRP Plan Name	U	No Default
MRP:Default Forecast Date	SAR-U	Default is Yes
MRP:Default Forecast Name	U	No Default
MRP:Default Plan Name	U	No Default
MRP:Default Schedule Name	U	No Default
MRP:Default Sourcing Assignment Set	SU	No Default
MRP:Demand Time Fence Days	S	No Default
MRP:Environment variable to set path for MRP files	S	No Default set for Profile. System will put the files in $MRP_TOP/ $APPLOUT by default.
MRP:Firm Planned Order Time Fence	S	Default is Yes
MRP:Include Scheduled Receipts in Use-up Calculation	S	Default is No
MRP:Interface Table History Days	S	Default is five days
MRP:Maintain Original Schedule Version	S	Default is No
MRP:MPS Relief Direction	SAR	Default is "Backward, then Forward". Stop and restart the planning manager if this profile is changed.
MRP:Perform Planning Manager Function in Loads	S	Default is Yes
MRP:Planning Manager Batch Size	S	Default is 250

TABLE 20.2 CONTINUED

Profile Option Name	Level*	Comment
MRP:MRP Planning Manager Max Workers	S	Default is 10
MRP:MRP Purchasing by Revision	S	No Default
MRP:MRP Purge Batch Size	S	Default is 25000
MRP:MRP Requisition Load Group Option	SRU	Default is Supplier
MRP:Retain Dates within Calendar Boundary	S	Default is Yes
MRP:Snapshot Pause for Lock (Minutes)	S	Default is 5 minutes
MRP:Snapshot Workers	S	Default is 5
MRP:Sourcing Rule Category Set	SU	No Default
MRP:Time Fence Warning	SARU	Default is Yes
MRP:Trace Mode	SARU	Default is No
MRP:Use Direct Load Option	SARU	Default is No
MRP:Use Ship Arrived Flag	SARU	Yes or No

*Levels can be **S**ite, **A**pplication, **R**esponsibility, or **U**ser. The system administrator sets most profile options.*

A value must be set for a profile option where a default is specified.

DEFINING FORECAST SETS

Individual forecasts can be grouped into a forecast set. Sets can be useful for combining forecast information that comes from related sources. An example would be to create a forecast set that consists of individual regional sales forecasts. At least one forecast set must be defined before an individual forecast is defined. There is no restriction on how many sets can be defined.

When you define a forecast set, you must select a *bucket* type to be used as the default for entering forecast information. Buckets can be days, weeks, or accounting periods. You must also indicate the level at which the forecast and consumption process will operate. If you are using Oracle Order Entry and Oracle Receivables, you have the option to define the forecast set at the customer, bill to, or ship to level. This option determines the sales orders that consume the forecast set. There is also an option to define the forecast set at the item level. If you do not have Oracle Order Entry or Oracle Accounts Receivable installed, this is the default.

For each forecast set (assuming you will use forecast consumption), you must specify the forward and backward consumption days that will be used. (Forecast consumption is discussed later in this chapter.)

DEFINING NAMES

This section covers the definition of Master Schedule and MRP plan names.

MASTER DEMAND SCHEDULE   The Master Demand Schedule (MDS) contains the demand for products supplied by your organization. Typically, the MDS consist of Sales Order and Forecast information. You can optionally associate an MDS with a demand class. Demand classes (discussed later) enable you to group similar demand types (for example, by customer).

The MDS can be relieved by sales order shipments. To allow this, you must set the MDS Relief option to Yes.

> **Note**   MDS relief will only happen if the MRP:Consume MDS profile option is set to Yes.

MASTER PRODUCTION SCHEDULE   The Master Production Schedule (MPS) contains the build schedule for your organization. This can consist of discrete quantities or build rates if you are using repetitive scheduling.

As with the MDS, you can choose to associate a demand class with the MPS. This ensures that only discrete jobs associated with the demand class can relieve the MPS. If you choose the Inventory ATP option, your MPS will be considered as supply in any ATP calculations carried out by Oracle Inventory. The Feedback option allows the Planner/Scheduler to see how much of a planned order has been implemented. When defining the MPS, you can choose the Production option to allow autorelease of planned orders against the schedule.

You can define multiple master production schedules, each with a unique name. The MPS relief option allows the original MPS quantities to be reduced when discrete jobs, interorganization shipments, purchase orders, or purchase requisitions are created. This prevents overstating requirements if Material Requirements Planning (MRP) is run between MPS runs. There is no MPS relief for repetitive items between MPS runs.

> **Tip**   For MPS relief to happen, the profile option MRP:Consume MPS must be set to Yes.

MATERIAL REQUIREMENTS PLAN   In the Material Requirements Planning (MRP) process, net requirements for material are calculated. The MRP contains planned orders/schedules to support the net requirements as well as recommendations for rescheduling or canceling existing orders. Any number of material requirements plan names can be defined. This enables you to generate multiple MRP plans, each with a unique name.

As with the MPS, you can select the feedback option to allow a planner to check the quantity of a planned order that has been implemented. You can also choose the Production option to enable autorelease of planned orders against the plan.

DISTRIBUTION REQUIREMENTS PLAN   Define any number of distribution requirements plans names. This enables you to generate multiple DRP plans, each with a unique name. The Distribution Requirements Plan (DRP) contains similar information to a material requirements plan, but it is based on the material requirements to support a distribution network (considering suppliers, manufacturing locations, warehouses, distribution centers, and customer locations).

The same setup options apply to a DRP and MRP.

DEFINING SOURCING RULES AND BILLS OF DISTRIBUTION

Sourcing rules and bills of distribution are associated with the operation of supply-chain planning. Sourcing rules define how an item will be replenished within a single organization or across all organizations. Bills of distribution can define replenishment across an entire enterprise, including supplier organizations, distribution centers or hubs, and manufacturing operations.

The operation of supply-chain planning is discussed later in this chapter.

CREATING ASSIGNMENT SETS

When the sourcing rules and bills of distribution have been defined, they need to be assigned. You have several options for assigning these:

- An item across all your organizations
- A single item in an organization
- All items in an organization
- A category or categories of items
- Categories of items in an organization
- All organizations

Assigning the sourcing rules and bills of distribution enables you to define the supply chain for your enterprise.

DEFINING INTERORGANIZATION SHIPPING NETWORK

In this setup step, you define how transfers of items between inventory organizations will operate. An organization can be a shipping organization, destination organization, or both. You can also decide whether you will use in-transit inventory. Part of the setup involves the assignment of accounting information to be used in recording charges associated with the transfer of items.

This setup step is typically completed in Oracle Inventory (see Chapter 16).

DEFINING SHIPPING METHODS AND IN-TRANSIT LEAD TIMES

You can define shipping methods as QuickCodes to be used with interorganization transfers. These could be a specific carrier or a description of a method (air, sea, and so on).

For use with supply-chain planning, you might want to associate a lead time to be used with each shipping method. This lead time can be defined when creating the interorganization shipping network. This step is also typically part of the Oracle Inventory setup (see Chapter 16).

RUNNING INFORMATION AUDIT

Oracle Master Scheduling/MRP provides an audit report to enable you to check the integrity of the data that will be used in the planning process. A series of predefined audit statements are provided to check for potential errors in the database (for example, items that are planned as buy but are not purchasable).

If you are converting data as part of your implementation, this report should be run after the conversion process has completed.

DEFINING PLANNING PARAMETERS

The planning parameters determine the basic defaults to be used in the planning process:

- *Snapshot Lock Tables*. Setting this parameter tells the planning process to lock tables when gathering on-hand order quantity information for the snapshot. If you set this parameter, you prevent certain transactions from taking place while the snapshot processes are running. The benefit is that you obtain more accurate order and inventory information for the planning process. With the memory-based planning engine, locking tables during the planning run is unlikely to have a significant impact on users performing transactions.

- *Default ABC Assignment Group*. This is required. Some organizations choose to implement their plans based on item ABC assignments.

- *Demand Time Fence Control.* You can determine whether demand time fences are honored in the planning process. If they are, forecast demand within the time is not considered. Sales order demand is still valid within the demand time fence.

- *Plan Safety Stock*. This tells the planning process to calculate safety stock for items when the plan is run. You must specify the safety stock parameters for your items if you need this planned.

- *Net Purchases*. You can choose to have your plan consider all purchases as supply. If you do not choose to net purchases, there will be no reschedule messages for your requisitions/orders, and the planning process will generate new planned orders to meet supply requirements.

- *Planning Time Fence Control*. This determines whether planning time fences are honored in the planning process. If this parameter is set and you have time fences specified for items, the planning process will not suggest new orders within the time

PART
III

CH
20

fence or provide reschedule-in suggestions for existing orders. You will still receive reschedule-out suggestions. If the parameter is not set, the planning process will plan new orders and create reschedule suggestions regardless of how the planning time fence is set for your items.

■ *Net WIP.* If this parameter is set, the planning process will consider existing discrete jobs and repetitive schedules as supply for an item. If the parameter is not set, there will be no reschedule suggestions for existing jobs, and new jobs will be planned to meet supply requirements.

■ *Net Reservations.* This determines whether existing reservations are netted off on-hand quantities when the plan is run. If this parameter is not set, the planning process will consider the on-hand quantity as being available regardless of reservations.

■ *Material Scheduling Method.* There are two options for this parameter. Operation Start Date schedules material to be available to meet the start date for a particular WIP operation. Order Start Date schedules material to be available for the start date of a discrete job.

■ *Planned Items.* You can specify whether the planning process considers all planned items, demand schedule items, or supply schedule items.

> **Tip**
>
> Although Oracle Master Scheduling/MRP provides these options, you will probably want to select All Planned Items for this parameter. This way, you include all possible sources of demand in your plan. If you want to exclude certain items from the planning process on an individual basis, you can set the MRP Planning Method attribute for these items to Not Planned. See Chapter 16 for an explanation of the item attributes.

■ *Include MDS Days.* You can optionally specify a number of days of past due MDS demand to include in the planning process. If you enter no value, the process will consider all MDS entries. A value of zero means that no past due MDS entries will be considered.

If you will be using repetitive schedules, you must also define default parameters at this step:

■ *Work dates or Calendar dates.* You can specify whether the dates for your repetitive schedules will be based on work dates or calendar dates. Using work dates forces your repetitive planning periods to follow the workday calendar. Choosing calendar dates enables your planning periods to include dates that are not part of the workday calendar.

■ *Anchor Date.* You can specify the date from which the repetitive planning periods start. You can anchor subsequent planning runs to this date or choose a new one.

■ *First Bucket Days, First Horizon, Second Bucket Days, Second Horizon, and Third Bucket Days.* You use buckets to define three time periods for your repetitive plans. This enables you to obtain better control of repetitive schedules in the near term and monitor overall changes in requirements further out. The periods are specified by selecting a bucket size (in days), which will be used as the basis for suggested schedules. The periods are bounded by the horizon, which is specified in days. The third period is bounded by the planning horizon you specify when you execute the plan.

> **Tip**
>
> The bucket days used in the first and second periods should be small to allow more finite control of suggested schedules. Consider using a higher number of bucket days for the third period where an overall picture of supply and demand is required.

STARTING THE PLANNING MANAGER

The planning manager process is responsible for the maintenance of a number of planning tasks including the following:

- Consumption of forecasts by sales orders
- Relief of the MDS by sales order shipments
- Relief of the MPS by the creation of purchase orders and discrete jobs
- Support of the MRP open interface routines

Although the planning manager is initiated from the Planning Manager window, it runs as a concurrent process based on the processing interval that you specify. You can also check the status of the planning manager from this window.

> **Tip**
>
> The default of 30 seconds for the processing interval seems to work well in most circumstances. In some situations, the planning manager process will fail. If users are vigilant, they will notice this through inconsistencies in the consumption or relief processes. However, it would be wise to create an Oracle Alert to monitor the status of the planning manager and notify an administrator if it should fail. You should also note that the processing interval is calculated based on the start time of the previous request.

PART

III

CH

20

DEFINING PLANNERS

Using the Planners window, you can define the planners for your organization. This enables you to group items by planner within planning reports and on the planner workbench. To assign a planner code to an item, you must update the Planner item attribute (see Chapter 16).

DEFINING PLANNING EXCEPTION SETS

Planning exception sets enable you to structure the way in which you view and implement planning exceptions related to items, orders, and resources. An exception set must be assigned to an item using the Exception Set item attribute (see Chapter 16 for an explanation of item attributes).

You can define exception parameters for the following situations:

- *Excess Quantities.* When the projected on-hand quantity exceeds zero or the safety stock for the item by more than the excess quantity you specify.

- *Repetitive Variance Exceptions.* When the suggested repetitive schedule exceeds the current schedule by more than the percentage you specify.

- *Resource Shortage.* When the capacity for a resource is overutilized by more than the percentage you specify.

- *Resource Excess.* When the capacity for a resource is under-utilized by more than the percentage you specify.

- *Over-promised Exceptions.* When the available-to-promise quantity falls below zero or the safety stock for the item.

- *Shortage Exceptions.* When the projected on-hand quantity falls below zero or the safety stock value you have specified for an item.

The exceptions are based on choosing a time period within which the exception condition is tested. The periods to choose from are the following:

- *Cumulative Manufacturing Lead Time.* This lead time can be calculated by Oracle Bills of Material. It is based on raw materials being in stock but requiring subassemblies to be manufactured.

- *Cumulative Total Lead Time.* This lead time can also be calculated by Oracle Bills of Material. It is based on raw materials being purchased and all subassemblies being manufactured.

- *Planning Time Fence.* This is based on the planning time fence defined for an item.

- *Total Lead Time.* This is the fixed lead time plus variable lead time multiplied by the order quantity.

- *User Defined Time Fence.* You can enter a number of days to be used as a user-defined time fence for exception reporting.

Tip

You can create a number of exception sets with different sensitivities that you can apply to different types of items. To do this, you can add the exception set name in an item template (or update an existing template) and then apply the template when you create an item. Item templates are explained in Chapter 16.

DEFINING DEMAND CLASSES

Demand classes enable you to group similar types of demand together. A typical application would be the creation of separate demand classes for a particular group of customers (for example, separate classes for retail customers and distributors).

Demand classes provide significant flexibility in the planning process:

- *Forecast Consumption.* You can assign a demand class to a forecast. This affects how forecast consumption operates. Sales orders can also have a demand class associated with them, and the planning manager uses this as part of the consumption logic.

- *Order Entry.* You can associate a demand class with an order type or with the ship-to address for a customer. When an order is entered, the relevant demand class is associated with the order.

- *Organization Demand Class.* A demand class can be associated with an organization. This has implications for forecast consumption and schedule relief if you are using supply-chain planning.

- *Master Schedules.* You can assign a demand class to an MDS or MPS. Sales orders with a demand class matching that of an MDS relieve it. Discrete jobs with a demand class matching that of an MPS relieve it.

- *Planning.* If a demand class is associated with an MPS, you can control the way that jobs, schedules, subinventories, and reservations are netted in the planning process by assigning demand classes to these entities.

CREATING SOURCE LISTS

Source lists provide a convenient way to group forecasts and master schedules for use in the planning process. They are of particular benefit when combining forecasts or master schedules from a number of sources into one single forecast or schedule that will be used for planning. With supply-chain planning, they provide a convenient way to pull together sources of forecasts or schedules from multiple organizations.

SETTING UP THE PLANNER WORKBENCH

The planner workbench is the basic tool that most organizations use to review and implement recommendations from the planning process. It is a common interface that is used with both Master Scheduling/MRP and Supply Chain Planning. There are some prerequisites to using the planner workbench:

- Define employees to enable you to load purchase orders. This step should already be complete.

- Define a deliver-to location to allow new requisitions to be loaded. This step should also be complete.

- Assign purchasing categories and list prices. The categories and list prices are assigned in the Oracle Inventory setup (see Chapter 16).

- Set requisition numbers to be automatically assigned. This is part of the Oracle Purchasing setup (see Chapter 15, "Using Oracle Purchasing") and is a prerequisite to implement planned orders as purchase requisitions from the workbench.

You can customize the display of information on the planner workbench by setting parameters for the horizontal plan and horizontal capacity views. You can also set some defaults to be used:

- *Supply/Demand.* You can assign a cutoff date to be used when displaying new orders and reschedule recommendations. You can also enter a default job class to be assigned to discrete jobs created from the workbench (see Chapter 21, "Using Oracle Work In Process," for an explanation of job classes).

- *Requisition Load Group.* You can assign a load group to be used when creating purchase requisitions from the workbench. The options are to group by buyer, item, category, supplier, individual requisitions per planned order, or all planned orders on one requisition.

> **Note**
> The requisition load group default can also be set at the site, responsibility, or user level using the MRP:Requisition Load Group Option profile option.

SETTING UP SUPPLIER-PLANNED INVENTORIES

If you are using supply-chain planning, you have the option to assign an inventory organization to a supplier. In this way, you can integrate the supplier organization into your planning process. You must first define a supplier, create a supplier organization, and then assign an inventory organization to that supplier.

In the same way, you can also assign an inventory organization to a customer, allowing integration of this organization into your supply chain.

CONVERTING DATA FOR MAJOR ENTITIES

If you are implementing Oracle Master Scheduling/MRP and want to move data from a legacy system, it needs to be converted. A number of open interfaces are provided with the applications that can assist with the conversion process.

> **Tip**
> Before converting any data using the open interfaces, ensure that all the setup steps in the relevant applications are complete. Data imported through the interfaces will be validated against your setups.

The two open interfaces directly relevant to Oracle Master Scheduling/MRP are the following:

- Open Forecast Interface
- Open Master Schedule Interface

Both interfaces are discussed in the section "Using Open Interfaces in This Application" later in this chapter.

You should also consider the conversion of Items and Bills of Material, particularly because many planning parameters are associated with item attributes or BOM structures. Conversion of item and BOM data is covered in Chapter 16 and Chapter 18.

As with all conversions, you need to assess the costs involved in developing programs to extract data from your legacy system and insert it in the relevant interface tables. In some cases, it might be more economical to create forecast and master schedule data using the Master Scheduling/MRP application, particularly if the volume is small.

PROCESSING TRANSACTIONS

The following section covers the main transactions involved in using Oracle Master Scheduling/MRP.

MAINTAINING FORECASTS

After you have created a forecast set with at least one forecast, you can create detailed entries for a forecast. Oracle Master Scheduling/MRP provides for manual entry of a forecast or for the creation of forecasts based on historical data.

MANUAL FORECAST ENTRY

To create a manual forecast entry, you need to select one of your previously defined forecasts. The forecast information is entered by item number. Each forecast entry is valid for a particular bucket. The buckets can be days, weeks, or accounting periods. The bucket type defaults from the information entered when the forecast set was created.

> **Tip**
>
> To speed up the entry and maintenance of forecast information, you can choose to enter a bucket type, a start date and end date for the forecast, and a quantity. This is useful if you have multiple identical forecast quantities over a number of identical periods (for example, 10,000 per week for 10 weeks).

For each forecast entry, you can also specify a confidence percentage that will be applied to the forecast. This percentage is used to calculate anticipated requirements when the forecast is loaded into an MDS or MPS.

FORECASTING BASED ON HISTORICAL DATA

In conjunction with Oracle Inventory, you can create a forecast rule, which can be used to generate forecasts based on historical data. Two methods are provided:

- *Focus forecasting.* Produces a forecast for a single period only.
- *Statistical forecasting.* Can be used for any number of periods.

You define forecast rules in Oracle Inventory. To do this, you must define a name for the rule and the bucket type to use. You must then specify which historical information should be considered in creating the forecast:

- Sales order shipments
- Issues to WIP
- Interorganization transfers
- Miscellaneous issues

You must also select the forecasting method that the rule will use. If you choose focus forecasting, the application will use focus forecasting algorithms to choose a best fit forecast based on historical transactions.

If you choose statistical forecasting, you can specify the following:

- The maximum number of historical periods to be considered in the calculations.
- The smoothing (alpha) factor.
- Use a trend model. You can also specify the amount of smoothing to be used in this model.
- Use a seasonality model. You can specify a smoothing factor to be used with the seasonality indexes.
- If you choose to use a seasonality model, you can enter a seasonality index by period.

When you create the forecast, you can choose to apply the forecast rule to all items, a specific item, a category of item, or all items in a category set (see Chapter 16 for an explanation of category sets).

Tip	It is unlikely that you would want to apply a forecast rule to *all* items in an organization. If you plan on using historical forecasting, consider creating item categories that will enable you to segregate the items that would benefit this method of creating forecasts.

You need to specify an overwrite option when generating a forecast using a forecast rule. This is explained in the next section.

COPYING AND MERGING FORECASTS

While maintaining separate forecasts for business reasons (by region, by customer, and so on), you might need to combine forecasts into one to be used in a subsequent planning operation. It might also be useful to copy an existing forecast (rather than manually re-create it) and then modify it to simulate a particular scenario.

Oracle Master Scheduling/MRP provides a tool to accomplish this. There are some critical parameters in the copy/merge process that you should consider:

- *Overwrite Option.* Selecting an incorrect option can cause problems that are difficult to undo. All Entries causes any existing forecast entries in the destination forecast to be *deleted* and replaced with the source forecast information. The No option means that any existing entries in the destination forecast are left as is, and the source forecast data is *appended*. Same Source Only means that any existing forecast entries that had previously been loaded from the same source forecast will be *deleted* and the newly copied or merged forecast entries will be added to the forecast.

- *Start and Cutoff dates.* You can choose how much of a forecast should be merged or copied. Forecast entries outside of this date range will not be merged or copied.

- *Explode.* If you are forecasting using planning bills of material (BOMs), you can use this function to create a forecast for the components of those BOMs. To do this, copy the forecast containing the planning items into another forecast with the Explode option enabled. The destination forecast will now contain forecast entries for the components. See Chapter 18 for an explanation of planning BOMs.

- *Current/Original Quantities and the Consume option.* See the next section of this chapter for a discussion of consumption.

- *Modification Percent.* You can choose to modify *all* entries in the source forecast by a percentage as they are merged or copied into the destination.

- *Carry Forward Days.* You can shift the dates on the source forecast entries by a number of days as they are merged or copied. This can be a positive number (shift forward) or a negative number (shift backward).

THE FORECAST CONSUMPTION PROCESS

Oracle Master Scheduling/MRP provides forecast consumption to replace forecasts with sales order demand as the sales orders are loaded. This prevents situations from arising where sales order plus forecast quantities overstate the true requirements. Consumption is enabled for a forecast set and applies to all forecasts within the set.

Other parameters associated with the forecast set affect the way that consumption operates:

- *Outlier Update Percent.* This is the maximum percentage of the original forecast quantity that a single sales order can consume. This prevents an unusually large or unanticipated sales order from consuming all the available forecast.
- *Forward and Backward Consumption Days.* These parameters tell the planning manager the number of days to look forward and backward from the sales order schedule date when locating forecast entries to consume. The planning manager will first look backward (if backward consumption days is greater than zero) and then forward (if forward consumption days is greater than zero) for a forecast to consume.

Tip

Forward and backward consumption days work with the bucket size you specify for your forecast entries. Choose the combination carefully! If you enter your entire forecast for a month with a bucket size of Day or Week and make the entry for one day or one week, this seriously reduces the chances of the planning manager finding a valid forecast to consume. You run the risk of overstating the demand when you load the forecast into an MDS along with sales orders. You should choose the combination of consumption days and bucket size that works best for your business. There are several examples in the Oracle reference documentation.

If you associate a demand class with a forecast, this also affects consumption. When a sales order is entered with an associated demand class, the planning manager looks for a forecast entry with the same demand class to consume. If it does not find one, it looks for a forecast with *no* demand class, and failing that, it overconsumes.

Overconsumption is a mechanism that provides feedback that the planning manager could not find adequate forecast quantities to consume. This process cannot physically consume more forecast than exists; however, it records the fact as Overconsumption. This entry shows as a zero original quantity and a negative current quantity.

You should also be aware of how consumption appears when you query a forecast. When a forecast entry is created, the quantity entered becomes the current quantity. This quantity also populates the original and total fields. When a sales order is loaded that consumes the forecast entry, querying the forecast shows that the current and original fields now reflect the fact that consumption has occurred. The current field is reduced by the quantity of the consuming sales order. The original field still shows the original forecast quantity.

Unconsumption is the process by which forecast consumption is reversed if there is a change in the sales order quantity or the sales order schedule date.

To further complicate the way in which consumption occurs, you have the option to consume forecasts as you use the forecast copy/merge process.

Tip

There are a lot of options available to manage forecast consumption. Ultimately, you will want to load forecast information into a master schedule. If this will be an MDS, you might also want to load sales orders. Using any or all of the options available (consuming forecast sets or consuming forecasts while copying or merging), you will need to get to a forecast that will represent anticipated demand for your products. In this way, you can be sure that adding sales orders to the MDS will not cause demand to be overstated.

MAINTAINING MASTER SCHEDULES

In the setup, you will have defined master schedule names. As described earlier, you can define Master Demand Schedules and Master Production Schedules. An MDS contains all sources of demand, including anticipated shipments. The Master Production Schedule (MPS) contains the supply to meet the demand in the MDS.

LOADING A MASTER SCHEDULE

You can load a master schedule from internal sources or with data from external sources through the Open Master Schedule Interface (see the section "Using Open Interfaces in This Application").

You can choose from a number of internal sources when loading a master schedule:

- *A forecast.* You can select a forecast to be used.
- *Interorganization Planned Orders.* These can be loaded from one or more of the organizations that are defined.
- *Sales Orders Only.* This can be all sales orders or only sales orders with scheduled dates from the load date forward.
- *Another MDS or MPS.* As with the forecast load process, you can apply a modification percentage to all entries in the source schedule when it is being loaded. You can also use carry-forward days (positive or negative) to shift the source schedule dates forward or backward by a specified number of days.
- *Source Lists.* These are described in the setup steps.

Some of the other options available when loading a schedule are the following:

- *Sales Order Demand Class.* You can limit the load to include sales orders with a specific demand class associated.
- *Demand Time Fence.* This gives you control over the loading of forecast and sales order entries using the demand time fence defined for an item (see the Material Requirements Planning section for a description of time fences).
- *Overwrite.* The overwrite options work in the same way as for merging and copying forecasts. The same warnings apply.
- *Start and Cutoff Date.* You can limit which forecast entries to load by specifying these dates.

- *Explode.* This determines whether the load process should explode items in an MDS. The level of explosion is set by the Max Bill Levels parameter in Oracle Bills of Material. This can be modified if you create manual MDS entries.

- *Consume, Backward Consumption Days, Forward Consumption Days, Outlier Percent and Quantity Type (original or current).* These options are related to the consumption of forecast during the load process. If you are loading sales orders and forecast, you can choose to consume during the load process or consume the forecast set and load the forecast with the consume option set to No.

MANUAL MASTER SCHEDULE ENTRIES

In every business situation, there will be exceptional requirements that are not driven by dependent demand. Typical examples would be the planning of spare requirements or manufacturing/engineering prototypes. In these cases, you have the option to load the demand into a forecast, or alternatively, you can create a manual master schedule entry (MDS or MPS).

> **Tip**
>
> Take care when using manual master schedule entries. If you create manual entries and then subsequently reload the schedule from forecasts/sales orders, there is a risk that you could overwrite the original manual entries. If this is not what you intend, choose the Overwrite option Same Source Only, which protects your entries with a manual source. Alternatively, you could keep your manual entries in a separate schedule and subsequently load them into the schedule you intend to use for planning.

SCHEDULE RELIEF

Schedule relief operates in a similar way to forecast consumption and is also controlled by the Planning Manager process. You control whether schedules should be relieved by setting the Relief flag when you define the schedule.

An MDS is relieved when sales order shipments occur. This prevents doubling-up of demand when sales orders are included in the MDS and it is used in a subsequent planning process. Every time a sales order shipment occurs, the planning manager relieves (reduces) the relevant MDS entry and flags it as having been relieved.

An MPS is relieved when a discrete job, interorganization shipment, purchase order, or purchase requisition is created. In the same way, this process prevents the MPS from overstating supply.

It is possible to stop the relief process by using the profile options MRP:Consume MDS and MRP:Consume MPS. By setting these profiles to No, you can temporarily prevent schedule relief from happening.

The MRP:MPS Relief Direction also affects the way in which MPS relief happens. The default on installation is Backward, then Forward. This means that the planning manager searches backward from the discrete job or purchase order date for the earliest quantity to relieve and then moves forward. You can change this profile to Forward Only, preventing earlier MPS entries from being relieved.

> **Tip**
>
> If you change this profile option, you need to stop the planning manager and restart it for the new profile setting to take effect.

REDUCE MPS

One additional tool to help maintain the MPS is the Reduce MPS item attribute, which assists with keeping the MPS quantities current. This attribute value is set in Oracle Inventory with the following values:

- *None*. The MPS is not reduced.
- *Past Due*. This reduces the MPS quantity to zero when the entry becomes past due.
- *Planning Time Fence*. This reduces the MPS quantity to zero if an entry violates the planning time fence set for the item.
- *Demand Time Fence*. This reduces the MPS quantity to zero if an entry violates the demand time fence set for the item.

GENERATING AN MPS PLAN

You can use an MDS or MPS as the source for an MPS planning run. The planning process uses the requirements in the source MPS/MDS to calculate the required supply. The output is an MPS plan with order and reschedule recommendations.

The process and options for generating an MPS plan are similar to those used for an MRP plan and are covered in the next section.

MATERIAL REQUIREMENTS PLANNING

The MRP planning process calculates net material requirements from gross requirements. The gross requirements can be obtained from an MPS or MDS. As mentioned earlier in this chapter, you might not require an MPS as part of your planning process if demand is stable and you do not need to manually control a production schedule. In this case, you can use an MDS as the source of requirements for the MRP planning process.

Deriving the time-phased net requirements in the MRP planning process involves considering on-hand quantities and scheduled receipts. The planning process also considers Master Scheduling/MRP item attributes and the BOM structure. The output from the planning process is an MRP plan containing planned orders, repetitive schedule suggestions, reschedule/cancellation recommendations for existing orders, and rate change suggestions for existing schedules.

GENERATING AN MRP

Use the Launch MRP or Launch MPS window to start the planning process. By default, the current date is displayed as the Anchor Date. You can select an earlier date to be used as the start of the repetitive planning periods. You can also choose a date for the plan horizon. By default, this date is derived using the number of months specified in the MRP:Cutoff Date Offset Months profile option. You can change this if you want.

You can set options that affect how the MRP planning (and MPS planning) process operates:

- *Overwrite.* You can choose All to generate a completely new plan. In this case, all firm planned orders and MPS entries are overwritten. If you choose None, firm planned orders are not overwritten. The third option is Outside Planning Time Fence, which overwrites firm planned orders outside the time fence for an item in an MRP plan. For an MPS plan, this option overwrites all MPS entries outside the planning time fence. Time fences are discussed in the next section.

- *Append Planned Orders.* This option has a significant effect on how much control is passed to the planning process to make recommendations. It works together with the Overwrite option. When you plan an MPS and choose not to overwrite entries, selecting Append Planned Orders does not generate reschedule recommendations or planned orders before the last date in the source schedule. You should only use this combination if you intend to manually manage the master schedule. In the case of MRP, this combination creates new planned orders but takes into account any firm planned orders that exist.

  If you choose the overwrite option to be All and select Append Planned Orders for an MPS or MRP plan, everything in the previous plan is deleted and replaced with new recommendations.

  Using the overwrite option Outside Planning Time Fence and selecting append planned orders means that the new plan only deletes planned entries beyond the planning time fence and replaces these with new recommendations.

  If you select None as the overwrite option and do not select append planned orders, the planning process does not generate new orders. With this combination, you decide how to best manage the MRP or MPS.

- *Demand Time Fence Control.* Select this option if you need to consider the demand time fence for items when generating the plan.

- *Net WIP.* Using this option enables you to consider discrete jobs or schedules in the planning process.

- *Net Reservations.* Selecting this option enables you to consider in the planning process inventory that has been reserved for orders.

- *Snapshot Lock Tables.* See the section "Defining Planning Parameters". You can override the default here.

- *Planning Time Fence Control.* If you choose this option, the planning process uses the planning time fences specified for items to control new order suggestions and reschedule recommendations.

- *Net Purchases.* Use this option to tell the planning process to consider existing purchase orders and requisitions when generating the plan.

- *Plan Safety Stock.* If you have set safety stock levels for your items and the stock will be MRP planned, you can choose this option. Item safety stock is controlled using the Safety Stock Method item attribute. It is either MRP planned as a percentage of gross requirements or manually specified through Oracle Inventory.

- *Plan Capacity.* You can choose this option to generate a capacity plan. You can also specify the bill of resources to be used and a simulation set (if you have created one). See the section "Using Oracle Capacity" later in this chapter.

- *Pegging.* If you need to use the graphical pegging features, select this option. The planning process generates the information required to peg supply back to the top level demand.

- *Material Scheduling Method.* See the section "Defining Planning Parameters." You can override the default here.

- *Planned Items.* See the section "Defining Planning Parameters." You can override the default here.

Order modifiers also affect how the planning process generates planned orders. By default, the planning process uses lot-for-lot sizing. This means that you get a single planned order to satisfy the net requirements for each day. Your business might already have planning policies established that dictate how orders should be created. Oracle Master Scheduling/MRP provides the following order modifiers to use in the planning process (which are set as item attributes; see Chapter 16):

- *Fixed Order Quantity.* You can manually assign an order quantity that will always be used for an item. If requirements on a single day fall short of this quantity, an order for the fixed quantity will be planned. If requirements on a single day are greater than the fixed quantity, two or more orders will be planned. You can use this attribute to set a fixed production rate for repetitive planned items.

- *Fixed Lot Multiplier.* You can assign a multiplier that will be used to create a single planned order. Requirements greater than or less than the multiplier will be rounded up to the next nearest multiple.

- *Minimum and Maximum Order Quantity.* You can use these attributes separately or together. With a minimum specified, when requirements are less than the minimum, a planned order is created for the minimum quantity. When requirements are greater than the maximum quantity on a single day, two or more orders are created with each order not exceeding the maximum quantity. For repetitive planned items, these attributes affect the daily rate.

■ *Fixed Days Supply.* When a number of days is specified for this attribute, the planning process aggregates requirements for this number of days into a single planned order.

■ *Round Order Quantities.* If you have fractional usage quantities for items, it is likely that the planning process will create planned orders with fractional quantities. By setting this attribute to Yes, the planning process will suggest a planned order quantity with the next largest whole number.

CONTROLLING THE PLAN

To assist with managing the planning process and reducing the amount of maintenance that is required, the Oracle Master Scheduling/MRP application includes some control options:

■ *Acceptable Early Days.* This control is set as an item attribute. You can specify a number of days that an order can be delivered before it is required. The planning process checks the value of this attribute and does not generate a reschedule-out recommendation if the early delivery date meets the value set in this attribute. Using this attribute, you can decide whether it is better to hold some extra inventory rather than continually review and implement reschedule recommendations.

■ *Time Fences.* Time fences enable you to protect portions of your plans based on policies you define. You specify time fences using item attributes. The time fence item attributes describe the limit of the time fence as being the plan date plus one of the following: cumulative manufacturing lead time, cumulative total lead time, total lead time, or a user defined number of days (see the section "Defining Planning Exception Sets" for a description of what these lead times mean). If you specify User Defined for a time fence, you must also specify the number of days using the time fence days attributes. There are three types of time fences available:

● *Demand Time Fence.* When you generate a plan and enable demand time fence control, the planning process only considers actual demand with the time fence. Forecast that falls within the time fence is ignored.

● *Planning Time Fence.* When planning time fence control is enabled, the planning process does not plan orders or make reschedule-in recommendations inside the planning time fence. You still receive reschedule-out recommendations.

● *Release Time Fence.* You can choose to have the planning process automatically release planned orders based on a release time fence. Within the time fence, purchase requirements are released as purchase requisitions and make requirements are released as discrete jobs. This process does not automatically release repetitive schedules.

■ *Firm Order Planning.* To further protect planned orders and actual orders, you can *firm* them. Firming an order fixes the quantity and date and, in most cases, prevents reschedule recommendations. Oracle Master Scheduling/MRP supports three types of firm order:

- *Firm Planned Order.* This is a planned order where the Firm flag set has been set using the planner workbench (see the section "Using the Planner Workbench"). When using firm planned orders, you can use the overwrite options during plan generation to prevent them from being overwritten. You do not receive reschedule recommendations for these orders if you rerun the planning process. By default, there is no time fence associated with firm planned orders. If you want to create a time fence for these types of orders, you should set the MRP:Firm Planned Order profile option to Yes.

- *Firm MRP Implemented Order.* When you use the planner workbench to implement planned orders as discrete jobs or purchase requisitions, you can choose to firm them without releasing them. If you rerun the planning process, you get reschedule recommendations for these orders until you release them.

- *Firm Scheduled Receipt.* When you release a firm implemented order, it becomes a firm scheduled receipt. Firm scheduled receipts cannot be affected by the overwrite options chosen when running the planning process. You do not receive reschedule recommendations for these orders if you rerun the planning process.

- Although you can firm purchase requisitions and discrete jobs through the planner workbench, you can also do this using the Oracle Purchasing and Oracle Work in Process applications.

If you are using Oracle Engineering, Engineering Change Orders (ECOs) can also affect the planning process. See Chapter 18 for an explanation of effective dates and use-up dates.

COPYING MPS AND MRP PLANS

You can copy MPS and MRP plans using the Copy Plan window. This provides you the flexibility to take a copy of a plan, modify it, and replan it while still maintaining the original. Using this approach, you can see the impact of changes to your plan and continue to modify it until you are satisfied with the results without changing the original.

USING THE PLANNER WORKBENCH

The planner workbench is provided with the Oracle Master Scheduling/MRP application to assist in the review of plan information and the implementation of plan recommendations.

REVIEWING PLAN INFORMATION

You can review the following plan information using the planner workbench:

■ *Resource.* You can review a plan's resource information by department or line.

- *Item On Hand Quantities.* You can verify the quantities on-hand for an item including nettable/non-nettable quantities and subinventory detail.

- *Item Supply/Demand.* With this view, you can see detailed supply and demand information generated for your plan.

- *Horizontal Plan View.* You can use this view to review your planning information in a horizontal format.

- *Enterprise Plan View.* The view provides an overview of all supply and demand for your items.

- *Graphical View.* You can graphically review supply and demand for items. You have the option to review supply and demand together or separately.

- *Snapshot versus Current.* When using the horizontal plan view, enterprise plan view, or graphical view, you can choose to use snapshot or current data. Snapshot data was valid at the time when the plan was generated. You can choose the current view option to see the effect of changes you have made since the plan was generated.

- *Planning Exceptions.* You can review a summary of exceptions created during the plan generation. Optionally, you can review detailed exceptions for items, orders, and resources. Some exceptions are only generated if an item has an exception set assigned. See the section "Defining Planning Exception Sets" for an explanation.

- *Graphical Pegging.* If you selected the pegging option when generating the plan, you trace the relationship between supply and demand and vice versa.

- *Available To Promise (ATP).* When you use the horizontal plan view, you can review ATP information for items. ATP is calculated for each item as: on hand inventory + supply˘ committed demand.

> **Note**
>
> This information is only calculated if the Calculate ATP item attribute is set to Yes for an item. The ATP information provided through Oracle Master Scheduling/MRP should be used for guidance only. It does not take account of any ATP rules that have been defined in Oracle Inventory and applied to an item (see Chapter 16). This ATP information is also available on the Planning Detail Report.

- *Capable To Promise (CTP).* CTP extends ATP by adding the availability of capacity to its calculation. You can review CTP information in your plan if you set the INV:Capable To Promise profile option in Oracle Inventory. You must also specify at the item level whether to check material and resource availability using the Check ATP item attribute. The item must also have a routing that specifies CTP.

NET CHANGE REPLAN

With the planner workbench, you also have the facility to replan changes to orders without generating a completely new MRP or MPS. This is called Net Change Replan. Oracle Master Scheduling/MRP offers two methods of doing this:

- *Batch Mode Planner.* This enables you to make all your changes and submit them for replanning as a batch. The advantage with this method is that while you are carrying out replanning, other users still have access to the plan information.

- *Online Planner.* The online planner enables you to replan changes by loading all plan data into memory while the session is active. Although this reduces the number of reads from the database tables during the session, it also prevents other users from accessing the plan data until you are finished.

IMPLEMENTING RECOMMENDATIONS

This section on the planner workbench has mostly concentrated on reviewing plan information. Most users spend the majority of their time doing this. When you are happy with the information in the plan, you can start to implement orders, schedules, and implement reschedule recommendations.

- *Firming planned orders.* You can use the workbench to firm planned orders. Order firming is discussed in the section "Generating an MRP."

- *Implementing a planned order.* Depending on how the Make or Buy item attribute is set, you can implement the order as a purchase requisition or discrete job. Planned orders for make items that are also purchasable can be implemented as discrete jobs or purchase requisitions. You select planned orders using the Supply/Demand window. For orders that are being implemented as discrete jobs, you can also modify the build sequence, schedule group, alternative BOM/routing, and demand class. The implemented orders can then be released using the Release Window.

- *Implementing Repetitive Schedules.* You can use the planner workbench to review suggested repetitive schedules and implement and release them. When selecting schedules to implement, you can modify the first and last unit completions dates, total schedule quantity, daily rate, and processing days. As you modify any of these values, the other values are automatically recalculated.

- *Releasing a Job or Schedule as Firm.* When releasing jobs or schedules, you can choose the firm option.

- *Rescheduling Scheduled Receipts.* During a planning run, there might be recommendations to reschedule existing purchase requisitions or discrete jobs. The reschedule recommendations are reschedule in, reschedule out, and cancel. Use the Supply/Demand window to select rescheduled jobs and requisitions for release. You cannot reschedule purchase order receipts from the planner workbench. This must be done in the Oracle Purchasing application (see Chapter 15, "Using Oracle Purchasing"). You can use the Order Reschedule Report to review purchase order reschedule recommendations.

USING SUPPLY CHAIN PLANNING

For organizations that consist of multiple manufacturing and distribution locations, Supply Chain Planning provides the capability to integrate planning across the entire enterprise.

With Supply Chain Planning, you can choose to generate plans for all organizations in the enterprise through one single planning run. You can optionally choose to have parts of the enterprise remain autonomous in the planning process.

Demand schedules for a supply-chain plan can include the Master Demand Schedules from all organizations. This incorporates all types of supply that are valid for an MDS (sales orders, forecasts, and so on). Supply schedules in a supply chain plan include Master Productions Schedules, Material Requirement Plans, and Distribution Requirement Plans from any or all organizations.

As mentioned earlier in the Setup section, you can create organizations to represent your customers and suppliers. In this way, supplier and customer organizations can be modeled and integrated in your supply chain. In the setup, you will also have considered the interorganization shipping network and the shipping methods. These affect how material moves between organizations within the supply chain. Supply-chain planning also provides sourcing rules and bills of distribution to define how replenishment takes place within the supply chain.

SOURCING RULES AND BILLS OF DISTRIBUTION

This section explains the use of sourcing rules and bills of distribution. These are used to describe the operation of your supply chain.

SOURCING RULES

Sourcing rules define how replenishment takes place in one organization or in all organizations. The replenishment source takes the form of one of the following:

- *Transfer From.* The item is sourced through an interorganization transfer from a specified organization.
- *Make At.* The item is manufactured at the organization.
- *Buy From.* The item is purchased from a supplier.

You can apply effective dates to the rule, but in the case of sourcing rules, this can only apply to the shipping organizations. Ranking can be used with sourcing rules to determine priorities. You can also assign an allocation percentage to be used when items are sourced from multiple organizations or suppliers. Time phasing can also be used to switch an item from make to buy within a sourcing rule. This is useful if you need to buy in or transfer an item from another organization while manufacturing is being started in the receiving organization.

BILLS OF DISTRIBUTION

Bills of distribution represent a combination of individual sourcing strategies that can be used across all organizations in the supply chain. Unlike sourcing rules, the sourcing strategies defined in bills of distribution can apply to different organizations at different times. As with sourcing rules, you can assign allocation percentages and rankings within a bill of distribution.

ASSIGNING SOURCING RULES AND BILLS OF DISTRIBUTION

To use sourcing rules and bills of distribution, you must create assignment sets to assign the rules to organizations and/or items in the organizations. Creating assignment sets is discussed in the section "Understanding Each Setup Task" at the start of this chapter.

GRAPHICAL VIEW

You can review assignment sets using an inquiry window. You can also view the indented where-used information and indented supply-chain bills for an item. This provides a graphical representation of the supply chain for an item.

MASTER SCHEDULING

Supply-chain master scheduling works in a similar way to the master scheduling process described earlier in this chapter. You can load a supply-chain MDS with multiple sources of demand from across the supply chain. You can use source lists (described in the Setup section) to specify the sources of data to be loaded into the supply-chain MDS.

A supply-chain MPS represents the supply required to meet the demand in a supply-chain MDS or another MPS. When you define a supply-chain MPS, you can specify whether it will be used to plan all organizations or specific organizations.

Supply-chain MPS plan generation works in a similar way to MRP/MPS plan generation. For the supply-chain MPS, you can specify organization-specific plan options if the plan covers multiple organizations.

MATERIAL REQUIREMENTS PLANNING AND DISTRIBUTION REQUIREMENTS PLANNING

The planning method for items is specified using the Planning Method item attribute (see Chapter 16). For any item, this enables you to specify whether it is any of the following:

- MRP Planned
- MPS Planned
- MRP/DRP Planned
- MPS/DRP Planned
- DRP Planned

When you define a supply-chain MRP or a DRP (see the Setup section), you can specify whether these plans apply to all organizations or specific organizations. As with supply-chain MPS generation, you can specify plan options that are specific to certain organizations. See the section "Material Requirements Planning" for a description of plan options.

SUPPLY CHAIN PLANNER WORKBENCH

When using supply-chain planning, the planner workbench provides you with additional options. Most of the information described in the section "Using the Planner Workbench" can be reviewed across all organizations, including the following:

- Horizontal Plan View
- Enterprise View
- Graphical Pegging

When implementing planned orders, suggested schedules, or reschedule recommendations, you can choose to do this across multiple organizations.

USING ORACLE ALERTS WITH THIS APPLICATION

Oracle Master Scheduling/MRP comes with two associated Oracle alerts. These alerts check forecast overconsumption based on a predetermined schedule. The alerts send an email message to a specified recipient or list of recipients when an overconsumption exception occurs.

You can use the Forecast Overconsumption—Summary alert to send a summary message or the Forecast Overconsumption—Detail alert to send detail information on the sales orders that caused the overconsumption.

To use either alert, it must be enabled and the alert scheduler must be running. Your system administrator can assist with the alert setup.

Tip	You should consider creating an additional alert to monitor the Planning Manager concurrent process. If this process fails, forecast consumption and schedule reliefs will not function. Although this was mentioned in the Setup section, it is important to repeat it here.

USING OPEN INTERFACES IN THIS APPLICATION

There are three open interfaces provided to work with the Oracle Master Scheduling/MRP application:

- *Open Forecast Interface*. You can import forecast entries from an external system into Oracle Master Scheduling/MRP using this interface. The entries are validated using your current setup.

- *Open Master Schedule Interface.*Master Schedule data can be imported into Oracle Master Scheduling/MRP using this interface. Again, the entries are validated using your current setup.

- *Open Forecast Entries Applications Program Interface.*This differs from the Open Forecast Interface in that it allows an external system to insert, update, or delete entries in an existing forecast.

As with all other open interfaces provided with the Oracle applications, you might need to write programs to do the following:

- Extract data from the external system

- Format it as required for use in the open interface tables

- Insert the data in the interface tables

Full details of the operation of the interfaces can be found in the Oracle reference *Oracle Manufacturing, Distribution, Sales and Service Open Interfaces Manual*.

TAKING ADVANTAGE OF BEST PRACTICES

In many organizations, master scheduling and material requirement planning generates a lot of information. Sometimes, this can become too much for a planner to review and analyze. There is always the risk that an important piece of information will be overlooked.

To minimize the effect of information overload, you should leverage some of the tools provided in the Oracle Master Scheduling/MRP application:

- *Planner Workbench*. Apart from the productivity benefit of being able to review and implement recommendations through a single common interface, the workbench also provides the capability to filter information using "finds." You should also consider placing items with common planning requirements under unique planner codes. The planner code does not have to be a person; it can be used to represent any particular grouping that you might need. You should also consider the planning horizon being used in plan generation. If it extends too far, there is a risk that too much data will be generated, and the information might also be unreliable.

- *Exception Sets.*You can minimize the volume of data to be reviewed in the planner workbench by creating and assigning exception sets. You can use the exception messages to search through the plan data to find exceptions that need to be dealt with as a priority.

- *Planning Reports.*Many of the planning reports provided with the application are most useful if you need to see detail for a particular forecast, schedule, plan, or item. The Planned Order report and Order Reschedule Report provide similar information to

PART
III

CH
20

that presented on the planner workbench. You can use the report parameters to limit the volume of data to be reviewed. For example, use the Out Days and In Days filters to limit orders being displayed on the Order Reschedule Report. Do you really need to see all orders that are being rescheduled out by one day?

UNDERSTANDING KEY REPORTS

Table 20.3 lists the reports provided with the Oracle Master Scheduling/MRP application.

TABLE 20.3 ORACLE MASTER SCHEDULING/MRP REPORTS

Report Name	Description
Audit Information Report	Shows exceptions generated when predefined audit criteria are applied to your data. See the Setup section.
Current Projected On Hand vs. Projected Available Graphical Report*	Use this report to produce agraphical display of the current projected on hand versus projected available inventory. You can use this report for MPS, MRP, and DRP plans.
Demand vs. Replenishment Graphical Report*	Shows a graphical summary of material availability for MPS, MRP, or DRP plans.
Financial Analysis Report*	Provides a costed summary of a DRP or MRP plan.
Forecast Comparison Report	Use this report to compare forecasts based on quantities or quantities and costs.
Forecast Detail Report	Shows the forecast detail for an individual forecast or a forecast set. You can display this report in a horizontal or vertical format.
Late Order Report*	This report shows planned or actual orders that are past due in a specified plan.
Master Schedule Comparison Report	Use this report to compare master schedules based on quantities or quantities and costs.
Master Schedule Detail Report	Provides a horizontal or vertical view of the detail within a master schedule.
Master Schedule Status Report*	Shows shipping activity for an MDS or production activity for an MPS.
Order Reschedule Report*	Use this report to view reschedule recommendations generated by an MPS, MRP, or DRP plan for discrete jobs, purchase orders, and purchase requisitions.
Planned Order Report*	This report shows planned orders recommended during plan generation.

TABLE 20.3   CONTINUED

Report Name	Description
Planning Detail Report*	Shows the detailed information related to an MPS, MRP, or DRP plan. You can choose to view this information in a horizontal or vertical format.
Planning Exception Sets Report	Lists the planning exception sets that you have defined.
Planning Manager Worker (once-a-day tasks)	Manually submits the planning manager worker. The planning manager also automatically submits this process.
Planning Parameters Report	Prints your planning parameters.
CRP Reports	You can submit the following capacity reports from Oracle Master Scheduling/MRP:
	CRP Rate Based Report
	CRP Routing Based Report
	RCCP Rate Based Report
	RCCP Routing Based Report

* These reports are also available as supply-chain versions.

FROM HERE

When implementing the Oracle Master Scheduling/MRP application, you should also review the material in the following sections or chapters:

- "Using Oracle Capacity" (the next section of this chapter)
- Chapter 16, "Using Oracle Inventory"
- Chapter 15, "Using Oracle Purchasing"
- Chapter 18, "Using Oracle Engineering and Bills of Material"
- Chapter 21, "Using Oracle Work in Process"

USING ORACLE CAPACITY

The Oracle Capacity application provides methods to enable you to monitor the utilization of available capacity. You can do this using the following:

- *Rough Cut Capacity Planning (RCCP).* This is used in conjunction with your master schedules. RCCP is typically used to check the utilization of critical resources over a long period.

- *Capacity Requirements Planning (CRP).* This is used with material requirements plans to check the utilization of resources. CRP considers scheduled receipts and on-hand inventory when calculating capacity requirements. It is typically used for reviewing capacity utilization in the near term.

For both RCCP and CRP, you can choose to plan capacity based on resources that have been assigned to operations on routings (routing-based) or by production lines (rate-based). Capacity for routing-based plans is in hours per resource per week. Capacity for rate-based plans is stated as production rate per week per production line.

Figure 20.2 shows the major relationships between Oracle Capacity and the other Oracle applications. The relationships affect the setup and operation of the Oracle Capacity application.

Figure 20.2
Capacity relationship to other applications.

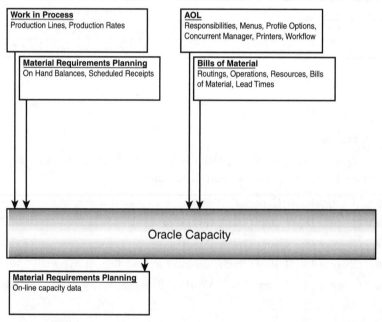

REVIEWING TOP ENHANCEMENT REQUESTS

Companies using the Oracle Capacity application have identified areas that could be improved. These are some of the enhancements that have been requested through the Oracle Applications User Group (OAUG):

- The process to load Bills of Resources automatically should also load assemblies that do not have an associated Bill of Material.

- The Rough Cut Capacity Planning (RCCP) process should consider Work In Process requirements as well as master schedule entries.

- Bills of Resources should not show phantom subassembly routing resources.

CONFIGURING THE APPLICATION

The following section describes the setup tasks required to configure the Oracle Capacity application. If you are implementing release 11 of the applications, you can use the Oracle Applications Implementation Wizard to manage the setup tasks.

UNDERSTANDING EACH SETUP TASK

This section provides detail on each of the setup tasks and the order in which they should be performed.

To use Oracle Capacity, you must first complete the setup for the following:

- *Oracle Inventory.* All required setups must be completed.

- *Oracle Bills of Material.* You should complete all the required setup steps. Define your Bills of Materials and routings. You should also calculate the routing lead times.

> **Tip**
>
> Completing the setup of these applications enables you to run some of the Oracle Capacity reports and use some of the online inquiries. To use all the available analysis tools, you should continue to complete the setup steps that follow.

DEFINING RESOURCE GROUPS (OPTIONAL)

You can create resource groups and assign resources to these groups in Oracle Bills of Material (see Chapter 18). Because resource groups can be used when loading a bill of resources to subsequently create an RCCP, you should group resources based on the way you intend to generate or use your capacity plans.

DEFINING SIMULATION SETS (OPTIONAL)

Simulation sets enable you to model the effect of resource changes on your plans by grouping the changes. When you have defined a set, you use it when assigning resources for a department in Oracle Bills of Material. You have the option to define capacity changes at this time. These can be the following:

- Add or delete a day

- Add or delete capacity for a shift

While making these changes, you can select a simulation set to associate with the capacity change. This simulation set can then be used when reviewing RCCP and CRP plans. You can

PART

III

CH

20

also specify the simulation set when generating an MRP or MPS plan if you choose the Plan Capacity option.

DEFINING MULTIDEPARTMENT RESOURCES (OPTIONAL)

When setting up resources in Oracle Bills of Material, you can assign a resource across multiple departments. When you generate an RCCP or CRP, you can choose to aggregate the resource usage across all departments using the resource. See Chapter 18 for information on defining resources.

HORIZONTAL PLAN DISPLAY OPTIONS

Options are available to control the way in which the horizontal plan display works for both CRP and RCCP. You can define the options using the Preferences window under View RCCP or View CRP.

SETTING PROFILE OPTIONS

The following profile options can be set for Oracle Capacity:

- *CRP:Default Bill of Resource Set Name.* This profile is set at the user level. You can enter a bill of resource set name that will default for the users any time they use a Bill of Resource window.

- *CRP:Spread Discrete Requirements.* You can select to have the discrete job load placed on the first day of an operation or spread over the total length of the operation. This profile is set at the site level. There is no default value when the application is installed.

Your system administrator typically maintains profile option settings.

PROCESSING TRANSACTIONS

The following section covers the main transactions involved in using Oracle Capacity.

ROUGH CUT CAPACITY PLANNING (RCCP)

As explained earlier, the intention of RCCP is to provide an overall picture of capacity utilization for critical resources. Unlike CRP, it does not include scheduled receipts and on-hand quantities when calculating capacity.

CREATING BILLS OF RESOURCES (OPTIONAL)

To gather resource requirements for RCCP, you must create a bill of resources. The bill of resources shows all resource required to manufacture a particular item. Bills of resources apply to both rate-based and routing-based capacity planning. You can choose to load the bill of resources automatically or add the items manually. The automatic process explodes through the BOM structure for an item and gathers all resource requirements. When using the load process, only current resources are considered.

The load process can be initiated for a single item or a range of items. If you have defined product families in Oracle Bills of Material, you can use these to load a bill of resources. The resource requirements for each of the family members is rolled up in the bill. You can then review capacity for the product family and the product family members.

You can use resource groups to limit the resources loaded into the bill to those that belong to a particular group.

ROUTING-BASED RCCP

Routing-based RCCP capacity utilization is calculated as follows:

Capacity utilization = Required Hours/Available Hours

The bill of resource information and the details for the master schedule entry are used to establish the required hours. Available hours are calculated using the resource information defined in Oracle Bills of Material (capacity units and availability).

RATE-BASED RCCP

Rate-based RCCP capacity utilization is calculated as follows:

Capacity utilization = Required Rate/Available Rate

Bill of resource information and the repetitive schedule allocation process are used to allocate the master schedule rate to production lines to arrive at a required rate. The available rate is calculated using the production line information set up in Oracle Work in Process (maximum hourly rate and line availability).

VIEWING RCCP

You can view RCCP capacity requirements for a selected master schedule. You can also use the simulation sets described earlier to see the effect of capacity changes for the schedule. If you choose the routing-based view, you can enter a resource and view its capacity utilization for the selected master schedule. Choosing the rate-based view enables you to specify a production line and view its capacity utilization for the selected master schedule. You can also view this information graphically by exporting the data to Excel.

USING RCCP DATA

When you review the data for rate-based or routing-based RCCP, you can determine situations where resources or production lines are underloaded or overloaded. You can use this information to balance capacity by modifying the usage of resources, adding additional resources, adding shifts, adding production lines, increasing production line rates, and so on.

PART

III

CH

20

CAPACITY REQUIREMENTS PLANNING (CRP)

CRP analyzes capacity utilization for short-term requirements, taking into account scheduled receipts and on-hand inventory balances.

ROUTING-BASED CRP

Routing-based CRP utilization is calculated as follows:

Capacity Utilization = Required Hours/Available Hours

The required hours are calculated using dates and quantities generated by the planning process for planned orders, discrete jobs, and repetitive schedules. The available hours are calculated based on the resource availability information defined in Oracle Bills of Material.

RATE-BASED CRP

Rate-based CRP utilization is calculated as follows:

Capacity Utilization = Required Rate/Available Rate

The required rate is calculated using actual rate information created by the planning process. The available rate uses the production line information that was defined in Oracle Bills of Material (maximum hourly rate and production line availability).

VIEWING CRP

Before you can review CRP data, you must generate a plan with the Plan Capacity option selected. When generating a plan, you can also choose to apply a simulation set. See the section "Generating an MRP" in "Using Oracle Master Scheduling/MRP."

The view options are similar to those used for RCCP. You can view information for resource utilization using the routing-based option and production line utilization using the rate-based option.

As with RCCP data, you can export your CRP data to Excel to view it graphically.

> **Tip**
>
> In release 11, you can also view capacity information online from the planner workbench. See "Using Oracle Master Scheduling/MRP" earlier in this chapter for an explanation.

UNDERSTANDING KEY REPORTS

Table 20.4 lists the reports provided with the Oracle Capacity application.

TABLE 20.4 ORACLE CAPACITY REPORTS

Report Name	Description
Bill of Resources Report	Prints your Bills of Resources.
CRP Rate-Based Report	Shows detailed capacity information for repetitively planned items that are manufactured on rate-based production lines for a selected material requirements plan.
CRP Routing-Based Report	Shows the detailed capacity plan and resource availability information for a selected material requirements plan.
RCCP Rate-Based Report	Prints a rough cut capacity plan for repetitively planned items that are manufactured on rate-based production lines for a selected master schedule and bill of resources.
RCCP Routing-Based Report	Shows the rough-cut capacity plan and resource availability information for a selected master schedule.

FROM HERE

When implementing the Oracle Capacity application, you should also review the material in the following section and chapter:

- "Using Oracle Master Scheduling/MRP" (the first section of this chapter)
- Chapter 18 "Using Oracle Engineering and Bills of Material"

TROUBLESHOOTING

- The memory-based planning engine can be problematic to set up and keep running consistently. It is worth the effort because it offers significant improvement in processing time over the standard planning engine, even with modest computing power. If you need assistance, Oracle Support can provide additional documentation to help with the configuration. Check the Oracle MetaLink Web site.
- If you are experiencing inconsistencies in master schedule relief or forecast consumption, you should verify that the Planning Manager is running. If not, you should investigate any errors and restart the Planning Manager.

CHAPTER 21

USING ORACLE WORK IN PROCESS

Oracle Work In Process provides a comprehensive set of tools to enable most organizations to manage their manufacturing operations. Over time, Oracle has expanded the capabilities of this application to provide support for "mixed mode" manufacturing. This enables organizations to continue to operate traditional discrete manufacturing (where appropriate) but also to incorporate elements of repetitive and flow manufacturing.

Figure 21.1 shows how Oracle Work In Process relates to the other Oracle Applications. These relationships affect the setup and operation of the Oracle Work In Process application.

Figure 21.1
This diagram shows how the Oracle Work In Process application interacts with the other Oracle Applications.

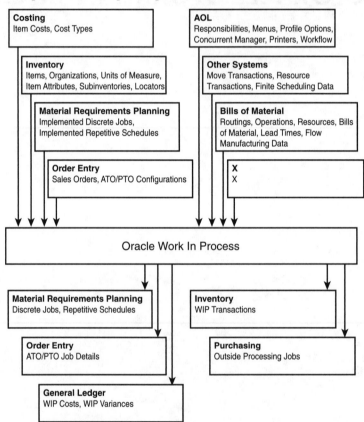

DISCOVERING NEW FEATURES IN RELEASE 11

Quite a number of new features have been added to release 11 of Oracle Work In Process (WIP):

■ *Integration with Projects and Tasks Set Up in Oracle Projects.* If you operate in a project-manufacturing environment, the application now enables you to define, track, and cost jobs by project. Projects and tasks are set up in Oracle Projects.

- *Average Costing in a Manufacturing Implementation.* Average costing for manufacturing transactions is available (See Chapter 19, "Using Oracle Cost Management").

- *Flow Manufacturing.* With release 11, Oracle has introduced tools to support flow manufacturing concepts. Flow manufacturing is based on "pulling" the product and material through the manufacturing operation. To ensure flexibility, manufacturing lines are created and balanced to support a changing mix of product. Manufacturing is organized by grouping products into families that require similar manufacturing processes. There is further discussion of flow manufacturing in Chapter 18, "Using Oracle Engineering and Bills of Material."

  To support this approach, Oracle has made available Work Orderless Completions. Rather than creating discrete jobs or repetitive schedules, you can base product manufacturing on a forecasted daily production rate and use work orderless completions to manage the backflush of pull *and* push components. (WIP supply types are discussed later in this chapter.) Any resource and overhead costs associated with the assembly can be collected from the flow routing when the backflush transaction occurs.

- *Saving Simulated Discrete Jobs.* In previous releases of Oracle Work In Process, you had the capability to simulate discrete jobs. Unfortunately, after the simulation was complete, the discrete job had to be created from scratch. In release 11, WIP now provides a facility to create discrete jobs from your simulations.

- *Viewing ATP Status of Discrete Job Component Requirements.* A facility is now available to check component ATP information when creating, simulating, or viewing a discrete job. In previous releases, checking of onhand balances was available, but this did not provide any visibility of quantities that were allocated to other jobs and schedules.

- *Job Details Can Be Viewed Online as Jobs Are Defined.* It is now possible to view component material requirements, operations, and resource requirements from the same window that is used to define and update jobs.

- *View Pending Job Transactions.* You can view pending discrete job transactions that could prevent you from purging, closing, or changing the status of a discrete job. Until now, the WIP application only provided a warning that there were pending transactions.

- *Restricted Delete on Outside Processing Resources when a PO Has Been Created.* WIP will prevent you from deleting resources in use at outside processing operations if a purchase requisition or purchase order has been created.

- *WIP Scheduling Interface.* An open interface has been added to allow information from external systems to schedule discrete jobs. This is discussed later in this chapter.

- *Improved Material Transaction Processing.* A number of improvements have been made to the way WIP material transactions work.

PART

III

CH

21

CRITICAL IMPLEMENTATION FACTORS

Before embarking on an implementation of Work In Process, the topics addressed in the following sections should be given consideration.

ISSUES AND GAPS

Companies implementing and using WIP have identified some issues and gaps with the application. With release 11, Oracle has incorporated additional functionality that addresses some of the gaps. Perhaps most notable is the introduction of functionality to allow organizations to use flow manufacturing techniques.

REVIEWING TOP ENHANCEMENT REQUESTS

Some of the concerns that are being addressed through the Oracle Applications User Group (OAUG) include

- There is no physical inventory facility available to use with Oracle Work In Process. This makes it tedious to count components and assemblies in a discrete manufacturing environment.

- It is not possible to create inventory reservations for WIP component requirements.

- Outside processing jobs do not complete or close automatically when assemblies are received from the supplier.

- There is currently no warning provided by the WIP application if assemblies are overcompleted on a discrete job. It is still possible to monitor the status of job completions using standard or custom developed reports. However, this requires frequent review by the Planner or Scheduler.

- The WIP application does not automatically consider substitute components when there is not adequate stock available of the primary component.

- If there are pull components on an assembly, there is no automated check of the onhand quantities before it is released. The Scheduler or Planner must review the balances onhand through an online inquiry.

- In an Assemble to Order (ATO) manufacturing environment, there is a significant amount of manual maintenance required to keep Sales Orders and Discrete Jobs synchronized.

REQUIRED SETUP TASKS

The following section describes the tasks required to set up the Work In Process application.

CONFIGURING THE APPLICATION

To ensure that the application works correctly for your business, it must be configured to suit your needs. Before configuring Work In Process, you should complete the required set up steps for Inventory, Bills Of Material, Engineering, Cost Management, Projects and MRP.

RESOLVING CRITICAL SETUP ISSUES

To set up the Work In Process application, you need to carefully consider the manufacturing approaches that exist in your organization. The Oracle WIP application will support the following:

- Discrete Manufacturing
- Repetitive Manufacturing
- Project Manufacturing
- Assemble To Order Manufacturing
- Flow Manufacturing

To further complicate things, WIP can also support combinations of these manufacturing approaches. The implementation team needs to find the best fit from these approaches and plan the setup accordingly.

The WIP application is tightly integrated with the Oracle Inventory and Oracle Cost Management applications. It is essential that there is adequate Cost Accounting input to the setup of this application.

TABLE SHOWING SETUP TASKS

Table 21.1 outlines the setup tasks to be completed for Oracle Work In Process.

TABLE 21.1   ORACLE WORK IN PROCESS SETUP TASKS

Setup Task Name	Required?
Define Work In Process Parameters	Yes
Define WIP Accounting Classes	Yes
Set WIP Profile Options	Yes
Define Production Lines	No
Associate Lines and Assemblies	No
Define Schedule Groups	No
Define Employees	No
Define Labor Rates	No
Define Shop Floor Statuses	No

PART

III

CH

21

TABLE 21.1   CONTINUED

Setup Task Name	Required?
Define Job and Schedule Documents	No
Define Operation Documents	No

Tip

Some of these steps are conditionally required based on the manufacturing approach that you decide to use. Further information on the dependencies is provided in the sections that follow.

UNDERSTANDING EACH SETUP TASK

This section describes in detail the tasks that need to be performed and some of the key decisions that you will need to make. Because of dependencies between setup steps, these need to be completed in the sequence outlined in the following sections.

DEFINING WORK IN PROCESS PARAMETERS

The selections made for the WIP parameters depend very much on how your organization runs its manufacturing operations.

For discrete manufacturing (for example, building product in batches or lots), the following need to be defined:

- *Default Discrete Class.* You can specify a WIP accounting class that will default when you create a discrete job without choosing a specific class. To set this value, you must first create the WIP accounting class you want to use as the default. The creation of WIP accounting classes is discussed in a subsequent setup step. This is the one case where you need to skip to a later step to complete the setup properly.

- *Default Lot Number Type Parameter.* If you are using lot numbers in association with your WIP jobs, you can specify how the lot number is determined. It can either be based on the job name or use the lot number rules that have been defined in Oracle Inventory (see Chapter 16, "Using Oracle Inventory").

- *Respond to Sales Orders.* This parameter works in conjunction with Assemble to Order (ATO) functionality. Sales Orders for Assemble to Order configurations are linked with discrete jobs. You can set this parameter to determine how your jobs will be affected by changes to the sales orders they are linked to:
  - *Never.* Jobs will not be affected.
  - *Always.* Unreleased jobs will be placed on hold if there are changes made to the sales order configuration.
  - *When Linked 1 to 1.* Changes to the sales order configuration will place the discrete job on hold, but only if the sales order-to-discrete job relationship is unique.

For Repetitive Schedules, you need to set the following parameters:

- *Recognize Period Variances.* You can determine which schedules qualify for having cost variances posted to the General Ledger. This can either be all repetitive schedules or just those that have a status of "Cancelled" or "Complete - No charges".

- *Autorelease Days.*This sets the timeframe that WIP uses to search for a schedule to automatically release when the previous schedule is completed.

If you will be using Available to Promise (ATP) checking for components, you should select the component ATP rule to be used. These rules are set up in Oracle Inventory (see Chapter 16).

If you have defined your inventory organization as an "Average Costing" organization (see Chapter 19, "Using Oracle Cost Management"), there are some additional WIP parameters that you can set:

- *Default Completion Cost Source.* This parameter determines how resource costs will be charged when assemblies are completed from a job into their completion inventory. This can be System Calculated, which is dependent on the setting of System Option (see the next parameter), or User Defined. User Defined enables you to choose a cost type that you have created. The value for this parameter is determined by the Cost Type parameter, which is explained later.

- *System Option.* If you have chosen System Calculated for Default Completion Cost Source, you must choose one of the following:
  - *Use Actual Resources.* The resource costs are calculated based on actual costs.
  - *Use Predefined Resources.* The resource costs are calculated based on predefined resource costs.

- *Cost Type.* If you have chosen User Defined for the Default Completion Cost Source, you need to select a cost type for this parameter. For an explanation of how to define a Cost Type, see Chapter 19.

- *Auto Compute Final Completion.* Setting this parameter to Yes sets the default for the WIP completion transaction. When the last assembly on a job is completed, choosing this option ensures that there is no positive cost balance left on the job. The default can be changed when the WIP transaction is being processed.

The following parameters also affect the way in which Move Transactions are processed:

PART
III

CH
21

- *Shop Floor Status for PO Move Resources.* This parameter affects the behavior of transactions for jobs with outside processing operations. You can assign a "no move" status to ensure that the only way assemblies can be moved from the queue of an outside processing operation is with a Purchase Order receipt. This ensures that quantities moved into and out of the queue step will match.

- *Require Scrap Account.* By setting this parameter to Yes, you can force the user to provide an account to be charged for scrap transactions from your discrete jobs. If you do not set this parameter, it becomes optional for the user to provide an account number.

> **Tip**
> If you process a scrap transaction without specifying an account, the value of the transaction will be associated with the job. You will have to treat this as a variance when the job is closed or at the end of an accounting period.

- *Allow Creation of New Operations.* You can determine whether additional operations can be added for a discrete job when a move transaction is being processed.

- *Allow Moves Over No Move Shop Floor Transactions.* You can prevent users from processing moves between "no move" intraoperation steps. The "Move Transactions: Allow Skipping Over No Move Statuses" security function can also be set for an individual user.

Backflush transactions will be affected by the settings of these parameters:

- *Supply Subinventory.* You can specify the default WIP supply subinventory to be used for backflush transactions.

> **Tip**
> Oracle Manufacturing provides a number of ways to specify the default WIP supply subinventory to be used. It can be set at the WIP application level, on the Bill of Material, or in the Item attributes. Consider carefully at which level you will set the default. In some cases, it might be appropriate to have all material pulled from one subinventory for a particular assembly, and this can be set on the BOM. In other cases, you might want to default the subinventory based on the type of component, and this can be set with the item attributes (see Chapter 16, "Using Oracle Inventory" and Chapter 18, "Using Oracle Engineering and Bills of Material").

- *Supply Locator.* This parameter applies to a subinventory that is under locator control (see Chapter 16). The same considerations apply as when setting up a default WIP supply subinventory.

- *Lot Selection Method.* If you are using lot control for items (see Chapter 16), you can determine how a backflush transaction will select the component lot to process. This can be manual, based on the lot expiration date, or First In First Out, using the receipt date.

- *Lot Verification.* Lots can be >verified when backflushing to ensure that the lots being selected are the ones that were actually used during the manufacturing process. This can be done for *all* lots, or you can choose to verify the *exceptions* only and assign lots to these manually.

You can set the intraoperation steps to be enabled for use in WIP. The "Queue" step is always enabled.

> **Tip**
> Regardless of how you set this parameter, the "To Move" step will be enabled at the last operation in a routing to allow completion of assemblies to inventory.

DEFINING WIP ACCOUNTING CLASSES

To collect job or schedule cost information and any cost variances that might arise during manufacture, you can create WIP accounting classes.

The classes themselves should be based on some logical grouping that makes sense in your business—for example, product families, subassemblies, final assemblies, and so on. These enable you to specify the valuation and variance accounts that should be used for a particular job or schedule. You must assign a WIP accounting class to all discrete jobs. As discussed previously, you can assign a default WIP accounting class to be used for discrete jobs. This can be changed when the job is being created.

> **Tip**
> In release 11 of Oracle Work In Process, you can use Product Line Accounting to link a default WIP accounting class with a product line category set. In this way, you can ensure that specific valuation and variance accounts are used when discrete jobs or schedules are created for a particular product line. For more information on this feature see Chapter 19.

> **Tip**
> You should complete the setup of WIP accounting classes with the assistance of a Cost Accountant. This step has significant implications for the operation of Oracle Cost Management.

PART
III

CH
21

WIP accounting classes use the following Valuation Accounts:

- *Material.* If you have set up a standard costing organization, this account will record WIP material transactions at standard cost. If your organization uses average costing, material transactions will be charged to this account based on the current average cost.

- *Material Overhead.* Using standard costing, this account will be charged based on standard cost when material with an associated overhead is issued to a schedule or job. With average costing, the current average cost will be used.

- *Resource.* This account is debited when resources are charged to a job or schedule and is credited when assemblies are completed. With standard costing, resources are charged based on the standard cost. If you are using average costing, they are charged based on the current resource rate.

- *Outside Processing.* In a standard costing organization, outside processing costs are charged to this account based on the purchase order price or the standard cost, depending on how you have set up outside processing. For average costing organizations, the current resource rate or the PO cost is used.

- *Overhead.* Any overhead costs associated with a resource or department are charged to this account. It is charged at standard cost when resources are used on a job or schedule and is credited when assemblies are completed from a job.

You also define variance accounts to track the cost differences that arise when costs charged to a valuation account do not match the credits to that account when assemblies are completed from a job or schedule. Oracle WIP supports variance accounts for the following:

- Material
- Resource
- Outside Processing
- Overhead
- Standard Cost

SETTING THE PROFILE OPTIONS

Table 21.2 shows the profile options that directly affect the operation of the Oracle Work In Process.

TABLE 21.2   ORACLE WORK IN PROCESS PROFILE OPTIONS

Profile Option Name	Required?	Manufacturing Approach*	Level**	Comment
TP:WIP Background Shop Floor Material Processing	Yes	ALL	SARU	Default is On-Line Processing.

TABLE 21.2 CONTINUED

Profile Option Name	Required?	Manufacturing Approach*	Level**	Comment
TP:WIP Completion Material Processing	Yes	Dis, Rep, Prj	SARU	Default is On-Line Processing.
TP:WIP Completion Transaction Form	Yes	Dis, Rep, Prj	SARU	Default is On-Line Processing.
TP:WIP Completion Transactions First Field	Yes	Dis, Rep, Prj	SARU	Default is Job.
TP:WIP Concurrent Message Level	Yes	Dis, Rep, Prj	SARU	Default is Message Level 0.
TP:WIP Material Transaction Form	Yes	Dis, Rep, Prj	SARU	Default is On-Line Processing.
TP:WIP Material Transactions First Field	Yes	Dis, Rep, Prj	SARU	Default is Job.
TP:WIP Move Transaction	Yes	Dis, Rep, Prj	SARU	Default is On-Line Processing.
TP:WIP Move Transactions First Field	Yes	Dis, Rep, Prj	SARU	Default is Job.
TP:WIP Move Transaction Quantity Default	Yes	Dis, Rep, Prj	SARU	Default is None.
TP:WIP Operation Backflush Setup	Yes	Dis, Rep, Prj	SARU	Default is On-Line Processing.
TP:WIP Resource Transactions First Field	Yes	ALL	SARU	Default is Job.
TP:WIP Shop Floor Material Processing	Yes	ALL	SARU	Default is On-Line Processing.

TABLE 21.2   CONTINUED

Profile Option Name	Required?	Manufacturing Approach*	Level**	Comment
TP:WIP:Work orderless Completion Default	Yes	WO	SARU	Default is Unscheduled. This profile option does not work with R11. It will be used in future releases.
WIP:Default Job Start Date	Yes	Dis, Prj	SARU	Default is No.
WIP:Define Discrete Job Form	Yes	Dis, Prj	SARU	Default is Interactive Definition.
WIP:Discrete Job Prefix	Yes	Dis, Prj, WO	SARU	Default is None.
WIP:Exclude Open ECOs	Yes	ALL	SARU	Default is Yes.
WIP:Job Name Updateable	Yes	Dis, Prj	SARU	Default is Yes. An individual user can not set this option himself. It can be set by the System Administrator for a specific user.
WIP:Move Completion Default	Yes	Dis, Rep, Prj	SARU	Default is No.
WIP:Requirement Nettable Option	Yes	ALL	SARU	Default is View all subinventories.
WIP:See Engineering Items	Yes	ALL	SARU	Default is Yes.

*Manufacturing Approach—Discrete, Repetitive, Project, Work Orderless. ** Levels can be Site, Application, Responsibility, or User. The system administrator sets most profile options.*

DEFINING PRODUCTION LINES

A production line represents a unique collection of departments, operations and/or manufacturing cells used to manufacture your products. Oracle WIP enables you to create production lines and then link them with repetitive schedules, discrete jobs, and work orderless completions.

The specifics of defining a production line to be used with repetitive schedules are covered later in this chapter.

Note Production lines can be assigned when you create a discrete job. This facility is available for information purposes only.

DEFINING REPETITIVE ASSEMBLIES

If you plan on using repetitive manufacturing, you must identify the repetitive assemblies and then assign them to one or more production lines. This is discussed later in this chapter.

Tip If you have installed Oracle Master Scheduling/MRP, you must set the Repetitive Planning item attribute to Yes in Oracle Inventory for your repetitive assemblies. This forces the planning process to plan your assemblies based on daily production rates rather than discrete quantities. Item attributes are discussed in Chapter 16. Repetitive Planning is discussed in Chapter 20.

DEFINING SCHEDULE GROUPS

You can create Schedule groups, which can be assigned to discrete jobs. Schedule groups can be a useful way to associate similar jobs with each other—for example, jobs being built to satisfy orders for a particular customer.

Note Schedule groups also have an application in Build Sequencing, which is available in release 11 of Oracle WIP. You can set a sequence for jobs that have been associated with a particular schedule group. One application would be to create a schedule group for jobs related to a customer and then use sequencing to prioritize the completion of these jobs.

DEFINING EMPLOYEES

If you need to collect labor costs based on "person" resources, you must define the employees. If you have installed Oracle Human Resources Management Systems, you can define the employees through that application; otherwise Oracle WIP provides a form to do this.

DEFINING LABOR RATES

For each employee that you define, you can enter an hourly labor rate. In fact, you can assign several hourly rates per employee with different effectivity dates. When you use actual costing, Oracle WIP uses the current rate when costing your person resource transactions.

PART

III

CH

21

DEFINING SHOP FLOOR STATUSES

Shop Floor Statuses can be created and used to control move transactions within your manufacturing operation. These statuses can be assigned to the intraoperation steps of a routing. A typical application would be to create a Quality Hold status. You can decide whether you want to prevent move transactions when this status is assigned or you want to use it for information only.

DEFINING JOB AND SCHEDULE DOCUMENTS

Release 11 of Oracle WIP provides the facility to attach a variety of file types to your discrete jobs and repetitive schedules. These could be drawings, images, flowcharts, manuals, and so on.

You also have the option to create a catalog of standard documents that you can choose from when defining a job or schedule. If these exist, you can assign them at this setup step.

DEFINING OPERATION DOCUMENTS

As with Job and Schedule Documents, you can assign documents to Operations. At this setup step, you can define standard documents that you can choose from when defining an operation. A typical application would be assigning operation instructions for a piece of equipment or a manual process that could be reused on several operations.

CONVERTING DATA FOR MAJOR ENTITIES

If you are implementing Oracle Work In Process and have been using another ERP system, you need to consider the conversion of your legacy data.

Oracle provides the basic tools to provide conversion of legacy data through the Oracle Manufacturing, Distribution, Sales, and Service Open Interfaces. The Oracle reference documentation explains the operation of the interfaces in detail.

Item and Bill of Material data are required to support your Work In Process implementation. There are two interfaces available to facilitate importing this data:

- *Open Item Interface.* Used for the import of Item Master data. This is covered in Chapter 16.
- *Open Bills of Material Interface.* Used for the import of BOM information. This is covered in Chapter 18.

Additionally, if you have existing routing information, this can be imported through the Open Routing Interface (see Chapter 18).

For importing Discrete Job and Repetitive Schedule information, Oracle provides an Open Job and Schedule Interface. Although this is designed to interface with other scheduling systems, it has applications in the conversion of WIP data from a legacy system. The WIP

Mass Load concurrent program reads data from the interface table and creates the discrete jobs and repetitive schedule.

The use of these interfaces requires development of programs to extract data from the legacy system, format it based on the open interface guidelines, and then insert rows in the interface tables. When the import programs are run, Oracle validates the data in the interface tables based on the current setup of the relevant application (Inventory, Bills of Material, or WIP).

> **Tip**
>
> Before you run any import program, ensure that *all* setup steps are complete. This will save you a lot of time in not having to manually sort through errors that have occurred because of an incomplete setup.

As with any data conversion effort, you need to assess the costs involved in developing custom software to extract and format your legacy data. With Items, Bills of Material, and Routings, the development cost will probably be justified. In many cases, it might be more cost-effective to create your discrete jobs and schedules manually at the time of conversion. Of course, this depends on the nature of your business.

PROCESSING TRANSACTIONS

This section covers the normal transaction activity that occurs within the Work In Process application.

WORK IN PROCESS TRANSACTIONS

The following sections cover the transactions that are involved in the operation of the Oracle Work in Process application.

PROCESSING SHOP FLOOR TRANSACTIONS

The shop floor transactions in WIP are typically related to routing-based manufacturing. Details of the creation of a routing are covered in Chapter 18.

INTRAOPERATION STEPS   Routings consist of operations that define the flow that an assembly will follow in manufacturing. For each of these operations, you can assign intraoperation steps that you can use to control transaction processing.

A summary of these steps is as follows:

- *Queue*. Assemblies in this step are typically awaiting processing.
- *Run*. Assemblies in this step are in process.
- *To Move*. Assemblies in this step have completed processing and are waiting for subsequent processing. If the assemblies are in the to move step of the last operation on a routing, they are available for completion.

PART

III

CH

21

- *Scrap.* Assemblies in this step are not considered available, but from a costing point of view, WIP considers them complete at the operation. Scrapping of assemblies is discussed later in this chapter. If you do succeed in salvaging assemblies at this step, you can move them to another step at this operation or to another operation.

- *Reject.* Assemblies in this step are not considered available. As with the scrap step, WIP does consider them complete at the operation. You can use this step to hold rejected assemblies that either require disposition or are awaiting rework. When you are sure what you need to do with these assemblies, you can move them to another intraoperation step at this operation or move them to another operation.

ADDING, UPDATING, AND DELETING OPERATIONS To maintain flexibility, you can add operations to your jobs and schedules. You can do this even if a routing does not exist. Discrete jobs must have a status of unreleased, released, on-hold, or complete. You can only add operations to repetitive schedules that are unreleased. Typically, this would enable you to add a temporary unplanned operation to a job or schedule.

> **Tip**
>
> WIP (depending on your security settings) will also allow the creation of ad hoc operations for discrete jobs while processing move transactions. This might be useful in creating temporary operations to allow processing of rework while a job is running.

You can also update operations on a job or schedule. An example would be the inclusion of revised work instructions that might be linked to an operation. Operations can be updated for discrete jobs with statuses of unreleased, released, on-hold, and complete. Operations on a repetitive schedule can be updated they have a status of released, on-hold, or complete. There must be only one active schedule for the assembly/line combination when the update happens.

Operations can also be deleted from a job or schedule if required. You cannot delete operations if there has been completion, move, or resource charging activity at that operation.

RESOURCES Resources are things that are required to perform an operation. These could include labor, equipment, outside processing services, and so on. Creating and assigning resources is discussed in Chapter 18.

When you create resources, you can define them to be automatically charged to a job or schedule when move or completion activity takes place either within WIP or as a result of outside processing PO activity. If required, resources can also be manually charged when moves take place or at any other time—for example, on completion of a job or schedule.

Resources can be added or updated while you are adding or updating operations (using the "Operations" window). It is possible to add a resource to a job or schedule that does not have any operations assigned. If you are adding a resource to a job or schedule that does have operations assigned, you must add the resource to the department that the operation is linked to (see Chapter 18).

If you delete an operation, the related resources are also deleted. You can delete resources while updating operations. Both transactions are carried out from the Operations window. WIP does not enable you to delete resources when there has been transaction activity on the schedule or job that has used the resources.

MOVE TRANSACTIONS   When using routings with operations assigned, product is moved through the sequence of operations using the Move Transactions window. There are two ways in which assemblies can move:

- *Intraoperation Moves.* Where assemblies move between the enabled intraoperation steps assigned within an operation (see Intraoperation Steps).

- *Interoperation Moves.* Where assemblies move between an intraoperation step of one operation and an intraoperation step of another operation.

Typically, product will move from the to move step of an operation to the queue step of a subsequent operation. In the case of rework and scrap, assemblies can move back to a previous step or indeed a prior operation.

The move transaction can also be used to perform a completion if the assemblies are at the to move step of the final operation (see the section on WIP Completion Transactions).

The effect of move transactions on material is discussed in the next section.

SHOP FLOOR STATUSES   Within the WIP application, you can set up any number of shop floor statuses that can be applied to the intraoperation steps used on a job or schedule. These statuses are used to prevent move transactions from taking place. In most organizations, this level of control is used to enforce a quality hold on a job or schedule. The statuses are defined and maintained using the Assign Shop Floor Statuses window.

> **Tip**
>
> Shop floor statuses are assigned to a specific discrete job or assembly/production line combination.

You cannot assign the same status to more than one intraoperation step at the same operation on a job. You can assign multiple statuses to the same step if this is required.

> **Tip**
>
> Oracle WIP provides additional controls for move transactions using the WIP parameter Allow Moves Over No Move Shop Floor Statuses(see the setup steps earlier in this chapter).

PART

III

CH

21

JOB AND REPETITIVE SCHEDULE STATUSES

Statuses can be assigned and maintained for jobs and schedules. These can be used to control the way in which the job is processed, and in some cases WIP automatically updates the status.

Tip

These statuses are not directly related to shop floor statuses, although in some cases they can have a similar effect.

The following is a summary of some of the more important statuses:

- *Unreleased.* The job or schedule has not yet been released for production. No transactions can be processed, although the job or schedule can be updated.

- *Released.* The job or schedule is available for production. Transactions can be made. This status is updated using the Discrete Jobs or Repetitive Schedules window.

- *Complete.* The total quantity on the job or schedule has been completed. WIP updates a job to this status automatically when the original job quantity has been completed. Transactions can still be processed against a job with this status, so it is possible to over-complete (see "WIP Completion Transactions"). How this status updates for repetitive schedules depends on the setting of the Autorelease Days parameter and the availability of an unreleased schedule (see the section "Autorelease of a Schedule").

- *Complete—No Charges.* The total quantity on the job or schedule has been completed. No further transactions can be processed on jobs or schedules with this status. Because this status is manually assigned by updating a job or schedule, you can use it to prevent any further transaction activity. For repetitive schedules, WIP can update a schedule to this status automatically (see the section "Autorelease of a Schedule").

- *On Hold.* The job or schedule can be updated, but no transactions are possible.

- *Cancelled.* The job or schedule has been cancelled, and no further update or transaction activity is possible. You can, however, change the status back to Released if necessary.

- *Closed.* This applies to a discrete job. The discrete job close process has been run, and no further update, transaction, or status change activity is possible. Closed does not apply to repetitive schedules because any costs and variances are posted to the general ledger as the financial period closes.

PROCESSING MATERIAL TRANSACTIONS

The following sections explain how typical material transactions are processed within the Work In Process application.

SUPPLY TYPES   Oracle uses supply types to determine how material is planned, supplied through the Work In Process application, and costed. You can set the supply type at the item level or on a particular Bill of Material.

> **Tip**
> The choice of setting the supply type at the item or Bill of Material level depends on how you want to manage the material flow through production. If it is likely that an item will have one supply type regardless of the assembly it is used on, setting this at the item level is adequate. However, if the supply of material changes depending on the assembly an item is use on, you must set the supply type on the BOM.

The following is a summary of the supply types from a WIP perspective:

- *Assembly Pull.* Component requirements are relieved from the supply subinventory when the assembly is completed.

> **Tip**
> Default supply subinventories are discussed in the setup section. You can assign the supply subinventory to a component on a Bill of Material, or it can be assigned at the item level (see Chapter 18 and Chapter 16).

- *Operation Pull.* Component requirements are relieved from the supply subinventory when the assembly completes a backflush operation.
- *Push.* Component requirements must be issued to the job or schedule.
- *Bulk.* Components with this supply type are not typically issued to jobs or schedules. The bulk designation is normally used for components that are expensed on receipt or on issue.
- *Supplier.* WIP creates requirements for components with this supply type when you create a job or schedule. They are not typically transacted.
- *Phantom.* This supply type is unique to phantom assemblies and has a significant impact on the planning process. When used as a subassembly within a BOM structure, phantom assemblies become transparent, and only their components are seen in the planning process. It is possible to treat a phantom assembly as a top level assembly and build it in WIP.
- *Based on Bill.* This is not a true supply type, but an indication that the supply type set on the Bill of Material will be used. For discrete jobs and repetitive schedules, this is the default supply type and can be changed when a discrete job is being created or when repetitive assemblies are being associated with production lines.

ISSUING/RETURNING MATERIAL   How Oracle WIP handles the issue and return of material depends on the supply type set for the components:

- *Issuing and returning specific components.* Using the WIP Material Transactions window, you can issue or return components of a job or schedule regardless of the supply type. This includes items with a supply type of bulk, supplier, and phantom. You must select the specific component option to do this. For jobs or schedules that have a routing, you can perform these transactions against components at any operation.

PART

III

CH

21

> **Tip**
>
> WIP enables you to transact ad hoc components to a job or schedule. These are component requirements that are not currently associated with the job or schedule. This option could save you the bother of having to update the material requirements on a job or schedule if a one-off component is required.

- *Issuing and returning all push components.* To simplify the issue or return of the push component requirements on a job or schedule, you can choose the All Material option. All push components can then be either issued or returned with one transaction.

The following transactions perform a backflush where the component requirements are deducted from the supply subinventory automatically. This eliminates the need for multiple transactions to issue the components to the job or schedule.

- *Completing assemblies to inventory using the Completion transaction.* Components with a supply-type of assembly pull are issued from the supply subinventory when the completion transaction takes place (backflush).

- *Moving and completing assemblies to inventory using the Move transaction.* This transaction is carried out using the Move Transaction window. Completing or moving assemblies to inventory causes components with a supply-type of assembly pull or operation pull to be relieved from the supply subinventory (backflush). You can determine when operation-pull components will be backflushed by assigning them to a particular operation when the Bill of Material is defined (see Chapter 18).

- *Completing assemblies at an operation.* Using the Move Transaction window, you can move assemblies through an operation. If there are components that have a supply type of operation pull and they are assigned to the operation, they will be relieved from the supply subinventory (backflush).

- *Receiving assemblies from outside processing operations.* This applies to outside processing assemblies that have pull components. When a Purchase Order receipt is performed, any pull components are relieved from the supply subinventory (backflush).

> **Tip**
>
> If the Allow Negative Inventory Balances parameter is set to Yes in Oracle Inventory, WIP enables you to process transactions that could drive an inventory location negative. You will receive a warning that this will happen. Even if this parameter is set to No, WIP will drive inventory locations negative for a backflush transaction if the onhand balance is not sufficient. See Chapter 16 for information on setting the organization parameters.

If you need to undo a backflush transaction that was processed in error, WIP provides a reverse backflush transaction. This can be processed from the Completion Transaction and Move Transaction windows. The assembly quantity in the completion subinventory is reduced and the balances of the component subinventories are increased based on the usage.

Oracle WIP enables you to replenish supply subinventories using the WIP Material Transactions window. This replenishment is based on the discrete job name or the repetitive schedule. You can also use a completion transaction to feed subassemblies to the supply subinventory of the next using assembly.

SCRAPPING MATERIAL/ASSEMBLIES   How you manage component and assembly scrap using WIP depends on a number of factors.

If you are using routings then you can enable the Scrap intraoperation step for any operation at which you anticipate scrapping. When you move assemblies to the scrap step of an operation, you can optionally enter an account code to collect the scrap cost. If you do not enter an account, the cost stays with the schedule or job until the accounting period closes or you close the job. For standard discrete jobs, MPS/MRP planning does not see any quantities in the scrap step as supply and replans accordingly. Scrap on repetitive schedules and nonstandard jobs is not netted from the supply quantity.

> **Tip**
>
> If an assembly has operation or assembly pull components and you attempt to move assemblies into the scrap step before a pending backflush has completed, you receive a warning. You risk a situation where the onhand quantities will not reconcile when the backflush transaction eventually completes. You can get around this problem by pushing the assembly pull or operation pull components onto the job or schedule to ensure that the subinventory balances remain correct.

In the absence of a routing, you can transact the assemblies to be scrapped to a completion subinventory and then scrap the assemblies using a miscellaneous issue to a scrap account. (See Chapter 16 for an explanation of miscellaneous transactions.)

Scrapping partially completed assemblies always causes a dilemma. Depending on the percentage of the assembly completed, you can choose to scrap the components only or to scrap the assembly and deal with any unused components as you see fit.

Scrapping assembly and operation pull components does not normally pose a problem. If there has not been a backflush transaction, you can scrap these components from the supply subinventory using a miscellaneous issue transaction.

Scrapping push components requires the return of the components to a subinventory (which could be any subinventory) where they can be scrapped using a miscellaneous issue transaction.

ADDING/UPDATING AND DELETING MATERIAL REQUIREMENTS   The material requirements on a discrete job or repetitive schedule can be updated if the status is released, unreleased, onhold, or complete. You can add components, change quantities, change supply type, and supply subinventories using the Material Requirements window. This provides for flexibility in the manufacturing process when additional material is required to complete a specific job or schedule or when substitutions need to be made.

PART

III

CH

21

Tip

> Although some organizations might prefer to control the material requirements through updating a job or schedule, WIP also enables you to issue ad hoc components (see the section "Issuing/Returning Material").

For nonstandard discrete jobs, you can use the Material Requirements window to add components and assemblies to your job. A typical use would be adding an assembly for rework and components that will be used in the rework.

There are no restrictions on deleting material requirements from jobs or schedules that have a status of unreleased. If the job or schedule has a status of released, onhold, or complete, you can delete requirements that have not yet been transacted.

WIP COMPLETION TRANSACTIONS

The topic of completion transactions is also discussed in the section "Issuing/Returning Material." Depending on the manufacturing approach you are taking, WIP provides different options for the completion of assemblies to inventory:

- *WIP completion for jobs and schedules with routings.* You need to ensure that the assemblies to be completed are in the to move step of the last operation. The completion transaction can either be done with the Completion Transactions window or the Move Transactions window. If you need to return assemblies from the completion subinventory to the job or schedule, you can do this using the return transaction type. This moves the assemblies back to the to move step of the last operation and reduces the completed quantity on the job or schedule. You cannot over-complete quantities on a job or schedule that has a routing without adjusting the job or schedule quantity.

Tip

> Completions and returns for repetitive schedules ensure that schedules are selected on a first-in, first-out basis.

- *WIP completion for jobs and schedules without routings.* These are completed using the Completion Transactions window. As with jobs and schedules that have routings, you can use the return transaction type to move assemblies back from inventory to the job or schedule. You can over-complete assemblies when there is no routing. This enables you to accommodate production overruns.

Tip

> Over-completions are not always a good thing. If you do not want to have quantities completed greater than the job or schedule quantity, you will need to monitor your

jobs and schedules closely. You can use the Complete - No Charges status to prevent further completions on a job.

■ *Work Orderless completions.* If you are using flow manufacturing methods, you can use work orderless completions to complete assemblies to inventory without the creation of a discrete job or repetitive schedule.

PURGING JOBS AND SCHEDULES

Oracle Work In Process provides a concurrent process to purge jobs and schedules that are no longer required. To be considered valid for purging, a discrete job must be closed in an accounting period that is also closed. Repetitive schedules can be purged if they have a status of Cancelled or Complete - No Charges and are also in an accounting period that has been closed.

You can review the jobs and schedules that would qualify for purging by choosing the Report Only option before proceeding with a purge.

Tip   When you purge discrete jobs and schedules using this program, *all* related data is removed from the database. If you need to retain information on jobs and schedules that you are about to purge, ensure that you have made alternative arrangements to store it.

MANAGING DISCRETE JOBS

This section covers the tasks associated with the creation and maintenance of discrete jobs.

DISCRETE JOB TYPES

Oracle Work In Process provides for two types of discrete jobs:

■ *Standard.* This is the most typical job type used in manufacturing. It provides for material requirements to be specified referencing a Bill of Material and to associate a routing with the job that will provide information on the operations and resources required to build the assembly.

■ *Nonstandard.* This job type is typically used to deal with exceptions in the normal manufacturing process. If necessary, you can add material requirements to a nonstandard job, or you can choose to use it to collect cost information for work performed only. Some applications for a nonstandard job could be rework, repair, prototypes, or project-related work.

DEFINING DISCRETE JOBS

When defining a standard discrete job, you need to consider the following:

■ The Job Name can be defaulted based on an internally generated sequence. If you have set a prefix using the WIP:Discrete Job Prefix profile option, this is used.

> **Tip**
>
> WIP uses an ASCII sequence for the job names if you take the default. You might need to choose a starting sequence number that allows for proper sorting in reports. You need a DBA to assist with setting the starting sequence.

■ WIP defaults the assembly's primary BOM and routing if they exist. You can choose an alternate for either the BOM or routing if one exists.

■ If you have set up a default WIP accounting class, it defaults on your job (see the setup steps earlier in this chapter). You can override the default if you need to.

■ The job status defaults to Unreleased. If you need to change it to a released or hold status, you can do this when you are defining the job. This depends on how you want to control your manufacturing operation (see the section "Processing Shop Floor Transactions").

■ There might be situations where you do not want to receive reschedule suggestions for a discrete job, and in this case, you should choose the firm option. Setting the firm option means that MRP planning does *not* create reschedule suggestions for your discrete job if there are changes in supply or demand. MRP creates additional planned orders if more supply is required.

■ Use the MRP Net Quantity with care. For standard discrete jobs, MPS and MRP consider any quantities scrapped off a job as being a reduction in the total supply. If you try to use the MRP Net Quantity to account for process yield losses and subsequently scrap assemblies, MRP over-plans.

■ If you associate a routing with a standard discrete job, you can enter either a start or completion date, and WIP forward schedules or backward schedules the job using the routing.

■ If you are not using a routing, you can enter the start or completion date, and WIP schedules the job based on the fixed and/or variable lead times for the assembly.

When you are defining nonstandard discrete jobs, you should consider the following points:

■ The use of an assembly with a nonstandard job is optional; however, if you are going to use a routing, you have to select an assembly.

■ Nonstandard jobs cannot be firmed.

■ You can use the MRP Net Quantity field to account for yield loss on nonstandard jobs. The MPS and MRP planning processes don't consider scrap on nonstandard jobs when calculating the supply.

■ If you have not assigned a routing reference to the nonstandard job, you must specify both the start and completion dates and times.

Both standard and nonstandard discrete jobs can be associated with projects. This enables you to track material and resource costs specific to a project.

> **Tip**
>
> You can only relate discrete jobs to projects if the Project References Enabled org parameter has been set to Yes in Oracle Inventory.

Discrete jobs can be linked to Sales Orders manually for Assemble to Order items. For Configure to Order Sales Orders, Final Assembly orders can also be created automatically (see Chapter 18, "Using Oracle Engineering and Bills of Material" for a discussion of the Assemble to Order process).

USING THE PLANNER WORKBENCH WITH DISCRETE JOBS

In the case of standard discrete jobs, WIP also enables you to create discrete jobs from the Planner Workbench. When the MPS and MRP planning processes are run, planned orders and reschedule suggestions are available through the Planner Workbench. This is part of the Oracle Master Scheduling/MRP application.

In a discrete manufacturing environment, using the Planner Workbench eliminates a lot of the tedious work involved in reviewing reschedule and planned order reports and then making the required changes by individually creating jobs or revising them.

There are two actions that would typically be carried out using the workbench:

■ *Implement Planned Orders.* Using this function, you can convert any or all of the planned orders into discrete jobs. The workbench can default the job name and WIP accounting class (if you have selected these to default in your setup). The job start date and the job quantity default to the MPS/MRP recommendation. These can be overwritten if you want. The job status defaults to unreleased. This can also be changed to released or hold from the workbench. Oracle uses the WIP Mass Load process to create discrete jobs from your selections on the workbench.

■ *Reschedule Scheduled Receipts.* This function enables you to execute reschedule recommendations for your discrete jobs. You can view and reschedule existing discrete jobs based on push-out, pull-in, and cancel recommendations. Again, changes are implemented using the WIP Mass Load process.

SIMULATING A DISCRETE JOB

You can simulate a discrete job to analyze any of the following:

- The effects of start and completion date changes.
- Variations in onhand and available-to-promise component quantities.
- Changing the Bill of Materials or individual components being used.

In release 11, you now also have the option to create a discrete job directly when you are happy with the simulation.

UPDATING A DISCRETE JOB

By querying an existing discrete job, WIP enables you to change certain information, depending on the status of the job:

- *Job Name.* If the WIP:Job Name Updateable profile option is set to Yes.
- *Job quantity.* There are no restrictions on changes for unreleased jobs; however, the quantity cannot be changed to less than the quantity that is in process. If the job is linked to a sales order, you cannot change the quantity to less than is on the sales order.
- *Schedule Dates.* You can change the start or completion dates and times.
- *Operations.* These can be added, changed, or deleted.
- *Resources.* These can be added, changed, or deleted.
- *Material Requirements.* These can be added, changed, or deleted.

MANAGING REPETITIVE SCHEDULES

This section covers the tasks that are associated with the creation and maintenance of repetitive schedules.

DEFINING A PRODUCTION LINE

As mentioned in the setup section, you must define production lines if you plan on using repetitive scheduling. You should give some thought to the following pieces of information that are required:

- *Hourly Rates.* A min and max rate should be specified. This information is used in scheduling.
- *Start and Stop Time.* This is used to calculate the availability of the production line. Making the start and stop times the same means that it has 24-hour availability.
- *Lead Time Basis.* This can be either fixed or routing-based. If the line has a fixed lead time basis (all assemblies take the same amount of time to run through the line), you need to specify in hours how long it will take to process the first assembly through the

line. If the lead time varies on the line depending on the assembly you are building, you can specify that a routing-based lead time is used. In this case, Oracle uses the assembly routing to calculate the lead time.

ASSIGNING AN ASSEMBLY TO A PRODUCTION LINE

After you have created a production line, you can associate your repetitive assemblies with it. Various combinations of production lines and repetitive assemblies are possible—for example, one assembly built on multiple lines or many assemblies built on one line.

When assigning a repetitive assembly to a production line, you need to consider the following:

- *Completion Subinventory.* You can assign a completion subinventory to be used for a particular production line and assembly combination. If the assembly has a routing assignment, the completion subinventory defaults from the routing. You need to set a value for this field if you will use Move transactions to complete assemblies.

- *WIP Supply Type.* The value here defaults to Based on Bill but can be overridden. See the section "Processing Material Transactions" for an explanation of supply types.

- *Accounting Class.* This can be defaulted based on the default accounting class associated with the Item (see the setup section "Defining WIP Accounting Classes"), or you can assign your own.

- *Line Priority.* You have to set a priority for the production line in each assembly/line combination you create. Master Scheduling/MRP uses this to select the lines for which to create repetitive schedules. It starts with priority 1 and works its way through other line priorities if additional lines are required.

- *Hourly Production Rate.* This defaults to the maximum rate that was defined for the production line when it was created. If you change this value, it must be less than the maximum value that has been set for the line.

- *Lead Time Line.* You can optionally select a line to be used in the calculation of lead time for a repetitive assembly. Oracle Master Scheduling/MRP uses the lead time to plan the repetitive schedules. If you do not select a line and you perform a lead time rollup, no lead time is assigned to your assembly.

DEFINING A REPETITIVE SCHEDULE

Repetitive schedules can either be created from planned schedules (using the Planner Workbench) or can be manually defined. You manually define repetitive schedules using the Repetitive Schedules window. Here, you can enter the line and assembly information as well as details of the daily quantity and the start and completion dates. Depending on whether the assembly has a routing or a fixed lead time has been assigned to the production line, WIP calculates the start and completion dates.

PART
III

CH
21

USING THE PLANNER WORKBENCH

As with discrete jobs, the Planner Workbench provides a useful tool to implement your repetitive schedules. The most significant differences are the following:

- Master Scheduling/MRP does not provide reschedule recommendations for repetitive schedules. Instead, it creates new repetitive schedules to match increases in requirements for a repetitive assembly.
- You can not "firm" a repetitive schedule from the workbench. You have to query the schedule using the Repetitive Schedules window and then firm it from there.
- When you implement repetitive schedules from the Planner Workbench, their status will be set to Pending - Mass Loaded. Before you can start building with these schedules, you must update their status to Released. You can do this in the Repetitive Schedules window, or you can use the Change Status option to update the status for a selected range of schedules.

UPDATING REPETITIVE SCHEDULES

Using the Repetitive Schedules window, you can make changes to existing schedules. These changes can include the following:

- Modifying the status of the schedule—for example, from Unreleased to Released for a manually defined schedule.
- Changing the total schedule quantity, daily quantity, or number of processing days.
- Changing the schedule dates. How this works depends on whether the assembly has a routing or the production line has a fixed lead time assigned. Depending on the dates being modified, you might have the option to select the *reschedule point*, which is the date WIP uses as the basis for rescheduling.

> **Tip**
>
> The mass change feature enables you to perform a status update on a range of schedules—for example, from Pending - Mass Loaded to Released.

PRODUCTION RATES AND CAPACITY

The WIP application provides you with a number of ways of permanently or temporarily adjusting repetitive scheduling to cope with capacity issues:

- You can increase the daily quantity on a repetitive schedule to account for overtime or an increase in resources on a line.
- Define an additional schedule to run on another line.
- For more permanent changes, you can change the start and stop times for a line, add more days to the workday calendar, or increase the production rate on a line.

Tip

If you need to protect your repetitive schedules from unrealistic changes in production rates, you can define a planning time fence and set acceptable rate increases and decreases using item attributes (see Chapter 16 for an explanation of Item Attributes).

AUTORELEASE OF A SCHEDULE

As discussed in the setup steps, it is possible to specify a window that WIP will use to look for schedules to release when the current schedule is completed. When this happens, the current schedule status is changed to Complete - No Charges and the next schedule within the autorelease timeframe is released.

If WIP cannot find a schedule within the autorelease timeframe, the current schedule status is changed to Complete, enabling further transactions and charges to occur on the schedule.

BALANCING THE SUBLEDGER TO THE GENERAL LEDGER

Every time a job or schedule is charged, relieved, or closed, WIP creates journal entries. You can choose to post these journal entries at the close of a financial period or post them more frequently (weekly, daily, and so on). Depending on your Inventory setup, these transactions are posted in summary, or the detail of every job or schedule related transaction can be posted (see Chapter 16).

Use the WIP Value Report to report the value of Work In Process inventory for an accounting period. Use the WIP Account Distribution and Inventory Account Distribution reports to reconcile the three reports to the General Ledger.

USING OPEN INTERFACES IN THIS APPLICATION

Oracle provides four open interfaces that can be used with the Work In Process application. These are explained in the *Oracle Manufacturing, Distribution, Sales and Service Open Interface Manual*:

- *Open Job and Schedule Interface.* Enables you to import job and schedule information from a variety of sources. A typical application would be the import of data from an external finite scheduling tool. The interface treats the data entered as planned orders, repetitive schedule suggestions, or update and reschedule recommendations. When data is imported through the interface, Oracle creates discrete jobs, creates repetitive schedules, or updates existing jobs and schedules.

- *Open Move Transaction Interface.*Provides for the import of move, completion, and return data. Typical sources of this data would be external shop floor control systems, test systems, or computer-integrated manufacturing (CIM) systems. When the transactions are imported through this interface, Oracle processes the relevant move, completion, or return transactions.

- *Open Resource Transaction Interface.*Enables the import of resource-related transactions from external systems. This data could be obtained from non-Oracle payroll or attendance recording systems. When data is imported through this interface, Oracle processes the relevant resource and overhead transactions.

- *WIP Scheduling Interface.*Enables detailed scheduling information for discrete jobs to be imported. This interface is designed to be used with third-party finite scheduling tools.

Note	You must ensure that *all* setup steps are complete before using any of the open interfaces. Oracle validates transactions created through the interfaces against the current system defaults and parameters.

UNDERSTANDING KEY REPORTS

In release 11, WIP now provides online inquiries from many transaction screens. This eliminates the need to run some reports or jump between windows to verify data. For example, job details can be viewed (material requirements, operations, and resources) when a job is being created.

Table 21.3 provides a summary of the standard reports and concurrent programs provided with the Work In Process application.

TABLE 21.3   ORACLE WORK IN PROCESS REPORTS

Report Name	Description
AutoCreate Final Assembly Orders	Is a concurrent program that is used to automatically create final assembly orders for assemble-to-order items (see Chapter 18).
Close Discrete Jobs	Is a concurrent program that can be scheduled to close jobs based on job number, class, or job status.
Discrete Job Data Report	Provides all job details including quantities, schedule, material requirements, operations, and resources.
Discrete Job Dispatch Report	Lists all jobs to be completed with a status of Released, Complete, and On Hold.
Discrete Job Listing Report	Lists all jobs, regardless of status. Can be run for all jobs with a status of Unreleased to show candidates for release.

TABLE 21.3   CONTINUED

Report Name	Description
Discrete Job Pick List Report	Is used to create a pick list of all components required to supply a job or range of jobs. Requirements are sorted by supply type.
Discrete Job Routing Sheet	Produces a listing of the operations and material requirements for a job or range of jobs. Can be used as a "traveler" to move with the job through the manufacturing process.
Discrete Job Shortage Report Has two uses: • It shows jobs with open material requirements (parts still to be issued). • It shows jobs with component shortages.	Please note that this report only reports shortages based on existing discrete jobs. Planned orders and reschedule recommendations from the planning process are not taken into account.
Discrete Job Value Report - Standard Costing	Shows variances and charges for discrete jobs in a standard costing organization. The report is automatically submitted when you close standard discrete jobs.
Discrete Job Packet	This report provides a convenient way to request the Discrete Job Pick List, Discrete Job Routing Sheet, and Discrete Job Shortage Report as a set.
Employee Rates Listing	Reports on employees and their hourly rates.
Expense Job Value Report	Shows summarized charge transaction information for expense jobs.
Import Jobs and Schedules	Submits the WIP Mass Load program to load transactions from the Open Job and Schedule Interface (see the section "Using Open Interfaces in This Application."
Job Lot Composition Report	Reports on the lot numbers assigned to components and assemblies on any discrete job.
Job and Schedule Interface Report	Is submitted when the WIP Mass Load program is run from the Import Jobs and Schedules screen. It produces a listing of jobs created, schedules created, and discrete jobs that were updated by the mass load. Information on failed transactions is included.
Move Transaction Report	Provides information on move transactions that can optionally include transaction details.
Production Line Report	Shows information on the production lines that have been defined, including the assemblies assigned.
Purge Jobs and Schedules	Is a concurrent program that purges jobs and schedules (see the section "Purging Jobs and Schedules").
Purge Report	Reports the results of a discrete job and/or repetitive schedule purge.
Repetitive Line Report	Shows the repetitive schedules that are assigned to a line or group of lines. Effective and pending schedules can be reported.

PART

III

CH

21

TABLE 21.3   CONTINUED

Report Name	Description
Repetitive Pick List Report	Similar to the Discrete Job Pick List Report. Reports on the components requirements for a schedule or range of schedules.
Repetitive Routing Sheet	Shows the operations, material requirements, and resources for schedules.
Repetitive Schedule Data Report	Lists complete information for repetitive schedules including schedule dates, quantities, material requirements, operations, and so on.
Repetitive Schedule Shortage Report	As with the equivalent report for discrete jobs, this lists either open material requirements or shortages based on available material.
Repetitive Shop Packet Runs a group of four reports: • Repetitive Pick List Report • Repetitive Routing Sheet • Repetitive Schedule Shortage Report • Repetitive Line Report	
Repetitive Value Report	Reports a summary of the charge transactions associated with a schedule or group of schedules.
Resource Performance Report	Shows resource efficiency by department.
Resource Transaction Report	Reports resource transactions for discrete jobs and schedules.
Shop Floor Statuses Report	Shows the detail of shop floor statuses that you have created.
Schedule Group Listing	Provides information on any schedule groups that have been defined.
WIP Account Distribution Report	Provides detailed account information for WIP cost transactions that are not material-related. There is a similar report in Oracle Inventory to provide information on the material cost transactions.
WIP Account Summary Report	Provides summary information on any WIP cost transactions. As with the previous report, this excludes material cost transactions that can be reported using an Oracle Inventory report.
WIP Accounting Classes Report	Reports on the WIP accounting classes that have been defined.
WIP Location Report	For jobs and schedules with associated routings, this report shows the location of the assemblies by operation.

TABLE 21.3 CONTINUED

Report Name	Description
WIP Offsetting Account Report	Lists WIP cost transaction detail by offsetting account.
WIP Outside Processing Report	Reports information for jobs and schedules that have outside processing resources.
WIP Parameters Report	Shows all WIP parameters with their values. This is useful in verifying the setup of Work In Process.
WIP Value Report	Reports in detail on the value of WIP inventory for a specified financial period.

TROUBLESHOOTING

■ Engineering Change Orders (ECOs) can have an impact on your jobs and schedules. By default, ECOs which have a status of Release, Schedule, or Implement, will update discrete jobs with a status of Unreleased. Repetitive schedules that have a status of Unreleased, Released, or On Hold will also be updated by these ECOs. You can optionally choose to have ECOs with a status of Open, update your jobs and schedules (by changing the profile option WIP:Exclude Open ECOs to No).

If there is a significant level of ECO activity in your organization, you should be cautious about releasing large numbers of jobs and schedules with future dates.

■ Some organizations find the planner workbench to be of limited use in its current form. Oracle plans to make this a more intuitive tool in future releases of the applications. In the meantime, your users may choose to use the Planned Order Report and Order Reschedule Report within the MRP application to manage Discrete Jobs or to supplement the workbench.

■ Many users find the shortage of reporting capabilities of the Work In Process application to be limited. While the reports within the WIP application will take account of actual jobs and schedules, they do not account for planned activity. You should consider using Planning Exception sets and the Shortage Exception to provide better visibility of requirements arising from actual and planned activity. Planning Exception Sets are discussed in Chapter 20 "Using Oracle Planning Applications."

PART

III

CH

21

CHAPTER 22

USING ORACLE WORKFLOW

SKILLS REQUIRED TO USE WORKFLOW

Oracle Workflow is a quasi-technical tool that enables users to graphically define rules to automate processes. The underlying PL/SQL statements allow the workflow module to translate the defined rules into automated activities.

To work with Oracle Workflow, there are two distinct skill sets required. The skill sets are the end user skill set and the technical skill set. It is best if the users have a combination of these two skill sets. If not, two or more users should work together to ensure the process flows realistically.

Caution

> No matter what the user's skill level, *always* back up the user's Oracle supplied workflow processes before making *any* changes within Oracle Workflow.

USER SKILL SET

The user skill set requires that the users be able to define a business process graphically. This includes the activities within the process, data attributes, and expected results of the process. All this can be done in a passive, off-line environment using the flat file component of Oracle Workflow.

TECHNICAL SKILL SET

The technical user assigned to Oracle Workflow must be proficient in PL/SQL and be able to transform user requirements into PL/SQL code.

Both skill sets can be easily learned at the Oracle education class (Oracle Workflow Release 11). This class is not a PL/SQL class; an introductory class to PL/SQL is required.

DISCOVERING NEW FEATURES IN RELEASE 11

Oracle Workflow Release 11.0 issubstantially more robust than its counterpart: Release 10.7. The changes and additions to Oracle Workflow are highlighted in the following sections.

NEW TABLES ENABLE MULTILINGUAL SUPPORT

Oracle Workflow can now support multilingual implementations. The Workflow notification process converts the message's language into the language conforming to the user's role and territory designation.

COMPLEX DOCUMENT REFERENCE

Complex documents generated by a PL/SQL procedure can now be referenced in a workflow process. The document can be displayed online in the text of the notification Web page or via an email notification.

ITEM TYPE CALLBACK FUNCTION

The Item Type Callback function provides the capability to run specific logic during the Workflow Engine's execution of a process.

AUTOMATIC NOTIFICATION HANDLING

The Notifications Routing Web page enables rules to be defined that automatically handle notifications in the role holder's scheduled absence.

DYNAMIC PRIORITY FOR NOTIFICATIONS

Multiple priority levels for the same notification can now be handled by defining a special notification attribute called #PRIORITY. This attribute creates a dynamic priority based on the value of the attribute.

If an attribute of #PRIORITY is not defined, the notification system assigns a priority to a notification based on the priority value set for the message associated with the notification.

NEW WORKFLOW HOME PAGE

A new Web page centralizes the links for all URLs that connect to Oracle Workflow.

NEW ATTRIBUTE TYPES: ROLE AND ITEM ATTRIBUTE

Oracle Workflow now contains two new attributes to aid in process flow. The *role* attribute is used to store the names of participants in a workflow process. The *item* attribute is used to store references to other item attributes in a process.

SEPARATE ICONS FOR SEND AND RESPOND MESSAGE ATTRIBUTES

The Workflow icons are now more easily distinguishable than ever. To eliminate the confusion between the Send and Respond message attribute icons, Release 11.0 provides two separate icons. The Send icon is the same as in Release 10.7. The Respond icon is the Send icon with a red arrow pointing back.

ENHANCED DEFAULT ERROR PROCESS

A new item attribute called ERROR_ACTIVITY_LABEL has been added to the WFERROR item type. Upon initiation of the default error process, this attribute is set to the instance label of the activity in error.

ENHANCED FIND INSTANCE WEB PAGE

The Find Instance Web page lets the users sign on to the current Web session with workflow administrator privileges. This allows the users to search for processes based on the process owner.

ENHANCED LOADING OF PROCESS DEFINITIONS

Process definitions can be opened from the database based on the definition's effective date.

ENHANCED WORKFLOW DEFINITIONS LOADER

The default mode of the Workflow Definitions Loader has been changed to UPGRADE from UPLOAD. When it runs, it now overwrites existing objects that have been modified.

ENHANCED EMAIL NOTIFICATIONS

The format of the response section of email notifications has been modified in order to provide the users with clear, concise instructions on how to respond to a notification.

ENHANCED NOTIFICATION VIEWER FORM

The users can now click individual icons that represent any form or URL reference.

ENHANCED BACKGROUND ENGINE

The Background Engine now processes only activities that have been deferred at the time of the run. Activities that have deferred or timed out after the beginning of the run must wait for the next call to the Background Engine.

UNDERSTANDING THE MAJOR COMPONENTS OF WORKFLOW

The major components of Oracle Workflow are the Oracle Workflow Builder, the Workflow Engine, the Workflow Definitions Loader, the Notification System, and the Workflow Monitor. Each is defined briefly here:

- *Oracle Workflow Builder* enables the users to graphically create and define processes.
- *Oracle Workflow Engine* holds all packages and procedures in a PL/SQL format.
- The *Workflow Definitions Loader* allows the users to go from a flat file to the database and back again.

- The *Notification System* begins with a notification from the Workflow engine, and then sends a message to users defined by roles. Any responses received from the notification recipients are validated and the engine is notified to resume processing according to the responses.
- The *Workflow Monitor* is a system-administration tool that monitors processes. It can be a great tool for maintaining and troubleshooting workflows after they are deployed.

WORKFLOW BUILDER

Oracle Workflow Builder is where the users create, view, and modify business process definitions. Using a navigator window, the users define the activities and underlying components of business processes. The users then graphically create a process diagram by assembling the activities in the process window.

Workflow Builder allows the users to save a process diagram to a database or a flat file by using the Workflow Definitions Loader utility. When saving the process to a flat file, Workflow Builder will validate some processes. In order to run the process, the users must save the process to the database.

In order to operate, Workflow Builder requires a PC running Windows 95 or Windows NT.

WORKFLOW ENGINE

The Workflow Engine is embedded in the Oracle 7/Oracle 8 server. It monitors workflow status and coordinates the routing of activities for a process. Calls to the Workflow Engine PL/SQL API (application programming interface) notify the engine of initiation and completion of workflow processes or of changes in the state of these processes.

The Workflow Engine determines the eligibility of activities to run. If it determines that an activity is eligible it then runs the activity. The Workflow Engine supports sophisticated workflow rules, including looping, results-based branching, parallel flows, rendezvous, voting, timeouts, and subprocesses.

WORKFLOW DEFINITIONS LOADER

The Oracle Workflow Definitions Loader is a utility program that allows the users to transfer process definitions between a database and a flat file. The utility runs on the server and is integrated with Oracle Workflow Builder. The users can upgrade the database with new versions of process definitions or upload existing process definitions after the database is upgraded. Because the Definitions Loader allows the users to source control process definitions in a flat file, they do not have to be online to work.

NOTIFICATION SYSTEM

The Oracle Workflow notification system enables users to receive and respond to notifications using email or a Web browser. In this way, activities that cannot be automated, such as requisition approvals, can be handled within the workflow process. Since Web functionality is available, all users with access to the Internet can be included in the workflow process.

The notification system routes electronic notifications to a user role. The role can encompass a single user or a group of users. Drilldown capability to Oracle application forms is also available through the notification system if the users have appropriate security access.

Each notification includes a detailed message to ensure that the users have all the information needed to make an informed decision. Included in all notifications requiring a response is a list of allowed responses. This list ensures that the response provided is understood by Workflow, thus allowing the process to continue to the next activity.

WORKFLOW MONITOR

The Workflow Monitor is a Java applet that allows users to graphically view the status of a single workflow process. The process can be displayed in detail or users can display the status of a specific activity of a process.

When the process or activity is viewed, Workflow places a box around the activity that is currently running. Green process connector lines indicate completed processes. Black connector lines have not been executed. If an error occurs in an activity, a red box appears around that activity's icon.

Tip

The system will appear to lock up after users tell the Workflow Monitor to retrieve a process. Have patience; it takes time for the process to load!

USING THE WORKFLOW ENGINE

Oracle's Workflow Engine is implemented in server-side PL/SQL. When a call is issued to one of its PL/SQL APIs, the Workflow Engine is executed. The Workflow Engine can run in real-time, or, if this is too costly, it can send the activity to the background engine to be run as a background task.

The Workflow Engine serves the client application by

- Managing the status of all activities for an item.
- Determining which new activity to transition to whenever an activity completes.
- Executing function activities automatically, whether real-time or through a background engine.
- Calling the Notifications System to send notifications.
- Maintaining an audit history of an activity's status.
- Detecting error conditions and executing error processes.

Additionally, the Oracle Workflow Engine supports results-based branches, parallel branches, rendezvous, loops, and subprocesses.

INITIATING A WORKFLOW PROCESS

> **Caution**
>
> Users can *add* processes and activities to an Oracle standard workflow but should *never delete anything*! If processes and activities are deleted, the standard Oracle application functionality could be impaired!

A Workflow process is initiated when an application executes a procedure that calls the WF_ENGINE.CreateProcess and WF_ENGINE.StartProcess APIs. These APIs are embedded in the application's code.

The application makes a call to the CreateProcess() API to create an instance of a Workflow process. The creation of the instance triggers the Workflow Engine and the Oracle Workflow APIs to set and get item type attributes for that process instance.

A call to the StartProcess() API starts the workflow process instance. Once the StartProcess() is started, the Workflow Engine identifies and executes the Start activity. It then follows the process to determine the next activity to transition to after completing the prerequisite activity. This process continues until the Workflow Engine comes to a notification or blocking activity. If a notification activity is encountered, the Notification System is called upon to notify the performer. The Workflow Engine continues following the workflow process until it encounters an End activity.

As the process runs, a savepoint is set for each completed function activity. When the commit process is initiated, all completed activities are saved as part of one commit cycle. If an error occurs during the commit process, the database can be set back to any previous save point.

ACTIVITY STATUS

At the time an activity is executed, its state is updated by the Workflow Engine to one of the following status types:

- *Active*: The activity is in the process of being executed.
- *Complete*: The activity executed successfully and is complete.
- *Deferred*: The activity has been moved to the background engine to be run.
- *Error*: The activity has encountered an error during execution.
- *Notified*: The activity is waiting for a response to a notification or from an external program.
- *Suspend*: The activity is placed on hold until released by the system administrator.

Only the system administrator can suspend a process. If a notification has been sent and is responded to while the process is suspended, the response will be saved and held until the system administrator removes the process from suspense mode.

■ *Waiting*: The activity is waiting for other activities to complete in order to continue processing.

CALLING THE WORKFLOW ENGINE

The Workflow Engine manages processes and applies Workflow Engine APIs to function activities. The engine must be informed when an activity completes. The WF_ENGINE.CompleteActivity() attribute automatically calls the engine when process, notification, and function activities complete.

If a response is required from a notification activity, users must be sure that the form or Web page calls the WF_ENGINE.CompleteActivity() attribute when the transaction is completed by the user's response. Also, if the function's activity calls an external program, be sure to code that program to call the engine when its processing completes.

WORKFLOW PROGRAM INTERFACES

Oracle APIs are grouped logically based on function. Engine APIs start or run processes, communicate attribute information, and state changes that take place. Each item is uniquely identified by its item type and key and are passed to subsequent API calls for each specific process.

UNDERSTANDING THE BACKGROUND ENGINE

The Background Engine runs processes and activities that are too costly to run in real-time and runs them in a batch process. All deferred or timed-out activities that satisfy the arguments of the procedure at the time the procedure is invoked are executed using the Background Engine. If new processes and activities are deferred or timed out, they are held until the next time the Background Engine is initiated.

The users must set up at least one Background Engine if any deferred processes or activities have been defined.

If the users set up only one Background Engine, be sure it is set to handle both deferred and timed-out processes and activities.

DEFERRED PROCESSING

The Oracle Workflow Engine uses a threshold cost to determine which activities are deferred and which are run in real-time. The default threshold cost is set at 50. The cost has no bearing on time or money but is an arbitrary scale defined by Oracle with 0 being the minimum and 100 being the maximum.

If the threshold cost is 50 or lower, the Workflow Engine determines that the activity is a real-time activity and processes it as such. If the threshold cost is over 50, the activity is routed to the background engine for processing. The Workflow Engine threshold is an externalized constant.

TIMED-OUT PROCESSING

When an activity times out, the Workflow Engine calls on the Notification System to deliver the notification. The activity's status is then updated to *notified*. The Background Engine assigned to timed-out processing monitors the system for activities having the notified status. If the activity's timeout values have been exceeded, it is marked as having timed out. The Workflow Engine is called to follow the timeout transition.

USING THE WORKFLOW DIRECTORY SERVICES

Oracle Workflow Directory Services enable Workflow users to define who users are and what roles they play in the process. The user creates a directory repository that is referenced by Oracle Workflow and that contains user and role information. The user repository is made up of three database tables with the following views: WF_ROLES, WF_USERS, and WF_USER_ROLES. Each view contains required information about a user or role.

An understanding of Workflow terms enables the user to better understand Workflow configuration:

- *Role*: One or more users who share a common bond such as a common responsibility.
- *Directory Repository*: A set of database tables and views that contains user information.
- *WF_ROLES*: Roles, responsibilities, or positions referenced in a directory repository. Currently maps to WF_USERS, Oracle HRMS positions, Oracle Applications responsibilities, Oracle engineering approval lists, and WF_LOCAL_ROLES.
- WF_USERS: Actual users of the system. Currently maps to Oracle HRMS employees, Oracle receivables, customer contacts, and WF_LOCAL_USERS.
- WF_USER_ROLES: Combines WF_ROLES and WF_USERS.

Three local tables are used when the Oracle Workflow cartridge is installed. They can be used to add information about users and roles that is not included in the existing directory repository. These local tables are WF_LOCAL_USERS, WF_LOCAL_ROLES, and WF_LOCAL_USER_ ROLES.

> **Tip**
>
> Local tables are optional and are generally used when utilizing Workflow as a standalone system with applications other than Oracle applications. In order to enter data into the WF_LOCAL tables, users must use SQL*PLUS or create a custom application interface.

CREATING A WORKFLOW PROCESS

A workflow process is made up of the following six components:

- *Item type*: A group of workflow components that must be associated with a specific item type.
- *Item type attribute*: A component of an item type that can be referenced by an activity.
- *Process activity*: The graphical diagram of a business process including function, notification, and process activities.
- *Function activity*: Actual automated running of a process as defined in a PL/SQL stored procedure.
- *Notification activity*: Activity that sends a message to a user and may require the user to respond.
- *Lookup type*: List of values.

USING THE WORKFLOW BUILDER

The Workflow Builder consists of a navigation tree containing a list of all process components needed to develop a workflow diagram. The users can drag and drop process, notification, and function activities from the navigation tree into a process window.

PLANNING THE PROCESS

The process should be planned thoroughly on paper before using Workflow Builder to create and diagram the process. Always look at a process as a work in progress and design it to be flexible to encompass future changes.

 Tip
> A process should be broken into key components in order to make modification easier.

When a process is being run by Workflow and changes are made to that process, the changes are not recognized until the process starts anew. If the users break the process into components, it then can be modified while the process is running and inserted before it reaches that point in the process. This will ensure the change is recognized during the current process run. Process planning steps should include the following:

1. Identify the business needs that the process encompasses.
2. Determine the activities needed for the process.
3. Determine how the process will be triggered. Is it triggered by a completed transaction or some other condition?
4. Identify the expected results of the process and define the possible results as lookup codes in a lookup type.

PROCESS ACTIVITIES

Process activities produce an expected result that users can then define as a lookup type. An example of this is the Employee Requisition Approval process, which can be completed with an approved or rejected result. Both codes, approved and rejected, are defined in the lookup type.

FUNCTION ACTIVITIES

Function activities return a result that determines the next transition in the Workflow process. The users define the result as a lookup code.

NOTIFICATION ACTIVITIES

Notification activities can be just an informational note or they can require a response from the recipient.

If the message sent by the notification activity is informational only, a response is not required. The users should create and include Send message attributes in the message.

If the message requires a response, users must create Send message attributes that provide adequate information so that the recipient can make a decision and respond. The user also creates Respond message attributes that prompt the user to respond. If the message requires a response, a particular response generally will define the route that the notification activity will take. This is called *branching activity* and the message attribute must have an internal name of RESULT.

DEFINING THE ITEM TYPE

Item types are defined in the data store or the workspace using the Item Type Properties page.

When defining a new item type, Workflow requires that the users give it a unique internal name. The internal name must be all uppercase and cannot have any spaces or colons. The maximum length is eight characters. Internal names are used by Oracle Workflow APIs, SQL scripts, and PL/SQL procedures to identify an attribute. Once an internal name is defined, users cannot change it. If the user deletes an item type the user also deletes the internal name.

The user next must assign a display name and optional description to the item type. The display name will appear in the navigator tree.

New to Oracle Workflow Release 11.0 is the item type selector/callback function. This function is a PL/SQL procedure that the Workflow Engine can call prior to executing an activity. It allows an item type to have multiple workflow processes associated with it. Based on the selector callback/function, an item type can determine the correct process to run. The command for this is RUN. It can also be used to reset (SET_CTX) or test (TEST_CTX) context information for an item type prior to running an activity.

DEFINING ITEM TYPE ATTRIBUTES

Item type attributes determine what values are valid and how the attribute is used. The following attribute types define the characteristics of your items:

- *Text*: Alpha text that has a specified character length.

- *Number*: A number can have an optional format mask.
- *Date*: A date can have an optional format mask.
- *Lookup*: One of the lookup values associated with a lookup type.
- *Role*: A role name from the list of role names defined in the directory service.
- *Attribute*: A reference of the name of an existing item type attribute used in a process in which the user wants to maintain references.
- *URL*: A uniform resource locator, which is an address to a network location. Allows users to access this address from the notifications Web page.
- *Form*: This includes the internal function name and optional form parameters of an Oracle applications form. Users might have access to these parameters from the Notification Viewer form.
- *Document*: This is an attached document defined by a document type. It includes the name of the document management system and a document reference.

DEFINING LOOKUP TYPES AND CODES

Within a process, lookup types provide a predefined list of values when referenced by activities, attributes, and notifications.

Although a lookup type must be associated with an item type, it can be referenced by components of other item types. Usually, lookup types are referenced as results types.

The lookup code is the internal name associated with the lookup type. Once an internal name is defined, the lookup code cannot be changed.

DEFINING MESSAGES AND MESSAGE ATTRIBUTES

Messages must be associated with an item type. When creating a message, the user provides an internal name, a display name, and a description of the message. The user also must specify the priority of the message. Each message has its own priority.

> **Tip**
>
> Oracle defaults the message sort based on priority. This functionality is available when the recipient uses the notifications summary or browser but is not accessible by email.

The Body Property page is where users define the message subject and text. Once a message is defined, users can assign message attributes.

> **Tip**
>
> Within the same data store, messages are not shared by item types. Lookup sets are shared by item types.

Linking an item attribute correctly is critical to your workflow performance.

> **Note**
>
> When defining item attributes, users must specify that they will be used elsewhere, such as in message notifications. If they aren't defined in item type attributes, they can't be called by the message notification system. The exception to this is when the RESULT attribute is used in messages.

MESSAGE ATTRIBUTES

Whenever the users create a message attribute, it must be associated with a message. A message attribute behaves differently depending on how the user defines the message source. A source of Send allows the users to reference a constant or the runtime value of an item type attribute. A source of Respond prompts the recipient to respond to the message. The Notification System uses a message's Respond attributes to generate the response section of a notification. A message can have multiple Respond attributes.

> **Note**
>
> To distinguish Send attributes from Respond attributes, Oracle as overlaid a red question mark on the Send icon to create the Respond icon.

If the users require a particular response to be the result of a notification activity, they must create a respond attribute with an internal name of RESULT.

DEFINING A FUNCTION ACTIVITY

Function activities are normally used to fully automate steps in a process and return a completion result. The function activity calls on a PL/SQL stored procedure to execute this activity. Each function activity must have a cost assigned to it.

ASSIGNING A COST TO A FUNCTION ACTIVITY

The cost of an activity determines whether a process is deferred, directed to the background engine for processing, or processed in real-time. Generally if a function activity requires a large amount of processing time or resources, users should assign a high cost to the activity.

Oracle's predefined threshold for activity cost is 50. If an activity is assigned a cost of 50 or less, the activity is performed in real-time. If the cost is over 50, the activity is deferred to the background engine for processing.

HANDLING EXCEPTIONS

When creating a process, the users should always model the exception handling process. This will enable Workflow to handle all defined exceptions automatically.

DEFINING A PROCESS ACTIVITY

Process activities must be defined before the users can diagram them. All process activities must be associated with an item type.

When defining the process activity, users must indicate whether the process is a top-level process, meaning a process that can be called directly, or a lower level process that must be executed by a top level process. A top level process is indicated by a check mark in the Runnable box on the Control Properties screen under the Activities tab.

Looping allows an activity to be visited more than once. When setting up a process activity, if the Loop Reset box is checked, the loop will continue to execute until a specific result is returned. If the loop reset button is unchecked and the activity is visited more than once, the specified activity is ignored by the process.

Tip

For the majority of process activities, you can leave the loop reset button CHECKED.

DIAGRAMMING THE WORKFLOW PROCESS

Diagramming a process entails no more than taking the activities the users have previously defined and using the icons to draw the process. If the process includes notification activities, before diagramming the process you must load all roles from the Oracle Workflow directory into Oracle Workflow Builder.

Note

A node is a single activity in a diagram. An activity may be repeated several times in a diagram and each iteration is considered a node.

DRAWING THE DIAGRAM

To open the process window, double-click the process activity for which the user is drawing the diagram.

To draw a diagram, the user simply drags and drops the activity icons into the process window. Each icon is considered a node of the process.

To create transitions, simply press and hold the right mouse button while moving the cursor from the source activity to the destination activity. The transition will follow the direction of the mouse. Each process must have at least one start and one end node.

EDITING A TRANSITION

A transition can be edited in several ways as follows.

- *Reposition a transition label*: Simply click the label and drag it to the new position.
- *Hide transition label*: Place the cursor on the transition, click the right mouse button, and select Hidden Label.
- *Bend a transition*: Click the transition and hold the left mouse button down. Drag the transition into the shape as required. This will create a vertex point in the transition. The user can reposition the vertex point to get the desired bend.
- *Loop transition back to its original activity*: Bend the transition as described previously. At the vertex point, select the transition arrowhead and, while holding down the right mouse button, drag it back to the original activity.
- *Remove a vertex point*: Select the vertex point and simply drag it to another vertex in the transition to combine the two points.
- *Straighten a transition*: Select the transition to be straightened and click the right mouse button. Select Straighten from the menu.
- *Alter transition result*: Select the transition and, using the right mouse button, select Results. (Used only when a transition has a result assigned to it.)
- *Lock a transition from further edits*: Select the transition and, using the right mouse button, select Locked from the menu. Be aware that any user with access to editing a diagram can release the lock.
- *Delete a transition*: Select the transition and, using the right mouse button, select Delete Transition from the menu.

CUSTOMIZING A NODE

The user can customize a node within a process by going into the Process Activity property page. Once the user customizes a node, its label name will be appended with an -N to identify it as a unique instance.

SETTING ACTIVITY ATTRIBUTE VALUES

An activity can be used many times within a process and the value of the activity attribute can vary from node to node. The user can change the attributes assigned to that activity in the Attribute Values control page.

REFERENCING STANDARD ACTIVITIES

Oracle Workflow provides a group of standard activities. Definitions of these standard activities follow.

- *Start*: Does not perform an action. Used as a designator to indicate the start of the process.
- *End*: Does not perform an action. Used as a designator to indicate the end of the process.
- *Noop*: Does not perform an action. Used as a placeholder in a process.

- *And/Or*: Used to converge branches of activities once those activities have completed.
- *Compare (Date, Number, or Text)*: When provided with a date, number, or text, compares the values in an item type attribute with the data provided.
- *Wait*: Pauses the process for the time period specified.
- *Block*: Pauses the process until a manual step or external process completes.
- *Wait for Flow*: Pauses a process until a designated process completes a specified activity.
- *Continue Flow*: Restarts the process paused by a Wait for Flow activity.
- *Role Resolution*: Determines a single user from a role that is comprised of many users.
- *Loop Counter*: Counts the number of times an activity has been visited or has looped.
- *Assign*: Assigns a value to an item attribute.
- *Get Monitor URL*: Gets and stores the Workflow Monitor URL in an item attribute.
- *Vote Yes/No*: Sends a notification to the users in a role and then tallies the Yes/No answers.

CREATING NOTIFICATION ACTIVITIES

A notification activity must be associated with an item type. Notification activities link the notification with the type of response expected. Notification activities also send notifications to all users who fit the role type.

When creating a notification activity, the default setup is to allow multiple users to be notified. Once a single user responds with a result, the notification is removed from all the other recipients' notification lists.

If voting is required, the Expand Roles box must be checked when setting up the notification activity. Voting requires all the recipients to respond to the message. The result is determined based on a user-defined formula and the process activity continues based on the result returned.

EMAIL

If a notification is sent to the users via email, the Respond attribute is written into the text of the email message.

Tip

When users respond to a message, they must be careful to use the exact response allowed or the response will error.

NOTIFICATIONS WEB PAGE

Notification via the Notifications Web page allows users to have access to lookup types in order to respond to them. Links to other Web pages can be provided within the notification as well.

NOTIFICATION VIEWER

The Notification Viewer provides the lookup type pick list so the recipient can respond to a notification. It also enables drill down capability so users can view Oracle application's forms.

AUTOMATIC PROCESSING RULES

The users can define rules for automatic notification handling. Each rule is specific to a role and can apply to any or all messages of a specific item type or message name. A rule can perform any one of the following actions: forward, respond, or no action.

Each time the Notification System sends or reassigns a notification to a role, the automatic notification handler tests the notification against that role's list of rules to find the most specific match.

MONITORING WORKFLOW PROCESSES

Oracle Workflow allows users to check the status of a process using the Status form or using the Java-based Workflow Monitor.

> **Tip**
>
> Using the Workflow Monitor is the best choice, when available, because it provides significantly more information regarding process status.

WORKFLOW STATUS FORM

The Workflow status form is a standard Oracle applications form that displays process status information. Oracle has developed this form as a folder form so that users can adapt the displayed information to suit their individual needs.

The form can be called from any Oracle application form by using `FND_FUNCTION.EXECUTE`. The developer form name is `FNDWFIAS` and the function name is `FND_FNDWFIAS`.

Users must provide the following parameter information in order to tell Oracle Workflow which process they want to review:

`ITEM_TYPE=<item_type>`

or

`ITEM_KEY=<item_key>`

The Workflow status form provides information about the process's activity, type, status, result, start date, and so on. All information is in character, not graphical, format.

USING THE WORKFLOW MONITOR

The Workflow Monitor graphically displays the called process. The users get detailed information about the process' or individual activity's status.

The form is divided into four areas—process title, process diagram window, detail tab window, and administration buttons—in order to give the users the most detail.

The process title provides the process name, item key, and user key that identifies the process the user is monitoring. The user can drill down to the subprocess level and the process title field will change to display the subprocess name.

The process diagram window graphically displays the process the user is monitoring. This is a read-only window, so there is no possibility of accidentally modifying the process from this form.

Oracle uses colored boxes to indicate the state of a process. Red means the activity has erred, green means the activity is in process or active, and yellow means the activity is suspended. A process can be suspended only using system administrator access and the user must be in administrator mode.

The transition arrows between the activities are color coded as well. A thick green line indicates that a transition path has been traveled, whereas a black line indicates it has not.

To receive more detail on an activity, you simply click the icon in the detail tab window. By clicking an empty space in the diagram, you can deselect any activity that was previously selected.

To drill down to the subprocesses, double-click an activity. The subprocess is then displayed and its information appears in the detail tab window.

The detail tab window provides detailed information about the process or activity. There are five tabs in which information may reside. They are as follows:

- *Definition*: Contains information about the processor activity's properties.
- *Usage*: Same as the definition but displays properties as a node in the process.
- *Status*: Shows status, result, and error information.
- *Notification*: Displays notification details if applicable for the activity.
- *Item*: Contains item type and attribute information.

The final section contains the administration buttons, which appear only when the user runs Workflow Monitor in administrator mode. Each button makes API calls when selected. The following six buttons may be available:

- *Abort Process*: Aborts the selected process, cancels any outstanding notifications, and prompts for a result to assign to the aborted process.
- *Suspend Process*: Suspends the selected process.
- *Resume Process*: Activates a suspended process.
- *Reassign*: Reassigns the notification to a different performer and requires the entry of a role name.
- *Expedite*: Allows the users to roll back a process that has erred. It provides two choices: skip the activity and assign it a specified result or try to execute the activity again.
- *Attribute*: Allows users to change an item attribute's value.

REVIEWING THE PROCESS LIST

The process list allows the users to find specific process instances based on search criteria. All processes listed are in ascending order by item type, and then item key. Each process instance is summarized.

REVIEWING THE NOTIFICATIONS LIST

The notifications list displays all processes that have been sent to a role and require a response.

If an error occurs because of a notification, you can click the Result column to get more details about the error.

You can select the user link in the WHO column to send email directly to the role that the notification was assigned to.

The Advanced Options button takes the users to the Activities List Web page, where they can specify filtering criteria to view other activities.

The View Diagram button brings the users to the Workflow Monitor to view the process diagram. This button can be used only when in administrator mode.

FILTERING THE ACTIVITIES LIST

The users can set up criteria to view specific process activities in the current process instance. The user can search by activity status—active, complete, error, or suspended—as well as by activity type—response notifications, FYI notifications, functions, and standard workflow items.

CONSIDERATIONS IN SETTING UP WORKFLOW

You should define and scheduleat least one background engine to handle deferred and timed-out activities. You also must determine where notifications will be sent. All notifications can go to email, which does not determine whose notification goes where. Additional considerations follow.

DEFINING THE WF_RESOURCES ENVIRONMENT VARIABLE

Be aware that if you are using the Workflow cartridge, you must customize the directory service views during setup. Workflow cartridge is installed when Workflow is a standalone system and is notbeing used with Oracle applications. The WF_RESOURCES environment variable is set up only when the user is using Workflow cartridge.

DEFINING A WEB AGENT

You cannot define a Web agent until you have installed Oracle Web Application Server. If you plan to use HTML statements, the Web agent is needed by the notifications mailer. The Web agent is also used by Oracle Workflow Web components.

ASSIGNING THE ADMINISTRATOR TO A ROLE

When assigning the Workflow Administrator to a role, you should map all users that will be given administration access into one group. This group should then be assigned to a single role in Oracle Workflow Directory Services.

CUSTOMIZING WEB PAGES

Oracle Workflow allows you to modify the Workflow's Web page to display the company's unique custom logo.

SECURING WEB PAGES

Securing the Web page when Oracle Workflow is embedded in Oracle applications is completed using the Oracle self-service Web applications security setup. This security is set up when completing the Release 11 installation. These setup steps do not require the purchase of Oracle self-service Web applications.

If the user is using the Oracle Workflow cartridge, secure the user Web pages with the authentication feature contained within Oracle Web Application Server.

USING NOTIFICATION MAILER

The Notification Mailer sends email messages and processes responses for the Workflow Notification System.

The Notification Mailer scans the database for messages to be sent. It then reconciles the recipient role with the email address, which is generally an email distribution list. To encompass multi-language processing, Notification Mailer changes its database session to the preferred language of the role using the role and territory settings. When compiling the message, it selects information based on the message attributes. It then creates the message using a message template. The message is then sent using the Oracle InterOffice, UNIX Sendmail, or a MAPI-compliant mail application. Responses are returned to a response account and the Notification Mailer calls the appropriate Notification API to complete the notification process.

SETTING UP MAIL ACCOUNTS

The user must have at least one mail account to send and receive responses. If preferred, the user can set up separate Send and Respond mail accounts.

Private folders should be set up in the Response account and named according to the value set for the discard, process, and unprocess Notification Mailer arguments. The process folder contains all processed responses; the unprocess folder contains unprocessed responses; and the discard folder contains discarded responses.

> **Note**
>
> Note that the Notification Mailer remains running unless there is a database failure or unless the PL/SQL package state changes for the session.

SETTING UP MESSAGE TEMPLATES

Templates are defined in the System: Mailer item type. The Notification Mailer has six predefined message templates, as follows.

- *Open Mail* is used for notifications that require a response.
- *Open FYI Mail* is used for notifications that do not require a response.
- *Canceled Mail* is used when a notification is canceled. It sends a message of cancellation to the recipient.
- *Invalid Mail* notifies appropriate recipients that their response is invalid.
- *Closed Mail* is used when a notification is closed. It sends a message to the recipients informing them that the notification is now closed.
- *Summary Mail* holds notification summaries.
- *Warning Mail* informs recipients of unsolicited mail they have sent.

ESTABLISHING ACCESS PROTECTION

Access protection does not provide security, per se. Workflow access protection prevents a user of a workflow definition from modifying seed data objects. Access protection enables users to control access to all workflow definitions except lookup codes, function attributes, and message attributes.

Oracle Workflow uses defined access levels as follows:

- Levels 0-9 are reserved for the Oracle internal workflow team.
- Levels 10-19 are reserved for the Oracle internal application object team.
- Levels 20-99 are reserved for Oracle applications and other Oracle product teams.
- Levels 100-999 are reserved for Oracle customers. On installation of Workflow Builder, the user is given a default access level of 100.
- Level 1000 is used for public access.

To protect an object from customization, the user assigns the object an access protection level equal to the user's current access level. If the user assigns the object an access level lower than the user's, the user will not be able to modify it. A level higher than the user's access level means another user can modify the object.

An object protected against customization is considered seed data.

> **Tip**
>
> A small lock appears on an object's icon to indicate that the object is read-only.

WORKFLOW DEFINITIONS LOADER

The Workflow Definitions Loader allows the user to transfer files between the database and a flat file (but don't tell your supervisor unless you want to bring work home!).

Use the loader to back up definitions prior to a database upgrade. Workflow Definition files have the .WFT extension.

The Workflow Definitions Loader involves a concurrent process that can be run in one of four modes: upgrade, upload, force, and download.

- The upgrade mode upgrades definitions from an input file and preserves customizations by using the access level defined in the input file.
- The upload mode uploads definitions from an input file while overwriting customizations using the default access code.
- The force mode uploads definitions from an input file disregarding access levels.
- The download mode downloads specified item type definitions to a flat file.

SETTING UP A DATA STORE

Setting up a data store is not difficult. It is critical that you build the data store step by step in the most logical manner. The following outline gives you the appropriate step-by-step process to follow to ensure that all components of a data store have been configured in the correct order. Following are the steps:

1. Set up Item Types
    1.1.   Internal Name (eight characters or fewer, no spaces)
    1.2   Display Name
    1.3.   Selector (if needed)
    1.3.1.   Set up Attributes
    1.3.2.   Internal Name (column name in an Oracle table)
    1.3.3   Display Name
    1.3.4.   Type (text, number, URL, and so on)
    1.4   Set up Lookup Types

1.4.1.	Internal Name
1.4.2.	Display Name
1.4.3.	Lookup Code (the expected results)
1.5.	Set up Messages
1.5.1.	Internal Name
1.5.2.	Display Name
1.5.3.	Subject
1.5.4.	Body (text and attributes)
1.5.5.	Drag down necessary item attributes and create message attributes out of them
1.5.5.1.	Send/Respond
1.5.5.2.	Lookup type
1.5.5.3.	Default value (item attribute)
1.5.5.3.1.	If the source is respond, the user must create a RESULT item attribute
1.5.5.3.2.	Send/Respond
1.5.5.3.3.	Lookup type
1.5.5.3.4.	Default value (a constant)
1.5.5.3.5.	Set up a RESULT for every message the user needs a response on
1.5.6.	Priority (set on properties of message)
1.6.	Set up Notifications
1.6.1.	Internal Name
1.6.2.	Display Name
1.6.3.	Result Type
1.6.4.	Message
1.6.5.	Timeouts
1.6.6.	Expand Roles (used in voting or FYI to more than one person)
1.6.7.	Change Icon
1.7.	Set up Functions
1.7.1	Internal Name
1.7.2.	Display Name
1.7.3.	Result Type
1.7.4	Cost (Determines whether the user will defer an activity. If cost is above 50, the user must set up a background engine.)
1.7.5	Error process/Timeout process
1.7.6.	Loop Reset
1.8.	Set up Processes
1.8.1.	Internal Name
1.8.2.	Display Name
1.8.3	Result Type
1.8.4.	Runnable?

2. Drag and Drop Icons from Navigator to Process Window

3. Draw Transitions

4. Customize Nodes (recipients for notifications, start and end nodes)

PREDEFINED WORKFLOWS EMBEDDED IN ORACLE APPLICATIONS

Table 22.1 describes the areas where Oracle has embedded the workflow functionality. Additional workflow processes can be developed as custom workflows and linked appropriately.

TABLE 22.1 PREDEFINED WORKFLOWS EMBEDDED IN ORACLE APPLICATIONS

Oracle Application	Workflow Process	Description
Application Implementation Wizard	Workflow is used throughout Wizard	A set of Workflow processes that walk users through the implementation and set up of Oracle applications
Oracle Web Employees	Expense Reporting Workflow	Review and management approval process of employee expense reports. Used by both Web employees and Oracle payables.
Oracle Web Employees	Candidate Offer Approval Process	Flows an employment offer through management approval hierarchy.
Oracle Web Employees	Employee Direct Access	Allows employees to review personnel data as well as make limited changes such as marital status and address changes.
Oracle Web Employees	Person Search Process	Controls navigation for entering search criteria and producing lists of people.
Oracle Web Employees	Person Suitability Match Process	Allows entering of matching criteria for search purposes. Provides list of employees who match criteria and produces a bar chart representing their skill sets.
Oracle Web Employees	Career Management Reviews Process	Sends notifications to reviewers for appraisals and assessments.
Oracle Web Employees	360 Degree Assessment Process	Sends notifications to a group of people that they are to perform an assessment as a group. Responses from the group are also handled by this workflow.
Oracle Web Employees	Receipt Confirmation Process	Allows the users to confirm receipts on the Web.

TABLE 22.1   CONTINUED

Oracle Application	Workflow Process	Description
Oracle Web Employees	Requisition Approval Process	An employee requisition is submitted through the appropriate manager approval hierarchy. The status of the requisition is also updated.
Oracle Web Customers	Customer Self-Service Registration Approval Process	Allows customers to receive authority, which consists of a username and password, for access to shipping information over the Web.
Oracle Web Customers	Order Entry Review Process	Allows orders to be reviewed and approved or rejected on-line. Notifies sales person and customer of approval or rejection decision.
Oracle Web Suppliers	Supplier Self-Service Registration Approval Process	Allows a supplier to receive authority, which consists of a username and password, for access to account and shipping information over the Web.
Oracle Engineering	Engineering Change Orders	Submits an engineering change order to the appropriate people for approval.
Oracle General Ledger	Journal Approval Process	Using an approval hierarchy and authorization limits, allows journal entries to be approved on-line prior to posting.
Oracle Payables	AP Open Interface Import Process	Based on setup, can verify and validate account code combinations in the open interface table. Used when importing invoice information from an outside system.
Oracle Payables	Credit Card Transaction Employee Workflow	After the Credit Card Transaction Validation and Exception Report has been run, Workflow notifies users of transactions against their credit cards and allows them to review and respond to charges.
Oracle Payables	Credit Card Transaction Manager Workflow	When the Credit Card Transaction Employee Workflow executes, Workflow also sends notification to the employee's manager for review and approval of the credit card charges.

TABLE 22.1 CONTINUED

Oracle Application	Workflow Process	Description
Oracle Payables	Expense Reporting Workflow	Review and management approval process of employee expense reports. Used by both Web employees and Oracle payables.
Oracle Projects	Project Approval and Status Change Process	Using the appropriate hierarchy, the project is routed to the correct managers for approvals and notification of status changes.
Oracle Projects	Budget Approval Process	Using the appropriate hierarchy, the project budget is routed to the correct managers for approvals and baselining of budget.
Oracle Purchasing	Document Approval Process	Performs all approval-related activities that exist in Oracle Purchasing based on the appropriate approval hierarchies and authorization limits.
Oracle Purchasing	Automatic Document Creation Process	Automatically creates standard purchase orders or releases against blanket agreements using approved purchase requisition lines, but only if the requisition lines have the required sourcing information.
Oracle Purchasing	Change Orders Process	Controls which change order documents must be re-approved. Routes appropriate change orders through the management approval process.
Oracle Service	Service Request Process	Routes a service request to individuals in the organization for resolution.
Oracle Service	Service Request Actions and Dispatch Process	Routes a service request action to individuals in the organization for resolution. Also notifies, with instructions, the appropriate service personnel who need to be dispatched to a field site.

SUMMARY

TROUBLESHOOTING

What does the check box Expand Roles do?

The Expand Roles check box, when checked, sends a notification to every user assigned to that role. Each user then gets to respond to the notification. This is critical for voting or FYI notifications. The Expand Roles check box, when unchecked, sends a single notification to all users assigned to that role, but when one user responds, the notification is closed to all other users responses.

Is there any debugging capability in Workflow?

Workflow currently does not debug PL/SQL activity functions. Future additions of Workflow should have some debugging capability. To debug a Workflow, make sure all function activities are working correctly before linking them into the process. If you continue to get error messages, you can always insert `dbms_output.put_line` to see more specifically what logic is being executed.

My process does not loop where it's supposed to; what's wrong?

Verify that the Loop Reset is checked in the check box. The definition for each workflow activity includes a property called Loop Reset which is a check box on the Details property page for the Activity definition. This box should always remain checked unless you are a Workflow expert. The Loop Reset property controls how the Workflow Engine behaves when it transitions back to part of a process that has already been executed. When a process transitions back over itself, it is called a loop.

CHAPTER 23

UNDERSTANDING MULTI-ORG

Multi-org functionality enables you to have multiple sets of books on one server. This not only saves on hardware costs; it provides the foundation for automated intercompany transactions and simplifies the financial consolidation process. In Oracle release 11, you can even create intercompany transactions across sets of books!

Oracle Applications and Multiple Organizations

Oracle applications that are directly impacted by the Multiple Organizational process are Oracle Cash Management, ORGer Entry/Shipping, Payables, Projects, Purchasing, Receivables, Sales Compensation, Sales and Marketing, and Service.

Discovering New Features in Release 11

Multiple Organizations in release 11 spans a broader range of applications and provides for some functionality across sets of books such as the ability to sell and ship products from different legal entities and across sets of books.

There are still some areas that do not provide automatic journal entries *across sets of books*. An example of this is entering purchase orders in one inventory organization and assigning the receipt of the inventory to another inventory organization. This can be an automatic process if the inventory organizations involved share the same set of books.

Understanding the Key Tables

The multiple organization structure simply partitions key tables to provide for an ORG_ID number per row. This, in turn, is used to provide security and data segregation. Criteria used to partition tables includes the following:

- The table contains a GL Account Code (code combination ID).
- There is a business reason for the table to be partitioned (for example, the entity should not be shared).
- The table contains transaction data.
- The table is an interface table where data being loaded is partitioned.
- The table includes a foreign key to a partitioned table and is accessed independently (in other words, not just as a child of a partitioned table).

The following Oracle Applications modules contain database tables that are secured by operating unit:

- Oracle Cash Management
- Oracle Order Entry/Shipping
- Oracle Payables
- Oracle Projects

- Oracle Purchasing
- Oracle Receivables
- Oracle Sales Compensation
- Oracle Sales and Marketing
- Oracle Service

CRITICAL IMPLEMENTATION FACTORS

The key to the implementation of a successful multiple organizational environment is in the planning. Organizational structure, responsibilities, security, and data replication are critical factors that must be taken into account.

UNDERSTANDING ORGANIZATION STRUCTURES

There are actually multiple dimensions at play within the multi-org structure. These are the business group, human resource organization, set of books, legal entity, operating unit, and inventory organization.

The first is the human resource dimension. It consists of the business group and the human resource organizations.

The business group is the consolidated enterprise, a major division, or an operating company. It's the highest level human resource organization and holds all employees of the enterprise.

You need more than one business group only if you segregate employees on an enterprise-by-enterprise basis. Oracle provides you with your first business group, which they have named Setup Business Group. You can change the name to be consistent with your company's naming conventions.

Under the business group are the Human Resources Organizations. These are used by the Human Resource module to segregate employees into reporting groups at levels lower than the business group, such as location or department. Refer to Figure 23.1 for a sample Business Group structure.

Figure 23.1
A Business
Group
Structure.

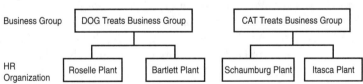

 Lay out your organizational structure before beginning setup in the system.

The next dimension of the multi-org structure is the set of books, legal entity, operating unit, and inventory organizations.

The first step is to determine how many sets of books your company requires. A set of books is defined by the three Cs: Calendar, Currency, and Chart of Accounts. Generally, if the three Cs are the same for each company you are setting up, they can share a set of books. If any one of the three Cs is different, you must have separate sets of books for each company that is different.

Security can be set up to ensure that each company's data integrity is maintained if multiple companies share a set of books. This can be done by setting up security rules based on the balancing segment within the key accounting flexfield.

The next step is to define a legal entity. Oracle's definition of a legal entity is that it represents a legal company for which you prepare fiscal or tax reports, *but*—and this is a big but—the organizational legal entity currently within the multi-org structure only supports automatic intercompany invoicing and movement statistics within the financials. Legal entity is used extensively for the Oracle Human Resource Management System. Oracle plans to use it for additional purposes in a future release. In the mean time, the legal entity designation requires you to assign a tax ID number to the legal entity. You will explore some issues with this concept shortly. A legal entity is assigned to a set of books.

Under the legal entity organization is the operating unit. The operating unit is an organization that uses any or all of the following: Oracle Payables, Receivables, Purchasing, Projects, Order Entry/Shipping, Sales Compensation, Sales and Marketing, Service, and Cash Management. Information is secured by Operating Unit, and each user sees information for only her own operating unit. A sample structure appears in Figure 23.2.

Figure 23.2
Information is secured by operating unit.

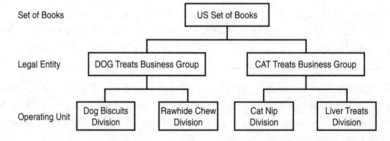

Within the Operating Unit are the Inventory Organizations. These organizations track inventory transactions, maintain inventory balances, and can manufacture or distribute products. You can have multiple inventory organizations that report to one or more operating units within the same set of books. Inventory Organizations have been inserted into the organizational structure in Figure 23.3.

As mentioned previously, the legal entity requires a tax identification number to be entered at time of setup.

Here's an example to illustrate how this works. If both the Dog Biscuit Division and the Rawhide Chew Division share the same tax ID number, they can be separate operating units under the legal entity. Figure 23.3 is an example of this type of structure.

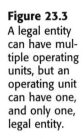

Figure 23.3
A legal entity can have multiple operating units, but an operating unit can have one, and only one, legal entity.

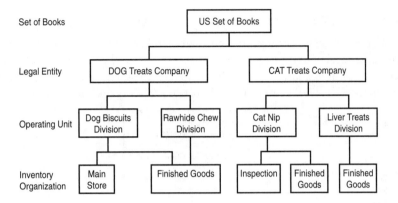

If they do not share the same tax identification number, you logically separate the legal entities into two separate legal entities. An example of this is provided in Figure 23.4.

Figure 23.4
Each legal entity has its own unique tax identification number.

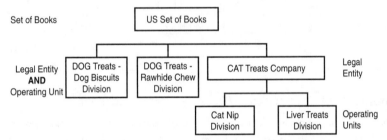

CENTRALIZED TRANSACTION PROCESSING WITHIN ORACLE APPLICATIONS

What about the company that wants centralized processing across legal companies? The solution is to create a single legal entity with one operating unit. Remember: At this time, Oracle uses the legal entity organization for automatic intercompany invoicing and movement statistics only. Tax and fiscal reporting at the legal entity level will be supported in a future release. Tax reporting by each legal company can still be maintained separately for general ledger reports and subledger purposes by using the balancing segment in your chart of accounts as your legal company designator. Oracle defines the balancing segment as an entity for which you provide a balance sheet.

Therefore, if you centralize processing, you can use your balancing segment within your chart of accounts to separate legal entity data within the ledger. To report and process 1099s in Payables, Oracle provides a mapping for tax identification numbers to balancing segments under the menu path Setup, Taxes, Reporting Entities. See Figure 23.5 for an example of centralized and decentralized organizational structures.

> **Tip**
> The key to setting up an effective multi-org structure is to determine whether you will have centralized or decentralized processing.

DECENTRALIZED TRANSACTION PROCESSING WITHIN ORACLE APPLICATIONS

If you decentralize processing, you must have an Operating Unit and, if necessary for taxing purposes, a legal entity for each group that processes any or all of the following: Payables, Receivables, Purchasing, Projects, Order Management, and Cash Management. See Figure 23.5 for an example of centralized and decentralized organizational structures.

Figure 23.5
The DOG Treats Company centralizes all of its Payables, Receivables, Purchasing, Projects, Order Entry, and Cash Management processes.

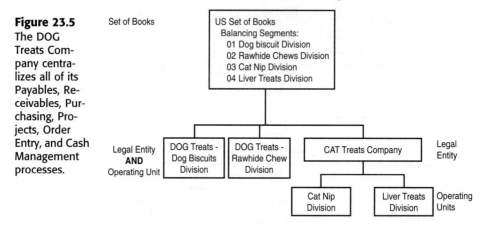

LIMITATIONS ON CENTRALIZATION/DECENTRALIZATION SUPPORT

Oracle does not support a combination of centralized and decentralized processes at this time. If you set up multi-org as a decentralized structure, you can give your users access to all responsibilities that represent all organizations to create a centralized capability in a decentralized environment.

You can set up a quasi-centralized/decentralized environment. An example would be a centralized payables department and decentralized purchasing department where the Payables Department handles all supplier invoices and payments and the Purchasing Departments are split among the various operating units.

The users for the Dog Treat Company would be given the following responsibilities:

TABLE 23.1   SAMPLE USER RESPONSIBILITIES

User Type	Responsibility
Centralized Payables User	
Payables Clerk1	AP Clerk—Dog Biscuit
	AP Clerk—Rawhide Chew
Decentralized Purchasing User	
Buyer1	Buyer—Dog Biscuits
Buyer2	Buyer—Rawhide Chew

This enables the payables clerk access to all accounts payable information by switching responsibilities to access the needed operating unit.

LINKING THE ORGANIZATIONAL STRUCTURES

You currently have a Human Resource structure and a Legal Entity structure. You now create the link between the two dimensions. This is done within the System Administration Responsibility and involves setting up Responsibilities and System Profile Options for each Operating Unit. Oracle states that a Responsibility defines what functionality of an application is available and that a Responsibility is assigned to users. Each Responsibility is assigned a set of System Profile Options. The System Profile Options link a Responsibility to a Business Group, Set of Books, and Operating Unit.

Figure 23.6 combines Figure 23.1 (the Business Group structure) and Figure 23.2 (the Legal Entity and Operating Unit structure).

> **Tip**
>
> Understand the link between your organizational structures and user Responsibilities before beginning setup in your system.

SECURITY

Data can be secured in several ways using Responsibilities within the Oracle Multi-Org structure.

Each Responsibility is linked to a set of books, a business group, and an operating unit. Each Responsibility also can have its own unique menu structure to allow access to only those areas of the menu tree applicable to the user's job requirements. To provide the most flexibility, the Responsibility is where data security is assigned.

Responsibilities can also be limited as to which Inventory Organizations they can view and enter data into. When the user goes to the Choose Inventory Organization window, she sees only those Inventory Organizations to which she has security access.

Oracle Multiple Organization structures do not allow viewing data across Operating Units. You can create custom reports to view this data.

SEED DATA REPLICATION

Data is replicated to multiple operating units when one of the following occurs:

1. When an installation or upgrade is the seed data, the replication process is run as part of the setup procedures.

2. When a new operating unit is created and saved, the seed data replication program runs automatically to replicate seed data in the new operating unit.

3. The AutoInstall adadmin option, Convert to Multiple Organization architecture, is manually run as a concurrent process.

Configure the Application

Before beginning system configuration and to ensure that your multi-org setup works as expected, you should always draw your organizational structure on paper before beginning setup, adding and revising components until it meets your company's present and future needs.

Setup Steps

The following steps represent the required setup sequence for multi-org functionality:

1. Develop the Organization Structure

   When developing your organizational structure, run through different process scenarios on paper before entering setup data in the system.

2. Define Sets of Books

   Each set of books you define requires that an accounting calendar, a chart of accounts consisting of your key accounting flexfield structure, and an active currency be set up prior to defining the set of books. Be sure to set up values for your retained earnings and intercompany accounts if you are using them because these will be required to complete your set of books' configuration.

3. Define Organizations

   Organizations are defined in the Human Resources tables. Always start by setting up your business group first. When you have the business groups entered, create a responsibility for each of the business groups. Link the responsibility to the business group using the System Profile Option HR: Business Group. This must be completed before setting up the remaining structure. Be sure to use the correct responsibility for each organization when proceeding with the remaining setup.

   Next, set up all legal entities and then finally your operating units. This ensures a streamlined configuration process when you define organizational relationships.

4. Define Organization Relationships

   Remember that Business Group and Legal Entities are separate structures. Business Group and Legal Entities are linked through Responsibilities using the System Profile Options. Legal Entities and Inventory Organizations are linked by Set of Books.

5. Define Responsibilities

   Responsibilities define what functionality of an application is available to a user.

6. Set the Operating Unit Profile Option for Each Responsibility

   The profile option is MO: Operating Unit.

7. Convert to Multiple Organization Architecture

When your setup is complete, have your database administrator run the Autoinstall utility adadmin. Be sure to choose the option to convert to multi-org. This process should only take a few minutes to run.

8. Define Inventory Organization Security (optional)

You can restrict your inventory users to selected inventory organizations by defining security based on responsibility.

9. Change Order Entry Profile Options (optional)

Order Entry Profile Options enable you to update each user's responsibility to enable different item validation organizations for your operating units.

10. Update Profile Options Specific to Operating Units

Certain profile options must be set at the Responsibility level. These include the following:

- AR: Receipt Batch Source
- AR: Transaction Batch Source
- OE: Item Validation Organization
- OE: Set of Books
- GL: Set of Books

11. Implement the Applications Products

You must set up Oracle er Entry/Shipping, Payables, Purchasing, Projects, Receivables, and Sales Compensation for each Operating Unit. This does not apply to Oracle General Ledger, Assets, Inventory, and the other manufacturing modules, which are only set up once (not per operating unit).

12. Secure Balancing Segment Values by Legal Entity (optional)

Security Rules control which Responsibilities have access to entering and viewing balancing segment data.

13. Run the Setup Validation Report (recommended)

Using the System Administrator Responsibility, run Setup Validation Report. This report gives you information on disabled fields on Enter Customer and Enter Supplier windows, verifies that you have set up consistent profile option values for all your responsibilities, and determines whether the item validation organizations are linked to the appropriate set of books within a responsibility.

TROUBLESHOOTING

If in doubt, call Oracle Support. Once in a while the multi-org functionality will not replicate set up data no matter what you do. Oracle Support should be able to help you out.

If user responsibilities suddenly begin to point to the wrong organization, check your site level profile options using the System Administration responsibility. If someone has changed the site level MO:Operating Unit value, and the responsibility level value has not been assigned, you will have this problem.

Never rearrange your organizational structure by reassigning operating units to different legal entities or business groups. Set up new operating units and new responsibilities pointing to them. Your historical data will remain available in the old organization, new data in the new organization.

CHAPTER 24

IMPLEMENTING ORACLE HUMAN RESOURCES AND ORACLE PAYROLL

If you are reading this chapter, you have likely decided to take on the challenge of implementing a new Human Resource Management System. This chapter presents an overview of issues to consider for such an implementation. Common issues affecting both HR and Payroll are addressed. Finally, a list of steps required for configuration of the Oracle HR/Payroll application is included. There are separate chapters regarding implementation of HR or Payroll (Chapter 25, "Using Oracle Human Resources," and Chapter 26, "Using Oracle Payroll") relating specifically to each module independently. Notes on Oracle Time Management are included with the Payroll chapter.

Another important note to consider when reading this chapter involves Human Resource and Payroll systems in general. Many of the issues addressed are not unique to Oracle and should certainly be considered for other HRMS package software such as SAP and PeopleSoft. For instance, consider the following:

Human Resource departments are loaded with government legislative and compliance reporting. Setup of an HRMS application directly affects the structure and content of data produced by these reports.

Payroll departments are required to transmit benefit files to and from third-party benefit administrators. These must be created based on the specific requirements of each administrator.

Historical data conversion and various approaches to conversion of HR/Payroll data have many common issues when dealing with packaged software.

Payroll systems that go live mid-year must have some mechanism for converting mid-year balances.

Integration testing and parallel testing requirements are certainly not unique requirements to Oracle.

CRITICAL HRMS IMPLEMENTATION FACTORS

This section addresses a number of critical implementation factors that should be addressed when implementing an Oracle HR/Payroll system. If you have already implemented Oracle Financials, some of these HR/Payroll issues will be common. However, beware. Human Resources and Payroll systems are quite different from Financial systems. Your success implementing a Financial system might not translate into a successful HR/Payroll implementation.

THE INITIAL PHASE

A detailed requirements analysis must be performed along with a high-level gaps analysis. This must occur early in the project to obtain good estimates of the expected project duration. This issue is closely tied to the next critical implementation factor of resources in that at least one experienced Oracle HR/Payroll resource should be involved. A solid project plan that identifies expected workload and assigns client resources to as many of the tasks that are reasonable should result from the requirements and gaps analyses. If this analysis is neglected, unpleasant surprises almost certainly will arise later in the project. The time to implement an HR/Payroll implementation (regardless of whether it is Oracle, SAP, or PeopleSoft) is often underestimated by a client.

RESOURCES

It is important to have a mix of functional and technical Oracle consultants as well as functional and technical personnel from the client. There is no perfect number of consultants. The scope of the project, number of employees, complexity of the client's business, time allotted before go-live date, and knowledge base of the users all factor into how many project-dedicated personnel are required.

Interaction between technical and functional project team members is necessary for project success. Although it might be important to have separate technical and functional teams, there should not be a permanent dividing line between these teams. Having good communication and cooperation between the technical and the functional personnel increases the chances of having a successful project and producing good results for the client.

FUNCTIONAL CONSULTANTS

The Oracle HRMS product is very flexible and highly configurable. The greater the flexibility of a product, the greater the number of decisions that must be made during the project. It is recommended that functional consultants in both Human Resources and Payroll be used, although this expertise might be achieved with one person. At least one consultant should have experience with the Oracle HR/Payroll products themselves. Again, this product is highly configurable. Experience with Human Resource and Payroll systems in general is not sufficient. The user community might have to live with setup decisions for years to come. The number of decision points is high. The cost of wrong or less-than-optimal decisions is high.

TECHNICAL CONSULTANTS

The Oracle HRMS database is somewhat complex. Two mistakes commonly made on projects are (1) assuming that experienced Oracle Financials technical consultants will easily translate into effective Oracle HR/Payroll technical consultants and (2) assuming that the client IT staff can handle these tasks without outside assistance. These issues are not about aptitude or potential. The issue is about experience.

An Oracle Financials consultant can be trained on Oracle HR/Payroll and certainly become effective. The mistake is to assume that the learning curve for the Oracle HR/Payroll database is the same as that of Oracle General Ledger. The result of this mistake is to significantly increase project duration, resulting in higher project costs possibly causing important deadlines to be missed.

The client IT staff must be represented and participate on the project. However, be careful not to assume that this staff will quickly master the Oracle HR/Payroll database. They will rely heavily on the experience of technical Oracle HR/Payroll consultants. If the learning curve for an experienced Oracle Financials consultant (who might already know the Oracle Tools of Forms and Reports) is high, the learning curve for an IT staff not previously exposed to Oracle will be higher.

It truly is a matter of spending the time and money to bring in experienced resources to help do the job right. The alternative is the increased price for bad, hastily made, or incomplete decisions.

Finally, the emphasis here has been on bringing in experienced functional and technical leadership. However, this leadership should not work in a vacuum. The user must be able to maintain the system after it goes live. Thus, it is imperative that clients have fulltime functional and technical staff to work on the project. This staff must become the experts so that dependence on consultants is not necessary for a long-term basis after the new systems go into production.

EXECUTIVE SPONSORSHIP

A vital component of the HR/Payroll implementation is the involvement and support of upper management. It is important for the team personnel to be able to rely on the support of management. The management team must be available to answer questions, make decisions, and communicate to other client management on the progress and impediments of the project.

This can be vitally important when the user community has used the same HR/Payroll systems for many years. Old habits die hard, and some users might refuse to assume tasks that they consider to not be their jobs. The new Oracle HRMS system brings much opportunity but also introduces potential frustrations as employees' roles might need to change. Upper management must remain involved to make decisions that affect employees' future responsibilities.

Part of this support by management is financial. Management needs to stay informed on where the project stands in relation to project timelines and allotted budget. The best consultants can resolve almost any business requirement. However, time and money add up. Management must be prepared to step in and make decisions and change business requirements or identify requirements of lower priority that can be solved in a future phase of implementation.

DOCUMENTATION

The user should keep thorough, accurate, and complete documents of processes, procedures, and decisions made during the project. If done correctly, this documentation can lead to enhancements and further refinement by client personnel (not consultants) after the project has completed and the new HR/Payroll system is live. Training manuals should be developed and constantly updated as testing is performed and changes are made to the system. Documents should be developed for the following categories:

User documentation

Solution design

Technical specifications

Training

It can be frustrating and frightening for a user to need to make changes to the system without sufficient documentation. The user might not fully understand why the system was set up in its current state. Thus, project documentation can provide not only the understanding of why the system was set up in the way that it was, but also what steps were necessary to provide the solution.

Documentation must be clear, concise, and accurate. It should be reviewed by the client during the project implementation. Proper documentation provides the roadmap to make new system decisions. Sticky notes posted on a wall do not stand the test of time.

PARALLEL TESTING

After rigorous system testing has occurred, parallel testing should occur on Oracle Payroll implementations. First, I'll define parallel testing. *Parallel testing* involves duplicating operations between the legacy system and the Oracle Payroll system. However, duplicate operations do not imply duplicate results. Duplicate results are certainly the goal. The parallel test is necessary to identify test results that do not match the results produced by the legacy system. Also, the parallel test is necessary to provide hands-on training for the actual users who will operate the eventual production system.

If sufficient payroll testing or conference room pilot testing has already occurred, parallel testing would not be necessary. This is true, but the keyword is sufficient. Some items can slip through rigorous payroll testing.

For example, a data conversion for tax information might have been tested for many employees. However, you will never really know whether the correct federal, state, and local taxes are being withheld until every employee has been tested. Various states have reciprocity laws for employees who work in one state but live in another. Because of these many combinations, parallel testing ensures that every combination has been met. Moreover, the tax information calculated during the parallel test might not match because Oracle Payroll calculates differently from the legacy system. Usually, the discrepancies are a result of incorrect legacy system calculations. However, nothing should be taken for granted.

The parallel test should be performed primarily by the actual endusers who will be operating the future production system. This gives the users hands-on, real-world scenario training to reinforce any user training classes that have been conducted. Certainly, this effort causes a burden on client staff because they are being asked to perform two jobs at once.

Some users simply do not have the manpower to handle data entry in two systems to run a true parallel of the one system and the new Oracle system. A good alternative to this is to use some kind of auditing tool. There are several tools of this kind on the market. The Implementation Team Leader would designate a Test Coordinator for each day that testing is being conducted. Having a Test Coordinator designated by day provides greater flexibility of scheduling, particularly if work is being done on more than a regular eight-hour day and through weekend and holiday time.

The role of the Test Coordinator is to prepare the testing document, hand out assignments to the testing team, assist individual team members with assignments, and log the results of the testing. The Test Coordinator gives problems identified by category to individuals knowledgeable in the area to resolve the problems. After a designated number of problems are found on one issue, no further testing on that function is done until the problem or problems are resolved. This eliminates valuable testing time being wasted on an already known problem. At the end of the testing period, the Test Coordinator documents the results of the test items and presents the findings to the Implementation Team Leader. It is recommended to have Subject Matter Experts from the various areas (Benefits, Compensation, Payroll, and so on) onhand to assist as members of the testing team and to answer questions regarding their areas of expertise. Support from the Technical function and DBAs is crucial.

How long should you parallel test? This answer varies from project to project. As a general rule, consider three full parallel runs over a three-month period. Essentially, you spend the first couple of weeks of each month performing the parallel test and the second couple of weeks of each month resolving problems and issues from the previous parallel test and preparing the system for the next parallel.

How should you structure and prepare for each parallel test? First, your DBA must establish a clean test database environment. Then, the DBA must prepare this environment to mimic a specific point in time that will correspond to the payroll period to be tested. The pay period to be paralleled does not have to be the current pay period. It can be a period back in time; however, this requires advance planning to ensure that the DBA has the appropriate production system backups and the client has the correct legacy system data backups prior to the desired payroll period dates. This is accomplished differently for different projects.

Some clients might already have a production Oracle system with Financials live. These same clients might have already converted some of their HR data into the Oracle production system prior to the official go-live date for HR/Payroll. In this situation, the DBA should perform a complete backup of code and data from the production system and refresh this information onto the test environment as of a specific point in time. Then, any other data conversions or migrations that are planned for the future HR/Payroll system must be performed. For example, the Oracle production system might already have employees, addresses, and assignments loaded in addition to the existence of other Oracle Application modules. After this information is refreshed into the test environment, other HR/Payroll scripts (or data entry) must occur (for example, Personal Payment Methods, Salary, and Element Entries). If a mid-year conversion is planned, the Balance Initialization routines must be initiated.

The Balance Initialization process should be elaborated on. On the first parallel test, the balance initialization might not provide as much value as it will on the future parallel tests. The first parallel test is likely to have many test results that are inaccurate. One small mistake can affect the results for numerous employees. These mistakes are often a result of user errors. Remember, this is a training exercise for the actual end users and provides an excellent learning experience for users without the risk of error to a real paycheck.

Other mistakes that can affect numerous employees involve data conversions. For example, one data conversion routine for benefits might have *operated* correctly to load employee bonuses; however, the correct operation might have been using an incorrect source data file for bonuses from another pay period. Another example could be a data conversion routine that incorrectly loaded pretax deductions for only one element. This one element causes the taxes and net pay to be incorrect for a large population of employees.

Thus, having correct balances prior to the first parallel test might not have improved the test results significantly. However, the Balance Initialization should seriously be considered by the time of the second parallel test.

After the parallel test has completed and after the project team has corrected programs, procedures, and so on, you are ready for the next parallel. It might be unlikely that you can reuse the same test environment. Thus, the DBA must again refresh this environment to mimic the specific point in time that will correspond to the payroll period to be tested. As you approach the second and third parallel test, you might have the opportunity to attempt back-to-back payroll period parallels without a refresh. This has an added advantage by allowing you to test month-to-date balances that are sometimes required in interface programs to third-party administrators.

If you want confidence when the new Oracle HR/Payroll system is ready to go live, you should have it after conducting parallel tests.

CELEBRATING SUCCESSES

An HR/Payroll implementation takes a significant amount of time to complete. The stress level will get high and it is vital to have a cohesive, productively functioning team. The difficulty is that there is only one finish line. The finish line is to successfully go live. However, this might be many months or even more than one year away. The team must recognize accomplishments along the way. There is no magical formula, but there are numerous small and large things that can be done to help the team feel motivated to continue their drive for success.

COMMON UNREALISTIC PROJECT EXPECTATIONS

One of the most common responses observed after a company purchases any new software package is the expectation that the new system will finally do everything they always wanted. It will also do all these tasks faster, simpler, and automatically. One of the hardest tasks a project manager must accomplish is to properly manage these expectations. This section will outline some of the more common surprises that can surface while implementing Oracle HR/Payroll.

HR/PAYROLL IS JUST ANOTHER ORACLE APPLICATION

This is generally the initial reaction of companies who have already implemented Oracle Financials and are preparing to implement HR/Payroll. They expect that the knowledge they have gained from the other applications will automatically transfer to the HR/Payroll modules. They also expect that any external resources they used for implementing the Financial modules will be equally experienced in implementing HR/Payroll.

You will quickly discover that the only areas that remain consistent in HR/Payroll are in constructing Key Flexfields and defining responsibilities and task flows. From there, the module takes on a life of its own. The HR/Payroll module was developed by a completely different development group located in the United Kingdom. Some of their unique terms show up every now and then, such as cheque and spinal points. The underlying HR/Payroll database table structures are very complex. At some implementations, we have developed SQL scripts to retrieve payroll results that required SQL Joins to 22 different tables.

Some companies plan to modify Oracle Payroll's Check Writer to conform to their own payroll check design. This is usually because they have been successful in completing this same task on their AP check form and do not expect any problems. Oracle Accounts Payable provides hooks in their check writing process that enable companies to insert the necessary escape sequences for the MICR coding. These same hooks do not appear in the Payroll Check Writer process. A simple task in AP can become a major modification in Payroll.

As stated before, successful Oracle Financials implementers do not automatically make successful Oracle HR/Payroll implementers. Many projects have missed implementation dates and exceeded budgets because the learning curve for HR/Payroll was grossly underestimated.

VERTEX WILL HANDLE ALL MY TAXING ISSUES

One of the key selling points of Oracle HR/Payroll is its tight integration with Vertex. Vertex refers to the payroll tax engine product produced by Vertex Corporation that is bundled with Oracle Payroll. Indeed, there is minimal setup required to have the proper taxes withheld in a normal payroll run. Vertex automatically recognizes the proper taxes to withhold based on the zip code of the employee's primary address and work location. Vertex also recognizes all full and partial reciprocity laws between states when employees work in one state and live in another.

Initially, this is a blessing to many payroll departments because they will no longer have to keep up with all the changing tax laws in all their jurisdictions. Some companies are surprised to discover that their legacy systems were not withholding all the proper taxes from their employees. Generally, this occurs at the local and school district levels. The initial reaction is to turn the tax off and continue to tax in the same manner as the legacy system. Until recently, the only way to turn the tax off was to navigate to the W4 window of all employees who have this tax and mark them exempt. This solution required careful monitoring of every payroll run because there is no easy way to identify these employees beforehand. A patch now enables companies to explicitly identify which local taxes to take at the GRE level. Before utilizing this solution, companies should research every tax body to determine whether they are required to withhold this tax.

The next area of frustration with the Vertex integration occurs when a tax has been withheld in error. This generally happens when a zip code was entered incorrectly and the problem was not discovered until the employee received her check. Oracle does not provide an easy method to return this amount back to the employee. You must make a balance adjustment to remove the withheld balance, as well as the Subject To tax balance. These adjustments can be complex and might cause problems later during the quarterly and year-end closes. The actual money is usually refunded to the employee through either an AP check or petty cash.

No More Manual Wage Attachment Calculations

Oracle HRMS provides an easy setup process to establish involuntary deduction elements for all the different wage attachments. The federal and state laws concerning wage attachments are complex, and Oracle HR/Payroll is designed to support all these laws. Once again, this is a blessing to the payroll department due to the complexity of these laws. However, Oracle does not provide any backup to support the calculation of a wage attachment. You have no idea what rule has applied when the amount is deducted from an employee's check. This can prove to be embarrassing and frustrating when an employee inquires about the calculation of the amount.

There are many stories where companies complete a parallel run and discover that the child-support calculations do not agree. After a detailed and time-consuming investigation, it has been discovered that court orders have been issued in violation of the law and that the judges needed to reissue new orders. The point here is that although Oracle was correct in applying the federal and state laws, it provided no backup to assist the payroll department in researching the issue.

Because of the ever-changing tax laws, there are many associated patches for wage attachments. As you go through your testing phase, do not assume that the Oracle calculation is always correct. You might need to contact Oracle Worldwide Support to discover that a missing patch is causing the calculations to be incorrect.

It Is Straightforward to Update the FIT Taxable Balance

One of the first tasks in preparing an implementation plan is to decide on a target implementation date. The easiest date to begin any new payroll system is the first paycheck of a new calendar year. All year-to-date totals start at zero on January 1, and there is no need to load balances from your legacy system. However, this is generally the busiest time of the year for a payroll department. Also, many companies want to phase different locations into the new system throughout the year. For many reasons, some companies have to transfer payroll balances from the legacy payroll system into Oracle Payroll.

Many companies assume that this will be a straightforward and simple task. They quickly discover, however, that their legacy tax balances do not map easily to the many components of the tax balances in Oracle. The FIT Taxable balance within Oracle Payroll is a good example of this challenge. To calculate the FIT Taxable balance, you must load in the following balances:

Gross Earnings

Supplemental Earnings for FIT

Supplemental Earnings for NWFIT

Def Comp 401K

Section 125

Clearly, there is not a one-to-one correspondence between the balances in the legacy system and in Oracle Payroll. Do not underestimate the time it will take to prepare the numbers that Oracle requires for a balance load. I recommend that you simulate a quarterly and year-end close during your testing of the balance loads. Many mistakes that are made during the balance load do not resurface until you attempt to create the necessary quarterly and year-end files and reports. Corrections to these balances can be complicated and time consuming.

WHEN WE ARE ON ORACLE, PAYROLL SHOULD RUN MUCH FASTER

This is a very delicate issue and there are no universal answers or predictions on how long a payroll will run in Oracle. One of the most powerful features of Oracle Payroll is that balances are not explicitly stored. Whenever a balance is referenced, Oracle dynamically calculatesthe balance by adding up all payroll run results for the requested period. This enables you to query on a year to date based on any date in the past through the power of DateTracking. Although this is a powerful feature not found in many payroll systems, it can have a negative effect on the processing times.

Because the early implementers of Oracle Payroll were unsatisfied about the processing times, Oracle instituted a process of storing the latest balances in tables to improve performance. This has improved processing times, but other performance-tuning might be necessary. One of the reasons I previously stressed the importance of performing complete parallel runs is to discover whether there will be any performance issues.

Some performance tips to try if you experience unsatisfactory run times include the following:

Summarize timecards. Instead of processing 5 timecards at 8 hours each, summarize this to one time card of 40 hours.

Experiment with the THREADS parameter of the PAY_PROCESSING_ PARAMETERS table. The general rule of thumb is two threads per CPU.

Any balances that are referenced in a Fast Formula are updated in the latest balances table. If you suspect that your processing times are spent calculating a particular balance, place a reference to this balance in a Fast Formula that will execute for every employee.

These are just a few of the more common techniques for improving performance. You might need to work closely with you DBA and MIS staff for any hardware performance solutions.

WHEN ORACLE IS IMPLEMENTED, WE WILL NOT HAVE TO RELY ON MIS SUPPORT ANYMORE

This comment comes from both the user and MIS departments. Most legacy systems require heavy MIS involvement to keep the system in compliance with tax laws. There is usually a backlog of enhancement requests from Payroll and Human Resources as well. Many companies elect to purchase these systems to lessen the burden on inhouse resources.

During the marketing phase, Oracle stresses the flexibility of Fast Formulas and the availability of easy-to-use reporting tools. Unfortunately, this is often interpreted to mean that an end user will be able to write her own reports or modify a Fast Formula. Granted, the tools being referenced are very easy to use. The problem centers on the complex structure of the Oracle HR/Payroll table design and detailed programming logic incorporated in the Fast Formulas.

As mentioned previously, a simple SQL query to retrieve a list of all employees with a United Way deduction might result in a complicated table join. At some implementations, we have observed complex Oracle Payroll joins through SQL requiring access to 22 tables. DateTracking also complicates simple queries because there can be multiple records in a table for the same employee. Clearly, preparing reports from payroll results require some extremely intense knowledge of table structures and SQL coding techniques.

The entire gross to net calculation in Oracle Payroll is accomplished with the use of Fast Formulas. One of the strongest assets of Oracle Payroll is that you can control this process by modifying or writing your own Fast Formulas. However, one look at an existing formula reveals that the everyday end user lacks the necessary skills needed to properly change a calculation.

MIS involvement during the implementation process is essential to the success of the project. This is especially important if you are using external consultants. MIS must be able to step in and support the system when it is time to let the consultants go. It is unwise to allow all of the knowledge gained from implementing your system to leave with the consultants when they walk out your door.

These are some of the recurring issues when implementing Oracle HR/Payroll. This section is not intended to scare you. Its purpose is to keep you from making some of the more common incorrect assumptions while you implement your system. Careful planning and constant testing yield a powerful and important tool in achieving the goals stated in your enterprise's mission statement.

HISTORICAL DATA CONVERSION APPROACHES

Conversion of legacy data is a major step in nearly all system implementation projects. With HR/Payroll systems, core employee data must be transferred from the current system to the new one. There are a few acceptable methods of accomplishing this with Oracle's HRMS. These will be outlined in the following sections along with advantages and disadvantages of each. Caution: Notice that none of the options in this overview suggests writing programs to load data directly into the application database tables. This is because the table structure and table interdependencies are quite complex due to a high level of normalization. Many tables can be impacted with the entry of a single record type. Using the application screens and/or available APIs guarantees that all appropriate tables are updated in the proper manner. Furthermore, direct table loading might void your Oracle Support agreement.

MANUAL ENTRY

With this approach, users actually key the data into the application windows. This is a very nontechnical method, but for some implementations, it might be the most preferred. If the current system contains a smaller, manageable number of records and technical resources are low or unavailable, manual data entry might be the way to go. Additionally, if a large user community were available for the task, it might take less time than you might expect, and it would be a great training exercise for those involved. Sometimes large record volumes in major implementation projects make this option unacceptable. Fortunately, there are other options.

SCREEN LOADER

A Visual Basic for Applications (VBA) script can be run to transfer data from a Microsoft Excel spreadsheet to GUI forms. This is an acceptable option if the conversion volumes are too large for actual manual entry and the user would prefer a semi-automated approach. It works by selecting certain data from the legacy system and importing it to an Excel spreadsheet. It can there be formatted in proper entry order with the required control commands and automatically written to the Oracle forms via the VBA script. The script includes looping logic to keep the process going until all data has been loaded. Think of this as robotic data entry. You can even watch the entry process on the PC screen as if a user were actually typing the information. The setup of the format can be tricky because you must consider all system responses and handle them in the controls. Field order and cursor movement must match the form exactly. Another caution is the load speed, which can be controlled. The PC can run the load script faster than the Oracle Application can respond in some cases, causing error conditions when fields get overwritten accidentally. Also, large volumes of records loaded in this fashion can tend to use a lot of PC memory resources, occasionally causing system lockups. It is best to run the loads in batches. For very large implementations, this option might not be the best. There are still two remaining methods for dealing with large volumes of data.

ORACLE APIS

Oracle provides callable Application Program Interfaces (APIs) that can be used to load the legacy data properly. An API is a stored PL/SQL Program/Package that resides in the database. This method works by selecting the appropriate data from the legacy system and loading a temporary table that will be processed by a program that calls the APIs using data from the temporary table. The API handles loading the data into the appropriate database tables in the same way the data would be loaded if it were entered manually through the

Oracle HRMS GUI forms. The APIs deal with much the same data as the forms, meaning that the data is grouped and loaded as if by form type (People, Assignment, and so on). This method is ideal for large numbers of records, but it requires technical resources with PL/SQL programming skills. Great care must be taken in testing the results of the load in a nonproduction environment because the records loaded cannot be rolled back or undone. Updating for corrections is possible, however. Additionally, you must also know the internal code designations for items that are loaded. Simply loading the user-readable value is not acceptable. The final method provides the added benefit of rolling back an unsatisfactory load.

Data Pump

This method uses the same APIs that you can call directly, but it requires less technical knowledge to operate. PL/SQL programs are provided (generated by running a process called the Meta Mapper) that will load data into the Data Pump tables. (You must still populate temporary tables with legacy data as a starting point.) When the Data Pump tables have been populated, you can then run the Data Pump to load the data into the application database tables. There are a number of advantages to using the Data Pump. First of all, it permits running in validation mode so that you can check for errors before actually running the load. If you discover errors after an actual load, you can rerun the Data Pump to correct the errors. The Data Pump process takes advantage of multithread environments, meaning that if you specified a multithread option for payroll processes, the Data Pump engine processes in the same manner. This means the Data Pump load process could potentially run many times faster than the normal API process. Another nice feature is the ability to load user values instead of internal code values. Data Pump handles the translation of the value to the code internally. The Data Pump process is submitted through Submit Reports & Processes like many other normal processes, so it is simpler to use for less technical individuals.

As you can see, there are a number of options available for loading legacy data into the Oracle HRMS. Each implementation project has its own unique parameters and constraints. These should be considered when making the decision on how to load legacy data. No single method is right for every implementation, but enough options exist to provide for a choice of the one that is the best fit.

Other Data Conversion Considerations

Now that you have an understanding of the approaches to Oracle HRMS data conversion, there are other issues to consider. This section focuses on issues regarding the types of data that you need to migrate into the new system.

Finding Oracle's Application Program Interfaces

APIs were introduced earlier. If you consider using APIs for data conversion, you will want to obtain a list of the APIs available within Oracle HR/Payroll. The name and type of the API and the PL/SQL code are stored in Oracle tables. By querying the tables, you can easily get the name, code, or type of an API.

Following are the relevant Oracle tables:

USER_SOURCE. All Database Objects created for the users.

DBA_SOURCE. All Database Objects created for the DBA.

ALL_SOURCE. All Database Objects.

Table 24.1 shows the table structure.

TABLE 24.1 TABLE STRUCTURE

Table Name	Column Name	Data Type	Description
USER_SOURCE	Name	Varchar2 (30)	Name of the API
	Type *	Varchar2 (12)	Type (procedure/package)
	Line	Number	Line Number (Each line of the PL/SQL code is stored as one record.)
	Text	Varchar2 (20000)	PL/SQL code
DBA_SOURCE	Owner	Varchar2 (30)	Owner name
	Name	Varchar2 (30)	Name of the API
	Type *	Varchar2 (12)	Type (procedure/package)
	Line	Number	Line number (Each line of the PL/SQL code is stored as one record.)
	Text	Varchar2 (2000)	PL/SQL code
ALL_SOURCE	Owner	Varchar2 (30)	Owner name
	Name	Varchar2 (30)	Name of the API
	Type *	Varchar2 (12)	Type (procedure/package)
	Line	Number	Line number (Each line of the PL/SQL code is stored as one record.)
	Text	Varchar(2000)	PL/SQL code

* Packages are stored as PACKAGE and PACKAGE BODY, where PACKAGE is the specification of the program and PACKAGE BODY is the actual program.

To identify the Oracle HR APIs, perform the following. In SQL*Plus, connect to the Oracle database as the APPS user and then issue the following query to find out the name of an API:

```
Select distinct NAME
From USER_SOURCE
Where NAME like 'HR_%'
```

```
And Type = 'PACKAGE';
```

In this code, the third line identifies packages starting with HR_. The last line is optional. In it, you can use either PACKAGE_BODY or PACKAGE.

After performing the preceding query, you should be able to identify the name of all APIs. Next, you will want to find out detailed information about specific APIs that can potentially be used by your data conversion team. You can use the following query to obtain a copy of the PL/SQL source code for any desire API. This query produces an output file named api.txt that contains a description of the API and corresponding comments retrieved from the API. This output file can be viewed in any text editor. The following is the PL/SQL code to produce this file:

```
SQL> Spool api.txt
SQL> Select TEXT
     from USER_SOURCE
     Where NAME = '{Name of the API}';
```

PART

III

CH

24

> **Note**   It is preferable not to use LIKE and % in the preceding SQL statement because each API has numerous lines of code.

```
SQL> Spool off;
```

CONVERSION OPTIONS: WHAT HISTORY SHOULD YOU MIGRATE TO ORACLE HRMS?

It is a common desire to convert as much information from your legacy system as possible into the Oracle HRMS system. However, practicality is necessary in addressing this issue. There are restrictions and data validation options with Oracle HRMS that might not have been met by your legacy system. Note that the method of conversion is addressed above under Conversion Methods. Following are a few of the types of data that you might want to convert:

Conversion of Employees. This refers to much of the basic information of an employee such as Name, Birth Date, Date of Hire, and so on. This is usually a good candidate for data conversion. I generally recommend that you convert only the most recent demographic information as opposed to the entire history. For instance, if a female employee has been married over the past few years, you should only concern yourself with her current last name. Otherwise, you will encounter date-tracking complications in converting the history of every date and name change that has occurred for this employee.

Conversion of Addresses. This is another good candidate for conversion; however, the conversion process is more involved than most people expect. Oracle HRMS requires an accurate county and zip code for each employee. This is required due to the impact an employee's residence has on Payroll taxation. Many legacy systems do not retain County information. Thus, your conversion must first derive the correct county for each employee. When more than one valid county exists for a given city, state, and zip code, you must contact your employees to determine the correct county.

Conversion of Assignments. This is a typical goal but one you must repeatedly review based on the various components of the employee assignment (organization, position, grade, and so on). For instance, many companies desire to convert job history into the Oracle HR assignment records. However, during your Oracle HRMS system design and configuration, you might have re-engineered your job naming strategy. Thus, there might not be a one-to-one correspondence between old job names and new job names. Moreover, if old job titles became obsolete but you still wanted to convert this job history information, you would first need to create the obsolete job title as a valid selection in Oracle before converting the jobs and subsequently end-dating the obsolete job names.

This same logic holds true for conversion of organizations. Due to buyouts, consolidation, restructuring, and so on, organization history might be difficult to convert. You would need to create all obsolete organizations before the conversion could succeed.

Thus, a more practical approach might be necessary. Consider converting assignment *history* into Special Information Types and converting only the latest information into the employee assignment. If your legacy system only has sufficient information to convert the employee's organization, payroll, and salary basis, prepare to update other information such as jobs and grades manually.

Conversion of Salary. This is usually a good candidate for conversion. Note that you must first convert an employee's assignment with a valid salary basis before attempting conversion of salary. Also, it is common to convert salary history using effective dates of each salary for each employee.

Conversion of Tax Information. Earlier releases of Oracle HRMS did not offer APIs for tax information. This was usually accomplished by screen keystroke emulation described earlier in this chapter. Now that APIs have become available, Tax Information is a good candidate for conversion.

Conversion of Earnings and Deductions. Consider using Batch Element Entry to accommodate this type of conversion, where you focus on one compensation or benefit element at a time. You can create batches by converting your information from the legacy system and then invoking the Oracle HRMS process to convert this information into the Element Entries tables.

Year to Date Balance Conversion. If you bring your new system live in the middle of a calendar year, this process is a must. Please see the section "Year to Date Balance Conversion" within Chapter 26, "Using Oracle Payroll," for details to approaching this process.

DATETRACK INFORMATION

DateTrack is an Oracle HRMS feature that enables you to view the system (employee, organizations, benefits, and so on) based on any desired snapshot in time. DateTrack enables you to establish an effective date to enter information that takes effect on your effective date (which could be a past, present, or future date) and to review HRMS information as of the effective date. DateTracking is Oracle's method of maintaining a continuous history of key information on employees such as salary, assignments, and benefits. This tracking can begin with the date the applicant is first interviewed, continuing with the hire date, tracking all events of the employee's work history, and culminating with the employee's retirement or termination.

DateTracking is one of the most helpful tools Oracle provides for tracking employee information. The DateTrack feature provides a means of knowing when records were changed by using DateTrack History. To access DateTrack History, choose the DateTrack icon from the Windows toolbar. This opens the Summary window with rows that show what employee information was changed and the date. You can use the option of a full history by clicking the Full History button in the DateTrack Window. This gives you a folder menu from which you can select specific information for review. It is also possible to customize this folder to fit individual user needs.

DateTracking is used when making additions, changes, or corrections to data. It is not used on all forms. Forms (such as Grades, Grade Rates, Jobs, People, and Position) opened directly from the Navigator Menu (sometimes referred to as top-level forms) access a common DateTracking date. This date remains in place until changed by the user. Forms opened from these forms (subsidiary forms) such as address, assignment, and element entries, have override ability from the top-level form. This allows different DateTracking dates to apply only while in these subsidiary forms. On returning to the higher level form, the DateTracked date reverts to the date on the top-level form.

For example, consider a situation where you were viewing Organizations from the Organization form. Assume now that you have changed your effective date to 01-JAN-2000 so that you can view the current organization definitions as of this date. Next, if you navigate to the Person form, your session date remains at 01-JAN-2000. You are not able to view information on an employee who was hired on or after 02-JAN-2000. This is because the employee does not exist as of your effective date. Now, assume that you have navigated to the Element Entries form for an employee. However, you desire to view the employee's element entries as of an earlier date such as 01-NOV-1999. You can change the system effective date to view these element entries. When this form is closed and you return to the Person or Assignment form, the system date changes back to 01-JAN-2000. This is because you changed the effective date while on a subsidiary (or child) form as opposed to changing the effective date on the top-level form (Person, Job, Organization, and so on).

The power of DateTracking can be observed during benefits enrollment time. Use of the DateTrack feature enables you to put in the new rates and coverage before year-end. For example, if the current day of the year is 01-DEC-2000, you can change your effective date to 01-JAN-2001 to allow entry of employee benefit changes scheduled to take place at the beginning of the next calendar year. Entry of these future changes will not affect payroll results from 01-DEC-2000 (assuming your payroll calendar does not have 01-DEC-2000 and 01-JAN-2001 within the same payroll period).

When logging on to Oracle HRMS, the effective date always defaults to today's date. When you have changed the DateTrack date to a past or future date and completed your transaction, you should reset the altered effective date. Not doing so could result in incorrect data for other transactions you enter. The following choices listed should be investigated thoroughly and the action to be changed should be analyzed closely to make the correct decision.

DateTrack Profile Options

There are profile options for DateTrack that can be configured for your specific implementation. The security options for DateTrack are usually set by the System Administrator, who would have knowledge of the user's level of proficiency.

As you establish a strategy for the following security options, consider starting with allowing users very limited ability to change DateTracked information; then, as users become more confident and knowledgeable, allow them to control this function by giving them unlimited ability to do so.

Options available from DateTrack security using the user profile option of DateTrack:Date Security include the following:

All. Allows the user to access past, present, and future dates. (Most typical selection.)

Past. Allows the user to only access past dates.

Present. Allows the user to only access current date.

Future. Allows the user to only access future dates.

Reminder options are the following:

Always. Causes pop-up dialog box reminder to the user of the current session date each time a top-level form is invoked from the Oracle HRMS Navigator.

Never. Does not require user acknowledgement of pop-up dialog box reminder for current session date.

Not Today. Causes pop-up dialog box reminder to the user of the current session date, if the current session date is not today, each time a top-level form is invoked from the Oracle HRMS Navigator.

DateTrack User Decisions

The user will encounter several types of DateTrack decisions while inserting, updating, and deleting records. Here are some the situations a user might encounter.

Typical options for deleting records consist of the following:

End Date. The user wants to establish a final date for the existence of the current record without actually deleting the history of the record itself. In essence the user wants to maintain history of the information up until the date of deletion.

Purge. The user wants to totally remove this record from the database without retaining the history of the record.

Deleting options when future records exist are as follows:

All. The user has requested to delete a record even though future dated records exist. The user wants to delete all occurrences of future records.

Next. The user has requested to delete a record even though future dated records exist. The user *only* wants to delete the next occurrence of this record without deleting further future occurrences of the record that exist after the next occurrence.

Typical options for modifying records include the following:

Update. The user wants the new record to add to, not destroy, historical records that exist. The new record becomes the active record as of the current DateTrack session date.

Correction. The user wants the new record to overwrite and destroy the current record that is displayed. (Note that multiple changes within the same day must always be a Correction.)

Modifying records when future records exist are as follows:

Insert. Insert the current record while retaining the future records. This causes the currently inserted record to remain active from the current session date until the date of the next future record.

Replace. Delete future records and replace those records with the current record.

REQUIRED ORACLE HRMS SETUP STEPS

Configuring the Oracle Human Resources and Payroll modules requires *analysis* of the various setup steps in a different order than is required for actual *configuration* of your production environment. For instance, the first few setup steps involve the creation of Key Flexfields. Until a detailed requirements analysis has occurred, the structures of these Key Flexfields cannot be established.

It is common to address certain details of this type of requirement analysis in a test database environment. This enables the user to test out the implications of setup decisions. Then, after the user is comfortable with the *requirements* for all setup steps, the actual setup steps can be followed in order in the production database. Following is a list of the setup steps, followed by a description of key issues associated with each step. Note that these steps are somewhat similar to what is documented by Oracle Corporation in *Oracle HRMS Implementation Guide Version 10SC*. However, I believe the following order of events and desired implementation tasks are slightly different and will result in a more efficient implementation:

- Define the Job Key Flexfield.
- Define the Position Key Flexfield.
- Define the Grade Key Flexfield.
- Define the People Group Key Flexfield.
- Define the Cost Allocation Key Flexfield.
- Define the Descriptive Flexfields.
- Enable Currencies.
- Define Users.
- Create Public Synonyms.
- Run Process Grant Permissions to Roles (ROLEGEN).
- Define Quick Code Types.
- Define Quick Code Values.
- Define Locations.
- Define Business Group Organization.
- Define View All Access to Business Group.
- Define Human Resource Organizations.
- Define Government Reporting Entity Organizations.
- Define Other Organizations.
- Define Organization Hierarchies.
- Define Jobs.
- Define Positions.
- Define Position Reporting Hierarchies.
- Define Career Paths for Jobs and Positions.
- Define Grades.
- Define Grade Rates.
- Define Pay Scales.
- Define Progression Point Values.
- Define Grade Steps and Points.
- Define Payment Methods.
- Define Consolidations Sets.
- Define Payrolls.
- Define Earnings.
- Define Deductions and Benefit Plans.
- Define Employer Liability Elements.
- Define Information Elements.

- Define Taxability Rules for Tax Categories.
- Define Input Values for Elements.
- Define Validation Formulas.
- Define Element Links for Earnings, Deductions, and Benefits.
- Define Taxation and Other Element Links.
- Define Payroll Balances.
- Define User Tables.
- Define Payroll Formulas.
- Define Payroll Formula Results.
- Define Salary Bases.
- Enable Salary Approvals.
- Define Proposal Reasons and Performance Ratings.
- Define Benefit Carriers.
- Define Benefit Coverages.
- Define Element Sets.
- Define Person Types.
- Define Assignment Statuses.
- Define Special Information Type Key Flexfields.
- Define Worker's Compensation Codes and Rates.
- Define Worker's Compensation Job Codes.
- Define Paid Time Off Accrual Plans.
- Define Human Resource Budgets.

PART

III

CH

24

DEFINING JOB, POSITION, GRADE, COST ALLOCATION, AND PEOPLE GROUP KEY FLEXFIELDS

Analysis for defining the Key Flexfields within Oracle HR and Payroll requires different timing depending on the Flexfield in question. The analysis for Job, Position, and Grade Key Flexfields typically occurs very early during the project implementation. The Cost Allocation Key Flexfield analysis occurs fairly early (sometime before Compensation and Benefits analysis). Note that the Cost Allocation Key Flexfield is usually structured in the same fashion as the Oracle General Ledger Accounting Key Flexfield. The People Group and Special Information Type Key Flexfields can occur any time within the project.

Each Flexfield with Oracle HR/Payroll must be set up via SYSADMIN responsibility. For each Key Flexfield, the following steps are required:

- Value Sets must first be created for each Flexfield segment where a predefined set of choices should be made available to the user.

- Value Set Values must be created to establish the specific predefined set of choices available to the user.

- Segments are created for each Flexfield. Generally, Dynamic Inserts should be set to Yes. If a predefined set of choices should be established for a given segment, Value Sets must be attached.

- Cross Validation Rules can be established to control the combination of segment values that a user can enter when selecting the values for all segments.

- Aliases can be established for providing shorthand user selections, which, in turn, imply a combination of values for several segments.

- Freeze and compile the Flexfields after all segments have been defined.

- Database Items can be created to allow access of individual segment values as opposed to only having access to the entire Flexfield (combination of all segments).

DEFINING DESCRIPTIVE FLEXFIELDS

Defining Descriptive Flexfields can occur any time within the project. The actual setup steps are similar to those of Key Flexfields. Note that each segment within a Descriptive Flexfield is generally viewed independently of the other segments. This is similar to the People Group Key Flexfield. In essence, a Descriptive Flexfield is generally not interpreted as a combination of values to establish one entity. By contrast, a Job Key Flexfield is interpreted as one job name regardless of the number of segments that were combined to create the job name.

ENABLING CURRENCIES

Enabling currencies might be necessary prior to setting up the Business Group organization. Each Business Group expresses compensation and benefits calculations in only one currency. Confirm through the SYSADMIN responsibility that the desired currency has been enabled.

DEFINING USERS

Defining users occurs later in the project when Oracle HRMS Security is implemented. For United States implementations, Oracle is seeded with default responsibilities US HRMS Manager, US HR Manager, and US Payroll Manager. These responsibilities are sufficient during the early phases of an implementation. At the time when salaries and compensation and benefits are loaded into the database, other security responsibilities should be defined.

PUBLIC SYNONYMS AND GRANT PERMISSIONS TO ROLES

The Database Administrator must create public synonyms and run the process Grant Permissions to Roles. This process must be run before running the process Generate Secure Users, which becomes necessary when Security has been implemented later in the project.

DEFINING QUICK CODE TYPES AND VALUES

Quick Codes are set up at various times throughout the project depending on specific user needs. For example, a Quick Code exists for organization types. This Quick Code is not required and can be set up at any time. Many other Quick Codes are predefined. Quick Code Values are the list of valid choices that exist within a Quick Code. Quick Codes can be System, Extensible, or User. Both System and Extensible Quick Codes have seeded values. Both Extensible and User Quick Codes can have values added by the user.

DEFINING LOCATIONS

Locations within Oracle HR are physical sites with unique mailing addresses. Oracle Payroll uses these locations to establish payroll taxation requirements. When an employee is assigned to work at a specific location, Oracle Payroll uses the address of that location to determine taxation rules and rates.

Consider the situation where a company has several buildings next to each other. If postal service mail generally arrives separately at each of these buildings, it is likely that each building will need to be set up as a separate location. Conversely, if the postal service generally delivers to one location, only one location will be required within Oracle Payroll.

Keep in mind that other Oracle modules share Locations with HR/Payroll. Thus, it might be necessary to define more locations than are required by Payroll. If the same Oracle Locations are to be used by Oracle Payroll and any other module, these locations should be defined within Oracle HR/Payroll to ensure that the address is set up with the appropriate payroll validation.

DEFINING BUSINESS GROUP ORGANIZATION

A Business Group is a special type of organization. Each Business Group has one government legislation. Thus, to pay employees from more than one country, multiple Business Groups are generally set up. An exception to this approach involves significant customization. Although Oracle Payroll is capable of paying different currencies for employees from other countries, the legislation that drives taxation must be overwritten using Fast Formula. The Business Group identifies the specific Key Flexfields that will be used. Also, the Business Group identifies how employee numbering occurs. Employee numbering can be manual entry, automatic system generation, or automatic use of the national identifier.

Oracle HR/Payroll comes delivered with a Setup Business Group. This Business Group can be reused. In this case, the name of the organization must be changed from Setup Business Group to a name corresponding to the company's top organization.

When you navigate to a Business Group organization, you will notice that the Others button has several choices. Work Day defaults can be established for the typical working day within the company. These defaults can be overwritten at lower levels for individual employees. Reporting Categories and Statuses can be enabled for the Business Group. Seeded Reporting Categories include Fulltime-Regular, Fulltime-Temporary, Parttime-Regular, and

Parttime-Temporary. PayMIX Information was a requirement in older versions of Oracle Payroll (release 10.5 and before) and can be ignored.

DEFINING VIEW ALL ACCESS TO BUSINESS GROUP

This is a SYSADMIN function. Navigate to the System Profile options and select the default responsibility (for example, US HRMS Manager). Ensure that the HR:Business Group option is set to the desired Business Group. By default, this is set to the Setup Business Group. Also, on this window, review the HR:User Type. For the responsibility US HRMS Manager, the HR:User Type should be set to HR with Payroll User. Also, if a Business Group is being used other than the Setup Business Group, this affects other Oracle modules. Within Accounts Payable, the Business Group must be set up within the Financials System Parameters. If there are no AP vendor employees or buyer employees already entered, modify the table FINANCIALS_SYSTEM_PARAMETERS.BUSINESS_GROUP_ID.

DEFINING HUMAN RESOURCE ORGANIZATIONS

Human Resource Organizations have an organization classification of HR Organization. These are the actual organizations to which employees are assigned. When determining the requirements for defining HR organizations, there are generally these competing agendas:

General Ledger Costing

Security and access to the HR/Payroll system

Management Reporting

Government Reporting (particularly AAP Reports)

Other Oracle modules (Projects, Purchasing, and so on)

Most clients take HR organizations as far down as the GL Cost Centers require. For other management reporting, you might need to take the organizations down further. Next, look at security requirements as far as who needs to access information. You might find that you have a satellite office where the HR manager should view or update employees from that site only. The organization hierarchy must be organized to enable this. Government Reporting (AAP, EEO-1, VETS-100, and so on) is the next challenge, particularly with AAP reports. Finally, consider what other Oracle modules share this information and how can you incorporate their requirements with HR.

DEFINING GOVERNMENT REPORTING ENTITY ORGANIZATIONS

At least one Government Reporting Entity (GRE) organization must be defined. The number of GREs required is based on the number of federal identification numbers within the company. Information that can be entered for a GRE includes the following:

Employer Identification Number

Government reporting information for EEO-1, VETS 100, and new hire reporting

Federal tax rules

State tax rules

Local tax rules

State Quarterly Wage Listings

W-2 reporting

Multiple Worksite reporting

Also keep in mind that organizations with multiple GREs can define a Tax Group when necessary for common reporting.

DEFINING OTHER ORGANIZATIONS

Oracle HR offers numerous other classifications for organizations that might require additional organization setup. The following organization classifications can be defined:

- Reporting Establishment
- Corporate Headquarters
- AAP Organization
- Benefits Carrier
- Workers Compensation Carrier
- Beneficiary Organization
- Payee Organization

DEFINING ORGANIZATION HIERARCHIES

Organization hierarchies are fairly straightforward to implement within Oracle HRMS. You can define one primary hierarchy and as many secondary hierarchies as desired. Because organization hierarchies are date-tracked, you can maintain a history of what your company looked like at any point in time. The main items that influence the structure of your organization hierarchies are the following:

- HRMS security requirements
- Management reporting requirements
- Government reporting requirements

It can be easier to maintain your system if the previously stated goals for organization hierarchies are combined into one hierarchy; however, there is no significant disadvantage to creating multiple hierarchies. Review each of hierarchical goals first in isolation, and then determine whether there are common goals between different hierarchies that will allow consolidation of multiple hierarchies.

DEFINING JOBS

Jobs are designed to be generic roles an employee can fill at a company. A given job name determines whether employees holding the job title are eligible for paid overtime. The job can be for either exempt employees or non-exempt employees but not both. The FLSA code will establish this status.

When setting up jobs, think carefully about government reporting requirements such as EEO-1, AAP, and VETS-100. Jobs within the United States can be associated with an Equal Employment Opportunity (EEO-1) Category. Oracle Human Resources has 10 seeded EEO-1 Categories that can be selected. Jobs can also be associated with job groups within an Affirmative Action Plan (AAP). The AAP codes are user-definable Quick Codes. Additional items to associate with a job include line of progression (which establishes the relationship from one job group to another) and Salary Code.

Management reporting requirements should also be considered when defining a job. This is often a major influence on the number of Key Flexfield segments that are established for a job. Each job name is a concatenation of each of the Job Key Flexfield segments. For example, if you desire to perform reports on all employees who are accountants regardless of whether they are cost accountants, senior accountants, tax accountants, and so on, the role of Accountant can be established as one segment, and the description or level of accountant (Cost, Senior, Tax, and so on) can be established as a preceding segment.

Although jobs are designed as generic roles within an organization, many organizations define Oracle HR jobs as if they are positions. Positions are discussed later. The reason for this strategy within implementation is because jobs are flexible. Whenever the organization restructures, jobs do not necessarily need to change. Positions must be changed within Oracle HR when the organizations change.

Finally, keep in mind that jobs are shared with other modules, such as Oracle Purchasing. Purchasing must establish its purchasing approvals using either jobs or positions. Thus, the setup of Oracle HR jobs must not be made in isolation by the Human Resources department.

DEFINING POSITIONS

A position is a distinct job within an organization. Like jobs, each position name is a concatenation of each of the Position Key Flexfield segments. Positions offer more features than jobs within Oracle but also have reduced flexibility.

A key feature of positions is the ability to define a position hierarchy. Another feature of positions involves vacancy management. When vacancies occur at a particular position, they must be filled by another employee with similar skills within the organization. Remember that a position is a specific job within a specific organization. One way to fill the vacancy is to review all other positions that exist for associated jobs. In essence, this is a review of employees in other organizations throughout the company that contain the same job.

Oracle HRMS security can be based on the position hierarchy. Thus, the use of positions adds more functionality than the use of jobs alone. The reverse argument of whether this security functionality is necessary involves whether organizations and the organization hierarchy can sufficiently meet security needs.

Positions are shared with other Oracle modules, such as Purchasing. Purchasing must establish its purchasing approvals using either jobs or positions.

DEFINING POSITION REPORTING HIERARCHIES

If positions have been defined, a position hierarchy almost certainly will be defined. Recall that most of the key reasons for defining positions involve the position hierarchy. In addition to the ability to define HRMS security using the position hierarchy, Oracle Purchasing often uses the same hierarchy to establish lines of approval.

Multiple position hierarchies can be defined, although one hierarchy must be the primary reporting hierarchy. Any position can exist in more than one hierarchy, but a position can appear only once within a given hierarchy. (This is the same case as with organization hierarchies.)

DEFINING CAREER PATHS FOR JOBS AND POSITIONS

A career path maps employee progression within the company from one job or position to another job or position. Note that career paths cannot be mixed between jobs and positions. An employee progresses from one job to another job or one position to another position but not from a job to a position.

When defining career paths based on positions, use the position hierarchy. Remember that multiple hierarchies can be created if multiple career paths are desired.

When defining career paths based on jobs, navigate to the career path window to define career path names. Next, define the jobs that are associated with each career path name. Finally, define lines of progression to show the relationship from one career path name to another. These lines of progression are used by AAP reports.

DEFINING GRADES

Grades are designed to establish relative compensation and benefits analysis among different employees within the company. Like jobs and positions, a grade name is the concatenation of each of the segments within the Grade Key Flexfield. Also, grades can be established as being valid for only certain jobs or positions.

DEFINING GRADE RATES

After establishing the grade names, you can associate values to each grade. These are called grade rates. The rates can be either a fixed value or a range of values. These grade rates can then be used to validate salary proposals. Oracle HR warns you if you attempt to assign an employee a salary that falls outside the parameters you established in your grade rates. Grade rates are date-tracked, which means you can keep a history of these rates. You can also enter values at a future date without affecting current values. If your organization desires to associate different grade rates to employees based on what region of the country in which they reside, you must set up distinctly different grades for each region. In this case, you could consider setup of your Grade Key Flexfield to have the first few segments the same for each region with a final segment indicating the region as the only difference from one grade name to the next.

DEFINING PAY SCALES

You can also use pay scales to establish values for your grade names. Pay scales are very common when pay levels are negotiated, as with union groups. These scales are a series of grade steps or points with specific values of pay for each step. You have the flexibility to establish different pay scales for different unions or one single set of pay points for all your employees. When established, employees are placed on a step within their grade. Employees move up the steps through an incrementing process. Note that pay scales are not tied to salary administration. For a detailed discussion of pay scales and progression point values, see the topic "Pay Scales and Pay Progression" in Chapter 25, "Using Oracle Human Resources."

DEFINING PROGRESSION POINT VALUES

The next step in the process is to assign rates to each of the progression points in the pay scale. Unlike grade rates, you must enter a fixed value for each point. These values are also date-tracked so that you can keep a history and enter future values. The rates are normally defined in monetary units, but they can also be defined as integers, days, or hours. An example of the use of hours would be to define a point value to signify the maximum number of overtime hours that can be worked in a week.

DEFINING GRADE STEPS AND POINTS

The final step in the process is to associate a subset of the progression points to each grade. Each point in the grade is considered a step. The steps of pay scales are normally followed in sequence; however, this window allows certain grades to be established where employees can skip the normal steps of a particular pay scale and jump several steps to the next step defined for the grade. Note within Oracle HR the fact that a grade can only be associated with one pay scale. Thus, each unique pay scale identified within your organization will require setup of a unique grade.

DEFINING PAYMENT METHODS

Payment methods define how an employee or third party is paid. There are three types: check, NACHA (direct deposit), and cash (which is rarely used). You can define as many payment methods as needed for each of these types. For example, you might have multiple payroll bank accounts throughout your organization. Each bank account would be set up as a separate payment method. You must select one of these methods as the default method for each of your payrolls.

DEFINING CONSOLIDATION SETS

Some of the post-payroll run processes can utilize consolidation sets, which group similar payrolls together. These processes include NACHA, Check Writer, Costing, and several of the standard payroll reports. This enables you to produce one NACHA file for all the payrolls in a consolidation set. Generally, these payrolls should have similar calendars to facilitate the scheduling of the processes. Consolidation sets are simply a list of payrolls that can be processed together after the payroll gross-to-net calculation has occurred for each payroll.

DEFINING PAYROLLS

You must define payrolls to pay your employees in Oracle HR/Payroll. Employees are assigned to payrolls on their assignment window. Payrolls can also be used to group like employees together for reporting purposes. Payrolls can be defined to limit employee eligibility to certain earnings, deductions, and benefit plans. Security definitions can be established based on payrolls to limit access to various windows within the Oracle HRMS product suite for certain groups of users. Normally, you define payrolls to establish different payment frequencies, such as your monthly payroll, your weekly payroll, your biweekly payroll, and so on. During the payroll definition, you must supply the first pay period ending date, day offsets from this date for cutoff, scheduled run and payment dates, and the default payment method. Other items established at payroll definition include the default consolidation set, NACHA bank information, valid payment methods, and costing information. Oracle Payroll then generates a payroll calendar.

DEFINING EARNINGS

Earning elements are used to represent compensation types such as salary, wages, and bonuses. Several salary elements are generated automatically by Oracle Payroll. They are Regular Salary, Regular Wages, Overtime, Time Entry Wages, Shift Pay, GTL Imputed Income, and Company Car. You can establish your own earnings element by using the Earnings window. There are three classifications that you can choose during the earning definition process. They are as follows:

> Earnings
>
> Supplemental Earnings
>
> Imputed Earnings

The Earnings classification generally represents earnings for time worked such as salary and hourly wages. Supplemental Earnings include a variety of special earnings paid to employees, such as bonuses and sick pay. Imputed Earnings are for noncash compensation such as personal use of a company car and company paid premiums for group term life insurance.

DEFINING DEDUCTIONS AND BENEFIT PLANS

Deduction elements fall into three main classifications. They are the following:

> Pre-Tax Deductions
>
> Involuntary Deductions
>
> Voluntary Deductions

Pre-Tax Deductions are further defined by category. The seeded categories for Pre-Tax Deductions are Deferred Comp 401k, Health Care 125, and Dependent Care 125. It is very important to use the correct category when establishing your pretax deductions. The category determines how your pretax deduction will be processed by the various federal, state, and local taxing authorities. If you need additional pretax deduction categories, you must update the QuickCode type US_PRE_TAX_DEDUCTIONS.

Involuntary Deductions are also further defined by category. They are defined in the QuickCode type US_INVOLUNTARY_DEDUCTIONS. Again, the category determines how the deduction will be processed. Involuntary deductions are highly structured and tightly controlled by various federal and state laws.

Voluntary Deductions can also be further defined by categories, but unlike the other two classifications, categories are not required. Voluntary deductions generally capture employee-requested deductions, such as United Way or any posttax benefit plan elections.

All deductions must have an amount rule to instruct Oracle Payroll on how to calculate the deduction. The rules are as follows:

> Flat Amount
> % of Earnings
> Payroll Table
> Benefits Table

The Flat Amount rule is the simplest. The generated element includes an input value called Amount, which gives the formula the deduction amount. The % of Earnings rule includes an input value called Percentage. This value gives the formula the percentage to use. The default formula uses the Regular Earnings balance as the base amount to apply the percentage. The rule Payroll Table enables you to look up the deduction amount in a pre-established payroll table. This table must be defined in the Table Structure window.

The final amount rule for deductions is Benefits Table. These tables are based on coverage levels to determine the amounts of employees' and/or employers' contributions toward a benefit plan. You establish the various coverage levels by updating the QuickCodes type US_BENEFIT_COVERAGE. When you have defined your deduction element for the benefit plan, use the Benefits Contributions window to populate the employee and employer contributions. Do not use the Table Structure window to establish the benefits table.

DEFINING EMPLOYER LIABILITY ELEMENTS

Oracle Payroll automatically generates employer liability elements that are used to capture the employer contribution amounts for benefit plans. All the employer tax liability elements are also automatically generated through the tight integration with Vertex. You might need to establish some additional employer liability elements for 401k employer match amounts or costs associated with required employee safety equipment. These elements are established directly with the Element Description window (bypassing the Earnings and Deductions windows). Create these elements using the classification called Employer Liabilities.

DEFINING INFORMATION ELEMENTS

Oracle HRMS provides an element classification called Information that enables you to hold almost any kind of information items issued to employees such as cellular phones, company cars, laptop computers, or identification badges. Generally, these elements are not processed during a payroll run, but they could be referenced in any Fast Formula.

Other uses for Information elements include accumulating hours for absence management and PTO (Paid Time Off) plans. Vertex uses information elements to feed various tax balances that appear in inquiry windows and on reports.

You define Information elements with the Element Description window using the classification called Information. The actual information being stored is defined in the Input Values, which you must also define.

DEFINING TAXABILITY RULES FOR TAX CATEGORIES

Oracle Payroll enables you to control the rules that Vertex will use when taxing the various earnings and deductions. The installation process populates these rules for a number of categories of supplemental earnings and imputed earnings. It also completes the rules for three of the pretax deduction categories. You should review these rules for all your taxing authorities including state, county, city, and school district. Vertex uses these rules to drive its tax calculations. You can add your own categories for supplemental earnings, imputed earnings, and pretax deductions to handle any unique tax requirements. This is also the place to maintain rules regarding the inclusion of categories of supplemental and imputed earnings in a state's payroll exposure to Workers Compensation. All these rules are maintained on the Taxability Rules window.

DEFINING INPUT VALUES FOR ELEMENTS

Oracle Payroll automatically creates the necessary Input Values for earnings and deductions based on the calculation and amount rules you select on the Earnings and Deductions definition windows. There are times, however, when you want to maintain some additional information on these elements or you have created your own Information element for a particular purpose. You can create your own input values through the Element Description window. You must add these values before linking and adding the element to any employees. When the element is in use, Oracle Payroll does not enable you to add any additional input values.

During the definition process of input values, enter a name for the input value and select a unit of measure (money, hours, character, date, number, or time). You can enter a number in the Sequence field to control the order in which the Element Entries window displays the input values. You can also require an entry for the value and/or restrict the values allowed by selecting a QuickCode type to act as a lookup for the input value. Fast Formulas can also be used to validate the entries as outlined in the following section.

DEFINING VALIDATION FORMULAS

Oracle Fast Formulas are powerful tools that can control the actual gross-to-net calculation of a payroll. They can also be used to validate entries into input values during the entry of an element in an employee's Element Entries window. For example, a formula could check an employee's length of service or salary before an amount is allowed to be entered into a bonus earning element. You must write the formula before you define the element and the corresponding input values.

Validation formulas are entered in the Formulas window using the formula type Element Input Validation. You must observe the following rules:

The formula must have one input value called entry_value.

The formula must set and return a local variable called formula_status. It must have the value of s for success or e for error.

The formula can return a text variable called formula_message that contains a text message. It can be used with either an s or e formula_status.

The formula cannot return any other values.

You cannot reference any other input value from another element in the formula.

You cannot return a value to any other input value.

DEFINING ELEMENT LINKS FOR EARNINGS, DEDUCTIONS, AND BENEFITS

When the element has been defined, input values established, and all validation rules applied, you are now ready to define eligibility and costing. You use the Link window to determine the groups of employees eligible for the element. You must also define a separate link for every costing combination for this element. The Link window can also be used to enter qualifying conditions such as age or length of service. You can also establish defaults, minimums, and maximums for each of your input values at the link level.

Obviously, you can create multiple links for the same element, but Oracle HR/Payroll enforces the rule that an employee cannot be eligible for an element more than once. The following is a list of components you can use to define eligibility:

Payroll

Salary Basis

Employment Category

Organization

Location

Job

Grade

People Group

Position

DEFINING TAXATION AND OTHER ELEMENTS

Oracle Payroll comes with all the necessary elements and calculations for tax deductions, tax credits, and employer liabilities already in place through its tight integration with Vertex, Inc. You must establish a separate support agreement with Vertex when you purchase Oracle Payroll. This enables you to receive monthly updates for any tax changes. These elements do require links to establish the costing matrix for your taxes. These links must be in place before you attempt your first pay run.

Oracle also includes two Workers Compensation elements (Workers Compensation and Workers Compensation Information) that also require links. These elements are created automatically by the installation process. The Workers Compensation element stores that amount of each employee's WC premium. The Workers Compensation Information element stores the Mod 1 Surcharge, Post Exp Mod 2 Surcharge, Post Prem Disc 1 Surcharge, and employee's payroll exposure.

You must also define the following tax information at the GRE level:

Federal-level supplemental withholding calculation method and any common paymaster for the GRE's employee

Self-adjust methods in use at the federal and state levels

State-level rates needed for calculation of SUI (state unemployment insurance)

Identifiers used at the state and local levels

DEFINING PAYROLL BALANCES

Oracle Payroll automatically creates balances for you when you define an earning or deduction. The name of the balance is the same as the name of the element. Oracle also creates all the necessary tax balances needed to support the Vertex integration.

There might be some special balances needed to support unique requirements that are specific to your enterprise. One of the most common user-defined balances is one to store pension eligible earnings. You define this balance through the Balance Window.

The definition process includes three steps. The first step is to uniquely name your balance. You also can supply a reporting name for your balance. This name will be used on reports and the statement of earnings.

The second step involves entering all the balance feeds for this balance. Here, you select one or more individual elements that feed the balance. You can only use those elements whose input values have the same unit of measure as the balance. Normally, this is the run result (Pay Value) of the element.

The final step is to list all the desired dimensions for this balance. Dimensions generally include Assignment Within GRE Year to Date, Assignment Within GRE Month to Date, and so on.

DEFINING USER TABLES

You can define your own tables within Oracle Payroll that store information such as wage codes, shift differentials, or any other amounts for your earnings and deductions. These tables are *not* created through SQL, but with the Table Structure window. Oracle FastFormula can access these tables through the GET_TABLE_VALUE statement. Do not use the Table Structure window to store rates for your medical and dental benefit plans. Oracle Payroll provides a special table for this purpose. Use the Benefits Contributions window to enter these rates.

After you define your rows and columns of the user table with the Table Structure window, use the Table Value window to enter values into the table.

You can also set up tables to support deductions that were defined with the amount rule Payroll Tables. The formula for the deduction uses a row type to help determine which row of the table to use to retrieve the deduction amount. There are three predefined row types:

> Age Range
>
> Salary Range
>
> Job Class

You can set up any additional types you require.

DEFINING PAYROLL FORMULAS

Oracle Payroll automatically creates a formula for every earning and deduction element you define through the Earnings and Deductions windows. Note that elements created directly from the Element Description window do not automatically create an associated formula. You can modify these formulas through the Write Formulas window. Remember to thoroughly test any changes you made to the generated formula.

Formulas can generate different types of run results. Direct Results normally update the input value Pay Value of the element containing the formula. You can only have one direct result per formula. The formula can also generate many indirect results. These results are passed to input values of other elements that will process further in the pay run. Formula results are covered in the next section.

DEFINING PAYROLL FORMULA RESULTS

As stated in the preceding section, formulas generate formula results. These results are defined in the Formula Results window. The different types of formula results include the following:

> *Direct Results.* Only one per formula, normally passed to the Pay Value input value of the element containing the formula.
>
> *Indirect Results.* Results that are passed to the input values of nonrecurring elements that will process later in the pay run. The priority number of the element that will receive this indirect result must be higher than the element that is passing the results.

Update. Results that are passed to recurring elements that will process later in the pay run. Like indirect results, the priority number of the receiving element must be higher than the passing element.

Message. Text message that you can pass from the formula to the Payroll Message report. You define on the Formula Results window whether the message is a warning or fatal error.

Stop. The formula can send stops to the calling element or other elements to prevent their processing in the run.

DEFINING SALARY BASIS

The salary basis is used to define how the salary is entered, such as hourly, monthly, or annually. For example, you can state an employee's salary in monthly terms but place her in a biweekly payroll. The salary basis does not have to match the pay periods.

Oracle Payroll generally expects you to use the basis of Monthly Salary for the seeded element Regular Salary and the basis of Hourly Salary for the seeded element Regular Wages. However, do not be deceived by the Input Value named Monthly Salary on the Regular Salary element. In actuality, you can associate any Salary Basis with this element. When you observe the element entries for an employee, the amount stored in the Monthly Salary input value might not actually be a monthly amount. However, Oracle has designed the Regular Salary formula to properly interpret this amount based on the employee's assigned salary basis.

Additionally, you can establish your own salary elements and associate any salary basis with them. Make sure you thoroughly test these elements with all your salary administration scenarios.

The salary basis is defined in the Salary Basis window. As stated previously, you associate a salary element with the salary basis. When you enter a salary proposal through the Salary Administration window, Oracle HR automatically updates the appropriate input value of the salary element. If you associate a grade rate with the salary basis, Oracle HR uses the grade rate to validate the salary proposals.

ENABLING SALARY APPROVALS

After you have defined your salary basis for each of your salary elements, you need to determine who can enter salary proposals and who can approve them. Salaries for new employees are automatically approved. However, all future salary changes must be approved after they have been entered. You can separate the approval process from the entry process by only adding the approval function to the menu of responsibilities for users who are authorized to perform approvals.

DEFINING PROPOSAL REASONS AND PERFORMANCE RATINGS

Oracle comes seeded with default proposal reasons and performance ratings. You should review the QuickCode types PROPOSAL_REASONS and PERFORMANCE_RATING for completeness. You can add other entries to these types to incorporate you own reasons and ratings.

Oracle HR enables you to break down a salary proposal into multiple components. For example, an employee might receive a raise that includes a 6 percent cost of living increase with a 10 percent performance increase. If you need to expand the salary components to include your proposal reasons, the system administrator must update the view for the Salary Management folder.

DEFINING BENEFIT CARRIERS

You can establish benefit carriers and associate them with your imputed earnings or pretax or voluntary deductions. The first step is to establish the address of the carrier in the Location window. You then set up the carrier in the Organization window using the location you just established. Make sure you use the classification Benefits Carrier. Navigate to the Element Description window for each of your benefits elements. Click the Further Information button and select your carrier in the field Benefits Carrier.

DEFINING BENEFIT COVERAGES

Benefit coverages are defined in the QuickCode type US_BENEFIT_COVERAGE. You establish the default employee and employer contribution amounts for the health care benefit plans using the Benefits Contributions window. Query the benefit plan, which is the element name for this plan. In the Coverage field, select from the pick list each of the coverages valid for this plan. For each coverage level, enter the employee and employer contribution amounts. If either component has no contribution, enter zero.

DEFINING ELEMENT SETS

Element sets are simply a collection of element names. Oracle HRMS uses element sets to enable you to restrict the elements that can be entered or viewed on a customized version of the Element Entries window. This is used to limit the elements that are processed by a particular payroll run. Finally, element sets can be used to define the elements over which the costs of other elements are to be distributed.

Element sets are defined with the Element and Distribution Set window. Enter a unique name and select the type: Distribution, Run, or Customization. Distribution sets are used for cost distribution, run sets for payroll runs, and customization sets for customizing the Element Entries window. You can select your elements by classification, such as Pre-Tax deductions, or by individual element name.

DEFINING PERSON TYPES

Person types are used to identify different groups of people. You might want to capture different types of information for different groups of people. You can also restrict access to certain sensitive groups of people. Person types can be used to accomplish these goals.

There are three main types of people you can maintain in your system. They are Employee, Applicants, and External. Oracle HR defines a special category of External called contact. These are people who are associated with employees or applicants, such as dependents.

Oracle HR comes seeded with default person types. These can be modified or added to. Use the Person Types window to make these modifications. During the definition process, you determine the name of the person type and the associated system name. The system name is used to define how Oracle should treat this person type.

DEFINING ASSIGNMENT STATUSES

Assignment statuses are used to record employee and applicant current statuses within the enterprise. You can use assignment statuses to track permanent or temporary separation from your company, such as paid or unpaid medical leave, family leave, or military service. There are four main system statuses for employees. They are the following:

Active

Suspend

Terminate

End

You assign your own names to these statuses through the Assignment Status window. Each system status can have several user statuses related to it.

Employee assignment statuses are used to control payroll processing. Each status has a payroll status of Process or Do Not Process assigned to it. You can also have different formulas execute for an employee when her status changes.

DEFINING SPECIAL INFORMATION TYPE KEY FLEXFIELD

Oracle HR delivers a Key Flexfield called Special Information Types, which enables you to store special personal information that is unique within your organization. Each type of information is a separate structure of the flexfield. Companies use this flexfield to store information such as skill requirements for jobs, pension-related information, and additional retiree information. Oracle delivers some of these structures automatically. They include ADA Disabilities, ADA Disability Accommodations, and OSHA Reportable Incidents.

Define your structures in the same manner as all your other Key Flexfields. When defined, you must enable your Special Information Type for the Business Group through the Special Information Types window. You use this window to define how the structure will be used. Make sure you check Other if you want to use this structure at the employee level.

One downside to Special Information Types is that you cannot create database items for this flexfield. Therefore, Oracle FastFormulas cannot access data stored in these flexfields. If your FastFormulas must reference this data, consider using either the People Group flexfield or one of the supported descriptive flexfields.

DEFINING WORKERS COMPENSATION CODES AND RATES

Workers Compensation is only valid for sites with Oracle Payroll installed. Each state has a workers' compensation program that provides insurance for employees with work-related injuries. The first step in the process is to define each of your Workers Compensation carriers through the Organization window. Make sure you use the Workers Compensation Carrier classification. At the GRE level, associate these carriers to each state through the State Tax Rules window. You also enter the Experience Modification rate and the Employer's Liability and Premium Discount rates, if applicable. Next, verify that the Taxability Rules for your Imputed and Supplemental Earnings properly represent earnings included in the employee's payroll exposure.

You must next define the WC codes and rates for each carrier and location in the state through the WC Codes and Rates window. This window enables you to query each state and carrier. If you leave the location field blank, the codes and rates you enter will be used for all locations in that state for that carrier. If you want to enter rates for a particular location, you must also query the location.

DEFINING WORKERS COMPENSATION JOB CODES

When you have defined all your Workers Compensation codes and rates, you must associate these codes to each of your jobs. At this time you also enter the Executive Weekly maximum (if one exists for this state), the state's rules regarding inclusion of overtime earnings in the payroll exposure, and any standard surcharges in use in this state.

Use the Workers Compensation Job Codes window to query each of the states. For each state, you must select the job titles and assign the corresponding Workers Compensation code. One of the most common error messages on the Payroll Message report is the dreaded "Cannot determine Workers Compensation rate for this employee." Generally, this means that you have not associated a Workers' Compensation code for this employee's job title in the work state for this employee.

DEFINING PAID TIME OFF ACCRUAL PLANS

Paid Time Off Accruals are important in tracking such benefit policies as vacation and sick time available for employees. Within Oracle HRMS, you must first set up one separate Hours Taken element for each accrual plan you create. For each accrual plan, you must establish a start rule for when the accrual should begin accruing for an employee. For each accrual plan, you must establish a period of ineligibility to identify when an employee is allowed to begin taking vacation/sick leave using the amount she has accrued. You must also establish bands identifying the accrual rates associated with each length of service.

Much attention is given to the subject of PTO Accruals in other chapters due to limitations in Oracle HRMS functionality. Also, note that significant enhancement to PTO Accruals are available using the Oracle Advanced Benefit (OAB) module.

DEFINING HUMAN RESOURCE BUDGETS

Human Resource budgets are a mechanism for monitoring work load requirements and work vacancy information throughout the year. Oracle HR can be set up to enable you to determine budget variances between budgeted and actual requirements for organizations, jobs, positions, and grades. To define budgets, navigate to the Budgets window. For each Budget Name you define, you must identify what Oracle Work Structure (jobs, grades, and so on) this budget is based on. Then, you must establish target goals for each Work Structure item within each period of time throughout the calendar year.

TROUBLESHOOTING

If you are planning to implement Oracle HR/Payroll, you are likely to obtain an excellent long-term solution. However, over the short-term, you are facing quite a challenge. Earlier in this chapter, there were numerous tips.

The earlier sections on Critical Implementation Factors and Unrealistic Project Expectations contain many tips. The biggest message from this chapter is that Oracle HR/Payroll is likely the most challenging to implement of the Oracle Applications. An experienced Oracle Financials consultant is usually *not* sufficient to meet the needs of an Oracle HR/Payroll project. It is highly advisable to establish project team members with specific experience on Oracle HR/Payroll. Your current project success and the likelihood of optimal long-term solutions will be greatly influenced by your decision.

CHAPTER 25

USING ORACLE HUMAN RESOURCES

The Oracle Human Resources (HR) Application is the foundational module for the Oracle Human Resource Management Systems (HRMS) product suite. Other Oracle HRMS modules that are built based on HR include Oracle Payroll, Training Administration, Time Management, and Advanced Benefits. This chapter focuses primarily on Oracle HR-specific issues. Before looking into specific Oracle HR issues, consider the following background as to why an organization might want to implement an HRMS system using Oracle HR.

In today's competitive business environment, many companies are recognizing that Human Resource management is vital. Although much attention has been given over the past decade to improving computer system productivity in financial and manufacturing systems, most top organizations are beginning to turn attention to an overlooked area: management of their employees. Employees are not listed on a balance sheet; however, the truly top organizations recognize that employees are a vital asset. Companies might ask simple questions such as the following:

Why aren't we able to retain top quality employees?

Are our salary and benefit plans sufficient to attract top quality employees?

Are our employees trained properly to play an optimal role in the creation or delivery of the products or services we provide?

Are there potential employees with a skill set that could improve our productivity or even revolutionize our current business? If so, how can we obtain this skill set or these employees?

With this perspective in mind, examine the issues in implementing the Oracle HRMS product suite, beginning with current features.

DISCOVERING NEW FEATURES IN RELEASE 11.0

Release 11.0 of Oracle HRMS provided a number of new features. Although not every feature is discussed in this chapter, please note a few of the ones that are of particular interest to Oracle Human Resources users:

Fast Path. This functionality applies to the entire Oracle HRMS product suite. The Find Person window, which pops up when you navigate to the Person window, is now used to access numerous other forms. For example, you can now use a Fast Path from the main Navigator to Find Person and jump directly to the Element Entries window without first navigating to both the Person and Assignment windows.

Batch Element Entry rollback. In previous releases, you could not roll back batches that had been transferred to Element Entries. With R11, you can, provided that you have not modified the element entry records.

Government reporting. Enhancements have been made to EEO-1 and VETS-100 Reporting.

Multiple Work Site reporting. This feature has been implemented.

Zip Codes entry enhanced. In R11, a range of zip codes can be entered on the Cities window. Additionally, new zip codes can be added to both predefined and user-created cities.

Salary Administration window updates. Several changes have been made, including the ability to view the maximum and minimum allowed salary based on the Grade Rates defined for the employee's Grade.

Career Management functionality. This has been introduced.

Work Telephone. This functionality has been moved from the Person window to the Phones window. The underlying database tables have moved this information as well.

Advertise job vacancies through HR Direct Access functionality. This has been added.

Assignment Budget Values window. This is now Date Tracked.

TABLES CHANGED IN RELEASE 11

Note that several Oracle HRMS tables have been changed in release 11. The majority of the table changes apply to the Oracle Human Resources module. Table 25.1 includes table names that have been changed.

TABLE 25.1 TABLE NAME CHANGES

Old Table Name	New Table Name
HR_ORGANIZATION_UNITS	HR_ALL_ORGANIZATION_UNITS
PER_PEOPLE_F	PER_ALL_PEOPLE_F
PER_ASSIGNMENTS_F	PER_ALL_ASSIGNMENTS_F
PER_POSITIONS	PER_ALL_POSITIONS
PER_VACANCIES	PER_ALL_VACANCIES
PAY_PAYROLLS_F	PAY_ALL_PAYROLLS_F

The Oracle HRMS Views that have been changed in release 11 are listed in Table 25.2.

TABLE 25.2 VIEW NAME CHANGES

Old View Name	New View Name
HR_ORGANIZATION_UNITS_SECV	HR_ORGANIZATION_UNITS
PAY_PAYROLLS_F_SECV	PAY_PAYROLLS_F
PER_ASSIGNMENTS_F_SECV	PER_ASSIGNMENTS_F
PER_PEOPLE_F_SECV	PER_PEOPLE_F
PER_POSITIONS_F_SECV	PER_POSITIONS
PER_VACANCIES_SECV	PER_VACANCIES
PER_PEOPLE_D	PER_ALL_PEOPLE_D
PER_ASSIGNMENTS_D	PER_ALL_ASSIGNMENTS_D
PAY_PAYROLLS_D	PAY_ALL_PAYROLLS_D

DISCOVERING NEW FEATURES IN RELEASE 11I

Release 11i includes several general new features:

Applications based on version 6 of both Forms and Report.

Oracle 8i. Features include capability to store embedded file types into the database.

Flexible dates. Such as MM/DD/YY.

Additional multilingual capabilities. Users have the capability to flip-flop between more than one language.

Third Party Administrator data export/import. This is configurable and provides for the run and rerun of processes to generate interface files.

Release 11i HR has the following new features:

Self-Service Enrollment

Premium Reconciliation Reporting

U.S. record-keeping for continuing benefits payments and family support orders (QDROs)

Enhanced Salary Planning capabilities (salary survey definition, import, and mapping)

Surveys (APIs will exist for upload of survey data for jobs.)

QuickHire (single, multipart form for all new-hire information)

QuickApplicant

Person Types (Multiple concurrent person types will be allowed; new seeded person types will exist.)

Release 11i HR paid time-off accruals enhancements that are planned include the following:

Flexible definition of plan start dates (not just January 1).

Flexible calculation of the rate of accrual.

Proration of accruals for part time employees.

Suspension rules for issues such as leave of absence.

Rules can be defined for accrual (for example, accruals can be defined based on hours worked).

Adjusted service dates will be recognized.

One set of Element Links for each plan. (Currently, there are several elements created for each accrual plan, including Carry Over Element, Residual Element, and more.)

HR Tips

This section contains various suggestions and tips to consider when implementing Oracle HR.

New Hire Reporting

Employees now must be reported in most states and Canada within the various regulated times (5-35 days), depending on the local legislation. All states at a minimum require the following:

> Employee addresses
>
> Date of birth
>
> Job
>
> Salary
>
> Hours normally worked per week
>
> Category of full- or part-time employment
>
> Indicator as to whether health care is available to employee and dependents
>
> Any existing child support obligations

New Hire Reports are submitted by Government Reporting Entity (GRE) Numbers and must include the following information:

> GRE legal name and address
>
> Federal Identification number (IRS issued number) or State Unemployment Insurance (SUI) Identification Number (some states require both numbers)
>
> Contact person's (person responsible for compilation of report) name, job, and work telephone number

This federally enacted law is due to national concerns over child welfare and fraud in programs such as workers compensation and unemployment. Exclusions to this report are employees with age, wages, or hours less than the state minimum. The Oracle-delivered New Hire Report is designed to meet the various formatting and data requirements of each state. The only state as of this writing that does not accept the Oracle New Hire Report as printed is Tennessee. Tennessee has its own form and the information must be copied onto that form. See Tennessee State Law for more details.

In most cases, the Payroll Department is the contact point for information on child support and other obligations of this type, and it therefore is usually responsible for submitting the New Hire Reports (one for each state in which employees are hired and one for each GRE).

Employee Hire Process

The new hire process consists of entering an employee into the system in order to pay the employee and to record information on the employee. One way to handle this task is through the Applicant Method of entering prospective new hires as Applicants during the interviewing process and then converting their employee type to Employee with the appropriate effective date or date of hire (DOH). Employee name and type at the minimum must be entered followed by address information, contact, beneficiary, and telephone numbers (work and home) to include all details that need to be recorded for an employee.

Ex-employees can also be rehired and classified as new hires. Caution should be exercised when entering the new "hire date" to maintain the integrity of the existing records. If using an adjusted service date, you should use a Descriptive Flexfield to put that date in. This is necessary when a rehired employee is to receive any credit for past years of service. Also, note that an employee cannot be rehired unless the termination for the employee's previous period of service includes a Final Process Date.

There is an option to Cancel if the employee has been entered in error. There are limitations on this function, and they should be reviewed carefully. These limitations exist if any of the following have occurred:

> Employee has been processed in a payroll run.
>
> Employee type has changed.
>
> New assignment has been made. (Giving an employee a new assignment creates a date tracked record and should not be deleted.)

The complexity of entering new hires is dictated by the amount of information a company maintains on its employees. This function is time-consuming to the new user but after gaining some proficiency becomes less cumbersome. The suggested method is to enter the company's necessary information before the employee's hire date and then enter the employee specific information (Ethnic Origin, I-9 status, Veteran Status, and so on) on the employee's first day at work from the documents the employee fills out.

The employee's address must be entered for a new hire. An employee can have only one primary address but can have more than one secondary address. The multiple addresses feature is helpful in organizations such as those in the public sector that hire large numbers of students. This feature is also helpful in industries that hire seasonal help. The first address you enter is listed by default as Primary. Clients using Oracle Payroll must note that the employee's primary address is used to maintain federal, state, and local tax rules. Thus, to have taxes calculated correctly, each employee must have a valid address. Additionally, Oracle HR provides numerous country address styles to enable all necessary address information to be entered based on each specific country's address requirements.

The employee assignment function in Oracle is a mandatory component of paying the employee. Components that must be present are the following:

> GRE
>
> Organization and Location with a physical street address (id: not a Post Office Box)
>
> Payroll
>
> Employment Category

W4 and other tax information as appropriate

Salary Basis

Approved Salary (All first time entry of salaries are automatically approved.)

Other common assignment information is entered for a new hire. Each employee is given a job or position title (See Chapter 24, "Implementing Oracle Human Resources and Oracle Payroll," for discussion on the uses of jobs versus positions). The employee job influences issues such as government reporting and whether an employee's job is eligible for overtime pay. Employees are often assigned grades to establish a relative basis of comparison of their salary to other employees in the same grade. The People Group functionality is commonly used on the assignment based on each customer's specific requirements. People Group Key Flexfield segments work independently from each other, providing specific methods of identifying employees that cannot be easily identified by merely referencing the employee's Organization, Job, Payroll, and so on.

Salary is the next item that should be entered for a new hire. As previously mentioned, to pay and report employee information, it is necessary for an employee to have an approved salary and a salary basis as a component of the employee assignment. Oracle has designed the salary function to automatically approve the initial salary entered for the new hire. All future salary entries after that are established as proposed salaries and must be approved before becoming effective. Some clients restrict the approval of salaries to higher management and/or Human Resource or Payroll personnel.

Tax information must also be entered for a new hire. Oracle provides a method for capturing federal, state, and local taxes, including tax credits and employer taxes that the company must pay and report on. Before an employee can be paid, it is necessary to have at least the Federal and State tax fields completed. Local, township, and school district taxes should be completed according to the laws in place for the locality. Earlier in the new hire discussion about addresses, the importance of having a correct primary address for each employee was stressed. This is imperative to ensure that the Vertex calculations for taxes and tax balances will be correct. The employee's home address and work location establish the state and locality tax information valid for the employee. In the event that there is an error in the taxes and tax balances, Oracle provides a means to make a manual adjustment (see "Tax Balance Adjustments" in Chapter 26, "Using Payroll").

To pay a new hire, a Personal Payment Method must be entered. Oracle Payroll enables the client to pay employees through the following methods:

Check

Direct Deposit (NACHA)

Combination of both Direct Deposit and Check

Oracle Payroll functionality provides for any combination that the client policy demands. Any employee not having a Personal Payment Method is paid by the default method chosen by the client, whether that be check, direct deposit, or a combination percentage of both. Earlier information on setting up new hire assignments stressed that each employee must have a valid GRE to be paid using any of these methods.

Finally, new hires should be assigned benefits and various benefit elections. This is accomplished through element entries. Oracle HR/Payroll defines elements as a means of holding information on employees for items such as compensation and benefits, employee absences, and other items distributed to employees, such as company cars. Although most element entries are created by manual entry in the Element Entries window, some element entries can be automatically generated based on the existence of other earnings, deductions, or employer liabilities.

EMPLOYEE TERMINATION

When an employee ends employment, you terminate her from Oracle HR. Oracle HR then establishes an end date to the employee's current period of service. To terminate an employee, keep in mind the following:

> If the employee is deceased, the Oracle system requires that you select Deceased in the Reason for Leaving field to provide for proper recording on the W2 Wage and Tax Statement.

> Actual Date is the only field required, and this is generally the date when the employee's person type changes to that of ex-employee.

> Notified and Projected dates are informational and can be used by the user depending on the level of reporting required on terminations.

> Final Process Date is the date after which no further processing can occur. This date is required if the employee is ever rehired. See the section "New Hire Reporting" earlier in the chapter.

A termination can be cancelled by selecting Reverse Termination if the employee decides not to leave or if the date of termination changes, as is often the case. Oracle HR accommodates this by changing the Person Type back to Employee. If any elements were end-dated due to the original termination date, they would have to be reinstated via the element entry form.

Oracle HR has provided a Termination Report that lists all the terminations and the reasons for leaving. The report can be run for any time period. Recruiting and other HR functions find this report very useful in analyzing turnover and retention. The accuracy of this report depends, of course, on the care used when choosing the leaving reasons. The user can add to the list of reasons for leaving by modifying the Quick Code LEAV_REAS. To realize optimum use of the leave reasons, the user should add those that will provide the most accurate description relating to her particular industry and business.

MANAGING EMPLOYEE ABSENCES

Human Resource departments must track employees' absences from work. They need to identify the types of absences that are allowable, track the dates and reasons for the absence, and group related absences together for reporting and analysis. They must also work closely with Payroll so that the employee is properly credited for paid time off. Oracle offers an absence management tool that is included with the base Human Resource module. This section describes its setup and use.

Oracle manages absence information at multiple levels. The top of this structure is called *absence category*. This enables you to group your related absences together. Examples of absence categories are the following:

> Medical Leave
>
> Family Leave
>
> Personal Leave
>
> Professional Leave

Within each of these categories, you establish *absence types*. For example, you can set up the following absence types under the category of Family Leave:

> Paid Maternity/Paternity
>
> Unpaid Maternity/Paternity
>
> Dependent Care

Finally, you can state a reason at the time you record the actual absence. For example, you can establish reasons such as Birth of a Child or Adoption of a Childas valid reasons. These reasons are established in the Quick Codes table ABSENCE_REASON.

The key setup steps for Absence Management are covered fairly well in the Oracle Human Resources U.S. User's Guide. There are a few things to keep in mind while you are completing the setup.

You set up a different nonrecurring absence element for each of your absence types. We recommend that you name the element the same as the absence type for clarity. Remember to set the Termination Rule to *Actual Termination*. Check the Multiple Entries Allowed box so that you can record multiple occurrences of this absence type in a pay period. Do not select the Process in Run box if this element will be used in a PTO (Paid Time Off) accrual plan. There must be at least one input value on this element. Generally, this input value will capture the hours associated with this absence type. If you plan to make entries to this element via PayMIX, you must also define an input value named Date Earned.

If only certain employees are eligible for certain absence types, use the Link window for this element to restrict this eligibility. For example, you can offer Paid Family Leave to only your full-time employees by utilizing the employment category on the Link window.

As stated previously, you can use PayMIX to record your absences. One drawback to this method is that you cannot review these occurrences in the Absence Attendance Detail window. Only entries made directly to the Absence Attendance Detail window can be reviewed.

PART

III

CH

25

PAID TIME OFF ACCRUALS

Many companies require their employees to earn their vacation and sick time through accruals. Oracle provides a standard mechanism that enables employees to accrue vacation and sick time on a pay-period basis. Many companies, however, accrue paid time off in ways that do not easily fit into Oracle's standard mechanism. For example, a company's accrual rate might be based on hire date, but carryovers occur on the anniversary date instead of January 1. Oracle's standard solution performs carryovers on January 1. Other business rules might require companies to develop their own accrual solutions.

One client of BOSS Corporation had a very complex vacation and sick-time accrual process. Our solution used standard Oracle functionality but still allowed the company to continue to support their unique business rules. The tools we used included Balance Creation, Table Structures, Fast Formulas, Formula Results, and Balance Feeds. I could present an entire paper on this topic alone. Instead, I will present a simplified example of the one we implemented and will only address the vacation time portion.

For the sample company, assume that they accrue vacation hours per pay period based on Table 25.3.

TABLE 25.3 VACATION HOUR RATE EXAMPLE

Years of Service	Vacation Rate
0 to 4 years	.33 days
5 to 10 years	.66 days

Next, employees can carry over up to 320 hours on their anniversary date. Any hours over this amount are lost. Finally, employees can "sell" vacation time back to the employer. The goal of the accrual process is to properly accrue at the rate described previously, carry over the allowed amount at their anniversary date, and properly decrement the balance when vacation is either taken or sold.

The first step is to create the balance that will hold the total hours available for vacation. Navigate to the Balance window (Navigation path: Compensation and Benefits, Balance) to define the balance. Make sure one of the dimensions includes Lifetime To Date (LTD). This will be the balance dimension that will track the total accrued hours because any year-to-date balances would be automatically zeroed out at the beginning of a new calendar year.

The next step is to define Table 25.3 using the Table Structure window (Navigation Path: Compensation and Benefits, Table Structure). The rows will contain the range of years of service, and the columns will have the corresponding accrual rates. Next, navigate to the Table Values window to log in the actual accrual rates.

Next, you need to define the element that will be assigned to each of the eligible employees. Define this element as an Information element and add any needed input values necessary. In this example, you will input a vacation date that the accruals should be based on. Generally, this is the same as the hire date, but it could be different if there was a break in service.

Now, you create the Fast Formula that will be attached to this element. It will use the vacation date and look up the accrual rate in our table. It will pass the results to an output variable on the RETURN statement.

The next element is the key to the solution, which you will call the Hold Element, which is another Information Element. You need an element that does nothing more than process the balance feeds. The accrual formula will pass its output as an indirect result to an input value on this Hold Element called Accrued Hours. The Balance Feeds for the Hold Element will use the Accrued Hours input value to add to the Vacation Hours Balance previously created.

You use the same approach for any vacation taken. The number of hours taken must be passed to another input value on the Hold Element called Taken Hours. Again, the Balance Feeds for the Hold Element will use the Taken Hours input value to subtract from the Vacation Hours Balance.

You will use the Formula Results window to create this link between the formula and the Hold Element. Navigate to the Formula Results window (Navigation Path: Compensation and Benefits, Formula Results) and select from the pick list the Accrual Element previously created. Assign the accrual formula previously created as a Standard formula. In the Formula Results region, define the output variable that has the accrual rate as an indirect result to the input value Accrued Hours in the Hold Element. Use the same approach for the formula that calculates the vacation. The output variable that has the total hours taken must be defined as an indirect result to the input value Taken Hours in the Hold Element.

PART
III

CH
25

The logic for the carryover process must be handled in the accrual formula. First, you must determine whether the anniversary date occurs during the period being processed. If so, then you must determine whether the life-to-date vacation balance will exceed the allowed limit of 320 hours. If so, you must adjust the Accrued Rate for this run so that the resultant balance equals 320 hours.

This discussion has outlined the approach we took at BOSS to solve this complex issue. We also developed several custom reports to document the results of the accrual process. *It is important to note that we met the client's requirements for their complex vacation accrual process without customization to standard Oracle functionality.*

GOVERNMENT REPORTING

The requirement by the United States government for employee reporting on companies is an important responsibility of a Human Resources department. Although in some companies, it is handled by Payroll, it is mostly considered a Human Resources function. As more and more government reporting requirements are given to U.S. companies, the need for purchasing packaged HR software such as Oracle Human Resources increases. Many companies realize that they will need to continue paying the costs of maintaining and reporting on this type of information. Although many companies toward the end of the 1990s were purchasing packaged software to obtain Year-2000 compliance, many of the HR package software purchases in the upcoming millennium will probably be influenced by the desire to remain compliant with government regulatory reports.

The Oracle HR product has been designed to handle this reporting necessity with as much flexibility as possible. The reports that can be produced with use of Oracle HR satisfy government reporting requirements and provide the information necessary for a client to review their practices and progress internally.

There are five main areas and reports to focus on:

EEO-1

AAP

VETS-100

ADA

OSHA

The EEO-1 (Equal Opportunity) and AAP (Affirmative Action Plan) reports are government-mandated reports that measure employment and advancement of employees by gender and ethnic origin within the client base.

The VETS-100 Report reports on the employment and advancement of Veterans in the categories of disabled and Vietnam-era Veterans.

ADA (American Disabilities Act) is reporting on those employees with disabilities and helps to monitor that employers are making reasonable accommodations for those employees identified as having discernable disabilities.

OSHA (Occupational Safety and Health Administration) records and reports workplace injuries and illnesses, including the number and severity of each.

All these reports should provide two things: compliance with government regulations and a means for clients to review their internal practices for fairness and safety. The first is required and the second recommended. This chapter will provide no in-depth discussion of the definitions and compliance-issues that encompass these items, but it will offer an overview of the functionality that Oracle HR provides to produce these reports and provide a tool to the client to use in monitoring these functions.

When planning all these reports, please read and make sure you understand how the Government Reporting Entity (GRE) Numbers factor into this reporting. The Oracle HR User's Guide gives detailed information on the reporting hierarchy. The reporting requirements for each company require customer-specific setup according to how their information should be reported. Before running these reports, the client must set up their reporting establishments, including Corporate headquarters and AAP Organizations along with the hierarchy and overrides for any individual employees as indicated.

Additionally, to support government reports, particularly EEO-1 and AAP, care must be given to the creation of Jobs and Grades within Oracle HR. Creating Job Groups and Lines of Career Progression is a functional issue that must be resolved by each company before the Oracle system can be set up and before you can ever hope to produce some of the government-mandated reports.

EEO-1 REPORTING SETUP STEPS

Follow these steps to set up EEO-1 Reporting:

1. For each GRE, enter information necessary for submission of the report.
2. Enter an EEO job category for each job.
3. Ensure each employee has the following recorded:

   Gender

   Ethnic origin

   An assignment to a GRE

   Job

4. Identify types of EEO-1 reporting to be submitted:

   Individual

   Headquarters Report

   Establishment

5. Determine establishment hierarchy; identify and define reporting organizations.
6. Build establishment hierarchies.
7. Enter any necessary overrides for employees.
8. Run the EEO-1 Report.

AAP REPORT SETUP STEPS

Follow these steps to set up AAP Reporting:

1. Ensure that each employee has the following:

   Gender

   Ethnic origin

   Been assigned to a GRE

   Job

2. Determine salary codes for jobs by selecting grades to represent each salary.
3. Define lines of progression for your jobs using Affirmative Action standards.
4. Determine job groups that jobs belong to.
5. Associate each job with your Affirmative Action Plan.
6. Define an AAP organization to represent each AA Plan.
7. Determine the AAP hierarchy.
8. Run the AAP Report.

VETS-100 Setup Steps

Follow these steps to set up VETS-100 Reporting:

1. Register Reporting Categories and Statuses for Business Group.
2. Enter information necessary for submission of VETS-100.
3. Record EEO job categories for jobs.
4. All employees with a qualifying Veteran status have been assigned to the following:

   Job

   Employment Category

   GRE

5. Determine establishment hierarchy required; identify and define the reporting organizations necessary.
6. Build establishment hierarchies.
7. Enter any necessary overrides.
8. Run VETS-100 Report.

ADA

The approach for ADA reports is the same as the preceding reports except with emphasis on identifying those employees who have disabilities and entering any pertinent information about them. Indicating an employee as disabled is accomplished by checking the Disabled Box when entering personal employee information. Oracle HR comes delivered with a predefined Special Information Type Key Flexfield for recording ADA information.

OSHA

Again, this report follows the same format as the others with the only difference being that information on work-related illnesses and injuries must be entered. Oracle HR comes delivered with a predefined Special Information Type Key Flexfield for recording OSHA events.

The flexibility of the Oracle HR functionality to support government reporting is demonstrated in the establishment of a correct reporting organizational hierarchy for one of these reports. When you have defined the organizational hierarchy for one report, you might have done the majority of the work for the others. This avoids repeating work and puts you on the road toward having correct, viable reports in a government-mandated format ready to be submitted with a minimum of effort required. Moreover, as the U.S. government institutes new reporting requirements, the Oracle HR system enables you to have a foundation so you can meet these new requirements more promptly and with less cost. If you speak with Compliance Officers for large corporations, you will quickly recognize the worth of these system-driven reports.

PAY SCALES AND PAY PROGRESSION

The use of Pay Scales is a common need when addressing union contracts. It is common to have an HR policy where various jobs have prenegotiated rates of pay based on duration of employee service. For example, after 6 months, the employee is paid $X, after 12 months, $Y, and so on.

There are two main obstacles to overcome in solving this problem via Oracle HR. First, Pay Scales are not tied to Salary Administration. Second, Oracle's implementation of automatic progression (how an employee's rate of pay is advanced from one step of the pay scale to the next) is not flexible. Automatic progression is not based on each individual employee's hire date, nor is it based on the amount of time an employee has occupied a specific step on a pay scale.

The following has not been implemented but is a proposed solution for these two issues. Oracle Pay Scales are used for data storage only. The automatic processes within Oracle HR should *not* be used to allow employee advancement to a new progression step. Custom processes are written to handle these situations. These custom processes, in turn, use the supported Salary Administration API to generate new salary proposals.

Consider a two-part solution. One solution solves the issue when an employee becomes eligible to advance to the next step on a pay scale. The second solution addresses the issue when there is an annual pay increase for all steps on a given pay scale.

The first solution addresses the advancement of an employee from one step to the next in a pay scale. The custom process performs the following activities:

1. Read the employee's records for assignment and underlying grade step point placement. Determine the employee's current *pay scale*, *step*, and *date* at that step. Note: A Descriptive Flexfield segment on the assignment form should be created to contain a Grade Step Override Date. This override date exists to handle issues such as unpaid leave. If a date value exists in this field, the program should ignore the effective date in the Grade Step form and use this override date (regardless of whether the override date is before or after the Grade Step's effective date).

2. Based on the employee's pay scale, read the table corresponding to the Grade Step Placement window to determine whether the employee is already at the *ceiling*. If so, stop.

3. Read the table corresponding to the Pay Scale window to determine the *frequency* at which an employee should progress to the next step.

4. Based on the date from step 1 and the frequency from step 3, if the employee is not eligible to advance to the next step, stop. If the employee is eligible to advance to the next step, write a SQL statement to update the table (no API is currently available) to place the employee at the next available step for the Progression Point Placement window.

Caution

There is significant risk in writing directly to database tables. We do not recommend this as a general practice. Because Oracle does not offer an API for this item, the only other alternative involves use of a report followed by a manual process. It is recommended that extensive testing occur on this step.

5. Clear the segment Grade Step Override Date from the employee assignment Descriptive Flexfield.

6. Generate a salary proposal using the Salary Admin API.

7. Payroll Manager must approve the proposed salary changes through the Oracle HR application.

The second solution addresses the issue when there is a pay increase (usually annual) for all steps on a given pay scale. The custom process performs the following activities:

1. Determine whether a new date tracked record exists in the progression point values table.

2. If a new entry is identified, search the employee assignment Grade Step Placement database table to find all employees who are at that specific progression-point step on that specific pay scale.

3. Write SQL statement to update the table (no API is available) to reflect that the employee's current progression point step has a new rate of pay. This step might not be required. The fact that they are already assigned to the step should automatically point them to the correct new rate of pay.

4. Repeat steps 6-7 from the previous solution.

On another issue, consider this suggestion. When naming the points to a pay scale, be descriptive. Instead of referring to pay scale points generically as 1, 2, 3, 4, and so on, use names such as 6 months, 12 months, 18 months, Temp Supervisor, Temp Maintenance, Temp Foreman, Temp Mechanic, and so on.

One last thing to help make things more confusing: If you begin looking at the database tables through SQL, you'll discover the terminology of *spines*. Progression points on the application windows are called *spinal points* in the database. Pay scales on the application windows are called *parent spines*.

SPECIAL BENEFIT ELIGIBILITY DATES

Most organizations administer benefits using eligibility criteria based on employee length of service using a special date that is other than the employee's most recent hire date. The Oracle Payroll Element Link window allows elements to be linked using employee qualifying conditions such as employee age and length of service following hire date. Here are a few examples of special dates:

Adjusted hire date for rehiring of previously employed employees to give credit for previous periods of service

Date that employee completed training or certification

Adjusted service date to account for company buyouts

Plant, unit, or other seniority dates

Job seniority dates

Oracle HR provides for special user-defined dates to be stored using flexfields. The most common placement of these dates is using either the Person Descriptive Flexfield or a Special Information Type. What are the advantages of using one versus the other? Your decision should be based primarily on how you want to retrieve this data.

The advantage of a Special Information Type is that there are an unlimited number of segments at your disposal. If you establish a Special Information Type Key Flexfield for special dates, there are 30 segments for data storage. Should you need more than 30, you can merely create a second Special Information Type Key Flexfield to store additional special dates. The disadvantage of using a Special Information Type is that these segments cannot be accessed using Oracle Fast Formula.

The primary advantage in using Descriptive Flexfield segments on the Person window is that these segments can be accessed using Fast Formula. A disadvantage to using the Person Descriptive Flexfield is that there are a limited number of segments. Additionally, these segments can be defined as required segments, which might or might not be a good idea. When a new employee is added, you would be forced to enter this information, which would prevent you from accidentally overlooking this information. However, this required entry would have a negative side effect when entering contacts or applicants because the Person window is also used for entry of people other than employees. Every person definition would require a value in these Descriptive Flexfield segments, which makes little sense.

Our conclusion: At BOSS, we prefer using the Person window Descriptive Flexfield as long as there are a sufficient number of segments available. If you intend to access these dates using Oracle Fast Formula, you should use the Descriptive Flexfield. If you intend to access these dates through a custom process (for example, a process that feeds time cards and other earnings to Oracle PayMIX), your placement of these dates is only a matter of personal preference.

Our wish: Wouldn't it be nice if a future release of the Oracle HR/Payroll product included a reserved flexfield on the Person window that was dedicated to special dates? Each segment would be a date format that provided for a user-definable name. Clearly, there is no way that Oracle or anyone else could create a hard-coded definition of every possible benefit eligibility date that a client needs. Every client has unique, and sometimes nonstandard, eligibility criteria. If these dates existed, the Element Link window could be slightly modified. Eligibility based on length of service could be modified to add a drop-down list containing the hire date plus all user eligibility dates. Then, the length of service (6 months, 3 years, and so on) would be based on the value from the selected date segment (or hire date). This functionality would enhance the product and not interfere with the goals of the future release of Oracle Advanced Benefits (OAB). Note that OAB is scheduled for release 11.5 of Oracle Applications.

BENEFICIARIES WITH ORACLE HR

During the benefit enrollment process, employees can name beneficiaries for benefits in these classifications:

> AD&D (insurance coverage for accidental death or dismemberment)
>
> Life Insurance
>
> 401(k)
>
> Pension
>
> Profit Sharing
>
> Stock Purchase

The beneficiaries are normally individuals who are entered into Oracle HR as contacts or organizations. When the beneficiary is set up, you can attach her to an employee's benefit element via the Beneficiaries window.

The first step in the process is to set up the beneficiary. If the beneficiary is an individual, navigate to the Person window of the employee to whom this beneficiary is to be associated (Navigation path: People, Enter and Maintain). Click the Others button and select Contact. Make sure you are date-tracked to the date the person becomes a beneficiary of the employee. Complete the window, making sure you include the name, gender, birth date, social security, and address (if different from employee). Be sure to check the Beneficiaries box.

If the beneficiary is an organization, such as an alumni association or local foundation, navigate to the Organization window (Navigation path: Work Structures, Organization, Description). As with all organizations, you must set up a Location record for the address of the organization before navigating to the organization window. Verify that you have set up the organization with the classification as *Beneficiary Organization*.

Now you are ready to record a beneficiary for a benefit. Set the effective date, via date-tracking, to the date the person or organization becomes a beneficiary of the benefit. Navigate to the Element Entries window of the employee (Navigation path: People, Enter and Maintain, Assignment, Entries). Place your cursor on the element representing the benefit. Click the Others button and select Beneficiaries to gain access to the Beneficiaries window. You can rank your beneficiaries in the Level field by selecting Primary, Second, Third, or Fourth. All primary-level beneficiaries who survive the employee become the actual beneficiary of the benefit. If all the primary beneficiaries do not survive the employee, the beneficiaries on the next level down become the actual beneficiary of the benefit, and so on. There is no limit to the number of beneficiaries you can enter at any one level.

You select the name of the beneficiary in the Name field. The pick list contains all contacts marked as beneficiaries for this employee and all organizations with the classification Beneficiary Organization. You can also divide the total benefit between multiple beneficiaries. In the percentage field, enter the percentage of the benefit to which this beneficiary is entitled. Oracle HR ensures that the total of percentages entered for beneficiaries at a level will total 100 percent.

BATCH ELEMENT ENTRY (BEE) USES

Batch Element Entry (BEE) is a means of entering mass information for elements for numerous employees. One of the most important uses is Benefits Enrollment.

BEE is used by many clients to accomplish the following Payroll functions:

Record timecard data

Enter special nonrecurring earnings or deductions

Enter one-time changes

BEE can be used for the following nonpayroll tasks:

Staff responsible for absence management

Benefits administration

Salary administration

After a Batch has been created, you validate the batch. See Table 25.4 for the different statuses a batch can have.

TABLE 25.4 BATCH STATUSES

Valid Mismatch	Transferred	Unprocessed	Error	Status
All headers, lines, and control totals are valid	All headers and lines have been transferred to Element Entries	One line, at a minimum, is unprocessed	One line, at a minimum, is in error	Combination of statuses in the batch, lines are not consistent

To enter batch headers and control totals, do the following:

1. Set the effective date desired.

2. Enter a name, reference number, and source of the batch.

3. Select the action to be taken if a batch line ends up matching an existing Element Entry. Actions are the following:

   Create new entry

   Reject entry

   Change existing entry

4. If Change entry is selected, indicate what type of change should be made to the existing Element Entry:

   Update

        Correct

        Override

5. If Reject is selected, you cannot select override.
6. If Purged after Transfer is desired, select this check box.
7. Choose the Totals button to validate the batch before transfer.

Enter Batch Lines by doing the following:

1. Choose the Line button and select the HR/Payroll element to which you want to make entries.
2. Choose the Default button to allow the default window to display the input values.
3. Enter default values.
4. Uncheck the Display check box for any field you do not want to display in the Lines window.
5. In the Lines window, enter data required for the batch.
6. Save your entries.
7. Batch lines can be retrieved and you can update a batch before you transfer it

Note also that Batch Element Entry can be used in interfaces to provide for the automated load of benefits enrollment. The interface needs to write to the following tables:

        PAY_BATCH_HEADERS

        PAY_BATCH_LINES

        PAY_BATCH_CONTROL_TOTALS

APPLICATION DATA EXPORT (ADE)

Application Data Export (ADE) is a powerful data extract tool specific to Oracle's HRMS application. Many users are not aware of what ADE is and what benefits it can provide. A common misunderstanding of ADE is that it is a separate program, possibly even a non-Oracle product, when in fact it is an Oracle product and is tightly integrated with the application. This misunderstanding is probably due to the fact that the program is not documented in the Human Resources or Payroll user manuals. In fact, the only comprehensive documentation is in the form of a 7MB (after extraction) MS Word document that is available on Oracle's FTP site:

```
ftp://external-ftp.us.oracle.com/apps/APPLICATIONS/HR_PAYROLL/
ADDITIONAL_FUNCTIONALITY/ADE/
```

ADE can be used from within the application by selecting the ADE button on the application toolbar at the appropriate time, or it can be run in standalone mode without the application running at the time. Most Human Resources and Payroll professionals know that they have unique needs for data, perhaps unlike any other groups in an organization. These people know that they receive many questions and are required to provide analysis on the organization's employee population and associated data. Employee lists, phone number listings, and birthday lists are just a few of the most basic requests. ADE puts power into their hands by providing them access to data without having to request a formal report from the MIS department. The users are not totally independent from MIS because technical skills are required to set up the ADE environment, but from that point the users can then generate data on their own.

The following are various topics and tips to consider when using ADE:

Running ADE from within Oracle HRMS. On most forms, the user is permitted to supply a value in a field and perform a query that returns matching data to that form. For example, one might go to the People form and query on all those employees with names beginning with "A" ("A%" in the Last field). When the data is returned, the user can invoke ADE by clicking the Data Export button on the toolbar (furthest button to the right). ADE starts up and enables the user to fetch the data and place it into a program on their desktop (for example, MS Word, MS Excel). All fields associated with that form are exported to the specified destination. All the folders within the application allow for ADE to be selected, exporting the contents of the folder to a selected destination. As you might imagine, when ADE is run in this manner, the data exported is limited to the data that can be viewed onscreen. Often, additional fields are required. In these cases, it is possible to run ADE in standalone mode.

Running ADE Standalone. ADE works by running established queries against the database and enables the user to place that extracted data into a program that he can use to further analyze or utilize the data. Microsoft Excel spreadsheets can be created as well as Microsoft Word documents. From that point, any sort of reports, graphics, form letters, or printed labels can be generated. The queries that ADE runs are based on database views. The views can be further refined with styles.

Views. Views are simply saved SQL statements that are normally created by MIS. SQL statements can be quite complex, joining many tables within the application. Most requests for information can be satisfied with a small number of well-designed views. These views can be further refined in ADE by creating Styles.

Styles. Styles can also be created by MIS, but they also can be created by HR or Payroll personnel who have some technical aptitude. A style can specify a subset of columns that are available in the view.

To run an ADE query in standalone mode, the user simply selects a style and specifies constraints at runtime to limit the query if necessary. At that point, ADE fetches the data and returns the results to a window for display. The user can then export the contents to another program if desired.

Other ADE Features. Security in ADE is controlled by application security. When using ADE, you select a responsibility the same way as within the application. Also, if configured to do so, ADE can be used to upload data to the application database. For example, the application provides for exporting of salary information and uploading of salary changes. This is actually accomplished using ADE, although it might not be

PART

III

CH

25

immediately apparent to the user. The same holds true for some of the letter-generation capabilities of the application (recruitment letters). ADE can also be used in conjunction with organization and position hierarchy diagrammers.

PRODUCING MS WORD DOCUMENTS USING ADE

Oracle HRMS provides a number of methods of automatically creating MS Word documents such as form letters or labels from Oracle data using ADE. It also enables creation of MS Excel spreadsheets, but because that is a more straightforward process and is well documented in other places, it is not covered in this discussion. Creation of MS Word documents is somewhat more involved and requires more setup.

There are four ways to produce Word documents using Oracle/ADE. They are as follows:

1. Use the recruitment letter form. This method enables you to place individuals into a form who are to receive letters. This is a fine choice for small numbers of recipients. This method can include functionality that would produce letters based on certain types of status changes of applicants. The database views that you base your letters on must contain certain columns for this method to work.

2. Generate letters with an export from a form. This method limits your person selection to queries that can be run on a form and columns that are available to that form. It is not a very flexible approach and therefore not recommended.

3. Generate letters using the MS Word Letter Request form. This method will be discontinued in future releases of Oracle HRMS (post 10.7).

4. Generate letters/labels using standalone ADE. This method is most flexible and is the recommended approach in most cases.

The remainder of this discussion contains details on the setup and processing of method 4.

RECOMMENDED SOLUTION

To use this method, you must modify an existing Style or create a new Style in ADE. To do this, you must have System Administrator rights to ADE, and you might need an available view that contains the data you need. The Styles you use are based on views or application forms. If you want to create a view, remember the naming convention "HRV_" should precede any view name that will be used by ADE. An MS Word merge document must be created and placed in the proper directory. The demonstration in the following section details a simple address label creation based on an existing view of all active employees. It shows how to use criteria to limit results of the process.

SETUP STEPS

The following steps show how to use an existing view of all employees to create a simple address label:

1. Create or modify a Style.

Start up ADE in standalone mode and sign in as system administrator. Select the Style tab and enter the following settings:

Form: GENERAL. Tells the system that this style is not based on a form.

View: HRV_CURRENT_EMPLOYEES_US. You can use or create any view that contains the data you want to include in your document. The name of the view *must* begin with HRV_.

Document: Address.doc. This is the actual name of the Word document that will be used. It should exist in the \APPLICATIONS\HRIO\LETTERS subdirectory of the drive on which ADE is installed. See step 2 for instructions to create the document.

2. Create a Word document.

   Go back to Paths tab in ADE. Click the Test button and select the style that you created in the prior step.

   Click OK, and MS Word is launched. A document is created with merge fields that equate to fields from the style. You can create the labels using these merge fields. Then create merge options by selecting Tools, Mail Merge menu options from within Word.

   Click the Create button, select the type of merge document (Mailing Labels, in this case) desired, and select Active Window.

   Click the Get Data button. Select Open Data Source. Use the Windows File Select facility to locate HRIO.XLS (usually in \APPLICATIONS\TEMP in the directory that ADE is installed into). Respond Entire Worksheet when the system prompts you for a range to include.

   Click the Setup button to select formatting options for your labels. Select the type of labels you want to use (5160 - Address, for this example). Then create the layout of your label by inserting merge fields in the way you want them to appear.

   Click OK. The layout of your document changes to reflect the appearance of your labels.

   Close the Merge Helper form and save the file using the same name that you specified in the "Document" setting for your style. Be certain to save the file in the \APPLICATIONS\HRIO\LETTERS subdirectory of the drive that ADE is installed into.

3. Run ADE query.

   Start ADE in standalone mode and choose the Style that was modified in the Query Details box.

   You can narrow the results of a query by selecting a field in the Criteria box and then clicking and dragging the button to the right of that box down to the Selection Details area. You are prompted to input your selection criteria. In this example, you want to see only those employees whose location begins with the number 951. Enter this value and click OK.

Then click the Fetch button to execute the query. The system runs the query and displays results in a spreadsheet-type format. Click the Word button to initiate the merge.

This launches MS Word with the data selected by the query formatted within the document that was created earlier.

You can print this document immediately or save it under a different name for later printing.

Please note that this final process might take several minutes to run depending upon the size of your query. Also, the seeded HRV_CURRENT_EMPLOYEES_US view, on which this example is based, contains a flaw that sends the County data to the State field.

IMPLEMENTING HR AFTER FINANCIALS

Many companies are faced with a situation in which they desire to implement Oracle HR/Payroll after they have previously implemented Oracle Financials. Because of shared tables between HRMS and Financials, there are often changes required to the Financial modules to accommodate the requirements of HRMS.

From an Oracle Payroll perspective, things are fairly easy. Generally, you should map segments of the Payroll Cost Allocation Key Flexfield to the corresponding segments of the Oracle General Ledger Accounting Key Flexfield. In essence, it is usually better if GL is implemented before Payroll.

When looking at issues affecting Oracle Human Resources, the issues are more challenges. The following areas of shared data must be addressed:

Organizations. Because these are used by Oracle Projects and other modules, you should prepare for additions and likely changes to organizations due to different HRMS security, costing, and reporting requirements. Note that it is not a requirement that HR use the exact same organizations that have been set up for the other modules. However, it does make good sense when a common organization is being represented.

Locations. If the same locations that were set up for Financials are planned for use by HRMS, you should assure the each location has an address. Moreover, prepare each address to obtain the appropriate Vertex validation by opening and saving each location from within HRMS. Otherwise, employees cannot be assigned and paid using this location.

Jobs/Positions. Oracle HR nearly always requires changes to jobs and positions that have been set up for use in Oracle Financials. This is because of management and government reporting requirements. In particular, implementers of Oracle Purchasing require either jobs or positions to identify buyers. However, if a position has been set up with one segment titled "Buyer," the HR department will almost assuredly require this to be changed.

People/Assignments. Some data within the underlying tables might need to be altered, depending on exactly how your data has been stored by Oracle Financials. These are usually more minor issues when compared to the other items of shared data. For instance, the last name and first name of employees might have been entered in uppercase. Because this is not as desirable for HR reports or Payroll checks, you might want to change items such as this.

Addresses. Employee addresses set up for use by Oracle AP require attention because AP does not establish the appropriate Vertex validations required by Payroll. You will likely need to write SQL scripts or prepare to delete and reenter certain addresses.

TROUBLESHOOTING

If you are planning to implement Oracle HR, consider that much of your upcoming challenge is an art. Sure, there are technical (or scientific) issues, such as the section earlier in this chapter discussing implementing Oracle HRMS after financials. Because Human Resources processes are often an art, most companies might never know whether they are obtaining a "good" implementation of Oracle HR. Troubleshooting HR processes and HR software implementation is thus generally not focused on getting the "right" answer. This is because there are often numerous answers with some degree of "correctness." The focus should be on whether you obtain solutions that make optimal use of the functionality of your Oracle Human Resources system.

At BOSS, we believe your best chances of obtaining optimal solutions are to work with heavily experienced individuals who know Oracle HR functionality thoroughly but who are not confined from creative thinking so that nonstandard solutions can be created based on your specific needs.

PART

III

CH

25

CHAPTER 26

Using Oracle Payroll

DISCOVERING NEW FEATURES IN RELEASE 11

Release 11.0 of Oracle Payroll provided a number of new features. Although not every feature will be discussed, please note a few of the ones that are of particular interest to Oracle Payroll users:

Latest Balances from Previous Payroll Run. In previous releases, if you ever rolled back a payroll, the following payroll run would take much longer to run. This is because the rollback would eliminate the values in the latest balances table. R11 improves this situation by retaining both the latest balances and the previous balances. Thus, a rollback will replace the latest balances with the previous balances, enabling your next payroll run to not require re-creation of these balances from scratch.

Costing of Balance Adjustments. Both the Adjust Balances and Adjust Tax Balances windows have been modified to provide costing of balance adjustments for purposes of transferring to the General Ledger.

Retro Pay by Run. Prior to R11, the Retro Pay process only enabled you to produce one Flat Amount of Retro Pay, which applied to the entire time period desired for the Retro Pay. In R11, you have the capability to see the separate effect that Retro Pay has on each individual pay period over the Retro time period. Oracle Payroll can produce individual run results for every payroll period being reprocessed. Note that these run results are still applied to the current payroll period.

Wage Attachment Earnings Rules. This is an R11 window created to enable you to create and update your own Wage Attachment rules affecting earnings income.

New reports include the following:

Employee Run Results. This identifies all payroll run results for an individual employee.

GRE Totals. This assists in balancing W-2s.

Invalid Address Information. This identifies incorrect addresses such as invalid GEO codes required in establishing proper payroll taxation.

Negative Balances. This enables you to identify negative employee payroll balances within a quarter or year prior to producing SQWL or W-2s.

SQWL Detail Report. This is a new report that is now produced as a part of the State Quarterly Wage Listing Process.

Taxable Balance Verification. This identifies incorrect tax withholdings for Medicare, Social Security, FUTA, SUI, and SDI.

940 Worksheet. This enables you to determine FUTA tax wages and tax liabilities.

941 Worksheet. This enables you to report on quarterly taxes.

CORBA functionality has been enhanced.

DISCOVERING NEW FEATURES IN RELEASE 11I

Release 11i Payroll new features include the following:

Oracle Cash Management integration provides for payroll check reconciliation.

Vertex Quantum Tax Engine is written in C, not Microfocus Cobol.

Category is expanded for 403.

Benefits enhancement support for OAB module.

Legislative payroll hooks enable you to enter extra Fast Formula checking in the Gross to Net calculation.

PayMIX and Batch Element Entry are consolidated. PayMIX is a U.S.-specific interface prior to release 11i. The PayMIX and Batch Element Entry windows are merged in 11i.

Performance is improved in the Transfer to GL process.

Performance is improved in Direct Deposit Advice process.

Performance is improved in various reports.

The payroll iterative engine aids in gross ups and pretax arrearage; note that these iterations occur in memory and do not result in additional run results in the database. The actual payroll process still creates the same number of Run Results as it does currently.

Oracle Time Management provides global support.

Business Intelligence System 1.3 is a cross-application function for issues such as revenue reporting.

A note if you are an Oracle Advanced Benefit (OAB) customer: Even though OAB takes a different approach to benefits enrollment/eligibility, your current HRMS setups for Elements, Element Links, and Element Entries will not be interrupted. You can continue to process Oracle Payroll as you have before. In fact, OAB makes extensive use of Elements and Element Entries. Note that there is no planned built-in migration of HR Element Links to OAB Benefits Enrollment/Eligibility for those customers who desire to convert their elements to the new OAB mechanisms for enrollment.

PAYROLL PROCESSING (FROM PAYMIX TO CHECKWRITER TO GL)

There are several operations that take place during a typical payroll process within Oracle Payroll:

PayMIX. Timecards are entered or are transferred from a timekeeping system.

Payroll Process. Calculation engine for Oracle Payroll.

Prepayments. Identifies payments as either check or direct deposit. It also prepares payments to third-party organizations for wage attachments.

Check Writer. Prepares file for printing payroll checks and any third-party payments.

NACHA. Prepares file for transfer to National Automated Clearing House.

Deposit Advice. Prepares file for printing deposit advices for employees receiving direct deposit.

Costing. Generates costing data to be transferred to General Ledger. It also prepares summarized costing reports based on actual payroll data.

Void Payments. Allows payments to be voided.

Transfer to GL. Transfers the costing data generated above to the General Ledger.

PAYROLL PROCESSING: PAYMIX

PayMIX (Payroll Mass Information Exchange) provides for rapid entry of data batches, including timecard data and one-time earnings or deductions. PayMIX is the interface that receives time cards from Oracle Time Management. Additionally, PayMIX is the interface used for receiving time cards in the United States from time and attendance systems (see the section titled "Time and Attendance Integration with PayMIX").

The existence of time cards within PayMIX has no effect on payroll processing. These time cards must be validated and transferred to the Element Entries tables before they can be processed.

There are four stages of a PayMIX batch:

Hold. Initial Entry is in progress. This is also the status the batches should be set to when a transfer of time cards has occurred from a time and attendance system.

Ready. Data has been entered and approved for validation or transfer.

Validated. The data is verified to contain no Oracle errors and can be transferred.

Transferred. Information has been successfully transferred to Element Entries. Note that the PayMIX Transfer process performs both a validation and a transfer.

A few more notes should be made about PayMIX validation.After information has been saved in PayMIX and the batch has been set to Ready, run the PayMIX Validation process to ensure that the entries are correct. Investigate and correct any that show errors. This process verifies the following:

The employee's assignment number exists in the database.

The employee is eligible for the earning or deduction.

Earnings or deduction element exists to receive the data entered.

Where values are entered as override, the original value is there to accept the override.

That no discrepancies exist with system-generated PayMIX batch totals.

When a batch is *not* in Transfer mode, you can still make additions and corrections to the batch. When the batch has been transferred, you can no longer change or delete the information in the batch. As of Oracle Applications 11.03, there was no PayMIX rollback process to undo batches that had been transferred to Element Entries. If you need to undo a transfer, you must go to each employee's Element Entry window and manually delete the offending timecard.

Payroll Processing: Payroll Processing

The Payroll Process is the primary calculation engine for Oracle Payroll. It processes all earnings, deductions, employer liabilities, and other payments that exist on an employee's Element Entries. When submitting the payroll process, you have the option to select the payroll period ending date and date of payment for a specifically defined payroll. (Note that a payroll is a group of employees designed to process together on a set frequency.) At times, you might want to submit subsets of employees for special payroll processing. Assignment Sets are a useful tool to help achieve this. Also, keep in mind that the QuickPay process is available when payroll processing is desired for only one employee at a time.

Payroll Processing: Processing Prepayments

The Prepayments process is run after the payroll is complete. The Prepayments process distributes the money in all the methods the user has defined. (Generally, this separates checks from direct deposits.) It also separates any third-party payments that were generated by wage attachments. Actual processing of payments is covered in the following section.

Payroll Processing: Payments Processing

The payments process consists of running three processes for paying employees: Check Writer, NACHA, and Deposit Advice. These are fairly straightforward processes. Check Writer produces checks to match each employee's Statement of Earnings (SOE). It also generates checks to third-party organizations for wage attachments. One drawback on third-party checks is that Oracle Payroll does not consolidate paychecks from multiple employees even when they have a common third-party organization. Oracle generates one check per employee. Many companies choose not to use this function for that reason. NACHA prepares an output file so that you can send money to the various banks and credit unions. Deposit Advice produces a file containing the Statement of Earnings from those employees using Direct Deposit.

Note that this Deposit Advice file can be used by your company's internal intranet to provide an online statement to the employee in addition to, or in place of, a printed statement. More users are investigating this means of making advice notices available to employees. Federal guidelines permit this but each state law needs to be investigated thoroughly if the user chooses an online method. Employees should be given ample notice that a new payroll system has been chosen, a sample copy of the SOE, and, if online, information on how to access the SOE. Recommendation is for a detailed memo with a sample copy of the SOE to include a telephone number and contact name to call if questions or concerns regarding their paycheck or direct deposit choice arise. If using an outside vendor to process paychecks, it is recommended that a backup payment source be identified. Identify either an inhouse printer or another outside source. This information is usually included in a disaster recovery plan.

PAYROLL PROCESSING: VOIDING PAYMENTS PROCESS

Oracle provides a method to void checks that were printed and need to be cancelled. This process can be useful in the case of printing errors, last minute terminations, or other reasons that necessitate the check being cancelled.

PAYROLL PROCESSING: COSTING

The Costing process converts the results from a payroll run into the appropriate debits and credits. This process is an important prerequisite to the Transfer to GL process. Even if payroll processing has already occurred for a payroll period, the costing data from the Element Links windows can be changed to apply to any payroll transactions that have not already been costed. Thus, running the Costing process provides verification of accurate costing before it is received by GL.

Many users are disturbed by the fact that the Costing reports only show the costing side of the journal entry without showing the balancing side of the journal entry. If you want to see both the costing and balancing sides of the journal entry, you must develop your own report from the data stored in the payroll costing tables.

PAYROLL PROCESSING: TRANSFERRING TO GL

The Transfer to GL process is initiated after you have verified that payroll costing is correct. This information is transferred to the GL_INTERFACE table and is, in turn, imported by users of Oracle General Ledger. Some clients desire additional manipulation of payroll costing data at this point. If so, carefully define your business rules and prepare to manipulate the payroll data in the GL_INTERFACE table prior to its import into GL.

QUICKPAY PROCESSING

The QuickPay process is a useful tool for calculating payroll payments outside of the normal payroll cycle. The process can be initiated at any time and processes pay for individual employees within a few minutes. The process is especially useful for processing payments for employees who have been paid incorrectly or for processing final payments for terminating employees residing in states requiring that final wages be paid within a specific time period. During implementation, QuickPay runs are an excellent method of testing earnings, deductions, and tax calculations.

The QuickPay process is initiated from the employee Assignment window. Identify the employee for which you will be processing a QuickPay. Navigate to the Assignment window. Choose Others and then QuickPay.

QuickPay runs accomplish the same results as the normal Oracle Payroll process submitted through Submit Processes and Reports. QuickPay runs calculate earnings, taxes, and deductions just as the normal payroll process runs. QuickPay runs can be specified as either regular or supplemental runs just as the normal payroll process runs. The distinction is that the QuickPay run is convenient and efficient for processing one employee. To process one employee through the normal payroll process runs, an Assignment Set of one employee needs to be created. Then, the Assignment Set needs to be referenced when submitting the payroll process through Submit Processes and Reports. Clearly, the QuickPay is less cumbersome than the normal payroll process.

When the QuickPay process is completed, the results can be reviewed immediately. This provides for the determination of the accuracy of the QuickPay run. The following review options are available from the View Results button:

> View Run Messages
>
> Run Results
>
> SOE Report
>
> Tax Balances
>
> Earning and Deduction Balances

View Run Messages displays system messages (warning or error) that occurred during the QuickPay run.

Run Results lists each element containing a Pay Value that was processed for the employee. This is particularly useful for viewing payroll elements that are not displayed on the employee's Statement of Earnings, such as Employer Liability elements.

SOE Report opens the Employee Statement of Earnings window to provide a view of all earnings and deductions and the resulting net pay that would be included on a paycheck.

Tax Balances displays federal, state, and local taxes. This is useful in viewing quarter-to-date and year-to-date tax balances for the employee.

Earning and Deduction Balances is similar to the Tax Balances button. This selection provides a review of employee balances of earnings and deductions for nontax elements.

If the payroll run results are satisfactory, a manual check can be issued, or the QuickPay can be included in the next scheduled Prepayments run. QuickPay gives the user the capability to override the employee's default payment method (Check or NACHA). After Prepayments has completed, the External/Manual Payments window can be invoked to establish the check number for the manual check.

OVERRIDING TAX INFORMATION

Some individuals, including highly compensated employees, request to withhold supplemental taxes at a higher rate than legally required. The Oracle Payroll System provides a method to do this at the state and federal level. The user can enter separate rates for state and federal in the employee tax information.

The three following conditions must be met to use a supplemental tax override rate:

> The GRE must have flat percentage override selection as a calculation method.
>
> A nonzero override rate must be specified.

A supplemental, not regular, payroll must be run.

The default withholding method is used if the three preceding conditions listed are not met.

To specify a Federal Income Tax (FIT) override, you select FIT override and enter the percentage in the Rate field. To withhold a Fixed FIT each period with no tax calculations occurring, enter the fixed amount. For Supplemental tax override, you enter a percentage in the Rate field to override the regular rate. The same procedure is used for State Income Tax override.

For state supplemental tax override, you must first specify a flat rate calculation method for the employer's GRE. Select the supplemental state withholding tax calculation method to be used for employees of this GRE.

Another note to consider when overriding tax information is the duration intended for the tax override. If the override is only intended for one pay period, you must remember to change the employee's W4 tax information back to its original values after the payroll run has been processed.

Other issues can arise requiring the override of tax information within Oracle Payroll due to tax rules when an employee works in one state and lives in another state. Similarly, these tax rules apply within certain states when an employee lives within one locality but works in another locality. In these situations, Oracle Payroll creates multiple tax records (multiple state tax records, multiple county tax records, or multiple locality tax records). If the user desires to force the taxation to be solely be from one state, county, or locality, the user can set the employee's tax information to 100 percent in the desired tax jurisdiction and 0 percent in the other tax jurisdiction record. A note of caution is necessary here.

Caution

Oracle Payroll is extremely flexible in the area of tax information to accommodate numerous issues, including sudden tax law changes. You should carefully research all relevant tax laws before overriding the defaults supplied by Oracle Payroll.

PROCESSING STATE QUARTERLY WAGE LISTINGS (SQWL)

One of the most important features of an automated payroll application is the ability to produce tax reports. Oracle HRMS provides for the production of required tax reporting. Some U.S. states require quarterly filings that give employment level and wage information for that employer within the state. The result of the process is a summary report and an associated electronic file that can be written to magnetic media and submitted to the state.

Running this process is simple. It is submitted for processing to the concurrent manager through the Submit Reports and Processes window, just like any other report or process. If the report ends in error, it can be rolled back using the standard Rollback process. If the report does err, it is most likely due to the fact that a balance adjustment has been made at some point that causes a balance to carry a negative value. The Request Log of the job in error contains an ASSIGNMENT_ID that enables you to identify the individual who is causing the error condition. Another balance adjustment can be made at that point to correct the negative condition. The SQWL job can then be run again. Oracle offers a Negative Balance Report that identifies potential problems. It is advisable to run this report just prior to running SQWLs.

SQWL Setup

Before successfully running the SQWLs, a number of parameters need to be set up. You need to identify any GREs in a state as a transmitter of the wage listing file and provide setup data. This is set up at the Organization level under the GRE/Legal Entity Organization Classification. There are four different groups of parameters there: SQWL Employer Rules (1), SQWL Employer Rules (2), SQWL Generic Transmitter Rules, SQWL State Transmitter Rules. You need to be familiar with the format requirements of the states with which you file and set those parameters accordingly. You also need to set up employer identification and contact information.

A few states (Alaska, California, and Missouri) request parameters to be set at the employee level. These are set in the alternative region of the person's Assignment window called GREs and Other Data.

SQWL Running

The SQWL jobs (called State Quarterly Wage Listing) are submitted individually by state. Parameters requested at runtime include state, quarter, format, and transmitter GRE. A summary page is produced that shows amounts that can be balanced to other reports for verification.

W-2 Year-End Processing

One of the most important tasks that must be completed by the payroll department is the preparation of W-2s and the supporting magnetic media. This section outlines the various steps to guide you in making the year-end process run smoothly.

Early in December each year, representatives from HR, Payroll, and MIS should meet to review the end-of-year schedule. During this meeting, members must map out the last payroll runs of the year and schedule the processing of year-end balance adjustments. Generally, these adjustments are for items such as relocation expenses, personal use of company cars, and education assistance. After the completion of the meeting, you should have a detailed calendar of all the year-end events.

Oracle strongly recommends that you run a series of year-end reports to validate the employees before beginning the year-end process. They are the following:

> *Taxable Balance Verification Report.* This report identifies incorrectly withheld amounts for Social Security, Medicare, FUTA, SUI, and SDI Taxes. This report is especially helpful if there were balance loads performed sometime during the year.

Invalid Address Report. This report lists people with invalid primary addresses.

GRE Totals Report. This report helps you balance W-2s. It lists totals for either selected GREs or all GREs. You should be able to balance this report with the year-to-date registers.

Negative Balances. This report lists negative year-to-date and/or quarter-to-date amounts in several tax balances. This can be very helpful if any of the tax balances were incorrectly loaded during an initial balance load procedure.

To demonstrate how you would correct a problem identified by one of the reports, assume that the Negative Balances Report listed negative amounts in the Excess balance for SUI ER in Massachusetts. According to the Tax Withholding rules, Section 125 deductions are subject to SUI. However, assume that you loaded the balances as if Section 125 deductions were not subject to SUI. The SUI ER Subj Whable balance was understated by the Section 125 amounts, and the SUI ER 125 Redns balance should have been zero. For this example, assume the YTD Section 125 amount was $56.10. Therefore, you needed to add 56.10 to the SUI ER Subj Whable balance and subtract 56.10 from the SUI ER 125 Redns balance.

The first step in the process is to determine what element to use to make the balance adjustment. During the initial balance load, Oracle generates elements to be used in balance initialization. These are created with the SRS process called Initial Balance Structure Creation. You can also use these elements to make balance adjustments. Navigate to the Balance window (navigation path: Compensation and Benefits, Balance) and query the name of the balance that needs to be adjusted. In this case, you need to adjust balances for SUI ER Subj Whable and SUI ER 125 Redns. Click the Initial Feed button and note the name of the element and input value. Table 26.1 outlines possible Initial Value Feeds for your balances.

TABLE 26.1   SUI ER BALANCE FEEDS

Balance	Initial Feed	Input Value
SUI ER Subj Whable	Initial_Value_Element_202_2_1	3
SUI ER 125 Redns	Initial_Value_Element_202_2_1	6

Now, you can create the balance adjustments. Navigate to the Adjust Balance window for the subject employee (navigation path: People, Enter and Maintain, Assignments, Other, Adjust Balance). Make sure you are date-tracked to the effective date of the balance adjustment. Select from the pick list the element Initial_Value_Element_202_2_1, and key in -56.10 in input value 3 and 56.10 in input value 6. Save your work. Other balance adjustments are performed in a similar manner.

The next step in the year-end process is to create the balance feeds for the various W-2 boxes. In the following example, assume that you plan to use W-2 Box 13C (cost of group-term life insurance over $50,000), W-2 Box 13D (elective deferrals to a section 401(k) cash or deferred arrangement), and the Pension Plan and Deferred Comp boxes in region 15. Table 26.2 contains possible balance feeds that need to be established.

TABLE 26.2 W-2 EXAMPLE BALANCE FEEDS

W-2 Box	Balance Feed	Input Value
W-2 Box 13C	Dependent Life Imputed. Employee Life Imputed.	Pay Value Pay Value
W-2 Box 13D	401(k) Pretax.	Pay Value
W-2 Pension Plan	All Pension Earnings.	Pay Value
Def Comp	This box is automatically checked if W-2 Box 13D is defined.	

The name in the Balance Feed column is the name of the element you created to calculate the earning or deduction. The phrase All Pension Earnings means that you add a balance feed for every earning element that should be included in pension-eligible earnings.

Now you are ready to run the first step of the year-end process, called the Year-End Pre-Process. The Year-End Pre-Process is the Oracle Payroll utility that archives the employee balances for a specific year and GRE. When archived, this data is available for end-of-year reporting. If an employee's record has changed after running the Year-End Pre-Process, you can retry the process for that employee. It is not necessary to rerun the entire process. In instances where multiple employee balances are changed, it might be easier to roll back the entire Year-End Pre-Process and rerun again from scratch. If you have generated any of the following reports, you must first roll them back (use the Rollback Process) prior to retrying the Year-End Pre-Process:

Federal W-2 Magnetic Media

State W-2 Magnetic Media

Federal 1099-R Magnetic Media

State 1099-R Magnetic Media

To retry selected employees in the Year-End Pre-Process, use the Retry Payroll Process (*not the Retry US Payroll Process*). To roll back the entire Year-End Pre-Process, use the Rollback Process.

When the Year-End Pre-Process is completed, you can then print the W-2 Register. This report can be printed in either detail or summary. This report prints the contents of each box for every employee (if the detail option is selected) and totals for the entire GRE. Balance these totals to the GRE Totals report and any year-to-date registers.

After performing the necessary balance adjustments, running the Year-End Pre-Process, and balancing the totals to the various registers, you are now ready to print the W-2 statements. Run the Employee W-2 report from the Submit Requests window. You can print W-2s for the entire GRE population or for a single organization, location, or employee. You can also sort the output by Employee Name, Social Security Number, Organization, Location,

Termination Reason, or Zip Code. Form W-2s are printed four copies per page, in accordance with the Evergreen #5206N preprinted laser form. This process is totally rerunnable and does not require you to retry the employee in the Year-End Pre-Process (unless you changed a balance).

The final step in year-end processing is to create the necessary magnetic tapes for the various federal and state agencies. These tapes contain the annual wage and tax statements of employee earnings and tax withholding for your enterprise. You must successfully run the Year-End Pre-Process for each GRE before running a federal or state magnetic W-2 report.

You run the Federal Magnetic W-2 Report from the Submit Requests window. In the Name field, select Federal W-2 Magnetic Media from the list of values. In the Year field, enter the tax year for the report. In the Transmitter GRE field, select the name of the GRE that functions as the transmitter of the W-2 report. This process creates the W-2 records for *all* GREs on one tape. It creates a file on the UNIX server that MIS needs to copy over to a tape.

The State Magnetic report is run in a similar manner. Once again, this process is run from the Submit Requests window. In the Name field, select State W-2 Magnetic Media from the list of values. In the State field, select the desired state. In the Year field, enter the tax year for the report. This process also creates State W-2 records for all GREs. MIS also has to copy the UNIX file to a tape.

This completes the synopsis of year-end processing. Clearly, the hardest part was performing the necessary balance adjustments and balancing the totals to the expected results. Some companies perform this task after every quarter in an effort to streamline the year-end process. They copy their production database instance to a test instance and balance the current YTD amounts to their quarterly reports. They also run the reports listed previously to catch any problems before they get to the crunch of year-end.

REGULAR VERSUS SUPPLEMENTAL PAY RUNS

Oracle offers two types of payroll runs to use when processing employee's earnings and deductions. They are the following:

> *Regular.* Is used to process employees' regular earnings along with their usual deductions. By definition, regular earnings are earnings for time worked, such as salary and overtime. Normally, you process only one regular run per pay period.

> *Supplemental.* Is used to process supplemental earnings such as bonuses, awards, sick pay, and any other special, one-time earnings. You can run as many supplemental payroll runs as necessary in a pay period.

The first step in understanding the ramifications of regular versus supplemental pay runs is to understand how these pay runs are structured. Regular runs process for each employee all recurring earnings and deductions not yet processed in the period. It also includes all nonrecurring earnings and deductions that currently exist in an employee's element entries that have not been processed. In both of these cases, regular runs process *supplemental* earnings that exist in the element entries and have yet to be processed. Oracle Payroll only allows one regular run per employee per period (with the exception described later in this section).

Supplemental runs process all supplemental earnings for an employee with unprocessed entries for the period. All deductions, whether recurring or nonrecurring, that have their processing type set to All are also processed in supplemental runs. Finally, supplemental runs process all unprocessed recurring earnings (regular or supplemental) and deductions for employees with a status of Terminated, for whom final pay has not yet been processed.

When you understand which elements are processed by regular and supplemental runs, you can turn your attention to tax withholding issues. The default income tax withholding method for regular runs is Regular withholding (also called Percentage or Annualized Wages withholding). Regular runs, by default, process any supplemental earnings with regular withholding rates. If you want to process supplemental earnings that exist in regular runs at supplemental rates, you must mark these earnings as Tax Separately. You accomplish this task by setting the input value called Tax Separately on the supplemental earning to Yes.

The default withholding method for supplemental runs is Supplemental Withholding. However, these runs apply regular withholding rates to any regular earnings included in final payments.

One other method that you can utilize is called Cumulative Withholding. This method applies to employees whose earnings occur unevenly during the year. Regular and supplemental runs both use this method for the regular earnings and commissions of those employees who qualify for and have requested it. Navigate to the Tax Information window of the requested employee and check the Cumulative Taxation box to turn on this method.

As mentioned previously, you can, in certain situations, process more than one regular run in a pay period for an employee. Generally, this is necessary when you have completed the normal pay process for a period and a stray timecard that must be processed arrives late. Assume also that the checks have been printed and the NACHA file has already been sent. Below are the steps to follow to process this additional check as a regular run in the same period:

PART

III

CH

26

> Enter the timecard in the requested period either through PayMIX or directly to the employee's Element Entry window.

> Navigate to the QuickPay window for this employee. Make sure to mark the pay run as a regular run.

> Click the Element Selection button and mark all the elements you want to process. This enables you to schedule the specific deductions you want to process with this additional timecard. Generally, any deduction that is calculated on a percent-of-earnings basis (such as a 401(k)) should be included, but flat amount deductions (such as medical and dental) should not be deducted again.

> Run the QuickPay and any associated postpayroll processing.

COSTING OF EARNINGS

Oracle Payroll is extremely flexible when it comes to costing of earnings. Cost information can be obtained at several levels within the Cost Allocation Key Flexfield: Payroll, Organization, Element Link, Assignment, Element Entry, and PayMIX. The valid cost levels are established when defining Flexfield Qualifiers for each segment of the Cost Allocation Key Flexfield.

How do you know which costing levels are appropriate for your implementation? Any time you are in doubt, open up the segment (via Flexfield Qualifiers) at a costing level. Just because the segment is opened, it does not imply that you ever have to fill in data at that level. Usually, General Ledger (GL) Accounts are only opened at the Element Link level, and GL Cost Centers are opened at all levels.

When preparing for the implementation of HR Organizations, it is recommended that you keep the GL requirements in mind. Costing defaults for earnings (and deductions) can be established based on HR Organizations. This aids in the future maintenance of employee information. The HR department does not have to concern itself with the GL cost segment values. The HR department merely needs to assign an employee to the correct organization. These costing defaults are particularly beneficial when an employee's earnings are costed the same way every pay period. Keep in mind that these costing defaults for an organization are flexible and can be overwritten during payroll processing. If Oracle Payroll retrieves costing information at a lower level, such as Element Entries, it overrides the defaults from the employee's organization.

Oracle Payroll is very flexible in dynamically changing a cost segment value from one payroll period to the next. Time card records can be entered into PayMIX using different cost segment values for each record. Consider a maintenance employee who works four hours at a cost center, two hours at another cost center, and still two more hours at a third cost center. The next day, this same employee works at other cost centers. For more details about the integration of cost data into PayMIX, please see the section of this chapter titled "Time and Attendance Integration with PayMIX."

What about cost defaults for groups of employees where the organizations of the employees do not apply? This is where the People Group Key Flexfield becomes particularly beneficial. Consider a situation where you want to separately obtain cost account information for employee Regular Salary using a distinction between executive and administration employees. In this example, executive and administration employees might be scattered throughout numerous organizations. You could set up a People Group Key Flexfield segment to distinguish these two groups and then establish two Element Links for Regular Salary based on the People Group segment value.

Caution

At the time of the writing of this book, a bug exists when salary changes are made in the middle of a payroll period. If Regular Salary has separate links based on People

> Group, you receive a payroll error that salary is not valid for the entire length of the period.

Here are a few thoughts that might influence your transfer of costing information for balancing/offsetting entries to the GL. At BOSS Corporation, we have observed that balancing segments behave as if they are fixed-costed even if the earnings element is defined as Costed. Consider setting up the Element Link with a fully qualified balancing segment. This works if you are balancing to only one account for cash. If you have multiple cash accounts, you need another solution. If you are too far into your implementation and cannot change your Element Links, be prepared for another solution. You need a customized process that is invoked after you have run the Transfer to GL process. You need to create a preprocess program that alters the data before the GL performs its import.

COSTING OF OVERTIME

Many times, companies want to separate out the premium portion of overtime to one GL account and the straight time portion to the normal straight time GL account. This allows the cost accountants to focus on the premium labor costs when overtime is required to complete a certain project or task.

This poses a problem for Oracle HR/Payroll because costing is performed at the element level. The standard Overtime element calculates the total overtime payment, including the straight time and the premium time. How can you separate this out to the two different GL accounts?

The key to the solution is to use two of the most powerful tools that Oracle gives you when implementing HR/Payroll: Fast Formulas and Indirect Formula Results. The first step in the solution is to create your own Overtime element because Oracle does not enable you to modify the seeded elements. Define the element with a Classification as Earnings and a Category as Overtime. Select HOURS_X_RATE_MULT_RECUR_V2 as the Calculation Rule. Oracle generates a formula called XXXXXXX_HOUR_X_RATE_MULT, where XXXXXXX is the name you gave your new Overtime element. You now need to make a copy of the formula used on the Overtime element and paste it into the generated formula. Make sure that you change all references of Overtime to XXXXXXX in the formula.

Study this new formula, and you will notice that Oracle has already separated out the straight time portion of the Overtime calculation into a variable called straight_OT. You only need to add a new statement that subtracts straight_OT from OT_pay to yield a new variable called premium_OT.

Oracle already sends the straight time portion of the overtime calculation to an Information element called Straight Time Overtime. Oracle uses this element for its Workers Compensation calculations. You need to create a new Information element called Premium Time Overtime, using the Oracle example as a guide.

Now navigate to the Formula Results Rules window and select from the pick list the name of the seeded Overtime element. Make note of the Formula Results region of the window. You need to set up your Overtime element exactly like the one you see here. Now select from the pick list your Overtime element, delete the Standard line in the Processing Rules region of the window, and save your work. Add the Standard line back in and make sure you specify the name of your formula. Down in the Formula Results region, add variable names exactly like the seeded Overtime element. Finally, add one more line using the premium_OT variable as an indirect result to the Information element you created previously.

The final step is to set up the Costing. The key to the solution is *not* to cost the Overtime element you created, but to cost the two Information elements. This enables you to specify different account numbers for each portion of the Overtime calculation.

There is one drawback to this solution that you must keep in mind. As stated previously, you establish the costing on the Element Link windows for the Information elements and not the Overtime element. There might be an occasion where you need to override this costing at element entry time. If you enter an override account number on the element entry for your overtime element, either through PayMIX or on the Element Entry window, the formula overrides both the straight time portion and the premium time portion with this override account. Oracle has stated that this is expected behavior and requires an enhancement request to modify it.

OVERTIME FLSA COMPLIANCE

As of release 11.0, Oracle Payroll is not Fair Labor Standards Act (FLSA)-compliant in the calculation of overtime. The seeded Oracle Payroll earning for Overtime does not properly calculate the adjusted overtime base rate of pay when the payroll frequency is greater than one week. The seeded Overtime earning calculates an average rate based on the entire payroll period, not on a separate week-by-week basis. Note that this implies that FLSA compliance can be met within the product if you define your payrolls with a frequency of weekly.

As an example, assume a biweekly payroll period from 01-DEC through 14-DEC for an employee making $10/hour (see Table 26.3). Note in this example that the earning Sales Commission was created with Overtime Base checked on the Earnings Form.

TABLE 26.3   ELEMENT ENTRIES

Date	Earning Element	Hrs	Multiple	Amt
Week 1				
07-DEC	Time Entry Wages	40	1	$400
07-DEC	Sales Commission			$200
07-DEC	Overtime	10	1.5	

TABLE 26.3   CONTINUED

Date	Earning Element	Hrs	Multiple	Amt
Week 2				
14-DEC	Time Entry Wages	40	1	$400
14-DEC	Overtime	1	1.5	

FLSA guidelines expect this overtime calculation:

Week 1 ($400 + $200) / 40 hours = $15/hour

$15/hour * 10 hours OT * 1.5 multiple = $225

Week 2 ($400) / 40 hours = $10/hour

$10/hour * 1 hour OT * 1.5 multiple = $15

FLSA Overtime = $225 + $15 = $240

Oracle Payroll calculates:

($400 + $200 + $400) / (40 hours + 40 hours) = $1,000 / 80 hours = $12.50/hour

$12.50/hour * 11 hrs OT * 1.5 multiple =

Oracle Payroll Overtime = $206.25

Thus: Employee is underpaid for the current payroll period by $33.75.

There are three different approaches to solving FLSA overtime-compliance calculations. Two of these solutions involve the use of Oracle PayMIX. These solutions involve the entry of an adjusted rate of pay into PayMIX for each overtime record. Approach #1 involves calculating the adjusted overtime rate before a record is inserted into PayMIX. Approach #2 involves calculating the adjusted overtime rate after records already exist in PayMIX. Approach #1 can only be used if you have an external Time & Attendance system. The integration program from Time & Attendance to PayMIX can include all the overtime rules. If you are using Oracle Time Management, you need to use Approach #2. If Approach #2 is used, it is vitally important that the PayMIX Transfer process, which transfers PayMIX batches to the Element Entries window, is not run before the overtime adjustment process is run.

Questions you must ask in implementing an adjusted overtime calculation are the following:

- Which earnings (Commission, Bonus, and so on) can influence an adjusted overtime rate of pay?

- Where do these adjustment earnings reside?

- Does the integration program have access to all earnings for the current pay period at the time that the integration is being run?

PART

III

CH

26

Some earnings can be set up in Oracle as recurring earnings. If so, the overtime calculation program must read an employee's Element Entries to determine whether the specific recurring earning exists. Other earnings, such as commissions, might have been previously fed through a different process into PayMIX. Thus, the overtime calculation program must read PayMIX to determine whether the specific nonrecurring earning exists. The integration gets complicated and is very rules-based, but the FLSA deficiency can be solved.

Approach #3 for solving FLSA overtime issues involves Fast Formula customization, careful setup of your Earning elements, and careful procedures for how these elements are used. Instead of using the seeded elements for Time Entry Wages and Overtime, create your own Earnings elements such as Week 1 Wages, Week 2 Wages, Week 1 Overtime, and Week 2 Overtime. Any earning that should be used to influence the adjusted overtime base rate of pay must be created in the same manner such as Week 1 Bonus and Week 2 Bonus.

Prepare to modify the formulas for Week 1 Overtime and Week 2 Overtime. Week 1 Overtime must calculate its adjusted overtime base rate based on the existence of Week 1 Wages, Week 1 Bonus, and so on within the current pay period. The formula for Week 2 Overtime must use similar logic.

Finally, if you use approach #3, be sure that interfaces between the time entry system and PayMIX are analyzed. The interface program must be customized to split week 1-related elements from week 2 if the source data from the time keeping system does not have these items already split.

Regardless of the current solution you choose, if the Oracle Payroll product is ever upgraded to become FLSA-compliant using the seeded Overtime element, take these steps to be prepared. All other earnings elements (Commission, Bonus, and so on) must be created carefully. On the Earnings window, select the appropriate check boxes for FLSA Hours and Overtime Base. Remember that if you fail to check these boxes appropriately, you cannot change the earnings' definitions later. In the meantime, your custom process to calculate an adjusted overtime-base rate of pay can use this information in establishing its rules for calculation.

401(K) CALCULATIONS/COMPANY MATCH

Oracle Payroll is now delivered to provide for the automatic creation through the Deductions window of a 401(k) company match element. However, earlier versions of the product did not have this functionality. The following discussion is still a useful learning tool regarding the flexibility and power of Fast Formula.

One of the most common benefit plans that companies offer employees is a 401(k) savings plan that usually includes a company match. This section outlines how at BOSS Corporation we used standard Oracle features to implement a typical 401(k) plan. The features we used include the following:

Balance Definitions

Global Values

Fast Formulas

Formula Results

The sample 401(k) plan has the following rules. Employees can elect to contribute up to 15 percent of their eligible earnings to the plan. The company matches 50 cents to every dollar, up to 10 percent of the eligible earnings. The deductions should stop when employees reach the IRS maximum amount allowed for 401(k) plans.

The first task is to set up a balance that will define eligible earnings. Use the Balance window to define this new balance (navigation path: Compensation and Benefits, Balance). In this example, name the balance 401K_Earnings. After completing the initial window, click the Feeds button and select from the pick list all the earnings that should be used when calculating the pretax deductions. Click the Dimensions button and select from the pick list the desired dimensions. Use Assignment within GRE Run in the formula. This balance will be used to calculate both the actual deduction and the company match.

Next, define a Global Value that will store the maximum year-to-date deduction allowed under the IRS rules. Navigate to the Global Values window (navigation path: Compensation and Benefits, Global Values) and define this amount. The 2000 amount is $10,000. Each year you can update this value using this window. In this example, name this value 401K_MAX.

Now define the Pre-Tax deduction. Navigate to the Deduction window (navigation path: Compensation and Benefits, Deductions) to set up this deduction. Use Pre-Tax Deduction as the classification and Deferred 401(k) as the category. In this example use Percent of Earnings as the Calculation Rule. This enables Oracle to generate a default formula that you can modify for your use.

Next, define the element that will store the company match portion of the 401(k) plan. Navigate to the Element Description (navigation path: Compensation and Benefits, Element Description) and set up this element as an Employer Liability. The formula passes the calculation results to this element.

Now make changes to the generated formula to calculate both the deduction and the company match. Navigate to the Write Formula window (navigation path: Compensation and Benefits, Write Formulas), and query the formula that Oracle created. Normally, the name of the formula is XXXXX_PERCENT_OF_EARNINGS, where XXXXX is the name of the deduction defined previously in the example. Click the Edit button to bring up the Edit window. Scroll down to the section where the actual deduction is calculated. Oracle inserts a comment right before the logic that instructs users where to put their custom modifications. The default formula uses the Regular Earnings balance. As the formula comments suggest, you want to replace the Regular Earnings balance with the one you created previously. Create a separate validation formula to validate the maximum 15 percent rule. You can also use the Maximum field on the Input Value to control the maximum allowed for the percentage.

The key modification to this formula is to include logic that calculates the company match. The results of this calculation should be stored in a variable that is included on the Return

PART

III

CH

26

statement. This enables you to pass this result to the Employer Liability element you created previously. To do this, navigate to the Formula Results window (navigation path: Compensation and Benefits, Formula Results), and select from the pick list the Pre-Tax deduction for our 401(k) plan. With the cursor down in the Formula Results region of the window, click the New Record icon to open up a new line. Select from the pick list the name of the variable that stored the result of the company match. In this example, use EMPL_CONTR. This automatically passes the results of the formula to the Employer Liability element.

After keying in the necessary links for each element, you are now ready to enroll people into the plan. You only have to add one element, the Pre-Tax deduction element, to Element Entries of participating employees. Enter the desired percentage in the corresponding input value. The formula handles the rest.

By using standard Oracle features, we were able to administer a typical 401(k) plan that can enforce IRS rules, calculate the company match, and enforce any special plan rules.

USING SPECIAL INPUTS ELEMENTS

Oracle has designed a method of making one-time changes to recurring earnings or deduction elements called Special Inputs. Special Inputs elements are automatically created for the earnings and deductions elements the user creates. These elements prevent the need to make manual calculations and to change recurring amounts. Moreover, if the recurring amounts themselves had to be changed, the user would need to remember to change the permanent amounts back.

Special Inputs elements enable you to do the following:

> Replace the normally calculated amount with another amount (using the Input Value: Replacement Amount)

> Provide a number to add to or subtract from the calculated amount (using the Input Value: Additional Amount)

Special Inputs elements can be entered either through PayMIX or through direct entry into the Element Entries window. The Special Inputs are named the same as their corresponding recurring element except that Special Inputs is added after the name. For example, a recurring element named Academic Housing Allowance would have a corresponding Special Inputs element named Academic Housing Allowance Special Inputs.

It is also possible to adjust arrearage balances for deductions when using Special Inputs. Special Input elements that are set up to allow for arrearage have an extra Input Value called Special Input Adjust Arrears. This makes it very easy for the user to correct an arrearage amount without requiring manual work and having to keep tally sheets of money owed to the employee or employer.

GENERATING ARREARS FOR NONRECURRING ELEMENTS (VIA RECURRING ZERO DOLLAR ELEMENTS)

Standard functionality of Oracle Payroll only enables arrears processing to occur on recurring elements. This can be set up in the Deductions window. There are check boxes for both Arrears and Partial Deduction that affect how Oracle Payroll handles insufficient funds.

Arrears occur on a deduction when an employee fails to have sufficient earnings within a particular pay period to satisfy all his required deductions. Oracle Payroll automatically transfers the unsatisfied deduction amount from one payroll period to the next. If the next period generates sufficient earnings to cover current pay period deductions, Oracle Payroll determines whether an arrears balance has been carried forward from a previous pay period.

This functionality is very powerful, but consider the situation where an organization wants to have Oracle Payroll automatically handle arrears processing for nonrecurring deduction elements. Unfortunately, arrears cannot occur unless the element is recurring. Thus, you must fake out the system.

Your requirements can be met by first setting up a recurring deduction and ensuring that the check box for arrears (and partial deductions, if desired) is checked. Then assign this deduction element to an employee's Element Entries. In the Element Entry Input Value for Amount (assuming this is a Flat Amount deduction), enter a value of zero.

If nothing else occurs after this point, Oracle Payroll attempts to process a zero dollar deduction, which fortunately has no affect on pay. Moreover, the resulting paycheck does not show the existence of this deduction.

Now, when the employee incurs a pay period where a one-time deduction amount should be assigned, use the corresponding Special Inputs element for that deduction. By feeding an Additional Amount to the Special Inputs element, the deduction itself changes from zero to this additional amount. Then, if there are insufficient funds within the pay period, the recurring deduction goes into arrears and attempts to satisfy itself in the next pay period.

What is the business case for such a scenario? Consider an organization that has a company store where employees can purchase its products. If an employee makes a purchase from the store, the company might have a policy to allow the amount of purchase to be deducted from the employee's next paycheck. This nonrecurring transaction can be fed to Oracle Payroll as the Special Inputs element described previously. After that, Oracle Payroll ensures that the money is recouped either in the next pay period or in a future pay period due to arrears processing.

RETRO PAY

The Retro Pay Process is used to adjust earnings or deductions in the current period for changes that should have taken place in the past (retroactively). Retro processing is usually required when items do not reach the payroll department in a timely fashion. Union negotiations sometimes result in a retroactive situation as well as changes in benefit tables. The effective date of the retroactive changes is crucial. After the effective date and affected employees are identified, you run the retroactive pay process and then run the current payroll.

Retroactive processing is usually not a result of payroll or management errors but changes to original entries such as those items listed previously. The system calculates the difference between the original entry and the retroactive entry and makes the adjustment. This eliminates manual calculation by payroll personnel and greatly reduces the margin for error.

Additional information on Retro Pay process follows:

> The process recognizes partial pay periods for salaried employees.
>
> Pay changes apply to all hours entered after start date for hourly employees.
>
> Calculation is based on balance differences, not run result.
>
> Use of YTD balance in Retro Set could cause problems when crossing year-end.
>
> Adjustments that cross year-end are recognized in the current pay period.
>
> Overtime for hourly employees is recognized by the process.
>
> Deductions can be adjusted retroactively.
>
> Make the End Date value at least one day into the current pay period when submitting the Retro Pay process.
>
> Input values on retro pay element are extremely important.

Retro Pay setup steps are as follow:

1. Navigate to Compensation and Benefits, Earnings.
2. Date-track to effective date of earning.
3. Create a Retro Pay Earning:

   Classification: Earning

   Category: Regular, Nonrecurring

   Calculation Rule: Flat Amount

   Save and close form.
4. Navigate to Compensation and Benefits, Element Description.
5. Query the Earning you just created. Verify Process in Run and Multiple Entries allowed. Navigate to Input Values.
6. Create two new input values: Start Date and End Date, with date format for units of measure. Save and close window.
7. Navigate to Compensation and Benefits, Link.
8. Link the Retro Pay Earning, save, and close.
9. Navigate to Payroll, Retro Pay Set.
10. Date-track to date of created earning.

11. Name the retro pay set, navigate to the lower part of the form, choose Gross Earnings_ASG_LTD for the balance, the retro pay element, and Pay Value as the input value, and save.

12. Navigate to Payroll, Assignment Set.

13. Create the name of the assignment set and the payroll for the employees who will receive retro pay and save.

14. Select the Amendment button and include all the people who need retro pay. Save and close.

15. Navigate to People, Enter and Maintain, and locate your person.

16. Navigate to the Salary Window, create a new record, and enter the new salary with the date it became effective. Save your record.

17. Navigate to Processes and Reports, Submit Processes and Reports.

18. Choose the Retro Pay Process and fill in the parameters with the name of the assignment set, retro pay set, and the start and end dates (start date should be when the increase occurred—end date should be period end date of the next unpaid payroll). Submit.

19. After the process is complete, you will be able to view the employees' entries and see the retro pay element with the retro amount.

20. Process the next payroll and see the retro pay paid to the employee.

TAX BALANCE ADJUSTMENTS

There are several occurrences that necessitate that Tax Balances be adjusted. For example, an employee might receive imputed income, such as stock options or relocation expenses outside of a regular payroll run. This would make it necessary to adjust tax balances including the Gross Earnings Subject to Tax Balance. Oracle Payroll has provided a means to adjust both of these Tax Balances through the Tax Balance Window.

To make adjustments to an employee's Gross Earnings Subject to Tax balance, you do the following:

> Select the name of the earnings type.

> Enter the gross amount of the change.

The system then locates the applicable balances and makes the adjustment.

To make adjustments to taxes withheld, you handle it in the same manner as listed previously. If you have defined the Tax Rules for the GRE to use the Self Adjust method, the calculation of employee withholding for Social Security, Medicare, State Unemployment Insurance, or State Disability Insurance is corrected with the next payroll run. This also corrects the Employer Liability balances for the same taxes.

It is important to have fully tested the operations of the Tax Balance window so that you do not endanger the accuracy of your tax balances.

Another common use for the Oracle Payroll Adjust Tax Balance window involves manual checks. Often, a company quickly hand-calculates the amount of tax required when preparing a manual check for an employee. Thus, these exact tax amounts must be entered along with the amount of gross pay through the Adjust Tax Balance window. If the tax amounts were manually calculated incorrectly, they might self-adjust during the next pay period as described earlier.

TAX BALANCE ADJUSTMENTS EXAMPLE

The following is a sample procedure for entering Stock Options for employees, where the taxes were paid externally to Oracle Payroll. You will use the Adjust Tax Balance to accomplish this task.

For this example, assume that an employee exercised a stock option and the corresponding taxes were either paid by the employee or were "grossed up" in the payment check. Following is the breakdown of the example:

> Gain on Stock Option exercise: $5,295.62
>
> FIT Taxes Withheld $1,482.77
>
> State Taxes Withheld $317.74
>
> Medicare Taxes Withheld $76.79
>
> Net Amount of exercise $3,418.32

Assume that you have already created an Imputed Earning element called Stock Options that will record the gross amount of the option.

The first step in entering the adjustment is to navigate to the employee's Adjust Tax Balance window (navigation path: People, Enter and Maintain, Assignment, Other, Adjust Tax Balances). Make sure you are date-tracked to the date when this adjustment occurred.

Select the earning named Stock Options and then fill in each of the dollar values as indicated previously.

The Work Address region of this window is completed automatically by the system. In this case, assume that the employee has already reached the limit for Social Security. Save your work. The system automatically creates balance adjustments for all the affected balances. You can review these adjustments in the Payroll Process Results window (navigation path: View, Payroll Process Results). Normally, this is all you need to record the event.

However, there previously existed a bug in Oracle Payroll that caused the Medicare EE Taxable, Medicare ER Taxable, and the SUI ER Taxable balances to be incorrect. Therefore, you needed to make some additional balance adjustments to correct this situation.

During the initial balance load of the YTD amounts, Oracle automatically created the necessary balance adjustment elements that you will use to fix this bug. You can determine the name of these elements by querying the balance via the Balance window (navigation path: Compensation and Benefits, Balance) and clicking the Initial Feed button. They are outlined in Table 26.4.

TABLE 26.4   INITIAL BALANCE FEEDS

Balance Name	Element Name	Input Value Name
Medicare EE Taxable	Initial_Value_Element_202_0_1	11
Medicare ER Taxable	Initial_Value_Element_202_0_1	14
SUI ER Taxable	Initial_Value_Element_202_2_1	7

Navigate to the employee's Adjust Balance window (navigation path: People, Enter and Maintain, Assignment, Others, Adjust Balance). Select from the pick list the first element name from the Table 26.4 (Initial_Value_Element_202_0_1). Tab over to the 11 input value name and key the Gross amount that was entered on the Adjust Tax Balance window. Put the same number in input value name 14. This adjustment adds the gross amount to the two Medicare taxable balances. Save your work.

The Status radio button should change to Completed. Click the New Record icon (the big green cross) and select from the pick list the next element name from the Table 26.4 (Initial_Value_Element_202_2_1). Tab over to the input value name 7 and key the negative of the gross amount ([ms]5295.62). This example assumes that the employee has already reached the SUI limit for his/her state. The Oracle bug assumes that all of this gross should be in the Taxable balance for SUI. This adjustment removes the gross. You also need to key the Jurisdiction code for the employee's work state. If it were Georgia, the Jurisdiction code would be 11-000-0000.

The Status radio button should change to Completed. This completes the process. You can review the results of this adjustment by reviewing the Tax Balance window for this employee (navigation path: View, Tax Information, Tax Balances).

TAX ONLY EARNINGS

Note that a side-effect exists when using Tax Only on the definition of earnings. There will be confusion as you review payroll results from the online Statement of Earnings (SOE) window. For each earning marked as Tax Only, Oracle Payroll displays a separate window on the SOE for the given pay period. This can get confusing because each individual SOE does not show all the tax deductions. However, the combination of all SOEs for the current payroll run, when added together, have the correct tax and deduction calculations. Fortunately, at the time of processing Checkwriter or NACHA, these items will be combined into one check or deposit advice (assuming that each earning has been defined without a requested Separate Check).

COSTING AND TRANSFER TO GENERAL LEDGER

Throughout this chapter, I have discussed various ways to set up your costing matrix for earnings and deductions. When this matrix is established and you have entered all your cost codes (at the Organization, Element Link, Assignment, or Element Entry level), you are ready to run the costing process.

The first step in running Costing is to decide how often you plan to send the costing data to GL. Some companies transfer costing data to GL after every payroll run, whereas others wait and transfer the data all at once at the end of the month. When you run the Costing process, you specify a starting and ending date and either a Payroll or Consolidation Set. The process then scans the payroll run results of the selected payroll or consolidation set and generates costing data for any run result within the date span that has not yet been costed. When the costing process has completed, you can run either of the two supplied cost summary reports. As noted in other sections of this chapter, these reports only show the costing side of the journal entry and do not show the balancing side entry.

After running the Costing process, if you discover that some of the cost codes were set up incorrectly, you can correct the codes at the Organization, Element Link, or Assignment level and retry the costing process for the effected employees. There is no need to rerun the corresponding payroll process. If you need to correct the coding at the Element Entry level, you need to roll back the costing process and rerun the payroll process of the affected employees. When this is completed, you then rerun the costing process.

The Transfer to GL process works in a similar manner. You specify a date range and either a payroll or consolidation set. The process scans the costing tables. It then transfers any costing records within the span and for the desired payroll or consolidation set that has not yet been transferred. All records are inserted into the GL interface table GL_INTERFACE. Oracle GL users then import the journal entries through the normal import process. You cannot retry individual employees on the Transfer to GL process. You can only roll back the entire run, make your corrections, and rerun the process.

Some companies must manipulate this data before it eventually lands in GL. Other companies still use legacy GL systems instead of Oracle GL. In either case, you can write customized code that accesses the data in either the costing tables in Payroll or the interface tables from Oracle GL. Do not modify the records in the costing tables because Oracle tightly controls the interactive action locks between the various payroll processes. You might want to create your own interface tables that would contain the modified tables. Currently, Oracle only supports an automated interface directly to Oracle GL. If you want to import payroll costing data to any other Oracle module, such as Project Accounting, you must write this interface yourself.

GL FLEXFIELD CHANGES: STEPS TO CHANGE PAYROLL COST ALLOCATION

What should you do if new costing requirements force changes to the structure of segments of the Oracle General Ledger Accounting Key Flexfield? For example, what if the old cost center was five digits and now it will be seven digits? Note that in this discussion, this is not merely referring to adding additional Value Set values to a Value Set for a given flexfield segment. The requirement is to change the structure of, or add segments to, the Cost Allocation Key Flexfield. Although there is much more thorough testing that should be conducted, consider following these steps to begin the process:

1. Change Cost Allocation Key Flexfield Value Sets to point to new GL value sets.

2. Ensure that the Oracle Payroll window GL Flexfield Map is now only referencing the newly desired Cost Allocation Key Flexfield segments. This implies that that some of the previously used segments might no longer be used.

3. Change Oracle HR/Payroll Organizations, Element Links, and Payrolls for every organization and element to ensure that the new GL costing values are selected.

4. Change Cost Allocation Key Flexfield Qualifiers.

5. Change Cost Allocation Key Flexfield displayable segments.

6. Confirm that Oracle HR/Payroll Organizations, Element Links, appear okay when you query them. In essence, confirm that there are no Form errors and that you can save simple changes to the records.

7. Run the Payroll process for one employee or small group of employees.

8. Run the Costing process.

9. Run the Transfer to GL process.

10. Analyze the GL_INTERFACE table.

11. Have General Ledger team import records to further identify problems.

LASER PRINTING OF PAYROLL CHECKS

The standard delivered solution for printing payroll checks is to spool the results of the Check Writer process to a printer that is mounted with preprinted forms. The user is responsible for providing the mechanism for getting this done. The easiest solution is to purchase the preprinted forms from an Oracle supported vendor, such as Evergreen. This solution, however, requires the user to match up the check numbers preprinted on the form with the check numbers generated by Check Writer. If the printer "eats" one of the forms, the check numbers can very easily get out of sync. Because it is undesirable to preprint signatures on the check form, you also have the issue of how to turn these unsigned checks into valid cashable documents.

At BOSS Corporation, we have observed solutions to this problem in two different ways. Neither of these solutions attempted to modify the results from the Oracle Check Writer process. Instead, processes were introduced that took the standard results from Check Writer and inserted the needed information.

The first solution uses the macro features of Microsoft Excel. If you are familiar with Excel, you can follow along. Make a bitmapped image of the check signature and store it on a controlled PC. Next, create an FTP script that prompts the user to key in the concurrent request ID of the Check Writer process. This script then copies the output file from the UNIX server to the controlled PC. The user then starts up Microsoft Excel and executes the specially designed macro. This macro steps through the copied file and inserts the signature into the appropriate spot. The final step is to spool the resultant spreadsheet to the laser printer where the Evergreen forms are already loaded. You still might have the problem of keeping the check numbers in sync. However, you have the advantage of not having to run the checks through a check signer.

This solution is easy to implement and uses tools that probably already exist. It does have its drawbacks. First, Excel can only handle approximately 450 checks in one spreadsheet at a time (memory constraint). The FTP process must recognize this limit and requires you to break up the Check Writer file into multiple import files. Each file has to be processed through the macro and printed separately. Obviously, this solution is unthinkable for check runs that number into the thousands. Additionally, it does not address the check number syncing issue.

The second solution provides a much cleaner approach to the problem. Again, we did not attempt to modify the standard Check Writer process. This time we used a third-party product called FormsXpress from Optio Software. This product is designed to receive output files and enable users to manipulate the results. By using this product, we totally redesigned the look and feel of the check document. Normally, the actual check prints at the top of the form, followed by the Statement of Earnings. Our client wanted to flip this around and print the actual check on the bottom of the form. We also inserted the company logo and signature. The biggest gain was that we were able to print the check number in the MICR format at the bottom of check document. This enabled us to use standard printer stock and not preprinted forms.

We were surprised with the ease of use of this product. It does require the use of a laser printer with the special MICR cartridge. There are also obvious control issues because this solution is very easy to implement. Most printers provide some hardware-locking features that enable you to physically control the use of the MICR cartridge. All in all, we feel this second solution offers the most flexibility without making any software changes to Check Writer.

ORACLE FAST FORMULA

Throughout this chapter, I have demonstrated the power of Fast Formulas and its capability to solve your special payroll calculation challenges. This section summarizes some recommendations for Fast Formulas.

The biggest advantage of Fast Formulas is the capability to access Database Items when performing payroll calculations. Database Items are pieces of information that Oracle automatically maintains for you. Examples of useful database items include the following:

Year-to-date 401(k) deduction amount

Total Regular Earnings for current pay run

An input value on another element

Global Values

Segments from a Key Flexfield

My first recommendation uses the last example from the preceding list. Many times, Oracle HR/Payroll users must decide where to store needed information. Do you use the People Group Flexfield, or should you use Special Information Types? If you need the information in a Fast Formula, use the People Group Flexfield. At the time of this writing, Oracle HR does not create a database item for information stored in a Special Information Type.

Several of our solutions at BOSS Corporation use the power of Indirect Results. This is where the results of one formula can be passed on to another element. When using this powerful feature, make sure that the receiving element processes *after* the generating element. You accomplish this task by assigning the receiving element a higher priority number than the generating element. We have used this feature to calculate imputed income and deduction amounts in the same formula and pass the results to the corresponding element. When doing this, do not forget to handle the situation when there is insufficient pay to cover a deduction.

Many times, we have created Table Structures to store necessary rates for payroll calculations. The Fast Formula statement GET_TABLE_VALUE can be used to retrieve these rates. We have used this feature when rates are different based on either a location or a value from one of the People Group Flexfield segments.

YEAR-TO-DATE BALANCE CONVERSION

During initial conversion and implementation, companies are faced with the decision of whether to implement in the middle of a calendar year or to wait until January 1. Clearly, the job is easier when you can wait until the start of a new calendar year. However, this is generally the busiest time of the year for a payroll department. Also, many companies want to phase different locations into the new system throughout the year. For many reasons, some companies have to transfer period balances from the current payroll system into Oracle.

One of the most unique features of Oracle Payroll is that it does not explicitly store year-to-date, quarter-to-date, and month-to-date balances. These numbers are automatically derived by calculating the balances as they would have appeared at the current session date. This date can be arbitrarily set by using a feature called date-tracking. You can literally see year-to-date, quarter-to-date, and month-to-date results for any date in the past, as long as the Oracle Payroll system was active on that date.

Although this feature is very powerful, it complicates mid-year conversions. Oracle needs to have a starting point to begin these calculations. Therefore, you must perform an initial balance load to establish this starting point. A good recommendation is to coincide the implementation date with the start of a quarter. This enables you to only need to provide the year-to-date balances as of the starting date. If the implementation date is not at the start of a quarter, you have to load quarter-to-date values additionally. Moreover, if your implementation date is not at the beginning of a month, you need to load month-to-date values.

Balance loads can be broken down into two parts. The first part is the easiest. This involves loading a balance for each earning and deduction element you defined in Oracle. Strangely enough, this part is not required. Oracle does not use any of these balances when calculating taxes or preparing the end-of-year W-2s.

The second and most difficult part requires that the tax balances must be addressed next. Oracle Payroll maintains many tax-related balances with its tight integration to Vertex. (For definition and description of Vertex, see the section "Vertex Will Handle All My Taxing Issues" in Chapter 24, "Implementing Oracle Human Resources and Oracle Payroll.") Because Vertex has no knowledge of how taxes were calculated in the legacy system, you must manually provide the numbers to populate the Vertex required balances. Following is a partial list of all the balances required just to calculate State Unemployment Insurance (SUI):

SUI EE Gross

SUI ER Gross

SUI ER Subj Whable

SUI ER Taxable

SUI ER Liability

There are many other tax bodies that must be loaded in a similar fashion. For companies with sites in different states, there might be different rules on what earnings should go in each balance.

How do you go about determining what should go in each balance? Oracle has published a white paper titled "Oracle HRMS TRM Supplement: US Legislative Balance Initialization" that lists the required balances. You must determine what numbers should go in each balance. Start with the Taxability Rules window to drive this process. This window (navigation path: Compensation and Benefits, Taxability Rules) outlines which earnings are taxable for each tax body. It also outlines which pretax deductions should be subject to each tax body. Use these rules to determine which earnings and deductions make up each balance. It is generally a good idea to produce a spreadsheet that explicitly provides a roadmap that a legacy programmer can use to prepare a file of these balances.

The next step is to load these numbers into the Oracle-provided interface tables. These tables are described in the Oracle HRMS Implementation Guide. When loaded, you must first run the Initial Balance Structure Creation process from the application. This process creates the necessary initial balance feed elements and links. When completed, the next step is to validate the table load by running the Initial Balance Load Process using the Validate option. This verifies that the interface table was loaded properly. When verified, rerun the Initial Balance Load Process with the Transfer option. This actually performs the balance load. You have the option to undo the entire process if you need to start from scratch.

When the load is completed, you can review the balances online using the Employee Balance window. (This functionality actually did not work for us at our last client site. Oracle has stated that this has since been fixed). The final task is to do a test parallel payroll run. Do this because many of the tax calculations are self-adjusting. This allows problems with the balance load to stick out like a sore thumb. For example, if you understated the subject wages for SUI, Vertex tries to self-adjust the SUI liability down using negative numbers. Likewise, if you did not properly load the Medicare Withheld balance, Vertex tries to catch up all of the deductions with one large deduction. Both of these deductions really do stick out.

Because of the complex nature of Oracle tax balances and the possibility of each state having unique subject tax rules, the balance load process is very complicated. It is also a very iterative process requiring many attempts before all the problems are ironed out. Do not underestimate the task involved, and prepare for significant payroll testing.

THIRD-PARTY ADMINISTRATOR TRANSFERS (PRO-C, PL/SQL)

Most organizations use outside administrators to handle the record keeping and processing of certain company benefits. Examples of these types of benefit plans include 401(k), Pension, Medical, Dental, and Supplemental Life Insurance.

Do not underestimate the time required to create these interface programs. First, every third-party vendor has a unique file format they require for receiving payroll data. The Oracle Payroll database is complex, so careful time must be taken to extract each item of information required by the vendor.

Regardless of whether the third-party administrator interface is written in Pro-C or PL/SQL, you must allow time for each interface for analysis, design, coding, unit testing, and integration testing. Depending on your number of interfaces, this can become a project in and of itself. Do not underestimate it.

However, in your desire to get a head start on third-party interfaces, be aware that full design and coding cannot be completed until after many system setup decisions have been made regarding your Compensation and Benefit elements. For example, a 401(k) interface might need to know the how much of an employee's 401(k) loan was repaid during the current pay period. Thus, the interface must be designed to identify the 401(k) deduction element and the 401(k) loan element.

Another example of this involves medical deductions. Most large companies offer several medical plans (PPO, HMO, and so on). Your third-party interface requirements for each medical plan must be designed to identify one medical plan element from another.

TIME AND ATTENDANCE INTEGRATION WITH PAYMIX

Prior to release 11i, an external Time and Attendance (T&A) system can be integrated with Oracle Payroll via PayMIX. To begin this process, an analysis must be done to map Oracle Payroll earnings to appropriate earning codes from the T&A system. Although it would be ideal for the T&A system earning codes to be named exactly the same as the earning elements in Oracle Payroll, this is often unrealistic. For example, the T&A system might have limitations on the number of characters allowed in an earnings code name.

The characteristics of the application program interface (API) from the T&A system can influence this mapping analysis. Consider a T&A API where a single output record contains hours and time worked. In this example, consider a record containing 12 hours worked from 10 p.m. to 10 a.m. The 12 hours worked might need to be split within Oracle as 8 hours Time Entry Wages and 4 hours Overtime. Moreover, a nighttime shift differential record might be necessary in Oracle for all, or a portion, of those 12 hours. Thus, one record from the T&A system could produce 3 records within Oracle PayMIX, as demonstrated in Table 26.5.

TABLE 26.5   EXAMPLE OF TIME WORKED

Oracle Earning Element	Hours
Time Entry Wages	8
Overtime	4
Shift Differential	8

Mapping can be affected by costing requirements. Within Oracle PayMIX, the costing on a single record cannot be split. Consider a variation from the previous example where the 12 hours should have been split evenly across two cost centers. This might cause a need for 6 records within PayMIX, as demonstrated in Table 26.6.

TABLE 26.6   EXAMPLE OF SPLIT COSTING

Oracle Earning Element	Hours	Cost Center
Time Entry Wages	4	100
Time Entry Wages	4	200
Overtime	2	100
Overtime	2	200
Shift Differential	6	100
Shift Differential	6	200

The frequency of data transfer should be considered. Determine how often batches should automatically be transferred into PayMIX. Over the course of a payroll period, it is not necessary to transfer data from the T&A system every minute. A transfer once per day is too infrequent. Consider an hourly transfer. This should be frequent enough, even during the final day of payroll close. Ensure that you have a manual capability to transfer batches into PayMIX. Determine when other network traffic (unrelated to payroll) occurs. Carefully coordinate the scheduled time for payroll transfers. If there is typically a peak of network traffic at the top of each hour, establish your automatic transfer at 15 minutes after each hour.

To organize PayMIX batches, determine who will review batches and establish a batch-naming convention for the Reference Name of a batch. Consider grouping batches weekly and by location to facilitate sorting for user access and for reporting. Table 26.7 shows the breakdown of a sample naming convention: YMMDDLLRRRRRR.

TABLE 26.7 SUGGESTED PAYMIX BATCH NAMING CONVENTION

Item	Description
Y	Year, expressed as only one digit (0 for 2000, 1 for 2001, and so on) to allow more text to be visible in the Reference field on the PayMIX Batch Information window
MM	Month
DD	Day
LL	Location
RR	Reference number identifying the original source of the data from the legacy system

Other issues for grouping of batches should be considered. PayMIX is designed so that separate batches exist for flat amount (Earnings) batches versus rate × time (Time) batches. You might want to create separate batches that are dedicated to exceptions (such as reduction in pay to recurring elements using Special Inputs elements).

The integration into PayMIX involves insertion into these primary tables:

> PAY_PDT_BATCH_HEADERS
>
> PAY_PDT_BATCH_LINES
>
> PAY_PDT_BATCH_CHECKS

If dynamic costing information is included in this integration, the integration accesses these tables:

> FND_ID_FLEX_SEGMENTS
>
> FND_FLEX_VALUES
>
> PAY_COST_ALLOCATIONS_F
>
> PAY_COST_ALLOCATION_ KEYFLEX

First, identify which cost segments (such as location and cost center) can dynamically change from one payment period to the next. There will be other segments, such as a cost account, which will probably not change. In this example, assume that cost center and location are segments 1 and 2, respectively. Also assume that these are the only segments that can dynamically change. For each time-entry record, verify that the values actually exist in the value set for segments 1 and 2 by accessing the following tables:

> FND_ID_FLEX_SEGMENTS
>
> FND_FLEX_VALUES

Second, now you know that each of the segment values is a valid value, but now you need to determine whether the code combination is valid. Determine whether the code combination exists for the business group within the following tables:

PAY_COST_ALLOCATIONS_F

PAY_COST_ALLOCATION_ KEYFLEX

If the code combination exists, retrieve cost_allocation_keyflex_id. If it does not exist, insert into these tables using the PYCSKFLI package and retrieve the newly created cost_allocation_keyflex_id.

Consider one final note on the integration from T&A to PayMIX. Keep in mind that Oracle Payroll is not Fair Labor Standards Act (FLSA)-compliant. The integration can be written to accommodate FLSA rules such that each overtime record within PayMIX can have an adjusted overtime rate.

OTHER INTERFACES

In this chapter, I have discussed various interfaces including interfaces to PayMIX (time cards), Oracle General Ledger (costing information), and Third-party Administrators (benefits information). Within payroll, this covers the most common interfaces that are required by an Oracle Payroll implementation.

However, other interfaces might be required. If Oracle Projects is being implemented, you might need to transfer payroll cost information to the Oracle Project Accounting modules. This is a customized interface and is usually designed to process during the Transfer to GL process.

Some implementations of Oracle HR/Payroll occur without the presence of the Oracle General Ledger module. In this case, a customized interface to a third-party GL system is required. This custom interface is usually implemented as a process to be run after the Oracle Payroll Costing process.

Interfaces for Benefits Enrollment and Salary Administration are discussed in Chapter 25, "Using Oracle Human Resources."

ESTABLISHING LATEST BALANCES

To improve performance when referencing a balance amount, the Oracle HRMS application balance call function is designed to first check for the presence of a figure in a table of latest balances and use it before dynamically generating the balance amount from historical detail. If the balance amount does not exist in the latest balance table, the balance must be generated. All balances that are referenced in Fast Formulas used in pay runs are automatically entered into the latest balances tables (PAY_ASSIGNMENT_LATEST_BALANCES, PAY_PER-SON_LATEST_BALANCES). If a user runs a report that references many balances that are not present in the latest balances table, the report could require significant processing time because the report must first cause each of the latest balances to first be generated. To help alleviate this problem, references to the required balances can be placed in a Fast Formula so that entries to the latest balances tables are created by the system. When dealing with balances that are related to tax jurisdictions (states, cities, and counties), a jurisdiction code must be supplied as an input value for the fast formula. The following setup shows the steps required to enable this functionality.

The first step is to create an element by navigating to the Compensation & Benefits, Element Description window. Create a nonrecurring element with Classification of Information. Turn on the check boxes for Multiple Entries Allowed, Process in Run, and Indirect Results.

Note

The Priority should be set so that the element processes after the VERTEX element, which normally has a priority of 4250.

Add an input value for the jurisdiction code by clicking the Input Values button. This Input Value should be defined with Name = Jurisdiction, Units = Character, and Sequence = 1. Also, be sure that the check boxes for User Enterable and Database Item have been checked.

Next, create your Element Link by navigating to the Compensation & Benefits, Link window. Remember to date-track to the appropriate start date for your implementation.

After linking the element, create a Fast Formula by navigating to the Compensation & Benefits, Write Formulas window. Include all appropriate balance names. Don't forget the Inputs Are and Return statements. The Fast Formula should look like this:

```
Inputs are jurisdiction (text)

LB1 = CITY_SUBJ_WHABLE_ASG_JD_GRE_QTD
LB2 = CITY_SUBJ_WHABLE_ASG_JD_GRE_RUN
LB3 = CITY_SUBJ_WHABLE_ASG_JD_GRE_YTD
LB4 = CITY_WITHHELD_ASG_JD_GRE_QTD
LB5 = CITY_WITHHELD_ASG_JD_GRE_RUN
LB6 = CITY_WITHHELD_ASG_JD_GRE_YTD
LB7 = COUNTY_SUBJ_WHABLE_ASG_JD_GRE_QTD
LB8 = COUNTY_SUBJ_WHABLE_ASG_JD_GRE_RUN
LB9 = COUNTY_SUBJ_WHABLE_ASG_JD_GRE_YTD
LB10 = COUNTY_WITHHELD_ASG_JD_GRE_QTD
  .

  .

LB47 = MEDICARE_ER_TAXABLE_ASG_GRE_RUN
LB48 = MEDICARE_ER_TAXABLE_ASG_GRE_YTD
LB49 = REGULAR_EARNINGS_ASG_GRE_QTD
LB50 = REGULAR_EARNINGS_ASG_GRE_YTD
return
```

Now that you have created the Fast Formula, you must associate your element with your Fast Formula. This can be accomplished by navigating to the Compensation & Benefits, Formula Results window. After saving your work, remain in the same window because you must feed the jurisdiction code to your custom element. Select the VERTEX element and add a formula result row that feeds Jurisdiction to your new element's input value, called Jurisdiction. Note that the Jurisdiction formula result from the VERTEX element now feeds both your new element and any other VERTEX elements that were previously associated with the VERTEX element.

HOW IT WORKS

Because your elements are information-type elements and are indirectly fed by another element (VERTEX) to which everyone will automatically be assigned, you do not have to explicitly assign your elements to employees. The element has been created with a priority level such that it will always be processed after the VERTEX element from which the jurisdiction code originates. Fast Formulas currently have a limitation of allowing no more than 64,000 characters, meaning if you have a lot of balances that you need to reference, you need to break up the references into more than one Fast Formula and element. This is not a problem. Simply be certain to include a jurisdiction code feed to each additional element as well.

In the preceding example, the jurisdiction code passed to the new element is the code for the employee's residence. It might be necessary to create an additional element attached to another Fast Formula that references the same jurisdiction-related balances but passes the jurisdiction of the work location to this element to establish balances for that particular jurisdiction. The work location jurisdiction code can be found in the VERTEX element as well (LOC_ADR_GEOCODE).

COMPENSATION APPROACHES

The main objective of a payroll system is to pay your employees with accurate and timely paychecks that include regular pay, any special pay, retro payments, and supplemental pay. For each of these pay types, the following sections explore some issues that need to be considered when setting up the Oracle HR/Payroll System. There might be other questions that pertain to your business, but these are the major ones. The Oracle system provides a method for handling most of these, but as is true with any system, it cannot provide a means for every pay factor for every client.

COMPENSATION APPROACHES: REGULAR PAY INCREASES

Regular pay increases are those that occur for merit increases, cost of living increases, recognized performance, and other company-specific reasons. Regular increases normally are submitted by the employee's manager with proper higher management approval with sufficient time to process them in a regular pay run on the effective date of the increase.

Some important factors to consider are the following:

Who can approve regular pay increases? Management, level of management, human resources, payroll, administration, or a combination of these?

Are mid-pay period increases allowed?

Are all increases effective on the first day of the pay period?

Are there any manual processes that will continue to be manual after the new Oracle system goes live?

Are there any functions being performed by your current system that will not be available with Oracle that will require manual workarounds?

Are pay increases annual, across-the-board, or on employee anniversary dates?

Are there any special considerations for overtime, double-time, and holiday pay?

COMPENSATION APPROACHES: ALLOWANCES/SPECIAL TYPES OF PAY

Special types of pay include items such as Housing Allowances, Relocation Allowances, Longevity Bonuses, and so on. These types of pay can be short term, one to two months, or ongoing for an unlimited amount of time.

Consider these points when planning how your Oracle system will be used to pay employees for these items:

If the user has allowances or special types of pay, do you create one element to handle all allowances or types or individual elements for each different allowance or type?

Are these pay types a percentage, a flat amount, or a combination of both?

Is your calculation of overtime a factor?

COMPENSATION APPROACHES: RETRO PAYMENTS

In a perfect payroll environment, there would be no retro payments because all increases would be received in Payroll with sufficient lead-time to include in the correct paycheck. Consultants and Human Resource and Payroll personnel know this is often not the case. Clients with unions often spend long amounts of time negotiating new contracts, usually after the present contract has expired. This would most likely result in retro payments for increased salary, deductions for increased benefits, and other negotiated items that would result in retro payments. Documents (both online and paper) to authorize increases often get delayed. Although it is not an easy issue to resolve, it is best to be realistic and plan for retro payments in the best, most efficient method possible. The Oracle system is designed to assist in this endeavor.

Listed following are some of the decisions that must be made when planning your Retro Pay Elements:

Are retro salary increases allowed, and if so, how will they be handled?

What level of approval is needed?

Are retro allowances and special pay types allowed?

How will overtime be handled in regards to retro payments?

Will manual work be involved?

How will retro payments affect costing?

For additional information on how to configure Oracle Payroll to allow for Retro Pay processing, see the section in this chapter titled "Retro Pay."

COMPENSATION APPROACHES: SUPPLEMENTAL

Supplemental payments are those items that are not a part of the regular pay given to employees. Supplemental pay is usually items above the normal salary. It is best to consult your Tax Advisor on whether items should be taxed as supplemental. The following list of questions to consider is not an exhaustive, complete list, but it should provide a head start:

What items (tuition, executive training, and so on) are considered supplemental wages and therefore subject to supplemental taxes?

Are supplemental wages to be issued in a separate check?

What is your company's policy regarding supplemental wages? Does it need to be revisited? Is compliance with tax regulations an issue?

COMPENSATION APPROACHES: SUMMARY

When planning your pay system using Oracle Payroll, it is recommended to review your pay policies for fairness and address any issues where compliance with federal, state, or local regulations is involved.

UNDERSTANDING KEY REPORTS

Oracle delivers standard key reports to document the Payroll process. This section discusses the use of each of these reports. They include the following:

Payroll Message Report

Gross to Net Summary Report

Payroll Register Report

Element Result Listing

Employee Deductions Taken

Employee Deductions Not Taken

NACHA Report

Federal, State, and Local Tax Remittance Reports

Costing Breakdown Summary reports

Before discussing these reports, you need to understand a feature of Oracle that causes great confusion throughout the Oracle Payroll world. When you define a Payroll during your initial implementation setup, you must state the first pay period ending date and a series of offsets from this date. These offsets are used to build a payroll calendar of dates and period names. For example, if during setup you stated that your first period end date was Sunday, December 26, 1999, your frequency was Weekly and your check offset was 5, this means that all your period ending dates will be Sundays and your payment dates will be Fridays. Oracle generates a calendar with all the dates completed for each of the years you specified in the Number of Years box. Also note that Oracle assigns a period name for each period. Generally, these are named 1 2000 Weekly for the first period, 2 2000 Weekly for the second period, and so on.

The feature occurs for companies that have payment dates greater than the period ending date (for example, the check offset is greater than zero). When you run a payroll, the Payroll Process requires that you state the period ending date and the check date. Assume that you want to run the payroll with a period ending date of 09-JAN-2000 and a check date of 14-JAN-2000. You would expect Oracle to assign this payroll run to the period named 2 2000 Weekly because this is the second payment date in 2000. (This assumes payments in 2000 on 07-JAN and 14-JAN; it also assumes that a previous payment on 31-DEC-1999 was associated with the payroll calendar of the previous year.) However, when reviewing the results of this payroll on the Payroll Run Results window, Oracle assigns this payroll run to 3 2000 Weekly! Apparently, Oracle takes the payment date, scans the calendar, finds the period in which this payment date falls between the period start date and the period end date, and assigns this period name to the payroll run. Because 14-JAN-2000 falls between 10-JAN-2000 and 16-JAN-2000, Oracle assigns 3 2000 Weekly to the payroll run in this example.

All the standard Oracle reports that list period names and dates use this confusing period name in its headings. You must use this name when running the standard Payroll reports, or you get erroneous results. Keep this in mind when you run the reports that require the period name in the selection window. This does not affect the actual checks, direct deposits, and NACHA files. It also has no negative effects on the State Quarterly reports or the Year End Processing. Oracle users have complained about this feature at user group meetings. Oracle has recognized the problem and has indicated plans to change this process in a future release.

After the successful completion of a payroll run, you should navigate to the Payroll Processing Results window and note the period name Oracle Payroll has assigned this run. Now, you are ready to run your reports. All these are run from the Submit Requests window. Generally, you run the reports in the following order:

> *Payroll Message Report.* This report lists any errors, warnings, or informational messages that were logged during the pay run. Use this report to locate employees with missing timecards, employees with no earnings, deductions that were automatically stopped by reaching a "towards owed" balance, or any other error situations that might arise during the gross-to-net calculation. Do not proceed to any other postprocessing steps until you are satisfied that all messages have been resolved or acknowledged.

> *Gross to Net Report.* Use this report to balance to any expected totals. It lists totals of each earning, deduction, and other elements of pay, including hours. One processing quirk is that you must be date-tracked to a date that is equal to or greater than the payment date before the pick list will include the period name you want to process. Remember to use the period name that Oracle Payroll assigned to this pay run. There have been several patches associated with this report. Your version of the report might not include all these patches. Some of the problems include the following:

Missing totals for involuntary deductions

Missing totals for wage attachment fees (no resolution at press time)

If you experience problems with this report, make sure you contact Oracle Support to receive the latest version of this useful report.

Payroll Registers. One of the most important reports out of a payroll run is a detail listing of the gross to net calculation for each employee. Originally, Oracle Payroll did not include a detail report by employee, assuming that companies would use the online review of a Statement of Earnings to resolve any problems. However, the user community consistently placed this report high on the desired list of enhancements. Therefore, Oracle responded by introducing their version of the detailed Payroll Register Report. It lists for each employee in the pay run the detailed gross-to-net calculation. It can also list year-to-date totals for these elements. There were performance problems with earlier versions of this report. Also, companies did not like the format of the report that lists one employee per page. Many companies have produced their own custom version of the payroll register.

The other two payroll registers that Oracle produces were the predecessors of the existing detailed report. They only list payment totals by employee and do not show the actual gross-to-net calculation. However, these reports are helpful for payroll check bank reconciliation:

Element Result Listing. When reviewing the Gross to Net report, you might need to know which employees have had payroll results for a particular earning or deduction total. The Element Result Listing is a very helpful report that lists every assignment that has the selected element in its run results. Use the payment date of the payroll run as the beginning and ending dates. Select a sort order that conforms to any source documents that you will use to reconcile the totals. The total listed for the selected element should match exactly to the total on the Gross to Net report.

Employee Deductions Taken. There is a summary and detail version of this report. It lists, for each employee, the deductions taken in a period together with a year-to-date balance for each deduction. The summary version of the report presents totals only. Remember to use the period name that Oracle assigned to the payroll run.

Employee Deductions Not Taken. These reports (summary and detail versions) are similar to the Employee Deductions Taken reports but also report on deduction amounts that went into arrears due to insufficient earnings. Use these reports to track arrears processing for deductions.

NACHA Report. After you have run the Prepayments process and the NACHA process, you can run the NACHA report. This is the only Oracle Payroll-supplied report that lists all the NACHA Payments by employee. The totals on the NACHA file should balance to the totals on this report.

Federal and State Tax Remittance Report/Local Tax Remittance Report. These reports are recent additions to Oracle's standard reports. They are replacements to the Tax Summary Listings that many companies had problems processing. Most of the problems were performance issues. These are the only Oracle Payroll-supplied reports you can use to pay the various taxes after each pay run. You select a check date range to process and, optionally, a GRE. If you leave the GRE blank, the report processes assignments for all GREs within the specified date range. You can also request MTD, QTD, or YTD totals along with the Check to Date totals.

One drawback to these new reports is that you cannot receive totals by payroll within a GRE. The previous Tax Summary listings did provide selection criteria by payroll.

Costing Breakdown Summary Reports. After you have run the Costing process, you can run the two Costing Breakdown Summary reports. One report enables you to select results by a date range (Cost Breakdown Report for Date Range), whereas the other enables you to select by costing runs (Cost Breakdown Report by Costing Run). They both show summarized totals from the select costing runs. As stated before, these reports only show the costing side of the journal entry. Not all the balancing entries show on these reports. Therefore, the report might not balance. Many companies design their own costing reports that show the complete balanced journal entry. Remember that any run results that could not be properly costed automatically end up in the suspense account that you established on your payroll definition window.

ORACLE TIME MANAGEMENT: TABLES AND POLICIES

Oracle Time Management (OTM) is designed to collect time and attendance data for processing through Oracle HRMS and Payroll. The ultimate goal of OTM is to produce time cards into Oracle Payroll. The use of OTM usually enables you to avoid a custom interface of time cards into Oracle Payroll's PayMIX.

Within OTM, Time and Attendance can be collected via one or a combination of the following methods: Autogen, Manual Entry, and Interfaces from time clocks. The Autogen method is the most efficient of the three. To utilize the Autogen process within OTM, the following tables need to defined:

Holiday Calendar. The Holiday Calendar defines paid and unpaid holidays. For a person to be paid for a holiday, the Holiday Calendar must be created, maintained, and assigned to an Earning Policy that has been assigned to the employee. The employee must have a time entry created for the pay period containing the holiday, and the information must be sent to PayMIX. If time worked is entered on a holiday or a holiday is entered on a date not listed on the Holiday Calendar, the system generates warnings during the Validate Timecards process.

Shifts. Shifts are defined based on standard Start and Stop work times. Shifts are used in defining Work Plans. Work Plans, in turn, are used in defining Rotation Plans. Thus, Shifts must be created prior to setting up Work or Rotation Plans.

Work Plans. Work Plans identify the applicable shifts for each day of week. Each Rotation Plan consists of at least one Work Plan. Work Plans are also used for the calculation of Off Shift Premiums and Shift Differential Overrides.

Rotation Plans. Rotation Plans are used to indicate dates when an employee moves from one Work Plan to another. If the employee does not change Work Plans, a Rotation Plan for the single Work Plan needs to be defined. The Rotation Plan is used for the Autogen process and calculates Off Shift Premiums and Shift Differential Overrides. *All employees are assigned to a Rotation Plan, even if the Rotation Plan consists of a single Work Plan.*

Project Accounts. Project Accounts are used to input time and/or dollar estimates for tasks or projects. This form applies only to manually input time.

Variance. Variance tables are used to define high and low levels of hours per period or hours by Organization, Location, or Earning.

Earnings Groups. Earnings Groups are used to group Earnings together for reporting purposes and for the accumulation of hours to be used in calculating weekly overtime caps on the Earning Policy.

The following Policies must be defined for OTM:

Hour Deduction. Used for the automatic deduction of hours for meals or breaks.

Shift Differential. Used to define the start and stop times and the corresponding premium to be calculated.

Premium Eligibility. Used to define the authorized premium associated with each Premium Eligibility Policy.

Premium Interaction. Used to define how Premiums relate to each other.

Earnings*. Defines daily/weekly base, overtime rules, holiday calendar, and premium policy assigned to each employee.

*It is not necessary to set up the Policies in the order listed. However, all other policies must be defined prior to defining Earning Policies.

Table 26.8 lists the Direct Links between an Oracle Time Management Table or Policy and the form it is assigned to.

TABLE 26.8   OTM TABLE/FORM RELATIONSHIPS

Table/Policy	Forms			
OTM Table/Policy	HRMS Person Assignment	OTM Earning Policy	OTM Work Plan	OTM Rotation Plan
Holiday Calendar		D		
Work Plan				D
Rotation Plan	D			
Shift			D	
Earning Group		D		
Earning Policy	D			

TABLE 26.8 CONTINUED

OTM Table/Policy	HRMS Person Assignment	OTM Earning Policy	OTM Work Plan	OTM Rotation Plan
Hour Deduction	D			
Shift Differential	D			
Premium Eligibility		D		
Premium Interaction		D		

Prior to setup, the various policies and inventory of your needs must be completed to ensure all areas have been considered and to avoid duplication.

TROUBLESHOOTING

This chapter has been loaded with various tips and techniques associated with implementing and using Oracle Payroll. In many cases, the specific solutions I have documented can be directly used by your implementation. However, the more important thing you should retain is the *approaches* I have taken to various solutions. It is quite likely that your implementation will require similar customer-specific solutions.

Oracle Payroll is considered by many consultants to be the most complex Application produced by Oracle Corporation. Do not underestimate the complexity of implementing any payroll system. If you have not read Chapter 24, "Implementing Oracle Human Resources and Oracle Payroll," you would be wise to do so. There are a number of important items in Chapter 24 that should influence your expectations of implementing Oracle Payroll. At BOSS Corporation, we have many customers who are both happy with the Oracle Payroll product and satisfied with our approach to implementation of this complex module.

PART

III

CH

26

CHAPTER **27**

ADMINISTERING THE ORACLE APPLICATIONS

As an Oracle Applications system administrator, you are responsible for defining and maintaining the following:

- The users of the system
- Users' responsibilities
- Reports and report sets a user can run
- System and user profiles
- Concurrent processes and processing
- Printers
- Alerts and workflow programs

In this chapter, you will study the setup and functionality of the Oracle Systems Administration module.

RELEASE 11 CHANGES

Release 11 of Oracle Applications incorporates a number of enhancements to the system administration function:

- The Application Object Library (AOL) provides multilingual support.
- Online documentation is in Hypertext Markup Language (HTML) Web format.
- Enhanced security allows vendors and customers to become users.
- Report request sets can be grouped and submitted in stages.
- An improved window lets you view concurrent requests.
- Concurrent request scheduling options have been improved.
- Flexbuilder is replaced with the account generator in Workflow.

UNDERSTANDING SECURITY

As the Oracle Applications system administrator, you define the users of Oracle Applications. Additionally, you assign each user responsibilities that give the user access to the Oracle Applications functions that are appropriate to his or her roles in the organization.

Each applications user requires a username and a password. An initial password is defined for them. The first time the applications user logs on, Oracle Applications requires her to enter a new (secret) password.

MENUS

A menu is a hierarchical arrangement of functions and submenus of functions. A menu is assigned to each responsibility.

Each Oracle Applications product has a Full Access responsibility with a menu that includes all the functions associated with that application. When you create a new responsibility, you can restrict the functionality of the responsibility by defining rules to exclude specific functions or menus of functions of the full access menu.

> **Note**
>
> Oracle recommends that you restrict a full access menu to certain responsibilities.

ANALYZING THE MENU REPORTS

The menu report documents the structure of character mode menus. This report is useful when defining new or editing existing character-based menus. You can use a hardcopy of this report to document your customized menus before upgrading your Oracle Applications.

The function security menu report set documents the structure of the menus you are using. This report set is useful when defining new menus. If you are upgrading from release 10, use the report set to document your existing menus. You can use a hardcopy of the output of this report set to document your customized menus before upgrading your Oracle Applications.

The function security menu report set consists of the function security functions report, the function security menu report, and the function security navigator report.

PROTECT YOURSELF DURING AN UPGRADE

To preserve your custom menus during an upgrade of the Oracle Applications, you should use unique names for your custom menus. As an example, you can start your custom menus' names with the three-letter code of your organization, such as XYZ_General_Ledger_ Super_User.

> **Note**
>
> Oracle Applications standard menus might be overwritten when the Oracle Applications are upgraded to a newer version.

MODIFYING EXISTING MENUS

You can modify an existing user-defined menu by either adding or eliminating functions and subfunctions from the menu hierarchy.

> **Note**
>
> It is recommended that you do not modify a standard menu delivered with the Oracle Applications because these menus can be overwritten when Oracle Applications are upgraded.

COMBINING PIECES OF SEVERAL MENUS You can create a new menu through combining other menus or submenus. You attach the menus you want to reuse to the new menu you are creating.

RESPONSIBILITIES

A responsibility is the level of authority you provide a user to give him access only to the data and functions appropriate to his roles in the organization. Each responsibility provides access to

- A specific application or applications
- A set of books or an organization
- A restricted list of windows that a user can navigate to
- A restricted list of functions a user can perform
- Reports in a specific application

Each user has at least one or more responsibilities, and several users can share the same responsibility.

DEFINING A RESPONSIBILITY

When you define a responsibility, you assign to it some or all of the following components:

- A data group determines which Oracle database accounts a responsibility's forms, concurrent programs, and reports connect to.
- A request security group defines the concurrent programs, including requests and request sets, that an applications user can run under a particular responsibility.
- Each responsibility is associated with a menu.
- A responsibility can have function and menu exclusion rules associated with it to restrict the application functionality.
- A responsibility can also include securing attributes to control access to Web applications in the self-service Web applications.

> **Note**
>
> If you do not assign a request security group to a responsibility, users working under that responsibility cannot run any reports, request sets, or other concurrent programs from a standard submission form.

REPORT GROUPS

A report group determines what reports and request sets a user is allowed to run with the responsibility the report group is associated with.

After you define a report group, you can run it as long as you have access to a standard Submit Requests window that does not limit access to specific requests.

Other users can also run the reports in the report group if you assign the report group to the users' responsibility.

DEFINING A REPORT GROUP

You assign a request security group to a responsibility when you define the responsibility. If the responsibility does not have a request security group, the user cannot run any reports using the Submit Requests window. You can add any request set to a request security group.

USERS

To log on to Oracle Applications, you need an Oracle Applications username and password. This logon is different from the username and password you use to log on to your computer or computer network. Your Oracle Applications logon connects you to your responsibilities, which controls your access to the Oracle applications, functions, reports, and data.

DEFINING A USER

An authorized user of Oracle Applications is known as an applications user identified by an applications username. A new applications user uses the applications username to log on to Oracle Applications and access data through Oracle Applications windows.

Consider the following items as you define your applications users:

- An applications user can work with only one responsibility at a time.
- The username must not contain more than one word.
- You should use only alphanumeric characters (A through Z and 0 through 9) in the username.
- You must limit your username to the set of characters that your operating system supports for filenames.
- A password must be at least 5 characters and can extend up to 100 characters.
- You should use alphanumeric characters (A through Z and 0 through 9) in a password. All other characters are invalid.

PART

III

CH

27

Note

It is recommended that you define meaningful usernames, such as the employee's first initial followed by her last name.

MAINTAINING PROFILE OPTIONS

You can set profile options for your user community through the System Profile window. If you change a user's profile option value, that change takes effect as soon as the user logs on again or changes responsibilities.

Profiles have four profile levels:

Site	Option settings pertain to all users at an installation site.
Application	Option settings pertain to all users of any responsibility associated with the application.
Responsibility	Option settings pertain to all users currently logged on under the responsibility.
User	Option settings pertain to an individual user, identified by his applications username.

The values that you set at each level provide the runtime values for each user's profile. When a profile option is set at more than one level, the site profile has the lowest priority. The site profile is superseded by the application profile. The application profile is superseded by the responsibility profile. The user profile has the highest priority.

Note   You should set site-level option values before specifying profile options at the other three levels after installing Oracle Applications. The options specified at the site level work as defaults until the same options are specified at the other levels.

UNDERSTANDING CONCURRENT PROCESSING

In Oracle Applications, online operations run simultaneously with programs that run in the background. This capability is known as concurrent processing. The system administrator manages when programs are run and how many operating-system processes are devoted to running programs in the background.

When a user runs a report, a request to run that report is inserted into a database table, and a unique identifier known as a request ID is assigned to the request. A concurrent manager reads requests from this table and runs the request if the manager's definition is satisfied about how many operating-system processes it can devote to running requests.

The following determines when a concurrent program actually starts running:

- When it is scheduled to start
- Whether it is placed on hold
- Whether it is incompatible (it cannot run) with other programs
- Its request priority

SETTING UP WORKERS AND SCHEDULES

You can activate and restart managers individually. A restart of a concurrent manager forces the internal concurrent manager to reread that concurrent manager's definition. Activating a manager allows the internal concurrent manager to start that manager when its work shift starts.

You should restart an individual manager for the following reasons:

- When you modify its work shift assignments
- When you modify a work shift's target number of processes
- When you modify its specialization rules
- When you change a concurrent program's incompatibility rules

When you shut down an individual manager, if you choose to deactivate the manager, all requests that are currently running are allowed to complete. If, on the other hand, you terminate the requests and deactivate the individual manager, all requests that are currently running are immediately stopped and marked for resubmission when the manager is later activated.

Note

You can also create a specialized concurrent manager for running all of your recurring periodic batch jobs.

You should never modify the standard manager because it is designed to pick up any jobs that are not sent to the specialized processor.

MANAGING FILES AND TABLES

You should identify your application tables and their associated primary key information to the Application Object Library. Primary keys should be identified before you begin auditing your application. AuditTrail does not maintain primary key information otherwise.

CONCURRENT PROGRAMS AND REPORTS

A concurrent program is a program that does not require continued interaction to perform a specific task. A concurrent program can be a report or a process such as the batch posting of journal entries to the general ledger.

Oracle Application-specific information can be organized and presented in what is known as a report. You can print reports or view them online. Reports can be as simple as summary information or as complex as a complete detailed listing.

You can group reports into a collection known as a request set. A request set submits all of the reports and programs as a single transaction. The individual reports and programs in a request set can be run serially or in parallel.

A report or request set provides different information each time it is run through report parameters. If the report or request set has parameters associated with it, the user is requested to provide input each time the report or request set is requested.

Additionally, you can set up a report or request set to resubmit itself on a regular basis. This feature is useful if you have a process that runs on a periodic basis and requires no parameters or static type parameters.

DEFINING AND REGISTERING EXECUTABLES

You are required to define a concurrent program executable for each executable source file used with concurrent programs. This concurrent program executable links the source file with the concurrent request users can submit.

Note

You cannot add new immediate programs to a concurrent manager program library. Oracle recommends that you use spawned concurrent programs instead.

The combination of application name plus program name uniquely identifies your concurrent program executable.

The concurrent managers use the application to determine in which directory structure to look for your execution file.

You cannot change the execution method once the concurrent program executable has been assigned to one or more concurrent programs in the Concurrent Programs window.

The maximum size of an execution filename is 30 characters.

DEFINING SETS

A request set lets you run several reports or concurrent programs conveniently and quickly. If you want to run the same report or process more than once with different parameters, you can include that report or process in the request set multiple times.

You can also run the reports and processes in a report set in a sequential or parallel order. If you create a request set where a report depends on the results of a prior report, run the reports in the request set in sequential order. You can also specify whether to stop processing if there is an error in any of the reports in the sequential request set.

You can select your printer options for a request set on a report-by-report basis. You can select a different printer for each report or any combination, including the same printer for all reports.

Note All concurrent programs that run request sets are titled Request Set *<name of request set>*.

UNDERSTANDING THE CONCSUB SYNTAX

You use the `concsub` utility to submit a concurrent request from the operating system prompt.

The syntax for the `concsub` utility follows:

```
CONCSUB applsys/pwd 'Responsibility application shortname'
'Responsibility name' 'Username' [WAIT={Y|N|n}] CONCURRENT
'Program application shortname' PROGRAM
```

The parameters associated with the `concsub` utility follow:

`applsys/pwd`	The Oracle username and password that connects to Oracle Application Object Library data.
`Responsibility application shortname`	The application shortname of the responsibility. For the system administrator responsibility, the application shortname is `SYSADMIN`.
`Responsibility name`	The name of the responsibility. For the system administrator responsibility, the responsibility name is `System Administrator`.
`Username`	The applications username of the person who submits the request. For example, `SYSADMIN` is the username of the system administrator.
`WAIT={Y|N|n}`	Set `WAIT` to `Y` if you want `concsub` to wait until the request you submit completes before `concsub` returns you to the operating system prompt. Set `WAIT` to `N` (the default value) if you do not want `concsub` to wait. You can also enter an integer value of n seconds for `concsub` to wait before it exits. When used, `WAIT` must be entered before `CONCURRENT`.
`Program application shortname`	The application shortname of the program. For the `deactivate`, `abort`, and `verify` programs, the application shortname is `FND`.
`PROGRAM`	To submit the Shutdown All Managers concurrent request, use the program `deactivate`. To submit the Shutdown Abort Managers concurrent request, use the program `abort`. To submit the Verify All Managers Status concurrent request, use the program `verify`.

You can hide the password when using `concsub`. If you supply only the username (no `/pwd` in the first argument), the system prompts you for the password. You can also put the password in a file and then redirect the password to standard input (`stdin`).

PART

III

CH

27

UNDERSTANDING PRINTERS

When you run a report in Oracle Applications, a report is generated and the output is formatted. Each report has associated with it a print style that defines the number of columns and rows it contains. Once the report is completed, a printer driver is attached to the report, providing the formatting instructions to the destination printer.

DEFINING STYLES

The look of the printed output depends on the print style. Additionally, your ability to print a report in a particular print style depends on the type of printer. A printer driver specific to the particular printer and the operating system is also required (in addition to the print style) for a report to properly print.

> **Note**
>
> You must assign both a print style and a printer driver to print that style to each printer type you want to use to print reports in that style.

Table 27.1 shows the standard printer styles available with the Oracle Applications. The column SRW refers to the name of the Oracle Reports printer driver (Oracle Reports used to be called SQL*ReportWriter), and the values in this column are names of print driver files for print styles such as portrait and landscape.

TABLE 27.1 PRINT STYLES

Name	User Name	Cols	Rows	Orientation	SRW
PORTRAIT	Portrait	80	65	Portrait	P
LANDSCAPE	Landscape	132	60	Landscape	L
LANDWIDE	Landwide	180	45	Landscape	W
DYNAMIC	Dynamic	0	0		
DYNAMIC PORTRAIT	Dynamic Portrait	80	66	Portrait	PD

DEFINING PRINTERS

The concurrent manager sends completed reports to the operating system. The operating system in turn issues a print command or calls a custom print program that issues an operating system print command.

The handling of page breaks, carriage returns, line feeds, bold text, and underlined text instructions are normally provided by the SRW file.

If you want to issue any page breaks, carriage returns, and line feed instructions before the output file is to be printed or after the output file is printed, you must enter the information in the printer driver's initialization or reset string.

The dimensions of a report are determined by the columns and rows values in the print style and override the width and height values provided in the SRW driver file.

DEFINING DRIVERS

A printer driver delivers commands to the operating system that tell the printer how to output the specified print style. The printer driver consists of a string of escape sequences as follows:

> **Note** The printer drivers use the HP Printer Control Language (PCL).

The following escape codes define the A4 initialization:

```
/eE/e&l1026a5.25C/e(s0t0p12h8.5V
    /eE        Esc E    Reset Printer
    /e&l10     Landscape
    /e&l26A    A4 Paper
    /e&l#C     VMI(#/26")
    /e(s0T     Typeface
    /e(s0P     Fixed Font
    /e(s12H    12 cpi
    /e(s#V     Font Size (# points)
```

This escape sequence sets up the landscape initialization:

```
/eE/e&l1o2a5.25C/e(s0t0p12h8.5V
```

Use these escape codes to define the landwide initialization:

```
/eE/e&k2G/e&l7h1o2a5.45C/e(s0p16.66H/e&k6.75H
```

The following escape codes define the portrait initialization:

```
/eE/e&l0o2a7C/e(s0t0p11H/e&a5L/e&k2G
```

To configure a printer for a 132-column landscape, use the following escape codes:

```
/eE/e&l10/e&l1E/e(oN/e(s0P/e(s8.5V/e(s0S/e(s0B/e(s0T/e
(s11H/e&k10H/e&l5.5C/e&k2G
```

To set up a portrait printout with 80 columns and 66 rows, use these escape codes:

```
/eE/e&l0O/e&l1E/e&a6L/e(0N/e(s0P/e(s8.5V/e(s0S/e(s0B/e(s0T/e
(s11H/e&k10H/e&l6D/e
```

You can set up a dynamic portrait printer with 80 columns and 66 rows with these escape codes:

```
/eE/e&l0O/e&l1E/e&a6L/e(0N/e(s0P/e(s8.5V/e(s0S/e(s0B/e(s0T/e
(s11H/e&k10H/e&l6D/e&k2G
```

Finally, you can use the following codes to configure a compressed print line of 180 characters per line in landscape orientation:

```
/eE/e&l10/e&l1E/e(0N/e(s0P/e(s8.5V/e(s0S/e(s0B/e(s0T/e(s14H/e&l5.5C/e&k2G
```

> **Note**
>
> In the printer escape code sequences, it is easy to confuse certain characters. Please note where l = lowercase L, 1 = digit one, O = uppercase O, and 0 = zero. Also, for your own printer and paper, you should verify each escape sequence with your printer documentation to verify correct usage of other common escape codes that control paper size, font, pitch, and so forth.

REGISTERING PRINTERS

You must register the printer with the Oracle Applications before the printer can be recognized by the system and output can be sent to the printer.

You register the individual printers by specifying the printer's operating system name, which is unique. You indicate the kind of printer it is by selecting a printer type.

ESCAPE CODES FOR HP LASERJET

When using PCL, any commands that use the same prefix can be strung together after the prefix. The concatenation is ended when a command ends in a capital letter. Following are the HP LaserJet printer PCL commands:

Reset

/eE	Reset
/e&l#X	Reset # of copies (1-99)
/e&u#D	Reset unit of measure (# = number of units per inch)

Print

/e&l0S	Simplex print operation
/e&l1S	Duplex print long-edge binding
/e&l2S	Duplex print short-edge binding

Offset

/e&l#U	Long-edge (left) offset registration print (# = number of decipoints, 1/720")
/e&l#Z	Short-edge (top) offset registration print (# = number of decipoints)

Page Side Selection

/e&a0G	Next side
/e&a1G	Front side
/e&a2G	Back side

Paper Destination

/e&l0G	Auto select
/e&l1G	Top output bin
/e&l2G	Left output bin

Optional Multi-Bin Mail Box

/e&l3G	Left bin face up
/e&l4G	Bin 1 face down
/e&l5G	Bin 2 face down
/e&l6G	Bin 3 face down
/e&l7G	Bin 4 face down
/e&l8G	Bin 5 face down
/e&l9G	Bin 6 face down
/e&l10G	Bin 7 face down
/e&l11G	Bin 8 face down

Paper Source

/e&l0H	Eject page
/e&l1H	Paper cassette
/e&l2H	Manual feed paper
/e&l3H	Manual feed envelope
/e&l8H	Tray 1
/e&l5H	Optional 500/2000 sheet lower cassette
/e&l4H	MP tray/tray 3
/e&l6H	Envelope feeder

Paper Size

/e&l1A	Executive
/e&l2A	Letter
/e&l3A	Legal
/e&l6A	Tabloid (11 × 17)
/e&l26A	A4
/e&l27A	A3
/e&l45A	JIS B5
/e&l46A	JIS B4
/e&l71A	JPOST
/e&l72A	JPOSTD
/e&l80A	Monarch
/e&l81A	COM 10
/e&l100A	B5
/e&l101A	Custom/Maximum
/e&l90A	DL
/e&l91A	C5

Page Length

/e&l#P	# of lines (5-128)

Orientation

/e&l0O	Portrait
/e&l1O	Landscape

PART

III

CH

27

| /e&l20 | Reverse portrait |
| /e&l30 | Reverse landscape |

Print Direction

| /e&a#P | # of degrees of rotation counter-clockwise (90 degree increments only). |

Margins

/e&l#E	Top margin, # of lines
/e&l#F	Text length, # of lines
/e&a#L	Left margin, # of columns
/e&a#M	Right margin, # of columns
/e9	Clear horizontal margins

Perforation Skip

| /e&l0L | Disable perforation skip |
| /e&l1L | Enable perforation skip |

Motion Index

| /e&k#H | Horizontal motion index, # of 1/120 inch increments |
| /e&l#C | Vertical motion index, # of 1/48 inch increments |

Line Spacing

/e&l1D	1 line/inch
/e&l2D	2 lines/inch
/e&l3D	3 lines/inch
/e&l4D	4 lines/inch
/e&l6D	6 lines/inch
/e&l8D	8 lines/inch
/e&l12D	12 lines/inch
/e&l16D	16 lines/inch
/e&l24D	24 lines/inch
/e&l48D	48 lines/inch

Vertical Position

/e&a#R	# of rows
/e*p#Y	# of dots
/e&a#V	# of decipoints

Horizontal Position

/e&a#C	# of columns
/e&*p#X	# of dots
/e&a#H	# of decipoints
/e=	Half line feed

Line Termination

| /e&k0G | CR=CR; LF=LF; FF=FF |
| /e&k1G | CR=CR+LF; LF=LF; FF=FF |

/e&k2G	CR=CR; LF=CR+LF; FF=CR+FF
/e&k3G	CR=CR+LF; LF=CR+LF; FF=CR+FF

Symbol Set

/e(0D	ISO 60: Norwegian
/e(1E	ISO 4: United Kingdom
/e(9E	Windows 3.1, Latin 2
/e(1F	ISO 69: French
/e(1G	ISO 21: German
/e(0I	ISO 15: Italian
/e(6J	Microsoft Publishing
/e(7J	Desktop
/e(10J	PS Text
/e(12J	MC Text
/e(13J	Ventura International
/e(14J	Ventura US
/e(579L	Wingdings
/e(5M	PS Math
/e(6M	Ventura Math
/e(8M	Math-8
/e(19M	Symbol
/e(0N	ISO 8859-1 (ECMA-94): Latin 1
/e(2N	ISO 8859-2: Latin 2
/e(5N	ISO 8859-9: Latin 5
/e(0S	ISO 11: Swedish
/e(2S	ISO 17: Spanish
/e(5T	Windows 3.1, Latin 5
/e(9T	PC Turkish
/e(0U	ISO 6: ASCII
/e(1U	Legal
/e(8U	Roman-8
/e(9U	Windows 3.0, Latin 1
/e(10U	PC-8
/e(11U	PC-8 D/N
/e(12U	PC 850
/e(15U	Pi Font
/e(17U	PC-852
/e(19U	Windows 3.1, Latin 1 (ANSI)

Spacing

/e(s0P	Fixed
/e(s1P	Proportional

PART
III

CH
27

Pitch

/e(s#H	# characters/inch
/e&k0S	10.0
/e&k2S	Compressed (16.5-16.7)
/e&k4S	Elite (12.0)

Point Size

/e(s#V	# of points

Style

/e(s0S	Upright (solid)
/e(s1S	Italic
/e(s4S	Condensed
/e(s5S	Condensed Italic
/e(s8S	Compressed (Extra Condensed)
/e(s24S	Expanded
/e(s32S	Outline
/e(s64S	Inline
/e(s128S	Shadowed
/e(s160S	Outline Shadowed

Stroke Weight

/e(s-7B	Ultra thin
/e(s-6B	Extra thin
/e(s-5B	Thin
/e(s-4B	Extra light
/e(s-3B	Light
/e(s-2B	Demi-light
/e(s-1B	Semi-light
/e(s0B	Medium (book or text)
/e(s1B	Semi bold
/e(s2B	Demi bold
/e(s3B	Bold
/e(s4B	Extra bold
/e(s5B	Black
/e(s6B	Extra black
/e(s7B	Ultra black

Typeface Family

/e(s0T	LinePrinter
/e(s4362T	Albertus
/e(s4168T	Antique Olive
/e(s4140T	Clarendon
/e(s4116T	Coronet
/e(s4099T	Courier

/e(s4197T	Garamond Antiqua
/e(s4102T	Letter Gothic
/e(s4297T	Marigold
/e(s4113T	CG Omega
/e(s4101T	CG Times
/e(s4148T	Univers
/e(s16602T	Arial
/e(s16901T	Times New Roman
/e(s16686T	Symbol
/e(s31402T	Wingdings

Underline

/e&d0D	Enable fixed
/e&d3D	Enable floating
/e&d@	Disable

> **Note**
>
> Any time you make a change to the printer driver, printer type, or printer definition, you should restart the concurrent manager for the changes to take effect.

TROUBLESHOOTING

System administration for the Oracle Applications is not difficult, but the work is not like other personal computer applications. The system administrator works with users, operating system administrators (UNIX or NT), database administrators, and network administrators to establish and secure the computing environment.

Consider the following items to administer the Oracle Applications effectively:

- Oracle Support can be very helpful. Don't hesitate to call them.
- Do not modify program definitions for Oracle concurrent programs. Copy the program, rename it, and make modifications to definitions for the copy.
- Be careful when you mark some program definitions with the run alone attribute. This program definition might block the transaction processors and cause the transactions to build up in the interfaces until the run alone program finishes.
- A concurrent report might finish completely but with a status of Warning when it failed to print. Check the end of the concurrent request log to see whether you should be working on a printer problem or a report problem.
- Do not alter the definition of the standard concurrent manager unless you are certain you have defined other concurrent managers to accept your requests.

PART
III

CH
27

- Changing passwords in the applications is tricky. If you change the password for the applsys user, you must not change passwords for any other usernames at the same time. You should log out and log on between changes.
- Printer definitions are cached in memory when the concurrent managers start up. If you change definitions, restart the concurrent managers to complete the change.
- Only the system administrator can create a new country code. Other responsibilities in the applications can access the countries but cannot create new records.

WORKING WITH PARTNERS

CHAPTER 28

WORKING WITH ORACLE SUPPORT

Your ability to work effectively with Oracle Support is a critical success factor for your implementation project. Working with Support is an acquired skill, and it is well worth your effort to develop this ability. This chapter shows you how to effectively get the most support for your time and money.

Because Oracle software runs on many different hardware platforms and operating system versions, Oracle Development freezes the code periodically for a specific release combination of hardware, operating system, database, and tools. This frozen version is labeled something like release 10.7 or release 11.02, and that is the code that Oracle ships to you. While your project to implement the Applications progresses, Oracle continues to modify and maintain the unfrozen versions of these programs. The frozen version that you have on your system can be as much as 12 to 14 months older than the current version. For each program, the unfrozen version that Support has might have 20 to 30 changes to it. When you hit a problem with your frozen version, Oracle Support can get you an updated copy via a patch.

Oracle Support has the following services:

- Provide remote telephone communications that support beta and production code released from Oracle Development.

- Isolate and verify problems with Oracle released code. Provide solutions for valid problems.

- Answer product usage questions. Note: support is not a substitute for a proper course of education or researching the reference manuals.

- Interpret error messages and conditions during installation or usage of the Oracle Applications.

PATCHES, MEGAPATCHES, AND UPGRADES

Patches can be new versions of the executable reports, forms, packages, procedures, triggers, and programs. Patches can also contain code to add or make changes to your data or the structure of the database.

You must test the results of a patch or upgrade. The law of unintended consequences says that you might cause a new problem when you apply a patch to fix an old problem. The most sophisticated and heavily customized Oracle customers create a suite of scripts of repeatable transactions and reports that can be run against a stable test database before and after the patch or upgrade. If the scripts don't produce identical results before and after the change, there is a business impact, and these customers are able to analyze the change.

The average Oracle customer analyzes the patch to see what might be affected, applies the patch in a test database, and asks the user to verify that results are acceptable. This approach has more risk than a full regression test suite. You must understand the impact of an incorrect patch on your production systems. What is your worst case scenario, and what are your recovery options?

DIAGNOSING THE PROBLEM

Before calling Support, you should have a good description of the problem and what caused it. Use of support is most effective when you know precisely what you want from them before you call.

> **Tip**
>
> When a problem surfaces during an implementation project, at BOSS we usually spend about a half hour defining and understanding the problem before calling Oracle Support. You can solve more problems on the first call if you understand what the system is doing.

CONCURRENT MANAGER LOGS AND MESSAGES

Problems with batch jobs and interfaces that are run by the concurrent manager can be investigated by looking at the run time log produced by these jobs.

For example, you run a concurrent process and the View My Requests form shows the job completed with an error. Before calling for support or investigating the executable or the data, which can be very involved, gather facts by reading the concurrent manager log. Usually, an important series of diagnostic error messages is near the end of the log. There are often several messages, and the trick is to pick out the ones with the highest odds of being the problem.

UNDERSTANDING THE SEQUENCE OF EVENTS

Understanding what happened and in what order is important to understanding and diagnosing the error. Document what happened and be prepared to lead the support analyst through exactly the same series of keystrokes to re-create the problem. Know the navigation path, the data that was entered, parameters and lists of values that were used, and so forth. Because an error might create several error messages, try to determine which event is the root cause because secondary messages might go away when you fix the basis of the problem.

REPEATING THE ERROR

If you can't re-create the problem consistently within a test database, calling Support and logging a Technical Assistance Request (TAR) might be a waste of time unless the problem is caused by a rare, one-time event.

Examine the parameters and user procedures that caused the problem. Collect error messages, logs, screen shots, and other output before calling Support. If you have them at hand, the conversation with the support analyst will be more efficient, and you might have to fax or email them to the analyst.

Also, try to understand enough about the problem to re-create the error on the support analyst's system. When you can create the problem on an Oracle system, you almost certainly prove that the problem is not caused by a customization you made and the problem is not caused by a data anomaly. If you can't re-create the problem on an Oracle system, the odds become good that the current version of the program will solve your problem.

USING DEDUCTIVE REASONING

Investigate the problem and use deductive reasoning to eliminate what the problem can't be and define what it is. On an established release of the software that has been in production for more than six months, proper definition of the problem might be 90 percent of the solution. Definition of the problem should be your responsibility. If you leave problem definition to the support analyst, you might spend a lot of time on the resolution.

Determine whether the program has ever worked. If it has, determine what is different this time. Suspect your procedures, the user, the data, or a system change. Involve the implementation team member in the problem statement. Gather facts about the problem.

Break the problem into parts. Determine which parts are working, and eliminate them from further analysis. This process directs your analysis to parts of the system that might be causing the error. Often, the project team spends a lot of time analyzing what they know about or just worked on simply because they think they understand it. The problem might be located elsewhere. Concentrate on what is not working and don't waste time analyzing what is working. If the problem is still not defined, subdivide the system further until you are working with a piece that is small enough to understand and diagnose.

LOGGING THE TECHNICAL ASSISTANCE REQUEST (TAR)

When you make a call to Oracle World Wide Support, you are connected to one of several support centers, and you begin an exercise in communication with a support analyst. The better you communicate the definition of the problem, the higher the odds are that you will find a solution. The TAR record is the minutes and permanent record of your conversations with the support analyst

In theory, this is the way the support process is supposed to work.

1. You contact Oracle World Wide Support and provide information for a TAR record. This information includes the version of the application, the platforms (database, middle-tier, and client), and the name and version of the form or report or process that is giving the error or the incorrect results. You can perform this step by phone or online at the MetaLink Web site. Because Oracle does not track your system configuration or upgrade projects, you must provide this information every time you initiate a new TAR.

2. The analyst gathers information and attempts an early statement and diagnosis of the problem.

3. The analyst reviews the existing knowledge base of previous problems with similar keywords. If the analyst cannot find references to similar TARs, you must decide to restate the problem, continue the diagnosis, or escalate to a more skilled analyst.

4. If the problem is identified, the analyst determines whether a solution is available. If a patch is required, the analyst sends the patch to you. You apply the solution to a test system and determine whether the problem is resolved. You close the TAR.

5. If the analyst can't identify the problem, you perform additional research and perhaps bring in additional resources. If progress becomes difficult, you must decide whether the business impact and experience level of the analyst justifies escalation of the problem.

6. If a solution is not available, the analyst creates a bug record and forwards the problem to Oracle Development. At this point, you loose visibility of the problem resolution because neither you nor the analyst can affect Development. Development might respond with a patch or a determination that the release works as designed. If the program works as designed, the issue must be processed as an enhancement request.

This process works pretty well, and your job is to lead Oracle Support through this process. Often in the real world, however, the analyst first determines your revision level of the executable causing the problem. He then recommends without further analysis that you upgrade to the latest certified revision for that executable.

This shortcut is often *not* in your best interest. When the analyst recommends an upgrade, it might involve multiple (dependent) patches or a megapatch. Although this strategy might work well for low severity problems, it represents a lot of work on your part and might not even make any sense. You get the latest version of a program, but you might patch and test for hours or days before realizing you didn't adequately diagnose the problem, and you must start all over again. This procedure can cause lots of stress in the case of an important problem.

> **Tip**
>
> If you are going to be doing complex weekend work and only have low-level support, log a TAR on Friday so that you can use that to get past the answering system.

WORKING WITH AN INEXPERIENCED ANALYST

The ERP applications business has been growing rapidly for the past five years, and the effort Oracle must make to support its customers is directly proportional to the number of customers and the quality of the software. This means Oracle's support staff has been growing rapidly, and if you have been working with the Applications for more than six months, you might get an analyst that knows less than you do about your problem.

However, the analyst has two big advantages. First, she works with only one application continuously. Second, she has access to the historical database of all TARs that might contain the solution you need.

Try to work with the novice analyst at her pace. Go slowly and be patient. If the analyst senses you are interested in helping her, she will often go above and beyond the call of duty to help you. However, you should know what you want from the TAR process. Use the analyst to access the knowledge base for you. Often, the novice analyst will try to go offline for further research, but don't let her get off the phone. She won't have a complete-enough definition of the problem to resolve the situation without you, and the next call she is assigned to will bump your problem to a lower priority. If you work with the novice analyst for about 40 minutes and you are not getting results, suggest escalation.

TECHNIQUES FOR WORKING WITH THE ANALYST

Working with an Oracle Support analyst is an acquired skill, but it can produce excellent results if you use a few simple techniques. The support analyst cares about your problem and has access to powerful tools that can solve most problems quickly. Remember, the analyst is *not* the person that caused the problem or who is responsible for the bug you are trying to fix.

> **Tip**
>
> Being polite works. Try not to transfer your stress to the analyst. You can still create a sense of urgency by briefly explaining the unfavorable impact the TAR is having on your business.

KEEPING THEM ON THE PHONE

If a support call lasts longer than about 50 minutes, the analyst might start to get very nervous. She might be under some measurement or instruction to keep calls under one hour. This can work to your advantage because you can use her urgency to move the solution along. If the analyst tries to take the call offline for further research, let her know that you will not abandon the problem and that this might be a good time to escalate it to a supervisor, commonly called the Duty Manager. Be polite but be firm that you are dedicated to defining and solving the problem. When she knows this problem is your top priority, she will have to stick with it or escalate the problem. Keep the deductive process going, introduce new evidence, and redefine the problem statement.

If the analyst convinces you there is nothing more that can be done without research, make sure the analyst can repeat the problem back to you and can re-create the problem on her own system. The analyst will show the problem to a supervisor or more experienced colleague. If they can't re-create or understand the problem, you must define it better.

> **Tip**
>
> If you do get off the phone, make sure you have an action plan for continuing to work toward a solution for your TAR. You and the analyst should know who is responsible for further action and when that action should take place.

It is your responsibility to follow up and get back on the analyst's priority list. Many new Oracle customers will wait for the analyst to call back and after three to five days become very frustrated by the poor service. The no-call-back problem is caused because customers abandon TARs without closing them, and the analysts work on their current problems before they work on the one you might have abandoned three days ago. Your goal is to always be a current problem.

If you have a problem that will take several days to reach a solution, know which support center is handling your call and the work schedule of your analyst. Call your analyst every morning (his time) and leave a voice mail if necessary. Let him know you are still working on the problem, and it is still unfavorably impacting your business. Try to submit new information or devise a tactical plan for closing the issue. The squeaky wheel does get the service.

SEARCHING FOR KEYWORDS IN THE KNOWLEDGE BASE

Understand and use the right vocabulary of the Oracle Applications. This technique will help you get a hit in the TAR history database. Try to think using the same terminology that Oracle or other customers with a similar problem would use to describe and define it. For example, all executable components of the applications have a module name. You should understand which module is misbehaving and search for references by module.

Also, use the documentation descriptions to describe what is happening. Be precise, but use general business terms as an outsider might describe your business. You are trying to find a match on a problem that some other business has already solved.

PARTITIONING THE PROBLEM

Breaking the problem into component parts often eliminates large parts of the system that are working and need no further investigation. For example, say that you have a printing problem with a report. If other reports are printing, you might be able to eliminate the hardware and the operating system as part of the problem. If the process worked earlier but is now broken, check out system changes, configuration parameters, the data, and user error.

Focus the analyst on where you think the problem is, and don't let him go astray. However, allow the analyst to introduce other areas for partitioning the problem. Your job is to know when he is just guessing and get the analysis back on track. Give the reason for your rationale—in this example, perhaps reports print just fine.

GETTING RESULTS

You can get good results from Oracle Support. It is your job to drive the process and know what results you want to obtain. It is time consuming, but the following techniques usually produce a solution.

RESEARCHING THE PROBLEM

Know how to obtain the version numbers of the program that is causing the problem. On a UNIX system, you can issue the following command to find out the module revision number of the badly behaving executable:

```
strings -a [filename] ¦ grep Header
```

To find the version information on the NT operating system, open a command window, change to the directory where the executible program is stored, and do a find `"Header"` `[filename]`.

> **Note**
>
> You should change directories to the location where the executable is stored, or `[filename]` should be the full path to the executable.

GIVING THE ANALYST FULL INFORMATION

Go slow enough for the analyst to type the details into the TAR record. Make sure everything you know about the problem is in the TAR record. Make sure you have the right database and applications version numbers.

BEING ABLE TO CREATE THE PROBLEM ON DEMAND

Demonstrating a problem on demand and showing in the documentation why the program is misbehaving are the two keys to getting fast results.

If you have customizations, make sure you can create the problem on Oracle's version of the program. Make sure it is an Oracle problem and not something you did locally.

If you are on Release 10SC, get PC Anywhere or Carbon Copy so that the support analyst can see issues that might exist only at your site. Remember, good support is all about good communication with your support analyst, and you can use these products to give a demonstration of what is happening to your analyst.

LOGGING ONE ISSUE PER TAR

Try to keep the problem simple, focused, and well-defined. Each unrelated problem should be reported and resolved on its own TAR. Oracle Support analysts are specialized by Oracle Application or technology. When you split apart unrelated problems, you can direct each TAR to the correct support group.

RESEARCHING UPGRADE ISSUES, BUGS, AND BULLETINS PROACTIVELY

The MetaLink pages on Oracle's Web site have a wealth of white papers, certified combinations, and search tools to assist you with administration of the applications. Why wait until the third week in January to discover that your version of the 1099 reporting program doesn't work the way you expect? Before conference room pilot activity, implementation project teams should research issues. Production systems administrators should research issues before applying major patches and before starting upgrade projects.

RESEARCHING THE DOCUMENTATION

The published documentation tells you how the program was designed and how the process is supposed to work. The documentation is right almost all of the time. If you find a function is performing differently from the description in the documentation, you are on the shortcut route to locating the patch you need or defining a bug.

> **Note**   Once, I spent about a half-day diagnosing a problem on the customer open interface. The client had an outdated version of the manuals and Support was able to provide photocopied manual pages rapidly to resolve the confusion.

USING THE DEBUG PROFILE OPTIONS WHERE AVAILABLE

Many applications have profile options that can be set to produce extra output in the concurrent request logs. For the Oracle Applications discussed in this book, the following release 11 profile options can help generate additional information about a problem:

- CST: Cost update debug level
- MRP: Debug Mode
- OE: Debug
- OE: Debug Level
- OE: Trans. Manager Debug Level
- OE: Debug Trace
- PO: Set Debug Concurrent ON
- PO: Set Debug Workflow ON
- AR: Debug Level for PostBatch
- FA: Print Debug
- HR: FastFormula debug level
- Concurrent: Debug Flags

CONTROLLING THE NUMBER OF PEOPLE FROM YOUR COMPANY THAT CONTACT SUPPORT

Because working with Support is an acquired skill, Oracle customers and Support often control the number of people who can initiate a TAR. This technique also helps to ensure that the people working the problem have the UNIX, database skills, and system security access to investigate the technical aspects of the problem. Unfortunately, this arrangement does not ensure the person contacting Support will have the business or applications skills to define the problem and re-create the error on demand.

> **Tip**
>
> If the points of contact with Oracle Support are technical people, make sure the end user who first identifies the problem participates in the initial support call when the TAR is opened and defined. This technique saves everyone a lot of time and establishes end user participation in the solution.

MAKING SURE IT IS EASY FOR THE SUPPORT ANALYST TO CONTACT YOU

Often, the analyst initiates a call to you when she needs more information or has a resolution. Make sure she can get in touch with you. Oracle can log contact information in the TAR definition, so make the following access methods available:

- Phone numbers
- Voice mail
- Pagers
- Email addresses

> **Tip**
>
> Let the support analyst know the hours you will be available and that you want to continue working on the problem. You can leave this information on the voice mail attached to the TAR number.

LEAVING VOICE MAIL ON THE TAR WHEN NEW DEVELOPMENTS ARISE

If you discover something new about the problem, call the support number and continue working on the existing TAR. The chances are high that your support analyst will not be available when you call. However, if you leave a voice mail with the new information, you can get back in the queue for service, and he will call you back. Also, if the problem goes away, close the TAR so everyone can focus on problems that are still open and important.

LOGGING TARS USING AN ELECTRONIC METHOD SUCH AS METALINK

You can control the accuracy and detail of the problem definition for a TAR by using electronic TAR creation mechanisms such as MetaLink. When you use this technique, you can influence the priority that is assigned. You don't have to wait for the analyst to come up to speed during the initial call.

ESTABLISHING AN INTERNET CONNECTION

A relatively high-speed Internet connection is important to working with Support. When a patch becomes available, the analyst can post it to the Oracle FTP site under your TAR number, and you can download it that same day. This technique is far superior to waiting for delivery of a tape by an express courier.

> **Note**
>
> A high-speed connection is desirable. Patches of more than 60MB are common, and you don't want to download that at 28.8KBPS.

ESTABLISHING YOUR DIAL-IN PROCEDURES IN ADVANCE

Occasionally, the support analyst wants to dial in to your system to run some ad hoc SQL queries on your data. If you are the first to discover a bug and Support is not able to reproduce it on an Oracle system, Oracle Development requires dial-in access to your database in most cases. If your company policy permits remote access by non-employees, you can save time by defining the connection process in advance.

Create a document of standard connection procedures for Support to use in advance. Test it by connecting to your system from the outside to make sure the modems and guest accounts are behaving correctly. Have the document ready to FAX or email so that Support will have an efficient method to connect to your system. If you enter the TAR electronically, do not paste the dial-in procedures into the body of the TAR because that is a security problem when the TAR is posted on MetaLink. Instead, have the support analyst enter the connection procedures and mark them to be unpublished.

HAVING ADEQUATE EXPERIENCE

Because working with Support is an acquired skill, training of contact people is worth the effort. Education and training improves diagnostic capability and speeds problem resolution. When you have a badly behaving application, it is helpful if you know what the correct behavior should be before you call Support. An inexperienced support analyst and a nontechnical, novice user have low odds of solving a problem. In a UNIX environment, someone at your site should have the following operating system and database skills:

- You need the ability to navigate through the UNIX file system. Understand where the Oracle programs are stored under the $APPL_TOP directory structure.
- You should be able to issue simple commands from the UNIX command-line prompt.
- You should be able to look at the data in the database tables with simple Structured Query Language (SQL) commands.
- You should be able to use the UNIX visual editor (vi).

> **Tip**
>
> If you don't have these skills, consider asking Support to dial in to your system early in the diagnosis of the problem.

ESCALATING ISSUES WHEN APPROPRIATE

There are two ways to affect the priority of your TAR. First, Oracle assigns severity levels based on business impact to each TAR. Second, if work is not progressing, you can escalate the TAR through the management hierarchy of Oracle Support.

Each TAR is classified by severity, and Support will act according to specified procedures:

- A severity 1 TAR is characterized by a complete loss of service and the mission-critical process is interrupted. The situation is a full emergency and usually has one or several of the following characteristics: data corruption, a critical function is not available, the system hangs indefinitely (causing unacceptable delays), or the system crashes repeatedly after restart attempts. Oracle Support is committed to work on these TARs continuously (twenty-four-seven) until the issue is resolved or as long as useful progress is being made. You must also be available to work on the problem on a continuous basis.

- The severity 2 problem is caused by a severe loss of service, and no acceptable workaround procedure is available. Oracle Support works on severity 2 TARs during normal business hours at the originating support center. If Oracle cannot duplicate the problem on their system, the analyst might request access to your system. Most TARs can be classified at this level.

- The severity 3 classification is used when there is a minor loss of service. There is some inconvenience, but a workaround procedure can compensate to restore functionality. The support analyst works on this classification of problems during normal business hours.

- The lowest level of classification is a severity 4 TAR. This level results in no loss of service, and the problem is a minor error that does not impede the operation of the system. This classification is good for making enhancement requests.

Oracle has established a five-level escalation process for severe TARs. Level 1 is the initial phone call and problem definition between you and the support analyst. You negotiate the severity level of the TAR with supporting business justification. You can request TAR reassignment, callback, or status of issues. If insufficient progress is being made, you can request to speak to a Duty Manager (level 2).

The second level of support is between you and the Duty Manager at the Oracle Support center. The analyst updates the escalation level field on the TAR to Duty Manager. The status of the TAR is set to Immediate Response Required. The analyst pages or personally hands off the TAR to the Duty Manager.

When the escalation has happened, the Duty Manager calls you within 30 minutes and determines with you an acceptable action plan. The Duty Manager documents the conversation and the plan in the TAR log. The Duty Manager follows up to ensure that the plan is followed and/or resets your expectations. The Duty Manager can assign more experienced analysts to the problem.

Level 3 support is between your project team leader and the Support Product Manager. If the level 1 and level 2 escalation processes fail, your project team leader might call and escalate the issue to the Support Product Manager. These two managers discuss and agree on an action plan to move the issue forward.

> **Note**
>
> We have resolved hundreds of support issues, and never have we had to raise a TAR to support level 3. The Duty Managers are very responsive. Descriptions of the procedures at level 3 through 5 are as provided by Oracle Support management.

After normal escalation at levels 1, 2, and 3, your project manager might escalate to the Applications Support Director. Presumably, there is a problem with the way the two organizations are working together, and these two managers must resolve those issues before work can proceed on the TAR.

The fifth and last level of escalation is between your CIO and the Support Site Director. If this level is needed, the Applications Support Director sets it up.

PLACING FULL DOCUMENTATION IN THE TAR

Include all relevant documents, reports, log files, and so forth in the body of the TAR. If you are escalating, new people become involved. If you are discovering a new bug, Development people become involved. If you have a severity 1 problem, other support centers might need to understand your comments to work continuously on the problem.

WHEN DEALING WITH BUGS, GIVING DETAILS TO THE DEVELOPER

When you are working with Development to diagnose and repair an official bug, make sure you understand the program specifications. At this point, you are helping to define the logic of the program. Try to determine how your problem fits within the original design of the system. Because Development is interested in making the program conform to the original design, you are not allowed to extend the original specifications or sneak in an enhancement request with this procedure.

ALLOWING TIME FOR TESTING

Perform the appropriate unit and integration tests on any materials you receive from Oracle Support. You should test module patches and megapatches before applying them to the production system. Most Oracle Application sites maintain at least one test database for this purpose. You should remain in control of your systems, and you should know the expected result of your tests. Don't compromise your production data, and know your recovery plan.

USING EXPERIENCED PEOPLE WHEN IN A RAPID IMPLEMENTATION SCENARIO

Working on a TAR and dealing with Oracle Support can be time-consuming. For an experienced user of support services, the shortest problem can easily take two hours to resolve:

- Half hour to detect the problem.
- Half hour to define the problem and initiate the call to Support.
- Three quarters of an hour to work with Support to document and diagnose the problem and find a solution.
- One quarter of an hour to implement the solution.

That two hours is about as good as it gets, and an inexperienced project team member can loose two or three times that much time.

More complex support issues can easily take 2-10 times the effort of the easy problems. Because a typical implementation for the core financial, distribution, and manufacturing applications might generate 50 to 100 TARs or more, this kind of activity can easily add more than a man-month of effort to a project.

BEING REASONABLE

Often, your issue with Support will not be resolved because Support cannot change the original design of the Applications. You might have to close your TAR by accepting an enhancement request when necessary. You have to know when to draw the line and be graceful about it. However, don't compromise if the documentation or common sense indicates that the software is misbehaving.

BEING PROFESSIONAL

Your professionalism will make working with Support much easier. Most of the support analysts are genuinely interested in helping you solve your software problems, and they have powerful tools to diagnose what is happening and find solutions. Work with the support analyst as a partner.

You might be under a lot of stress during the support call, but it is your job to relieve stress and move the TAR forward. You might be mad at Oracle Corporation in general for shipping you buggy software, but don't transfer that anger to the support analyst who is the one person who can solve the problem.

I have seen analysts verbally abused many times, and it never accomplished anything. Stick to the diagnostic facts, and be constructive and polite. You will be rewarded with a cooperative and concerned analyst. If you don't get the results you deserve, you can easily get a new and more experienced analyst by escalating the problem to the Duty Manager.

TRACKING PROGRESS AND CLOSING THE TAR

You must drive the TAR resolution process. If you can't solve a problem in the first phone call, make sure your issues are being worked every day. Establish a log and update the status of open TARs after each phone call. Follow up on each open TAR every day. You can use voice mail, email, or other methods. When you finish work on a TAR, make sure it is closed so all will understand the status of the issue. Soft-closing a TAR with a future date is available if you just need to test a solution.

DOCUMENTING YOUR SYSTEM

Keep track of the patches, changes, and revision levels of your system. If you have multiple instances at various stages of testing, training, development, and production, you will want to know the state of each implementation. You need to have this information for several reasons:

- The support analyst needs to know the state of your system, and Oracle can't keep track of the patches and changes you apply.
- You can use this information again on an upgrade.
- Sometimes patches don't fix problems. It is helpful to know which ones didn't work so you won't waste time on them on other instances.
- Rarely, but unfortunately, a patch can make a problem worse or change the problem to something else. You need to know the history to unwind the problem.

THE BUG DATABASE

If you are working with an established release level of the application, the odds are high that some other Oracle customer will have discovered the same problem that is plaguing you. If Oracle Development has resolved the problem, there will be a bug number, and the solution will be available to you as a patch. Your ultimate goal is to diagnose your problem and get to the patch as soon as possible.

Oracle does not publish comprehensive lists of bugs that have been fixed. You must work with your support analyst to determine which bugs and patches apply to your implementation, hardware/software combination, and business requirement. Use the techniques outlined in this chapter to define which items in the bug database are needed for your production systems.

THE BUG PROCESS

If you are working with a new release of the applications, be aware that you might find programs that misbehave or act differently than the documentation would suggest. If Oracle Development has not yet produced a solution to the problem, the support analyst will start the process with Oracle Development to get a solution.

PART
IV

CH
28

There are slightly different procedures for different kinds of problems. A bug in a form must document the specific keystrokes, mouse clicks, and error messages. A problem with performance must document the number of records in the table, the execution time, and how the performance degraded. A bug in a report shows whether the report will run from the operating system, the log file, and a copy of the output report. The goal is to create a reproducible case for Oracle Development.

When a bug report has been filed with Oracle Development, both you and the support analyst lose visibility of the problem. Oracle Development usually works anonymously, and you won't know how the problem is progressing until a solution is available. Occasionally, Development will ask for additional information, and that will be a clue that something is happening. You can still call your analyst daily to keep the activity level high, and you can try to escalate by pleading severe business impact. However, realize that Support is only able to give to you what Development gives to it.

Development might produce a patch to resolve your problem, or it might determine the application is behaving as designed. In the latter case, you will be able to file an enhancement request, but this means that you will not get a solution to this problem in the current release of the applications.

In Conclusion

Oracle Support is an important partner in your implementation and usage of the ERP applications. The services provided by Support are critical to your ability to operate the applications software, and it is worth the effort to learn and develop the skills to resolve problems. Your organization pays a lot of money for support services, and this chapter shows several techniques for maximizing the benefits that you get from this service.

CHAPTER 29

WORKING WITH CONSULTANTS

INTRODUCTION

The decision to work with consultants can be a costly, yet necessary, decision. Almost every ERP project uses outside help during the implementation. This chapter is designed to help you understand issues involved in selecting and contracting with consultants. There are important parallel chapters that should be read in conjunction with this chapter.

Appendix A, "The Oracle Employment Market," offers a significant discussion regarding the different types of skill sets that are required of consultants. It is vital that a hiring company understand the different types of consulting skill sets that might be required on a project because one size does not fit all. The skill sets of functional consultants are quite different from those of technical consultants. Consulting project management skills are a totally different discipline. Moreover, functional and technical consultants might have applied their skills only to particular disciplines. A hiring company must recognize that a functional Oracle Payroll consultant has entirely different skills from a functional Oracle Accounts Payable consultant. Before researching consulting firms, read Appendix A to establish an understanding of the different types of consulting skill sets.

Appendix B, "The State of the Oracle Consulting Market," provides a detailed summary of the different types of consulting organizations available in the Oracle market. This analysis reviews independent consultants; smaller, more specialized consulting companies; larger, diversified consulting companies; and Oracle Corporation consulting. Although Appendix B includes a perspective of advantages and disadvantages to the consultant, be sure to study the advantages and disadvantages to the hiring firm.

WORKING WITH CONSULTANTS

This chapter discusses issues in working with consultants as well as a few additional tips in the selection process of the best consultant for your needs.

WHAT ARE YOUR NEEDS?

Before you bring consultants into your business operations, start by asking yourself some basic questions:

> What is the project? Define each project.
>
> What are the goals of the project?
>
> What roles and skill sets do we need in order to staff this project?
>
> What are the deadlines and corresponding risks of missed deadlines?
>
> Do we need to bring in consultants simply to help us determine our needs?

At a minimum, your company should begin the process internally by documenting requirements, as you understand them. Clearly, the products being implemented can have an influence on your requirements, and opportunities for business reengineering can influence your requirements. However, you must start from somewhere.

Documenting your requirements establishes a tangible point of origin for the project. Even if you bring in consultants to assist with a formal requirements analysis, they will need access to a great deal of your information. In essence, you will need to gather much, if not all, of this information later anyway. Thus, it is advisable to start now.

This process allows your various departments to begin thinking about the details of their future system needs. This process causes them to be involved early in the process and will be a significant momentum boost when the project implementation itself begins. This process helps your various departments to feel an ownership of the upcoming project.

At some point in this process, it is usually advisable to bring in experienced consulting leadership for a formal requirements analysis and gap analysis. Consultants, if they are sufficiently experienced, should be able to bring in special knowledge and experience that complement the operational experiences of the internal staff of most companies. Consultants can help by demonstrating core functionality of the Oracle Applications.

Consultants can bring the experience of a variety of past implementations in the specific application areas desired by your project. The concept of best practices is often overused as sales hype. However, the origins of this concept have substance. An experienced consultant can bring her knowledge of the best (and worst) practices and procedures that she has observed from other companies. Moreover, consultants can bring industry-specific experience. This can be an important aspect in refining your needs during the requirements analysis.

Consultants can bring specific product knowledge that benefits the requirements and gap analysis process. Consultants can communicate these experiences to a client to determine whether the product's gap in requirements is a true gap that must be solved. Consultants can present alternative solutions with associated costs so that the client can understand the cost implications of their requirements. Some companies are wise in recognizing that their view of their true requirements can be altered during this process. Just because the existing business operation has worked the same way for 25 or 30 years, that does not imply that there are not other equal or better ways to accomplish the same tasks. This argument can be exaggerated because a company should not arbitrarily change for the sake of change. However, the point remains that you should take a fresh look at what you perceived to be your requirements.

This leads into another point. Outside consultants should be able to bring a fresh perspective. They have no baggage based on your past 25 to 30 years of specific business operations. They have not been caught in the politics of why the past business operations have occurred in the current fashion. They should not be afraid to ask the question, "Why? What makes that past requirement a vital requirement in the future?"

The point to this discussion is to gain a grasp of your needs and requirements before and during the process of engaging consultants. Without doing so, a project implementation will have difficulty in being a success and will certainly cost more later than you now realize.

PROJECT MANAGER AND LEADERSHIP

A project's success is vitally influenced by the success of the project manager. If an outside consultant is being considered for this role, plan to select a heavily experienced consultant. The selection of this individual can perhaps have the greatest influence on the overall cost of the project. These costs include short-term costs for the cost of the initial implementation itself and long-term costs for the ongoing maintenance of the future systems.

The short-term costs often involve a misunderstanding of scope and an inability to minimize scope creep. However, long-term costs can involve increasing current scope to decrease long-term maintenance costs. This is a careful balancing act that is both art and science. Look for a project manager who has extensive experience implementing projects of similar sizes to yours.

A successful programmer or consultant does not necessarily make a successful project manager. These are separate disciplines that require separate time and experience. Of course, the ideal situation is to find a project manager who is both an effective manager and an effective implementer.

Look for a project manager who has experience managing the implementation of the specific products you are encountering. This can reduce the number of surprises that new products can bring. Although the manager might not know the solutions to the specific products, the hope is that the manager has experience hearing about and correcting the problems that your specific products can introduce. In essence, you need a project manager who is experienced enough to understand whether the problems on the project are typical or abnormal. Additionally, your project manager should be an effective leader who has the respect of both the consultant and client project teams.

For example, a general ERP project manager might be effective in understanding many of the industry issues and process issues that could affect your Oracle implementation. However, the best experience is likely to come from the "school of hard knocks." This school is based on direct experience. The ERP project manager might be effective in correcting problems after they have occurred but might not proactively correct the problems before they occur.

A similar example is to review an Oracle project manager who is managing new projects within the Oracle Applications arena. A past manager of Oracle Financials or Manufacturing might be unprepared for the product idiosyncrasies of Oracle HR/Payroll or of an Oracle Data Warehouse.

SELECTING INDIVIDUAL CONSULTANTS

After the manager has been selected, it is time to identify the specific consultants who will participate on the project team. Direct product experience again is emphasized here. Additionally, you will review other aspects of the selection process itself.

If you are new to the Oracle world, be careful about assuming that you need x number of Oracle consultants (where Oracle here is defined as anyone who has implemented a project on an Oracle database). The questions should be the following:

- How many Oracle Accounts Receivable consultants do we need?

- Should these consultants be functional or technical consultants?

- What are the differences between an Oracle HR/Payroll consultant and an Oracle Manufacturing consultant?

- Do these different products truly require a different skill set from different consultants?

The answer to these questions is that different projects require different types of consultants. By defining your project goals and requirements as described earlier, you can better attempt to match individual consultant skills with your specific requirements. Please refer to Appendix A for a further elaboration on the many types of Oracle Application skill sets that will need to be orchestrated on your project.

After you identified the skill sets required by your consultants, you are better able to select your specific consultants. You should establish an interview process that includes both the consulting project manager and the end client himself. Be careful about a blanket acceptance of any consultants your consulting organization presents. At least be careful at first.

If this is a long term, multiyear project (or projects), there might come a point where you have built up enough trust in the selecting abilities of the consulting project manager. However, at the onset of the project, it is recommended that the client remain involved in the selection process.

Some clients might not feel they have enough product experience to know whether the consultant in question has the appropriate experience. However, you can often pick up on various character traits of the consultant. You can learn what to look for in the event that you must interview other consultants later in the project. You can determine whether the consulting company is trying to load your project with green kids fresh out of boot camp. (Please see Appendix B, "The State of the Oracle Consulting Market," for further elaboration on this issue.)

Also, consider having the consulting project manager interview each candidate as well. To have a maximum efficiency team, it is desirable that the project manager and subordinate consultants have a common set of goals and understandings. Assuming that the project manager is well experienced in managing projects, she will recognize skills and traits that might not be conducive to a productive implementation.

Finally, check references on the each individual consultant where possible. What the consultants' references are saying is probably what you will be saying in the upcoming months.

WORK ETHIC AND ATTITUDE

As your project progresses, you will observe that the success of the project is influenced by every single team member. When observing your consulting team members, be proactive in understanding issues in which the consultant is involved. Trust your instincts and be prepared to pull the plug on individual consultants.

The goal here is not be divisive and adversarial. Clearly, this can stifle the overall morale and productivity of the project team and, in turn, cause you added cost that is difficult to attribute to decreased morale. However, you are paying the bills and deserve a quality of service consistent with what you are paying.

If a consultant seems to have a lax work ethic, this is a warning sign. Consultants should be highly self-motivated, or they are perhaps in the wrong industry. A good attitude is a must. If you observe a consultant who is not a good team player to either your employees or to other consultants, get rid of him. Again, trust your instincts.

There might be a tendency to believe that these character traits are simply an aberration and will blow over soon. Besides, you do not know the consultant well enough to understand the dynamics of her personality or the consistency of her character. There will be a tendency to believe that there is too much cost to start the search process over for a new consultant, so you might decide to continue using the questionable consultant. Be careful with this line of reasoning.

Quite frankly, your project will probably cost more than anyone previously estimated anyway. Your project timeline will probably take longer than anyone previously estimated. Thus, you will be stuck with your bad attitude, low work ethic consultant much longer than you previously estimated. Remember that the cost of retaining this consultant will usually go underestimated.

Please note that I am not condoning a flippant and knee-jerk reaction to swapping out consultants. You should work very closely with the project manager and all team members so that your needs are met. Because you were involved in the selection process of the individual consultant (assuming you followed the advice in this chapter!), you are partially to blame for the selection of this consultant as well. Now is not the time to blame yourself and not necessarily the time to blame your project manager. Now is the time to have a productive project. Cut your losses by removing the consultant, but prepare to do damage control immediately.

LARGE SCALE PROJECT TEAM STRUCTURE

Large projects require additional attention when assembling the team. The layers of project management might need to increase. However, the issues discussed earlier regarding project management and selecting individual consultants should still hold true. Just because the project is big, that does not mean you remove your requirement to help select every individual project member for the team.

It is important that the hiring company maintain an active role in as many aspects of the project as is possible. All projects should be approached with a partnership mentality. Large projects are an excellent example of how the partnership can be most effective.

Consider a peer management style, where a client manager and a consulting manager operate as peers. For example, there might be an overall project manager covering all aspects of the project. Both the client and the consultants should mirror this role. Midlevel managers might be needed for the implementations of Oracle Manufacturing, Financials, and HR/Payroll. Functional managers for each individual module might be required to report to the midlevel managers. In each case, it is advisable to create a team where the consulting manager is matched with a manager from the client.

Another benefit of the peer management project team structure involves knowledge transfer. If the client has functional and technical team members in addition to managers working alongside the consultants, on-going training will occur. This will be much more advantageous than attempting a go-live training course at the end of the project. The client will already have an operational understanding of the individual Oracle Application products and will understand the business decisions that influenced particular setup and configuration solutions.

PREPARATION FOR CONSULTANT: CONTRACTS

Every company and industry has different legal requirements. Nevertheless, in preparing contracts for consultants, following are a few suggestions to aid the contract preparation process. Throughout the process, remember that you are entering into a partnering relationship on the project. Clearly, your main goal is to protect your company's interests. A good contract should be able to protect both your and the consulting company's interests. DISCLAIMER: Please consult with your legal department before following the suggestions outlined in this section.

Termination. Identify clear rules for termination of the project both for Cause and Not for Cause. Design these rules so that they apply equally to both parties. If one party must provide *x* weeks of notice to terminate a contract, the other party must maintain the same standards.

Relationship. Although the spirit of the working relationship should be a partnering relationship, the terminology in the contract should clearly state this contract does not constitute a partnership or joint venture. You do not want to open your risk to include the bad decisions of your consulting organization.

Confidentiality. Your confidential material must be protected. Ensure that the contract clearly identifies confidentiality. In some cases, there might be need to have joint confidentiality to protect the consulting organization's proprietary tools.

Ownership. Oracle Applications Consultants are in the software business. Generally, the client is not. As SQL scripts and project plans are prepared, they should generally remain in the ownership of the consulting company (although joint ownership is also an option). After all, your project should have the opportunity to benefit from other companies' past projects. You are already protected by confidentiality so ownership of the tools and methods should be less of an issue to the client. If a client requires sole ownership of all project deliverables, prepare for increased project costs without the benefit of the increased expenditures. In this situation, the consultant should start all project plan tasks from scratch and not reuse past scripts, technical design documents, project plans, and so on. When used, their ownership rights have been transferred to the client, so the consultant should prepare to reinvent the wheel from scratch.

Work Requests. Even if an overall Services Agreement exists between the two companies, it is advisable to have additional Work Orders or Work Requests that address every single consultant on the project. If any specific arrangements need to be applied to a particular consultant or group of consultants, they can be addressed in the Work Request without compromising the overall Services Agreement.

PREPARATION FOR CONSULTANT: RATES AND FEES

When administered and managed properly, a time and material contract provides greater long-term benefit and lower long-term cost to a client. Management issues necessary in a time and materials contract include careful change management and high-level consulting management experience.

Typical expenses that a client must budget for include the billing rate, plus the travel-related costs for airlines, hotels, transportation, and meals.

PREPARATION FOR CONSULTANT: FIXED PRICE CONTRACTS

Some companies desire to pursue fixed price contracts with a goal to minimize and control the capital expenditure. Now pursue some of the hidden negative side effects that many clients have observed with a fixed price contract.

A fixed price contract creates an environment that reduces the common goals of a project team. Relatively speaking, the following two dynamics exist:

■ The primary goal of the consultant organization is to perform as little work as necessary to successfully call the job complete.

■ The primary goal of the client is contribute as little effort as possible to the project because the consultants, not the client, have the responsibility to deliver.

Sure, everyone will give lip service that these two dynamics will not apply to her. Everyone can be a clever salesperson and say the right things before the project begins. People can genuinely convince themselves that this approach is the best idea. The bottom line is that the dynamics above are human nature and affect the business tendencies of both clients and consultants alike.

The peer management implementation approach described earlier in this chapter becomes an unlikely solution with a fixed price contract. The consulting organization needs to control scope and change management to keep costs low because the project cost (not price) remains fixed. A peer manager from the client is still a good idea for the project but has competing goals to the consulting project manager. The focus on implementation has moved away from implementing the most efficient long-term solutions. The focus is now on ensuring that a solution is achieved with minimal calendar time effort with the hopes that the solution will still be acceptable. With peer management and peer functional roles from all levels of the client, the client many times considers long-term solutions where reasonably possible. (As a side note, controlling scope creep with consultants is a different issue and can be solved in different ways.)

With fixed price contracts, there is generally a sharp reduction in user involvement. The client does not have the ultimate responsibility for delivery in this case. The consultants do. Even when the client attempts to have its users involved in the data gathering and other related processes, problems arise. In any business, operational emergencies arise that require employees to address these issues. Time spent addressing these emergency issues takes time away from the implementation project. Because of the fixed price contract, there is less incentive for the client's users to hurry back to the implementation project. If the consultants are working on a time and materials basis, the client will have a greater incentive to hurry back to the project because time away from the project costs money.

With fixed price contracts, there is a tendency to staff with lesser-qualified consultants. The best consultants are usually staffed on a Time and Materials contract.

Philosophically, consider an example where you are a consulting firm with two projects, each requiring five consultants. One project is fixed price, and one is time & materials (T&M). Now assume that you have six heavily experienced consultants and four junior consultants at your disposal. You will likely assign five of your best consultants to the T&M project, leaving the fixed price project with one of your best consultants. Thus, the fixed price project will contain four junior consultants.

If you were a *T&M client* who was selecting individual consultants through the interview process (see interview recommendations earlier this chapter), you would select five of the six available experienced consultants. The T&M client will not accept the junior consultants because you share in the risk of the project implementation. The *Fixed Price client* will desire five of the top consultants but will probably only receive one of them. This is because if you are paying a fixed price, you have agreed that the consulting organization is taking the risk. You have trusted that they will supply sufficient resources to complete the job. If they can't complete the job on time, they incur the additional expense.

In this example, the reason the consulting organization will take the risk of overloading your fixed price project with junior consultants is simple. The junior consultants are lower cost, plus they are harder to sell to other clients who will pay time and materials. If these lesser-experienced consultants are out of work and on the consulting firm's bench, these consultants will make the company zero dollars in revenue. Even if the junior consultants prolong the fixed price project duration, they have still generated some revenue. Some revenue is better than the zero revenue of sitting on the bench. The fixed price project has become a research and development project for the consulting organization. When the consultants have made enough mistakes at your long-term expense and gained a little experience, they are ready to work on a time and materials basis, and the process starts over. The consulting firm can now hire and train some new kids and provide them to the next fixed price project.

Even if you disagree with the volume of junior consultants in the preceding example that are selected for a fixed price project, you must accept the statistical likelihood that you will not have as many top-level consultants on your project. This likely fact will create the two greatest costs you will encounter:

- Medium-term maintenance costs because many project solutions were not implemented correctly
- Long-term opportunity cost because better, more powerful, and more efficient solutions were missed

The medium-term maintenance costs are hidden when you go live with your new system. These can prove to be enormous. For example, consider a new Oracle Payroll system that has been "correctly" producing paychecks. The client might have signed off on this implementation and not realized that there are employees who are currently being taxed in wrong tax jurisdictions or not even being taxed at all. Sure, detailed payroll testing should have identified these types of issues. However, if the consulting firm provided less experienced consultants, the consultants might not have even recognized the problems.

The client cost is now more expensive than if they had implemented it correctly the first time. Not only do you now have to pay for the correction to ensure proper future calculations, you now need to perform tax balance adjustments to correct past incorrect calculations.

There is a long-term opportunity cost that is lost due to non-optimal, long-term project decisions. First, without knowledge of more efficient and more powerful solutions, the client will not recognize the better solutions that could have been chosen. If a better solution is truly more efficient, it involves a truly lower cost each time the solution is processed. Secondly, some project setup and configuration decisions are binding. If you observe a future fabulous idea that can save the company money but you find out that the system has been set up and configured without appropriate flexibility, you will now lose the opportunity of your new cost savings idea. Alternatively, you could re-implement the system at a huge cost to design in the system flexibility that will allow your cost saving idea to be implemented.

A few people might read this section and conclude that you can outsmart the system by purchasing a fixed price implementation but demanding only the best consultants. Nothing is impossible. But buyer beware, you have probably outsmarted yourself. Of course, if a higher level of management does not give you a vote in this decision, do not lose your job! Just remember that the human nature of the consulting organization's staffing decisions is not a fictitious item. Besides, if it takes 6 or 12 months after the new system goes live to finally conclude that the implementation was a disaster, you will have plenty of time to find a new job!

CONTROLLING CONSULTING PROJECT COSTS: CHANGE MANAGEMENT

Controlling project costs is usually a challenge on any new software implementation project. The same challenge holds true when working with consultants.

At the beginning of the project, define project goals and project scope. During the requirements and gap analysis phases of the project, prepare to define a more detailed definition of project scope. This is a vital first step in controlling consulting costs on the project. New potential scope items will likely be identified throughout the project. Without a clear up-front definition of scope, it will be more difficult to resist the urge of adding functionality to address new scope.

Change management and appropriate change control tools should be used throughout a project. A good change control document will include a clear description of the following:

- The change requested.
- The business rule or need being solved.
- The expected implications of never implementing this change.
- An identification of potential workaround solutions.
- The expected implications of implementing a workaround, followed by the future implementation of the desired change. (In essence, will the change be more difficult to implement in the future than it is to implement now?)
- The expected difficulty level in providing a solution to this change.
- The priority level of whether this change should become a requirement during this phase of the project.

Change control is an important step and reminder to the entire project team. Both consultants and client staff should understand the implications on project cost of new desired project functionality. Numerous small changes add up to one big change. It is very easy for scope creep to get out of hand without good change management.

CONTROLLING CONSULTING PROJECT COSTS: CLIENT INVOLVEMENT

Change management is better implemented when both the client and consulting project management are involved in the review of change requests. Both the client and consulting managers should maintain updates with client executive management.

Executive management does not want surprises. Too often, software implementations bring too many unwanted changes. By administering the type of change control documents described earlier, it becomes easier for project managers to summarize and communicate scope changes to executive management. Also, because the client has been involved throughout the project, executive management needs to know that scope changes are not merely a creation of the consultants. The client's own people have been involved every step of the way.

Often, executive management is more concerned about observing a project out-of-control than they are about authorizing additional budget expenditures. Executive management needs to know that the project is under control, its people are influencing decisions, and that future scope changes will be controlled. At least if the project is under control, the likely volume of other future scope changes can be estimated.

CONTROLLING CONSULTING PROJECT COSTS: REVIEWING THE ORIGINAL REQUIREMENTS

No plan can perfectly identify all new variables that arise on a project. A good project plan should allow for a certain amount of unexpected and newly identified project tasks. Allowing for a certain amount of unexpected change can actually be good in the long-term. Recall the discussion earlier regarding long-term opportunity costs lost during fixed price projects. Be careful about curbing scope to achieve short-term cost savings when long-term negative effects exist.

On the other hand, if the volume of change requests remains high, this might point to other problems on the project. It is possible that the original requirements definitions need to be revisited in certain areas to provide a more detailed and thorough outline of the project requirements. This might seem like needless repeat work, but by revisiting the requirements, you have a better chance of reviewing and possibly redefining project scope in certain areas. From that point, you have a better chance of controlling scope because scope probably wasn't fairly identified to begin with.

Many times, the scope creep is directly attributable to department personnel not being thorough enough with their requirements. It is easy for departmental personnel to forget about special reports and other departmental procedures that typically occur at another time during the calendar year. These types of oversights become exaggerated when the consultants engaged during the requirements gathering phases do not have extensive experience with the product being implemented. The consultant should know to ask the client about different types of procedures and solutions they have implemented in the past. The consultant should have the experience to ask the client about areas that seem to have something missing.

CONTROLLING CONSULTING PROJECT COSTS: WEEKLY STATUS REPORTS

When working with consultants, the use of weekly status reports is an important tool. Status reports help remind the consultant to remain goal-oriented. Status reports require accountability for how project time has been spent. A good status report covers more than identification of tasks accomplished during the week. A status report should identify work completed that was beyond what the consultant expected to encounter during the week. This type of item is important so that a project manager can understand why certain consultants seem to fall behind schedule. If they are solving problems outside of their originally intended scope, the manager early in the project can address this.

The status report should also include an identification of the expected tasks to be accomplished in the upcoming week or period. This will confirm that the consultant plans to work on the same priorities as expected by the client. Finally, a status report should identify issues and concerns that could affect future time lines or scope.

A side benefit of status reports is observed during turnover of consultants. If a previous consultant has left the project, her past status reports are an excellent starting point for the next consultant.

The client should review these reports and not necessarily place a blind trust on the priorities of the consultants. The point here is not to be adversarial. The point is for the clients to remain informed and continue to educate themselves throughout the project. The goal here is to help reduce the risk of being blindsided by major project problems by addressing them early enough before they can become big problems.

CONTROLLING CONSULTING PROJECT COSTS: IMPORTANCE OF DATABASE ADMINISTRATOR

When implementing an Oracle Applications project, do not diminish the importance of obtaining experienced database administration services. Moreover, it is advisable that the database administrator has applied his experience to the Oracle Applications themselves as opposed to merely managing an Oracle database without the Applications installed.

Careful management of the various Oracle Application patches and product upgrades can greatly influence project costs. If the database goes down for a significant time during the implementation, the consultants and client staff might literally be out of work, depending on their current assignments. Even a skilled database administrator will apply patches from Oracle that bring down the database. However, the goal here is to have a DBA on the project who is skilled in troubleshooting a database and even in restoring a database from the previous night's backup.

The expense of the consultants becomes keenly apparent when many consultants are waiting on the return of a downed database. The cost of several consultants waiting around can be much more than the cost of paying for a more experienced Oracle Applications DBA (assuming that the higher cost truly obtains higher experience).

CONSULTING WORK ENVIRONMENT

The subject of the consulting work environment can be a touchy subject. There are all kinds of competing schools of thought here.

Some companies maintain that they must ensure that consultants must not have a better work environment than their actual employees. Although this point is quite valid, the best solution might actually involve upgrading the work environment of the existing employees! Clearly, this costs money, and a careful research should occur regarding the expected productivity gains that can be obtained. Research in this area is extensive if you find this subject debatable.

Another school of thought involves a goal to "encourage" the consultants to want to finish the job sooner rather than later. The distorted implementation of this goal is to make the environment moderately uncomfortable for the consultant. That way she will not become complacent and remain onsite for any longer than is necessary.

Before discussing this subject further, a practical note should be interjected. There is sometimes a limit to what a company can do in this area. The suggestion here is not to build a multimillion dollar consulting complex! Having said this, consider the following.

Because you are paying a premium rate for consultants, it is vital that you obtain premium performance. You might have addressed the performance in such ways as described in other sections within this chapter and within Appendixes A and B such as the following: obtaining heavily experienced consultants with direct experience on the specific Oracle Applications being implemented; requiring weekly status reports; avoiding fixed price contracts; remaining involved in the project yourself; and so on. However, human performance can definitely be influenced by work environment.

It is important to find out what items the consultants feel are necessary to help improve performance. I will not discuss the merits (or lack thereof) of a mahogany desk or of the studies showing the simple influence of office lighting on human productivity and behavior. The point is that different projects have different needs.

Assume that elaborate documentation is required for the project. The primary consultants themselves must initiate much of this; however, some documentation can be identified for processing by the technical writer or by the clients themselves. A $40/hour technical writer is less expensive than a $160/hour consultant, even if the technical writer is marginally less productive.

Consider a simple example of a printer. If the consultant must walk up a flight of stairs to obtain a printout, how much time is being spent on this activity? Clearly, this example is a bit exaggerated, but the point is still valid. Assume that the round-trip to the printer takes four minutes on average. Do not forget about the times that you get to a printer and find you are waiting on someone else's 80-page document. In this example, what is the cost of the purchase of an additional printer as well as the additional network drops necessary to support the printer?

Does a faster computer containing more memory enable the consultant to process more testing results? If the consultant spends 10 percent of his time processing, 70 percent of his time analyzing, and 20 percent of his time documenting, the answer here is likely no. No, the consultant does not need a faster computer. The point here is to consider whether you as a client have asked yourself the question.

Again, you must be practical here, but the point is important. If a manufacturing line can produce 20 widgets an hour in environment A and 15 widgets an hour in environment B, environment A makes much more sense if the cost is not prohibitive. The problem with consultants is that they are not building easily quantifiable widgets. But they darn sure are costing you much money.

One problem that actually occurs here involves the company's various budgets. The preceding printer example might have involved expenditure from an equipment capital budget, whereas the project team has a separate budget. As a client, do not let this kind of red-tape stand in the way of proven science and even common sense.

Hopefully, the point here has inspired some practical thought. Human behavior and employee productivity are corporate issues that happen to apply to consultants as much as they do to employees. The goal is not to see how nice you can make the environment. The goal is to determine how to get the highest level of performance while maintaining solid fiscal responsibility along the way.

CONSULTANT TRAVEL AND COSTS

One area where a client can gain greater productivity from their consultants involves travel requirements. It is generally necessary for most functional consultants to spend a high percentage of their time on-site at the client site. This is because of the high level of interaction between the consultant the functional user. However, there are some situations where these consultants can productively work remotely if they have conference calls, email, a fax machine, and dial-up access to your system.

With technical consultants, there are more opportunities for remote work. If a consultant is implementing new reports and if a detailed reports requirements analysis has already occurred, the technical consultant can document, design, and develop reports remotely.

Of course, careful management should occur when consultants work remotely. Not every human is trustworthy. You really need to address each situation on a case-by-case basis. However, many consultants can work remotely with great success. When this occurs, the client saves more than the time and expense of travel-related costs. The client can gain in productivity if the consultant can manage her time without typical office distractions (assuming that these distractions have not merely been replaced by other distractions at home).

Another area that can affect productivity involves the four-day workweek. Most consultants respond positively when they can work hard and focus over four days to produce 40 hours of work. By traveling home, they have one weekday at home to handle typical family issues such as doctor and dentist appointments. Then, they actually have a weekend like normal working Americans. Why is this important to the client? This is important because you are reducing the likelihood that your consultant will achieve project/travel burnout. At least you are delaying when the effects will set in.

CASE STUDIES OF CONSULTANT BEHAVIOR

This section takes a look at different types of issues that arise when working with consultants. Later in the chapter are some case examples of client behavior. Review some of the following behavior patterns and see which ones apply to your project. In some cases, I have described some recommended approaches to dealing with these issues.

CASE STUDY: THE PRIMA DONNA CONSULTANT

The prima donna consultant is usually a quite knowledgeable consultant. The problem with this consultant is that he has forgotten that he puts his pants on one leg at a time just like every other human. When dealing with a prima donna consultant, closely review the responses of other team members. For a period of time, the superior performance and knowledge of the Prima donna might outweigh the negative impact on surrounding team members.

There is a difference between solid self-confidence and downright arrogance. The prima donna most certainly will cause damage at some point on the project in terms of how he has affected other consultants or employees. You are likely better off long-term with an energetic and hard-working consultant even if another consultant might have less product knowledge. Use the prima donna to your advantage, but do not let your luck run out.

Long term, you are usually better off sending this guy to the exit. Do not worry if the door hits him on the way out. His ego cannot be bruised easily anyway.

CASE STUDY: THE WORN-OUT CONSULTANT

The worn-out consultant can feel drained for any of a number of reasons. Perhaps the consultant has been traveling for several consecutive projects. Moreover, long work hours on your project will likely become necessary at certain stages of the project. This can be quite tiring both physically and mentally. There is a positive way to view this consultant. If she has been involved in a number a high-energy projects, each requiring travel, she might have demonstrated commitment to help other clients succeed. This same type of commitment might see you through to a successful project finish as well. Moreover, her experience level might be high if she has been involved in several projects.

What you must assess is whether this consultant is merely tired or is experiencing genuine burnout. A burned out consultant might not make it to the finish line. However, if she truly has the skill set, she might be worth the risk of retaining on the project. A reduction in productivity here is probably not a result of a poor character trait.

CASE STUDY: THE QUICK AND DIRTY CONSULTANT

The quick and dirty consultant becomes identified as someone who finishes quickly but often due to being less concerned with quality. This activity is actually to the delight of some fixed price consulting managers. You do not often have to worry about scope creep with this person. You simply need to watch out for sloppiness and insufficient software testing. Also, you do have to worry about whether you are obtaining the best long-term solutions.

This consultant is probably a risk to your project depending on the degree to which he makes haphazard decisions. Try to observe the consultant closely. If he is simply trying to hurry up so that he moves on to the next project, make sure that he first puts closure to your needs and requirements.

CASE STUDY: THE TURF-PROTECTING CONSULTANT

The turf-protecting consultant causes many of the same negative side effects as the prima donna consultant discussed earlier. However, this consultant is likely not as good as the prima donna, so your leash should be short.

The turf protector is a threatened consultant. Often, he is threatened by the presence of other good consultants. He is worried that someone will be better than him, which will cause him to lose his job or position.

Sometimes, he has become a product of his company's consulting environment. There are some recognized (particularly larger) consulting organizations out there that instruct their people to avoid sharing information with consultants from other firms even though they work on the same project. These consultants and their consulting firm have lost track of a valuable lesson. The lesson is that the client is paying them big dollars to help this project become a success.

Do not belabor the point by focusing on all the investment you have placed in the consultant over the course of the project. You will be surprised how quickly a good team-playing consultant can come in and get up to speed. The other team members will benefit from a change as well.

Note that the end client has to look closely sometimes to observe this behavior between different consulting firms. Do not become detached to what is happening under your own roof. Stay in close touch with your team members.

The turf protector cannot be rehabilitated (or at least, you should not spend the future time and money to attempt the rehabilitation). This is a character flaw deep within the consultant. His best therapy is if you help him out of the door as soon as possible.

If the turf-protecting consultant is actually a product of a turf-protecting consulting firm, you have already lost a great deal of money, but you do not know it yet. Go find someone who will remember that you are the client and your needs must be first and foremost on the agenda of the project team.

CASE STUDY: THE CONSULTANT AFRAID OF MISTAKES

No employee or consultant is perfect. Clearly, you do not want to pay big dollars to a consulting firm whose consultants continually make mistakes and poor decisions. However, much of your implementation involves solving problems and evaluating alternatives. The best consultants are willing to explore multiple solution alternatives. However, they should not be afraid of an occasional mistake. The only real problem is if the consultants fail to acknowledge and correct their mistakes. Overall, these consultants can be productive team members. They might simply need a little encouragement now and then.

CASE STUDY: THE CONSULTANT AFRAID TO DISAGREE

Somewhat related to the previous consultant is the consultant who is afraid to disagree. You are paying big dollars for consultants to provide quality solutions. At the end of the day, you are better off if you've been able to select solutions based on multiple potential options.

Some consultants do not want to disrupt other team members by suggesting that better, alternative solutions could exist because this is challenging someone else's solution. Similarly, they might be afraid because they do not have the confidence that their solutions could be any better.

Issues such as this are always a balancing act. Communicating a disagreement does not have to imply that you are condoning disagreeable behavior. The focus should be on providing the best solution and not looking negatively at the team members who suggested less optimal solutions. Encourage creative thinking. Encourage different solutions if necessary but still maintain the importance of rallying the team to one solution at the end of the day.

Quite frankly, a consultant needs to be willing to tell the client things that the client does not care to hear. It is in a client's best interests to review its processes from a fresh and different perspective. If the consultant believes an existing business process is inefficient, he is doing the client a disservice by not communicating his recommendation.

CASE STUDY: THE CONSULTANT WHO CAN'T ACCEPT POOR CLIENT DECISIONS

If a consultant is really effective and has good experience, she will attempt to convince the client to alter certain business decisions throughout the project. Most projects finish with at least one solution that a well-experienced consultant would say was not the best decision. What the consultants must remember is that they are not paid to make the final decision. They are paid to provide alternatives and produce solutions. It is the client's job to make the final decision on the various alternatives.

The consultant does not have to live with a decision long-term even if she believes it is the wrong one. It can be important in these situations for the consultant to document their concerns and communicate these to the client. This is actually a consulting trait when she feels strongly that a decision is not in best interests of the client. However, at the end of the day, the consultant must realize that she does not get a vote. If she has communicated her concern clearly, that is all she should do. At that point, encourage her to get over it. Encourage her to continue to communicate her concerns as long as they are with a productive and team-oriented attitude.

In fact, this is actually an aspect that attracts many people into consulting. Consider the situation where you work for a company that has made several "bad" decisions. At least, these decisions seem horribly bad in your sight. If you must work for this company for the next 20 years, you will always be reminded of the less than optimal decisions you've watched your company make. However, if you are a consultant, you get to leave the project when it is over. If the client's decisions were truly poor, you do not have to live with them!

CASE STUDY: THE "REINVENT THE WHEEL" CONSULTANT

This type of consultant is actually someone who tends to over-engineer a solution. This consultant is actually a good person to have on your project team. However, he requires some checks and balances. The advantage of this consultant is that he is quality driven. He wants his client to know that they have received the best solution.

What the client must do and what the consulting managers must do is evaluate when a good solution is good enough. There are certainly times when the absolute best alternative is needed, and you will be glad this consultant was around. However, there are times when you must clearly communicate that a simple solution is sufficient.

Try not to stifle this consultant's creativity; he will hit a home run for you sometimes. At the same time, remind him that you are paying the bills and that you will be truly satisfied with his performance using the less than optimal solution.

CASE STUDY: GOOD CONSULTANT, WRONG FIRM SYNDROME

Occasionally, you will observe an excellent consultant who seems to be working for the wrong firm. Perhaps the firm is not meeting her needs in some way. Perhaps the consultant is unhappy with the ethical standards and practices of the firm. Perhaps the consultant has a specialized skill that really does not offer a clear career path within the consulting firm.

As an end-client, you need this consultant to remain with your project until you obtain completion. Unfortunately, you do not have much leverage. If you sense that a consultant is unhappy with her firm, try to maintain open communication with her. Encourage her to stick with you through the end of the project. Encourage her that you will provide an excellent reference for her at her future clients based on her willingness to sacrifice her needs for the good of your project.

CASE STUDY: THE 40-HOUR MAX CONSULTANT

The demands of consulting consist of periods of time on a project requiring long hours. In this section, I am not referring to the consultant who has worked long hours for an extended period of time and then suddenly refuses to do so. I am not referring to any consultant who establishes his normal workweek at 40 hours. I am referring to the consultant who will never go the extra mile for your project when you have a special time of need.

If the consultant typically produces good work, all is not lost. This is probably not a reason to send the consultant packing. However, it will cause some pains at certain times in your project. Ensure that you have others on the project team who have obtained some of the skill sets of this consultant. That way, you have an alternative if extra hours are truly needed. Quite honestly, if a consultant falls within this category, he might not remain a consultant long-term. He really needs to return to a "normal" desk job. This situation is unusual in consulting.

CASE STUDY: THE GREAT ATTITUDE, HARD-WORKING, BUT WRONG EXPERIENCE CONSULTANT

Generally, a consultant without sufficient experience should be sent home. After all, the client is paying top dollar to obtain outside consulting experience. However, sometimes you encounter a hard-working consulting with a great attitude but insufficient experience.

These situations should be judged on a case-by-case basis. You are likely to pay more long-term based on the inexperienced decisions made by this consultant. Even if you like the consultant, be prepared to make a change.

On the other hand, you might want to take a chance with this consultant. This is a difficult situation. If this consultant is a quick learner, you might benefit long-term. The teamworking attitude and hard-working approach are character traits that should not be overlooked. This person is going to be a great consultant one day. You have to judge whether he is ready to be a good enough consultant now.

CASE STUDY: THE WRONG EXPERIENCE CONSULTANT AND DECEITFUL ABOUT IT ALSO

Beware of this person. Some consultants will say anything on a resume and in an interview just to get the job. Then, when they get the job, they will actually be very hard-working to learn the job so that they can earn their stay. These folks are sometimes hard to identify during the interview process. Checking past client references is one of your best bets.

However, now that your project has begun, you might observe that the consultant was not forthcoming with her true Oracle Applications experience in a particular product area. If you conclude that the consultant was deceitful, cut your losses now. No matter how hard she works to demonstrate her value, she cannot be trusted. Perhaps you have heard the old saying, "Burn me once, shame on you. Burn me twice, shame on me."

CASE STUDY: THE LEGITIMATE FAMILY CRISIS

When you engaged your consultants, you probably had carefully laid out assignments on your project plan. Sometimes, legitimate family crises occur, and a consultant must leave the project for a short term. Unfortunately, this is the real world, and this consultant might need your understanding and support just as your own employees will.

Your best preparation for this type of activity involves items discussed earlier in the project: weekly status reports and peer client involvement at all levels of the project.

CASE STUDY: THE CONTINUAL CRISIS CONSULTANT

How do you know whether a consultant is simply having a string of bad luck or is an unstable person in general? Many times, you do not know because you have not had years to get to know this person as an employee. You might have only known him briefly as a consultant. Your sympathy and flexibility is admirable for a human who really is a good person but is having a string of bad luck. The problem is that you have a project with real deadlines. It might be tough making a decision to change your selection to a replacement consultant, but it might be necessary for you to complete the job before the deadlines. I do not suggest a lack of compassion for this person. However, I suggest that you do not sacrifice your entire project wondering and waiting for these crises to end. If you feel this person's substandard productivity or high level of absences will truly sacrifice the positive results of the rest of the team, you need to let this consultant go.

CASE STUDY: OVERBOOKED CONSULTANT

The overbooked consultant is often the consultant who cannot say, "No". This consultant might be working on several projects for several different clients at once. Every time an existing or new client contacts this consultant, she readily agrees to accept the extra work. Although some people can successfully manage multiple part-time consulting assignments simultaneously, the overbooked consultant cannot. This consultant cannot manage her own workload. This consultant will likely not be reliable at critical times during your project.

CASE STUDY: CONSULTANT LOOKING FOR FIRST U.S. EXPERIENCE

This consultant is a person who is new to the United States. A consultant new to the U.S. can have his advantages. Many times, he is hard-working and can be obtained for extremely cheap billing rates. The hiring firm must recognize that this consultant is often high-maintenance. Note here that I am not referring to consultants who have had experience with several U.S. projects.

This consultant might bring some skills to your project that can be put to productive use. For instance, he might be quite effective using PL/SQL. However, if his communication skills are poor, this will require a high level of maintenance by the client or project managers. When managed correctly, you can obtain good return on your lower cost investment. When not managed correctly, you will spend much more than you might have expected.

CASE STUDY: CONTRACT PROGRAMMERS WHO THINK THEY ARE CONSULTANTS

Contract programmers are difficult to identify during the interview process. Contract programmers are often successful software developers. They can be skilled in the full cycle of design, development, testing, and documentation of software systems. They are capable of playing important roles on your project implementation.

The problem occurs when a contract programmer believes she is also a consultant. A good consultant can review several business issues and present alternatives to the client. An effective functional consultant must clearly understand more than the technology being used for the solution. Some contract programmers are capable of becoming excellent consultants. As a hiring firm, you should look closely at the consultant's background. You will need key team members who can understand your different business decisions.

This group of programmers is quite confident in their abilities. They can be quite convincing in describing their abilities. If you are unsure about a person, check out her references carefully. Try to determine whether this person is really a consultant or just a contract programmer is disguise.

CASE STUDIES OF CLIENT BEHAVIOR

I have focused on sharing examples of consultant issues and behavior. However, the employees of the hiring firm can have a vital influence on cost. How the employee responds to and works with the consultants can have a direct affect on the consultants' productivity. Because the consultants' time is expensive, the hiring firm should clearly communicate to its employees regarding the importance of responsiveness to the consultants. Please keep this in mind as you review the following case studies. Additionally, you will probably know your existing employee behavior patterns before consultants arrive on the project. Try to head off problems in advance where reasonably possible.

CASE STUDY: THE "I CAN FIGURE IT OUT" EMPLOYEE

Some employees might resent the fact that a high-dollar consultant is being brought into the project. These employees might strongly feel that they are capable of accomplishing everything the consultant can. Of course, if the consultant does not have extensive experience, the employees might have a point. However, it is the employees' attitude toward the project that can become detrimental.

Sometimes an employee's resentment will become a measure of pride. The employee might spend extra time trying to solve certain problems without seeking help from the consultants. The employee avoids seeking help so as not to be perceived as inferior to the consultant. This is quite inefficient in two ways. First, the consultant might have some direct experience with specific problems that the employee is trying to solve. Second, the cohesiveness of the team suffers because various team members are not working together for the common good of the project.

The fact that certain employees want to solve problems themselves is a good quality. This is a much better situation than an employee who refuses to contribute anything productive. The problem is when the employee does not want to use the best available tools (in this case the availability of an experienced consultant) to help achieve success.

CASE STUDY: "DON'T ASK ME, YOU'RE THE EXPERT"

This type of behavior in certain employees is quite similar to the issue with the "I can figure it out" employee. The root of this problem is generally resentment.

This employee would relish the opportunity to publicly demonstrate his worth. This employee is quite pleased when the consultant seeks his advice on a particular solution. Occasionally, an employee will respond to the consultant, "Don't ask me. You're the expert." A similar response might be, "I thought we were paying you the big bucks to know this stuff." There is clear resentment in this situation.

A good consultant in this situation will ignore her own pride. You will never win this employee's trust with a fight.

CASE STUDY: THE "IT'S NOT MY JOB" EMPLOYEE

A project implementation can be quite grueling. Many unexpected challenges can arise. The client needs a hard-working project team that can be flexible. Sometimes a new item of work is identified that really does not seem to fall in anybody's specific project plan. Here is a good time to have a consultant who will roll up his sleeves and not be afraid to get his hands dirty.

If you identify a consultant with this type of behavior, you do not have a team player who is looking after your best interests. More often, this type of behavior is observed of the end client themselves, not by the consultants. Sometimes this is a corporate squabble between different departments. No one wants to take responsibility, and everyone else is always the bad guy. If you fall into this category, please give us all a break and lend a helping hand.

CASE STUDY: THE SNIPER EMPLOYEE

The sniper employee is the person who is always looking for something wrong. This employee has characteristics similar to those described in the previous two sections, but this employee is a bigger problem and can be destructive to the project. The sniper makes special effort to undermine the efforts of employees and consultants alike on the implementation. His criticism is clearly not intended to be constructive. Many years ago, we worked for a client who assigned to a large project team several employees who would lose their jobs when the implementation finished. The project did finish eventually, but that client spent an extra $300,000 caused by snipers.

If management keeps a hands-on approach to the project, this type of employee will be easily identifiable. This employee is not subtle about his opinions and is on a mission. If your project is forced to depend on information that requires interaction with the sniper, start your efforts as early as possible. This employee will find every excuse in the book as to why he cannot produce the necessary and complete information in a timely fashion.

CASE STUDY: "I'M TOO BUSY (IT'S MONTH-END CLOSE, YOU KNOW)"

Many employees can fall into this category during the course of project implementation. These employees are usually required to work full-time on both the project implementation and on their existing jobs. Consultants can become quite unproductive and cost the company money when information is needed that only these employees can provide.

This employee always seems to be too busy. Sometimes, there are legitimate excuses, such as operational requirements for month-end close or for employee new hires. However, as the project progresses, you can determine whether this same employee always seems to have a scheduling conflict or other crisis.

This situation should be viewed as more of a management issue. It is quite likely that the employee is genuinely overloaded with her normal full-time duties. It is also possible that the employee does not have full appreciation for the priority of the ERP implementation project. If the client's management is involved in the project, they should communicate priorities to the employees. Management might need to reshuffle other employees' work assignments to offload the overloaded employee.

IN SUMMARY

If you have worked with consultants for any length of time, I suspect you have nodded in agreement to many of the subjects addressed in this chapter and in Appendixes A and B. Software implementation projects often cost much more than most companies originally plan. You, the client, should remain active and assertive on the project to maintain as much control as possible.

CHAPTER 30

ALLIANCE PARTNERS

INTRODUCTION

In 1994, Oracle released version 10 of the Applications with greatly expanded use of Application Program Interfaces (APIs). The Applications were opened and standardized for extension and enhancement of function. These APIs and the opening of many entry points to the Oracle functions spawned a mini-industry of extending and expanding the applications. Soon, Oracle and many software vendors formed the Cooperative Applications Initiative (CAI) to coordinate the delivery of extended business solutions to customers.

In this book, we want to give you solutions to business problems in addition to Oracle Applications reference material. This chapter presents solutions from the vendors in the Oracle Applications industry. These solutions are software you buy from companies other than Oracle. Many of these companies are Oracle Partners in the CAI programs. Others were showing solutions at the fall 1998 OAUG conference.

> **Note**
>
> The marketing departments of these companies wrote much of the content of this chapter, and we present this material as it was given to us. Please carefully evaluate for yourself whether the product or service really is unique, unparalleled, strategic, efficient, and so forth.

ADMINISTRATION UTILITIES

The following sections describe the administration utilities available from third-party vendors.

FIRSTSENSE SOFTWARE, INC.

Product Name: FirstSense Enterprise

Product Category: Application Performance and Service Level Management

Contact Name: Margaret Rimmler

Contact Phone: (781) 685-1171

Contact Email: mrimmler@firstsense.com

Web Page: http://www.firstsense.com

FirstSense Software provides applications performance and service-level management software for Oracle Applications and other key enterprisewide distributed applications, including client/server, intranet, and extranet environments. The company's flagship product, FirstSense Enterprise, is the first applications management product that continuously monitors application performance and availability from the end users' perspective and delivers Just-In-Time Applications Performance Management. This new technology captures detailed diagnostic information at the precise moment when a performance degradation occurs. This enables IT staffs to efficiently pinpoint the source of application performance problems, whether they originate with the client, network, server, or database. FirstSense arms IT management with the information necessary for application service-level reporting, trend-lining, and analysis. By shifting from infrastructure monitoring to understanding the application service levels delivered to end users, IT can more directly align its operations with business unit objectives.

PRECISE SOFTWARE SOLUTIONS

Product Name: Precise/Interpoint

Product Category: Administration Utilities

Contact Phone: (781) 380-3300

Contact FAX: (781) 380-3349

Contact Email: info@precisesoft.com

Web Page: http://www.precisesoft.com

Precise/Interpoint is an integrated tuning solution for Oracle Applications that has the following features:

- Pinpointing the exact origin of problematic SQL statements—ERP users, transactions, modules, and reports.
- Locating the source of problems—the core application or customized extensions.
- Very high sampling rates with no Oracle overhead.
- 24×7 performance monitoring.

The multitiered and flexible architecture of an Oracle application makes it difficult to identify and locate the exact source of database performance problems. Moreover, Oracle Applications use one or several user IDs and program names. These user IDs or program names do not identify the real user or transaction executing the problematic SQL statement, making it impossible for the DBA to detect the actual user running the specific problematic transaction. Therefore, when a problematic statement is located, the DBA has no way to determine the source of the problem.

Precise/Interpoint is a unique application performance-tuning solution that is tailored for Oracle Applications running on an Oracle database. Using the core technology of Precise/SQL, Precise/Interpoint manages ERP performance by automatically identifying and tracking problematic resource-consuming SQL statements back to their point of origin—the users, modules, transactions, programs, screens, reports, and requests.

By monitoring both the Oracle database and the Oracle Application, Precise/Interpoint can locate the exact cause of a database performance problem, regardless of where the problem occurs within the core application, user customizations, or extensions.

Unlike other performance management solutions, Precise/Interpoint collects performance data from the database at very high sampling rates without connecting to Oracle or consuming any Oracle resources. Using this unique technology, data analysis reflects actual application resource consumption and ensures that Precise/Interpoint can safely be used on a 24×7 basis in a production environment.

SUPPORTED PLATFORMS

Precise/Interpoint supports Oracle Applications 10.7 and higher.

Oracle 7.1.6 and higher are supported running on the following:

- AIX 4.1 and higher
- DEC Alpha 4 and higher
- HP/UX 10.0 and higher
- Microsoft Windows NT 4.0
- Sequent 4.2, Sequent 4.4.1
- Sun/Solaris 2.5, Sun/Solaris 2.6

The following client operating systems are supported:

- Windows 3.X
- Windows 95
- Windows NT

ABOUT PRECISE SOFTWARE SOLUTIONS

Precise Software Solutions is the leading provider of application performance management solutions for Oracle-based systems. The Precise Enterprise product suite, comprising Precise/SQL, Precise/Interpoint, Precise/Presto, and Precise/Presto!, provides comprehensive solutions that increase IT ROI by detecting and solving performance problems throughout the enterprise—in databases, data warehousing environments, ERP applications, and storage systems. Precise Enterprise enables users to find database performance bottlenecks, focus on key performance areas, and improve overall application and system performance. With headquarters in Braintree, Massachusetts, Precise Software Solutions services clients worldwide through its offices in the United States and Israel and through an international network of resellers and distributors.

CHAIN LINK TECHNOLOGIES, INC.

Product Name: IS*Integrity

Product Category: System Administration Utility

Contact Name: Greg Matheny

Contact Phone: (408) 543-4413

Contact Email: Gmatheny@CLTI.com

Web Page: `http://www.clti.com`

IS*Integrity is approved by the Cooperative Applications Initiative CAI program of Oracle Applications. Components of the IS*Integrity product suite are the following:

Resolve*Integrity (An intelligent Issue Resolution system)

Apps*Integrity (An Integrated Change Management and Application Deployment system)

Object*Migrator (Oracle Applications AOL setup management system)

GL*Migrator (Oracle Applications GL setup management system)

Resolve*Integrity enables end users to document an issue they encountered with a software application. The built-in workflow engine routes issues for quick resolution. Intelligent, knowledge-based searches are performed to expedite the resolution process. When an issue is resolved and requires software fixes, a software change request is automatically created in Apps*Integrity.

Apps*Integrity (A*I) automates the Software Change Deployment process. Developers or IS analysts can create a Software Change Request (CR) for *Software Changes*. CRs are routed using the built-in workflow engine for online approvals. When approved, the changes are automatically deployed. A typical automated deployment process could involve checking out files from a version control repository (for example, ClearCase, PVCS, RCS, and so on), moving the files to the target environments using any file transfer utilities (for example, rcp, ftp, and so on), and performing postmove steps (for example, compile programs, run scripts, relink executables, and so on).

Key features of Apps*Integrity include the following:

- Workflow-based routing and notification
- An execution engine that completely automates deployment of Software Changes
- Automated postdeployment steps (compilations/linking of source code, execution of scripts, and so on)
- Complete enforcement of security
- 100 percent audit trail for all software changes
- Platform independence with Java interface

A*I is a 100 percent Pure Java application that is platform-independent. Users access A*I from any Java-enabled Web browsers to control any ERP, home-grown, or third-party applications. The Patch*Applicator extension to A*I enables you to automate the patch application and management process for Oracle Application.

Object*Migrator & GL*Migrator enable you to manage Oracle Applications setups for AOL and GL modules in the following ways:

- Migrate setups between database instances.
- Archive setups and rollback changes at any time.

- Compare setups between database instances.
- Simulate setup changes to identify problems early.
- Report changes with audit trail reports.

TRILLIUM SOFTWARE

Product Name: Change Management Suite

Product Category: Change Management Software Version Control Software

Contact Name: Virgil Flack

Contact Phone: (612) 924-2422

Contact Email: vflack@TrilliumSoftware.com

Web Page: http://www.TrilliumSoftware.com

Trillium Software provides integrated Change Management and Version Control software to enable companies running Oracle Applications to manage software and change that occurs to their Oracle environments. Oracle Applications customers continually have changes that occur to their Oracle Applications environments due to patches, new releases, customizations, software enhancements, bug fixes, and database modifications. CMS detects changes, versions the software, and reports changes automatically in all your environments. CMS also interrogates every software program, database object, and databases schema, and it reports on changes that have occurred in your environments. This includes forms, reports, libraries, SQL scripts, UNIX scripts, packages, procedures, functions, tables, indexes, views, sequences, synonyms, constraints, grants, triggers, and so on. This enables DBAs and developers to see the impact of change to their software environments. Software customizations can be quickly identified and migrated via drag-and-drop technology to new Oracle versions. Differences between test and production can quickly be identified to resolve problems such as "it works in test, but not in production."

The Change Management Suite (CMS) consists of five integrated products: the Change Finder, Automated Change Finder, Object Finder, Automated Generation, and Automated Versioning software. The CMS contains drill-down, context-sensitive reports that are immediately available online, showing every line of software code and database object that has been added, changed, or deleted in your environments. Every change is stored and available online in easy-to-read reports that can be kept for an indefinite time period. CMS is completely integrated with most version control systems. Automated Versioning is also available in CMS to eliminate the check-in/check-out overhead experienced with other version control systems. There is no need to check-in/check-out or manually register your software code with CMS. CMS automatically and continuously monitors your environments to detect when change occurs. You can manually register different versions of software if you prefer; however, this is not required due to Automated Versioning's sophisticated monitoring capabilities. You can also perform impact analysis to determine what software and database objects would be affected by proposed software changes. Performing "where-used" analysis against the entire Oracle Applications software and database easily determines where every program, procedure, function, library, text string, or database object is used. CMS performs code promotion, installation, and generation of Oracle Applications software. No longer is there a need to have to coordinate the installation of database objects, code promotion, generation of the executable code, and the installation of the software between several people during off-peak hours. CMS does all these tasks automatically. Installation statuses are available online, and any module affected by a customization, patch, or new release is highlighted. Email notification is given after the software is correctly installed. CMS performs complete Change Management and Version Control for Oracle Applications.

ULTIMEDIA, INC.

Product Name: Migrator Plus

Product Category: Implementation Tools

Contact Name: Sudhir Saxena

Contact Phone: (510) 438-6841

Contact Email: `mktg@ultimedia-us.com`

Web Page: `http://www.ultimedia-us.com`

What is it? Migrator Plus is a comprehensive productivity tool that allows selective migration of setups and data from one Oracle Applications instance to another—for example, from Test to Production. Web-based, it enforces data integrity by migrating all related objects, including children. Therefore, migrating Users also migrates associated Profile Option Values, associated Responsibilities, and so on.

Who can use it? All companies and organizations currently using, implementing, or upgrading Oracle Applications.

How can you use it?

1. *During implementation.* Synchronizes setups in multiple Oracle application databases. Enables quicker rollout of Applications to other installations from the Production instance.

2. *In Production.* Facilitates debugging problems by bringing subsets of Production data to test. Helps debug problems by enabling users to simulate a small portion of the production environment in test. Enables users to test out Security Rules, Budgets, FSGs, Allocation formulas, and so on in Test before moving them to Production.

3. *Multiple Installations.* Helps maintain centralized control on master data such as Chart Of Accounts, Cross Validation rules, and so on by entering once and migrating it to all other installations. Very useful in a global installation. Helps downsize databases. Is excellent for downsizing the Production database, and rolling out to multiple sites.

REDWOOD SOFTWARE & SERVICES

Product Name: Redwood4 for Oracle Applications

Product Category: System Administration Utility

Contact Name: Uzi Yair (USA) or Geoff Hornsby (UK)

Contact Phone: (800) 438-3515 (toll free) or (949) 425-8800

Contact Email: `info@us.redwoodsw.com` or `info@nl.redwoodsw.com`

Web Page: `http://www.redwoodsw.com/`

Redwood4 for Oracle Applications is fully integrated with Oracle's Concurrent Manager and enables process-centric as well as information-centric users to take full advantage of the Oracle Applications environments. The added benefits of controlling the Concurrent Manager with Redwood4 include complex, multistep, multiplatform job streams and distributed processing to multiple hosts with load balancing, as well as a comprehensive Publish/Subscribe solution for Output Management. Oracle SQL*Net is used to communicate with all managed hosts that schedule and process jobs with Redwood4. Oracle's PL/SQL is used to manipulate the execution of all jobs within Redwood4 according to complex rules stored in an Oracle database. Complex job definitions, job submission, status monitoring, and viewing of production job output is done with the Redwood4 Information Explorer client available in both Windows and HTML GUI formats. All functionality within Redwood4 is used to extend the basic job control offered by the Concurrent Manager.

Information-centric users access the results of job processing stored in the Redwood Information Warehouse and are logically organized into various user-managed infomarts via the Redwood Information Explorer client interface, also available in both Windows and HTML GUI formats. The integration between Redwood4 and Oracle Applications is achieved through a series of Application Program Interfaces (APIs). These APIs enable a single Information Management and Planning (IMP) solution across the enterprise. They also allow the combination of Oracle Applications and Redwood4 to smoothly provide access to newly processed and archived information critical to production Oracle Applications users for decision-support purposes.

A supplied import facility is used to gather all existing Concurrent Manager job definitions into the Redwood4 Repository. When collected, additional processing rules such as the configuration of multistep, multiplatform, multihost job streams with processing dependencies and extensive job parameter validation rules can be applied. Most importantly, all aspects of the integration effort are automated, and no modifications to the Concurrent Manager are necessary to accomplish the related tasks.

PHOENIX SOLUTIONS

Product Name: WorkBench

Product Category: System/Database Management

Contact Name: Mark Wittkopp

Contact Phone: (678) 443-9359 ext. 204

Contact Email: karraUD@msn.com

Web Page: http://www.phoenix-solutions.com

Phoenix WorkBench is an integrated solution to automate the workflow of data warehousing, data mining, data scrubbing, and systems integration. WorkBench eliminates bottlenecks caused by complex data analysis because it provides an all-encompassing solution. WorkBench is comprised of six modules that cover the entire business analysis cycle, including the following:

- Query Manager
- Reports Manager
- Process Manager

WorkBench was built to perform analysis on data housed in various locations and on different systems.

AppWorx Corporation

Product Name: AppWorx Oracle Applications Extension

Product Category: System Management

Contact Name: Dan McCall

Contact Phone: (425) 644-2121

Contact Email: dmccall@appworx.com

Web Page: http://www.appworx.com

The AppWorx Oracle Applications Extension (OAE) is an Oracle-approved software solution that extends the capabilities of Concurrent Manager by providing automated business process automation, job scheduling, workload balancing, and output management in the Oracle Applications environment. With AppWorx and OAE as their single point of control, Oracle Applications customers can manage their job streams as business processes, implementing multijob and multi-instance dependencies and providing conditional logic to their processing. The product is designed for use by both end users and systems personnel.

AppWorx/OAE has a full-featured output viewer to examine data online. It also provides enterprise-caliber output management, distributing data to remote printers, email addresses, printer lists, or data files. AppWorx/OAE can be configured to send email notifications of job status, issue alerts via pager, or run custom scripts based on job outcome. AppWorx/OAE is tightly integrated with the Oracle Applications module, concurrent manager, and the Oracle database, and can accept nonstandard inputs, simplifying the automation of complex processing routines including FSG Generation, MRP planning, Mass Allocations, and G/L Importing and Posting.

ONWIRE TECHNOLOGIES, INC.

Product Name: NetRecorder

Product Category: Network and Application Monitoring Tool

Contact Name: Per Brondum

Contact Phone: (781) 449-7799

Contact Email: pbrondum@onwiretech.com

Web Page: http://onwiretech.com

NetRecorder Server monitors performance of any application using SQL*Net V2 or V8, including NCA and Oracle Applications. It inspects and enforces service-level agreements and detects/terminates security violations. It enables SQL Diagnostics with full access to SQL and bind variables/values (including a reproducible test case) and maintains and monitors service levels of applications or individual transactions.

NetRecorder delivers real-time data as well as historical data of all transactions, with no impact on the network or production systems being monitored and with no software installed on servers or clients.

QUEST SOFTWARE

Product Name: SQL Impact

Product Category: System Administration, Data Conversion, and Implementation

Contact Name: Gil Asherie

Contact Phone: (949) 720-1434

Contact Email: gasherie@quests.com

Web Page: http://www.quests.com/

SQL Impact allows changes to be made to a database with proper impact analysis. This software provides documentation and auditing capabilities to manage the interdependencies between the application source code and all database objects. Developers use SQL Impact to identify that all programs impacted are verified. SQL Impacts' impact analysis process determines precisely which components of an application are affected by structural changes to the database.

SQL Impact drills down to the individual lines of source code affected. SQL Impact can initiate an editing session to perform and test the required changes. This software provides important application documentation on how each application uses the database and the interdependencies between application objects. By automating the tedious and error-prone task of impact analysis, SQL Impact enhances the productivity of DBAs and developers while improving the overall reliability of the system.

Product Name: I/Watch

Product Category: System Administration Utility

Contact Name: John McIlwain

Contact Phone: (949) 720-1434

Contact Email: jmcilwain@quests.com

Web Page: http://www.quests.com/

I/Watch monitors both the database and operating system. It runs unattended and alerts the DBA or system administrator of impending problems. When notification of the problem is received, I/Watch takes the DBA through the necessary steps to respond from pinpointing the problem all the way to its final resolution. I/Watch provides sophisticated historical replay and analysis capabilities to identify the causes of the problem.

I/Watch can be configured to provide early notification, should the same conditions recur. If practical, I/Watch can even be programmed to take automatic corrective action, thus minimizing the chances of the problem reccurring. Other features include a capacity to help tune the environment for optimal performance, recommendations for configuration changes, and identification of bottlenecks.

Product Name: SQLab Monitor

Product Category: System Administration Utility

Contact Name: John McIlwain

Contact Phone: (949) 720-1434

Contact Email: jmcilwain@quests.com

Web Page: http://www.quests.com/

SQLab Monitor is a Windows-based, real-time monitoring and diagnostic solution for Oracle databases. This software provides detailed information about user activity, I/O activity, and database operational overhead across multiple database instances. SQLab Monitor's features include an intuitive drill-down architecture, comprehensive color-coded diagnostics, a user activity monitor, a user lock monitor, and a User Table Access monitor.

SQLab Monitor has the capability of recording and playing back historical data so that it can be reviewed later. DBAs also have the ability to monitor and control several Oracle instances from a single interface.

The information supplied by SQLab Monitor enables DBAs to quickly identify database performance exception conditions and, in turn, take appropriate corrective action.

Product Name: SQL Navigator

Product Category: System Administration Utility

Contact Name: Darin Pendergraft

Contact Phone: (949) 720-1434

Contact Email: dpendergraft@quests.com

Web Page: http://www.quests.com/

The SQL Navigator family is a complete development environment for Oracle PL/SQL and SQL server-side development and management. It provides an integrated environment for development and testing of stored procedures, schemas, SQL scripts, and more, all from an easy-to-use graphical user interface. This solution suite was conceived, designed, and developed by Oracle developers and DBAs who have hands-on experience with the most typical problems faced by Oracle developers. SQL Navigator has set new standards in the complex process of developing, testing, and managing applications that interface with Oracle databases.

SQL Navigator's user-friendly design is helping Oracle development and administration teams achieve unprecedented productivity gains worldwide.

The SQL Navigator family also includes optional modules for PL/SQL debugging, SQL tuning with Xpert advice, integrated version control with InterSolv PVCS and Microsoft SourceSafe, integrated impact analysis, and Oracle Web development.

Product Name: Schema Manager

Product Category: System Administration Utility, Implementation Tools

Contact Name: Gil Asherie

Contact Phone: (949) 720-1434

Contact Email: gasherie@quests.com

Web Page: http://www.quests.com/

Schema Manager provides a comprehensive repository that supports all object types and dependencies. Simple drag-and-drop capabilities enable a DBA to quickly populate the repository from an existing database environment, creating a baseline version. Using the baseline version, Schema Manager can support schema changes in both development and production modes.

During development, frequent schema changes can be made directly to the development database. In contrast, in production mode schema changes must be carefully orchestrated. Schema Manager calculates the delta and captures all the changes made during development and then automatically generates the corresponding upgrade script to apply the changes to the target database. With pre-audit and post-audit features, if the deployment is unsuccessful, a rollback script is provided to undo all changes with loss of user data.

Product Name: SharePlex for Oracle

Product Category: Enhanced Reporting, System Administration, and E-commerce

Contact Name: Melanie Kacerek

Contact Phone: (800) 306-9329

Contact Email: mkacerek@quests.com

Web Page: http://www.quests.com

SharePlex for Oracle is a high-speed, log-based replication software solution that continuously replicates changes from a production instance to multiple, fully accessible target Oracle instances. The target instances can be used daily for reports and queries, and as needed for high availability and disaster recovery (planned and unplanned outages of the production system). Offloading the reports improves the general performance for an OLTP environment. Relocating ad hoc queries eliminates spikes in OLTP performance. Target instances can be local or remote because SharePlex for Oracle supports both LAN and WAN environments. Consequently, you can use SharePlex for Oracle to get the data to the users, wherever they might be.

SharePlex for Oracle is designed to handle business volumes of data—thousands of transactions per second for thousands of tables without the overhead costs associated with trigger-based solutions. By monitoring the redo logs, replicating the changes via memory as much as possible, and using a continuous, high-speed network protocol over TCP/IP (not SQL*Net), SharePlex for Oracle is able to replicate quickly with a very small footprint on the source system, source instance, and the network. Its comprehensive and flexible nature enables SharePlex to replicate complete ERP applications because it replicates long columns and sequences in addition to tables. SharePlex for Oracle provides continually updated and accessible targets that offer options for reporting, high availability, and disaster recovery, without the drawbacks of trigger-based solutions.

Product Name: Space Manager

Product Category: System Administration Utility

Contact Name: Gil Asherie

Contact Phone: (949) 720-1434

Contact Email: gasherie@quests.com

Web Page: http://www.quests.com/

Space Manager provides a comprehensive solution for space management and reorganization. This software offers preventative maintenance, problem detection and resolution, and capacity planning across any number of databases. In correct object sizing and reorganization, Space Manager can provide both defragmentation and relocation, features designed to improve access times and have minimal impact on application availability.

Space Manager's capacity-planning feature can prevent problems such as running out of space by predicting the future size of individual objects, groups of objects, or even the entire database. The software automates the space management process, thus increasing DBA productivity and significantly enhancing the performance and overall quality of the Oracle database environment.

Product Name: SQLab Tuner

Product Category: System Administration Utility

Contact Name: John McIlwain

Contact Phone: (949) 720-1434

Contact Email: jmcilwain@quests.com

Web Page: http://www.quests.com

SQLab Tuner provides an in-depth analysis of SQL activity, enabling DBAs to identify the most offensive SQL statements that consume much of a system's resources. This data is presented in a SQL activity graph. SQLab Tuner can define Collectors to record and capture many statements over time. With SQLab Tuner's filtering capabilities, users can set threshold levels for buffer-gets and disk-reads to collect only the most offensive statements.

The most offensive statements, when identified, can be tuned by SQLab Tuner's built-in tuning feature. This provides the user with the most comprehensive explain plan and the chance to view complete describe information, including the structure of tables and indexing scheme and analyze statistics. SQLab Tuner provides comprehensive statistics for each object in the database to find those that get the highest number of hits. This facilitates the resolution of I/O bottlenecks.

Product Name: SQLab Xpert

Product Category: System Administration Utility

Contact Name: John McIlwain

Contact Phone: (949) 720-1434

Contact Email: jmcilwain@quests.com

Web Page: http://www.quests.com/

SQLab Xpert provides context-sensitive tuning advice for SQL statements based on the Oracle execution plan and the database structure. The software identifies offensive SQL statements, provides EXPLAIN information, tunes the SQL and the Indexing scheme, and as a result resolves I/O bottlenecks.

When the offensive SQL statements have been identified, SQLab Xpert provides fast, intelligent advice on how to improve response time, substantially improving productivity. With a click of a button, SQLab Xpert can then rewrite SQL statements to implement the advice that is selected. This software provides for a comparison of several possible tuning scenarios simultaneously across multiple databases and enables the user to select the solution that provides the best results.

Product Name: TOAD

Product Category: System Administration Utility

Contact Name: Darin Pendergraft

Contact Phone: (949) 720-1434

Contact Email: dpendergraft@quests.com

Web Page: http://www.quests.com/

TOAD is a lightweight, powerful tool built around an advanced PL/SQL editor. Object browsers give users quick access to database objects. Hotkeys, auto-correct, and type-ahead features make PL/SQL editing and testing fast and effortless. Registered users get Web access to bug fixes and enhancements. Licensed TOAD users get bug fixes, regular enhancements, and new features, such as Oracle8 and 8i object support and more.

TOAD users also benefit from email access to Quest Software Technical Support Staff. All features in the licensed version will be Y2K-compliant.

IMPLEMENTATION AND INTERFACE TOOLS

The following sections describe the implementation and interface tools available from third-party vendors.

LOTUS DEVELOPMENT CORPORATION

Product Name: Domino Connector for Oracle Applications

Product Category: Implementation Tools

Contact Name: Bart Lautenbach

Contact Phone: (617) 693-7280

Contact Email: John_Lautenbach@Lotus.com

Web Page: http://www.eicentral.lotus.com

The Lotus Domino Connector for Oracle Applications enables Lotus Domino applications to exchange data with Oracle Applications, Business Modules to seamlessly combine Oracle Applications, and Business Module data to exchange with Domino applications. Lotus Domino Connectors are system files developed to allow Domino Server applications to connect, authenticate, and translate data between Domino and external RDBMS, ERP, Transaction System, Directory, and Text/File source data, thus extending the value of Domino applications by providing interactive access to enterprise source data. Using the Lotus Domino Connector for Oracle Applications, Oracle application data can be seamlessly integrated into Lotus Domino environments, providing Domino clients with live access and update capabilities, or scheduled, high-volume transfer between Domino and Oracle Applications' business data.

Lotus Domino Enterprise Integration technologies offer developers a choice of visual and programmatic tools for integrating Lotus Domino applications with enterprise Connector source data, including Oracle Applications and other enterprise systems. Lotus's Domino Enterprise Connection Services (DECS), a technology currently provided with the Lotus Domino Server, offers developers a visual tool and high performance server environment to create Lotus Domino applications that provide live, native access to enterprise data and applications. The visual tool presents an application wizard and online documentation to easily assist the application developer in defining external data source connections, which currently include RDBMS, file/text and ERP Connector source selections (including Oracle RDBMS and Oracle Applications), and other ERP systems. Lotus Domino Connector object classes (LotusScript or Java) can be used to programmatically access Connector source data from Domino applications, permitting extensive, customized, and highly specific control of data exchange between Domino and Domino Connector source data.

In addition, Lotus Enterprise Integrator is a server-based data distribution technology provided by Lotus, offering scheduled transfer or synchronization of Domino Connector source data. Data transfer across Connector sources, including Oracle Applications sources, is defined and scheduled within Lotus Enterprise Integrator without programming. The result is rapid, secure, and scheduled exchange of data between Domino and Oracle Applications, as well as Oracle RDBMS and other ERP, Transaction, and DBMS systems.

The Domino Connector object classes enable application developers to include process-specific, customized business rules and data transfer functions to help finely control transfer processing between Domino and external Connector sources. The Domino Connector for Oracle Applications, used within the wide range of Domino Enterprise Integration Tools, including DECS, LotusScript and Java classes, and Lotus Enterprise Integrator, provides a flexible application development framework and the capability to access the data stored in Oracle Applications or the Oracle RDBMS.

OnDisplay

Product Name: CenterStage

Product Category: Application Integration, Implementation Tools, and Data Conversion Utility

Contact Name: Charles Owen, Director, Product Marketing

Contact Phone: (925) 355-3212

Contact Email: charleso@ondisplay.com

Web Page: http://www.ondisplay.com

Company Phone: (925) 355-3200

Company Email: info@ondisplay.com

OnDisplay, Inc., is a member of the Oracle Partner Program. OnDisplay provides a unique approach to content migration and integration, enabling organizations to convert and integrate content into their operational systems faster and more completely than other products. OnDisplay's premier product, CenterStage ERP, incorporates a rapid integration architecture, which employs a unique iterative, intuitive, and graphical solution for ERP conversions and interfaces. In contrast to competing products, CenterStage is not a one-to-one, code-generating transformation tool that maps data from the database layer. Instead, CenterStage ERP gathers the information from the content layer, so there is no need to write program code to reassemble the business logic. OnDisplay CenterStage ERP products reduce the risk of conversion and integration by giving complete control of the conversion process and access to the information, enabling corporations to reduce implementation and application interface timeframes considerably.

Following is a listing of OnDisplay CenterStage ERP products and benefits.

Benefits of CenterStage ERP Migrate include the following:

- Accesses data at the business content layer
- No need to write programming logic to re-create business rules
- Uses any input source including unstructured text and Web data
- Rapid approach and methodology for data conversion

Benefits of CenterStage ERP Integrate include the following:

- Nonintrusive approach to system interfaces
- Requires no change to existing programs or IT infrastructure
- Single vendor solution for bridging the gap between old and new systems
- Many-to-many rapid application integration solution

EVOKE SOFTWARE CORP

Product Name: Migration Architect

Product Category: Implementation Tools

Contact Name: Barbara LaVigna

Contact Phone: (415) 512-0300 ext. 143

Evoke Software's Migration Architect is a powerful Data Profiling and Mapping solution that utilizes a combination of automated discovery and interactive analysis to provide data and business analysts with a thorough understanding of their legacy data prior to implementing ERP, data warehouse, or data consolidation projects.

Migration Architect uses inference-based Data Profiling technology to analyze data across disparate sources, revealing the content, structure, quality, and integrity of existing data. Profiling is performed in three dimensions: down columns (column profiling), across rows (dependency profiling), and across tables (redundancy profiling). The resulting profile forms the basis for developing a consolidated data model and set of source-to-target transformation maps that are 100 percent supported by the data. This model is automatically available to Oracle's Designer 2000 to support accurate target database design. All of Migration Architect's profiling analysis, in turn, is used with third-party data migration tools (such as Oracle's EDMS) to extract, scrub, transform, and load the data from one system to another.

Migration Architect accelerates project completion time and lowers the risk and cost of packaged application implementations (such as Oracle Applications) while providing higher levels of data and application quality.

CONSTELLAR CORPORATION

Product Name: Constellar Hub, Constellar WarehouseBuilder, and Constellar Oracle Applications Toolkit

Product Category: Implementation & Integration Tools

Contact Name: Melanie Flanigan

Contact Phone: (650) 631-4863

Contact Email: mflanigan@constellar.com

Web Page: http://www.constellar.com

Constellar offers three products for Oracle Applications users:

1. Constellar Hub
2. Constellar WarehouseBuilder
3. Constellar's Oracle Applications Toolkit

Constellar Corporation provides companies with a centralized, high-performance solution for integrating Oracle Applications, legacy systems, and data warehouses. The solution is Constellar Hub, powerful enterprise application integration (EAI) software. By utilizing a hub architecture and an underlying Oracle database, Constellar Hub offers a faster, more manageable and flexible approach for implementing Oracle Applications. Constellar centrally stores and manages all the metadata and business rules for each source and target system. Constellar Hub greatly facilitates the interface development process and eliminates the need for point-to-point, hand-coded interface programs. In addition, because all data flows through the Hub, Constellar can perform very sophisticated data transformations, including merging multiple data streams, data cleansing, aggregations, staging, and so on, for a standardized approach to EAI.

In addition to Constellar Hub, Constellar offers Constellar WarehouseBuilder, which provides high-performance, single-pass acquisition, aggregation, and loading of large data volumes into a wide range of data warehouses and data marts. This enables Oracle users to leverage the same solution for integrating Oracle Applications and loading Oracle- or non-Oracle-based data warehouses. What's unique about Constellar WarehouseBuilder is its dimensional reference model—the Dimensional Framework—to centrally manage each dimension used in all OLAP systems across the enterprise. This enables Constellar WarehouseBuilder to manage distributed data warehouses and marts from a single point; respond to changing business needs quickly; and, above all, produce large volumes of aggregated, multidimensional data faster than any other tool on the market.

Constellar also offers an Oracle Applications Toolkit to enable organizations to easily consolidate data from multiple source systems into Oracle Applications by simplifying interface development and deployment into Oracle Applications Open Interface. Existing legacy host systems, with their complex file designs, can easily be mapped onto the prebuilt Oracle Applications interface. Constellar's Oracle Applications Toolkit also enables users to leverage the same business rules and transformation across varying sources and to effectively manage production interfaces with integrated scheduling, exception handling, and monitoring.

SmartDB Corporation

Product Name: SmartDB Workbench and SmartDB Templates for Oracle Applications

Product Category: Application Integration, Data Conversion, and Interfacing

Contact Name: Shirley Kumamoto

Contact Phone: (650) 988-8996 ext. 238

Contact Email: skumamoto@smartdb.com

Web Page: http://www.smartdb.com

SmartDB is the leader in providing easy-to-use and comprehensive visual data conversion and interfacing software solutions for enterprise application integration. Its newest release, SmartDB Workbench 4.1, a data conversion and data interfacing software solution, is based on a unique, visual, template-based transformation engine. It enables rapid, error-free data conversion, including data transformation and validation, with all functions integrated into one user environment. SmartDB Workbench Data Conversion Templates for Oracle Applications extend the popular SmartDB Workbench product by providing a faster and more complete implementation of Oracle Financial and Manufacturing Applications.

SmartDB's customers include Toshiba, ALCOA, Siemens, Motorola, and General Electric among others. As a result of SmartDB Corporation's commitment to excellence, Oracle's Worldwide Alliance Program has named the company "The Americas Partner of the Year as a Complementary Software Provider" and has certified SmartDB products as part of the CAI program.

Mercury Interactive Corporation

Product Name: WinRunner for Oracle Applications

Product Category: Automated Testing Tools

Contact Name: Jim Hare

Contact Phone: (408) 822-5303

Contact Email: jhare@merc-int.com

Web Page: http://merc-int.com

WinRunner provides the fastest, easiest way to perform testing of business processes. WinRunner for Oracle Applications is architected specifically to test Oracle Applications NCA, SmartClient, and character-mode architectures. It simplifies test automation, providing the most powerful and productive functional test solution for Oracle Applications. Testers and developers can ensure high quality implementations without compromising ontime deployment. WinRunner's integrated scripting environment takes a visual approach to creating scripts quickly and easily. This unique environment combines recording, point-and-click, and test script logic in a single environment while giving all the benefits of exception handling, verification, and extensive test reporting.

Product Name: LoadRunner for Oracle Applications

Product Category: Automated Testing Tools

Contact Name: Jim Hare

Contact Phone: (408) 822-5303

Contact Email: jhare@merc-int.com

Web Page: http://merc-int.com

LoadRunner enables IS groups to deploy their mission-critical Oracle Applications with confidence. LoadRunner for Oracle Applications is architected specifically to load and stress test Oracle Applications NCA, SmartClient, and character-mode architectures. From a single, centralized point of control, it stresses Oracle Applications GUI and Web clients, application and database servers, and the system as a whole. LoadRunner emulates thousands of Oracle Applications virtual users with just a few machines, minimizing hardware resource requirements for testing. LoadRunner for Oracle Applications measures the performance of various business transactions, tests distributed scenarios, and verifies system integrity. By running the same transactions at both local and remote sites, LoadRunner also exercises the entire infrastructure to identify network issues.

Product Name: TestDirector

Product Category: Test Management Tools

Contact Name: Jim Hare

Contact Phone: (408) 822-5303

Contact Email: jhare@merc-int.com

Web Page: http://merc-int.com

TestDirector, Mercury Interactive's companion product to LoadRunner and WinRunner, is the scalable test management solution for planning, executing, and communicating quality control during the entire development process. TestDirector enables testers to rapidly translate business processes into a comprehensive test plan that acts as a central point of control for all aspects of the test. With the flexibility to support both manual and automated testing, TestDirector is scalable to keep hundreds of users informed of the entire project status. TestDirector is an essential tool to guarantee the highest level of quality.

SOFTWARE TECHNOLOGIES CORPORATION (STC)

Product Name: DataGate

Contact Name: Amy Hale

Contact Phone: (408) 730-2640

Contact Email: ahale@stc.com

Web Page: www.stc.com

The DataGate product suite enables organizations to integrate Oracle Applications across the entire enterprise regardless of the network, platform, operating system, or language environment of the individual systems. DataGate is comprehensive, addressing the largest number of data access obstacles of any integration solution available. It is real-time, enabling the highest event-driven performance possible with integration technology, but also can handle batch store-and-forward activity. It is automated, minimizing user setup and administration by providing ready-made connectivity modules, proactive alerting on detection of user-defined conditions, and the power to create reusable templates at all levels of configuration. It is intelligent, with a powerful internal scripting language that can be used to define complex transformation, routing, and polling logic through conventional point-and-click GUI dialogs.

The DataGate product suite comprises the following:

- DataGate server, which performs message identification, transformation, routing, queuing, journalizing, monitoring, and alerting
- DataGateWays, the point of contact between specific business systems and DataGate
- DataCast, a specialized network interface based on IP Multicast and publish/subscribe technologies
- Alert Notifier, providing enterprisewide, proactive monitoring and alert features
- ScreenScripter, a screen-based data transfer mechanism for communicating with applications lacking conventional APIs
- Universal Index, which creates a single identifier across an enterprise so that identification and demographic information are centralized in one shared index

ASSET MANAGEMENT

The following section describes the asset management solutions Indus International provides.

INDUS INTERNATIONAL, INC.

Product Name: PassPort/EMPAC

Product Category: Enterprise Asset Management

Contact Name: Kerry Lamson

Contact Phone: (415) 904-5000

Contact Email: kerry.lamson@iint.com

Web Page: http://www.indusworld.com

The Indus Solution Series for Enterprise Asset Management (EAM) addresses the entire life cycle of securing, maintaining, and optimizing your enterprisewide assets. The system goes beyond automated record-keeping or reactive maintenance management. Instead of discretely managing resources for labor, material, tools, and equipment, the Indus Solution Series optimizes your capacity and efficiency by integrating all plant processes. EAM includes asset performance methodologies such as Benchmarking, Total Productive Maintenance (TPM), Reliability Centered Maintenance (RCM), and Total Quality Management (TQM).

Indus EAM solutions are an integral part of the supply chain and interact seamlessly with production planning, ERP, DRP, logistics, and manufacturing execution systems. Information from the Indus Solution Series integrates with Oracle Applications such as Financials and Human Resources, as well as external systems such as supplier inventory and pricing systems. This enterprisewide integration is vital to achieving optimal plant floor productivity, reduced lead times and inventories, and increased production efficiencies and throughput.

BUSINESS TO CONSUMER COMMERCE

The following section describes the business to consumer commerce solutions provided by HighTouch Technologies.

HIGHTOUCH TECHNOLOGIES, INC.

Product Name: HighTouch Consumer Commerce suite

Product Category: Business to Consumer Commerce, Marketing, Business to Consumer Order Entry, Customer Service, Call Center, Direct Selling Software, Customer Loyalty & Retention, Direct Marketing

Contact Name: Jim Fry

Contact Phone: (888) 780-5001

Contact Email: jfry@hightouch.net

Web Page: http://www.hightouch.net

Our HighTouch Consumer Commerce suite provides you with a completely integrated, Oracle-based, enterprisewide solution for all of your direct-to-customer marketing needs, as well as front and back office operations. HighTouch software integrates state-of-the-art marketing, call handling, order entry, customer service, fulfillment, and accounting functions through a seamless, unified real-time process. Developed with Oracle's Designer 2000 tools, our system integrates with Oracle Applications and is designed to operate in a standalone configuration enabling 24 × 7 operations. Our totally integrated system encompasses a vast array of robust functionality to meet all your consumer sales, service, fulfillment, and marketing needs. The HighTouch suite is comprised of the following modules.

ORDER ENTRY

A complete order management module designed to process incoming sales from the Internet, mail, telephone, or POS, HighTouch Order Entry is a high-speed, high-volume, sales processing system. It features the following:

- Real-time sales activity reporting
- Scripting
- Profiling
- Online payment processing
- Event pricing and discounting
- Customer and order holds
- Returns processing
- Auto-ship and continuity programs
- Suggestion selling
- Dynamic product linkage
- Substitution
- Product upselling
- Real-time inventory and sales allocation with oversell capability
- Flexible product discounting
- Outsourcing fulfillment
- Other robust features designed to maximize the potential of every transaction

CUSTOMER SERVICE

Our Customer Service program keeps your agents and representatives totally in touch with your customers' needs. Your agents are empowered with real-time online ordering, billing and shipping status, product and marketing information, and a complete, detailed transactional history at their fingertips on the front line, when your customers need to know.

REAL-TIME INFORMATION

Real-time information exploits the full potential of electronic media by constantly capturing, massaging, and summarizing data from sales and service sessions, thereby optimizing business decisions. Real-time graphical product sales and customer call information is accessible via the World Wide Web including end-of-segment/event/day sales reporting and P&L by segment/event/day.

ELECTRONIC COMMERCE

Designed from the ground up as an e-commerce system, HighTouch Electronic Commerce software fully exploits the potential of the Internet and other electronic media as a standalone 24×7 virtual sales machine. Our system provides a complete electronic commerce solution deploying all facets of the sales and fulfillment process from order entry through inventory reservation, delivery, and automated follow-up.

GLOBAL COMMISSIONING

Global Commissioning is capable of single and simultaneous genealogy management in multiple countries using appropriate languages and currencies. This facilitates creative distributor compensation plans within direct selling or multilevel marketing enterprises without limit to the depth or breadth of the down-line organization.

DIRECT MARKETING

Our Direct Marketing data mart collects and analyzes all customer and transactional data to facilitate creation of pinpoint-targeted, consumer-oriented promotions and campaigns. It then executes acquisition and cross-selling programs through automatic mail, email, fax, and outbound call queues. It utilizes predictive modeling tools including multidimensional queries, response forecasting, financial modeling, and "what if" analysis. The Direct Marketing module provides advanced Internet marketing features covering the spectrum from online customer profiling to targeted promotional activities.

CUSTOMER RELATIONSHIP MANAGEMENT

Customer Relationship Management (CRM) provides the most advanced tools on the market today for managing comprehensive customer loyalty and retention programs and relationships with customers. CRM satisfies the growing need among almost all businesses to maximize ongoing relationships with their customers. CRM uses a powerful database system that maintains a full customer history detailing all of a customer's interactions with a company and demographic characteristics. It delivers a wide range of marketing applications for running loyalty programs and building long-term customer relationships, including sophisticated retention and frequency (points and rewards) programs, targeted retention promotions, and customer profitability tracking and modeling.

ELECTRONIC COMMERCE AND DATA INTERCHANGE

The following sections describe various e-commerce and data interchange solutions offered by third-party vendors.

CONCUR TECHNOLOGIES, INC.

Product Name: Employee Desktop

Product Category: Electronic Commerce

Contact Name: Natalie Hadfield

Contact Phone: (425) 702-8808

Contact Email: natalieh@concur.com

Web Page: www.concur.com

Concur's Employee Desktop serves as the access portal and activity manager for all employee-facing applications—solutions developed to automate time-consuming, paper-laden business processes, such as procurement and travel expense management. Employee Desktop creates a home base where employees have immediate access to an integrated suite of products that automate the core business processes that impact their day-to-day work. Running in a standard browser over the corporate intranet, Employee Desktop collects all employee-facing applications within a single interface. It then flags, reports, and organizes the pending activities for each one.

Direct links from Employee Desktop into Oracle Financials provide for account code validation from every employee-facing application, maintaining only a single set of accounting codes within the system. Data is captured once at its source and passes through the system smoothly, maintaining data accuracy at every step, with no need to rekey information. The integration of Employee Desktop with Oracle Financials is designed to eliminate hours of data entry, auditing, and compliance monitoring to provide organizations with a cost-effective way to manage redundant administrative tasks across the entire enterprise.

ST. PAUL SOFTWARE

Product Name: eVision Application Integration Module for Oracle Applications

Product Category: Electronic Commerce/EDI (Electronic Data Interchange)

Contact Name: Gina L. Sandon

Contact Phone: (651) 603-4400

Contact Email: gsandon@stpaulsoftware.com

Web Page: http://www.stpaulsoftware

St. Paul Software's eVision Application Integration Module (AIM) provides EDI transactions not currently supported by Oracle's EDI Gateway. eVision AIM replaces custom programs and interfaces that integrate EDI. The version 10.7 EDI Gateway supports purchase order (850) outbound, purchase order (850) inbound, invoice (810) outbound, and advance shipment notices (856) outbound. For Oracle users, this creates a unique challenge in how to integrate other EDI transactions. Several companies have developed custom-coded interfaces to integrate the required transactions. Considerations in developing custom code include internal Oracle expertise, development resources available, EDI transaction expertise, and—most importantly—long-term code maintenance, upgrade, and migration efforts. By utilizing eVision AIM, Oracle Applications users take advantage of enhancements and maintenance provided by St. Paul Software and avoid the costly maintenance of custom code.

St. Paul Software developed eVision AIM to integrate EDI transactions with a rapid implementation and to avoid custom code issues. It is a powerful GUI integration tool with direct connect to Oracle Applications data tables. eVision AIM controls the post and extract processes and provides data validation according to customer-defined business rules.

Validation of the data prior to posting or extraction, and audit trail reporting, ensure data integrity in the application data tables. In addition, eVision AIM accesses cross-referenced data already maintained in the Oracle Applications and supports turnaround data storage required for certain EDI documents. The base module provides the processing engine with kits available by EDI transaction. For transactions not currently supported in Oracle, the tool enables faster integration, enhancements, migration support, and EDI transaction management.

GE INFORMATION SERVICES, INC.

Product Name: Enterprise System and Application Integrator

Product Category: Electronic Commerce and Enterprise Application Integration

Contact Name: Jeffery R. Eck

Contact Phone: (301) 340-5419

Contact Email: jeffery.eck@geis.ge.com

Web Page: http://www.geis.com

GE Information Services is committed to providing business-to-business solutions that solve both electronic commerce and enterprise application integration challenges in one solution. GE provides a single solution for companywide integration requirements. For business to business (B2B) and application to application (A2A) situations, whether they be legacy application to ERP, EDI to ERP, or any combination, the GE solution is a proven, capable, single solution for companywide integration requirements. It just makes sense to use a common framework to integrate both your external business partner applications and your internal applications. GE software products work together to provide that common, extensible framework.

GE's solution for Oracle Applications includes the Enterprise and Application Integrator products, which are integrated together and provide a comprehensive solution for integrating inbound/outbound EDI with the Oracle Applications, as well as integrating legacy applications with the Oracle Applications. GE's Enterprise System acts as a gateway between Oracle Applications and legacy applications, as well as a gateway between Oracle Applications and external EDI requirements. GE's Enterprise System provides all the technical know-how to communicate using Internet technology as well as more traditional communication pathways such as VANs and numerous other communications protocols. The Application Integrator component of the solution provides the actual data manipulation and transformation capabilities. The Application Integrator component is capable of "any-to-any" data transformation. Therefore, it can translate between inbound EDI to Oracle EDI Gateway, Oracle EDI Gateway to outbound EDI, legacy application to Oracle Application and vice versa, or even EDI to EDI.

GLOBAL COMMERCE AND IMPORT/EXPORT

The following sections describe the global commerce and import/export solutions available from third-party vendors.

VASTERA

Product Name: EMS-2000

Product Category: Import/Export Regulatory Compliance

Contact Name: AJ Bosk

Contact Phone: (703) 661-9006

Contact Email: aj.bosk@vastera.com

Web Page: http://www.vastera.com

Vastera is a complementary Oracle Alliance Partner that provides services, content, and software for export and import regulatory compliance, customs clearance, and international documentation. When offered together, the joint Oracle/Vastera solution provides complete functionality for international requirements not found in other ERP solutions. The EMS-2000 solution by Vastera complements Oracle's applications by addressing the complex requirements for country-specific trade regulations.

The Export compliance solution analyzes order, item, and customer information to determine whether the order can proceed through the order workflow cycle. Thus, Oracle Order Entry, in conjunction with EMS-2000, addresses the specific business requirements of export regulatory compliance and required international documentation.

The Import compliance solution in EMS-2000 performs a number of checks and calculations for customs' pre-entries, commercial invoices, and entries to help ensure that transactions comply with import laws and trade agreements before goods are imported.

The integration of these products with Oracle occurs through a series of standard open Application Program Interfaces (APIs) that enable Oracle Applications, release 10, to support complete export and import regulatory compliance coupled with Oracle Applications. This integration allows data to be shared between Oracle Applications and EMS-2000, giving users the capability to hold and verify orders that have failed to meet criteria designated in the Export Determination and Import Determination requirements at any point in the workflow cycle. Compliance checks can be done at any stage in the order cycle.

SYNTRA

Product Name: Global Logistics System (GLS)

Product Category: International Trade Logistics

Contact Name: Martha Urscheler, Director of Marketing

Contact Phone: (212) 714-0440

Contact Email: info@syntra.com

Web Page: http://www.syntra.com

The Global Logistics System is a comprehensive and fully scalable software solution that automates every step of the global trade logistics process: order processing, document generation, regulatory compliance, in-transit inventory management, global Track and Trace, and data communications. More than 500 multinational companies—including Lucent Technologies Microelectronics Group, GE Medical, and BASF—use GLS to manage their global commerce operations in the most timely, efficient, and cost-effective manner possible.

GLS was developed in close cooperation with Oracle Corporation; it is NCA 10.7-certified and is also certified for the CAI program. Because of SYNTRA's close development relationship with Oracle, GLS integrates seamlessly with Oracle Applications, extending their ERP/supply-chain functionality into the complex, highly specialized, and risk-intensive area of global trade logistics. This enables the end user to reduce supply-chain inefficiencies, cut inventory management costs, avoid regulatory compliance difficulties, and improve customer service and satisfaction.

NEXTLINX (FORMERLY EXPOSOFT, INC.)

Product Name: Velocity

Product Category: Additional Integrated Application (Trade Management Software)

Contact Name: Ned Merrill

Contact Phone: (301) 565-4334 or (800) 237-2552

Contact Email: sales@nextlinx.com

Web Page: http://nextlinx.com

Velocity is an automated international trade management software product. This system "bolts-on" to the Oracle Application Order Management module. Functionality includes export, import, and logistics management that enables companies to maintain compliance with domestic and international regulations as well as move their goods around the world more efficiently. It is a state-of-the-art solution available in three scalable architectures: 2-tier, 3-tier, and Web-enabled. Velocity is extremely flexible, configurable, customizable, and available in various foreign languages. It is a proven product installed at over 100 locations supporting thousands of users. It has been successfully put into production for many of Oracle's largest international customers.

Export functionality included in the Velocity software suite includes denied-party screening, export license application and management, shipping documentation (over 80 forms), and audit trail creation and management. NextLinx also updates the system weekly with the most current governmental regulations. The Import module provides vendor screening, duty drawback, tariff reduction and preferential trade program management, valuation alerts, and customs pending actions. The suite also includes full letter of credit and logistics management.

DATA COLLECTION AND BAR CODES

The following sections describe the solutions for facilitating data collection and bar codes available from third-party vendors.

CONNECTWARE

Product Name: Connectware for Oracle Applications

Product Category: Automated Data Collection, Bar Coding, Business Process Automation, Data Collection, and/or Integrated Applications

Contact Name: Gordon Graham, VP Marketing

Contact Phone: (514) 287-1854

Contact Email: info@connectware.ca

Web Page: http://www.connectware.ca

Connectware for Oracle Application provides seamless integration of bar coding with all popular transactions for manufacturing and distribution. Connectware can reduce the average time to complete an Oracle transaction by 88 percent, cut keystrokes by 76 percent, and virtually reduce data entry errors.

To safeguard your corporate database, Connectware follows all of Oracle's rules for data integrity and is 100 percent certified under Oracle's Cooperative Applications Initiative (CAI).

DATA NET CORPORATION

Product Name: DataBridge for Oracle

Product Category: Automated Data Collection For Shop Floor and Distribution Applications

Contact Phone: (954) 437-3535 ext. 15

Contact Email: jweiss@datanetcorp.com

Web Page: http://www.datanetcorp.com

Data Net Corporation, a CAI-approved partner, has created an integrated solution for automatically collecting data from shop floor applications and updating Oracle. DataBridge, Data Net's NT-based solution, validates and updates data on a real-time basis. DataBridge allows multiple vendors' data collection hardware to be integrated in an open system by creating the terminal prompts in HTML code. A full suite of off-the-shelf transactions is available for rapid implementation. Examples of transactions that are in the library include Sub-Inventory Transfer, WIP Assembly Completion, Purchase Order Receipt, Sales Order Shipment, In-Transit Shipment, and Account Receipt.

Data Net also offers a library of complementary software products to enhance the functionality of Oracle Applications. These packages are fully integrated with DataBridge, which in turn seamlessly passes the pertinent data to Oracle Applications. These complementary packages include Time and Attendance, Labor Management, Warehouse Management, and Quality. In addition, DataBridge provides for custom complementary products to be developed to meet specific customer requirements. Data Net has also interfaced to the Oracle Process Applications formally known as GEMMS.

BPA Systems, Inc.

Product Name: BP*LINK/APPS

Product Category: Bar Coding, Integrated Applications, Supply Chain Automation, and Warehouse Management

Contact Name: Paul Palmer

Contact Phone: (512) 231-8191 ext. 1017

Contact Email: paul@bpasystems.com

Web Page: http://www.bpasystems.com

BPA Systems provides supply-chain automation solutions, mobile user interfaces, and bar code technology for the Oracle Applications. BPA's BP*LINK/APPS products automate and simplify transactions in Oracle Applications modules for Purchasing, Work In Process, Inventory, Order Entry (Shipping), Assets, and Warehouse Management by using state-of-the-art, wireless data collection devices and bar code technology. Compliance bar code label printing is fully supported. BP*LINK/APPS are approved by Oracle's Cooperative Applications Initiative for release 10.7 and release 11.

The key to BP*LINK's family of products is BPA's Mobile User Interface for Oracle Applications. BPA's Mobile UI is an alternative interface for Oracle Applications that is optimized for use on mobile devices such as personal RF bar code scanners and fork truck-mounted VMUs. Receiving, material movement, Work In Process, Warehouse Management, product labeling, and Shipping are effectively performed from mobile devices using BP*LINK. The combination of BPA's Mobile UI, Oracle Applications and mobile bar code devices creates a powerful supply-chain automation platform.

USDATA CORPORATION

Product Name: FactoryLink

Product Category: (Manufacturing Software) Human-Machine Interface/ Data Acquisition Software

Contact Name: Mike Goeke

Contact Phone: (972) 497-0337

Contact Email: mgoeke@usdata.com

Web Page: http://usdata.com

USDATA FactoryLink provides the tools for building real-time systems to consolidate data from automated and non-automated sources into a real-time database. Then, this real-time data is correlated with production data in the Oracle WIP, Inventory, Cost, and Quality modules through the Oracle Applications interface. The primary strengths of USDATA FactoryLink are its speed, industrial robustness, and connectivity capabilities.

FactoryLink applications run as compiled systems on Microsoft Windows NT and can be edited while monitoring production equipment for process interruptions and anomalies. The product provides alarming, event notification, historical data storage, trending, scripting, process graphics, and numerous communication methods. The product has been applied in many industries around the world over the last 20 years.

Product Name: WebClient

Product Category: (Manufacturing Software) Human-Machine Interface Visualization Client Software

Contact Name: Mike Goeke

Contact Phone: (972) 497-0337

Contact Email: mgoeke@usdata.com

Web Page: http://usdata.com

USDATA WebClient provides remote visualization of FactoryLink systems via Internet connections and standard HTML browsers. The current status of the production equipment or historical performance data can be monitored, and changes can be made to the FactoryLink settings with proper authority.

WebClient allows associated disciplines to browse the internal status of production equipment without traveling or even walking around the floor. The production equipment can be thoroughly examined or diagnosed without interrupting current production operations. Up to 99 WebClients can be connected to a single FactoryLink server, which can be monitoring numerous machines on the plant floor.

Product Name: Xfactory

Product Category: (Manufacturing Software) Manufacturing Execution System

Contact Name: Mike Goeke

Contact Phone: (972) 497-0337

Contact Email: mgoeke@usdata.com

Web Page: http://usdata.com

USDATA Xfactory is a visual modeling MES system built on the Microsoft DNA architecture. The three-tier architecture provides levels of manufacturing agility and adaptability not previously available. The architecture isolates the business rules to the middle tier, independent of a static database schema. This allows the system to be modified and extended by the users without specialized technology expertise.

Standard system views are provided for production planners, production operators, and operations managers, along with a standard set of production reports. All production reports remain accurate without regard to any changes made to the application rules on the middle tier. The system enables operation personnel to see the queue, routing, work order information, instructions, and so on for each process; any changes in the system are immediately available to all clients viewing that information. High-speed automated and semiautomated applications in automotive, semiconductor, and electronics assembly have been the primary focus.

TEKLYNX INTERNATIONAL

Product Name: Sentinel Print Pack

Product Category: Enhanced Reporting, Electronic Commerce, and Additional Integrated Applications, Bar Code, Bar Code Labeling

Contact Name: Lee Patty

Contact Email: lee_patty@teklynx.com

Web Page: www.teklynx.com

Sentinel Print Pack is a 32-bit, multithreaded print spooler for bar code label printing to over 500 thermal label printers as well as any Windows printer driver. Sentinel Print Pack is a Windows NT service to provide for full automation in any labeling application. Output from any Oracle application can be utilized into variable data to be printed on any label printer throughout the network enterprise.

Sentinel Print Pack's graphical user interface makes creation and editing of label formats seamless. Time-consuming, text-based editing of formats is replaced by point-and-click movements.

EXPENSE MANAGEMENT

The following section describes the Necho Systems solution for expense management.

NECHO SYSTEMS CORP.

Product Name: NavigatER

Product Category: Expense Management Software/Enhanced Reporting

Contact Name: Sarah Spence

Contact Email: sarah.spence@necho.com

Web Page: http://www.necho.com

Necho is a strategic partner for organizations wanting best-of-breed T&E processing software that delivers robust functionality and information reporting. NavigatER automates every activity within T&E processing from expense claim creation through verification, audit, payment, and corporate card prepopulation; it also integrates with all key Oracle enterprise applications to reduce costs and increase efficiencies.

The AdministratER module within NavigatER gives organizations control over configuring the system (for example, organizations gain a fast turn-around time on adding, deleting, or changing financial codes and policies), based on their preferred practices, via the easy-to-use Windows-based tools. This means lower maintenance and upgrade costs and immediate software conformity with business policies and processes. The latest Java version, NavigatER 4, has offline capability—employees use the same application whether they are on the corporate LAN/WAN, intranet, or offline (for example, on a plane). Users only have to be trained on one application, and the IT department only maintains one version of the software.

Product Name: FinancER

Product Category: Expense Management Software/Enhanced Reporting

Contact Name: Sarah Spence

Contact Email: sarah.spence@necho.com

Web Page: http://www.necho.com

Necho is a strategic partner for organizations wanting best-of-breed T&E functionality and information reporting for infrequent travelers with FinancER software. FinancER is a Web-based solution that streamlines the processing of business expenditures within the finance/accounting operations resulting in cost savings and increased efficiencies.

FinancER includes a shared services robot that electronically generates EZ-ER expense reports that integrate charge card transactions detail with corporate business rules. The pregenerated EZ-ER reports can be easily distributed to employees for verification, explanation, or the addition of out-of-pocket items for a streamlined expense management process and consolidated data capturing and reporting.

Product Name: ProcurER

Product Category: Expense Management Software/Enhanced Reporting

Contact Name: Sarah Spence

Contact Email: sarah.spence@necho.com

Web Page: http://www.necho.com

Necho Systems Corp. is a developer of Web-based, global software solutions for business expense processing. Through automation, Necho delivers return-on-investment solutions for corporate operations, including travel and entertainment (T&E) and procurement that integrates with Oracle systems (including HR, Financial, and so on). Necho is a strategic partner for organizations wanting best-of-breed robust functionality with ProcurER software. ProcurER captures procurement card transactions making them accessible to card holders for verification and detailed financial coding.

ProcurER integrates with all key Oracle enterprise applications to reduce costs and increase efficiencies.

DOCUMENT MANAGEMENT AND WORKFLOW

The following section describes the Feith Systems and Software solution for document management and workflow.

FEITH SYSTEMS AND SOFTWARE, INC.

Product Name: Feith Document Database (FDD)

Product Category: Document Imaging, Document Management, COLD, and Workflow

Contact Name: Mitch Farbstein

Contact Phone: (215) 646-8000

Contact Email: mitch@feith.com

Web Page: http://www.feith.com

Feith Document Database (FDD) is a complete Document Imaging, Document Management, COLD, and Workflow solution. It runs on Oracle and other standard SQL databases and on all popular UNIX and NT platforms. Full-text indexing is available. FDD operates in client/server and Web modes and seamlessly integrates with Oracle Financials and other host-based applications.

Feith Systems is based in the Philadelphia suburb of Fort Washington, with offices in Atlanta and Southern California. Founded in 1979, the company has been providing imaging and document management solutions since 1986.

PAYROLL PROCESSING

The following section describes the Ceridian Employer Services solution for payroll processing.

CERIDIAN EMPLOYER SERVICES

Product Name: Payroll and Payroll Tax Outsourcing Services

Product Category: Additional Integrated Applications

Contact Name: Candy Patrin, Public Relations Manager

Contact Phone: (612) 853-4380

Contact Email: (612) 853-4430

Web Page: http://ces.ceridian.com

PART

IV

CH

30

Ceridian Employer Services, a business unit of Ceridian Corporation, provides outsourced payroll and tax filing solutions. The Ceridian Source product suite also includes payroll tax filing services that complement inhouse payroll processing, and time and attendance solutions—currently available for Windows, SQL Server, and Oracle environments. The outsourcing of noncore functions, such as payroll processing and tax reporting, is a logical complement to the ERP strategy. Outsourcing minimizes the resources devoted to noncore business functions, which allows organizations to maximize the return from their ERP investment.

The integration solution offered for users of Oracle HR provides a standardized and supported interface between Oracle HR and various Ceridian payroll solutions. The interface was developed jointly by Ceridian and the Oracle HR development staff. When the interface is implemented, changed data is transferred from the Oracle HR application to the Ceridian Interface, where audit and validation procedures are applied to the data. When validated, data is passed to the Ceridian payroll application and subsequently to the Ceridian processing center for gross-to-net calculation and associated payroll and tax services. Oracle HR is used as the primary repository of employee HR data, whereas the Ceridian payroll application is utilized for hours and earning entries, payroll exceptions such as off-cycle or void checks, temporary deductions, and communication with the Ceridian processing center. Ceridian's integration is certified by Oracle's Cooperative Applications Initiative.

TREASURY MANAGEMENT

The following section describes the SunGard Treasury Systems solution for treasury management.

SUNGARD TREASURY SYSTEMS

Product Name: ICMS Treasury System

Product Category: Financial Apps/Enterprise Treasury Solutions

Contact Name: Sue Singh

Contact Phone: (650) 244-4200 ext. 209

Contact Email: sue_singh@sungardtreasury.com

Web Page: http://www.sungardtreasury.com

The ICMS/TS extends the utility of Oracle Financial Applications by providing an interface directly from the Treasury System database to the Oracle General Ledger. Treasury transactions captured in ICMS/TS are transmitted to the Oracle G/L on a regular basis. Chart-of-Accounts information is transmitted directly into ICMS/TS so that Treasury transactions can automatically be journalized to the proper G/L line for accounting.

The ICMS/TS is a scalable, modular package that corporate treasurers use to track, execute, monitor, and report the full range of cash and treasury activities with a minimum of rekeying. These activities include daily cash position, cash forecasting, debt and investment portfolio management, foreign exchange transaction management, financial risk scenario modeling and tracking, comprehensive inhouse bank functionality, and external bank relationship management. The ICMS/TS is a 32-bit Treasury package that can be configured to run on the Oracle database engine in a standalone or network environment. SunGard Treasury Systems' ICMS/TS is certified "ON Oracle."

PROJECT MANAGEMENT

The following sections describe the project management solutions provided by third-party vendors.

PRIMAVERA SYSTEMS, INC.

Product Name: Primavera Project Planner (P3)

Product Category: Project Management

Contact Name: John Garay

Contact Phone: (610) 949-6922

Contact Email: jgaray@primavera.com

Web Page: http://www.primavera.com

Primavera Project Planner (P3) gives today's project managers and schedulers the one thing they value most: control. As a member of Oracle's Cooperative Applications Initiative (CAI) program, Primavera offers PEAK, an interface between P3 and the Projects module of Oracle Applications. By using the two products together, companies realize the benefits of using best-of-breed products without having to worry about data synchronization. PEAK is a CAI-approved interface.

About Primavera: Primavera delivers innovative software products and services to help customers successfully manage all their projects and resources. As a leading developer of project management software, Primavera stands alone as the only vendor to provide their clients with software for every aspect of the project managing process: risk analysis, large-scale projects, small to mid-size projects, contract management, team communication, remote real-time updating, and so on. With an installed base of more than 100,000 customers, Primavera software operates in a broad range of businesses: manufacturing, construction, information systems, development, engineering, utilities, and telecommunications.

MANTIX SYSTEMS, INC.

Product Name: Cascade PgM

Product Category: Additional Integrated Applications (Program/Project Management)

Contact Name: Tom Isaac

Contact Phone: (703) 904-7969

Contact Email: tisaac@mantix.com

Web Page: http://www.mantix.com

Cascade PgM is a comprehensive suite of software that supports best practice program management by integrating cost, schedule, resource, and time management. It is an enterprisewide system for project-oriented organizations providing top-down control and assignment of targets, budgets, and resources throughout a program. It can also track benefits and link these to associated costs for better business control.

Cascade PgM is completely integrated with Oracle Projects via Oracle's Activity Management Gateway and has been certified on Oracle Applications V10.7 and V11 through Oracle's Cooperative Applications Initiative (CAI) Program. This integration of Cascade PgM and Oracle Projects provides complementary project management (planning, scheduling, budgeting, cost management, resource management, and earned value analysis) and cost accounting functions in a single, integrated business solution. Cascade PgM is also completely integrated with Microsoft Project 98 for detailed scheduling, resource assignments, and activity tracking and statusing.

Product Name: Cascade WEBTime

Product Category: Additional Integrated Applications (Time and Progress Recording)

Contact Name: Tom Isaac

Contact Phone: (703) 904-7969

Contact Email: tisaac@mantix.com

Web Page: http://www.mantix.com

Cascade WEBTime is a Web-based, project-oriented, time and progress recording system. WEBTime is completely integrated with Cascade PgM and Oracle Projects, providing for automatic comparisons of planned and actual hours and dollars at any stage of a project. Work assignments created in Cascade PgM are automatically transferred to each employee's electronic timesheet. Employees then book actual hours against these chargeable tasks and enter progress such as remaining effort or percent complete.

Approved timesheet information is automatically transferred to Oracle Projects via Oracle's external PA transaction interface table, ensuring consistency between the project management and accounting systems.

ARTEMIS MANAGEMENT SYSTEMS

Product Name: Artemis Views

Product Category: Project Management

Contact Name: Patrick Perugini

Contact Phone: (303) 531-3102

Contact Email: patrick_perugini@artemispm.com

Web Page: http://www.artemispm.com

Artemis Views is an enterprise project management software solution that extends the functionality and capability of Oracle Applications. Artemis Views is a set of integrated applications for complex project planning, resource scheduling and tracking, project budgeting and earned value reporting, and executive dashboard-style project analysis and reporting. These applications integrate directly to Oracle Applications through the Oracle Projects Gateway to exchange critical project, resource, and cost data directly with the Oracle Applications system.

As the world's largest project management software vendor and an approved Cooperative Applications Initiative partner, Artemis brings a wealth of project and process management experience to Oracle Applications users. By combining the sophistication of the Artemis Views project management solution with the enterprise capabilities of the Oracle Applications suite, businesses can more accurately and efficiently create, track, and measure their critical projects, budgets, and resources.

ENGINEERING MANAGEMENT

The next section describes the MatrixOne solution for engineering management.

MATRIXONE, INC.

Product Name: Matrix Global Advantage

Product Category: Product Development Management (PDM)

Contact Name: Jim McCallum

Contact Phone: (888) 508-1695

Contact Email: info@matrix-one.com

Web Page: http://www.matrix-one.com

The Matrix Global Advantage product development management (PDM) solution helps companies redefine product development and turn their efforts into unique, competitive advantage. At the core is Matrix, a highly flexible and scalable, Web-centric PDM backbone designed to meet the needs of the largest enterprises. Matrix's support of loosely coupled federated databases is a powerful feature that enables the seamless sharing of Matrix-based information, regardless of its location or data model type, further enhancing access across the enterprise and among supply-chain partners. The product's flexible business modeling provides for the quick mapping and evolution of business definitions, roles, and processes as they change over time.

Implementations are expedited through business applications for domain-specific product development processes such as change, structure and BOM management. Integration to CAD, CAE, viewer mark-up, and visualization applications and other legacy systems are offered, as well as integration to enterprise resource planning (ERP) systems, including Oracle Manufacturing. The Matrix Oracle Manufacturing integration automates the format, sharing, and management of product development information throughout the product lifecycle. This eliminates redundant processes and inconsistencies in BOMs and Item Masters. It also improves workflow across the enterprise.

QUALITY MANAGEMENT

The next section describes the IQS solution for quality management.

IQS, INC.

Product Name: IQS Business System

Product Category: Quality Management

Contact Name: Sales Manager

Contact Phone: (440) 333-1344

Contact Email: sales@iqs.com

Web Page: http://www.iqs.com

The IQS Business System is a powerful and proven solution that offers a unique model for integrating quality systems and Oracle Applications to achieve superior enterprisewide performance. It enables companies to become more competitive and profitable and to achieve and maintain ISO 9000, QS-9000, AS 9000, and ISO 14000 registration faster and at a lower cost than other systems. Instead of being built around the specific characteristics of any one of a number of general and/or industry-specific quality standards, the IQS unique solution is designed around the needs of complex business processes. This unique and comprehensive approach ensures that you meet—and exceed—the quality standards you set out to achieve, as well as improving your productivity, throughput, and revenue.

The model used in building the system begins with functions for managing supplier, customer, and employee information and activities. It continues with components designed to administer documentation relevant to quality systems and manufacturing processes, as well as product data management and analysis and FMEAs. On the operations level, it includes modules for preventative maintenance and gauge calibration, as well as complete inspection, data collection, and reporting with full SPC capabilities. The system provides tracking of nonconformances (NCMs) and the means for issuing and handling corrective actions (CARs). The IQS Business System integrates systemwide audit management capabilities and makes available a number of application-specific modules to help meet PPAP and APQP requirements, common to the automotive industry. Complete quality cost tracking embedded throughout the IQS Business System provides the capability to view the positive results of operational changes that result from continual improvement efforts.

TAXATION

The following sections describe the taxation solutions provided by third-party vendors.

TAX COMPLIANCE, INC.

Product Name: Property Tax Management System (PTMS)

Product Category: Tax Software

Contact Name: Michael Dobbins

Contact Phone: (619) 547-4100 ext. 318

Contact Email: mdobbins@taxcomp.com

Web Page: http://www.taxcomp.com

Tax Compliance, Inc., has developed and supports an easy-to-use, fully automated, property tax software system called Property Tax Management System or PTMS. PTMS handles personal and real property as well as inventory reporting. PTMS imports data from Oracle's Assets Enterprise Solution and creates tax renditions on paper or disk that are guaranteed acceptable to all assessors. Also included is an extensive database of important tax-related information, such as state classifications, percent good tables, and assessor/collector information. The system compares owner's rendered values with assessor's values for easy identification of over-valued assets. PTMS also handles tax payments and creates check requests that can either be printed or exported electronically to accounts payable. Relevant payment information can be imported back into PTMS for complete tax payment tracking. PTMS is currently in use by more than 200 corporations, including Oracle Corporation,

AT&T, Dean Witter Reynolds, Consolidated Freightways, General Motors, The Gymboree Corporation, National City Corporation, Banc One, and Borders Group.

TCI is a Cooperative Applications Initiative (CAI) Partner. Through the Cooperative Applications Initiative, Tax Compliance, Inc., provides its property tax compliance customers with the capability to integrate Oracle Applications with PTMS. The integration between the products is achieved through an exchange of data, enabling a smooth transition of vital asset information via PTMS's built-in import utility. The integration allows Oracle Assets and PTMS to seamlessly exchange information critical to corporate tax departments.

TAXWARE INTERNATIONAL, INC.

Product Name: Company Overview

Product Category: Sales and Use Tax Calculation and Reporting

Contact Name: Suzanne Hawkins, Editorial questions

Contact Phone: (650) 961-4473

Contact Email: suzanneh@taxware.com

Web Page: http://www.taxware.com

TAXWARE International, Inc., (founded in 1964) is a tax software developer of worldwide tax systems. A sales/use tax software pioneer, TAXWARE offers a family of products for mainframe, midrange, and PC computer platforms—including client/server, network computing, and electronic commerce environments. Providing a global tax solution, the company's systems for automated tax compliance include modules that address sales/use, consumer's use, Internet, international taxation, address verification, exemption processing, automated returns, property, and payroll taxes. TAXWARE is privately held with headquarters in Salem, Massachusetts and has regional offices in Los Angeles, Mountain View, Cincinnati, Chicago, Atlanta, and London.

Product Name: TAXWARE SALES/USE Tax System

Product Category: Third Party Sales Tax Application for Oracle Financials

Contact Name: TAXWARE International Marketing Services

Contact Phone: (978) 741-0101

Contact Email: info@taxware.com

Web Page: http://www.taxware.com

The SALES/USE Tax System automatically calculates accurate sales, use, and consumer's use taxes and operates as an integral part of Oracle Financials 10.4.2 and higher. The Tax Master File provides rates for all U.S. tax jurisdictions and Canadian provinces.
TAXWARE's prepopulated Product Taxability Matrix provides for product-specific taxation. Taxware's Tax Management Database (TMD), part of the SALES/USE Tax System, enables users to access tax rate information, as well as verify the last line of the address information

for a given location. In addition, TMD can be used to find a city name for a Zip code, find a Zip code for a city, or verify a Zip code and a city name, as well as being used to retrieve up-to-date tax rate information for sale and use taxes. Using verified address information, a TMD client can retrieve tax rates for state, county, city, or part of city, find information on current and prior tax rates, and verify effective dates for tax rates. STEP (Sales Tax Exemption Processing) optionally interfaces with the SALES/USE Tax System for error-free handling of tax-exempt sale and purchase transactions, generating reports as needed. The STEP System processes, stores, tracks, and maintains tax exemption certificates. The system singles out certificates that are nearing expiration and flags them in advance of the expiration date. STEP enables users to automate tax calculations, allowing decision-making by product, by cost center, by project, or by vendor. Finally, the ReMIT System (Returns Module for International Taxation) produces facsimile tax returns for the most commonly required sales and use tax returns, including key supplemental forms, for each state that it supports. The system accepts data that has been imported from the SALES/USE Tax System or entered directly onto the ReMIT tax return preview screen. ReMIT merges the data with a scanned image of tax return forms. A menu-driven system, ReMIT greatly simplifies and shortens the tax compliance process.

The system, available in both Character Mode and Smart Client or NCA environments, is linked to the Order Entry and Accounts Receivable modules of Oracle Financials. The integration of these products is through a series of open Application Program Interfaces (APIs) that enable Oracle Applications, release 10.4.2 and higher, to transparently access tax rate and address information from TAXWARE during sales transaction processing. TAXWARE, in turn, automatically receives detail transaction information from Oracle Applications for its own auditing and reporting purposes. This tight integration creates a seamless flow of Oracle data across the enterprise and allows instant access to time-critical data with a single point of data entry.

Product Name: TAXWARE INTERNET Tax System

Product Category: Electronic Commerce

Contact Name: Don Burns

Contact Phone: (978) 741-0101

Contact Email: donb@taxware.com

Web Page: http://www.taxware.com

The INTERNET Tax System, which has been benchmark-tested as the fastest processing tax calculation software in the industry, offers Web mall owners and merchants a way to automate the calculation of sales/use and international tax for online transactions in both the Windows and UNIX environments. TAXWARE's INTERNET Tax System for Oracle Internet Commerce Server was designed specifically to run as a cartridge on Oracle's universal server, and when installed, the TAXWARE cartridge can be called automatically via Oracle's interface to TAXWARE. By sending address and product details to TAXWARE, users automatically receive accurate tax rates and amounts for most European and many Asian-Pacific and South American countries.

Based on Zip codes or VAT registration and country code for address verification, the system includes the following functionality: merchant profile creation, customer address verification, exemption processing, product taxation, jurisdiction logic, tax calculation, transaction tracking, nexus administration, and international taxation and reporting with WORLDTAX. WORLDTAX provides compliance with the reporting requirements in over 20 countries for cross-border transactions, detailed calculation for commodities and services, and triangular trade processing.

Product Name: TAXWARE PROPERTY Tax System (PTR)

Product Category: Third Party Property Tax Application for Oracle Fixed Assets

Contact Name: Jack Spicer

Contact Phone: (978) 741-0101

Contact Email: jacks@taxware.com

Web Page: http://www.taxware.com

TAXWARE's PROPERTY Tax System (PTR) is a Windows-based corporate property tax reporting system that enables firms to create property tax reporting renditions valid in almost all U.S. jurisdictions. (PTR-OH produces forms for inter-county and single-county returns and all required rendition attachments in Ohio.) It enables users to create what-if scenarios and management reports and to track real and personal property tax bills. PTR interfaces with fixed asset, spreadsheet, or database systems and provides multiple company and location reporting in all states.

The system is available in both the Character Mode and Smart Client or NCA environments. The integration is enabled by Oracle's Request Center, available with Application Desktop Integrator (ADI) 4.0. Oracle's Request Center provides a user-friendly mechanism to retrieve data from Oracle Assets in a multitude of data formats. The data file is easily configurable by the user to contain specific asset data such as the following: asset number; serial number; tag number; category; description; the date and year the asset was placed in service; the state, county, and city in which the asset is located; asset quantity; asset cost information; general ledger accounts to which the asset is assigned; and so on. This data file can be easily imported into PTR for detailed property tax processing/reporting.

VERTEX, INC.

Product Names: Quantum for Sales and Use Tax, Quantum Returns, Quantum for Payroll Tax, Quantum for Property Tax

Product Category: Tax

Contact Name: Oracle Account Manager

Contact Phone: (610) 640-4200

Contact Email: info@vertexinc.com

Web Page: http://www.vertexinc.com

Vertex and Oracle have partnered to create a complete multistate tax compliance suite that includes sales/use tax, property tax, and payroll tax. The Oracle interfaces to Vertex's Quantum family of solutions mean faster, more efficient, and accurate tax compliance so that tax professionals can focus on more strategic activities. Vertex's full suite of compliance products simplifies relationships with third-party providers.

Oracle Financials is integrated with the PL/SQL version of Quantum for Sales and Use Tax. Quantum automates sales and use tax compliance through the research of rules and rates and the accurate calculation of tax amounts.

Quantum Returns completes the compliance process by automatically importing tax data from a summary file and entering it onto exact replicas of state and locally administered return forms, ready for signature and filing.

Oracle Assets is integrated with Quantum for Property Tax. Quantum automates the property tax compliance process by tracking dates, providing for review and adjustment of property valuations, estimating property tax based on jurisdictional requirements, and generating signature-ready returns. It then compares estimated with actual assessed values and processes tax bills, payments, and billbacks.

Quantum for Payroll Tax is a fully integrated component of the Oracle Human Resource Management System (HRMS). The full integration of these products enables users to transparently calculate and record correct payroll tax amounts during payroll processing.

FEDERAL LIAISON SERVICES, INC.

Product Name: FLS Payroll Tax System, FLS Wage Attachment System

Product Category: Payroll Applications, Tax Applications

Contact Name: Dave Mayo, VP, Sales & Marketing

Contact Phone: (972) 239-8881

Contact Email: dmayo@flsinc.com

Web Page: http://www.FLSPayrollTax.com

Federal Liaison Services, Inc., provides software solutions, outsourcing, and professional services to employers for government reporting and compliance—automating the tasks associated with payroll tax payments and filing, wage garnishment, W-2, and 1099 processing. FLS solutions are Windows-based, Web-enabled, and scalable to enterprises of all sizes.

FLS currently offers two products for the Oracle application platform. The FLS Payroll Tax System provides employers with direct control over their payroll tax responsibilities and automates the preparation of payroll tax deposits and returns. The FLS Wage Attachment

System enables employers to easily comply with changing government regulations for garnishments, protecting privileged information, and eliminating penalties.

AUTOMOTIVE INDUSTRY

The following section describes the manufacturing solution for the automotive industry provided by Radley Corporation.

RADLEY CORPORATION

Product Name: Oracle CARaS

Product Category: Applications—Industrial Vertical-Automotive

Contact Name: Lydia Maes

Contact Phone: (248) 559-6858 ext. 170

Contact Email: lmaes@radley.com

Web Page: http://www.radley.com

Radley has been delivering manufacturing solutions since 1974. The company has grown by implementing turnkey systems (including MRPII and accounting), EDI, automotive release accounting, and bar code data collection solutions for manufacturers and distributors. Radley is a member of the Oracle Business Alliance Program (BAP) as well as the Cooperative Applications Initiative (CAI). Data collection designed for Oracle is ConnectSIP, which utilizes Oracle open API interfaces, Intermec Hardware, and network products and resides on the Oracle host or PC front end.

The most recent version of CARaS (6.3) is designed to extend the capabilities of the Oracle Automotive Demand Management solution to handle the inbound 830/862/866/850/ DELFOR/DELJIT/DELINS EDI translations and do release management of the demand transmitted via EDI. CARaS is a complete CUM management system for the automotive industry and is a third-party product separate from Oracle Applications. However, it is part of the Oracle Automotive solution suite and does share some data with the Oracle Automotive Demand Management Solution. We provide functionality in the following areas: Customer EDI demand is received, translated, and maintained within CARaS. An export function provides this demand to Oracle for all trading partners in a common file format. The 830 material release, 862 shipping schedule, 866 production sequencing, and 850 purchase order transaction sets are translated, demand is calculated, and data is exported from CARaS and loaded into the Oracle demand stream processor. Data flagged as sales orders gets routed to the Order Entry application. Data flagged as Forecast gets routed to the Forecast application. Incoming daily and weekly schedules (ANSI ASC X12 or EDIFACT) are interpreted, taking into consideration trading partner CUMs (or quantities) and in-transit shipments. Standard pack quantities, in-transit times, daily/JIT schedules, and release ship codes are also used to calculate production quantities and shipment dates to meet customers' schedules. When processed, this demand information is exported to the Oracle demand management solution. Extensive reporting, online history, and Automotive style shipping are provided.

This is available with Oracle Automotive, effective with release 11. The inbound 830, 862, and 866 transactions are not supported by the standard Oracle EDI gateway. These transactions can only be received and processed into Oracle when Oracle Automotive has been installed. Oracle CARaS release 6.3 is Y2K-compliant.

PLANNING AND SUPPLY CHAIN MANAGEMENT

The following sectionsdescribe planning and supply chain management solutions available from third-party vendors.

OPTUM, INC.

Product Name: Optum SCE Series

Product Category: Supply Chain

Contact Name: Sally Perkinson

Contact Phone: (800) 561-0462

Contact Email: sperkins@optum.com

Web Page: http://www.optum.com

Optum, Inc., with headquarters in White Plains, N.Y., and offices in Charlotte, NC and Costa Mesa, CA, provides the first strategic supply-chain execution series for manufacturers, distributors, and retailers. Its software integrates demand fulfillment—from order to delivery—optimizing the flow of goods and information through global distribution networks. Optum provides companies with strategic advantage by improving customer responsiveness in logistics and increasing service levels without increasing inventory.

Optum products complement Oracle's applications by addressing the complex requirements for supply-chain execution in manufacturing, retail, and distribution organizations. This integration provides Oracle customers with a leading SCE solution, tightly integrated with Oracle Order Entry, Inventory, Purchasing, Work in Process, and Bills of Material. Optum products are used in a variety of industries, including automotive, electronics and high technology, and consumer and industrial products. Included among the company's customer base are market leaders such as Motorola, Invacare, Russ Berrie, United Natural Foods, Anixter, Caliber Logistics, and Xerox. For additional information, visit Optum on the Web at http://www.optum.com.

MANUGISTICS, INC.

Product Name: Manugistics6

Product Category: Supply Chain Management, Electronic Commerce

Contact Name: Tricia Sale

Contact: Phone: (301) 984-5000

Contact Email: info@manu.com

Web Page: http://www.manugistics.com

Manugistics6 uses customer-centric supply-chain optimization to enable companies to create and optimize their supply chains around their customers. It is quick to implement, adapts easily to change, and delivers rapid results. Manugistics6 includes configurable modules for Network Design and Optimization, Constraint-Based Master Planning, Demand Management, Real-Time ATP+, Distribution Planning, Transportation Management, Manufacturing Planning & Scheduling, Material Planning, Configuration, Collaboration, Monitoring, Measuring, and Open Application Integration.

Manugistics6 is easily integrated with Oracle's ERP applications through a preconfigured integration flow, called an auto plug-in. The auto plug-in utilizes Manugistics Open Application Integration to enable companies to reduce the time, cost, and risk of integration. Manugistics6 is also part of the Oracle CPG solution and is integrated with Oracle Manufacturing as part of Oracle's Cooperative Applications Integration (CAI) program.

PARAGON MANAGEMENT SYSTEMS, INC.

Product Name: Paragon Applications

Product Category: Advanced Planning and Scheduling (APS)/Supply Chain Management (SCM)

Contact Name: Ken Peterson

Contact Phone: (310) 642-2121

Contact Email: kpeterson@paragonms.com

Web Page: http://www.paragonms.com

The Paragon Applications decision-support suite—Global Strategic Planner, Demand Planner, Global Real-time ATP, Supply Chain Planner, Material & Capacity Planner, Reactive & Dynamic Scheduler, and Web-Based Agents—provides a fully certified integration with Oracle Manufacturing Applications. The integration provides small, medium, and large enterprises with a robust solution for supply-chain planning and scheduling, directly linked to the following Oracle Applications: Oracle MPS/MRP, Oracle Inventory, Oracle BOM, Oracle Engineering, Oracle Purchasing, Oracle Order Entry, and Oracle WIP. Paragon's planning and scheduling software, together with Oracle's enterprise resource planning applications, provides an integrated system for global supply-chain management, simultaneous material and capacity planning, real-time ATP/CTP, and operation sequencing. This capability can be deployed to do the following:

- Respond to demand changes

- Perform capacity and material allocation
- Perform real-time quotes and order entries
- Adjust to manufacturing events
- Generate and update purchase requisitions for material supplies
- Dynamically reschedule work-in-progress (WIP) on the shop floor
- Perform real-time ATP/CTP allocation and reallocation based on user-defined business rules

Following is a summary of the functional interfaces between Paragon's APS/SCM system and Oracle Applications.

PARAGON APPLICATIONS AND ORACLE MPS/MRP

Paragon imports a statement of forecast demand in terms of daily, weekly, or periodic time buckets from Oracle's MPS/MRP module. Paragon calculates the consumption of this forecast based on customer orders received from Oracle Order Entry.

PARAGON APPLICATIONS AND ORACLE PURCHASING

Oracle Purchasing provides Paragon with scheduled receipts of supply orders. Paragon determines the available material needed to execute the purchasing plan and directly feeds planned supply orders for those material requirements to Oracle Purchasing through purchase requisitions. Paragon can also automatically modify or cancel existing purchase requisitions contained in the Oracle Purchasing system.

PARAGON APPLICATIONS AND ORACLE WIP

Oracle WIP provides Paragon with both planned and actual data for work-in-process. Paragon generates optimal work orders based on planned objectives and forwards these work orders automatically to Oracle WIP. Paragon can also cancel, reschedule, or insert new work orders into Oracle WIP. Paragon schedules each operation needed to execute the job called out in the work order and communicate its schedule to Oracle WIP.

PARAGON APPLICATIONS AND ORACLE ORDER ENTRY

Customer orders are communicated from Oracle Order Entry to Paragon. Paragon results can be used to determine accurate and reliable promise dates and to support customer service in providing status updates on orders as well as early warning notifications to customers.

PARAGON APPLICATIONS AND ORACLE INVENTORY

Oracle Inventory provides Paragon with the Item Master, on-hand inventory, safety stock requirements, and organizational department information. Paragon uses this information to perform a supply/demand and netting calculation to determine the exact requirements for manufacturing.

PARAGON APPLICATIONS AND ORACLE BOM/ENGINEERING

Paragon imports resource definitions, resource calendars, bill-of-material, and routing information from Oracle BOM. The Paragon interface then builds manufacturing methods matching the appropriate BOM and routing alternatives and revisions (from Oracle Engineering).

I2 TECHNOLOGIES, INC.

Product Name: RHYTHM Factory Planner, RHYTHM Demand Planner, and RHYTHM Supply Chain Planner

Product Category: Additional Integrated Applications

Contact Name: Norm Mueller

Contact Phone: (847) 685-8008

Contact Email: norman_mueller@i2.com

Web Page: http://www.i2.com

i2 Technologies, Inc., is the leading developer of supply-chain optimization and decision support solutions. i2's solutions are in use across a variety of industries, including consumer packaged goods, automotive, metals, high technology, and electronics. The RHYTHM family of solutions provides complete supply-chain management from sourcing and manufacturing to distribution, logistics, and transportation planning. i2's comprehensive product development strategy for providing solutions across the total business enterprise is known as eBusiness Process Optimization (eBPO). With eBPO, i2's widely used RHYTHM product suite is being expanded in response to the requirements of high-velocity businesses that want to accelerate their business cycles, from customer to supplier.

i2 and Oracle have a joint development and worldwide distribution partnership to deliver Architected Best in Class capability for advanced supply-chain planning as part of Oracle Applications. The seamless integration of Oracle's enterprise applications with i2's advanced planning tools yields an industry first: enabling ERP customers with complex planning requirements to make real-time optimization decisions. The Oracle/i2 RHYTHM alliance delivers a broad solution that integrates all operational elements of an enterprise, from product development to the management of the entire supply chain. Oracle's RHYTHM solution enables companies to generate significant economic value through increased market share, higher quality and productivity, streamlined business operations, and lower costs. As an integral part of Oracle's Application solution suite, i2's unique portfolio of supply-chain solutions provides comprehensive, intelligent support for planning and scheduling functions across both inter-enterprise and intra-enterprise supply chains, bringing unique capabilities to the market, including Real Time Available-To-Promise, Constraint Based Planning, and Integrated Advanced Scheduling.

WAREHOUSE AND DISTRIBUTION MANAGEMENT

The following sections describe warehouse and distribution management solutions available from third-party vendors.

CATALYST INTERNATIONAL

Product Name: Catalyst WMS

Product Category: Warehouse & Distribution Center Management Applications

Contact Name: Scott Rishel

Contact Phone: (414) 362-6723

Contact Email: srishel@mke.catalystwms.com

Web Page: http://www.catalystwms.com

The Catalyst Warehouse Management System (WMS) is a client/server based solution designed to increase productivity, inventory accuracy, and customer service within the warehouse and distribution center. The system provides new insights into managing your personnel, space, and equipment, thus enabling you to control and monitor every operation within your warehouse. As a full-functioning WMS solution, the system supports receiving, put away, inventory management, picking, and loading all in real-time, utilizing the latest bar code and radio frequency technology. Along with the preceding functionality, Catalyst provides advanced functionality such as transaction history analysis, advanced wave planning and order selection, yard management, task interleaving, cycle counting, opportunistic cross-docking, and value-added processing, including kiting and QA processes.

The integration between the products is achieved through a series of Application Program Interfaces (APIs), which enables rapid data access between the applications leveraging a single point of data maintenance. The integration allows Oracle Applications and Catalyst Warehouse Management System to seamlessly provide information critical to warehouse management system customers. This integration supports interfaces between Oracle Supply Chain, Oracle Financials, and Oracle Manufacturing.

TRW INTEGRATED SUPPLY CHAIN SOLUTIONS

Product Name: Logistics Execution Systems

Product Category: Logistics Execution Systems

Contact Name: MARC Sales

Contact Phone: (800) 876-3667

Contact Email: MARC@trw.com

Web Page: http://www.trw.com/MARC

TRW's LES (Logistics Execution Systems) offers a complete suite of packaged warehouse management and logistics products under the MARC (Material and Resource Control) logo. Our MARC-CS (Configured Solution) and MARC-ES (Engineered Solution) are standard WMS packages that can be easily configured and tailored to meet unique warehouse or distribution requirements. All TRW MARC products utilize the latest in RF and Automatic ID technologies and easily integrate with automated material-handling equipment and logistics subsystems for complete end-to-end warehouse control. MARC systems communicate to ERP or legacy host systems and support version migratable interfaces to Oracle, SAP, BAAN, QAD, PeopleSoft, and other host applications. TRW's MARC systems have been proven across multiple industries, including pharmaceuticals, automotive, retail, apparel, publishing, catalog/mail order, grocery, food, semiconductors, consumer packaged goods, and utilities. TRW provides multiple system implementation and customer support packages, including 24-hour, 7-day support. The hardware used to support the MARC systems is DEC VAX DEC Alpha, HP 9000, IBM RS/6000, and Sun Solaris in conjunction with UNIX or VMS/Open VMS and IBM operating systems. MARC-ES and MARC-CS are the cornerstones of the MARC product family.

Complementary products, such as MARC-Vision (Decision Support), MARC-WC (Warehouse Control), MARC-RM (Resource Management), MARC-ConfiguratorPlus, MARC-Customs, MARC-LS (Labor Standards), MARC-AC (Accounts), and MARC-MN (Monitor), offer value-added solutions that differentiate TRW from its competitors.

GENCO DISTRIBUTION SYSTEM

Product Name: R-Log

Product Category: Reverse Logistics

Contact Name: Don Rombach

Contact Phone: (412) 820-3752

Contact Email: don127@genco.com

Web Page: http://www.genco.com

GENCO Distribution System's R-Log software package is an Oracle-based application that efficiently handles the processing of returned goods. The R-Log package is the most sophisticated of its type, including modules for receiving, scanning put-away, shipping, management reporting, and disposition management. GENCO's installed base of the R-Log Package includes industry leaders such as Wal-Mart, Sears, Kmart, Target, and many other retailers.

CIM VISION INTERNATIONAL

Product Name: CIM+ Warehouse Management System

Product Category: Integrated Applications—Warehouse Management

Contact Name: Carl Hunt

Contact Phone: (562) 951-8000

Contact Email: carl@cimvision.com

Web Page: http://www.cimvision.com

With a rules-based architecture, the CIM+ Warehouse Management System supports a high degree of flexibility and intelligent messaging for warehouse personnel. It utilizes paperless processing for Oracle Applications by using RF handheld units to automate material receipts, put-away, picking, and palletizing processes.

Product Name: CIM+ Manufacturing Execution System

Product Category: Integrated Applications—Manufacturing Execution

Contact Name: Carl Hunt

Contact Phone: (562) 951-8000

Contact Email: carl@cimvision.com

Web Page: http://www.cimvision.com

This system supports real-time dispatching, labor management, quality control, product tracking, and genealogy for Oracle Applications. Information is provided for comprehensive serial or lot control with dynamic label generation for product identification. Information collected on scrap, machine time, rework, and actual labor provide for more accurate productivity and cost analysis.

Product Name: CIM+ Time & Attendance

Product Category: Integrated Applications—Time and Attendance

Contact Name: Carl Hunt

Contact Phone: (562) 951-8000

Contact Email: carl@cimvision.com

Web Page: http://www.cimvision.com

Collect and manage Oracle Applications time-based data in real-time. Perform employee scheduling and attendance tracking with a flexible architecture that can adapt to processing your organization's Oracle Applications payroll. This system also supports interfaces to other leading payroll systems.

Product Name: CIM+ Bar Code Data Collection

Product Category: Integrated Applications—Bar Code Middleware

Contact Name: Carl Hunt

Contact Phone: (562) 951-8000

Contact Email: carl@cimvision.com

Web Page: http://www.cimvision.com

Oracle Applications transactions are automated with badges, bar code documents, and labels. Our open architecture supports multiple data collection equipment providers and offers configurable data collection prompts in a Windows point-and-click environment. User-defined label formats can be triggered to print out dynamically while performing specific Oracle Applications transactions.

Manhattan Associates

Product Name: PkMS

Product Category: Warehouse Management Systems

Contact Name: Michelle Houde

Contact Phone: (770) 955-5533 ext. 1530

Contact Email: mhoude@manhattanassociates.com

Web Page: http://www.manhattanassociates.com

We're removing the barriers to peak performance—the drag on business velocity that occurs when your supply chain doesn't work cohesively. With our total systems solution, the supply chain moves faster to meet customer demands. By synchronizing information flow, we're helping industries creatively collaborate to make the supply chain seamless and efficient for everyone. Ask our clients—over 375 industry leaders representing more than $200 billion in global annual shipments. We've helped them set new standards of performance in the world marketplace. They've achieved new levels of supply-chain integration and competitive advantage—reaping the benefits of moving information and products through the supply chain more efficiently and more rapidly. Supply-chain momentum is building, and Manhattan Associates is a driving force.

Today's distribution center is more than just a storage facility that manages inventory levels, customer orders, labor productivity, and material handling/packaging equipment. It must now manage value-added services, as well as capture and communicate information throughout the increasingly complex supply chain. Today, you need a supply-chain execution system that reaches far beyond the four walls of your distribution facility, integrating the movement of information and product to meet customer demand and helping you comply with supply-chain industry initiatives to increase product momentum. You need Manhattan Associates' PkMS warehouse management solution to help you put the information gears in motion, building momentum throughout a community of manufacturers, distributors, retailers, suppliers, transportation providers, and customers.

REPORTING ENHANCEMENTS AND BUSINESS INTELLIGENCE

The following sections describe the solutions for reporting enhancements and business intelligence available from third-party vendors.

ARIS SOFTWARE

Product Name: NoetixDW

Product Category: Enhanced Reporting

Contact Name: Lisa Robinson

Contact Phone: (425) 372-2721

Contact Email: lisa.robinson@aris.com

Web Page: http://www.noetix.com

NoetixDW adds value to Oracle Application installations by simplifying the task of implementing a data warehouse. On the Oracle Application server, NoetixDW builds a set of data-warehouse-ready views that can then be used as the data source for third-party data warehouse tools. Data warehouse designers no longer need to understand the complicated structure of the Oracle Application data. With NoetixDW, many data warehousing factors are taken into consideration including security, aggregation, performance, and functional value. Whether your implementation is a data warehouse or an OLAP server, NoetixDW views can be used as the data source greatly reducing the cost of a new data warehouse project.

Product Name: NoetixViews

Product Category: Enhanced Reporting

Contact Name: Lisa Robinson

Contact Phone: (425) 372-2721

Contact Email: lisa.robinson@aris.com

Web Page: http://www.noetix.com

The NoetixViews product line adds value to Oracle Application installations by organizing complicated underlying data into business views that enable you to quickly roll out decision support solutions. NoetixViews eliminates the need for the end user to have knowledge of database relationships, complex joins, and flexfield values. During installation, the Noetix-Views online Help is automatically generated and is tailored to each Oracle Application configuration. The online Help explains the type of information found in each view. The examples in online Help instruct the user on which views to select for the desired information. Online Help also assists the end user with query construction by providing hints on how to properly build a query step-by-step. Additionally, indexed columns are clearly identified, helping to produce optimal query times. The end user can employ his favorite query or reporting tool to access a view along with the online Help and gain access to meaningful business information quickly and easily.

In summary, NoetixViews provides the following benefits:

- Easy information access for fast rollout of end user and ad-hoc reporting.

- Automatic customization of the business views and online help to reflect your unique Oracle Application implementation.

- Online Help & Hints guide you to the answers you need.

- Optimized views return results quickly.

- Can be used with any query or reporting tool.

- Automatic upgrade protection keeps pace with Oracle Application releases.

- Supports char-mode, SC, NCA. Release 9-11.

CorVu Corporation

Product Name: CorVu Integrated Business Intelligence Suite

Product Category: Business Intelligence/Balanced Scorecard

Contact Name: Alan Missroon

Contact Phone: (770) 993-5995

Contact Email: amissroon@corvu.com

Web Page: http://www.corvu.com

Combining end user query, production reporting, executive alerting, OLAP analysis, forecasting, what-if analysis (simulated business modeling), balanced scorecard, and business performance management applications, CorVu provides the only complete and fully integrated business intelligence solution for the Oracle community. The latest version of CorVu's Balanced Scorecard offers direct connectivity to the database, communication, feedback, integration of quantitative and qualitative measures, direct input of performance results, and object-oriented design. In addition, this functionality can be deployed over the Web via CorVu's Web server.

Product Name: CorVu Balanced Scorecard Gold Edition

Product Category: Balanced Scorecard

Contact Name: Alan Missroon

Contact Phone: (770) 993-5995

Contact Email: amissroon@corvu.com

Web Page: http://www.corvu.com

The Balanced Scorecard Gold Edition offers a powerful framework for measuring and analyzing business performance. In fact, with the exception of a live database connection, it provides features similar to that of CorVu's flagship Platinum Edition. Among others, these include the following:

- Integration of both quantitative and qualitative measures
- Robust communication facilities
- Component-based scorecard design
- Integration with desktop and Web applications
- Flexible performance target settings
- Comparative performance analysis
- Ease of use

CorVu has exerted great effort and care to provide the simplest and most intuitive environment for scorecard development and deployment. Complete with extensive "bubble help" facilities, the Gold Edition employs standard Windows drag-and-drop.

DecisionPoint Applications

Product Name: DecisionPoint

Product Category: Packaged Data Warehouse

Contact Name: Marc Demarest, CEO

Contact Phone: (503) 768-3612

Contact Email: marc@dpapplications.com

Web Page: http://www.dpapplications.com

DecisionPoint Applications, Inc., is the market leader in packaged data warehousing applications. DP Application's DecisionPoint family of packaged data warehouse environments materially improve the quality, speed, and effectiveness of decision-making processes. The DecisionPoint product family provides customers with pre-integrated, end-to-end, data warehousing infrastructure and applications, installed in eight weeks or less at a fixed cost and with guaranteed returned business value.

The enterprisewide decision support systems combine the following:

- Speed, simplicity, and legibility of a data mart
- Scalability, robustness, and extensibility of an enterprisewide data warehouse
- Ease-of-use of integrated OLAP tools

The DecisionPoint product family provides commercial organizations committed to providing decision makers with integrated, fully-extensible enterprisewide data warehousing infrastructure that can be deployed in weeks at a fixed cost with returned business value. Guaranteed.

THE END OF THE DATA DEFICIT

The fiduciary data set—detailed operational data that the firm uses to report to external regulatory agencies, its shareholders, trading partners, and internal organizations—ought to be the basis of every enterprisewide commercial decision support system or data warehouse. Yet, this kind of detailed data, across industries, is the most difficult kind of data for decision-makers to obtain.

To solve the data deficit, the DecisionPoint product family does the following:

- Extracts the detailed financial, human resources, and distribution data stored in ERP production environments such as Oracle, PeopleSoft, SAP, and heritage systems.

- Automatically extracts, cleanses, and reformats those data sets, in all their detail and richness, using intelligent DecisionPoint Source Experts.

- Stores those data sets in query-ready DecisionPoint Analytical Domains in the DecisionPoint Warehouse on an enterprise DSS server that is based on industry-leading relational database management system technology, and that includes complete metadata management and graphical operations and management (O&M) interfaces.

- Exposes those Analytical Domains, subject to security profiles, to any ODBC-compliant desktop DSS tool, as well as making data in analytical domains available to proprietary multidimensional OLAP tools.

Rather than complicating the decision support systems problem by introducing yet another stove-piped technology component that requires integration, management, and support resources, the DecisionPoint product family offers a complete, end-to-end, pre-integrated data warehousing infrastructure, prebuilt data extraction and cleansing technology, predefined analytical domains, and preconstructed client/server access, at a fraction of the cost of custom-built and integrated data warehouses. Because DecisionPoint is a pre-integrated, packaged data warehousing infrastructure, it can be installed and in production in any organization in eight weeks or less.

PHOENIX SOLUTIONS

Product Name: WorkBench

Product Category: System/Database Management

Contact Name: Mark Wittkopp

Contact Phone: (678) 443-9359 ext. 204

Contact Email: karraUD@msn.com

Web Page: http://www.phoenix-solutions.com

MarketsManager provides the analytical tools to respond to market/business trends and opportunities by putting the entire market process in one place. The Phoenix MarketsManager enables the qualifications, targeting, and management of Sales/Marketing programs and tracks customers through the whole process, including operations, contracts, billing, and collections. It provides the company with the capability to use both internal and external data, providing the complete availability of data necessary to manage projects and help personnel focus on relationship management. It provides access to data so different groups can use the same data to perform different functions.

HUMMINGBIRD COMMUNICATIONS LTD.

Product Name: BI/Suite

Product Category: Business Intelligence

Contact Name: Lucinda Brommersma

Contact Phone: (613) 548-4355

Contact Email: `lbrommersma@kingston.hummingbird.com`

Web Page: `http://www.hummingbird.com`

BI/Suite, the Hummingbird business intelligence product offering, enables end users to access and analyze information stored in transactional databases, data marts, and data warehouses both on and off the Web. BI/Suite includes the following:

- BI/Query, an enterprise query and reporting application
- BI/Web, a thin client solution for performing query and reporting tasks on the Web
- BI/Analyze, an enterprise OLAP application that enables users to analyze information in multidimensional databases to spot trends, relationships, and patterns in their business
- BI/Broker, an enterprise application server designed to provide scheduling, security, distribution, notification, and centralized administration services to all of Hummingbird's business intelligence applications

BI/Suite offers organizations a complete, integrated, enterprise business intelligence solution with the lowest cost of ownership.

Hummingbird delivers end user access to Oracle Applications data. The combination of Hummingbird business intelligence and Oracle Applications data gives users the capability to query, report, and do sophisticated analysis of strategic data collected through Oracle Applications. With the graphical interface of both Hummingbird BI/Query and BI/Analyze, business users can query and analyze Oracle data to answer critical business questions and make informed decisions. The tools enable the dissemination of valuable data to the entire corporation, not just IT staff or front-line application users.

PRINTING AND OUTPUT ENHANCEMENT

The following sections describe solutions for printing and output enhancement available from third-party vendors.

SIGFORMS

Product Name: Jetform Central 5.2 and Design 5.2

Product Category: Electronic Forms

Contact Name: Randy Steyer

Contact Phone: (800) 338-3676

Contact Email: Randys@sigforms.com

Web Page: http://www.sigforms.com

Within the Standard Oracle Applications, users are unable to customize their forms output. Application users can now eliminate the rising costs of preprinted forms and custom programming changes and have the flexibility to make changes and control the appearance and format of business documents. SigForms provides a software-integrated solution for production laser printing that enables an Oracle Application user to create any type of customized documents, forms, checks, reports, and bar codes. This solution has several unique advantages: The software is server-based, requires no reprogramming of Oracle, and has the capability to create dynamic forms. This feature is ideal for multiple-page documents and multiple PC forms per page and provides a very professional, highly customized look. The check-printing solution requires no special printers, keeps secure measures intact, and automatically applies conditional signatures and logos. Bar coding printing supports all major formats, prints multiple bar codes per page, and is dynamically driven by data. All customer's Oracle forms are printed to laser printers on blank laser paper.

SigForms provides solutions to meet your global needs in the event that you require multiple languages, multiple logs, previewing of the documents, or back-printing of multiple terms and conditions. Consulting services by SigForms can customize the suite of products to produce individualized forms that generate the look and feel on your desired forms. (A client also has the ability to create or customize their forms through the PC design tool.) After receipt of specific customer data streams, the trained consultants provide rapid-prototyping of forms to the customer. The final forms can be implemented remotely or onsite at the customer's facility. This robust electronic form solution, combined with the expertise of the SigForms consultants, provides an end-to-end form solution that completes your automated ERP implementation.

STR SOFTWARE COMPANY

Product Name: FaxCommander for Oracle Applications

Product Category: Document Delivery (Fax and Email)

Contact Name: Gretchen Moen, Marketing Manager

Contact Phone: (804) 897-1600 ext. 111

Contact Email: gretchen@strsoftware.com

Web Page: http://www.strsoftware.com

STR Software Company offers FaxCommander for Oracle Applications, a scalable document delivery solution for UNIX systems. With FaxCommander for Oracle Applications, users can fax or email any document that they can print. FaxCommander automates the delivery of mission-critical documents such as purchase orders, order acknowledgements, and more. The user simply selects a report, enters the fax or email parameters, and submits the request to the concurrent manager. The concurrent manager runs the report in the background and then "prints" the output to FaxCommander.

Integration with forms packages, one-button faxing, and batch transmission capability are included in this full-featured solution that follows Oracle Applications coding standards. By faxing and emailing mission-critical documents from Oracle Applications, companies save time and money while increasing productivity. To help guarantee these results, STR Software Company offers the FaxCommander Pilot Program, a 30-day, risk-free evaluation of FaxCommander for Oracle Applications.

OPTIO SOFTWARE, INC.

Product Name: OptioDCS (Document Customization Server)

Product Category: Output Customization, Output Management, Electronic Forms, and Document Customization

Contact Name: Kim George

Contact Phone: (770) 283-8500 ext. 576

Contact Email: Kimg@optiosoftware.com

Web Page: http://www.optiosoftware.com

As a certified CAI partner for Oracle releases 10.7 and 11.0, Optio Software provides Oracle Applications users with a rules-based document formatting and delivery solution. Available for Windows NT, UNIX, and AS/400 environments, OptioDCS (Document Customization Server) accepts standard print streams generated by Oracle Applications, enabling the creation of custom documents without custom programming. Built-in, rules-based intelligence enables users to produce and deliver customized business and production documents based on the business processes and requirements.

Oracle Applications users can create, customize, electronically deliver, and access mission-critical documents and automatically deliver documents via multiple output devices, including departmental laser or thermal printers, fax servers, email systems, the Internet, or desktops. Users increase enterprise efficiency and improve business processes through gaining control over the appearance and delivery of Oracle Application output. Through the seamless integration with Oracle Applications, users are ensured rapid, on-time implementations, scalable systems, improved portability, and increased flexibility to support dynamic, ever-changing business requirements.

Product Name: OptioFAX

Product Category: Fax Server/Output Customization/Output Management

Contact Name: Kim George

Contact Phone: (770) 283-8500

Contact Email: Kimg@optiosoftware.com

Web Page: http://www.optiosoftware.com

Optio Software, a certified CAI partner for Oracle releases 10.7 and 11.0, provides Oracle Applications users with a high-performance UNIX and Windows NT-based facsimile software system—OptioFAX. The solution enables users to automate the process of sending, receiving, viewing, and routing faxed business documents right from the desktop—without any changes to Oracle Applications. Ideal for enterprises with high fax volumes, OptioFAX includes such features as fax broadcast, annotation, multiple "phone book" creation/storage, and built-in diagnostics and reporting to monitor and manage faxes across an organization. OptioFAX integrates seamlessly with OptioDCS, enabling you to automatically fax customized documents created from DCS without ever having to print a hardcopy, helping to improve productivity throughout the organization and optimizing the output of Oracle Application information. OptioFAX can also be used as a standalone faxing solution.

Product Name: OptioDesigner

Product Category: Output Customization, Output Management, Electronic Forms, and Document Customization

Contact Name: Kim George

Contact Phone: (770) 283-8500 ext. 576

Contact Email: Kimg@optiosoftware.com

Web Page: http://www.optiosoftware.com

OptioDesigner from Optio Software, a certified CAI Partner on releases 10.7 and 11.0 for output customization, is a Windows-based graphical user interface (GUI), providing easy creation of document and report templates. OptioDesigner, used in conjunction with OptioDCS, offers unparalleled flexibility in designing and individualizing the appearance of important documents produced from Oracle Applications. The interface provides the ability to easily integrate graphical content, such as bar codes, diagrams, and logos, with output from Oracle Applications, giving users complete automatic document layout capabilities.

ACOM COMPUTER, INC.

Product Name: ACOM Integrated Check Processing Solution

Product Category: Integrated Applications

Contact Name: Bill Cropley

Contact Phone: (800) 347-3638

Contact Email: bcropley@acom.com

Web Page: http://www.acom.com

Integrated MICR Laser Check Processing Solutions from ACOM provide accounting and payroll departments with significantly enhanced security, efficiency, and control. They also satisfy "Ordinary Care" standards of the Uniform Commercial Code (UCC) for avoidance of liability in the event of check fraud. ACOM's integrated solutions generate the entire check, including company and payee information, logos, amounts, MICR lines and signatures, on blank safety-check stock, in a single pass through a MICR-enhanced laser printer. ACOM is a single-source vendor of check processing solutions, providing not only the systems, but also secure check stock and supplies for ongoing operations.

ACOM solutions are fully compatible with Oracle business management software and are comprised of both software and hardware. QuickCheck check-processing software receives check files from the database, formats them using stored electronic check forms, and spools them out to one or more MICR laser printers for production. The QuickForm forms design module enables users to create or modify electronic check forms quickly and easily. A comprehensive selection of midrange MICR-enhanced network laser printers provides performance rates of from 17 to 40 pages per minute. Stuffer-sealer equipment enables automated postprocessing. ACOM offers its own line of Secure-A-Check safety check stock, with several types of security features available, and laser printer consumables. Maintenance contracts are available.

FRx SOFTWARE CORPORATION

Product Name: Visual Financial Reporting

Product Category: Enhanced Reporting

Contact Name: Wendy Barnhart

Contact Phone: (303) 741-8000

Contact Email: wbarnhart@frxsoft.com

Web Page: http://www.frxsoft.com

FRx is an advanced Visual Financial Reporting software application that interfaces with leading ERP and accounting systems. FRx features automatic creation of complex financial reports with rollups through multiple reporting hierarchies. The FRx DrillDown Viewer enables users to drill from summary financial information to underlying transaction detail. Presentation quality reports can be printed, exported to spreadsheets, or emailed for remote viewing or printing. FRx Report Servers provide high-throughput production financial reporting. Multicompany consolidations are easily accomplished, even when companies use different account structures, fiscal years, or accounting systems. FRx is used in over 65,000 sites worldwide and provides a direct interface to over 30 leading accounting systems.

DATALINE SYSTEMS

Product Name: RTD 5000 Series

Product Category: Addition Integrated Applications

Contact Name: Scott Hunt

Contact Phone: (770) 992-6144 ext. 228

Contact Email: shunt@dlsys.com

Web Page: http://dlsys.com

Dataline's RTD 5000 suite of software provides Oracle users an easy-to-use output development and management system. RTD 5000 provides Oracle users a powerful set of development tools that enables companies to create electronic documents for laser printing or for electronic distribution. This includes the ability to create forms and graphics and to reformat the existing data. The data can be a delimited data file, a CRLF (Print Image file), or a file acquired using SQL queries. Users can develop dynamic forms by testing the Oracle Application data for certain conditions and building the form based on those rules. RTD 5000 enables Oracle users to implement data-driven forms.

Dataline's RTD 5000 suite includes an output server (DARTServer). DARTServer is used to automate the output process. Just as the RTD 5000 Development System can create data-driven forms, the RTD 5000 DARTServer provides data-driven distribution. The RTD 5000/DARTServer contains the electronic forms library with all resources. The data generated by your Oracle Application system determines the form to be used, the output device, and the location. The RTD 5000 Output Server (DARTServer) supports Postscript/PCL, PDF, or HTML, enabling users to output to printers, COLD, email, or Internet servers.

BOTTOMLINE TECHNOLOGIES, INC.

Product Name: PayBase Payment Management Software

Product Category: Oracle Product Enhancement—Financials

Contact Name: Suzanne Hurt

Contact Phone: (603) 436-0700 ext. 5203

Contact Email: shurt@bottomline.com

Web Page: http://www.bottomline.com

PayBase Payment Management software is a full, 32-bit product that enables organizations to manage all their payments across the enterprise and access payment data from a single, comprehensive database. Utilizing a modular design, PayBase does the following: creates laser checks, supported by full-function Check Fraud Avoidance (positive pay); produces NACHA-compliant electronic payments, including both ACH and financial EDI; and offers electronic remittance advice delivery; all from the same payment file. Full-system security, a comprehensive audit trail, and reporting are also components of PayBase.

Specific features of each module include the following:

- Laser Check prints A/P and payroll checks, as well as any year-end requirements (W-2s and 1099s), using blank stock.

- Two forms of check recovery are supported in PayBase: printer restart and log spoil/secure reprint, done by individual check instead of rerunning the entire file.

- The sort feature reformats a data file from any sequence without changing original data file.

- Manual or on-demand checks can be requested locally or from any authorized remote site.

- You can maintain multiple bank accounts, change the account for different check runs, switch bank, logo, signature and MICR information dynamically during the run.

- Check Fraud Avoidance (Positive Pay) receives files from non-PayBase applications for the central storage of all issued checks.

- The wizard helps build interface to major banking institutions.

- Integral communications software automates transfer of information to the bank.

- A complete modem setup and configuration simplifies operation.

- Data is reformatted to meet the bank's required specifications.

- You can receive files from the bank to compare issued with cashed checks; include stops, manuals, and voids; and use "appends" to enable multifile transfer with a single bank communication.

- Electronic Payments is a single system that creates both ACH and more complicated financial EDI payments.

- Creation of NACHA standard electronic payment files accepted through the national ACH network is possible.

- The software supports large and variable length addenda records in a single transaction.

- The optional ability is available to translate an FEDI payment record for mapping to A/R system.

- Electronic Remittance Advice Delivery is a single system that delivers remittance advice as email, fax, or in printed format.

- The integral database houses recipient information.

- On-the-fly updating of the database can be done from the payment file.
- Email deliveries can be encrypted.

EVERGREEN DATA SYSTEMS

Product Name: LaserForms.Plus

Product Category: Electronic Document Solution

Contact Name: Andee Chin

Contact Phone: (800) 248-2898

Contact Email: andee@evergrn.com

Web Page: http://www.evergrn.com

Add powerful new electronic document management functions for your Oracle reports. In addition to printing your reports on demand on plain paper, LaserForms.Plus can automatically fax and email Oracle documents directly from your workstation, saving time and money. Print AP Checks on demand for the latest in convenience, cost-savings, and security.

LaserForms.Plus eliminates the expense and hassle of obsolete forms. When your enterprise changes, whether it's a new logo or a reengineered workflow, Evergreen can remotely update your LaserForms.Plus system for the latest in convenience, cost-savings, and security.

Product Name: IntelliFlow

Product Category: Integrated Software Application

Contact Name: W. Miller

Contact Phone: (702) 365-9755 ext. 111

Contact Email: wmiller@synapsis.com

Web Page: http://www.synapsis.com/Pages/IntFlo1.htm

IntelliFlow is an enterprisewide e-forms automation solution for managing documents and forms. It utilizes email transport across TCP/IP networks and PPP-based modem remote clients. The client/server architecture supports clients on various Windows platforms and supports both NT and UNIX servers. The system uses an Oracle RDBMS for document storage and management and manages data, voice, forms, and email as documents.

IntelliFlow supports conventional as well as Web-based forms distributed and processed as email forms. This allows workflow to be managed with data-capture geographically disbursed. Fixed and mobile clients can input and manage forms data against back-end Oracle databases. IntelliFlow subsystems include forms, document management, email, security, and workflow management. Digital signatures and encryption provide secure access for e-commerce usage.

PART V

APPENDIXES

THE ORACLE EMPLOYMENT MARKET

INTRODUCTION

The employment market for skilled Oracle professionals has been quite robust throughout the 1990s. To understand the Oracle market, you must first understand what the varied skills that establish a person as an Oracle professional are. It is interesting to see how the demands for Oracle professionals have changed over time.

Recall that Oracle Corporation changed information system departments within corporate America, and throughout the world, by creating superior relational database products and tools. Many companies, such as SAP and PeopleSoft, approached the information technology market by building solid HRMS, Manufacturing, and Financial applications that were built on a relational database. The relational database of choice was often Oracle.

Thus, there were heavy technical "roots" in the early Oracle professionals. These individuals often were known for strong database administration skills. They had to understand how to manage the intense database system requirements of products that were created by companies such as SAP and PeopleSoft. In addition, strong data architecting (modeling skills) were needed for customizations to these products.

Next, Oracle Corporation began to make an aggressive push into the applications market, most notably in the financial area. Based on the success of Oracle Financial applications, Oracle began creating Manufacturing applications and finally Human Resource Management System (HRMS) applications.

This push by Oracle into the packaged application solutions market created new opportunities for IT professionals. A new need arose for functional consultants who understood the business issues of a financial institution. For instance, accounting professionals were needed to help provide advice regarding the configuration of the Oracle Financial products. Technical consultants were needed to prepare customizations, write reports, and write trigger code at the form and database level for specific Oracle Applications. These technical consultants became proficient in SQL (structured query language), PL/SQL (procedural SQL), and SQL*Loader.

This created a new distinction in identifying skills for an "Oracle professional". The skills of the functional accountant are fairly easy to distinguish from the skills of a technical database administrator (DBA). However, there was now a new classification of technical skills that had arisen. These were technical experts who had obtained a thorough understanding of the exact tables and table relationships within and between the various Oracle Application modules. The database administrator was no longer the only type of technical Oracle professional. Whereas the DBA might often have had the technical expertise to become a strong technical Oracle Applications professional, the DBA often found that she did not have time to become an expert of both disciplines. Thus, technical Application experts emerged.

The problem-solving products most commonly used by the technical Application experts were Oracle Forms and Oracle Reports. Many technical application specialists took their knowledge of the Oracle tools and transitioned fairly easily in problem solving between the various Oracle Financial modules. Additionally, the database schemas among the various

Oracle Financial modules were very similar. It was, and still is, common for a strong Oracle Accounts Receivable or Fixed Asset expert to become proficient on Oracle General Ledger or Accounts Payable in a short amount of time.

During the second half of '90s, Oracle Corporation threw a curve ball at the packaged applications industry with the creation of the Oracle Human Resources Management Suite. This is described as a curve ball because intricacy of the database design was more complex than the Oracle Financial modules. The emergence of Oracle HRMS created two new types of experts: functional HRMS professionals and technical HRMS professionals. Thus, at this point, it would be fair to classify the different types of Oracle Professionals as follows:

Database Administrators

Technical Financial/Manufacturing Experts

Technical Human Resource Management System Experts

Functional Manufacturing Experts

Functional Financial Experts

Functional Human Resource Management System Experts

The question often arises: Why is Oracle HRMS so much more complex? For starters, the Oracle HRMS development created a new approach to interfaces for data conversion and migration. Previous Oracle Applications used "Interface" tables to receive and provide import for data. The Oracle HRMS Applications included numerous application program interfaces (APIs).

However, the HRMS technical complexity did not stop there. Understanding the Oracle HR tables is not overly difficult, but understanding the Oracle Payroll tables is. Many strong technical Oracle Financial developers discovered that a significant learning curve exists in Oracle HRMS, primarily due to Oracle Payroll complexity.

Throughout this discussion of the development market, there were other skills that became important. The tools mentioned earlier, such as Oracle Forms and Oracle Reports, did not have to be used only on Oracle Applications. Custom software applications can be created with these Oracle tools used for user interface and data retrieval. Thus, there were Oracle technical experts who were skilled with Oracle tools but with no exposure to database administration nor to the Oracle Applications.

Oracle Forms did not overwhelm various business professionals as a user interface. The standards within the Oracle Forms product were usually not compliant with CUA (Common User Access). Recall that CUA was established in the 1980s primarily due to the influence of Microsoft with its Windows Operating System and IBM with its OS/2 Presentation Manager Operating System. Oracle Forms was far less robust and user-friendly than Presentation Manager, Windows, and even PowerBuilder. Thus, the demand for Oracle tools experts did not become overwhelmingly high if these professionals did not have associated Oracle Applications experience. The demand did exist, but not to the extent of the functional and technical disciplines addressed earlier.

As the late '90s arrived, still new technical experts were required. These professionals were Web experts. The Oracle Applications became Web-enabled, requiring new training and new disciplines even for Oracle Applications technical specialists.

I have progressed through the entire decade and certainly left out numerous other skills and employment opportunities that were influenced by the Oracle market. Consider the following.

Programmers were necessary. Managers, designers, developers, and testers were necessary to create each of the Oracle products. As the Oracle products (from the database to the tools to the applications) became more popular, Oracle needed to greatly expand its Sales and Marketing staffs. Moreover, as the various Oracle products gained industry momentum, the need for experienced consultants grew. Thus, skilled recruiters found significant work in locating and matching talented consultants with clients in need of assistance for their implementations.

SKILLS NEEDED TO BECOME A CONSULTANT

The high demands for skilled consultants often inspire individuals to ask, "What must I do to become an Oracle Consultant?" First, as you read the section in this chapter on how the Oracle market developed, you must first identify what type of Oracle professional you want to be. There are functional, technical, and project management disciplines that can be pursued.

Technical Consultants. A technical consultant must have a strong knowledge of relational database concepts (for example, operational primitives, functional dependencies, normalization forms) and the Oracle tools (particularly Oracle Reports). If the technical consultant desires to be a DBA, there are specific relational database skills related to sizing a database and tuning a database that must be learned. If the technical consultant desires to assist with implementations of the Oracle Applications, he needs to master the database model for the appropriate models desired.

Functional Consultants. A functional consultant must have a strong knowledge of the business discipline associated with a particular Oracle Application. For instance, a Payroll professional must fully learn how Oracle Payroll performs its calculations. The Payroll professional should establish a solid understanding of tax rules and laws within the various government legislative bodies where the professional desires to implement Oracle Payroll.

However, the functional consultant generally must obtain some moderate technical understanding of Oracle. A basic understanding of SQL is helpful to the functional consultant. Even if you have no plans to write intricate SQL scripts, it is helpful to understand basic methods for extracting or reviewing data that exists in the database.

One of the most overlooked skills of aspiring functional consultants is the need to be a problem solver. Technical consultants are generally trained to continually solve new problems. This is not always the case for functional professionals. For example, consider a solid accounting professional with 15 years of Accounts Receivable and Accounts Payable experience. This professional certainly understands many overall AR and AP issues. However, if this professional has worked for only one corporation during these years, it is possible that this professional has not been required to solve different industry approaches to paying or receiving payment from customers. Every new Oracle Application implementation offers some new variation of business problem solving.

Project Management. Another important discipline needed in some consultants is project management skills. Being a good functional consultant or a good technical consultant does not necessarily make the consultant a candidate to be a good project manager. Although project management techniques are a separate discipline, it is generally advisable for an aspiring Oracle project manager to also establish either a strong technical or functional background with various Oracle modules.

Database Administrator. Solid database administration is crucial for the operation of Oracle Applications. The database administrator must become an expert in the overall understanding of relational databases. The DBA should be responsible for installation, configuration, backup/recovery, and troubleshooting problems. The DBA must learn advanced SQL to help tune the database. The DBA, or other properly trained technical consultants, should be involved with the design review of any customizations, as they may affect database performance.

The DBA must be well organized to prepare strategies for system backup and restore. The nature of the assignments for a DBA requires an individual who can often work off-hours on a regular basis. To install new patches or perform backups and restores to an Oracle database, the DBA must minimize the business impact to users. Time left out of the system for a user can mean money lost for the business. The DBA's requirement for off-hours is added to by the emergency needs of a system during the normal business day. If the Oracle system is not responding, the DBA must be available to bring the system back up as efficiently as possible.

A good DBA is easy to justify because an excellent one can easily improve performance and reliability of an ERP system by three to five percent. If you have 100 users on the system and they are three percent more efficient because you have a good administrator, that is the equivalent savings of three full-time employees.

CHARACTER TRAITS OF A GOOD CONSULTANT

Character traits might seem like an insignificant issue when dealing with the complex world of Oracle technology. There are many quality people in this world who do not have qualities to be a good Oracle applications consultant. Clearly, a good consultant must have solid Oracle skills. However, good skills alone are generally not sufficient to be a good long-term consultant. In the consulting industry, you basically have no assets (unless you are selling a product). The main thing that a consultant has is her reputation.

Here are some suggested character traits that you might want to consider if you desire to establish an excellent long-term reputation as a quality consultant:

Clarity

Accuracy

Passion for the Product or Service

Genuine Concern for the Client

Clarity implies good communication skills. Can you clearly communicate your suggested solutions to the client? Can you clearly understand the business needs being expressed to you by your client? Can you clearly communicate with written documentation to allow future employees of your client to understand how you solved their problem?

Accuracy is primarily built upon both knowledge and an honest communication of that knowledge. To be accurate about a subject, you must first fully understand the subject. When you understand the subject, you must communicate the correct answers to your client and not just the easy answer or the answer that you believe the customer wants to hear.

A passion for the service you are providing might not be necessary on a short-term basis. However, if you do not have a strong belief (or passion) that the service you are providing will bring significant value to your client, you will have difficulty maintaining a high motivation level long-term. If you do not have a passion believing that the products you are implementing are good, you will not maintain a high motivation long-term. Not every client will be excited about his Oracle implementation. It will often be necessary for the consultant to bring some enthusiasm and excitement to project that is not superficial.

A concern for the client might seem obvious, but it still should be addressed. If you do not genuinely have a concern for your client, it will be difficult for you to maintain a high motivation level throughout a long implementation project. Moreover, it will be difficult for you to maintain a cohesive environment for project decision-making. It is really important to understand and actually care about the needs, emotions, and concerns of your client. An Oracle implementation can be overwhelming for many clients who have grown accustomed to doing business in only one fashion for their entire career. It can be challenging for a heavily experienced consultant, who "knows" the best answer based on her many implementations, to remain patient and accept that the best answer might not be chosen by your client. Without a genuine concern for your client, you find it difficult to be patient when you feel your experienced solutions are not being properly received and accepted.

CONSULTING ADVANTAGES

There are many advantages that consulting can offer. The challenging lifestyle of a consultant is worth a premium salary. The most visible advantage of consulting is the money. The financial advantages of consulting often extend well beyond the higher salaries. If the consulting engagement requires travel, you can build up frequent flyer miles quickly. Cashing in frequent flyer miles to an airline for free travel is real money savings to the consultant. Frequent guest programs at hotels offer similar financial advantages. Other financial advantages to travel involve expense reimbursement. If the consultant worked in his hometown, he would have to incur a cost to eat anyway. With expenses being reimbursed, this is a cost savings to the consultant, which further improves his financial situation.

Perhaps the greatest advantage to consulting is that the job rarely becomes stagnant. If a person is a problem solver, consulting offers the potential to continually solve new problems at the next consulting assignment. The consultant has the opportunity to avoid maintenance mode of a system. While the client obtains a production system with procedures to handle the normal repetitive business, the consultant leaves to a fresh, new engagement. It is difficult for a consultant to become bored from a repetitive job.

There is another advantage to avoiding maintenance mode on a system. After the consultant leaves the project, he does not have to continually live with poor implementation decisions that were made by the client (although he might have to live with knowledge of any poor decisions that he personally made). The consultant gets to leave and tackle new challenges. If the consultant made mistakes on the previous job, as any human will do, he has the opportunity learn from these mistakes and do an even better overall job on the next project. Every person will observe business-world decisions that he disagrees with. If a poor, or less than optimal, solution is made by the client, the consultant will not have to spend years in maintenance mode being reminded of a decision that was made against his recommendation. He simply moves on and solves new challenges on the next implementation.

The consultant often has the advantage of retaining expert knowledge. As you continually solve new problems for new businesses, you should learn from your successes and mistakes. As you implement Oracle systems, you will continually see the changing technology. This will allow you to stay current with new Oracle technology and further help you to remain an expert in your area of operation.

There are lifestyle advantages that a consultant can observe. The hotel lifestyle can offer many nice conveniences including a freshly cleaned room everyday. The hotel is often located near the client's place of business, so long commutes to the office are not necessary. The opportunity to see new places is a big advantage. Every area of the world has its own unique features and personality. Many times you cannot truly appreciate the region of the country or of the world until you have had an opportunity to spend time there.

CONSULTING DISADVANTAGES

There are disadvantages to accepting a job in consulting. The biggest disadvantage is the impact on families. When consulting requires travel, there is less time to build those vital relationships with family members. Even when the consultant does not travel, long hours are often required on projects. If the in-town consultant comes home late from the project every night, a similar strain occurs on the family. All the advantages listed earlier will not equal the pain encountered if a marriage suffers. If you are considering a consulting job that requires extensive travel and you are married, make this a team decision. Here are a few suggestions to ease this lifestyle:

Communicate. Call home. Stay in communication regularly (preferably daily) with your spouse and family.

Communicate. Don't put things off. Communicate just as you would if you were at home. If there are important family subjects, don't wait for the weekend to address everything face-to-face. Otherwise, you will spend the entire weekend problem solving.

Maximize the quality of time together. Because the weekend is your only time together, make sure it is quality time.

Remember the long hours. Many nonconsulting jobs or in-town consulting jobs require long hours. Remember that even if you remained in town, you might often be working long hours anyway. Thus, the quantity of your lost time together might not be as much as you think.

Go on vacation. You are building up frequent flyer miles and frequent hotel stays. Let your family be the recipient of these benefits. Travel for free, and allow the family to look forward to these vacations!

Other disadvantages exist in consulting. Your consulting job will require enormous flexibility. Airport delays cannot be easily planned for. You are continually required to learn a new business and new business culture. You will not remain settled in because you always feel as if you are changing jobs. If a business culture allows for numerous competing agendas, you must be prepared that your issues might be neglected. This is difficult for a problem-solving consultant to accept; however, it is vital for the consultant to remain mature and adept in whatever environment exists. The work environment might not always be optimal and can impact your performance. You simply have to learn to deal with it. You have accepted this high-powered job as a problem-solver and should do so to the best of your abilities based on the constraints of the project. Remember, if a particular project has a poor work environment, you get to leave after the project is over.

Another disadvantage to consulting is the overwhelming pressure to perform. The client looks to the consultants as the experts. There are many project challenges that require detailed investigation and creative solutions. Being an expert consultant is not as simple as memorizing a book or memorizing a few implementation steps. There is pressure not only to come up with a solution for difficult challenges, but also to determine whether this is the best solution available. And if this were not enough, there is pressure to produce these solutions in a timely manner. The client pays dearly for your time, and you will want them to feel the value of their investment.

Burnout is another disadvantage of consulting. The high energy and hard work required to solve a client's problems does not subside when the project is over. It all starts over again. Many people only do one ERP implementation in a lifetime and barely survive. I know consultants who have done two projects a year for five years and are still alive to tell about it. This work pattern, combined with the other disadvantages mentioned in this section, can wear a person down. Many consultants will experience burnout and need to take a break.

SUPPORT JOBS

The Oracle Applications market has created the need for product support specialists. Some developers and consultants choose to work for Oracle Worldwide Support. There are several advantages to this type of position. Travel requirements are minimal. The opportunity for fresh problem-solving activities exists. Working for Oracle Worldwide Support allows employees to keep up with current releases of the Oracle products. In some ways, a support specialist is like a consultant because they are both solving customer-specific problems. The support personnel will often need to re-create the customer's scenarios on their own systems before recommending a course of action for correction.

There are some difficulties in playing a support role for any product, and Oracle is no different. The problems called in by clients are often some of the more difficult ones that the client has encountered. These can be issues where the client and consultants have not identified a solution that is acceptable to the client. Other problems called in by the clients are often product deficiencies or bugs. Identifying bugs to the client is not usually a glamorous position. Tension can be high when the client calls Oracle WWS to have a bug addressed. The client wants things fixed and wants them fixed right away. It is not as simple as looking up the error message in a reference manual and telling the client how to fix it. If the errors are due to bugs, support personnel can be caught in the middle of tension between the development group and the client. The development group might require significant time to design an appropriate long-term solution for the bug that meets the needs of all clients. Sometimes, the development group will review the issue as being lower priority than other development issues. These are difficult issues to communicate to a client, and they add challenge to the job of Oracle support specialists.

PRODUCT DEVELOPMENT JOBS

"Creating a better mousetrap." That is the goal of most software developers. There are many software development opportunities available at Oracle, software companies, consulting firms, and your own IT department. Developers are needed to create new products and to prepare upgraded functionality to existing products. Seeing the latest and greatest functionality can be very appealing. Moreover, being able to influence the direction of technology and product functionality can be even more appealing.

Oracle Corporation has been very innovative with creating new products. This challenge should continue to attract new jobs for top-notch developers. A successful product development effort also requires good management and solid quality assurance (QA) testing. Thus, project manager jobs are necessary to support product development.

Product development jobs are not limited to Oracle Corporation. Some companies review Oracle product functionality and focus on a particular area where they feel the product is deficient. These companies hire developers to create their own products, which can be interfaced to the Oracle products. Thus, new product development and consulting jobs can be created from third-party organizations.

SALES/MARKETING JOBS

What good is a superior product if no one knows about it? Oracle Corporation does an effective job of heavily promoting its products to new and existing clients through the Sales and Marketing staff. These jobs are available to people with good marketing skills. However, these jobs also require a desire to understand and learn the various Oracle products.

Sales and marketing are important in the consulting world, particularly for large-scale implementations. Rather than market the merits of the Oracle products, a third-party organization must be able to market its services. These companies must be able to demonstrate how they will add value to implementations through product expertise, implementation methodology, and many other distinguishing factors.

RECRUITING JOBS

The wide variety of Oracle-related job opportunities that have been described in this chapter creates the need for recruiters who are industry specialists. Recruiters must learn which of the particular skills (technical consulting, functional consulting, sales, and so on) are needed by Oracle Corporation, consulting organizations, and end-clients of Oracle. Then, the recruiters must identify where the best talent exists. Many companies do not have the time to keep an Oracle industry-specific expert employed who knows instantly where to find the best talent. Thus, recruiting jobs are an offset of the Oracle product growth.

WORKING FOR ORACLE CORPORATION

One way of keeping up with the latest Oracle-related technology is to work for Oracle Corporation itself. Oracle offers a wide variety of job opportunities similar to those that have been discussed earlier in this chapter.

Oracle Corporation employees have access to training classes that are generally offered prior to the public availability to outside companies. This provides Oracle employees (sales staff, consultants, support staff, and so on) with the most current technological information. Although having this advanced technological knowledge prior to the outside world is usually short-lived, the advantage should not be overlooked. There is always excitement and certainly value in having an up-front look at technology in any industry.

Oracle Corporation developers actually have the opportunity to shape future project direction. This is an intriguing opportunity that is worth consideration of top software developers.

Perhaps one of biggest disadvantages in working at Oracle involves the overall company size. With corporate success comes growth, and Oracle has certainly grown at an impressive rate. However, growth causes problems at many large organizations, including Oracle. Large companies usually have added bureaucracy, which can hinder responsive decision-making.

Other advantages and disadvantages can be reviewed in Appendix B, "The State of the Oracle Consulting Market," under the section "Larger Diversified Consulting Firms."

WORKING FOR ORACLE CUSTOMERS

One way to gain access to Oracle technology is to work for a client company that has implemented Oracle products. Numerous companies have installed Oracle databases. Many of these companies also use Oracle technologies for custom Reports and Forms development. Many other companies have installed various Oracle Applications on top of the Oracle database.

What are the advantages in working for a customer of Oracle? First, as stated previously, you have the opportunity work with state-of-art technologies. You have the opportunity to monitor upcoming releases of the various Oracle products to help ensure that your organization is maintaining a competitive advantage in the marketplace.

Avoiding travel is another advantage. Many Oracle experts (whether they are Oracle Corporation employees or third-party consultants) have a requirement for a high level of travel. Some Oracle experts choose to work for clients of Oracle so that they can avoid the burnout of a prolonged travel schedule.

Job stability is also an advantage of working for a client of Oracle. The job responsibilities and assignments are more likely to be consistent from one day to the next when compared to typical job responsibilities of a consultant. Also, many clients realize their dependence on Oracle-trained employees and this brings longer-term stability. Most clients desire to keep their top Oracle-trained employees happy to avoid the costs of higher paid outside consultants.

There are disadvantages in working for Oracle customers. For starters, not every Oracle customer desires to stay current on all of the latest Oracle products. Of course, this might not be a disadvantage to some people who prefer to avoid the headaches associated with bleeding-edge technologies. Another disadvantage involves the potential for routine. Many Oracle professionals desire new problem-solving opportunities on a regular basis. However, Oracle clients are involved or will eventually be involved in a maintenance mode. Maintenance mode of any system can become monotonous.

Another disadvantage involves the likelihood of less compensation. The value of a consultant trained on state-of-the-art Oracle technologies is heavily inflated over the typical value of an IT staff member responsible for maintaining an Oracle system or any other system. The Oracle client company must justify and balance the salaries paid to its Oracle-trained employees to the overall salary structure and policies of the organization.

WHAT HAPPENS AFTER YEAR 2000?

This is a common question that is asked by many within the Enterprise Applications industry and certainly will influence the Oracle employment market in upcoming years. Year 2000

PART

V

APP

A

system compliance was a major motive during the late 1990s for corporations to consider implementing Oracle Applications. However, Y2K compliance was not the only reason customers turned to Oracle. If Y2K compliance were the only issue, corporations would have spent all their money updating existing in-house financial, manufacturing, HR/payroll, and other database applications.

Packaged software from companies such as Oracle, PeopleSoft, and SAP were selected in the late 1990s for additional reasons. Companies such as Oracle can devote numerous man-years of effort to developing applications that they believe will meet the needs of the vast majority of their customers. Not every company has the ongoing budget to spend on many man-years worth of development. Moreover, even if companies have the budget, they must hire and retain a sufficient number of properly trained employees if they desire a high quality in their homegrown systems. They must hire sufficient numbers of people to cover both ongoing maintenance of the existing systems and future software development.

The issue of maintenance and upgrade of a company's existing systems should be discussed further. Legislative issues must be kept up-to-date. Suppose that the government establishes new reporting requirements for Human Resource reports for Equal Employment Opportunity or Affirmative Action Planning. These must be created in the homegrown system. However, if you owned the Oracle HRMS product suite, you could expect that Oracle will create a solution in a future release. Consider sales tax and payroll tax changes. If a company owns Oracle Financials and HR/Payroll, it can expect that the Oracle product suite, through its relationships with Vertex, will include the latest tax legislation.

The point is that there were significant reasons why companies purchased Oracle products late in the 1990s. Sure, Y2K caused a spike in demand because Y2K compliance caused many companies to react to a problem sooner than they would have liked to. However, now that many companies have accessed new technologies from Oracle, they often recognize that this was a great long-term decision. There is likely to be demand for either future new Oracle products or for future upgrades to existing products. Moreover, many companies who solved their Y2K problems by "patching" their homegrown system must still battle the numerous maintenance issues in keeping the system current.

There is also a competitive fear that many companies will experience within their respective industries. No company wants to feel that it is losing ground to the competition or is less flexible in responding to the continually changing needs of its customers. If a company knows that its key competitors have installed the latest technologies from Oracle, that can influence the company to consider the same. Just because your competition makes a decision to purchase Oracle products, that does not mean that it is the best decision for you. However, any successful company will monitor the actions and directions of its competitors and will desire to avoid being at a competitive disadvantage in any area of its business.

The Oracle employment market encountered a significant decrease in demand in the spring and summer of 1999. I believe that this was an aberration. Just as the mid-90s produced an inordinately high demand, 1999 produced an inordinately low demand. If a company had Information Technology budget money allocated to solving any issues, the Y2K problem had to be solved before any other budget money was spent. Moreover, even if the company desired a strategic long-term solution, it would not be wise to start an Oracle Applications project. There simply was not enough calendar time left before January 1, 2000. Thus, new Oracle project implementations during late 1998 and 1999 were far fewer.

It is my expectation that future demand will be very solid for Oracle products, and thus, future Oracle-related jobs should be plentiful. The Oracle market will probably not grow as explosively as it did in the mid-90s but probably will not remain as slow as it did in 1999.

UPGRADES TO R11, R11I, R12

Companies will choose to upgrade for a variety of reasons. New technological improvements at the database level could inspire clients to want to increase the processing speeds of reports and processes. New functionality for Oracle Applications that target specific business industries such as public sector, higher education, and other vertical markets might influence existing customers to want to upgrade their Applications. New legislative product releases or changes to the Oracle products to accommodate new legislative changes will also influence many clients to need to upgrade.

The message here is that Oracle database and application specialists will be needed over the upcoming years to assist clients with upgrades to Applications release 11, release 11i, and release 12. As the existing installed base of Oracle products grows, the market for upgrades to existing installations will also grow.

PHASE II APPLICATIONS/FUNCTIONALITY

There will be other Oracle employment opportunities that arise from current Oracle clients. Many new Oracle implementations have focused, and will continue to focus, on implementing core and "necessary" functionality. There might be many desired functions that have been identified during a requirements analysis that will need to be implemented in the future.

This desire for Phase II functionality or Phase II secondary applications constitutes a demand for skilled Oracle professionals. This demand is not likely to create as many new job opportunities as have other Oracle employment opportunities. However, the demand still exists and will create employment and other consulting opportunities. The Phase II project team sizes are likely to be a subset of the sizes of the original project teams as a general rule.

Many companies will attempt to solve Phase II issues using existing company staff that has worked on the initial implementation of the products. This is because the paradigm shift of learning new technology will be less of a hurdle. For example, consider a client that had identified many Phase II issues associated with desired reports. During Phase I, this existing client staff might have successfully learned the tools for Oracle Reports and the appropriate database model (AP, AR, and so on) from which the reports should be created. For more complex features and truly new features, there should still be need for outside consulting assistance to augment client staff, depending on the complexity of requirements.

ORACLE CORPORATION IS AN ENGINE OF GROWTH

It is worth noting that there will be Oracle-influenced employment opportunities in areas not discussed in this chapter. Oracle Corporation can be viewed as an engine of growth. As the volume of Oracle product sales continues to grow, there will continue to be demand for more industry experts to satisfy that demand. As Oracle creates new products, there will be need for new product specialists.

APPENDIX **B**

THE STATE OF THE ORACLE CONSULTING MARKET

The consulting market for Oracle opportunities has experienced explosive growth in recent years. Solid opportunities still exist over the upcoming years. The nature of these opportunities will differ based on the type of consulting organization involved. The following includes an in-depth analysis of the types of consulting firms who specialize in Oracle expertise. This analysis reviews independent consultants; smaller, more specialized consulting companies; larger, diversified consulting companies; and Oracle Corporation consulting. The following analysis reviews advantages and disadvantages to consultants at each of these different types of consulting arrangements. The analysis also addresses advantages and disadvantages to the employing organizations that desire to hire Oracle-skilled consultants.

INDEPENDENT CONSULTING

Some heavily Oracle-experienced consultants choose to work independently of other consulting firms. In certain cases, these consultants are some of the most heavily experienced consultants available. This opportunity can be really appealing to the consultant who desires to maximize his earnings potential. These consultants tend to be quite confident and willing to take risks. In return, they have the opportunity to make more money than other non-independent consultants with similar skills do because there are no middlemen in their own corporation sharing in the revenues they generate.

INDEPENDENT CONSULTING: ADVANTAGES TO CONSULTANT

There are advantages for consultants who desire to remain or become independent. As mentioned in the introduction, money is a big motivator. If the consultant is confident that she can continually find new work, she will likely be able to make more money. An end client can pay the consultant much less than they pay a larger firm. Yet, the individual consultant can make more because there are no marketing costs or corporate overheard. Additionally, there is no intercompany revenue sharing and so on to be satisfied.

Independent consultants have the advantage of significant freedom. They are not weighed down by corporate politics. They are free to move from one project to the next based on their own timing. They are free to research job opportunities anywhere in the world. Some independent consultants enjoy the opportunity to relocate for a project to minimize travel requirements.

Independent consultants have tremendous flexibility for vacations. It is not uncommon for a consultant who has finished a long-term project to desire a longer-term vacation. The independent consultant has no vacation requests or approvals needed from her own company.

Independent consultants have flexibility of work environment. There are some consultants who do not work well in teams; however, these same consultants might have a wealth of knowledge about a particular Oracle product. It can be their desire to deliver the absolute best services available with no one looking over their shoulders and micromanaging their efforts. If these types of consultants remain independent, they do not have to deal with the same co-workers from project to project. Moreover, they do not have to deal with the same managers and supervisors from project to project. These consultants have great flexibility in making their own project decisions. Then, when the project is over, they can leave and not have to deal with the same co-workers or team members on a longer-term basis.

INDEPENDENT CONSULTING: ADVANTAGES TO EMPLOYING COMPANY

The greatest advantage to a company that chooses to offer contracts to independent consultants is financial. The opportunity exists to find the most heavily qualified individual consultant at the absolute lowest price. This can be very tempting for companies that are overwhelmed by the typical consulting rates charged by larger consulting organizations. Another advantage to the employing company is that they receive just-in-time help on projects, using consultants who are experts in the specific functional and technical areas required by the company.

INDEPENDENT CONSULTING: RISKS TO CONSULTANT

There are considerable risks to a consultant who works independently. First, the consultant has no other marketing department following up on other Oracle consulting opportunities. Thus, there is little or no opportunity to establish a backlog of work. His company does not have other existing projects in progress where the consultant could choose between one of these at the completion of the current project.

Another risk of independent consulting involves project duration. It is always more desirable to obtain a longer-term project as opposed to a shorter-term project. However, if a consultant is between assignments and out of work, he can accept a short-term assignment even though he did not want to. The bills still have to be paid. The problem with the short-term assignment is that the consultant needs to spend time searching and interviewing for new job opportunities. This is a difficult thing to do if you have made a commitment to your current short-term employer to deliver a high quality level of service. It is difficult to remain focused to your current client if you know you must almost immediately search for another job.

There is a timing risk due to unexpected project terminations. In this day and age where mergers and acquisitions are common, the independent can be caught in the middle. Many companies proceed through an Oracle, PeopleSoft, or SAP implementation and suddenly terminate the entire project. Sometimes, this is due to a buyout or merger. Sometimes, it is due to an internal power struggle. Sometimes, it is because the company is enduring new financial pressures from industry that affect their budget. If the project abruptly stops, the independent consultant might have had zero time to be prepared.

Independent consultants face risks to their individual reputation. If a project does not go well, it cannot be blamed on their firm. The consultants receive full blame, regardless of whether they agree with the assessment.

The other reputation issue deals with project completion and short-term project extensions. Consider the situation where the consultant has signed a six-month project. Assume that the consultant has delivered top-quality service during these six months. When the six months nears its end, the consultant must look for other work. The problem exists when the existing client desires an extension. If the extension is longer term, the decision to stay remains fairly easy.

However, what if the existing client only needs three or four more weeks of support, while a new prospective client offers a one-year project? Here is the dilemma. From a legal perspective, the consultant has completed his term and does not have to stay. From a short-term or medium-term job stability perspective, the new opportunity is difficult to turn down (particularly in a market where consulting opportunities have become scarce). What if leaving the existing client puts their business in jeopardy? How important is it to take the client all the way to finish line? Clearly, if the consultant chooses to leave, the existing client can become quite upset. The consultant might have lost any opportunity for future, repeat business or, most importantly, the opportunity to have a good client reference.

Maintaining skills through adequate personal training is another risk to the independent consultant. The Oracle technologies are rapidly changing. It is difficult for the independent consultant to schedule regular training due to responsibilities from his current project. The consultant must maintain the full burden of off-hours training or training in between projects.

Finally, there is a significant risk in the recent ERP market due to the decease of Oracle jobs related to Y2K backlash. Many consultants who had found smooth sailing in the mid to late 1990s found themselves out of work in 1999 with little prospect for finding good, long-term opportunities.

INDEPENDENT CONSULTING: RISKS TO EMPLOYING COMPANIES

Employing companies face many risks when attempting to employ independent consultants. The first risk involves knowing whether you have found the best available consultant. Did you have the time to research numerous consultants and check references? It takes time to research good ones.

Loyalty is a big risk. If an independent consultant is motivated primarily by money, how will she react if another firm offers her more money to do the same thing she is currently doing? Some independent consultants can resist this urge. Others cannot. The example in the previous section is worth noting here also. What if your implementation was only expected to cover a six-month period? When you offered the contract to the consultant, there was no way of knowing every variable and risk that the project faced. Thus, six months was only an estimate of need. What if you near the end of six months and determine that you desperately need three or four more weeks' effort? Will the consultant remain loyal to you if another company offers her more money with a one-year contract?

Related to the loyalty issue are the client's best interests in general. The independent consultants are in business to make money for themselves and not for their firm. Some independent consultants might want to protect their best interests and minimize the level of assistance and support they provide to fellow team members with similar skill levels. The client should monitor reactions by inhouse team members and other consultants to determine whether the independent consultant is a prima donna as described in Chapter 29, "Working with Consultants." Establishing the best team players in this type environment is difficult for the employing company and requires careful management by the client.

Finally, consider that the independent consultant is also her own marketing department. Her attention will lose focus at times because she must continually search for her next project.

SMALLER, SPECIALIZED CONSULTING FIRMS

Many heavily Oracle experienced consultants choose to work for smaller, specialized consulting firms. These consultants often share similarities to independent consultants in that they desire to make more money than they can at larger, more bureaucratic organizations. Many consultants at these firms are often quite entrepreneurial in nature and desire to avoid the largest consulting organizations. However, they know that to grow a successful business, they need a team working for their same goals, so they do not want to work as independent consultants. These consultants also prefer the idea of a smaller team where their individual success can influence the success and direction of the company.

SMALLER, SPECIALIZED CONSULTING FIRMS: ADVANTAGES TO CONSULTANT

As is the case for independent consultants, money is a big motivator for consultants who work for smaller consulting firms. The smaller company has fewer layers of management and smaller overall marketing staff. Thus, there are fewer numbers of people who must share in the profits being generated by each consultant. This allows for significantly higher salaries. Yet, along with these higher salaries, there is a greater stability of income.

Consultants of smaller firms do not share the same level of anxiety near the end of a project that an independent consultant experiences. The consultant at these firms has an easier opportunity to accept short-term extensions at the end of a project. The consultant can continue to work on project completion until the client is satisfied without wondering whether he will have a job when the project is over. The consultant does not need to worry about the financial impact of missing other long-term opportunities because there are usually other heavily experienced consultants within the firm to satisfy other opportunities.

Minimal corporate bureaucracy is a huge reason why many consultants prefer smaller consulting firms. The red tape and political infighting that can occur in large organizations can sap the creative energy of a consultant. A top-notch consultant usually prefers exerting energy to solve client business issues. These consultants often state they do not desire to exert energy related to internal fighting between various regional or vertical business units within a large consulting firm.

Visibility is a big advantage to consultants at smaller specialized consulting firms. It is difficult for a consultant's good deeds to get lost in the shuffle. The best performers in any type of business want to be recognized and made to feel that contributions are genuinely important. Greater corporate visibility makes these types of firms attractive to some of the most heavily experienced consultants.

PART

V

APP

B

SMALLER, SPECIALIZED CONSULTING FIRMS: ADVANTAGES TO EMPLOYING COMPANY

Many firms that have hired consultants to assist with implementations believe the best value exists with smaller, specialized consulting organizations. These firms tend to offer some of the most heavily experienced consultants at rates cheaper than the largest consulting companies, yet with greater stability than can be obtained with independent companies.

The smaller, specialized consulting firms tend to have the most experienced consultants for the reasons stated in the previous section. It is worth noting again that the primary reason is because they can afford to pay their employees more than larger, more bureaucratic organizations. Many of these consultants have been trained in implementation methodologies when at the larger consulting firms.

By definition, a specialized consulting firm is specialized. Thus, they tend to focus their energies on a specific discipline or niche. There is usually some consulting company that happens to specialize in the exact product or service desired by the employing company. Consider a company that specializes only in providing Oracle-skilled functional and technical consultants. This company does not exert energy trying to market and support other ERP products such as PeopleSoft or SAP. This company does not hire COBOL programmers to assist organizations in outsourcing or fixing old legacy systems. This type of smaller consulting firm cannot meet all business needs. However, its energies and business can be focused on exactly what the employing company needs to succeed with an Oracle implementation.

The costs of contracting with smaller company consultants are usually cheaper when comparing comparable talent at the Big 5 or Oracle. This is a big advantage to the employing company.

SMALLER, SPECIALIZED CONSULTING FIRMS: DISADVANTAGES TO CONSULTANT

There are disadvantages to consultants who choose to work for smaller, more specialized consulting firms. These consultants cannot maintain the same comfort zone that a larger company such as the Big 5 or Oracle can offer. These consultants are less able to put their jobs into "cruise control" as they can at the larger companies. Because the organization is smaller, there are fewer overall consultants who can help pick up the slack.

Related to this issue is the fact that a consultant's weaknesses can be more easily exposed. The consultant can no longer sit back and hope that some someone else within the organization can solve the big problems. Consultants at these smaller firms must usually take more responsibility and be more flexible in solving the needs of their clients.

There can be less job stability in some specialized consulting firms. If the market slows in the area where the company has established its specialty, the company can come under greater pressure to survive. Some companies will not be able to overcome this situation due to a lack of diversity in other product and service offerings.

Related to the job stability issue is the quality of the management at the smaller, specialized consulting organization. You should thoroughly research the reputation and quality of management of a smaller firm. Because there are fewer layers of corporate management and bureaucracy, there are fewer places to hide poor management with poor market vision.

SMALLER, SPECIALIZED CONSULTING FIRMS: DISADVANTAGES TO EMPLOYING COMPANY

Smaller consulting firms can pose disadvantages to companies employing Oracle-skilled consultants. Sure, these consulting companies can usually offer higher experienced consultants at a less expensive price. However, what kind of backup plan can the consulting firm offer if something negative happens to top quality consultants who have been offered to the employing company? Does the smaller firm have the presence within the industry to respond with the same level of quality and experience with future consultants? Does the smaller firm have a suitable implementation methodology, or is it more of a body shop? As a result, checking out references should be imperative for the employing company.

Smaller consulting firms desire to grow. The desire for growth can inspire some companies to sell you services in new product/service areas. For instance, a company with a historical track record of helping companies implement Oracle Financials from both a functional and technical perspective might attempt to translate that Oracle experience into future implementations of Oracle HR/Payroll. In this example, the company's past Oracle implementation successes could deceive the employing company into believing that the new Oracle modules are simply an extension of their previous experience. In reality, the functional and technical issues of Oracle Payroll are dramatically different from Oracle Financials. Issues such as this have burned many hiring organizations.

A further example involves the assumption that a good Oracle Manufacturing technical consultant quickly translates into a good Oracle Manufacturing functional consultant. This, too, is incorrect. The message is that a hiring company must be prepared to shop around more than once depending on the exact, particular disciplines they need to solve their specific business issues. Shopping around takes time.

Another disadvantage to using smaller consulting firms involves project team size. If your project has the potential to grow quite large, research to determine the breadth of experience that the consulting firm can offer.

Finally, there is a disadvantage for an employing organization in that they must expend more effort to shop around to find the best-specialized firm to meet each of their various Oracle product implementation needs. By definition, a specialized consulting firm is distinguished in one or a few areas but not in every area needed to meet all the business needs of the client.

LARGER, DIVERSIFIED CONSULTING FIRMS

Many consultants learn and develop solid skills and business practices at larger, diversified consulting organizations. Examples of companies referred to here include the Big 5 firms, Oracle Corporation, EDS, CSC, and other large, diversified service providers. These and other similar large firms offer many employment opportunities to Oracle-skilled professionals.

LARGER, DIVERSIFIED CONSULTING FIRMS: ADVANTAGES TO CONSULTANT

Consultants who choose to work for larger, diversified consulting firms obtain a number of positive factors. These larger firms already have a large account base. The Big 5 already has a large number of relationships based on years of accounting relationships. The larger companies have better brand recognition than do smaller firms. Because the larger firms are by definition larger, they are better able to win large consulting contracts that employ many consultants. These consulting firms have brand recognition out in the market place. When they arrive at a prospective client, they have less need to introduce themselves simply to prove to the prospective client that they are a credible organization. This brand recognition brings greater job security to Oracle-skilled consultants.

Larger consulting firms have the opportunity to support more-extensive training programs. This can be particularly attractive to younger, developing consultants who have great potential but need more experience and training. When Oracle Corporation creates new training courses, it is common for the Big 5 and similar corporations to send some consultants to these classes.

Consultants often gain good habits when working for the Big 5 and other diversified consulting companies. Most of the companies have well-documented implementation methods. If the consultant works on a project where the organization is actually making good use of the methods, there is a tremendous opportunity to learn. A younger consultant can learn proper documentation standards and proper project estimation/tracking methods. The advantage to the consultant is usually not the specific method being used, but the fact that a thorough, organized series of methods is being followed. These types of methods and the requirement for meticulous organization will be invaluable as the consultant progresses through his career.

Finally, the opportunity for local work is a little higher. Most consultants are required to travel, and this remains the case for large consulting firms. However, if the big consulting company has a larger number of Oracle-related projects than does a smaller company then statistically the odds are in greater favor that one of these projects will be in the hometown of the consultant.

LARGER, DIVERSIFIED CONSULTING FIRMS: ADVANTAGES TO EMPLOYING COMPANY

A company that is considering an ERP system implementation has good reasons to consider employing the Big 5 and other large, diversified consulting organizations. Larger consulting companies offer financial stability. There is less likelihood that the consulting firm being engaged will go out of business before the project is complete.

Larger, diversified consulting firms usually bring local executive account management. Some hiring organizations feel more secure when they know they can drive across town to speak to a partner or principal of the organization. Sure, a hiring firm of a smaller, more specialized consulting organization could have the opportunity to pick up a phone or send an email.

However, there is a tangible security when you know that you can meet face-to-face with an executive who has the power and influence to make changes when a project has begun seeing difficult times.

Larger consulting firms often bring solid project methodologies that are designed to help maintain control of larger projects. Moreover, these methodologies have often been used with many other clients. Even in cases where the method has been somewhat inferior for other clients, the larger consulting firm has had opportunities to document and learn from critical mistakes. The method does not ensure project success, but it offers a higher probability of success.

Related to the methodologies is project management in general. The Big 5 and similarly sized organizations often have senior project managers who have direct experience managing large-scale implementations.

Larger consulting organizations have more historical documentation and best practices information that can potentially be used by the consultants to benefit the employing company. This can be an advantage, although it often becomes a more neutral factor than it should be. If the large consulting firm does not have a truly centralized mechanism for sharing information across its various regional and vertical business lines, the client will never benefit from this past project information. Certainly, this issue is not a negative factor to the employing organization and, at worst, is a non-issue. The question is whether these potential advantages for the client can be actually realized due to the consulting company's internal organizational structure.

Larger consulting firms offer the potential for one-stop shopping for solving the entire setup software needs of a client. They have access to more resources in more product areas than do smaller firms. However, although this is definitely an advantage, the advantage might not be as large as it seems. No firm has the time or the resources to properly research the best solution for every business need. Even though the employing organization might not obtain the *best* solution in the arrangement, the odds are greater that a *good* solution will still be recommended.

Finally, larger consulting firms, by definition, have more employees. If a sizable number of these employees have direct, hands-on skills in the particular Oracle discipline, the hiring firm has a little more project stability. Turnover can be high when dealing with experienced IT professionals and particularly when the professionals have Oracle-related skills. If your project were to lose key consultants before completion, the larger consulting firms have a chance to be well equipped to provide a suitable replacement.

LARGER, DIVERSIFIED CONSULTING FIRMS: DISADVANTAGES TO CONSULTANT

There are disadvantages to consultants who choose to work for larger, diversified consulting companies. Working for any large company involves a much higher incidence of company politics. Playing company politics has helped many professionals advance their careers more quickly when compared with consultants and other professionals who did not want to "play the game."

There are other political issues that are often influenced and exaggerated by the internal structure of a large firm. To satisfy numerous types of clients, large consulting firms will often align business services based on regional or industry-specific vertical markets. Although this is a good goal for certain disciplines (such as COBOL or C programmers), it often produces problems in disciplines (such as Oracle) where there are not excessive numbers of highly skilled professionals.

For instance, it might make great strategic sense for the organization as a whole to attempt to meet the needs of a particular automotive firm who is implementing an Oracle ERP system. However, assume that the large consulting firm has a Business Line or Service Line designed to exclusively work with automotive companies. Now assume that the client desires to put in Oracle GEMMS for process manufacturing. It might happen that most of the skilled GEMMS consultants report to different regions of the country or the world. The managers of these consultants often resist "giving" their skilled consultants to another internal branch unless they can obtain the full revenue that they would observe in the open market. On the other hand, the vertical-market executive might scoff at the idea of paying high interbranch rates for using these consultants. The automotive vertical-market executive in this example can be faced with the dilemma: "Do I forego revenue and pay the high interbranch rate, or do I attempt to train someone who really does not have the appropriate experience so that I can make my profit margin?" Even executives and managers who desire to work well together between business units will face disincentives to do so because of the financial incentives of the business structure.

What is the message? In this example, a consultant with all the necessary skills might live in the exact same town where the business opportunity exists; however, because the consultant "belongs" to a different region or vertical unit, she might miss the opportunity for an assignment that is both exciting and local. This can leave a real sour taste in the mouth of a consultant who missed opportunities simply due to organizational politics.

Related to the politics issue is the issue of the overall bureaucracy of larger consulting organizations. A consultant can experience frustration when attempting to accomplish certain tasks because of the red tape and number of approvals necessary to ensure that all company policies have been satisfied. Because many business policies are firmly entrenched, the consultant has much less opportunity to make changes to business philosophy and direction. There is less visibility, which can influence opportunities for advancement. Certainly, there are more numerous corporate levels required to advance through to get near the top of this type of company.

Finally, less pay is the biggest disadvantage to consultants working at larger consulting firms. Because of the greater number of levels of management and the much higher corporate overhead, it is more difficult for the highest salaries to trickle down to the actual consultant. As the consultant becomes more and more experienced, there is a much greater financial temptation to consider working for smaller, more specialized firms that focus on her particular type of skill.

LARGER, DIVERSIFIED CONSULTING FIRMS: DISADVANTAGES TO EMPLOYING COMPANY

Disadvantages exist to employing companies that choose to contract the services of larger, diversified consulting firms. There is a general perception that bigger implies better. Although this can be true on the management front, it is often not true from the perspective of experience levels supplied by consulting organization.

Consider the disincentives for the best Oracle-skilled consultants to remain with the large consulting organization. These disincentive issues were discussed in the preceding section and include issues such as lack of top salaries, less corporate visibility, and higher corporate politics and bureaucracy. If you were a consultant and felt that you could make more money, endure less corporate bureaucracy, and still do the exact same Oracle-related work at a smaller, more specialized firm, how long would you continue to work under your existing arrangement? Now that you are a hiring manager who is about to employ the services of a large firm, what indications do you have that the actual consultants who are coming to your project are actually some of the most highly skilled in the industry?

There are occasions when this environment can be turned into a positive by the large, diversified consulting organizations. Most of these firms believe that they have good management and good methodologies; however, they inwardly know that they do not have enough of the most highly skilled and experienced resources. Many of their consultants have been groomed through solid internal training programs, yet they might still be younger with less experience.

There are large consulting organizations that solve this issue by subcontracting Oracle-specific work to independent consultants or to smaller, more specialized firms. This enables the larger consulting company to bring in the most experienced talent, yet still take advantage of the corporate methodologies they already have in place. If the large, consulting firm is resistant to this type of subcontracting business arrangement, they still have the potential to create good project teams. However, the risk to the client is tremendously higher than expected.

It is recommended that the hiring organization do more than simply check the overall references of the large, consulting firm. References should be checked based on the individual project team members assigned to a particular client. This keeps pressure on the large consulting organization to supply a higher quality and greater experienced level of talent. It is recommended that references be checked for most résumés that are being proposed for the project. After all, are you purchasing the name of a firm or purchasing the skills of the individual consultants that you will see on a daily basis?

The final disadvantage is the higher cost of big company consultants, although this issue can be exaggerated. Overall, it costs an employing company more to hire equivalently trained consultants at a large organization than at a small organization. This is usually the case over the short term. However, this cost can be exaggerated in the long term. If the larger firm brings the overall management and experience to increase the probability of project success, the higher cost of consultants can be justified.

PART

V

APP

B

ORACLE CORPORATION CONSULTING

A large number of consultants choose to work for Oracle Corporation itself. Oracle Corporation consultants can be found all over the world. As can be expected, these consultants usually focus exclusively on consulting related to products produced by Oracle Corporation.

ORACLE CORPORATION CONSULTING: ADVANTAGES TO CONSULTANT

Advantages for consultants at Oracle Corporation are significant. Perhaps the biggest advantage that Oracle Corporation can offer its consultants is state-of-the-art training. Oracle Corporation is continually creating new and more exciting products. Consultants at Oracle often get to hear about the products before they are officially released to the public. Oracle Corporation invests significantly to keep its consultants well-trained on functionality of relevant Oracle products. A consultant has the advantage in some cases to stay ahead of industry peers regarding exposure and training to the latest and greatest products.

The number of consultants who are trained on any given Oracle product is usually higher at Oracle Corporation than at any other company in the world. Because there are more trained consultants on a particular Oracle module, there are more inhouse contacts for an Oracle Corporation consultant to contact when they experience challenges and problems on a project. However, this advantage can be exaggerated. On some occasions, there can be so many consultants asking so many internal questions that an overload occurs. The strongest consultants with the most knowledge to answer these questions can only answer so many questions in a week while still providing adequate value to their own clients. Nevertheless, this communication environment is still an advantage.

Because Oracle Corporation Consulting has assisted in many past projects, a great deal of project documentation exists. This can be particularly helpful to younger consultants who desire to learn from the experiences from past projects within the firm.

Oracle Corporation consultants have the ability to contact fellow employees within Oracle Corporation development organizations. This can be advantageous when product documentation is insufficient in describing all the intended uses of particular software. Oracle Corporation consultants can use this pipeline to the development organizations to obtain valuable information that could influence their decisions at a client site.

Consultants at Oracle Corporation have the ability learn a method that is tailored specifically for implementing Oracle Applications. Oracle AIM (Application Implementation Method) is the standard used by most Oracle Corporation consultants. Knowledge of this method is particularly advantageous to younger consultants who are learning proper project standards and techniques. (See similar discussion in the section "Larger, Diversified Consulting Firms: Advantages to Consultant.")

Finally, because of the large number of consulting projects being implemented by Oracle, there might be an opportunity for the consultant to find work that is closer to home. Most consultants have 100 percent travel requirements, but the chances are at least higher that local work can be obtained.

ORACLE CORPORATION CONSULTING: ADVANTAGES TO EMPLOYING COMPANY

Companies that choose to employ Oracle Corporation consultants have several potential advantages. First is the potential pipeline of information to the product development groups and to other Oracle Corporation employees. If there is a critical decision that needs to be made on a project, the Oracle Corporation consultant is likely to have the best access to an internal decision-maker at Oracle.

The use of Oracle's Application Implementation Method is an advantage to employing companies. It is critical that a client uses a structured and methodical approach to increase the chances of long-term project success. Most Oracle Corporation consultants are trained on this method and bring this knowledge to their clients.

A more subtle advantage to employing companies who choose to use Oracle Corporation consultants involves the overall negotiation of product purchases. Depending on the number of products being purchased and many other factors, a company facing an upcoming implementation can sometimes use this as bargaining power with Oracle Corporation. The potential for moderately discounted consulting rates might be obtained in exchange for agreement for a full-scale product suite purchase.

Employing companies generally obtain consultants from Oracle Corporation who have been trained on the critical Oracle products required for the project. This level of training is advantageous particularly when new product versions arrive. The Oracle Corporation consultants have the potential to be well-informed from a training class on all the latest and greatest product features.

ORACLE CORPORATION CONSULTING: DISADVANTAGES TO CONSULTANT

Disadvantages exist for consultants who choose to work for Oracle Corporation. For starters, corporate bureaucracy at Oracle Corporation can cause much inefficiency. Note the write-up in the section "Larger, Diversified Consulting Firms: Disadvantages to Consultant." There is an example of a skilled Oracle GEMMS expert who is forced to miss a fabulous local opportunity due to big company politics. Oracle Corporation is very similar to these other big companies when dealing with the political infighting of various regional and vertically aligned business units. A consultant can find her personal goals compromised and ignored due to this type of bureaucracy.

For equivalent skills and experience, many Oracle Corporation consultants observe lower pay in relation to other Oracle-skilled consultants. This disadvantage to the consultant is very much similar to the issues discussed with larger, diversified consulting firms. There is simply a great deal of corporation overhead and many layers of management who must share in the profits generated by each consultant.

Oracle Corporation consultants sometimes observe disadvantages in the project environment because they work for Oracle. Many clients find some area that they perceive to be deficient within the particular Oracle products that they have purchased. The client will often desire the consultant to pressure Oracle to "fix" problems with the product. Although the Oracle Corporation consultant was not responsible for creating the products herself, the client will expect her to put pressure on others within Oracle to improve or fix the product. This implied responsibility and pressure on the consultant could be counterproductive. The consultant would be better utilized designing new solutions to meet the specific customer's needs instead of trying to defend her organization on the merits of the product.

Another disadvantage that influences the growth of Oracle Corporation consultants involves objectivity in decision-making. Although Oracle products tend to be very reputable in the marketplace, not every item created by Oracle is superior in every single niche. A consultant at Oracle might feel implied pressure to "sing the company tune" and promote products with an Oracle brand name even when competing products exist that might better serve her client. This does not mean that a consultant at Oracle will compromise her client's best interests. The message is that there are certainly pressure and challenges that must be overcome to obtain true objectivity.

Related to this issue is that Oracle Corporation consultants might lose out on the opportunity to learn about new non-Oracle products. Regardless of the merits of the following products, it would take extremely unusual circumstances for an Oracle Corporation consultant to be allowed to spend significant consulting time assisting with SAP HR/Payroll, PeopleSoft General Ledger, Microsoft SQL Server, and so on. Thus, the Oracle Corporation consultant might not be developing the most diversified industry skills.

ORACLE CORPORATION CONSULTING: DISADVANTAGES TO EMPLOYING COMPANY

Companies that choose to employ Oracle Corporation consultants often observe disadvantages. Many clients feel that they pay higher consulting rates for lower levels of Oracle product experience. The client assumes that the most heavily Oracle experienced consultants should logically come from Oracle itself. This is not necessarily the case.

The client might actually receive more junior consultants in some cases who are fresh out of Oracle boot camp. Thus, the consultants are well-trained but not necessarily well-experienced. This situation can occur for several reasons. First, some of the best Oracle Corporation consultants might be engaged in long-term projects with existing customers. These consultants who have gained the most hands-on experience are not available to leave their current client in the middle of the project. Others of the most heavily experienced consultants leave the company because of big-company politics or other issues. These consultants can usually obtain more money doing the same work with a specialized, smaller consulting firm. As a result, some clients observe higher costs for equivalent, or even lower, levels of experience.

Finally, corporations who choose to use Oracle Corporation consultants sometimes loose the ability for objectivity or experience in choosing the best overall solutions. In particular, if their consultants continue to be trained on only Oracle products, what other non-Oracle solutions might best meet the client's needs? In many cases, out-of-the-box solutions using the Oracle products are the best choice. However, are the particular Oracle Corporation consultants assigned to each project always equipped to recommend or design the best industry solution?

SUMMARY OF THE ORACLE CONSULTING MARKET

Each of the types of consulting alternatives described in this chapter can offer special opportunities to consultants depending on where you are in your career and what your specific needs are. You should not focus too much on any one section in this chapter. All should be considered together to help have a more objective assessment of the industry as a whole. It can be easy to overlook the various disadvantages discussed. Yet, the disadvantages are real, and every type of consulting opportunity has a downside.

PART

V

APP

B

An Oracle Applications Implementation Checklist

The purpose of this appendix is to provide a checklist of things that typically occur during an Oracle Applications implementation. Each implementation is unique, and you will want to adapt this list to your own project requirements.

PLAN AND INITIATE THE PROJECT

Every implementation requires substantial planning prior to beginning the implementation process. It is critical to know the scope, resources, timeline, and final objectives for your project. You should consider allocating between three and five percent of your total budget to planning activities. However, don't look at that budget allocation as a cost or overhead to the project. If you don't plan well, you will surely lose three to five percent in project team efficiency. Create a realistic project plan that will ultimately result in a successful, timely implementation. Use this phase of the project to establish the plan, controls, and procedures.

PLANNING

This list shows items you might want to consider as you prepare the software implementation project plans:

- Evaluate various implementation methods: rapid, preconfigured, phased, big bang, reengineered, customized, and so forth.
- Develop a high-level project work plan. Don't lock in your detailed project plan until you finish the analysis phase of the project. Don't let a project sponsor or steering committee lock in a budget until the analysis phase is complete.
- Determine time and cost criteria for the project. Try not to lock into a firm production date until you complete the analysis phase.
- Determine and document the assumptions that are in effect at the time the project is initiated.
- Create a risk assessment deliverable and a plan to mitigate risks.
- Document anything that is out of scope for the project.
- Conduct a high-level review of business requirements.
- Review data conversion methods available and determine which method is best for each module.
- Determine test plans and the degree of effort required.
- Develop a high-level reporting strategy. Estimate the volume of custom reports to be written for each module.
- Define transition policies after reviewing business constraints.
- Estimate the time required to complete tasks. Decompose tasks longer than four days into shorter subtasks.
- Load the implementation plan into the Project Management software tool.

- Establish a working budget and understand the planned return on investment.
- The project plan remains a living document as revisions are made, new tasks are added, tasks are deleted, and resources are added or deleted.

STAFFING

Staffing your project is the process of bringing resources and skills to the project team. Most companies must form an implementation team of functional, technical, managerial, and consulting resources and skills. Consider the following:

- Identify the project manager, internal sponsors, steering committee, and managers, both technical and functional.
- Identify internal technical and functional resources for each module. Form a project team. Establish an organization chart for the implementation team and end users.
- Determine the technical and functional skill sets needed by members of the project team.
- Make sure project team members can make decisions about business processes, requirements, and policies.
- Identify technical and functional external resources.
- Select at least one database administrator and system administrator.
- Develop an education plan for the project team. Analyze educational needs for internal resources and identify the classes each team member will attend.

CONTROLS

Project controls are the procedures, practices, and policies you use to govern the software implementation activities. Tight controls can stifle and delay the work. However, a lack of control is almost always expensive and risky. Project controls include the following:

- Define scope, goals, and terms for the project.
- If you think you need it, develop a project quality plan.
- Establish an issue tracking and resolution process.
- Define policy and justification criteria for modifications to the Oracle applications.
- Define custom report policy and justification criteria.
- Define a policy and justification for custom interfaces.
- Define acceptance criteria for the Oracle Applications software.
- Define a policy for implementation of noncore business requirements.
- Determine the impact of other corporate projects and initiatives on the Oracle Applications project.
- Define a policy and justification for creation of custom reports.

COMMUNICATION

When a small implementation team makes enterprisewide decisions about future business processes, communication helps the organization accept the change to the new software. Following are aspects of communication to consider:

- Review project goals, scope and deliverables with the project team.
- Tell the implementation team, the project sponsor, and the steering committee about your implementation strategy.
- Obtain a sign-off of the project plan by project team members.
- Determine communication methods for project stakeholders.
- Determine the frequency and locations of project status meetings for the project teams, project managers, and steering committee.
- Schedule and conduct a kickoff meeting for the project team.

LOGISTICS

The implementation project will last from four months to more than a year. Take the time at the beginning to set up a decent work area and make the team comfortable, efficient, and productive:

- Obtain workspace, equipment, and supplies needed for the project team.
- Set up a project war room. Ensure everything necessary is present to make the implementation team efficient.

ANALYZE THE BUSINESS AND THE TECHNOLOGY

You need to define high-level business requirements during the planning and initiation phase of the project for planning purposes. However, when the project has started, it is critical to perform an in-depth analysis of the business requirements to ensure that all the details of the requirement are understood and documented. When the detailed analysis has been performed, you should have an accurate definition of the scope. Project scope and the work plan will continue to change until the analysis is complete.

The following list shows many of the activities of the analysis phase of the implementation project:

- Document current business operating processes, policies, and requirements.
- Determine special business requirements for transition to new systems.
- Inventory the current technical architecture.
- Identify discussion materials needed for review during analysis meetings. Gather copies of all current reports.
- Define all integration points among Oracle modules.

- Determine the fit between Oracle Applications and non-Oracle systems at all integration points.

- Define and estimate the scope of custom interfaces.

- Obtain file specifications for all interfaces.

- Design custom interface programs.

- Determine future business processes and detailed requirements.

- Determine future technical architecture requirements.

- Document contingency plans and requirements.

- Gather information about processing volumes and frequencies.

- Assess risks and variables affecting system performance, fault tolerance, availability, and response time.

- Establish policies and procedures for working with Oracle Support. Create a TAR tracking log.

- Define and document all setup information choices. Define Key and Descriptive Flexfields.

- Perform detailed analysis of legacy reports. Construct a matrix to compare Oracle and legacy reports.

- Design custom reports.

- Design conversion programs for legacy data.

- Document gaps and the proposed resolution for each.

- Define and estimate the cost of custom extensions to the applications.

- Document any policy changes.

- Define all data loads for each module.

- Verify accuracy of all legacy data that will be loaded into the Oracle Applications.

- Identify any balance loads.

- Define test plans.

- Review transaction volumes and frequencies.

- Complete the estimating spreadsheet for hardware sizing.

- Review system-sizing estimates from the planning phase of the project to ensure original estimates were accurate. Adjust if necessary.

- Determine security requirements.

- Determine Responsibilities and User Profiles.

- Determine audit and control requirements.

- Update the project plan to reflect changes.

- Audit your project for red flags.

- Define and confirm new business policies and procedures.

PART

V

APP

C

BUILD AND CONFIGURE YOUR SYSTEM

At this stage of the project, the installation process should be complete and development/test instances will be created. When the business requirements have been clearly defined, the process of building, configuring, and testing the system can begin:

- Create responsibilities and users.
- Configure the system from setup documents completed during business analysis. Make sure to document any changes or fine-tuning of the configuration parameters.
- Map business requirements to Oracle Application function points.
- Load data manually and through open interfaces into the test instance.
- Map legacy data to be converted to Oracle Application Program Interfaces (APIs).
- Build, balance, and unit test legacy data conversions, initializations, and loads.
- Code and test custom reports.
- Code and unit test custom interfaces.
- Use the Optimal Flexible Architecture (OFA) when you install the applications.
- Implement a backup, recovery, and fault tolerance strategy.
- Conduct a conference room pilot test of the fully integrated system. Document a test plan, verify results, and repeat until results meet business requirements.
- Configure the production system when you have determined the freeze point for Oracle patches and integration tests.
- Always analyze build activities and decisions for their impact on future upgrades.
- Make sure you document all spontaneous changes in the setup documents.

TRANSITION TO THE NEW SYSTEM

When the system has been configured, built, and tested, the next step toward final implementation is to perform transition tasks. These tasks prepare the system for production use by the users:

- Prepare training materials.
- Create user procedure and system operation manuals.
- Identify end users for training and schedule classes.
- Conduct user-training classes.
- Load data and beginning balances into the production database manually or programmatically through open interfaces.
- Enable end user support capability.
- Make sure project documentation reflects the system as built.

- Audit your project for red flags.
- Achieve a team consensus on the go/no-go decision.

SUPPORT THE PRODUCTION SYSTEMS

The production Oracle system requires administration and support. There might be a formal hand off from the implementation team to the support organization, or some of the project team members might remain involved as power users and administration staff. When the system stabilizes, start improving and refining the system to keep moving forward.

This list shows supporting activities required for Oracle ERP systems after users begin making production transactions:

- Make sure the system is fault tolerant and the database backups are reliable.
- Verify that end users are capable of operating the system. Conduct additional training and support as required.
- Apply patches carefully after testing. Test everything you get from Oracle before applying it to your production system.
- Monitor the use of free space within the database.
- Monitor system response time and tune concurrent processes that consume the most system resources.
- Identify disk I/O hot spots and redistribute I/O across the physical disk drives.
- Conduct a postimplementation audit to verify that business requirements were met, measure user satisfaction, and create the basis for continuous process improvement based on the new applications.

PART

V

APP

C

INDEX

I

Y

BOSS Corporation is a service company devoted exclusively to Oracle Applications and Technology. **BOSS** was founded in 1995 on the premise that, in the Oracle Applications service marketplace, there should be something **BETTER**. The founders of **BOSS** were simply not satisfied with the level of service seen in our market, and they left employment at Oracle Corporation with the purpose of providing **BETTER** services to Oracle Applications customers...hence, **B**etter **O**rganization **S**ervice **S**olutions was formed and became known as **BOSS**. Since **BOSS** founders wanted to set a precedent in providing solutions to customers of the Oracle Applications, what difference does **BOSS** make in being **BETTER**?

Experience is the Difference
At **BOSS** Corporation, we hire and retain some of the highest qualified consultants in our profession, with strong functional, technical, and project management skills. We have simply found that being more experienced is **BETTER**.

Services and Rates
BOSS Consultants are experienced business professionals with Oracle Application and Technology expertise and the know-how to effectively design, manage, and execute the project plan. **BOSS** offers the highest level of service at more competitive rates than "big 5" firms and Oracle Services.

BOSS Expert Services
- ❏ Oracle Human Resource Management Applications Implementation (HR, PAY, OTM, OTA, OAB)
- ❏ Oracle Financial Applications Implementation (GL, AP, PO, FA, AR, PA)
- ❏ Oracle Distribution Applications Implementation (PO, INV, AR, OE)
- ❏ Oracle Manufacturing Applications Implementation (MRP, MPS, OE, INV, BOM, ENG, CPP, OPM/GEMMS)
- ❏ Remote and on-site Oracle Database Administration Services
- ❏ Oracle Education and Training
- ❏ Data Warehousing

Application Specialists
HR and Payroll
Financials and Manufacturing
Upgrades and DBA Services
Data Warehousing

BOSS
CORPORATION
Atlanta • Dallas • Raleigh

Voice 770-662-5500 Fax 770-622-5400
info@bosscorporation.com
www.bosscorporation.com

Applications Implementation
- ❑ Proven, successful, and economical project work plans
- ❑ Business process analysis for application fit and function
- ❑ System build to configure, convert legacy data, interface to foreign systems, and customize or extend the applications
- ❑ Transition planning and support while migrating to the Oracle Applications
- ❑ Post launch support for the user group and the IS organization

Database Administration
- ❑ Oracle Applications installations and upgrades
- ❑ Remote support
- ❑ Database tuning and performance

Education and Training
- ❑ Education for the Applications implementation project team
- ❑ End user training during transition to Oracle Applications
- ❑ New features training for upgrade clients

Technical Services
- ❑ Applications extensions and customizations (SQL*Forms 4.5 & 2.3, SQL*Reports 2.5, PL/SQL, SQL*Plus, Interfaces, and Data Conversion)
- ❑ Database Administration (Installation, Upgrade, Tuning, Remote Support)
- ❑ Data Warehousing

BOSS Corporation offers a complete set of implementation and support services for a **B**etter **O**racle **S**ervice **S**olution. **BOSS**'s focus on each Oracle service line helps you achieve the highest return on investment from your Oracle Applications.
BETTER does make a difference...

Please visit us at www.bosscorporation.com

Voice 770-622-5500 Fax 770-622-5400
info@bosscorporation.com
www.bosscorporation.com

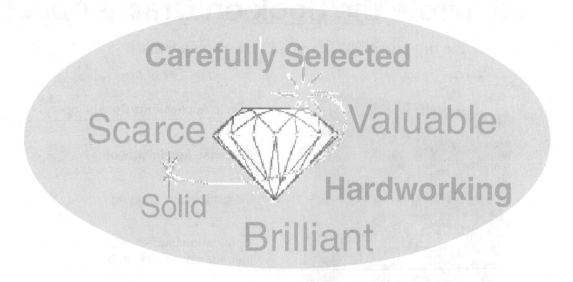